TRIUMPH IN ADVERSITY

Studies in Hungarian Civilization
in Honor of
Professor Ferenc Somogyi
on the Occasion of his Eightieth Birthday

Edited by

Steven Béla Várdy
and
Ágnes Huszár Várdy

EAST EUROPEAN MONOGRAPHS, BOULDER
DISTRIBUTED BY COLUMBIA UNIVERSITY PRESS
NEW YORK

1988

EAST EUROPEAN MONOGRAPHS, NO. CCLIII

*The Columbia University Press is Responsible Only
for the Marketing and Distribution of This Book*

Printed in the United States of America

Professor Ferenc Somogyi

The publication of this Work
was made possible
through the financial support
of the

HUNGARIAN ASSOCIATION,
Cleveland, Ohio
Dr. John Nádas, President

the

UNITED HUNGARIAN FUND,
Cleveland, Ohio
Dr. Gábor Papp, President

and

by a number of
Professor Somogyi's friends

TABLE OF CONTENTS

Editors' Preface xi

I. PROFESSOR FERENC SOMOGYI

1. Professor Ferenc Somogyi: Man, Scholar, and Publicist 2
   Steven Béla Várdy, *Duquesne University*
   Agnes Huszár Várdy, *Robert Morris College*

2. Frank, Francis, Ferenc: A Linguistic Analysis of Ferenc
   Somogyi's First Name 15
   Gyula Décsy, *Indiana University*

3. Ferenc Somogyi's Publications 19
   Sarolta B. Somogyi, *Árpád Federation, Cleveland*

II. FROM THE EARLY ÁRPÁDS TO THE AGE OF RÁKÓCZI

4. Early Twelfth-Century German Politics in the
   Background of Hungarian History 61
   Z. J. Kosztolnyik, *Texas A & M University*

5. Images of Woman and Love in the Poetry of Janus
   Pannonius, 1434-1472 77
   Katherine Gyékényesi Gatto, *John Carroll University*

6. The Hungarian Royal Chancery, 1458-1490: Was it
   a Center of Humanism? 97
   L. S. Domonkos, *Youngstown State University*

7. Markus Mark de Kémes: Hungarian Master at the
University of Paris, ca. 1521-1523 113
  Astrik L. Gabriel, *University of Notre Dame*

8. The Institution of Licentiatus: Hungarian Experiment
with the Laity's Participation in Ministry during the
Sixteenth and Seventeenth Centuries 125
  Gilbert E. Mihályi, O. Praem., Norbertine Fathers
  St. Joseph Priory, De Pere, Wisconsin

9. Prince Ferenc Rákóczi and the Hungarian Historical
Mission... 139
  Lél F. Somogyi, *Árpád Academy, Cleveland*

III. FROM ROMANTICISM TO THE AGE OF REFORM

10. Mihály Vörösmarty and the Development of Romanticism in Hungary 155
  Thomas Szendrey, *Gannon University*

11. Baron Joseph Eötvös's Political Essays in the Cause of
Reform during the 1840s 179
  Steven Béla Várdy, *Duquesne University*

12. Hungary's Tax System and the Issue of Tax Reform
in the 1840s 195
  Edsel Walter Stroup, *University of Akron*

IV. FROM TRIANON TO WORLD WAR II

13. Hungary's Road to Trianon 235
  Sándor Szilassy, *Glassboro State College*

14. The Hungarian Gendarmerie: Its Tragic Role in
World War II.. 273
  B. A. Rektor, *University of Arizona*

15. Bárdossy Reconsidered: Hungary's Entrance into

World War II 297
Botond R. Clementis-Záhony, *John Ashbrook Center, Ashland College*

V. NATIONAL MINORITIES IN HUNGARY AND IN THE SURROUNDING STATES

16. Regionalism in Practice: The Ethnoprotective Role of the Semi-Autonomous County System of Historic Hungary 323
Julius Varsányi,* *University of Adelaide, Australia*

17. Ethnic Minorities in Hungary since World War II........ 367
Francis S. Wagner, *The Library of Congress (Ret.)*

18. The Hungarian Minority in Czechoslovakia: A Status Report.. 389
Edward Chászár, *Indiana University of Pennsylvania*

VI. SOCIAL AND ECONOMIC DEVELOPMENTS IN TWENTIETH-CENTURY HUNGARY

19. The Development of Social Politics in Hungary during the Interwar Era...435
Andor Csizmadia,* *University of Pécs, Hungary*
Translated by Thomas Szendrey, *Gannon University*

20. Social Work in Hungary between 1940 and 1945 411
Sarolta B. Somogyi, *Árpád Federation, Cleveland*

21. The Pillar of Hungarian Society: The "Good Peasant" ...447
Michael Sozan,* *Slippery Rock University*

*Deceased

22. Hungarian Foreign Trade under the New Economic
    Mechanism, 1968-1980 473
       Nicholas A. Vardy, *Stanford University and
       Harvard University*

VII. HUNGARIAN-AMERICAN LIFE, CULTURE, AND POLITICS

23. Alexander Asbóth: Hungarian General in the
    American Civil War 499
       Ferenc Tar, *Balatoni Museum, Keszthely, Hungary*

24. The Legacy of Alexander Finta 527
       Leslie Konnyu, *The American-Hungarian Review,
       St. Louis*

25. Documenting Hungarian-American Immigration
    History: The Ruzsa Collection and its Significance 553
       Susan M. Papp, *Hungarian Studies Review,
       University of Toronto and Canadian Broad-
       casting Company*

26. The "Justice for Hungary" Ocean Flight: The Trianon
    Syndrome in Immigrant Hungarian Society 573
       N. F. Dreisziger, *Royal Military College of Canada*

27. Character and Role of Hungarian Literary and Critical
    Journals in North America in the 1970s and 1980s........591
       Ágnes Huszár Várdy, *Robert Morris College*

Contributing Scholars...607

Financial Contributors...617

MAPS AND ILLUSTRATIONS

I. Asztrik L. Gabriel: *Marcus Mark de Kémes:*

1. The first page of the Records of Marcus Mark
   de Kémes 120

II. Julius Varsányi: *Regionalism in Practice*:

1. Ethnographical map of Upper Hungary in the
   9th Century.. 364

2. Historic frontiers and Trianon frontiers of
   Upper Hungary.. 365

3. Ethnographical map of Upper Hungary at the
   time of Trianon... 366

III. Ferenc Tar: *Alexander Asbóth*:

1. Asbóth's house of birth in Keszthely, Hungary 521

2. Asbóth during his exile in Kütahya, Turkey......... 521

3. One of the "Kossuth Dollars" issued in New
   York in 1852 522

4. One of the illegal "Kossuth Forints" issued in
   London in 1860... 522

5. General Asbóth in the Battle of Pea Ridge in the
   Civil War, March 7, 1862 523

6. General Asbóth in uniform during the Civil War...524

7. General Asbóth's gravestone in the Old English
   Cemetery in Buenos Aires, Argentina................. 525

IV. Leslie Konnyu: *The Legacy of Alexander Finta*:

1. Alexander Finta (1881-1958) 539

2. Cardinal Patrick Hayes 540

3. Hungarian Poet, Sándor Petőfi (1823-1849)......... 541

4. Bronze plaque of Colonel Michael de Kováts
   (1724-1779).. 542

5. Bronze plaque of Colonel Michael de Kováts
before his death 543

6. Model of the proposed "Spirit of Columbia" 544

7. Hungarian poet and dramatist Imre Madách
(1823-1864) 545

8. Bronze plaque of Louis Kossuth (1802-1894) 546

9. Bronze bust of Louis Kossuth 547

10. Bronze plaque of Ágoston Haraszthy (1812-1869). 548

11. "The Faun and the Nymph" in wood 549

12. "The Pacific Ocean" in bronze 550

13. The Finta Museum in Túrkeve, Hungary 551

EDITORS' PREFACE

This book is the result of the joint efforts of twenty-five scholars from twelve disciplines and three continents. Although a large number of them are historians from the United States, the majority represent such diverse fields as cultural anthropology, economics, law, library science, linguistics, literature, military science, political science, social work, and theology, and live in such countries as Australia, Canada, Hungary, and the United States.

The contributors and their studies are bound together first of all be their respect for Professor Ferenc Somogyi, as well as by their interest in the Hungarian past, present, and future. They wish to honor Professor Somogyi with these contributions, and hope that by doing so they will also add to knowledge about Hungary and the Hungarians in the English speaking world.

Although the editors have undertaken this project already in the spring of 1983, for various reasons — including delays in receiving the enclosed essays, extensive editorial work, search for funds, and other obligations — have prevented them from delivering the finished manuscript to the publisher until the late summer of 1987. This puts the publication date of this work well beyond the target date of 1986, but it is hoped that the resulting book will be judged so as to have warranted this delay.

As is inevitable in a work of this nature, the enclosed essays do not center on a single topic and do not represent a homogeneous view of Hungarian Civilization. They mirror the distinct views, diverse methodological approaches, and varied scholarly or creative abilities of their respective authors. As such, they are bound together only by their concentration on Hungarian history, culture, and various manifestations of Hungarian life. Even so, however, they represent a kind of whole, and are well within the confines of the discipline called Hungarian Studies.

The editors made a distinct effort to synchronize to some degree the system of documentation of the enclosed studies, but — as is inevitable in cases when contributions come from so many countries and disciplines — this was not always possible. A number of contributions had to be translated into English, while others required extensive revisions and rewritings. In each instance this was done simply to make the enclosed essays more readable. No attempt was made to change the basic conclusions and ideological orientations of the respective authors. For this very reason the editors do not wish to be held responsible for the conclusions and orientations found in this work, some of which they may not fully share.

This work could not have been completed without the encouragement and moral support of Professor Somogyi's wife, Sarolta B. Somogyi, and the financial support of Dr. John B. Nádas, and Dr. Gábor Papp, presidents respectively of the Hungarian Association and the United Hungarian Fund, both of Cleveland, Ohio.

We are also grateful to a number of Professor Somogyi's friends who have likewise contributed to this project, at least to the tune of the price of a single volume of this work; as well as to Professor Stephen Fischer-Galati of the University of Colorado, the editor of the "East European Monographs" of Columbia University Press, for undertaking the publication of this work.

S. B. Várdy & A. H. Várdy
Pittsburgh, Pennsylvania
August, 1987

I.

PROFESSOR FERENC SOMOGYI

Steven Béla Várdy &

Ágnes Huszár Várdy:

1 / PROFESSOR FERENC SOMOGYI: MAN, SCHOLAR, AND PUBLICIST

The 20th century is an age of wars and revolutions. In the course of the past seven or eight decades or so we have fought two "world wars" and many lesser ones that are interspersed before, after, and in between these two global conflicts. As a matter of fact, the belligerency of our age is so pervasive that from the perspective of a later century the period of the two world wars will probably appear simply as a new "Thirty Years War," and the century as a whole will in all likelihood seem like the age of a second "Hundred Years War."

Given the above realities and the resulting mass social upheavals and dislocations throughout the world, it is almost unavoidable that a sizable segment of the intelligentsia of many nations should find themselves compelled to leave their native environment and be forced to find their livelihood in alien lands under strange and unusual circumstances.

While in some cases such an uprooting has led to rapid readjustment, acclimatization, and even improvement in one's social and economic position, in most instances—especially in the case of established scholars in the humanities and social sciences from non-English speaking countries—such transplantations produced traumas, personal tragedies, and breaks in the continuity of their life and scholarly endeavors. As such, a significant portion of such displaced scholars ended up either in a dead end street, or on a road that was the result of personal and career compromises and far removed from the path they have initially chosen for themselves.

Of those who came after World War II—particularly from countries that were on the wrong side of the political—military alignment during the war—only a minority of displaced European intellectuals was able to avoid such a fate. This was the case with most of the Hungarian intelligentsia who arrived on America's shores between 1948 and 1952. Because of their strong anti-communist political convictions, they were haunted and persecuted back home by Hungary's new masters; because of their country's past alliance with Germany, they were barely tolerated here by the strongly anti-German American public; because of their humanistic, legal, or military education, they had no transferable skills in this land of practical knowledge; and because of their "strange" social customs and seemingly "extreme" political views expressed emphatically in an accented English, they were deeply distrusted by the man on the street who had a natural distaste for intellectuals anyway. As such, their fate was far from enviable. Only the most fortunate among them were able to go through the appropriate adjustments quickly enough to "make it" in American society on their own terms and in their own special fields of preparation. [1]

Given the above realities, it is no wonder that Professor Somogyi's life and scholarly career in the United States also took a somewhat different turn than what one would have expected on the basis of his achievements in Hungary. Under normal circumstances, the latter should have landed him in a top position at one of America's respected universities, without all the vicissitudes he was subjected to before finding a small niche in the American academic world.

Back home he had devoted his life primarily to legal scholarship in the area of inheritance and social welfare legislation, while also serving as one of the noted advocates and administrators of his country's social welfare system. Here in the United States he was forced to diffuse his scholarship in accordance with the needs and limited opportunities of the post-World War II political immigrants from Hungary, as well as to devote much of his knowledge, dedication, and energy to publicistic and cultural activities connected with the cultural-intellectual-political aspirations of his fellow immigrants. The results are undoubtedly different from what they would have been had he remained at home, or had he been given the chance to develop his potential fully in an American, rather than in a Hungarian-American environment. As to whether these results would be preferable to his current achievements, is a matter of pure conjecture. Only the foolhardy would dare to compare the quality and quantity of known achievements with results that never came to be.

* * *

Ferenc Somogyi, the future constitutional historian, legal scholar, social welfare administrator, cultural politician, publicist, and cultural historian was born over eight decades ago on June 25, 1906. He came into this world in the Trans-Danubian town of Nárai as the oldest son of a non-titled noble family. After completing primary school in his native town, he finished his secondary education at the Preparatory School of the Premonstratensian Order (*premontrei gimnázium*) in the city of Szombathely, from where—much earlier—József Cardinal Mindszenty, the future staunchly anticommunist Primate of the Hungarian Catholic Church graduated.

Following his graduation in 1927, Ferenc Somogyi enrolled at the Royal Hungarian Elizabeth University of Pécs, from where he received his doctorate in political science in 1932 and his law degree (Doctor Juris) in 1934. During these years he won five separate awards for scholarly excellence from the University. [2]

Even before receiving his degrees, Somogyi was employed by his alma mater; first as a librarian at the School of Law (1931-1936), and then—for a while simultaneously—as an Assistant to Professor Zoltán Kérészy (1933-1938), the Director of the Institute of Legal History. In the latter capacity, Somogyi participated extensively in the instructional and scholarly work of the Institute. As an example, starting with 1933, he edited the Institute's publication series,[3] as well as the legal journal *Pécsi Jogász* (Jurist of Pécs),[4] while at the same time summarizing and publishing the activities of the Institute for the years 1932-1936.[5] Moreover, during the same period, he authored a number of significant studies on such topics as the institution of entailment,[6] the history of Hungary's Jewish laws,[7] and the question of inheritance in medieval and early modern Hungary.[8]

In 1937, on the basis of his scholarly achievements, Somogyi was habilitated a "Private Professor" (*egyetemi magántanár*) at the University of Pécs. [9] In the following year he was also named the Social Councellor of Baranya County, and in 1939 he was elected one of his city's two representatives to the Hungarian Parliament.

In 1940, Somogyi was one of the top contenders to the Chair of Hungarian Legal and Constitutional History at the newly re-established University of Kolozsvár (Cluj) in Transylvania. Only his unexpected drafting into the Hungarian Army, in conjunction with the territorial revisions taking place at that very time, prevented his appointment to the post, which had to be filled immediately. [10]

In October 1940, while retaining his association with the University of Pécs, Professor Somogyi was also appointed Assistant to the Executive President of the National Foundation for Folk and Family Protection (*Országos Nép- és Családvédelmi Alap*), and then the Director of the Social Welfare Section of the Ministry of Interior, as well as the Executive Vice President of the National Social Welfare Superintendency (*Országos Szociális Felügyelőség*).

The end of World War II found Professor Somogyi in Austria, along with many other political immigrants from the devastated countries of Central and Eastern Europe. After five years in Austrian emigré camps (Kellerberg, Spittal an der Drau)—where he served in such diverse capacities as teacher, theater manager, director, and journal editor—he arrived in the United States in late 1950. He settled down in Cleveland, Ohio, where he immediately became one of the most prominent, trusted, and respected spokesmen of the Hungarian immigrant community, as well as the voice of moderation, cultural distinction, and scholarly detachment in that sea of distress and political emotionalism. [11]

While continuing to edit his journal *Vagyunk* (We Exist) [12] until 1956, in 1952 he became one of the founders of the still existing Cleveland Hungarian Association (*Magyar Társaság*), an organization of national scope and influence, as well as of the more scholarly Danubian Institute (*Dunai Intézet*) whose goal was to examine and to find solutions to the historical, political, economic, and social problems of the Danube region. [13]

In 1953, Professor Somogyi cofounded and codirected the St. Stephen Free University (*Szent István Szabadegyetem*), where he lectured on Hungarian history and Hungarian constitutional history. A decade later in 1962 he became the Director of the Hungarian Studies Program at Western Reserve University, where he taught courses on Hungarian Cultural History. [14]

In addition to the intrinsic merits of these undertakings for Hungarian Studies in the United States and for a whole generation of young Hungarian-Americans—including one of the authors of this essay—one of the important and lasting results of these activities was Professor Somogyi's publications of four separate major volumes on Hungarian history, cultural history, and literature, totalling more than 2,000 pages. [15] And he produced all of these works while being engaged in extensive publicistic activities in half a dozen newspapers and periodicals throughout North America; while helping to organize the annual Hungarian Congresses (*Magyar Találkozó* or *Magyar Kongresszus*) that draw their participants from all over the world (1961-); while editing the proceedings of these congresses (1965-); [16] and while serving as the General Secretary of the Árpád Academy of Hungarian Scientists, Writers and Artists Abroad (*Árpád Akadémia*) (1966-)—an institution that embraces a significant portion of the traditional-conservative emigré Hungarians with scientific and scholarly distinctions from around the world. [17]

* * *

Although fate has compelled Professor Somogyi to devote over half of his life and well over half of his energies to activities that were not part of his original career goals, and although a significant portion of his writings—particularly his articles in periodicals—are publicistic in nature, in the depth of his heart he always remained a scholar, and his scholarly works have much to offer both to generalists and to specialists.

During the early phase of his career in the 1930s, Somogyi's most significant work was undoubtedly his study on inheritance in pre-modern Hungary: *Végrendelkezés nemesi ma-*

gánjogunk szerint 1000-től 1715-ig (Testamentary Disposition According to the Civil Law of Our Nobility from 1000 A.D. to 1715). [18] In this work—in line with the views of his mentor at the University of Pécs, Professor Zoltán Kérészy [19] —he championed the uniqueness of Hungarian legal-constitutional developments. As such, he became embroiled in a major controversy with the noted constitutional historian, Professor Ferenc Eckhart and his disciples at the University of Budapest, [20] who viewed Hungary's evolution simply as a component part and a reflection of East Central European and general European developments. It was to defend his views that Somogyi wrote his related study entitled *Családiság és ősiség* (Patrimony `and Entailment) in 1938, [21] which turned out to be another significant treatment of this issue.

Somogyi's increased involvement in social welfare activities during the late 1930s and early 1940s also directed his scholarly interests from the history of entailment and inheritance toward the history and current status of social welfare in Hungary. The results were three important studies on Hungarian social welfare legislation from medieval times to his own age, two major co-edited and co-authored volumes on the status and goals of social welfare activities in contemporary Hungary, and a number of related scholarly articles in various periodicals.

In his *Társadalompolitikai törvényalkotás Werbőczy előtt* (Sociopolitical Legislation before the Age of Werbőczy) (1943), [22] and his *Társadalompolitikai törvényalkotás Werbőczy után* (Sociopolitical Legislation after the Age of Werbőczy) (1944) [23] Somogyi summarized and analyzed— for the first time in the history of this discipline—Hungary's laws and legal traditions for their "social welfare content." In a more extensive study entitled *Szociális törvényalkotásunk fejlődése* (The Development of Our Social Welfare Legislation) (1944), [24] he synthesized the results of his research on this topic into a coherent and pathbreaking work on the history of social legislation in Hungary.

Along the same lines, Somogyi coedited and coauthored a major work on the goals and obligations of the budding Hungarian social welfare system: *A magyar szociálpolitika feladatai* (The Tasks of Hungarian Social Welfare Policy (1940), [25] as well as a similar work on the achievements of that policy during the early 1940s: *Nép- és családvédelem az 1940-42. évben* (Folk and Family Protection in the Years 1940-1942) (1943). [26] During the same period, he also elaborated his views concerning the origins, current status, and goals of social welfare policies in Hungary in such periodicals as *Nép- és Családvédelem* (Folk and Family Protection) and *Donaueuropa* (Danubian Europe), as well as in a number of collective volumes. [27]

For a number of years following his departure from Hungary in 1945, conditions made it impossible for Professor Somogyi to continue his academic and scholarly work. It was during these early years of exile that he turned to publicistic and editorial activities, so as to utilize his knowledge, dedication, and energy for the enlightenment of his fellow immigrants.

Not until the mid-1950s was Professor Somogyi able to return to a limited amount of academic work and to resume his scholarly research and writings. The most important results of the latter include his history of Hungary, *Küldetés: A magyarság története* (Mission: The History of the Hungarian People) (1973), [28] a shorter English version of the same work entitled *Faith and Fate* (1977), [29] and a two-volume synthesis of Hungarian literary and cultural developments, *Magyar nyelv és irodalom* (Hungarian Language and Literature (1975-1977), [30]

Of these three works, the *Küldetés* is undoubtedly the most significant publication. As observed by a reviewer, it is an "objective..., well researched, and beautifully written"[31] synthesis with a flavor of its own. It explores a number of new theories, especially in conjunction with the proto-history of the Magyars, yet at the same time it reflects the pedantic scholarship and traditional historical philosophy of its author, as well as his belief in the unique mission of his people in the Carpathian Basin.[32] As such, it is a well-balanced and welcome alternative to the multi-authored, dry, and often spiritless syntheses produced in Hungary during the same period.

Naturally, the shorter English language version of this work cannot fully duplicate the content, spirit, and atmosphere of the original. And this also holds true for the two-volume literary history, where Somogyi is somewhat removed from his own field of specialization. Even so, his *Magyar nyelv és irodalom* — which is also the product of his lectures in Hungarian cultural history at Western Reserve University — has become a handbook for many who view it as a respectable alternative to the Marxist syntheses published in Hungary during the last few decades.

In addition to producing these syntheses, since 1965 Professor Somogyi was also the primary editor of twenty-six volumes of the proceedings of the annual Hungarian Congresses that drew their participants from all over the world. Entitled *Magyar Találkozó Krónikája* (Proceedings of the Hungarian Congress), [33] one day these twenty-seven volumes and their sequels will undoubtedly be among the most important sources for the portrayal of the history, politics, and inner life of the Hungarian-American community. [34]

Mention should also be made of Somogyi's reassessment of the role of Hungary's first Christian king, *Szent István a magyar nemzeti élet központjában* (St. Stephen in the Focus of Hungarian Public Life) (1970); [35] of his Hungarian-American institutional history, *A Magyar Társaság három évtizedének vázlatos története* (The Outline History of the Hungarian Association's Three Decades) (1983); [36] of his compilation of a biographical handbook on the members of the Árpád Academy, *Az Árpád Akadémia tagjainak tevékenysége* (Activity of the Members of the Árpád Academy) (1982); [37] as well as of his scholarly contributions to the memorial volume published on the occasion of the death of King Louis the Great of Hungary, *Louis the Great, King of Hungary and Poland* (1986). [38] The latter include a significant study on the origins of Hungary's first institution of higher learning, the University of Pécs (1367), which is Somogyi's own alma mater and the scene of his early scholarly activities; a detailed analysis of King Louis's Constitutional Decree of 1351 (*Decretum unicum de anno 1351*) which is one of the foundation stones of Hungarian constitutionalism; and a translation of the same Decree of 1351. [39] With these publications Professor Somogyi demonstrated again and again his continued and unabated dedication to historical scholarship — in spite of the everpresent obligation to engage in publicistic activities.

* * *

If initially Professor Somogyi's scholarly works centered on the development of Hungarian entail, inheritance, and social welfare laws, and later on the broad interpretation of Hungarian historical and cultural developments, his publicistic works dealt with many diverse topics, as demanded by the exigencies of the age.

During the 1930s and early 1940s, for example, the majority of his over four score articles, which appeared in Hungary's prominent national and regional newspapers, concentrated primarily on social issues. These included the examination of the lifestyles and problems of the country's rural population, and the advocacy of general social transformation and social welfare reform in Hungary. In the course of those years, he spoke up for the need of land reform, against the evils of social polarization, for the necessity of folk and family protection, against the abuse of Hungary's national and religious minorities, as well as for the need of educational reforms, with particular attention to the training of social workers at Hungary's institutions of higher learning. [40]

Naturally, the subject of his articles changed immediately as soon as he was forced to leave Hungary in 1945. Emigré life produced new circumstances and new realities. All at once, the number one problem he and his compatriots faced, was not the transformation of Hungarian society—which at that very moment was being forcibly transformed under the shadows of the occupying Soviet Army—but the preservation of the sanity of the dejected emigrants, and the continuation of Hungarian culture and way of life in the alien world of the displaced persons' camps across Austria and Germany. [41]

To advance the cause of sanity and the yearning for a better future, Professor Somogyi founded and edited the journal *Vagyunk* (We Exist), which for nearly a decade (1948-1956) became an instrument of hope among the emigrants—both by its very existence and assertive title, as well as through the articles of its learned and prolific editor. While educating the emigrés about their rich cultural heritage and historical traditions, these articles effused optimism and a belief in the re-emergence of a new and better Hungary. [42]

Professor Somogyi, however, did not limit his literary creativity to his own journal. He contributed to over a dozen other significant emigré publications—both before and after, as well as during the existence of his own periodical. Among others, these periodicals included the pioneering *Magyar Út* (Hungarian Path) and *Fáklya* (Torch) published in Austria in the years immediately after World War II, [43] as well as such well-known Hungarian-American newspapers, journals, and yearbooks as the *Katolikus Magyarok Vasárnapja* (Catholic Hungarians' Sunday), *Kárpát* (Carpathians), *Az Újság* (News), *Magyar Újság* (Hungarian News), *Kanadai Magyar Újság* (Canadian Hungarian News), *Amerikai Magyar Élet* (American Hungarian Life), *Detroiti Újság* (Detroit News), *Amerikai-Kanadai Magyar Élet* (American-Canadian Hungarian Life), *Őrszem* (Guardian), *Hungarian Insights*, and the already mentioned *Magyar Találkozó Krónikája* (Proceedings of the Hungarian Congress) which he cofounded and edited yearly since 1965. [44]

In the course of the past four decades, Professor Somogyi wrote several hundred studies, articles, and reviews in these publications. Together they represent a significant and revealing slice of Hungarian emigré life in Europe and in America—with all its vicissitudes, failures, hopes, and achievements of such an existence.

During the same period, he also contributed to a number of independent volumes dealing with such diverse topics as Cardinal Mindszenty's visit to the United States, [45] the return of the Hungarian Holy Crown—St. Stephen's Crown—to the motherland, [46] the role of such Hungarian heroes in American history as Colonel Michael Kováts (1778-79) and Louis Kossuth (1851-52), [47] and various aspects of Hungarian education in the United States. [48]

Virtually all of Professor Somogyi's contributions were written in an informed, reasoned, and detached tone, which is more characteristic of a scholar than of a journalist. Along with the wide scope of his topics and unusual depth of his learning, this unique feature of his publicistic writings makes him into one of the most prolific, authoritative, and dispassionate practitioners of Hungarian-American journalism. He stands way out from the ranks of emigré journalists and pseudo-journalists, a significant number of whom tend to give vent to their personal and political disappointments through political extremism and personal attacks against those who disagree with them or who are willing to come to terms with the realities of the day. This is one of the reasons Professor Somogyi enjoys such wide respect among Hungarian-Americans—even among those who do not necessarily agree with him and or know him personally.

* * *

Those who know him personally, respect him even more. They respect him as a man of learning and cultural sophistication; they respect him as a scholar of considerable achievements; and a number of them—including the authors of the present study [49]—also respect him as the prototype of the ideal professor of the old school who used to command respect and attention by their very presence, not to speak of their knowledge, sophistication, moral courage, tolerance, and their willingness to exchange views and to agree or to disagree on the level of a man of culture and learning—as did Sophocles in Plato's *Dialogues.*

In retrospect, these are precisely the type of professors who seem to be absent in this age of mass education and technological progress, and who are sorely missed by those of us whose fate has bound them permanently to the world of humanistic learning and to the ideals of a broadly interpreted "classical" culture. However short the time may have been that we have spent under Professor Somogyi's tutelage, his influence is still with us after three decades of "struggle for existence" in a world that is far different from the ideal world of our youth while reading Plato and listening to Professor Somogyi's polished lectures about the origins of the Hungarian nation and the details of Hungarian constitutional developments. And without that influence, today we too would be different: more empoverished intellectually, less sensitive to the finer aspects of human existence, and far less willing to be tolerant of others who hold divergent views and unorthodox ideas. This may be his greatest gift to those of us who had the good fortune to be associated with him during a short period of our formative years.

* * *

Notes

1. Concerning this strange fate of the post-World War II immigrants, see especially Kázmér Nagy, *Elveszett alkotmány* (The Lost Constitution) (Munich: Auróra Könyvek, 1974; 2d ed., London, 1982; 3rd ed., Budapest, 1983); Gyula Borbándi, *A magyar emigráció életrajza, 1945-1985* (The Biography of the Hungarian Emigration, 1945-1985) (Munich: Az Európai Protestáns Magyar Szabadegyetem Kiadása, 1985); and S. B. Várdy, *The Hungarian-Americans* (Boston: Twayne Publishers, 1985), pp. 113-150.

2. Cf. "Somogyi Ferenc," in Pál Szabó (vitéz), *A m. kir. Erzsébet tudományegyetem és irodalmi munkássága* (The Hung. Roy. Elizabeth University and Its Scholarly Activities) (Pécs: Dunántúl Pécsi Egyetemi Könyvkiadó, 1940), pt. I, 137, and pt. II, pp. 864-868.

3. See "Ferenc Somogyi's Publications," no. 28, in this work. Hereafter cited as *FSP*.

4. *FSP*, no. 29.

5. *FSP*, nos. 2, 5, 42.

6. *FSP*, nos. 1, 7, 44.

7. *FSP*, nos. 3, 38.

8. *FSP*, nos. 6, 43.

9. For Somogyi's "Habilitation Dissertation" see *FSP*, no. 6. For additional information on Somogyi's activities at the University of Pécs, see Andor Csizmadia, "A jogtörténeti oktatás a pécsi tudományegyetemen a két világháború között" (The Instruction of Legal History at the University of Pécs between the Two World Wars), in *Jubileumi tanulmányok* (Anniversary Studies), eds. Andor Csizmadia and Tibor Papp, 2 vols. (Pécs: Pécsi Tudományegyetem, 1967), II, pp. 107-128; and *idem*, "A jog- és államtudományi kar, 1923-1951" (The School of Law and Political Science, 1923-1951), in *Fejezetek a pécsi egyetem történetéből* (Chapters from the History of the University of Pécs), ed. Andor Csizmadia (Pécs: Pécsi Szikra Nyomda, 1980), pp. 35-64.

10. In 1940, György Bónis (1914-) was appointed to the Chair of Legal History at the University of Kolozsvár, a position which he held only until 1944.

11. See especially "Somogyi Ferenc," in *A IV-V. Magyar Találkozó Krónikája* (Proceedings of the 4th and 5th Hungarian Congress) (Cleveland: Árpád Könyvkiadó, 1966), p. 259-260. Hereafter cited as *Krónika*.

12. *FSP*, no. 34.

13. Ferenc Somogyi, *A Magyar Társaság három évtizedének vázlatos története* (The Outline History of Three Decades of the Hungarian Association) (Cleveland: Magyar Társaság, 1983), pp. 12-14.

14. *Ibid.*, p. 12; (Steven) Béla Várdy, "Magyarságtudomány az észak-amerikai egyetemeken és főiskolákon" (Hungarian Studies at North American Colleges and Universities), in *Krónika*, XII (1973), pp. 102-132, especially p. 10; and *idem*, "Hungarian Studies at American and Canadian Universities," in *The Canadian-American Review of Hungarian Studies*, II/2 (Fall 1975), pp. 91-121, especially p. 104. See also (Steven) Béla Várdy, "Az észak-amerikai magyarságtudomány mai helyzete" (The Current Status of Hungarian Studies in North America), in *Hungarológiai oktatás régen és ma* (Hungarian Studies in the Past and Today), ed. Judit M. Róna (Budapest: Tankönyvkiadó, 1983), pp. 165-173; and Steven Béla Várdy and Agnes Huszár Várdy, "Historical, Literary, Linguistic, and Eth-

nographic Research on Hungarian-Americans: A Historiographical Assessment,"
in *Hungarian Studies* (Budapest), I/1 (1985), pp. 77-122.

15. *FSP*, nos. 21-24.

16. *FSP*, no. 35.

17. Somogyi, *A Magyar Társaság*, pp. 33-35; and *FSP*, no. 25.

18. *FSP*, no. 6.

19. On Zoltán Kérészy, see S. B. Várdy, *Modern Hungarian Historiography* (New York & Boulder: East European Monographs, Columbia University Press, 1976), pp. 191-192, 273-274. On Somogyi's other noted professors—József Holub and Antal Hodinka—see *ibid.*, pp., 141-144; and *idem, Clio's Art in Hungary and in Hungarian-America* (New York & Boulder: East European Monographs, Columbia University Press, 1986), pp. 81-82, and 121-127.

20. On Eckhart and his school of legal history, see Várdy, *Modern Hungarian Historiography*, pp. 185-190.

21. *FSP*, no. 7.

22. *FSP*, no. 8.

23. *FSP*, no. 9.

24. *FSP*, no. 10.

25. *FSP*, no. 31.

26. *FSP*, no. 32.

27. *FSP*, nos. 45-58.

28. *FSP*, no. 21.

29. *FSP*, no. 24.

30. *FSP*, no. 22-23.

31. See Zoltán Kosztolnyik's review in *Austrian History Yearbook*, XVII-XVIII (1981-1982), pp. 349-350.

32. See S. B. Várdy, "A Traditional Historian's View of Hungarian History," *The Canadian-American Review of Hungarian Studies*, 4/1 (Spring 1979), pp. 59-65.

33. *FSP*, no. 35.

34. For a brief portrayal of this series, see Várdy, *The Hungarian-Americans*, pp. 138-141.

35. *FSP*, no. 20.

36. *FSP*, no. 26, and note 13, above.

37. *FSP*, no. 25.

38. *Louis the Great, King of Hungary and Poland*, eds. S. B. Várdy, G. Grosschmid, and L. S. Domonkos (New York & Boulder: East European Monographs, Columbia University Press, 1986).

39. For Somogyi's contributions to the above work, see *ibid.*, pp. 221-236, 429-451, 453-467; and *FSP*, nos. 80-82.

40. *FSP*, nos. 83-171.

41. See Nagy, *Az elveszett alkotmány* (1974), pp. 29-45; and Várdy, *The Hungarian-Americans*, pp. 133-141.

42. See the articles under *FSP*, nos. 183-230.

43. *FSP*, nos. 171-182.

44. *FSP*, nos. 231ff.

45. *FSP*, nos. 337-338.

46. *FSP*, no. 68.

47. *FSP*, nos. 66, 374.

48. *FSP*, nos. 36-37.

49. Having been a student of Professor Somogyi's in Cleveland, I am well aware of his influence on his students. (S. B. Várdy).

2 / FRANK, FRANCIS, FERENC: A LINGUISTIC ANALYSIS OF FERENC SOMOGYI'S FIRST NAME

The word "Frank" originally referred to a member of a Germanic tribe of the Franks; and perhaps it also meant "javelin," i.e. a light spear, carried and thrown by hand. This root word has no correspondences outside the Germanic branch of the Indo-European linguistic family. It is thus to be regarded as a Germanic innovation. The Germanic adjective derivative of this term is *frankiskaz* = "of the Franks," which in Old English became *frencisc* = "name of the French."[1] This *frankiskaz* was borrowed from Germanic into Late Latin, where — after adaptation to the adjective ending set *-iscus/-isca/-iscum* — it took on the form *franciscus/francisca/franciscum*, i.e. "a member of one of the Germanic tribes of the Rhine region in the early Christian era; especially one of the Salian Franks who conquered Gaul about 500 A.D."[2] At this time the name also received the appellative meaning "generous, free, sincere, straightforward," because in Frankish Gaul full freedom was possessed only by the conquerors and those native peoples who stood under their protection.

In Latin, in addition to the adjective *Franciscus/Francisca/Franciscum*, the substantive form *Francus/Franca/Francum* was also known in the meaning "French," which is used both as an adjective and as a noun. The Latin masculine adjective *Franciscus* became a personal name only in 1181, when the father of the future St. Francis of Assisi named his newborn son *Francis* because his wife was of French origin. It was this *Francis(cus) of Assisi* (1181-1226)

15

who founded the medicant order of the *Franciscans* (Grey Friers) in 1209, and then in 1212 also the Clarissin Order for women.

After the 13th century, the name of this popular saint was given to millions of Christian children. During the next few centuries, the basic Latin form of *Franciscus* was changed in the various European languages according to local habits and needs of pronunciation. In Italy it became *Francesco* (*c* pronounced as *ch*), while in France and England it became *Francis* (*c* pronounced as *s*). This *Francis* is used today in the English speaking world both as a masculine and as a feminine name. As a masculine name, it is a shorter version of *Franciscus*; while as a feminine name, it is a pet form of *Francisca*.

* * *

The earliest Hungarian form of *Franciscus* was most certainly *Ferencs* (*cs* pronounced as *ch* in English). The initial consonant cluster of *Franciscus* was abolished by the insertion of an *e*. Because of the *cs* (= *ch*) pronunciation, this earliest Hungarian form can only be regarded as a borrowing from Italian. This archaic form had been preserved in a number of Hungarian family names, especially in the northern part of Historic Hungary with many families of Slovak origin, such as *Ferencsik*, and *Ferjenčík*—the latter being, among others, the name of a member of the Slovak cabinet in 1946-1948.

The original Hungarian variation (with *cs* pronounced as *ch*) was soon replaced by *Ferencz—Ferenc* in its more modern form—which seems to be a borrowing from German. The German pronunciation of *c* is *ts* or *tz*, in place of the Latin-Italian *c* (= *ch*). It is also possible, however, that the later Hungarian pronunciation of the Italian-based *Ferencs* was simply altered under the influence of the newer German pronunciation, which used *z* (*tz, c*) at the end of the name.

Frenc(*z*) then became the commonly used Hungarian variation. The earlier *Ferencs* was either forgotten, or only used in various forms as an archaic family name. This could only have happened under Germanic linguistic influence, a phenomenon that became increasingly prevalent in and after the 16th century. A systematic research into the origins of Hungarian family names could perhaps disclose new data concerning the spread of *cs* (=*ch*) form, not only in former Upper Hungary, but also in various other sections of the country.

St. Francis is a canonized saint only of the Roman Catholic Church, for the Eastern Orthodox Church does not venerate him. His day of remembrance is the 4th of October. Apparently, it is well known throughout the Western Christian World that *Frank/Francis* (masculine) and *Franz/Ferenc* belong together etymologically.

Frank as a given name became popular in the United States only in the course of the last hundred or so years. It is often regarded as a good pre-Christian Germanic name with pointed Anglo-Saxon traditions. Yet, many people of non-Anglo-Saxons roots are also known by this name (e.g. Frank Sinatra, who is of Italian extraction).

In Germany, the name became widespread in honor of *Frank Wedekind* (1864-1918), a popular poet in the late 19th century. Following World War II, it became even more common in West Germany, in all probability under American influence. In East Germany, however, it does not belong among the preferred given names,[3] undoubtedly precisely because of its American connotation.

Hungarian immigrants with the name *Ferenc* often translate their names either to *Frank* (as the poet Frank Mózsi, or the State Department personnel Frank Földváry) or to *Francis* (as the historian/bibliographer Francis Wagner). The *Francis/Ferenc* version of this name has basically a strong Catholic appellation, for which reason it is seldom given to children in Protestant Northern Europe.[4]

Notes

1. See the term "Frankon" in *The American Heritage Dictionary of the English Language*, ed. William Morris (Boston-New York-Palo Alto: American Heritage Publishing Co. Inc. and Houghton Mifflin Co., 1969), p. 1515.

2. *Ibid.*, p. 522.

3. Lutz Mackensen, *3876 Fornamen* (München: Südwest Verlag, 1983), p. 58.
4. Ee. Kiviniemi, *Rakkaan lapsen monet nimet* (Espoo: Weilin-Göös, 1982), p. 70.

Sarolta B. Somogyi:

3 / FERENC SOMOGYI'S PUBLICATIONS

CATEGORIES OF PUBLICATIONS:

I.   Books, Textbooks, and Pamphlets

II.   Editorial Work

III.   Scholarly Studies, Eassays, and Research Reports

IV.   Newspaper and Periodical Articles

V.   Obituaries

VI.   Book Reviews

ABBREVIATIONS USED IN THE BIBLIOGRAPHY:

AKME — *Amerikai-Kanadai Magyar Élet* (American-Canadian Hungarian Life)

KMV — *Katolikus Magyarok Vasárnapja* (Catholic Hungarians' Sunday)

MTK — *A Magyar Találkozó Krónikája* (Proceedings of the Hungarian Congress).

NCsV — *Nép- és Családvédelem* (Folk and Family
Protection)

I. BOOKS, TEXTBOOKS, AND PAMPHLETS:

1. *Az ősiség intézménye és a hűbéri vagyonjog* (The
Institute of Entailment and the Feudal Property Law) (Pécs:
Taizs József Könyvnyomdája, 1931), 29 pp.

2. *A jogtörténeti szeminárium 1932-33. tanévi tevé-
kenysége a m. kir. Erzsébet Tudományegyetemen* (The
Activities of the Legal History Seminar in the Academic
Year 1932-33 at the Roy. Hung. Elizabeth University) (Pécs:
A Pécsi m. kir. Erzsébet Tudományegyetem Kiadványai,
1933), 20 pp.

3. *Zsidójogunk fejlődésének áttekintése* (The Outline
History of Our Jewish Laws) (Pécs: Haladás Nyomda, Rt.,
1936), 46 pp.

4. *Jogtörténet és jogpolitika. Válasz Hegedüs Ferencnek*
(Legal History and Legal Politics. Reply to Ferenc Hegedüs)
(Szombathely: Összetartás Keresztény Sajtóiroda, Hajnal
Ferenc Könyvnyomdája, 1936) 8 pp.

5. *Három év (1933-36) a pécsi egyetem jogtörténeti sze-
mináriumában* (Three Years (1933-36) in the Legal History
Seminar at the University of Pécs) (Pécs: A pécsi m. kir.
Erzsébet Tudományegyetem jogtörténeti szemináriumának
kiadványai, 1936), 36 pp.

6. *Végrendelkezés nemesi magánjogunk szerint 1000-től
1715-ig* (Testamentary Disposition According to the Civil
Law of Our Nobility from the Year 1000 to 1715) (Pécs:
Dunántúl Pécsi Egyetemi Nyomda Rt., 1937), 100 pp.

7. *Családiság és ősiség. Válasz Eckhart Ferenc ny. r.
tanár bírálatára* (Patrimony and Entailment. Reply to the
Critique of University Professor Ferenc Eckhart) (Pécs: Haladás Nyomda Rt., 1938), 48 pp.

8. *Társadalompolitikai törvényalkotás Werbőczy előtt*
(Socio-Political Legislation before Werbőczy) (Kassa: Szent
Erzsébet Nyomda, 1943), 64 pp.

9. *Társadalompolitikai törvényalkotás Werbőczy után* (Socio-Political Legislation after Werbőczy) (Kassa: Szent Erzsébet Nyomda, 1944), 56 pp.

10. *Szociális törvényalkotásunk fejlődése* (The Evolution of Our Social Welfare Legislation) (Budapest: Az Országos Szociális Felügyelőség Könyvei, 1944), 200 pp.

11. *A legújabb kor története. A francia forradalomtól a második világháború kitöréséig (1789-től 1939-ig) vázlatosan* (The History of the Most Recent Age. From the French Revolution to the Outbreak of World War II (1789-1939) in Outline Form) (Spittal an der Drau, Austria: Vagyunk Kiadó, 1950), 13 pp.

12. *A stilisztika szabályai* (The Rules of Style) (Spittal an der Drau: Vagyunk Kiadó, 1950), 13 pp.

13. *A retorika vázlata* (An Outline of Rhetoric) (Spittal an der Drau, Austria: Vagyunk Kiadó, 1950), 10 pp.

14. *A poetika — költészettan — elemei* (The Elements of Poetics) (Spittal an der Drau, Austria: Vagyunk Kiadó, 1950), 23 pp.

15. *Útmutató a magyar művelődés történelmi tanulmányozásához* (Guide to the Historical Study of Hungarian Culture) (Cleveland, Ohio: Vagyunk Kiadó, 1963), 142 pp.

16. *Készülés a küldetésre. A magyar történet. I. rész. Kr. e. 209-től Kr. u. 1038-ig* (Preparation for the Mission. Hungarian History. Part I. From 209 B.C. to 1038 A.D.) (Cleveland, Ohio: Vagyunk Kiadó, 1967), 25 pp.

17. *A küldetés vállalása. A magyar történet. II. rész. 1038-tól 1437-ig* (Acceptance of the Mission. Hungarian History. Part II. From 1038 to 1437) (Vagyunk, 1968), 25 pp.

18. *Helytállás. A magyar történet. III. rész. 1437-től 1699-ig* (Standing Firm. Hungarian History. Part III. From 1437 to 1699) (Vagyunk, 1968), 27 pl .

19. *Küzdelem a szabadságért. A magyar történet IV. rész. 1699-től 1956-ig* (Struggle for Freedom. Hungarian History, Part IV. From 1699 to 1956) (Cleveland, Ohio: Vagyunk Kiadó, 1968), 26 pp.

20. *Szent István a magyar nemzeti élet központjában* (Saint Stephen in the Focus of Hungarian Public Life) (Cleveland, Ohio: Árpád Könyvkiadó Vállalat, 1970), 64 pp.

21. *Küldetés. A magyarság története* (Mission. History of the Hungarian People), 2d ed. (Cleveland, Ohio: Kárpát Publishing Company, 1973; reprinted 1978), 656 pp. with 75 illustrations and 25 maps.

22. *Magyar nyelv és irodalom 1825-ig* (Hungarian Language and Literature to 1825) (Cleveland, Ohio: Kárpát Publishing Company, 1975), 442 pp. with 55 illustrations.

23. *Magyar nyelv és irodalom 1825-től 1925-ig. I. rész. Hagyományok* (Hungarian Language and Literature from 1825 to 1925. Part I. Traditions) (Cleveland, Ohio: Kárpát Publishing Company, 1977), 512 pp. with 33 illustrations.

24. *Faith and Fate. A Short Cultural History of the Hungarian People through a Millennium*, with Lél F. Somogyi (Cleveland, Ohio: Kárpát Publishing Company, 1977), 208 pp. with 34 illustrations and 11 maps.

25. *Az Árpád Akadémia tagjainak tevékenysége.* (Activity of the Members of the Árpád Academy), ed. and comp. Ferenc Somogyi (Cleveland, Ohio: Árpád Akadémia, 1982), xxxviii, 404 pp.

26. *A Magyar Társaság három évtizedének vázlatos története* (The Outline History of Three Decades of the Hungarian Association) (Cleveland, Ohio: Magyar Társaság, 1983), 96 pp.

27. *Hungarian Historical Calendar 1984* (Cleveland, Ohio: St. Margaret Hungarian Federal Credit Union, 1984), 12 pp.

II. EDITORIAL WORK:

28. *A pécsi m. kir. Erzsébet tudományegyetem jogtörténeti szemináriumának kiadványai* (Publications of the Legal History Seminar of the Hung. Roy. Elizabeth University of Pécs) (Pécs: Dunántúl Pécsi Egyetemi Könyvkiadó és Nyomda Rt.) vol. I (1933), 20 pp., vol. II (1936), 36 pp.

29. *Pécsi Jogász* (Jurist of Pécs) (Pécs: Haladás Nyomda Rt., 1935-1938), vols. I-IV, pp. 64, 116, 148, 80.

30. *Ifjúságunk időszerű sorskérdései. Dél ifjúságának 1937. december 1-én, 2-án, és 3-án tartott ankétján elhangzott bevezető előadások és felszólalások* (Timely Vital Questions of Our Youth. Introductory Lectures and Remarks at the Youth Conference of the Southern Region Held on December 1st, 2d, and 3d, 1937), 2d ed. (Pécs: Nemzetvédő Sorozat, 1939), 64 pp.

31. *A magyar szociálpolitika feladatai. A vármegyei szociális tanácsadók és közjóléti előadók pécsi országos értekezletén elhangzott előadások* (The Tasks of Hungarian Social Welfare Policy. Presentations at the National Conference of County Social Welfare Counselors and Referees at Pécs), eds. Lajos Esztergár and Ferenc Somogyi, 2 parts (Pécs: Kultúra Könyvnyomdai Műintézet, 1940), vi, 744 pp.

32. *Nép- és családvédelem az 1940-1942. évben* (Folk and Family Protection in the Years 1940-1942) (Budapest: Magyar Királyi Állami Nyomda, 1943), 290 pp.

33. *A legszebb magyar költemények* (The Most Beautiful Hungarian Poems). I. rész: *Haza, otthon, család* (Part I: Motherland, Home, Family) (Spittal and der Drau, Austria: Vagyunk Kiadó, 1950), 19 pp; II. rész: *Küzdelem, bujdosás, remény* (Part II: Struggle, Exile, Hope) (Spittal an der Drau, Austria: Vagyunk Kiadó, 1950), 15 pp; III. rész: *Hit, szeretet, elszántság* (Part III: Faith, Love, Determination) (Cleveland, Ohio: Vagyunk Kiadó, 1953), 18 pp.

34. *Vagyunk. A külföldi magyarok ausztriai közlönye* (We Exist. Journal of Emigrant Hungarians in Austria) (Kellerberg; later Spittal an der Drau, Austria: Vagyunk Kiadó, 1948-50), vols. I-III, nos. 1-54, pp. 150, 342, 248; (Cleveland, Ohio: Vagyunk Kiadó, 1950-1956), vols. IV-IX, nos. 55-118, pp. 222, 174, 226, 108, 142, 96. Up to October 5, 1950, this journal was published twice a month in Kellerberg, and then at Spittal an der Drau, Austria; starting with December 25, 1950 it was published once a month in Cleveland, Ohio, with the altered subtitle: *Szociális és kulturális magyar szemle* (Social and Cultural Hungarian Review).

35. *A II-XXVI. Magyar Találkozó krónikája* (Proceedings of the 2d to 26th Hungarian Congress), eds. Ferenc Somogyi and János Nádas, 23 vols. (Cleveland: Árpád Könyvkiadó, 1966-1987), vols. II-III, IV-V, and VI-XXVI, 228, 279, 200, 207, 274, 309, 248, 256, 328, 222, 254, 336, 296, 295, 296, 288, 320, 240, 240, 352, 256, 352, 352, 352, 320. Vols. II-III and IV-V were published as joint volumes; VI to XXVI were published individually. Vol I of the series was edited by Béla Béldy, and published in Buenos Aires, Argentina, by Editorial Pannonia, 1962.

36. *Emlékkönyv. A clevelandi magyar nyelvoktatás, 1958-1978* (Memorial Album. Hungarian Language Instruction in Cleveland, 1958-1978) (Cleveland, Ohio: Hungarian School Care Club, 1978), 56 pp.

37. *Magyar földrajz* (Hungarian Geography), by Pál Bolváry and Ernő Kálnoky; eds. Gábor Papp and Ferenc Somogyi (Cleveland, Ohio: A Magyar Iskola kiadása, 1979), 80 pp.

III. SCHOLARLY STUDIES, ESSAYS, AND RESEARCH REPORTS:

38. *"A zsidóság az ezeréves magyar jogban"* (Jews in Hungary's Millennial Law), in *Turul Évkönyv* (Turul Yearbook) (Pécs: Haladás Nyomda Rt., 1936), pp. 49-80.

39. *"Levéltári kutatásomról"* (About My Archival Research), in *Pécsi Jogász* (Jurist of Pécs), II (Pécs, 1936), pp. 79-80.

40. *"A jogtörténeti vizsgálódások végső, jogászi célja"* (The Final Juristic Goal of Research in Legal History), in *Pécsi Jogász*. II (1936), pp. 107-109.

41. *"Ifjúságunk a világnézetek harcában"* (Our Youth in the Midst of Ideological Conflicts), in *Pécsi Jogász*, III (1937), pp. 21-33.

42. *"Jogtörténet (szemináriumi élet)"* (Legal History. Functioning of a Seminar), in *Pécsi Jogász*, III (1937), pp. 89-91.

43. "Az örökösödési szerződés szabályai 1351-től 1526-ig oklevelek alapján" (Rules of Contracts of Inheritance from 1351 to 1526, on the Basis of Documents), in *Pécsi Jogász*, III (1937), pp. 97-103.

44. "Családiság és ősiség" (Patrimony and Entailment), in *Pécsi Jogász*, IV (1938), pp. 29-72.

45. "A dunántúli földbirtokforgalom szociális kihatásai" (The Social Implications of the Sale of Estates in Transdanubia), in *A mai magyar szociálpolitika* (Hungarian Social Welfare Policy Today) (Budapest: A Korszerű Közszolgálat Útja, 1939), pp. 622-629.

46. "Társadalmi kérdések keletkezése és megoldása elvi alapon" (The Roots and Solutions of Social Problems on the Basis of Principles), in *A magyar szociálpolitika feladatai* (The Tasks of Hungarian Social Welfare Policy), eds. Lajos Esztergár and Ferenc Somogyi (Pécs: Kultúra Könyvnyomdai Műintézet, 1940), pp. 24-33.

47. "Intézményes nép- és családvédelem" (Institutional Folk and Family Protection), in *Nép- és Családvédelem* (Folk and Family Protection), I (Budapest, 1941), pp. 2-10. Hereafter cited as *NCsV*.

48. "A nép- és családvédelem, mint különleges magyar hivatás" (Folk and Family Protection as a Unique Hungarian Mission), in *NCsV*, I (1941), pp. 121-114.

49. "Ungarische Armen- and Volksfürsorge" (Hungarian Poor Relief and Folk Protection), in *Donaueuropa* (Danubian Europe), I (Budapest, 1941), pp. 387-394.

50. "Szociális jogszabályaink ősi nyomain" (In the Ancient Footsteps of Our Social Welfare Laws), in *NCsV*, II (1942), pp. 202-206.

51. "Az aranybulla elveinek társadalmi érvényesülése" (The Social Impact of the Principles of the Hungarian Golden Bull), in *NCsV*, II (1942), pp. 361-367.

52. "Nemességünk és a jobbágyság szabad költözködése" (Our Nobility and the Freedom of Movement of the Serfs), in *NCsV*, II (1942), pp. 449-456.

53. "Jobbágyvédelmi törvények a mohácsi vész után" (Serf Protection Laws after the Battle of Mohács), in *NCsV*, III (1943), pp. 162-169.

54. "Örökös jobbágyság és magyarságvédelem" (Perpetual Serfdom and the Protection of the Hungarian People), in *NCsV*, III (1943), pp. 365-370, and 405-409.

55. "A magyar szociálpolitika története" (The History of Hungarian Social Welfare Policy), in *Szociális Magyarország* (Social Hungary), ed. Ede v. Faragó (Budapest: Athenaeum, 1943), pp. 15-46.

56. "Szervezés, igazgatás" (Organization, Administration), in *Nép- és Családvédelem az 1940-1942. évben* (Folk and Family Protection in the Years 1940-1942), ed. Ferenc Somogyi (Budapest: Magyar Királyi Állami Nyomda, 1943), pp. 32-47.

57. "Magyar szociálpolitikai törvényalkotások" (Hungarian Social Welfare Legislation), in *Szociális Magyarország*, pp. 47-70.

58. "Ipari munkásvédelem Trianon előtt" (Protection of Industrial Workers before Trianon), in *NCsV*, IV (1944), pp. 1-4.

59. "Demokrácia" (Democracy), in *Fáklya* (Torch) (Kellerberg, Austria), II/6-12 (February 17-March 31, and April 14, 1946), 8 pp.

60. "A magyar parasztság eredete és fejlődése" (The Origin and Development of the Hungarian Peasantry), in *Fáklya*, II/43 (October 20, 1946), pp. 4-6.

60a. "A szociális gondolat érvényesülése" (The Success of the Social Idea), in *Magyar Harangok, Hontalan magyarok lapja* (Hungarian Bells, Magazine of Hungarian Emigrants) (Rome, Milan, Geneva), II/2 (May 1947), pp. 14-16.

61. "A magyar századok évszámokban" (Hungarian Centuries in Yearly Chronology), *Vagyunk* (We Exist) (Cleveland), V (1952), pp. 105-109, 121; and VI (1953), pp. 46-47, 59-61.

62. "Magyar urbárium-könyv 1770-ből" (Hungarian

Socage Book from the Year 1770), in *Vagyunk*, VII (1954), pp. 85-106.

63. "A kereszténység pajzsa. I. Az Árpádházi királyok. II. A vegyes házbeli királyok" (The Shield of Christianity. I. Kings of the Árpád Dynasty. II. Kings of Mixed Dynasties), in *Históriás Kalendárium* (Historical Calendar) (Cleveland, Ohio: Katolikus Magyarok Vasárnapja, 1952), pp. 9-27.

64. "Szociális törekvések és eredmények Trianon után" (Social Aspirations and Accomplishments after Trianon), in *Históriás Kalendárium* (1953), pp. 33-48; reprinted in *Vagyunk*, IX (1956), pp. 97-112.

65. "A magyar Szent Korona" (Holy Crown of Hungary), in *Krónika, A Kanadai Magyar Kultúrközpont Lapja* (Chronicle. Publication of the Canadian Hungarian Cultural Centre) (Toronto), III/12 (December 1977), pp. 4-7.

66. "A magyar Kováts Mihály amerikai érdemei" (The American Merits of the Hungarian Michael Kováts), in *Fabriczy Kováts Mihály almanach* (Almanach of Michael Kováts de Fabriczy), ed. Géza Szentmiklósy Éles (Cleveland, Ohio: A Clevelandi Kováts Emlékbizottság Kiadása, 1979), pp. 21-25.

67. "Nyelvtani áttekintés (Grammatical Review), in *Szép magyar világ* (Beautiful Hungarian World), ed. Jenő Pohárnok, 2d ed. (Cleveland, Ohio: Árpád Könyvkiadó Vállalat, 1981), pp. 209-232.

68. "The Hungarian Holy Crown," in *The Last Battle for Saint Stephen's Crown*, ed. Attila Simontsits (Toronto: Weller Publishing Co., 1983), pp. 5-11.

69. "A magyarság kulturális szerepe az emigrációban" (The Cultural Role of Hungarians in Emigration), in *Az I. Magyar Találkozó Krónikája* (Proceeding of the First Hungarian Congress), ed. Béla Béldy (Buenos Aires, Argentina: Editorial Pannonia, 1962), pp. 117-130.

70. "Magyar szemlélet Zrínyi példája nyomán" (Hungarian Ideology on the Basis of Zrínyi's View), in *A IV-V. Magyar Találkozó Krónikája* (Proceedings of the Fourth and Fifth Hungarian Congresses), eds. Ferenc Somogyi and

János Nádas (Cleveland: Árpád Könyvkiadó Vállalat, 1966),
pp. 12-23. Hereafter cited as *MTK*.

71. "Megemlékezés a pécsi egyetem alapításának hat-
századik és a pozsonyi egyetem megnyitásának ötszázadik
évfordulójáról" (Commemoration of the 600th Anniversary
of the Foundation of the University of Pécs, and of the 500th
Anniversary of the Opening of the University of Pozsony),
in *MTK*, VII (1968), pp. 85-93.

72. "Szent István a magyar nemzeti élet központjában"
(Saint Stephen in the Focus of Hungarian Public Life), in
MTK, IX (1970), pp. 80-109.

73. "A clevelandi Magyar Társaság húszéves működése"
(Twenty Years of Activity by the Hungarian Association of
Cleveland), in *MTK*, XII (1973), pp. 167-172.

74. "Az akadémia eszméjének magyar megvalósulása"
(The Realization of the Idea of an Academy in Hungary),
in *MTK*, XV (1976), pp. 151-162.

75. "Rákóczi születésének 300. évfordulója" (300th Anniversary of Rákóczi's Birth), in *MTK*, XV (1976), pp.
293-298.

76. "Megemlékezés az Egyesült Államok fennállásának
200. évfordulójáról" (Commemorating the 200th Anniversary of the Foundation of the United States), in *MTK*, XVI
(1977), pp. 161-165.

77. "Nagy volt. Megemlékezés Nagy Lajos király halálának 600. évfordulójáról" (He Was Great Indeed. Commemorating the 600th Anniversary of the Death of King Louis
the Great), in *MTK*, XXI (1982), pp. 210-222.

78. "Hogyan lett Magyarország a szentek országa?" (How
did Hungary Become the Land of Saints?), in *MTK*, XXII
(1983), pp. 200-210.

79. "A nemzetiségi törvény és a kisebbségi kérdés"
(Hungary's Nationality Law and the Minority Question),
in *MTK*, XXIII (1984), pp. 32-40.

80. "The Medieval University of Pécs," in *Louis the Great,
King of Hungary and Poland*, eds. S. B. Várdy, G.

Grosschmid, and L. S. Domonkos (New York: East European Monographs, Columbia University Press, 1986), pp. 221-236. Translated from Hungarian by Lél F. Somogyi.

81. "The Constitutional Guarantee of 1351: The Decree of Louis the Great," in *Louis the Great, King of Hungary and Poland*, pp. 429-451. Translated from Hungarian by Lél F. Somogyi.

82. "King Louis's *Decretum unicum*, Prepared in the Year 1351," in *Louis the Great, King of Hungary and Poland*, pp. 453-467. Translated from Latin by Ferenc Somogyi and Lél F. Somogyi.

IV. NEWSPAPER AND PERIODICAL ARTICLES:

83. "Nyugat-Magyarország Ausztriában" (Western Hungary in Austria), in *Vasvármegye* (Vas County) (Szombathely, February 9, 1932).

84. "Viribus unitis" (With United Power), in *Pécsi Napló* (Pécs Diary) (Pécs, February 10, 1932), p. 3.

85. "Újabb jogászi szempontok" (Recent Legal Views), in *Nemzetvédő* (Defender of the Nation) (Pécs, November 1933), pp. 7-8.

86. "Jogi oktatás. Jogászi alap- és szakműveltség" (Legal Education. Basic and Specialized Training), in *Hajnal* (Dawn) (Pécs, March 1934), pp. 4-6; and (April 1934), pp. 4-6.

87. "A 'Pécsi Széchenyi Szövetség' faluszemináriumának munkamódszere és eddigi eredményei" (The Work Methods and Achievements of the Seminar on Village Research of the Széchenyi Federation of Pécs), in *Széchenyista Ifjúság* (Széchenyi's Young Followers), no. 2 (Budapest, 1935), pp. 3-5.

88. "A román falumunka kiállítása" (Exhibition of Romanian Village Research), in *Széchenyista Ifjúság*, nos. 3-4 (1935), p. 16.

89. "A faluszeminárium tevékenysége" (The Activities

of the Seminar on Village Research), in *Széchenyista Ifjúság*, nos. 9-10 (1936), pp. 6-7.

90. "Gazdaöntudat és proletárlelkület" (Small Farmers' Pride and Proletarian Psychology), in *Széchenyista Ifjúság*, no. 8 (1937), pp. 6-7.

91. "Új szavak és fogalmak a falu körül" (New Words and Definitions about the Village), in *Széchenyista Ifjúság*, no. 9 (1937), pp. 12-13.

92. "A pécsi példa" (The Example of Pécs), in *Széchenyista Ifjúság*, no. 10 (1937), pp. 12-13.

93. "Az eredményes falumunka első feltétele" (The Primary Condition of Successful Village Research), in *Széchenyista Ifjúság*, no. 2 (1938), pp. 2-3.

94. "A bakonyi falunap" (Village Day of Bakony), in *Széchenyista Ifjúság*, nos. 5-6 (1938), pp. 29-30.

95. "A magyar föld sorsa és fajtánk jövője" (The Fate of the Hungarian Village and Future of Our Nationality), in *Széchenyista Ifjúság*, nos. 9-10 (1938), pp. 4-5.

96. "Jogászi feladatok" (Legal Tasks), in *Pécsi Jogász*, I (1935), pp. 5-8.

97. "A sterilizációról" (About Sterilization), in *Pécsi Jogász*, I (1935), pp. 9-12.

98. "Fonákságok" (Absurdities), in *Pécsi Jogász*, II (1936), pp. 11-12.

99. "Párviadal és lovagias elégtétel" (Duelling and Chivalrious Reparations), in *Pécsi Jogász*, III (1937), pp. 84-85.

100. "Ifjúsági ankét" (Youth Conference), in *Pécsi Jogász*, III (1937), p. 129.

101. "Közelebb az élethez" (Closer to Life), in *Pécsi Jogász*, IV (1938), pp. 1-2.

102. "Falumunka" (Village Research), in *Turul Évkönyv* (Turul Yearbook) (Pécs: Haladás Nyomda, 1936), pp. 45-48.

103. "A pécsi egyetem és a dunántúli középosztály" (The University of Pécs and the Transdanubian Middle Class), in *Fáklya* (Torch), II/11 (Budapest, 1936), pp. 31-32.

104. "A falumunka jelentőségéről" (On the Significance of Village Research), in *Fáklya*, II/12 (1936), pp. 25-26.

105. "A pécsi példa" (The Example of Pécs), in *Fáklya*, III/1 (1937), pp. 25-26.

106. "A jogi oktatás reformjáról" (On the Reform of Legal Education), in *Fáklya*, III/2-3 (1937), pp. 47-48.

107. "Sváb Törökország — Magyarországon" (Swabian Turkey in Hungary), in *Fáklya*, III (1937), pp. 84-85.

108. "Az ifjúság és a sajtó" (The Youth and the Press), in *Fáklya*, IV/5-6 (1938), pp. 32-33.

109. "Hídverés. Középosztályunk és a magyar falu propagálása" (Bridge Building. Our Middle Class and the Propagation of the Hungarian Village), in *Fáklya*, IV/9 (1938), pp. 18-19.

110. "Fenn és lenn" (Up and Down), in *Korunk Szava*, VI (Voice of Our Age) (1936), p. 494.

111. "A szekták vidékén" (In the Region of the Sects), in *Pécsi Katolikus Tudósító* (Catholic Informer of Pécs), XV (Pécs, 1937), pp. 159-160.

112. "Falusi népünk vallásossága" (Religiosity of Our Rural Population), in *Pécsi Katolikus Tudósító*, XV (1937), p. 185.

113. "Destrukció" (Destruction), in *Pécsi Katolikus Tudósító*, XVI (1938), p. 6.

114. "És az Ige testté lőn" (And the Word Became a Body), in *Pécsi Katolikus Tudósító*, XVII (1939), pp. 2-3.

115. "Beteg-e a magyar falu?" (Is the Hungarian Village Ill?), in *Pécsi Katolikus Tudósító*, XVII (1939), pp. 22-23.

116. "A társadalmi akarat megtestesítése" (The Embodiment of the Social Will), in *Szociális Gondozás* (Social Care), IV (Pécs, 1938), pp. 85-91.

117. "A falu meg a város" (The Village and the City), in *Kisgazdaság* (Small Farmstead), no. 17 (Pécs, 1939), pp. 1-3.

118. "A magyar szociálpolitika főbb irányai" (The Main Directions of Hungarian Social Welfare Policy), in *A magyar szociálpolitika feladatai*, (Pécs, 1940), pp. 728-731.

119. "Szociálpolitikai szemle" (Review of Social Politics), in *Az Ország Útja* (The Country's Highway), IV (Budapest, 1940), pp. 22-25, 55-57, 106-111, 137-141, 174-178, 237-242, 350-354, 392-395, 444-449; and V (1941), pp. 17-20, 53-56, 150-153, 184-186, 211-216, 244-248, 277-281, 313-317, 342-344, 367-370.

120. "Egyetemi szociális képzés" (University-Level Social Education), in *Az Ország Útja*, IV (1940), pp. 243-246.

121. "Vidéki közigazgatásunk csak szociális közigazgatás lehet" (Our Local Administration Can Only Be Social Administration), in *Egyedül Vagyunk* (We Are all Alone), III/2 (Budapest, 1940), pp. 27-28.

122. "Az Országos Nép- és Családvédelmi Alap létesítésének előzményei, szervezete, és működése" (Antecedents, Organization, and Functioning of the National Foundation for Folk and Family Protection), in *Munkaügyi Szemle* (Review of Labor Affairs), XV (Budapest, 1941), pp. 169-175.

123. "Szociális védelem" (Social Protection), in *Sorsunk* (Our Fate), II (Pécs, 1942), pp. 374-378.

124. "Egyetemeink a szociális képzésről" (Our Universities on Social Welfare Education), in *NCsV*, II (1942), pp. 241-246.

125. "Alföldi Dezső előadása" (Dezső Alföldi's Lecture), in *NCsV*, II (1942), pp. 308-309.

126. "Társadalmi munkaközösségek" (Social Working Teams), in *NCsV*, II (1942), 308-309.

127. "Vándorülés Pécsett" (Regional Conference at Pécs), in *NCsV*, III (1943), pp. 180-181.

128. "Szociális munka és hivatás" (Social Work and Calling), in *Szociális Értesítő* (Social Bulletin), III (Pécs, 1944), pp. 1-2.

129. "Falumunka" (Village Research), in *Nemzetvédő* (October, 1935), p. 4.

130. "Egészségügy, étkezés, ruházkodás, lakás falun" (Hygiene, Eating Habits, Clothing, Housing in the Village), in *Nemzetvédő* (November 1935), p. 5.

131. "A falu társadalmi tagozódása" (Social Stratification in the Village) in *Nemzetvédő* (December 1935), p. 7.

132. "Kereskedelem, ipar, és hitelügy falun" (Commerce, Industry, and Credit in the Village), in *Nemzetvédő* (February 1936), p. 7.

133. "Egységet!" (Let's Have Unity!), in *Nemzetvédő* (April 1936), pp. 2-3.

134. "Elnémult harangok" (The Silenced Bells), in *Nemzetvédő* (April 1936), pp. 4-5.

135. "A megoldatlan zsidókérdés a magyar társadalom pusztulása" (The Unsolved Jewish Question Is a Crisis Point in Hungarian Society), in *Nemzetvédő* (November 1936), pp. 3-4.

136. "A hazai német kisebbségek problémáinak margójára" (Concerning the Problems of Hungary's German Minority), in *Nemzetvédő* (December 1936), pp. 3-4.

137. "A kisebbségi kérdés magyar nemzeti szempontból" (The Minority Question from the Vantage Point of Hungarian National Interests), in *Nemzetvédő* (March 1937), pp. 1-2.

138. "Mi pogányok?" (Are We Pagans?), in *Nemzetvédő* (August 1937), p. 6.

139. "A tettek ünnepe" (The Feast of Actions), in *Nemzetvédő* (September 1937), p. 1.

140. "Utat a magyar őserőnek!" (Give Way to Hungarian Talent!), in *Nemzetvédő* (September 1937), pp. 1-2.

141. "Hát ez mi? Osztályszelekció?" (What is this? Class Distinction?), in *Nemzetvédő* (September 1937), p. 2.

142. "A 'Viharsarok' földjén, Magyarország felfedezőinek nyomában" (On the Lands of the 'Stormy Corner' in the Footsteps of Hungary's Explorers), in *Nemzetvédő* (September 1937), p. 4.

143. "Adjon Isten!" (May God Grant it!) in *Nemzetvédő* (January 1938), p. 3.

144. "Okuljunk! Az ifjúsági ankét után" (Let Us Learn! In the Wake of the Youth Conference), in *Nemzetvédő* (January 1938), p. 8.

145. "Csak percek és pillanatok" (Only Minutes and Seconds), in *Nemzetvédő* (April 1938), pp. 3-4.

146. "Munkára ismét!" (To Work Once More!), in *Nemzetvédő* (September 1938), pp. 1-2.

147. "Széteső társadalom — egységes világnézet" (Disintegrating Society — Unified Ideology), in *Nemzetvédő* (December 1938), pp. 1-2.

148. "A pécsi kerület bajtársi munkája" (Fraternal Work in the District of Pécs), in *Nemzetvédő* (January 1939), pp. 9-12.

149. "Falukutatás Baranyában" (Village Research in the County of Baranya), in *Dunántúl* (Transdanubia) (Pécs, September 11, 1935), p. 5.

150. "A falumunka lehetőségei Baranyában" (Possibilities of Village Research in Baranya), in *Dunántúl* (October 20, 1935), p. 6.

151. "Küzdelem az elhagyott népért" (Struggle for the Abandoned Population), in *Dunántúl* (July 10, 1936), p. 4.

152. "A belügyi tárca költségvetéséről" (On the Budget of the Ministry of Interior), in *Dunántúl* (November 19, 1939), p. 4.

153. "Szerzetesi alázattal tekintsük szent hivatásunkat" (Let's View Our Sacred Mission with Monastic Humility), in *Dunántúl* (May 11, 1943), p. 5.

154. "Sehol a világon" (Nowhere in the World), in *Nemzetvédő* (January 1938), p. 8; reprinted in *Bajtárs* (Comrade) (Pécs, January 10, 1938), p. 6.

155. "Keresztény vallás és nacionalizmus" (Christianity and Nationalism), in *Bajtárs* (January 15, 1938), p. 1.

156. "Ezerarcú társadalmunk egysége" (The Unity of Our Multifaceted Society), in *Bajtárs* (December 1938), p. 2.

157. "Magyarnak a magyar földet!" (Hungarian Lands for Hungarians), in *Bajtárs* (January 1939), pp. 1-2.

158. "Új honfoglalás" (New Land Conquest), in *Baranya* (Pécs, December 24, 1938), p. 3.

159. "Megindul a munka" (The Work Begins), in *Baranya* (April 8, 1939), pp. 1-2.

160. "Turáni átok?" (The Curse of Turan?), in *Turul Követtábori Újság* (Turul Camp News) (Szeged, September 10, 1938), p. 2.

161. "A földbirtokreformról" (About Land Reform), in *Pécsi Napló* (Pécs Diary) (October 31, 1939), p. 4; (November 3, 1939), p. 5; and (November 4, 1939), p. 5.

162. "Embert a gátra!" (Men to the Dikes!), in *Pécsi Napló* (March 6, 1940), p. 6.

163. "Mire tanít március 15?" (What Does March 15th Teach Us?), in *Pécsi Napló* (March 19, 1940), pp. 4-5.

164. "A földbirtokreform és a felsőház" (Land Reform and the Upper House), in *Nemzetőr* (National Guardian) (Pécs, November 27, 1939), p. 3.

165. "Tandíj és tehetség" (Tuition and Talent), in *Nemzetőr* (April 8, 1940), p. 3.

166. "Szavak és tettek" (Words and Deeds), in *Pest* (Budapest, July 5, 1940), p. 7.

167. "A közigazgatás és a társadalom" (Public Administration and Society), in *Magyarország* (Hungary) (Budapest, March 20, 1940), p. 5.

168. "A családvédelem anyagi eszközei" (The Financial Resources of Family Protection), in *Kis Újság* (Little News) (Budapest, July 7, 1940), p. 7.

169. "Bajtársi szolgálat" (Fraternal Service), in *Nemzeti Újság* (National News) (Budapest, May 10, 1942), p. 6.

170. "Szociális képzés az egyetemeken" (Social Education

at the Universities), in *Függetlenség* (Independence) (Budapest, July 12, 1942), p. 13.

171. "Pécstől Szentesig" (From Pécs to Szentes), in *Szentesi Napló* (Szentes Diary) (Szentes, August 2, 1942), p. 3.

172. "Országépítő első szent királyunk emlékének időszerűsége" (The Timeliness of the Memory of Our First Saintly King), in *Magyar Út* (Hungarian Path), II/25 (Kellerberg, Austria, 1947), pp. 2-5.

173. "Szociális" (Social), in *Fáklya* (Torch), II/11 (Kellerberg, Austria, March 24, 1946), p. 6.

174. "Szociális szellemű életünk új záloga" (The New Pledge of Our Social Life), *Fáklya*, II/13 (April 7, 1946), pp. 3-4.

175. "Őszintén" (Frankly), in *Fáklya*, II/13 (April 7, 1946), p. 5.

176. "Szálljunk magunkba!" (Let Us Examine Ourselves!), in *Fáklya*, II/14 (April 14, 1946), p. 5.

177. "Kezdjük magunkon!" (Let Us Begin with Ourselves!), in *Fáklya*, II/18 (May 5, 1946), pp. 3-4.

178. "Táborunk szociográfiája" (The Sociography of Our Camp), in *Fáklya*, II/51-52 (December 25, 1946), pp. 8-9.

179. "Osztályharc és kereszténység" (Class Struggle and Christianity), in *Fáklya*, III/25 (July 6, 1947), pp. 8-9.

180. "Politika és társadalomtan" (Politics and Sociology), in *Fáklya*, III/26 (July 13, 1947), pp. 9-12.

181. "A konzervatív Egyház haladó szelleme" (The Progressive Spirit of the Conservative Church), in *Fáklya*, III/29 (August 24, 1947), pp. 5-9.

182. "Számkivetésünk igazi értelme" (The True Meaning of Our Exile), in *Fáklya*, III/33-34 (September 21, 1947), pp. 6-9.

183. "Szétszórtan is" (Even in the Diaspora), in *Vagyunk* (We Exist), I (Kellerberg, Austria, 1948), pp. 1-2.

184. "Szent István öröksége" (Saint Stephen's Heritage), in *Vagyunk*, I (1948), p. 1.

185. "Veni, Sancte" (Come, Holy Spirit), in *Vagyunk*, I (1948), p. 33.

186. "Vigyázzunk!" (Let's Watch Out!), in *Vagyunk*, I (1948), p. 47.

187. "Demokratikus és szociális Magyarország" (Democratic and Social Hungary), in *Vagyunk*, I (1948), pp. 133-137.

188. "A jogalap tisztázása" (Clarification of the Legal Foundations), in *Vagyunk*, II (1949), pp. 27-28, 59-62.

189. "Régi jog és új kötelesség" (Old Laws and New Obligations), in *Vagyunk*, II (1949), p. 165.

190. "Fürtszedés" (Gleanings), in *Vagyunk*, II (1949), p. 179.

191. "Petőfi Sándor" (Sándor Petőfi), in *Vagyunk*, II (1949), II, p. 210.

192. "Küldetésünk" (Our Mission), in *Vagyunk*, II (1949), p. 223.

193. "Nincs kibúvó!" (There is No Excuse!), in *Vagyunk*, II (1949), p. 237.

194. "A szeretet" (Love), in *Vagyunk*, II (1949), p. 301.

195. "Trianon. Justice for Hungary," in *Vagyunk*, III (1950), pp. 121-123.

196. "Szent László király" (King Saint Ladislas), in *Vagyunk*, III (1950), pp. 133-135.

197. "Évforduló" (Anniversary), in *Vagyunk*, III (1950), p. 167.

198. "És leszünk is!" (And We Shall Survive!), in *Vagyunk*, III (1950), p. 199.

199. "Mindenütt magyarok" (Hungarians Everywhere), in *Vagyunk*, III (1950), pp. 223-225.

200. "Tíz éve" (Ten Years Ago), in *Vagyunk*, III (1950), pp. 239-240.

201. "Töretlenül" (Unbroken), in *Vagyunk*, IV (1951), p. 1.

202. "A végeken" (On the Frontiers), in *Vagyunk*, IV (1951), p. 5.

203. "Néhány szó a politikáról" (Some Words About Politics), in *Vagyunk*, IV (1951), pp. 43-44.

204. "Verhovay szellemében" (In the Spirit of Verhovay), in *Vagyunk*, IV (1951), pp. 61-62.

205. "A szociális gondolat érvényesülése" (The Triumph of the Social Idea), in *Vagyunk*, IV (1951), pp. 69-70.

206. "A hősök napján" (On Memorial Day), in *Vagyunk*, IV (1951), p. 74.

207. "A szociális Magyarország aranybullája" (The Golden Bull of Social Hungary), in *Vagyunk*, IV (1951), pp. 85-87.

208. "Nincs alku" (There is No Bargaining), in *Vagyunk*, IV (1951), pp. 97-98.

209. "A legnépszerűbb új amerikás magyar Clevelandben" (The Most Popular New American Hungarian in Cleveland), in *Vagyunk*, IV (1951), pp. 107-108.

210. "Lesz még egyszer ünnep a világon" (There Will Once More be a Holiday in the World), in *Vagyunk*, IV (1951), pp. 135-136.

211. "Tanuljatok!" (Learn!), in *Vagyunk*, IV (1951), p. 155.

212. "Vigyázzatok!" (Look Out!) in *Vagyunk*, IV (1951), pp. 171-172.

213. "A magyarság első évezrede" (The First Millennium of the Hungarian People), in *Vagyunk*, IV (1951), pp. 192-195; and VIII, pp. 63-66, 115-120.

214. "Vitam et sanguinem" (Our Life and Blood), in *Vagyunk*, IV (1951), pp. 201-202.

215. "Ötéves a 'béke' " (The 'Peace' is Five Years Old), in *Vagyunk*, V (1952), pp. 13-14.

216. "Teleki Pál tanítása" (The Teachings of Paul Teleki), in *Vagyunk*, V (1952), pp. 45-46.

217. "Színvonal és magyarság" (Quality and the Hungarian People), in *Vagyunk*, V (1952), pp. 148-149.

218. "Nyelvünk védelmében" (In Defense of Our Language), in *Vagyunk*, VI (1953), p. 154.

219. "Az aradi tizenhárom emléke" (The Memory of the Thirteen Martyrs of Arad), in *Vagyunk*, VI (1953), pp. 155-156.

220. "Tartsák meg magyarságukat!" (Keep Your Hungarian Heritage!), in *Vagyunk*, VIII (1955), pp. 9-11.

221. "Magyar láng" (Hungarian Flame), in *Vagyunk*, VIII (1955), p. 12.

222. "Hőseinkről" (About Our Heroes), in *Vagyunk*, VIII (1955), pp. 42-44.

223. "Megemlékezés Szent László királyról" (Remembering King Saint Ladislas), in *Vagyunk*, VIII (1955), pp. 53-54.

224. "Bevezetés. Történetírás" (Introduction. Historiography), in *Vagyunk*, VIII (1955), pp. 57-62.

225. "Örökbefogadás formaságok nélkül" (Adoption without Formalities), in *Vagyunk*, VIII (1955), pp. 94-96.

226. "Vörösmarty" (M. Vörösmarty), in *Vagyunk*, VIII (1955), pp. 121-125.

227. "Érdekes" (Interesting), in *Vagyunk*, IX (1956), pp. 24 and 44.

228. "A déli harangszó" (The Angelus), in *Vagyunk*, IX (1956), pp. 69-75.

229. "Boldogasszony Anyánk" (Our Blessed Virgin of Hungary), in *Vagyunk*, IX (1956), pp. 91-93.

230. "A Szent Jobb" (The Holy Right Hand of King Saint Stephen), in *Vagyunk*, IX (1956), p. 96.

231. "Az ipari kultúra fokmérője: a munkás biztosí-

tottsága" (The Measure of Industrial Culture is the Security of the Worker), in *Katolikus Magyarok Vasárnapja* (Catholic Hungarians' Sunday) (Cleveland-Youngstown), 58/3 (January 19, 1951), p. 6. Hereafter, this paper is cited as *KMV*.

232. "Kocsiút - gyalogút" (Highway - Pathway), in *KMV*, 58/5 (February 2, 1951), p. 7.

233. "Szociális Magyarország" (Social Hungary), in *KMV*, 58/20 (May 18, 1951), p. 6.

234. "Ez is hajt, mint az öreg Vissy!" (He Drives Like Old Man Vissy!), in *KMV*, 58/21 (May 25, 1951), p. 7.

235. "Gondoljunk csak Szombathelyre" (Let's Just Think about Szombathely), in *KMV*, 58/24 (June 15, 1951), p. 2.

236. "Kutyafacsarók" (Dog Wringlers), in *KMV*, 58/25 (June 29, 1951), p. 8.

237. "A dobzósok" (Plum Pickers), in *KMV*, 58/28 (July 13, 1951), p. 5.

238. "A kis kévekötőlány" (The Little Sheafbinder Girl), in *KMV*, 58/31 (August 31, 1951), p. 5.

239. "Szent István intelmei és a kisebbségi jog" (Saint Stephen's Admonitions and Minority Rights), in *KMV*, 58/32 (August 10, 1951), p. 6.

240. "Az első koronázás" (The First Coronation), in *KMV*, 58/33 (August 17, 1951), p. 6.

241. "Szent István intelmei" (Saint Stephen's Admonitions), in *KMV*, 58/34 (August 24, 1951), p. 6.

242. "Király a teknő alatt" (King under the Wash Tub), in *KMV*, 59/2 (January 11, 1952), p. 5.

243. "Égi küldött" (Messenger of Heaven), in *KMV*, 59/4 (January 25, 1952), p. 5.

244. "A magyar Szent Korona és annak elmélete" (The Hungarian Holy Crown and Its Doctrine), in *KMV*, 59/33 (August 17, 1952), p. 6.

245. "Legyen szabadság a Duna-Tisza táján" (Let Freedom Reign on the Shores of the Danube and the Tisza), in *KMV*, 60/11 (March 29, 1953), p. 6.

246. "A Szent István Szabadegyetem első féléve" (The First Semester of Saint Stephen Free University), in *KMV*, 60/33 (August 16, 1953), p. 6.

247. "A legnagyobb magyar" (The Greatest Hungarian), in *KMV*, 67/26 (July 21, 1960), p. 5.

248. "Magyar gondolatok július 4-én" (Hungarian Thoughts on the 4th of July), in *KMV*, 91/27 (July 22, 1984), p. 3.

249. "A világosi fegyverletétel" (Capitulation at Világos), in *KMV*, 91/21 (August 26, 1984), p. 6.

250. "Tanúságtétel. Megjelent a XXIII. Krónika" (Testimony. Volume XXIII of the 'Chronicle' has Appeared in Print), in *KMV*, 91/33 (September 2, 1984), p. 2.

251. "El akarták oltani a holdvilágot" (They Wanted to Extinguish the Moonlight), in *Históriás Kalendárium* (Historical Calendar) (Cleveland, Ohio: Katolikus Magyarok Vasárnapja, 1952), pp. 9-17.

252. "A magyar tudományos társaság megszervezése" (Foundation of the Hungarian Scientific Society), in *MTK*, IV-V (1966), pp. 214-215.

253. "Felterjesztés-tervezet VI. Pál pápa őszentségéhez" (Petition Draft to His Holiness, Pope Paul VI), in *MTK*, IX (1970), pp. 110-111.

254. "Lelki és szellemi egység. Megnyitó" (Spiritual and Intellectual Unity. Opening Speech), in *MTK*, XI (1972), pp. 12-14.

255. "A fejlődés folytonossága" (The Continuity of Progress), in *MTK*, XI (1972), pp. 113-114.

256. "Ideológia-mentes állam" (State without Ideology), in *MTK*, XII (1973), pp. 251-252.

257. "Igazunkért" (For Our Truth), in *MTK*, XV (1976), pp. 15-16.

258. "Megoldatlan kérdések, elodázhatatlan feladatok" (Unsolved Questions, Unavoidable Obligations), in *MTK*, XVIII (1979), pp. 105-106.

259. "Nemzeti hagyományaink szellemében és a jövő szolgálatában" (In the Spirit of Our National Heritage, and in the Service of the Future), in *MTK*, XIX (1980), pp. 17-20.

260. "Trianon 60 év után is igazságtalan" (Trianon Is Unjust Even after 60 Years), in *MTK*, XX (1981), pp. 69-73.

261. "Előszó" (Forword), in *MTK*, II-III, pp. 7-8; VI, pp. 7-8; IX, pp. 7-8; XIV, pp. 7-8; XV, pp. 7-8; XXII, pp. 7-8.

262. "Az Árpád-pályázatok eredménye" (Results of the Árpád Competitions), in *MTK*, II-III, pp. 81-83, 171-174; IV-V, pp. 91-93, 202-204; VI, pp. 134-137; VII, pp. 136-138; VIII, pp. 228-230; IX, pp. 246-247; X, pp. 194-196; XI, pp. 195-197; XII, pp. 158-160; XIII, pp. 108-111; XIV, pp. 109-111; XV, pp. 124-126; XVI, pp. 203-206; XVII, pp. 184-188; XVIII, pp. 138-139; XIX, pp. 158-160; XX, pp. 118-120; XXI, pp. 102-103; XXII, pp. 100-103; XXIII, pp. 164-167; XXIV, pp. 142-145; XXV, pp. 71-73; XXVI, pp. 155-156;.

263. "Az Árpád Akadémia működéséről" (About the Activities of the Árpád Academy), in *MTK*, VI, pp. 178-183; VII, pp. 79-83; VIII, pp. 233-238; IX, pp. 254-260; X, pp. 198-205; XI, pp. 199-209; XII, pp. 253-261; XIII, pp. 136-138; XIV, pp. 127-132; XV, pp. 141-148; XVI, pp. 237-245; XVII, pp. 192-202; XVIII, pp. 149-150, 154-164; XIX, pp. 175-187; XX, pp. 129-139; XXI, pp. 116-128; XXIII, pp. 109-121; XXIII, pp. 177-190; XXIV, pp. 187-202; XXV, pp. 165-179; XXVI, pp. 173-185.

264. "Szent István születésének ezredik évfordulója után" (In Wake of the Millennium of the Birth of Saint Stephen), in *Kárpát* (Carpathians), VI/4 (Cleveland, April 1970), pp. 607.

265. "Trianon - Európa tragédiája" (Trianon, the Tragedy of Europe), in *Kárpát*, VII/1 (May 1970-February 1971), pp. 5-6.

266. "A szociális Magyarország aranybullája" (The Golden Bull of Social Hungary), in *Kárpát*, VII/2 (March-May, 1971), pp. 1-2.

267. "Zrínyi küldetése és példája" (Zrínyi's Mission and Example), in *Kárpát*, VII/3 (June-September 1971), pp. 7-10.

268. "Az aranybulla kiadása" (The Issuance of the Golden Bull), in *Kárpát*, VIII/2 (May-December, 1972), pp. 1-5.

269. "A Szent Korona" (The Holy Crown), in *Kárpát*, IX/1 (January-March, 1973), pp. 1-4.

270. "A prímási méltóság" (The Office of the Primate), in *Kárpát*, IX/2 (April-December, 1973), pp. 1-3.

271. "A magyar Szent Korona jelentősége" (The Significance of the Hungarian Holy Crown), in *Az Újság* (News) (Cleveland, May 7, 1970), p. 1; and in *Magyarság* (Pittsburgh, May 8, 1970), p. 5.

272. "Nincs alku. Emlékezzünk Trianonra" (There Is No Deal. Let Us Remember Trianon), in *Az Újság*, 55/23 (June 5, 1975), p. 1.

273. "Függetlenségi nyilatkozat" (Declaration of Independence), in *Az Újság*, 55/27 (July 3, 1975), p. 1.

274. "Nagy-Boldogasszony napján" (On the Day of Our Lady of Hungary), in *Az Újság*, 55/31 (August 14, 1975), p. 1.

275. "Szent István napján" (On the Day of Saint Stephen), in *Az Újság*, 55/32 (August 21, 1975), p. 1.

276. "Tanuljunk!" (Let Us Learn!), in *Az Újság*, 55/34 (September 4, 1975), p. 1.

277. "Az aradi tizenhárom" (The Thirteen Martyrs of Arad), in *Az Újság*, 55/38 (October 2, 1975), p. 1.

278. "Magyar művészek 'Bicentennial' kiállítása" (The 'Bicentennial' Exhibit of Hungarian Artists), in *Az Újság*, 55/44 (October 23, 1975), p. 1.

279. "Borúra derű. A Magyar Tudományos Akadémia megalapítása" (After Rain Comes Shine. The Foundation of the Hungarian Academy of Sciences), in *Az Újság*, 55/42 (October 30, 1975), p. 1.

280. "Magyar Találkozó" (Hungarian Congress), in *Az Újság*, 55/43 (November 6, 1975), p. 1.

281. "Sorskérdések" (Vital Questions), in *Az Újság*, 55/44 (November 13, 1975), p. 1.

282. "Az Árpád-pályázatok" (Árpád Competitions), in *Az Újság*, 55/45 (November 20, 1975), p. 1.

283. "Az Árpád Akadémia" (The Árpád Academy), in *Az Újság*, 55/46 (November 27, 1975), p. 1.

284. "Csoda lesz!" (There Will Be a Miracle!), in *Magyar Újság* (Hungarian News), 66/11 m(Cleveland, March 11, 1976), p. 1.

285. "Rákóczi születésének 300. évfordulója, hazatérésének 70. évfordulója" (300th Anniversary of Rákóczi's Birth, 70th Anniversary of the Repatriation of his Remains), in *Magyar Újság*, 66/13 (March 25, 1976), p. 1.

286. "Április 4. magyar gyásznap" (April 4th, a Hungarian Day of Mourning), in *Magyar Újság*, 66/14 (April 1, 1976), p. 1.

287. "Hősök napján" (On Memorial Day), in *Magyar Újság*, 66/21 (May 27, 1976), p. 1.

288. "Trianon," in *Magyar Újság*, 66/22 (June 5, 1976), p. 1.

289. "Szent László" (Saint Ladislas), in *Magyar Újság*, 66/25 (June 24, 1976), p. 1.

290. "Amerika, 1776-1976," in *Magyar Újság*, 66/26 (July 1, 1976), p. 1.

291. "Szent István ünnepe" (The Feast of Saint Stephen), in *Magyar Újság*, 66/31 (August 19, 1976), p. 1.

292. "Zászlónk" (Our Flag), in *Magyar Újság*, 66/33 (September 2, 1976), p. 1.

293. "Október 6," in *Magyar Újság*, 66/38 (October 6, 1976), p. 1.

294. "Öntudatunk ébrentartása" (Keeping Our Consciousness Alive), in *Magyar Újság*, 66/42 (November 4, 1976), p. 1.

295. "Nem hadizsákmány és nemcsak ereklye" (It's Not

a Booty, and Not Only a Relic), in *Magyar Újság*, 67/12 (March 31, 1977), p. 1.

296. "Hőseinkről (About Our Heroes), in *Magyar Újság*, 67/20 (May 26, 1977), p. 1.

297. "Igazságot!" (Justice!), in *Magyar Újság*, 67/21 (June 2, 1977), p. 1.

298. "Szent László ünnepe" (The Feast of Saint Ladislas), in *Magyar Újság*, 67/24 (June 25, 1977), p. 1.

299. "Két nap emléke" (The Memory of Two Days), in *Magyar Újság*, 67/25 (June 30, 1977), p. 1.

300. "Kövessük Szent István példáját" (Let Us Follow Saint Stephen's Example), in *Magyar Újság*, 67/30 (August 18, 1977), p. 1.

301. "Arad," in *Magyar Újság*, 67/37 (October 6, 1977), p. 1.

302. "1956 október 23 emléke" (The Memory of October 23, 1956), in *Magyar Újság*, 67/39 (October 20, 1977), p. 1.

303. "November elején" (At the Beginning of November), in *Magyar Újság*, 67/41 (November 5, 1977), p. 1.

304. "Nádas János dr. köszöntése" (Salute to Dr. János Nádas), in *Magyar Újság*, 68/5 (February 2, 1978), p. 1.

305. "A magyar április: halálos tavasz" (Hungarian April: A Deadly Spring), in *Magyar Újság*, 68/13 (April 6, 1978), p. 1.

306. "Hőseink" (Our Heroes), in *Magyar Újság*, 68/20 (May 25, 1978), p. 1.

307. "Szent László" (Saint Ladislas), in *Magyar Újság*, 68/25 (June 29, 1978), p. 1.

308. "Két győzelem emléke" (The Memory of Two Victories), in *Magyar Újság*, 68/32 (August 31, 1978), p. 1.

309. "Tetemrehívás október 6-án" (Called to the Ordeal of the Bier on October 6th), in *Magyar Újság*, 68/37 (October 3, 1978), p. 1.

310. "Maradéktalanul" (Entirely), in *Magyar Újság*, 69/3 (January 19, 1979), p. 1.

311. "Mind hősök" (All Are Heroes), in *Magyar Újság*, 69/22 (May 31, 1979), p. 1.

312. "Szent István ünnepe" (The Feast of Saint Stephen), in *Magyar Újság*, 69/30 (August 10, 1979), p. 1.

313. "Mohácstól Mohácsig (From Mohács to Mohács), in *Magyar Újság*, 69/32 (August 30, 1979), p. 1.

314. "A szabadságharc emléke utat mutat" (The Memory of the Fight for Freedom Shows the Way), in *Magyar Újság*, 69/40 (October 25, 1979), p. 1.

315. "A hálaadás ünnepe és a Magyar Találkozó" (Thanksgiving Day and the Hungarian Congress), in *Magyar Újság*, 69/44 (November 22, 1979), p. 1.

316. "December 6-án" (On December 6th), in *Magyar Újság*, 69/46 (December 6, 1979), p. 1.

317. "Faludi Ferenc halálának 200. évfordulója" (The 200th Anniversary of the Death of Ferenc Faludi), in *Magyar Újság*, 69/47 (December 13, 1979), p. 1.

318. "Bethlen Gábor emléke" (The Memory of Gábor Bethlen), in *Magyar Újság*, 69/49 (December 27, 1979), p. 1.

319. "Második 'fekete péntek' " (Second 'Black Friday'), in *Magyar Újság*, 70/3 (January 17, 1980), p. 1.

320. "Szent Benedek születésének 1500. évfordulója" (The 1500th Anniversary of Saint Benedict's Birth), in *Magyar Újság*, 70/7 (February 21, 1980), p. 1.

321. "Emlékezzünk Trianonra" (Let Us Remember Trianon), in *Magyar Újság*, 70/8 (February 29, 1980), p. 1.

322. "Hősi erőfeszítés korszaka kezdődött" (The Age of Heroic Efforts Began), in *Magyar Újság*, 70/9 (March 6, 1980), p. 1.

323. "Mindszenty," in *Magyar Újság*, 70/17 (May 1, 1980), p. 1.

324. "Hősök napján" (On Memorial Day), in *Magyar Újság*, 70/20 (May 29, 1980), p. 1.

325. "Osztatlanul" (Undivided), in *Magyar Újság*, 70/21 (June 5, 1980), p. 1.

326. "Apák napján" (On Fathers' Day), in *Magyar Újság*, 70/22 (June 12, 1980), p. 1.

327. "Magyar maradt" (He Remained Hungarian), in *Magyar Újság*, 70/24 (June 26, 1980), p. 1.

328. "Kosztolányi-est Clevelandben" (Kosztolányi Evening in Cleveland), in *Magyar Újság*, 70/23 (June 19, 1980), p. 1.

329. "Mindszenty bíboros kaliforniai látogatása" (Cardinal Mindszenty's visit to California), in *Magyar Újság*, 70/23 (June 19, 1980), p. 4.

330. "A függetlenség napja" (Independence Day), in *Magyar Újság*, 70/25 (July 3, 1980), p. 1.

331. "Rab nemzetek hetén" (The Week of the Captive Nations), in *Magyar Újság*, 70/27 (July 17, 1980), p. 1.

332. "Szent István születésének éve" (The Year of the Birth of King Saint Stephen), in *Kanadai Magyar Újság* (Canadian Hungarian News) (Winnipeg, Ontario), March 11, 1969; and in *Magyarság* (March 14, 1969), pp. 1-3.

333. "Szent István intelme az emigrációban" (The Admonitions of Saint Stephen for Those in Exile), in *The Chariot*, LXIII/5 (Crawfordsville, Indiana, 1970), appendix, p. 1.

334. "A függetlenség ünnepe" (Independence Day), in *Detroiti Újság* (Detroit News), 59/27 (July 3, 1969), p. 1.

335. "Néhány kérdés tisztázása. Mindszenty védelmében" (Clarification of a Few Questions in Defense of Mindszenty), in *Detroiti Újság*, 63/18 (May 11, 1973), p. 5.

336. "Szent István" (Saint Stephen), in *Detroiti Újság*, 64/32 (August 23, 1974), p. 1.

337. "Symbol of Freedom," in *Our Hero. Program of Mindszenty's Visit to Cleveland, Ohio* (Cleveland: The Mindszenty Committee, 1972), pp. 1-3.

338. "A szabadság eszméjének megtestesítője" (The Personification of the Idea of Freedom), in *Mindszenty József bíboros érsek-prímás látogatása 1974 tavaszán Cleveland egyházmegyében* (The Visit of Primate Archbishop Cardinal Jóseph Mindszenty to the Diocese of Cleveland in the Spring of 1974) (Cleveland: Kárpát Publishing, 1975), pp. 4-5.

339. "A 'Bicentennial' és mi magyarok" (The 'Bicentennial' and We Hungarians), in *Amerikai Magyar Élet* (American Hungarian Life) (Chicago, October 4, 1975), p. 9; and (October 11, 1975), p. 9.

340. "A magyar Szent Korona" (The Hungarian Holy Crown), in *Krónika*, 3/12 (December 1977), pp. 5-7.

341. "A magyarok tündöklő csillaga" (The Guiding Star of the Hungarians), in *Őrszem* (Guardian), I/1 (Cleveland, September 1981), p. 2.

342. "Saint Gerard and His Mountain," in *Hungarian Insights*, II/1 (Cleveland, 1981), p. 7.

343. "Saint Stephen. The Splendid Star of the Hungarians," in *Hungarian Insights*, II/2 (1981), p. 1.

344. "The Noon Bells Toll: The Forgotten Feast Day," in *Hungarian Insights*, II/2 (1981), pp. 9-10.

345. "With Pride, Gratitude, and Respect We Celebrate with the Hungarian School," in *Hungarian Insights*, IV/2 (1983), pp. 3-4.

346. "Magyarságismeret" (Hungarian Studies), in *Open Door*, XVIII/4 (Cleveland: St. Margaret Federal Credit Union, 1983), p. 2.

347. "Az Árpád Akadémiáról" (About the Árpád Academy), in *Magyarság*, 60/2 (January 30, 1985), p. 4.

348. "Hittel és hűséggel" (With Faith and Fidelity), in *Amerikai-Kanadai Magyar Élet* (American-Canadian Hungarian Life) (August 21, 1982), p. 1. Hereafter cited as *AKME*.

349. "Az 1956-os magyar szabadságharc történelmi jelentősége" (The Historical Significance of the Hungarian

Fight for Freedom of 1956), in *AKME* (November 6, 1982), p.11.

350. "Miért éppen Pécsettt?" (Why in Pécs of All Places?), in *AKME* (November 20, 1982), pp. 12-13.

351. "A maga erejéből" (On His Own Power), in *AKME* (November 27, 1982), p. 10.

352. "Magyarságtudatunk fokmérője" (The Measure of Our Hungarian Consciousness), in *AKME* (December 4, 1982), p. 9.

353. "Két magyar est" (Two Hungarian Evenings), in *AKME* (December 11, 1982), pp. 10-11.

354. "Jövőnk szellemi záloga" (The Spiritual Assurance of Our Future), in *AKME* (December 18, 1982), p. 9.

355. "Irodalmi magaslat" (Literary Heights), in *AKME* (January 1, 1983), p. 9.

356. "Az Amerikai-Kanadai Magyar Élet 25 éves fennállását ünnepli" (The American-Canadian Hungarian Life is Celebrating Its 25th Anniversary), in *AKME* (March 25, 1983), pp. 11.

357. "Bélyeggyűjtés és bélyegkiállítás" (Collection and Exhibition of Stamps), in *AKME* (January 8, 1983), p. 9.

358. "Figyelemreméltó megállapítások" (Statemets Worthy of Attention), in *AKME* (January 29, 1983), p. 8.

359. "Magyar szent év: 900. évforduló" (Hungarian Holy Year: 900th Anniversary), in *AKME* (April 30, 1983), p. 8.

360. "Az aradi tizenhárom" (The Thirteen Martyrs of Arad), in *AKME* (October 8, 1983), p. 8.

361. "Hol vagy, István király?" (Where Are You, King Stephen?), in *AKME* (August 20, 1983), pp. 1-2.

362. "November 4, a magyar nemzeti gyász napja" (November 4th, Day of Hungarian National Mourning), in *AKME* (October 29, 1983), p. 3.

363. "A XXIII. Magyar Találkozó" (The 23rd Hungarian Congress), in *AKME* (December 31, 1983), p. 9.

364. "A Szent Jobb" (The Holy Right Hand of King Saint Stephen), in *AKME*, 27/32 (August 24, 1985), p. 2.

365. "Mennyei" (Heavenly), in *AKME*, 28/25 (June 28, 1986), p. 5.

366. "A clevelandi ekumenikus istentisztelet és múzeumi kiállítás értékelése" (Report on the Ecumenical Service and Museum Exhibit of Cleveland), in *AKME*, 28/26 (July 12, 1986), p. 8.

367. "Hol vagy, István király?" (Where Are You, King Stephen?", in *AKME*, 28/32 (August 23, 1986), p. 11.

368. "Húsvétkor" (At Easter Time), in *AKME*, 29/15 (April 18, 1987), p. 1.

369. "A magyar öntudat megnyilvánulása" (Manifestation of Hungarian Consciousness), in *KMV*, 93/28 (July 13, 1986), p. 9.

370. "Budavár visszavétele, 1686" (The Reconquest of the Fortress of Buda, 1686), in *KMV*, 93/36 (September 7, 1986), p. 8. Reprinted in *A Szív* (The Heart), 72/9 (September 1986), pp. 401-402. Map on p. 399.

371. "A Horthy-korszak méltatása" (Assessing the Period of the Horthy Regime), in *KMV*, 94/3 (January 18, 1987), p. 8.

372. "Beköszöntő" (Introduction), in *Review* (Cleveland), I/1 (November 1986), pp. 1-2.

373. "Képek a könyvben" (Illustrations in the Book), in *Review*, II/1 (April 1987), pp. 3-4.

374. "Miről tanúskodik a clevelandi Kossuth-szobor? (What Does the Kossuth Statue of Cleveland Tell Us?), in *A clevelandi restaurált Kossuth-szobor újraavató ünnepélyére készült emlékkönyv, 1985. október 27* (Memorial Volume for the Occasion of the Rededication of the Cleveland Kossuth Statue, October 27, 1985), ed. Sándor Szabadkai (Cleveland, 1985), pp. 25-26 and 49.

375. "Évfordulók és korhadt fakeresztek" (Anniversaries and Decaying Wooden Crosses), introduction to Viktor Rákosi's volume of short stories entitled *Korhadt fakeresztek* (Decaying Wooden Crosses) (Garfield, NJ: Turan Printing, 1986), pp. 2-3.

376. "A szerző" (About the Author), in *ibid.* p. 1.

377. "Királygyilkosság?" (Regicide?), in *Hazánk*, III/6-7 (June-July, 1987), p. 6.

377a. "The Second One Hundred Years." *Review*, II/2 (August 1987), pp. 4-5.

V. OBITUARIES:

378. "Tolnai Lajos" (Lajos Tolnai), in *NCsV*, II (1942), p. 320.

379. "Vitéz Kovács Dezső" (Dezső v. Kovács), in *NCsV*, II (1942), p. 321.

380. "Radnóti István" (István Radnóti), in *NCsV*, III (1942), p. 161.

381. "Kós Károly" (Károly Kós), in *Magyar Újság*, 67/35 (September 22, 1977), p. 1.

382. "Béky Zoltán halála" (The Death of Zoltán Béky), in *Magyar Újság*, 68/45 (November 30, 1978), p. 1.

383. "Sheen érsek" (Archbishop Sheen), in *Magyar Újság*, 69/47 (December 13, 1979), p. 1 and 3.

384. "A nemzeti emigráció gyásza. Kótai Zoltán halála" (The Mourning of the National Emigration. The Death of Rev. Zoltán Kótai), in *AKME* (August 16, 1980), pp. 9-10.

385. "A magyar emigráció gyásza" (The Mourning of the Hungarian Emigration), in *KMV* (August 24, 1980), p. 7.

386. "Tripolszky András búcsúztatása" (Farewell to András Tripolszky), in *AKME* (October 2, 1982), p. 9.

387. "Meghalt Gábor Áron. Isten nyugosztalja" (Áron

Gábor Died. May He Rest in Peace), in *AKME* (January 15, 1983), p. 6.

388. "Gyászmise Irányi püspökért" (Memorial Mass for Bishop Irányi), in *KMV*, 94/19 (May 10, 1987), p. 8. Signed as "s- f-."

389. "Meghalt Nyeste János" (János Nyeste Died), in *KMV*, 94/23 (June 7, 1987), p. 7.

VI. BOOK REVIEWS:

390. "Nagy Iván: Nyugat-Magyarország Ausztriában (Iván Nagy: Western Hungary in Austria), in *Külügyi Szemle* (Foreign Affairs Review) (Budapest, 1932), pp. 339-340; and in *Magyar Külpolitika* (Hungarian Foreign Affairs) (Budapest, March 1932), p. 11.

391. "Kérészy Zoltán: A Corpus Juris Hungarici, mint írott kútfő" (Zoltán Kérészy: The Corpus Juris Hungarici as a Written Legal Source), in *Jog* (Law), II (Budapest, 1935), pp. 151-152; and in *Jogállam* (Legal State) (Budapest, 1935), pp. 82-843.

392. "Viczián István: A Quadripartitum eltérései a Tripartítumtól a nemesi magánjogban (István Viczián: The Differences between the Quadripartitum and the Tripartitum in the Civil Law of the Nobility), in *Jogállam* (1925), p. 310; and in *Polgári Jog* (Civil Law) (Budapest, 1935), p. 507.

393. "Lajos Iván: IV. Károly király élete és politikája" (Iván Lajos: The Life and Politics of King Charles IV), in *Pécsi Jogász*, I (1935), pp. 11-12.

394. "Degré Alajos: A Négyeskönyv perjogi anyaga" (Alajos Degré: The Litigative Features of the Quadripartitum), in *Pécsi Jogász*, II (1936), pp. 43-47.

395. "Sándorfy Kamill: Törvényhozásunk hőskora" (Kamill Sándorfy: The Heroic Age of Our Legislation), in *Pécsi Jogász*, II (1936), pp. 47-48.

396. "Dávid Tibor: Regöly," in *Pécsi Jogász*, II (1936), pp. 90-91.

397. "Földmunkáskérdés, munkástelepítés, munkaalkalmak. Szabados Mihály könyve" (The Problems of the Day Laborers, Resettlement of Laborers, Opportunities for Work. A Book by Mihály Szabados), in *Dunántúl* (December 13, 1936), p. 11.

398. "Bozóky Géza: Nemzetközi váltójog" (Géza Bozóky: International Law of Exchange), in *Pécsi Jogász*, III (1937), p. 107; and in *Pannonia*, nos. 1-6 (Pécs, 1937), p. iii.

399. "Kun Lajos: Egy baranyai falu földműves és bányásznépének szociális hygiénéje" (Lajos Kun: The Social Hygiene of the Peasant and Miner Population of a Village in Baranya), in *Széchenyista Ifjúság*, no. 8 (1937), p. 16.

400. "Babics András: A kamarai igazgatás Pécs városában 1686-1703" (The Fiscal Administration of the City of Pécs in 1686-1703), in *Nemzetvédő* (September 17, 1937), p. 8.

401. "Losonczy István: A mulasztás. I. A mulasztási bűncselekmény okozatossága" (Negligence. I. Casuality in the Crime of Negligence), in *Pécsi Jogász*, III (1937), p. 123.

402. "Szilágyi László: A székely nemesi rendi társadalom" (László Szilágyi: The Székely Noble Feudal Society), in *Pécsi Jogász*, III (1937), p. 123.

403. "Székely István: Házasságjogi reformgondolatok" (Reform Ideas Concerning Marriage Law), in *Pécsi Jogász*, III (1937), p. 123.

404. "Natkó Gyula: Mérlegen Magyarország politikai pártjai és politikusai (Gyula Natkó: Hungary's Political Parties and Politicians are Being Weighed), in *Nemzetvédő* (December 8, 1937), p. 8.

405. "Gárdos Miklós: A szociális gondoskodás főbb kérdései" (Miklós Gárdos: The Main Questions of Social Thought), in *NCsV*, II (1942), p. 104.

406. "Nagy Mózes Erzsébet: A szociálpolitika bibliai alapjai és történeti fejlődése" (Erzsébet Nagy Mózes: The

Biblical Basis and Historical Evolution of Social Welfare Policy), in *NCsV*, III (1943), p. 63.

407. "Kornis Gyula: Tudós fejek" (Gyula Kornis: Scholarly Heads), in *NCsV*, III (1943), pp. 193-194.

408. "Egyed István: Magyar államélet (István Egyed: Life of the Hungarian State), in *NCsV*, III (1943), p. 194.

409. "Magyarország hatályos törvényei" (Hungary's Effective Laws), in *NCsV*, III (1943), pp. 268-269, and 346.

410. "Berze Nagy János: Baranyai magyar néphagyományok" (János Berze Nagy: Hungarian Folklore Traditions of Baranya County), 3 vols., in *NCsV*, III (1943), p. 298.

411. "Weis István: Hazánk társadalomrajza" (István Weis: Sociography of Our Homeland), in *NCsV*, III (1943), p. 346.

412. "Gajzágó László: A nemzetközi jog eredete" (László Gajzágó: The Origin of International Law), in *NCsV*, III (1943), pp. 424-425.

413. "Emlékkönyv dr. viski Illés József ny. r. egyetemi tanár tanári működésének 40. évfordulójára" (Memorial Volume on the Occasion of the 40th Anniversary of the Appointment of Dr. József viski Illés as a University Professor), in *NCsV*, III (1943), pp. 425-426.

414. "Túry Sándor Kornél: Vallás, erkölcs, és vagyonjog" (Sándor K. Túry: Religion, Ethics, and Property Law), in *NCsV*, IV (1944), pp. 24-25.

415. "Badacsonyi József: A magyar ipartörvény gyakorlati kézikönyve (József Badacsonyi: Practical Handbook of Hungarian Trade Laws), in *NCsV*, IV (1944), p. 25.

416. "Georg Rácz: Die neue Rechtsentwicklung in Ungarn" (Georg Rácz: Recent Legal Evolution in Hungary), in *NCsV*, IV (1944), pp. 25-26.

417. "A magyar szociális jogszabályok ismertetése" (Review of Hungarian Social Welfare Laws), in *NCsV*, IV (1944), pp. 65-66.

418. "Tettek - Tervek" (Deeds - Plans), in *NCsV*, IV (1944), pp. 68-69.

419. "Kornis Gyula: Tudomány és társadalom" (Gyula Kornis: Science and Society), in *NCsV*, IV (1944), pp. 141-143.

420. "Egyed István: A mi alkotmányunk" (István Egyed: Our Constitution), in *NCsV*, IV (1944), p. 143.

421. "Társadalomtudomány" (Social Sciences), in *NCsV*, IV (1944), pp. 147-148.

422. "Kovrig Béla: A munka védelme a dunai államokban" (Béla Kovrig: The Protection of Work in the Danubian Countries), in *NCsV*, IV (1944), p. 278.

423. "Mártonyi-Ottlik-Szászy: Jogi előadások II" (Mártonyi-Ottlik-Szászy: Legal Lectures II), in *NCsV*, IV (1944), pp. 278-279.

424. "Bárdossy László: Magyar politika a mohácsi vész után" (László Bárdossy: Hungarian Politics after the Battle of Mohács), in *Sorsunk* (Our Fate), IV (Pécs, 1944), pp. 191-192.

425. "A besúgó és az apostol. Eszterhás István új regénye" (The Denouncer and the Apostle. A New Novel by István Eszterhás), in *Vagyunk*, IV (1951), pp. 141-142.

426. "A magyar katona a második világháborúban. Írta vitéz Adonyi Ferenc" (The Hungarian Soldier in the Second World War. By Ferenc v. Adonyi), in *Vagyunk*, VIII (1955), p. 39.

427. "Árnyékban a dóm. Irta Bognár Ágnes Erzsébet" (The Cathedral under Shadow. By Ágnes Erzsébet Bognár), in *Vagyunk*, VIII (1955), pp. 39-40.

428. "Hungary by Imre Dittrich," in *Vagyunk*, VIII (1955), p. 40.

429. "Bognár Ágnes Erzsébet: Istenhordozók" (Ágnes Erzsébet Bognár: God-Bearers), in *Vagyunk*, VIII (1955), p. 135. Signed as "Vassy Lél."

430. "Búzakereszt. Emigrációs novella antológia. Szerk. Kisjókai Erzsébet" (Shock of Wheat. An Anthology of Emigrant Short Stories. Ed. Erzsébet Kisjókai), in *Vagyunk*, VIII (1955), pp. 36-37. Signes as "-i -c."

431. "Czermann Antal: Vértanú Szent Gellért nemzeti szentélye" (Antal Czermann: The National Shrine of the Martyr Saint Gerard), in *Vagyunk*, VIII (1955), p. 137. Signed as "Szeghy Csaba."

432. "Padányi Viktor: Vérbúlcsú (Viktor Padányi: Vérulcsú), in *Vagyunk*, VIII (1955), p. 138. Signed as "Historicus."

433. "A diadalmas világnézet. Prohászka Ottokár könyvének új kiadása" (The Triumphant World View. The Republication of Ottokár Prohászka's Book), in *Magyar Újság*, 66/6 (February 5, 1976), p. 1.

434. "Géniusz. Ágoston Ede verses regénye Petőfiről (Genius. Ede Ágoston's Poetic Novel about Petőfi), in *Magyar Újság*, 68/45 (1978), p. 6.

435. "Bemutatás és ajánlás" (Presentation and Recommendation), in T. Dombrády Dóra, *Őrkő. Elbeszélések* (Guardian Rock. Short Stories) (Cleveland: Kárpát Publishers, 1978), pp. 7-8.

436. "Előszó" (Preface), in Béla Rektor, *A magyar királyi csendőrség oknyomozó története* (The History of the Royal Hungarian Gendarmerie) (Cleveland: Árpád Könyvkiadó Vállalat, 1980), pp. 7-8.

437. "Előszó" (Preface), in *The Árpád Academy. The Activities of the Members* (Cleveland: Árpád Academy, 1982), pp. vii-xvi. (Preface in English, French, German, Hungarian, and Spanish.)

438. "Korai magyarokról" (About Ancient Hungarians), in *AKME* (March 12, 1983), p. 9. Review of Tibor Baráth's book published without the name of the reviewer.

439. "Az amerikai magyar színjátszásról" (About American Hungarian Theater), in *AKME* (March 26, 1983), pp. 12-13. Review of Mihály Sárossy Szüle's book.

440. "Amerikai küzdelem a magyar Szent Koronáért" (American Struggle for the Hungarian Holy Crown), in *AKME* (May 14, 1983), p. 9. Review of Attila Simontsits' documentary book on the return of the Holy Crown to Hungary.

441. "1000 év magyar művészei egy festő életrajzában"
(Hungarian Artists of One-Thousand Years in the Biography
of a Painter), in *AKME* (March 17, 1984), p. 9. Review of
a book by Ernő Gyimesy Kásás.

442. "New Book on Louis the Great," in *Hungarian
Insights* VIII/1 (March, 1987), p. 4. Unsigned.

443. "Új könyv. Kostya Sándor: Ősi földünk, a Felvidék"
(A New Book. Sándor Kostya's Our Ancient Land, Upper
Hungary), *KMV*, 94/19 (May 10, 1987), p. 7.

VII. NOTE:

The bibliographical entries above do not represent
Professor Somogyi's complete works. There are those whose
existence is known, but without specific bibliographical
data; while others — published mostly in diverse Hungarian
emigré newspapers around the world — are simply inaccessible at this time. Nor does this bibliography contain
the serialized versions of four of his books, which first appeared as series of articles in such newspapers as the Cleve-
land-based *Az Újság* (News) and *Magyar Újság* (Hungarian News), and the Detroit-based (*Detroiti Magyar
Újság* (Detroit Hungarian News). The books in question
are: *Küldetés. A magyarság története* (Mission. History
of the Hungarian People) (1973), *Magyar nyelv és irodalom
1825-ig* (Hungarian Language and Literature to 1825)
(1975), *Magyar nyelv és irodalom 1825-től 1925-ig* (Hungarian Language and Literature from 1825 to 1925) (1977),
and *Faith and Fate. A short Cultural History of the Hungarian People through a Millennium* (1977).

Even though an octogenarian, Ferenc Somogyi still
publishes regularly in a number of Hungarian-American
papers, and he is also one of the principal contributors to
the Chicago-based *Amerikai-Kanadai Magyar Élet* (American-Canadian Hungarian Life), where he writes regularly
news articles, obituaries, and short book reviews every week.

II.

FROM THE EARLY ÁRPÁDS TO THE
AGE OF RÁKÓCZI

Z. J. Kosztolnyik:

4 / EARLY TWELFTH-CENTURY GERMAN POLITICS IN THE BACKGROUND OF HUNGARIAN HISTORY

Das Wormser Konkordat tragt den Charakter
des Kompromisses an den Stirn.
                                    Karl Hampe

The Concordat of Worms, 1122, did have a lasting impact for over a period of thirty-five years in German politics and diplomacy in that it had altered the formerly hostile relationship between the papal curia and the imperial court by establishing friendly cooperation between them.[1] The Pope had now become predominant in ecclesiastical affairs of the Empire and expected political support from its court circles. Such cooperation would have made the previous papal-Norman alliance unnecessary in the Italian south; the Germans, too, disliked the Normans. Indeed, the anti-German tendencies of the earlier papal-Norman understanding had, in fact, changed at this stage to a papal-German diplomatic association with strong anti-Norman bias. The new diplomatic situation did not lead, however, to a new anti-Norman papal policy on the grounds that the renewal of Guelph-Ghibelline controversy in the empire prevented the pontiff from having German support for creating a diplomatic front against the Normans. The Pope had to recognize the royal title of the Norman ruler after the latter had unified Sicily with Southern Italy. Because of renewed party strife on German soil, the north Italian cities expected more independence of imperial influence.[2]

In examining the politics of the period, it will be necessary to pay some attention to the election of 1125. Lothair, Duke of

Saxony, was elected king. The electors would not elect Frederick of Swabia for the reason that by selecting a *homo novus* they were able to show independence the late Henry V and his advisers refused to believe they had. The chroniclers say that the Archbishop of Mainz had, by refusing to vote for the son of Henry V's younger sister, influenced the outcome of the 1125 election. The late Henry V and his friends had not been allies of the Church. The archbishop initiated the election struggle for Lothair and obtained the support of the Archbishop of Cologne together with the adherence of ecclesiastics who had been playing a lead in public life, for Supplinburg. The Archbishop of Mainz intervened in the political interests of his friend and former ally because in his opinion only Lothair of Supplinburg could carry on a fight on equal terms with the anti-ecclesiastical Hohenstaufen, and bring the struggle to a successful conclusion.[3]

The behavior of Henry the Black of Bavaria must also have contributed to the outcome of the 1125 election. The duke maintained good relations with Henry V. His daughter, Julia, was married to Frederick of Swabia despite the political enmity shown toward Henry by Archbishop Conrad of Salzburg, front runner of church reforms in Bavaria. What happened was that the archbishop persuaded the duke to alter his political views and agree to the support of Lothair's candidacy. Through the influence of Conrad a strong Saxon-Bavarian coalition came into being, strengthened by the marriage of Gertrude, Supplinburg's only child, to Henry the Proud, son of Henry the Black.[4]

Lothair III was strong in personality and was a protector of the Church. Earlier, as duke of Saxony, he had supported the papal party against the emperor. This new Saxon-Bavarian alliance created by the election had led, however, to the Guelph-Ghibelline confrontation in earnest, so characteristic of German politics during the twelfth century. The Hohenstaufen were the opposition, though their leader, Frederick of Swabia, was not an overly ambitious person; he was satisfied with his dukedom. Frederick strenghtened his authority in Swabia and in the attached Rhineland until Lothair III suddenly demanded from him the surrender of the Rhinish city of Spires and its surroundings on the grounds that they had been adjudged to him by the Diet of Regensburg in

1125. Frederick refused even to discuss the surrender of the territory in question, but, because of an unexpected emergence in 1126 of the Czech question that now preoccupied the king's attention, a direct military confrontation between Lothair and Frederick was avoided.[5]

Lothair III forced the resignation of Sobieslav, Duke of Bohemia, in favor of Otto, Duke of Moravia; however, his troops were beaten back by Sobieslav on Czech soil, and the king had to acknowledge Sobieslav as Duke of Bohemia. Lothair III had suffered a thorough defeat and could not think of an anti-Hohenstaufen campaign. The situation was improved by 1127, when Henry the Black died, and his son, Henry the Proud, inherited his share of Saxon territory and Bavaria, though a smaller portion of the latter, together with Swabia, was inherited by Welf /VI/, younger brother of Henry the Proud. It was at this time that Gertrude became the wife of Henry the Proud.[6]

How complicated the German domestic situation really must have been is shown by the fact that the Hohenstaufen had to face Bavarian and Czech resistance because they wanted to occupy the city of Nuremberg. The city resisted the planned takeover; and, because Conrad of Swabia, brother of Frederick, revolted against him, Lothair III sought refuge in Würzburg. In December, 1127, Conrad's troops proclaimed him "king." Regardless of church opposition Conrad /now "king"/ moved to Italy to intervene in Milanese politics. Milan supported its archbishop against the Pope in the controversy over an old custom that Rome always sent the Pallium to the new Milanese archbishop, but Honorius II refused this. The pontiff dispatched a message instead to the archbishop telling him to visit Rome and receive in person the pallium.[7]

Conrad of Swabia continued to play politics. Archbishop Anselm of Milan crowned him with the iron crown of Lombardy, whereby Conrad gained a territorial foothold on the peninsula and demanded that Matilda of Tuscany's patrimony be handed over to him. The Holy See could not comply with such a demand, and the Milanese sensing a confrontation developing between Rome and Conrad, concluded peace with the former; the "king" had to leave Italian soil. Back at home, his brother Frederick had lost the city of Nuremberg to the coordinated attack of Lothair III and Henry the Proud (Lothair's son-in-law). Only the revolt against Lothair III in 1130 saved the cause of Frederick of Swabia.[8]

In 1130, a papal schism occurred in Rome on account of a double papal election. The Frangipani and Pierleoni families vied for the papal throne, and the cardinals were divided. The candidate of the Frangipani faction, George Prareschi, was elected pope under the name of Innocent II, and Peter Pierleoni assumed the title of Anacletus II.[9] One ought to realize, of course, that Pope Honorius II, who died in 1130, was the former Cardinal Lamberti of Ostia, who played an important role in arranging for the Settlement of Worms in 1122. He was elected pope in 1124 with the support of the Frangipani faction at a time, when, under pressure from the Frangipani, the already chosen pontiff, Celestine II, had to step down.[10]

Sixteen Frangipani cardinals, among them the majority of cardinal-bishops, elected Cardinal George as Innocent II in a hurry. On the same day, but four hours later, twenty-four electors chose Peter as Anacletus II. In other words, Innocent II was elected first, and Anacletus II by the majority vote of the Cardinals.[11] Both elections were held within the guidelines of the 1059 papal election decree, and both of the pope-elects were chosen by other cardinals; therefore, neither of them wished to step down. The elects now appealed to Lothair III for recognition, but he, in agreement with the decree of Nicholas II, refused to intervene in the papal electoral process.[12]

Rome sided with Anacletus II, a descendant of a Roman Jewish family, and Innocent II fled the city.[13] To Pisa he went, and from there to the Frankish kingdom,[14] where he obtained the support of Bernard of Clairvaux.[15] Abbot Bernard persuaded the Frankish[16] and English monarchs to recognize Innocent II as pope, in 1130, and in 1131.[17] And, at the ecclesiastical assembly at Lieg, Lothair III held the stirrup of Innocent II's horse when he descended from it. Under the influence of Norbert of Xanten, the German king, too, acknowledged Innocent II as the legitimate pontiff.[18]

The strong group of supporters of Anacletus II included Roger II of Sicily who, in return for his services, demanded from him papal recognition of his royal title. (Roger's correct title should have been King of Sicily and Duke of Apulia and Calabria). Indeed, on Christmas day, 1130, they crowned Roger II King of Sicily in Palermo. He held an empty title. His nobles, hostile to each other, were also unhappy with their monarch, a descendant of a mere noble family. When it became known that the North decided to support Innocent II and Lothair III was going to visit Italy to install Innocent II on the papal throne, the Normans turned against their "king" and defeated his army.[19]

Pope Innocent II was installed in 1132; on June, 1133, he anointed and crowned Lothair II Holy Roman Emperor. It must have been characteristic of the conditions surrounding the coronation that it had to take place in the Lateran because St. Peter's was occupied by troops loyal to the anti-pope. The Emperor now confirmed the Concordat of Worms: bishop-elects would receive from the emperor, but before their consecration, temporal insignia /of the episcopate/. He also recognized the rights of the Holy See over Tuscany (donated by Matilda of Tuscany to St. Peter, but) confiscated by Henry V. Lothair III obtained Tuscany as a fief from the hands of the Pope, but allowed its use and income to go to Henry the Proud, his son-in-law. (In the Vatican, there is a wall painting of the scene, where Lothair III kneels in front of the Pope receiving his crown from the pontiff's hands; the caption under the painting reads that now Lothair was the vassal of the Pope).[20]

Anacletus II once again gained the upper hand in Rome upon the departure of Lothair III. He received help from Roger II, after the latter had successfully subdued his unruly vassals. Innocent II left for Pisa; Lothair returned to the Empire to restore order. Both Frederick and Conrad of Swabia had submitted to him, together with Eric, king of Denmark. The Czech and Polish courts, too, acknowledged him as their feudal overlord.[21]

Lothair III visited Rome again in 1136. By then, the Pope had persuaded both Pisa and Genoa to cease fighting each other and turn instead on their common enemy, the Normans, who had been endangering merchant shipping on the Mediterranean. Milan, too, joined the papal alliance even though its archbishop had received his pallium from Anacletus II. The Emperor publicly recognized the privileges of the

Italian city states; moved freely toward Rome, and took Bari and Salerno. (Roger II left for Sicily). Lothair III named Alife of Ranulf as duke of Apulia, but because Innocent II had insisted that it was within his jurisdiction to name the duke, it was both the Pope and the Emperor who had Alife installed in his position. Understandably, when the German decided to go home, the pontiff did not restrain him. Lothair III, by then a very sick man, died on German Soil in 1137. [22]

The events discussed here coincide in Hungarian history with the period of Stephen II (1116-31), son of Coloman the Learned, [23] and of Béla II the Blind (1131-41), son of Álmos, younger brother of Coloman, who, for political and dynastic reasons was blinded by his brother, the king. [24] The reign of Stephen II was described at some length in the *Chronicon pictum* [25], whose chronicler emphasized the point of view that it was the *potentiores regni*: powerful nobles of the realm, who had crowned Stephen, the naive young son of the book-lover king. [26] Because he wanted to appease the nobles, Stephen II had, after a peaceful visit to Dalmatia, scheduled talks with the Duke of Bohemia, but the talks were aborted before they began. Instead of a cordial discussion, an armed clash took place on the Hungaro-Czech border on the Olsava river. It was the young and thoughtless monarch's fault, the chronicler wrote, because he, "ut fuit impetuosus," being of evil temper, acted hurriedly, without consulting with his advisers in the matter. [27]

Realization of the planned Hungaro-Czech talks was prevented by the scheming of the traitor named Solt, [28] though, in order to understand the background of Solt's behavior and to analyze his motives, one has to turn to non-Hungarian sources for information. It was the biographer of Archbishop Conrad of Salzburg who reported that, earlier, Hungarian troops broke into German /Austrian/ territory, whereupon the margrave in charge of the region, Leopold of Babenberg, obtained Bohemian aid and counter-attacked Hungarian lands occupying *castrum ferreum* (a place that can be identified as Vasvár, or as Eisenstadt /Kismárton/, today). [29]

It is here that one may find the clue for Solt's plan to keep the king from meeting peacefully with the Duke of Bohemia. Solt did not act on his own, but upon encouragement he must have received from the advisers of the Czech duke, whose interests—both, the duke's and the advisers'—must have been served by preventing Stephen II from having a talk with the Duke of Bohemia. [30] The clerical biographer of Salzburg recorded that the king had under the influence of Archbishop Conrad surrendered the prisoners of war and booty captured in the campaign on German (Austrian) lands to the margrave. [31] However, it was not the margrave concerned, but the Archbishop of Salzburg who, through his legate, had talks with the Hungarians, as if to imply that someone had to have a bad conscience. After all, it was Margrave Leopold and not the archbishop who had invaded Hungarian territory with Czech aid. At the scheduled Hungaro-Czech meeting on the Olsava, the background of the Hungaro-German (Austrian) encounter, carried out with Czech help, would certainly have come up for a clarifying discussion. [32]

Nor ought one leave out of consideration the Salzburg biographer's remark that the king had made peace only after Archbishop Conrad had a considerable force move in against him. [33] The archbishop would not leave his protegee, the margrave, in the lurch, but the Hungarian ruler must have thought it too daring to face a prince of the Church in a military situation. Indeed, when the Salzburg cathedral, burned down, the Hungarian king hurried to the aid of the archbishop. [34]

And yet, Stephen II did not enjoy a good reputation before his nobles; they decided to keep a close eye on him and had asked for the hand in marriage of the daughter of the Duke of Apulia on his behalf. [35]

The fiasco of the 1123 military expedition against Kiev likewise made no contribution to the prestige of the young monarch. [36] Following the invitation of the Ruthenian duke Bezen and of Yaroslav, Duke of Vladimir, Stephen II invaded Russian soil in order to "avenge the disgrace his father had earlier suffered there." [37] The campaign was not popular with the nobles who, in fact, refused obedience to the king in a hastily summoned meeting (*ad consilium regis*). They threatened the monarch that they would elect another ruler instead of him, were he to continue the campaign. [38] Today's Hungarian researchers speak of the sad ending of the ill-fated Kiev campaign in terms of a two-party confrontation between the anti-royal party of Álmos (whose supporters were sworn enemies of Coloman the Learned and of his son, Stephen II), and of the group loyal to the king, though critical of him. [39]

And yet, one has to consider the fact that the nobles already on Kievan soil refused obedience to the monarch only after the death of Duke Bezen, when they (had felt that they) were lacking legal justification for their being there. [40] This is quite evident from the conversation of the king with Kozma of the clan of Pázmány, leader of the opposition. The latter was perturbed that the king would, like his father before him, attempt to extend his authority over Ruthenian-Kievan lands, thereby increasing his power base at the expense of the nobles of the opposition. The latter could not approve of such an ambitious plan.[41] Angrily, Stephen II had ordered upon his return from Kiev — the chronicler said, three years later — that the Polish (Ruthenian) frontier be devastated, but his troops also invaded Serbian and Bulgarian lands. [42] The chronicler insisted that only because of his descent from the House of Árpád did the nobles of the opposition tolerate Stephen II as their king.[43]

In spite of his legitimate constituency on the throne, or because of it, the king relied upon some awful measures to deal with his enemies. The chronicler says that Stephen II saw in every human being either a traitor or an opponent. [44] He had a noble woman, Christina, burnt to death [45] — though the Byzantine sources reveal that he had condemned her for a very good reason. [46] The king had fire built out of horse manure under (the text reads over the heads of) some persons enclosed in narrow compartments, and burned them to death. [47] He punished individuals by having burning candles dripping hot wax into their rectum, until the candles burned down. [48] The two-party opposition must have used selective means to bring their victims to talk.

The question must be asked, of course, how and from where did the chronicler obtain his information? Did he arrange his report according to written evidence, or after hearsay? Did he talk with eyewitnesses? If he reported events correctly, he did it with joy and satisfaction in order to chronicle the evil deeds done by the least civilized son of the learned book-lover king, who held the throne by constituent rights. [49] Álmos himself, fearing for his life, had fled to

Byzantium, where they had extended protection to him and to the many refugees gathering about him.[50]

Stephen II regarded it as *casus belli* that the Byzantine court granted political asylum to both Álmos and Béla the Blind, though the chronicler recorded, the king lost this war and many good people perished in it.[51] But the chronicler writes with a voice choked by emotion and hatred; his main theme is, that, aside from being the descendant of Árpád, Stephen II had no other claim to the throne. Therefore, he did not report that the king's *Greek* campaign had started because of the influence of the Hungarian political refugees at the Byzantine court—Álmos among them—who, in spite of his blind state (or, perhaps, because of it), did not cease agitating against his own uncle and king.[52] When the prince died in Byzantium, and his body was taken home upon royal orders so that he may receive an honorable burial at Fehérvár, the cause of the war ceased to exist, and the campaign came to an end.[53]

Stephen II had no heirs, and earnestly wanted peace. When Bishop Paul and Othmar the Reeve had told him that Béla, Álmos's son, was alive, he ordered that Béla succeed him on the throne.[54] He also obtained for his new heir on the throne the hand in marriage of Ilona Helena, daughter of Uroš, grand župan of Serbia. He assigned a place to reside to the young couple, and assured them an annual pension.[55] It may be, of course, that the king had taken this action not so much out of respect toward his own family, but because he wished to irritate the opposition: those nobles who let him down during the Kiev campaign, and who had threatened him with deposition.[56]

The chronicler reports that before Stephen II had received news about Béla the Blind, the nobles (of the opposition) decided that after the death of the king, he should be succeeded by Saul, who was the son of his sister, Sophia.[57] The king must have been wary about the behavior of the nobles who could hardly wait for his death so that they could elect one of themselves, or someone else to the throne.[58] At this time the monarch appeared to be close to death, and the "traitors" (a term used for the first time by the chronicler) held an election.[59] When Stephen II recovered from his illness, he had one of the royal electors beheaded, and an other one exiled to the Byzantine court. There are also indications that this second elector may have gone into self-exile.[60]

After this hysterical and by all account unconstitutional election (carried out by members of the opposition), the loyal nobles made security around the monarch so strict that not even members of the family were allowed to enter the royal household grounds without permission.[61] The chronicler reporting this revealed, incidentally, that the electors came from the king's closest circle.[62] On the other hand, the fact that Stephen II without further delay accepted the succession of Béla the Blind to the throne shows that he listened to the advice of his loyal barons and agreed with their opinion.[63]

The previous blinding of Béla II did, however, disturb the chronicler much.[64] He reported that Queen Ilona had, with the consent of her husband and the barons, summoned a meeting of a General Assembly at Arad-Ónod, in order to ask its members, why, and upon whose advice had her husband been blinded?[65] Although the chronicler here expressed his own opinion by placing words into the mouth of the Queen, he added that, then and there, sixty-eight of the conspirators /gathered in the Assembly/ were killed.[66]

From the remark of the chronicler that the Queen had appeared before the Assembly with her children, it becomes evident that it was not held at the beginning of Béla II's reign.[67] It took time to determine the king's position among the nobles of the realm, the hierarchy, and the population. Only when the Queen felt reasonably certain that the barons in attendance and the people would support her, did she summon the Assembly. She wanted to find out about the opposition still unknown to her, but most probably well known to the barons and people gathered in the Assembly.[68]

Queen Ilona did not know at the beginning of the Assembly who exactly had formed her husband's opposition, and her concern was not baseless. The Hungarians were like a stormy sea[69] because they called in Boris, Coloman the Learned's illegitimate son and pretender to the throne, to occupy the country with Ruthenian and Polish aid.[70] When Boris appeared at the Sajó river (which, at this time, had formed the Hungarian border), many of the nobles went over to him).[71]

Béla II the Blind had no other choice but to take up arms

against the intruder.[72] Before he gave battle to Boris, the king arranged for a special meeting with the nobles, in order to convince himself of their loyalty.[73] At this gathering there appeared, next to the nobles loyal to the king (*fideles regni*: loyal to the cause), members of the less loyal element (*infideles et contradictores*), who, the chronicler added, had evil intentions.[74] The loyalists decided right there and then to separate the sheep from the goats and to kill the traitors, lest they join Boris's forces and endanger the existence of their country.[75]

The King's disloyal opponents now staged a revolt, but his supporters oppressed it by killing its leaders. One of the traitors, Samson by name, was still able to enter the royal tent and orally abuse the monarch to his face[76], but, when the momentarily surprised loyalist went into action, Samson had to flee for his life. Being pursued to the Sajó, he fell into the river, and because of the heavy armor under his cloak, he drowned.[77]

Béla II's supporters did not do an unfinished job. They dispatched delegates to the leader of Boris's Ruthenian and Polish troops to tell him that the King reigned with the approval and consent of the entire country, and held the crown of the realm by right; *quod de iure regnum tenere debeat*.[78]

The delegates carried out their mission well. The Polish leader withdrew his troops and returned home.[79] In turn, the abandoned Boris was, with some of his troops still at his side, defeated in a battle on the feast of Mary Magdalene.[80] The determination of Queen Ilona and the loyalty of the monarch's nobles saved the throne for Béla II the Blind and assured the royal children's succession to the crown.

Notes

1. On Worms, see *Monumenta Germaniae historica, Legum collectio*, cited hereafter as *MGHLL*, sectio IV, Const. 1, 107; M. Doeberl, ed., *Monumenta Germaniae historica selecta*, vol. III (Munich, 1889), nos. 21a and 21b; J. D. Mansi, ed., *Sacrorum concilorum nova et amplissima collectio*, 31 vols. (Florence-Venice, 1759-98; 54 vol. repr., Osnabrück, 1968), XXI, 273ff.; E. Bernheim, "Das Wormser Konkordat und seine Vorurkunden," *Historische Vierteljahrschrift*, 10 (1907), 196ff.; F. X. Seppelt, *Geschichte der Päpste*, 5 vols., rev. ed. (Munich, 1949-57),

III, 159ff. For detail on background, cf. Anselmi Gemblacensis *Continuatio*, anno 1122, in G. H. Pertz, ed., *Monumenta Germaniae historica, Scriptores*, 32 vols. (Hanover, 1854—), cited hereafter as *MGHSS*, VI, 378; J. Haller, *Das Papsttum: Idee und Wirklichkeit*, 5 vols., rev. ed. (Stuttgart, 1952-59), III, 25ff.; I. Ott, "Der Regalienbegriff im 12. Jahrhundert," *Zeitschrift der Savigny Stiftung für Rechtsgeschichte*, kan. Abt., 35 (1948), 234ff.

2. Cf. K. Hampe, *Deutsche Kaisergeschichte*, 12th rev. ed., ed. F. Baethgen (Heidelberg, 1968), 109ff.; B. Gebhardt, *Handbuch der deutschen Geschichte*, 4 vols., 8th ed. (Stuttgart, 1954-60), I, 284ff; Z. J. Kosztolnyik, *From Coloman the Learned to Béla III (1095-1196): Hungarian Domestic Policies and Their Impact Upon Foreign Affairs* (New York: East European Monographs, Columbia University Press, 1987), 41ff.

3. On the background, cf. *Vita Norberti*, c. 21, *MGHSS*, XII, 700ff.; also, *Narratio de electione Lotharii, ibid.*, XII, 511, to the effect that Lothair had renounced investiture prior to his election. A Hofmeister, "Das Wormser Konkordat: zur Streit um seine Bedeutung," *Festschrift B. Schäfer* (Jena, 1915), 64ff.

4. Cf. W. Bernhardi, *Lothar von Supplinburg* (Berlin, 1879; rep. Berlin, 1975), 39f., and 44.

5. Cf. Annalista Saxo, *Chronicon regum Francorum*, a. 1127, *MGHSS*, VI, 764; Otto of Freising, *Gesta Friderici Imperatoris*, i:16, *ibid.*, XX, 347ff.

6. Cosmas Pragensis, *Chronica Bohemorum*, iii:13: "Justicia enim erat Boemorum, ut semper inter principes eorum maior natu solio potiretur in principatu," *ibid.*, IX, 105; *idem*, iii:56 and 58; Canon of Wishegrad, *Continuatio Cosmae Pragensis*, anno 1126, *ibid.*, IX, 123.

7. Cf. Ph. Jaffé, ed., *Regesta pontificum Romanorum*, 2 vols. (Leipzig, 1885), I, no. 906; Landulph de s. Paulo, *Historia Mediolanensis*, c. 52, in *MGHSS*, XX, 44.

8. Landulph, c. 53; Otto of Freising, *Chronicon*, vii:17, *MGHSS*, XX, 256f.; Bernhardi, 238ff.

9. Jaffé, *Regesta*, I, nos. 5928, 5931, 5939 and 5944; F. X. von Funk-K. Bihlmeyer, *Kirchengeschichte*, 2 vols., 8th rev. ed. (Paderborn, 1926-30), II, 114f.; Bernhardi, 297ff.

10. *Annales Ceccanses*, aa. 1125 and 1126, *MGHSS*, XIX, 275ff. The events of the papal election of 1130 date back to 1124, when Cardinal Frangipani acclaimed Cardinal Lampert as pope instead of the already elected Celestine II, cf. L. Duchesne, ed., *Liber pontificalis*, 2 vols. (Paris, 1886-92), 306, n. 4. Celestine II resigned, but was reelected.

11. Cf. J. Watterich, *Vitae pontificum Romanorum ab ex saeculo IX usque ad saeculum XIII* (Leipzig, 1862), II, 185f. The election of Innocent II is mentioned in a writ of Walter of Ravenna to Norbert of Kanten, cf. J. P. Migne, ed., *Patrologiae cursus completus, series latina*, 224 vols. (Paris, 1844-55), cited hereafter *MPL*, 179, 39, and discussed in the *Chronicon s. Andreae*, iii:37, in *MGHSS*, VII, 549; and by John of Salisbury, *Policraticus*, ed. C. C. J. Webb, 2 vols. (Oxford, 1909), viii:3. Duchesne, *Liber pontificalis*, II, 379.

12. On the 1059 papal election decree, see Doeberl, III, no. 4; W. Ullmann, "Zum Papstwahldekret von 1059," *Zeitschrift der Savigny Stiftung für Rechtsgeschichte*, kan. Abt., 68 (1982), 32ff.

13. It must have been the intention of Pierleoni to be pope after Honorius II, cf. *MGHSS*, XXVI, 39. On his Jewish descent, see Ordericus Vitalis, *Historia ecclesiastica*, xii:21, in *MPL*, 188, 914f. It was the Cardinal-Bishops of Albano and of Ostia who had elected Innocent II, cf. *Annales Reichersbergenses*, anno 1130, *MGHSS*, XVII, 454.

14. *Ibid.*; *Romoualdi Annales, ibid.*, XIX, 420; *Annales Casinenses*, a. 1130, *ibid.*, XIX, 309; Ordericus Vitalis, xiii:3; Rodulphi, *Vita Petri Venerabilis*, c. 4, in E. Martene and U. Durand, eds., *Veterum scriptorum et monumentorum collectio*, 9 vols. (repr. New York, 1968), VI, 1187.

15. Cf. the abbot's correspondence, in *MPL*, 182, 293ff.; also, Doeberl, IV (Munich, 1891), no 7; J. Sydow, "Bernard von Clairvaux und die römische Kurie," *Citeaux in de Nederlanden*, 6 (1955), 5ff., in ref. to two of Bernard's letters, in Doeberl, IV, ep. 126 and 127. On Innocent II allegedly being a Prareschi, see Duchesne, *Liber pontificalis*, II, 385; Arnulf of Lisieux held a good opinion of the family, cf. *MPL*, 201, 18f. According to Gerhoch of Reichersberg, Innocent II was the rightfully elected pontiff, "universitas Ecclesiae propter electio et eligentium potiorem partem in Innocentium consensit," *ibid.*, 194, 1445; or, in E. Dümmler, ed., *MGH Libelli de lite*, 3 vols. (Hanover, 1891-97), III, 305.

16. Innocent II celebrated Easter, 1130, at St. Denis de l'estree, cf. R. Molinier, ed., Suger, *Vita Ludovici VI* (Paris, 1887), c. 21, or *MPL*, 186, 1330f.; fled to Paris, Duchesne, *Liber pontificalis*, II, 381; also Peter Venerabilis, *De miraculis*, ii:16, *MPL*, 189,. 928; and participated in the Synod of Étemps, cf. Suger, c. 21; Ordericus Vitalis, xiii:1, *MPL*, 188, 923ff.; insisted that Cluny did influence the royal court's decision in recognizing Innocent II; also, *Annales Blandinenses*, a. 1130, *MGHSS*, V, 28; Bernhardi, 327ff.

17. Cf. *Annales Magdeburgenses*, anno 1131, *ibid.*, XVI, 183f. Ordericus Vitalis, xiii:3, though his report on attendance is different; also, *Vita Norberti*, c. 19, *MGHSS*, XII, 697ff. The Reims, 1131, synod excommunicated Anacletus II, *ibid.*, XII, 697, n. 57. English recognition mentioned by Suger, c. 31; and Ordericus Vitalis, xiii:11.

18. Norbert of Xanten did intercede with the emperor's court, cf. *MGHSS*, XII, 700f.; Annalista Saxo, anno 1130, *ibid.*, VI, 766f.; for inside information, see Otto of Freising, *Chronicon*, vii:18 etc., *ibid.*, XX, 257.; F. J. Schmale, "Die Bemühungen Innozenz II um seine Anerkennung in Deutschland," *Zeitschrift für Kirchengeschichte*, 65 (1953), 240ff.

19. Analectus II obtained the support of Roger II of Sicily, cf. *MPL*, 179, 689ff.; the contemporaries could not understand the behavior of Roger II, see M. Bouquet, ed., *Rerum Gallicarum et Franciarum Scriptores*, 23 vols. (Paris, 1738-1876), XV, 366. Analectus II did recognize Roger II as king, cf. Ordericus Vitalis, xiii:23, *MPL*, 188, 922. On the other hand, Anacletus II did not know how to behave himself, cf. Duchesne, *Liber pontificalis*, II, 380; but gained control of Rome, cf. *Annales Reichersbergenses*, anno 1130, *MGHSS*, XVII, 454; H. W. Klewitz, "Das Ende des Reformpapsttums," *Deutsches Archiv*, 3 (1939), 371ff.

20. Lothair III did, before his coronation, renounce investiture, cf. *Narratio de electione Lotharii*, *MGHSS*, XII, 511; the new emperor received as a fief the duchy of Tuscany from the Pope, cf. *Annales Magdeburgenses*, a. 1133, *ibid.*, XVI, 184; *MGHLL*, II, 75; Jaffé, *Regesta*, I, no. 5962; Romualdi Annales, in *MGHSS*, XIX, 420. Wall painting mentioned in *Chronica regis Coloniensis*, a. 1156, *ibid.*, XVII, 766f.; Otto of Freising, *Gesta Friderici Imperatoris*, iii:10, did say that the painting symbolized the fact that the emperor "homo sit papae." Cf. *ibid.*, XX, 421f.

21. *Annales Magdeburgenses*, anno 1135.

22. Annalista Saxo, anno 1137, *MGHSS*, VI, 775; *ibid.*, XIX, 422; Freising, *Chronicon*, vii:20, Bernhardi, 783ff.

23. Cf. E. Szentpétery, ed., *Scriptores rerum Hungaricarum* 2 vols. (Budapest, 1937-38), cited hereafter as *SSH*, I, 434,4-6.

24. *Ibid.*, I, 429,10-13; *Annales Aegidi Brunsvicenses*, a. 1135, *MGHSS*, XXI, 13; on his reign, *Chronicon pictum*, cc. 160-63, in *SSH*, I, 446ff.; Gy. Kristó-F. Makk, "Krónikáink keletkezéstörténetéhez" /Remarks on the Origins of Hungarian Chronicles/, *Történelmi Szemle*, 15 (1972), 198ff.

25. *Chronicon pictum*, cc. 153-59; J. Horváth, *Az Árpád-kori latin nyelvű történeti irodalom stílusproblémái* /Stylistic Questions Concerning the Latin Language Historical Literature of the Arpadian Age/ (Budapest, 1954), 270ff. Kosztolnyik, 79 ff., and 93, n. 1; 94, n. 8.

26. *SSH*, I, 434,6-8, possibly in ref. to Ps. 118, 109 (Vulgate).

27. *SSH*, I, 434f.; Cosmas of Prague, *Chronica Bohemorum*, iii:42, *MGHSS*, IX, 123,4: "...unde dux ille ad placitum distulit ire." F. Makk, "Megjegyzések II István történetéhez" /Some Comments on the Reign of Stephen II/, *Memoria saeculorum Hungariae*, ed. J. Horváth, *et al.*, (Budapest, 1974), I, 167ff.

28. *SSH*, I, 435,7-10.

29. Cf. *Vita Conradi archiepiscopi Salzburgensis*, c. 18, *MGHSS*, XI, 63ff., and 73f., composed in the 1170's, cf. W. Wattenbach, *Deutschlands Geschichtsquellen im Mittelalter*, 2 vols., 6th ed. (Berlin, 1893-95), II, 299f.

30. *MGHSS*, IX, 123,1-8.

31. *Ibid.*, XI, 74,2-7.

32. Gy. Pauler, *A magyar nemzet története az árpádházi királyok alatt* /The History of the Hungarian Nation under the Árpád Kings/, 2 vols. (Budapest, 1893-95), I, 227ff.

33. *MGHSS*, XI, 74,12-20. "Er zuerst brachte durch seine Festigkeit und sein persönliches Ansehen einen daurenden Frieden mit den Ungarn zu Stande." Cf. Wattenbach, II, 300; Bernhardi, 528f.

34. *MGHSS*, XI, 75 (c. 20); the cathedral burnt down on May 4, 1127, cf. *Annales s. Rudberti Salisburgensis, ibid.*, IX, 774, and note 67.

35. *Chronicon pictum*, c. 154; B. Hóman *Geschichte des ungarischen Mittelalters*, 2 vols. (Berlin, 1940-43), I, 381, spoke of the daughter of *an* Italian Norman count; Pauler, II, 231 and 473f., wrote that Stephen II had married a daughter of Robert of Capua. See also Cosmas of Prague, *Chronica*, iii:51.

36. *SSH*, I, 437,14-16; Kievan Annals, a. 1123; Moscow Annals, a. 1123; Tverj Annals, a. 1123, in A. Hodinka, *Az orosz évkönyvek magyar vonatkozásai* /Data Concerning Hungary in the Russian Annals/ (Budapest, 1916), 96Af., 200ABff., and 266Af., respectively; Pauler, I, 231f.

37. *SSH*, I, 437.; Gy. Moravcsik, *Byzantium and the Magyars* (Amsterdam-Budapest, 1970), 78f.

38. *SSH*, I, 439,9-11; the meeting, *ibid.*, I, 438,31, was different from the one held by "principes Hungariae," *ibid.*, I, 438,20-22.

39. F. Makk, "Megjegyzések II. István történetéhez" /Comments on the Reign of Stephen II/, in J. Horváth, *et al.*, ed., *Memoria saeculorum Hungariae*, I (Budapest, 1974), 251ff. F. Makk, *Magyarország a 12. században* /Hungary in the Twelfth Century/, in *Magyar História* series (Budapest, 1986), 60ff.

41. *Ibid.*, I, 438,30-439,5.

42. *Ibid.*, I, 439,18-24; Pauler, I, 233.

43. *Ibid.*, I, 437,11-14.

44. *Ibid.*, I, 442,13-15; F. Makk, "Megjegyzések II. Béla történetéhez" /Comments on the Reign of Béla II/, *Acta historica Universitatis Szegediensis*, 40 (1972), 31ff., spoke of two parties (=interest groups), the one supportive of Álmos and Béla /II/ the Blind; the other, of Coloman the Learned and his son, Stephen II, cf. L. Elekes *et al.*, *Magyarország története 1526-ig* /Hungarian History until 1526/ (Budapest, 1961), 93.

45. *SSH*, I, 442,16-17.

46. Cf. A. Meineke, ed., Iohannes Cinnamus: *Epitomae rerum ab Ioanna et Alexio Comnenis gestarum* (Bonn, 1836), cited hereafter as Cinnamus, i:5 (12,18-21); Gy. Moravcsik, ed., *Fontes byzantini historiae Hungaricae aevo ducum et regum ex stirpe Arpad descendentium* (Budapest, 1984), cited hereafter as Moravcsik, *Fontes,* 194ff.; *idem,* "Les sources byzantines de l'histoire hongroise," *Byzantion,* 9 (1934), 663ff.; K. Krumbacher, *Geschichte der byzantinischen Literatur,* 2nd ed. (Munich, 1897), 279ff.

47. *SSH*, I, 442,17-19.

48. "Cereos magnos ardentes in fundamentum hominis stillare faciebat," *ibid.,* I, 442,19-21.

49. B. Hóman and Gy. Szekfű, *Magyar történet,* 5 vols., 6th ed. (Budapest, 1939), I, 297f.; compare with F. Heer, *Geistesgeschichte,* 2nd ed. (Stuttgart, 1965), 90ff.

50. Cinnamus, i:4.

51. *Chronicon pictum,* c. 156; Cinnamus, i:4 (CB, 10); I. Bekker, ed., Nicetas Choniates, *Historia: De imperio Iohannis Comneni Porphyrogeniti* (Bonn, 1837), cited hereafter as Choniates, *Iohannis Comneni,* c. 5 (CB, 24); recent edition of Greek text by I. A. von Dieten, ed., *Nicetae Choniatae Historia* (Berlin-New York, 1975), cited hereafter as Dieten, 17,39-19,2; Moravcsik, *Fontes,* 257ff.; Krumbacher, 281ff.

52. Álmos has been a dangerous enemy, cf. *SSH*, I, 442f.; Cinnamus, i:4; Choniates, *Iohannis Comneni* c. 5 (Dieten, 17).

53. *Chronicon pictum,* end of c. 156; Canonicus Wissegradensis, *Continuatio Cosmae Pragensis Chronica,* anno 1137, *MGHSS,* IX, 143.

54. *SSH*, I, 443,9-21.

55. *Ibid.,* I, 443,21-27, 29-31.

56. *Ibid.,* c. 155.

57. *Chronicon pictum,* c. 158; Sophia had married Lampert of Hunt-Pázmány who established a monastery at Bozók in about 1135; cf. E. Szentpétery, ed., *Regesta regum stirpis Arpadianae critico-diplomatica,* 2 vols. (Budapest, 1923-61), I, no. 59.

58. L. Erdélyi, *Árpádkor* /Age of the Árpáds/ (Budapest, 1922), 147, supported by A. Bonfini, *Rerum Ungaricarum decades quattuor,* ed. J. Fógel *et al.,* 4 vols. (Leipzig-Budapest, 1936-41), I, 117; one is to remember, of course, that Bonfini "war unkritisch, nur für die Zeit Matthias (=Corvinus) glaubwürdig." Cf. A. Potthast, *Bibliotheca historica medii aevi,* 2 vols., rev. ed. (Berlin, 1896), I, 163. Pauler, I, 237, expressed a different view.

59. *SSH*, I, 444,9-11.

60. He had a German name, *ibid.,* I, 441,14; Pauler, I, 235; was a misguided person, *SSH*, I, 444,9-11.

61. *Ibid.,* I, 444,17-19.

62. *Ibid.,* I, 444,11 and 16.

63. *Ibid.,* I, 444,16-23.

64. *Chronicon pictum,* c. 150; Alberici Trium Fontium, *Chronica,* anno 1135, *MGHSS,* XXIII, 832; as to the reason why? see *SSH*, I, 429,10-13; and *Annales Aegidi Brunsvicenses,* anno 1135, *MGHSS,* XXI, 13.

65. *SSH*, I, 447,1-14; the scene has some similarity with III Kings, 16, 11 (Vulgate). The chronicler spoke of a special meeting, *SSH*, I, 446f., and not of the gathering on St. Stephen's Day. Concerning this, see the Hungarian Golden Bull of 1222, art. 1, in H. Marczali, *et al.,* eds., *Enchiridion fontium historiae*

Hungarorum (Budapest, 1901), 134f. According to Gy. Kristó - F. Makk, "Krónikáink keletkezéstörténetéhez" /Remarks on the Origins of Hungarian Chronicles/, *Történelmi Szemle*, 15 (1972), 198ff., the *Chronicon pictum* cc. 160 and 161, represent two strands, providing conflicting information.

66. *SSH*, I, 447,19-25, a serious blow to the opposition?

67. *Ibid.*, I, 443,21-26.

68. "...quorum consilio hoc sit actum?" *Ibid.*, I, 447,14; Béla the Blind lived in constant fear for his life, *ibid.*, I, 443,9-12.

69. "Quia Hungari semper fluctuant iniuria, sicut mare salsum," *ibid.*, I, 447,28-30; F. Makk, "Megjegyzések Kálmán külpolitikájához" /Comments on the Foreign Policy of Coloman the Learned/, *Acta historica Szegediensis*, 67 (1980), 21ff.; *idem*, on Béla II, *art. cit.*, *ibid.*, 40 (1972), 31ff.

70. Albericus, *Chronica*, anno 1135, *MGHSS*, XXIII, 832; on Boris, see Otto of Freising, *Chronicon*, vii:21, *ibid.*, XX, 259,30-35; A. Lhotsky, "Otto von Freising: seine Weltanschauung," in his *Europäisches Mittelalter* (Vienna, 1970), 64ff.; furthermore, Canon of Wishegrad, *Continuatio*, anno 1132, *MGHSS*, IX, 138; Moravcsik, *Byzantium*, 78.

71. "Plurimi autem ex nobilibus," *SSH*, I, 447f.

72. He requested and obtained military aid from his brother-in-law, Adalbert, cf. *MGHSS*, XX, 259,35-37; Cosmas of Prague, *Chronica*, iii:51, *ibid.*, IX, 126,6-8; Bernhardi, *Lothar III*, 530, and 539ff.

73. *SSH*, I, 448,17-19; in the background, Choniates, *Iohannis Comneni*, c. 5 (Dieten, 17); the Hungarian chronicler emphasized loyalty to the cause: *fideles regni* (that is, the realm), and not to the King! Cf. *SSH*, I, 448,19-20.

74. *Ibid.*, I, 448,25-27.

75. *Ibid.*, I, 448,27-35.

76. *Ibid.*, I, 450,7-13.

77. *Ibid.*, I, 450f.

78. *Ibid.*, I, 451,17-18. The leader was the Polish monarch himself, Boleslaw III, cf. *Chronicon principum Poloniae*, c. 15, in A. Bielowski, ed., *Monumenta Poloniae historica*, 6 vols. (Lvov-Cracow, 1864-93; repr. Warsaw, 1960-61), III, 457ff.; *Annales Polonorum*, in *MGHSS*, XIX, 624.

79. "Cum suis perterritus, expectata nocte fugam iniit." Cf. *ibid.*, IX, 138,23-24.

80. *SSH*, I, 451f.; *Continuatio Claustroneuburgensis I*, anno 1134, *MGHSS*, IX, 612. After the battle, the king had richly rewarded the loyalty of his supporters, cf. *SSH*, I, 452,2-16.

Katherine Gyékényesi Gatto:

5 / IMAGES OF WOMAN AND LOVE IN THE POETRY OF JANUS PANNONIUS, 1434-1472

Critics and historians of Hungarian literature have long acknowledged Janus Pannonius (1434-1472) to be the greatest poet of the early Hungarian Renaissance. [1] With a classical Latin vocabulary and grammatical structure, enriched by the liberal use of mythological allusions, Pannonius's verse magically conveys the age's vision of a man-centered universe. Innumerable books, monographs and articles have explored the political and humanist aspects of Pannonius's life and ouevre, [2] but none have examined his concept of woman and love. Although his career as a powerful church official and politician in the court of Matthias Corvinus (1458-1490) left little room for romantic dalliances, [3] there is evidence in the poetry, especially in his early epigrams, that Pannonius was no stranger to women nor to love. Furthermore, in some of the longer poems, namely the epithalamia and elegies, Pannonius reveals in sharp contrast to his erotic and many times sexually explicit epigrams, an idealized view of woman in her roles of wife and mother. The purpose of this essay, therefore, is to reflect on Pannonius's images of woman, and indirectly on love, and to elucidate how these evolved from an hedonistic portrayal in which woman was perceived as an object for man's pleasure, to an appreciation of woman as spouse and companion, and ultimately her idealization in what Pannonius deemed her most perfected and valuable role—that of nurturer and mother.

The poems of Janus Pannonius that treat the themes of woman and love can be divided into three types: epigram, epithalamium, and elegy. While cultivating the epigram, a form in which he excelled, Pannonius was not only imitating Martial as well as Catullus,[4] but was also employing one of the oldest literary forms noted for its brevity and wit. Essentially in its earliest form, the Greek epigram served as an inscription, like epitaphs, dedications or sentiments put on gifts—it was a distillment of the lyric impulse to its tiniest tangible drop. Later the Roman epigram became an invective, sacrificing the flavor to the sting. This sting, or unexpected surprise ending, many times was a personal judgment or a verdict on a certain predicament or situation.[5] Hence, for Pannonius as for Martial, the epigram is autobiographical and occasional in mode, and almost always possesses a provocative tone.[6] It is a poetry of experience insofar as it depicts the author's reactions to the foibles and follies of human nature, especially those related to man's sexual exploits.[7] Conversely, one must bear in mind that the epigram traditionally and actually has its own artistic purpose and shape, and as such, does not need an immediate connection with reality. It can merely suggest a conventional form, such as a party, or an escapade in a house of ill repute in order to create a poetic situation.[8] This fact becomes particularly important in light of some of Pannonius's more obscene and tasteless epigrams. To paraphrase the words of Ovid, Pannonius's life was probably chaste, only his Muse was naughty.[9] Catullus expressed the same thought in a slightly different manner: a poet must be *castus* but not his verses if they hope to interest and excite readers.[10]

All of the epigrams in question were written during Pannonius's extensive stay and studies in Italy, first at the Humanist academy of Guarino da Verona in Ferrara (1447-1454) and later at the University of Padua (1454-1458).[11] In these surroundings and imbued with the Renaissance spirit, it was only natural that Pannonius expressed with his poetic first person the thematic concerns of the age, among them man's relationship with woman. His early approach was primarily an outpouring of an adolescent's obsessive preoccupation with sex and the inner turmoil created by unfulfilled desire. In two of the epigrams addressed to Agnes, "De Agnete" (*Ágneshez*) /To Agnes/ and "Optat Coitum Puellae" (*Szeretkezni vágyik*) /He wishes to Make Love/,[12] Pannonius first eulogizes the fiery brilliance of Agnes's eyes which reminds him of the effulgent magnificence of the stars and then proceeds in the second poem, in the most casual tone, to invite her to bed with him. The first epigram's metaphoric description of Agnes's eyes as a pair of stars is punctuated with adjectives that connotatively are applicable to both: *"ragyogó," "legragyogóbbja," "tüzel," "lobogó," "szikrázik"* /shining, shiniest, burns, flaming, sparks/ (69). When the poet glances at Agnes's eyes, he sees not only a pair of shining stars but the hidden depths of her burning passion. The use of the mythological figures of Venus and Jupiter, Sirius and Arcturus, first of all reflect Pannonius's familiarity with classical literature and astrology. Secondly, the mythological figures as poetic devices have their own distinct function within the parameters of the poem, namely to add greater resonance to the metaphor, to embellish the verse, and to draw a parallel between the myth and the actual situation in order to give the latter greater importance and transcendence. Thus Pannonius desires to unite with Agnes in a heated embrace as to equal the blazing splendor of the intertwined planetary and stellar figures of the evening sky:

> Vénusz anyánk tüzel így égi helyén, lobogó
> Karjai közt Jupiternek. S így szikrázik az éjben
> Arcturusát ölelő távoli Sírius is.

> /Thus Venus our mother burns in her heavenly home,
> within the flaming arms of Jupiter.
> And thus sparks distant Sirius in the night
> while embracing Arcturus./ (69)

Agnes's eyes, her and the poet's passion, the stars and planets fuse into one fiery image before the reader's eyes.

The second poem, "Optat Coitum Puellae" (*Szeretkezni vágyik*) /He Wishes to Make Love/, is an invitation to love. Again the poet addresses Agnes, cautiously at first because she is married,[13] yet armed with a series of arguments favoring his cause: woman was created for this act, without sex there would be no propagation of the race, she won't wear it out, she would make both of them happy, her mother gave it to her father, otherwise she, i.e. Agnes would not exist, nor would her beautiful eyes, whose passionate gaze sears his flesh and spirit. The sex act, the poet continues, affords great pleasure for both the man and the woman, its only negative aspect being abstention from it. He subduedly pokes fun at the virgins who at first reluctantly and measuredly succumb and afterwards cannot control their own desires. Mythological references to Juno and Jupiter, Mars and Venus reinforce and lend an authoritative tone to his reasoning. The contrapuntal structuring of his arguments and wordplay, for example, *"sok eföldi-égi nőktől,"* /from many earthly-heavenly women/, *"ezt ha adni fogod, javadra válik/ hogyha meg nem adod, gyötör sokáig,"* /if you give this, it will be to your benefit/ if you don't give it, it will torment you for a long time/ (69), comes to a climax in the last two lines, a technique reminiscent of Martial's style. The repetition and emphasis on the word *"nyilván"* in a multi-meaningful context gives the last line its punch:

> Nem szól semmit, aj-aj! nem adja nyilván,
> ám mégis: mosolyog, odaadja nyilván.
>
> /She speaks not, oh-oh! surely she does not give it,
> But still: she smiles, certainly she gives it./ (69/

The conquest of the woman initially out of reach, is now within the grasp of the poet, her submission intimated by her smile. The suspenseful moment of Agnes's vacillation is skillfully captured in the poet's brilliant manipulation of a few words that give one pause, and then proceed to resolve the dilemma with a quiet bang.

Written in the same vein the epigram, "Ad Magdalenam" (*Magdolnához*) /To Magdalene/ (71), [14] also introduces the classical figure of the go-between. [15] The poet once again suffers and despairs because of unfulfilled desire and seeks the intervention of his beloved's confidante, named Magdalene, in order to win her favor. He is in need of someone to intercede on his behalf, and in exchange is willing to do anything and everything.

> Unszold szép rokonod, hogy meg ne vessen,
> És majd, hogyha elérnél nála többet,
> Melyről szólani tilt a bölcs szemérem,
> Meglásd, teljesitem, ha bármit óhajtsz.
>
> /Urge your beautiful relative, not to ignore me,
> And, if you attain more with her than that which

wise modesty prohibits mention,
You'll see, I'll do anything you wish./ (71/

Youth's insatiable lust is the theme of two brief, related epigrams, "De Se Ipso" (*Saját magáról*) /About Himself/ and "De Amica Sua" (*Barátnőjéről*) /About His Girlfriend/ (73). In the former Pannonius reproaches himself for his uncontrollable lust when confronted by the appealing curves of the female body. In the latter he complains to his mistress about her voracious appetite for sex, regardless of his almost superhuman sexual virtuosity.

"De Silvia" (*Szilviáról*) /About Sylvia/ (75) is a humorous, witty, epigrammatic treatment of the theme of the unwed, promiscuous, pregnant lover, who tries to pinpoint a father in order to legitimize her baby. Pannonius's reactions to her charge that he is the father border on being the most succinctly clever and spontaneously funny of his amatory poems, with the sting occurring in the last line. Sardonically he likens her predicament to that of one traversing a field of thorny bushes and emerging with a bloody leg, only to proclaim that it was this particular thorn that pricked her.

> Mert ha te dús tövisek közt jársz, mondd, így keseregsz-e:
> Vérzik a lábam s jaj, épp ez a tüske hibás!

> /Because if you wander through a thicket,
> tell me, do you lament thus:
> My foot is bleeding and ouch, this
> precise thorn is the culprit!/ (75)

Pannonius's penchant for the occasional obscene imagery of Martial is evident in the two epigrams directed to Laelia, most likely a pseudonym for another mistress. In the short, two-lined epigram, "De Laelia" (*Laeliáról*) /About Laelia/ (75), the poet stoops to prurient *double entendres*, while in the follow-up poem, "Ad Eandem" (*Ugyanahhoz*) /**To the Same**/ (75), Pannonius juxtaposes the vision of a pair of copulating snakes with only the two heads distinguishable, to his own dream of passionate union with Laelia with one exception—their two heads are also fused. The comparison is very striking by virtue of a complex, emotional situation being grasped by a most revealing and shocking reptilic act.

Egybefonódik a párzó kígyópár s oly erősen
minthacsak egy testből nőne a két kicsi fej.
Én meg, Laelia, úgy vágyom veled összetapadni
hogy ne legyen többé még a fejünk se külön.

/The copulating pair of snakes clings together so tightly
as if their two little heads grew out of the same body.
And I, Laelia, desire to stick to you
so that not even our heads are two./ (75)

"Quaestio Ardua et Difficilis" (*Súlyos és kellemetlen kérdés*)
/A Serious and Unpleasant Question/ (87) explores the nature of
the sexual relationship between men and women. The poem
commences with a simple query about a biological reality — the
why and wherefore of intercourse — and concludes with an answer
bound in myth. Sexual desire has been with us ever since
Prometheus formed man out of clay and realized that he had to
provide for procreation in the physical make-up of the human
species.

S mert a leány ágyékából tépett ki kevéskét,
s rakta a másik lény lába közé e csomót:
most az a vájat folyton kergeti hajdani részét,
és ez a rész folyton visszakivánja helyét.

/And because he tore a small part from the girl's groin,
and placed this lump between another creature's legs:
now that cavity constantly chases its former part,
and the same part constantly desires its original place./ (87)

The sex act, the poet asserts, is a most natural result of two bodily
parts seeking the primeval union that was once theirs.

Repeatedly we have seen in these early epigrams that
Pannonius placed great emphasis on the purely erotic essence of
woman and love. Ideally he tells us, in yet another epigram, "Ad
Amicam" (*Barátnőjéhez*) /To His Mistress/ (89), that he desires
an everlasting, physical union with woman in which the pleasure
of the moment supersedes all else, and time is suspended:

Haj pedig én, kicsikém, addig vágynálak ölelni
míg csak a zöld repkény fogja a tölgy derekát;

S akkor végeznék csak a csókkal, hogyha a csúszós
kagyló kagylóját önmaga hagyja oda. (89) [16]

/Oh but I, little one, would desire to embrace you
as long as the green ivy clings to the oak tree's waist;
And I would only end our kiss, when the slippery
conch abandons its shell./ (89)

As the poet verbalizes his wishful thinking regarding the
permanence of their affair, the *dénoûement* jars the mind with its
earthy imagery:

Bár úgy kötnék Vénusz láncai a szeretőket
mint ahogy a nőstény s kan kutya összeragad!

/If only Venus's chains would bind lovers as closely
as a bitch and male dog stick together!/ (89)

The picture of two dogs in heat mating defeats our expectation of
a more romantic ending and leaves a lasting impression on the
reader's mind. [17]

The oft-quoted myth of Leda and the swan serves as the basis
for the epigram, "De Amore Suo In Ledam Puellam" (*Lédához
fűződő szerelméről*) /About His Love For Leda/ (91). In this
instance the poet is infatuated with a golden haired Leda, and
challenged by the prospect of her seduction. Inspired by
the example of Zeus he realizes that he too must resort to
deception and force in his conquest of her. The inner world
of the poet's desire, the outer world of an impossible situation, and the mythological world converge within the poem
to create a tri-dimensional, elastic reality.

A false sense of modesty and feigned shock provide the
tongue-in-cheek humor of the epigram, "Conqueritur, Quod se
Socii ad Lupanar Seduxissent" (*Panaszkodik, hogy társai
bordélyházba csalták*) /He Complains That His Companions
Lured Him to a Bordello/ (95). Images of bedecked, bejewelled,
partly nude females in varying erotic poses present themselves to
the poet within the confines of a paltry dwelling at the edge of
civilization. He berates his companions for having dragged him
under false pretenses to such a place, yet all the while fully
cognizant of the circumstances and anticipatory of the impending adventure.

The female ideal of Pannonius's youth is best summed up in the poem, "Qualem Optet Amicam" (*Milyen barátnőt szeretne*) /The Kind of Mistress He'd Like to Have/ (97). When in bed (almost always a given condition), she should be the perfect mistress, fetching, witty, good-humored, and most importantly uninhibited, almost licentious in her love-making: *"mindennél inkább kell bujasága nekem"* /more than anything I want her passion/ (97).

To conclude the overview of Pannonius's early amatory epigrams, one might mention two more which incorporate aspects of the Ovidian and the courtly love traditions. In "Ad Iustinam" (*Justinához*) /To Justina/ (105), he sends a token of his love to Justina who interprets the gesture as if he were trying to buy her love, and returns the gift to the poet. Angrily the poet challenges her to send him a gift and in the last line threatens not to accept it in order that she too suffer the pain of humiliation and rejection. "De Se Quod Amare Coepisset" (*Mikor szerelembe esett*) /When He Fell In Love/ (109) discusses the madness and delirium of unrequited love. Addressing his friend Michael, the poet begs for his assistance and understanding since he too had undergone the same experience earlier, but with little sympathy from the poet. Love is metaphorically portrayed as an all-consuming fire that through an act of fate, destroys first man's body and ultimately his soul: *"Fogva vagyok, lángok mardosnak minden izemben, / S végül a tűzbe merész szellemem is belehull"* /I'm captive, the flames sear my every being,/ And finally, my brave spirit too falls into the fire/ (109). Thus love for Pannonius, at least erotic love, is in the long run a destructive rather than a constructive force in man's life: *"Emberi vágyakozás Ámor s kín—nem pedig 'isten'"* /Love is a human longing and suffering—not a god./ (155)

As we have seen, the epigrammatic mode is Pannonius's vehicle for the direct, sometimes startlingly coarse depictions of his youthful emotions and reactions to romantic liaisons and fantasies. It becomes clear that for Pannonius, woman, at least within the poetic parameters, represents mainly a beautiful, sexual object. At times she can be playful, sensual, matching her partner's eroticism; other times she is cold, selfish, withholding sex from her lover. The question still remains however, what exactly was the relationship between passion and poetry for Pannonius. The answer probably lies within the poetic traditions of his era. Pannonius like the other neo-Latin poets had literary consciousness and the need to immortalize that self-awareness through deed and word. Since the Christian sense of the universe had been weakened by the queries of the age, man no longer knew where time was leading him. In this particular poetic tradition physical passion makes time cease, at least while the couple are in the throes of that love. On the other hand, a better way to conquer death was through poetry and Pannonius fully discerned this fact. He knew that by imitating the classical writers he linked what was alive for him now with what was alive in the past, and this too represented a major victory over time. [18] Thus Pannonius's images of woman and love in at least the early period seem to have served this dual purpose.

The remaining body of poems that involve images of woman and love evidence the poet's recovery from his adolescent sexual obsession and point to a maturation process resulting in the idealization of both subjects. No longer do we encounter only female types or unidentified individuals; rather we are confronted with historically accurate female personages who are eulogized in their queenly, motherly or wifely roles. [19] The epithalamia comprise the second category of poems, and while the epigrams were born of moments of inspiration, these were mainly written for political and social aims. [20] The epithalamia or wedding songs extol the virtues of the bride who is always matched up with a groom who is himself a paragon. In the tradition of Catullus, Pannonius's nuptial odes deal with the praise of the highborn and are written for special occasions to express his feelings about the families, [21] and like his predecessor, Pannonius celebrates marriage as the fulfillment of the woman's life. [22] The female profile that emerges from his wedding songs is that of the dutiful wife, initially always a virgin, dedicated to ennobling and honoring her already model of a husband.

In the ode, "Ad Antonium Mariam, De Coniuge Ducenda" (*Antonius Máriához a nősülésről*) /To Maria Antonius about Marriage/ (295), the poet petitions the gods so that Antonius's future wife may never tarnish his name. In his prayer to Venus he begs her to find a pure virgin for Antonius and to unite the young couple forever with an everlasting and true love. As the goddess of love, Venus is beseeched by the poet to provide his friend with the perfect girl, whom he proceeds to describe from three perspectives: her character, her life's work, and her appearance.

The ideal wife according to Pannonius and the mores of the times, should be wise, serious, honest, kind, modest, and above all pure in heart. She should be whole, untouched and possess innocence of body and soul and a light, refined temperament. Her daily labor should consist of female handiwork, namely embroidery and weaving. Physically she should have a pretty face with sparkling eyes, a shining, milk-white countenance accentuated by rosy lips. Her shape should equal that of Venus. In conclusion, Pannonius promises Venus eternal homage if she grants his request on behalf of his friend.

In another epithalamium, dedicated to Gulielmo Calefino and Flordemilia Guarina's wedding, Pannonius exploits the occasion to praise the Calefino dynasty and the Guarino family tree.[23] After enumerating the honors bestowed on the Calefinos throughout their history and their claim to fame and fortune, the poet extols the bride, using a litany of mythological comparisons:

> **Bája a szépalakú Cytherea csodás adománya,**
> szende erénye pedig szűz Dianára utal.
> Phoebus ajándékát Pallas plántálta szívébe,
> s mesterségedet is, Penelope, ügyesen
> megtanította a lánynak: a hímzésére ha néznek,
> elbujhatnak Kos vagy Szidon asszonyai.
> Néki arany Juno, Jupiter felesége adott szent
> méltóságot, a fent legmagasabban ülő; (303)

> /Her charm is the shapely Cytherea's wonderful gift,
> and her coy virtue points to the virgin Diana.
> Phoebus's gift was planted by Pallas in her heart,
> Who also skillfully taught her your craftmanship, Penelope:
> the women of Kos and Sidon would do well to hide as they
> view her embroidery.
> Golden Juno, Jupiter's wife, the one who sits on high, blessed
> her with saintly dignity;/ (303)

Her physical beauty and her snowy face, he continues, are no less finer than her spirit. She possesses nobility of body and soul, and respects God and her parents. All that she is, declares the poet, is due to the fact that her father is Guarino, the silver-tongued orator and prodigious writer of prose and verse whose name is immortalized in his multifarious literary output. Thus Flordemilia's worth is measured by her relationship to her famous father. His identity gives value to her before marriage, while that of her husband's will do so afterwards. In either case, Pannonius sees woman strictly as a correlative of man.

In a joyful hymn dedicated to Hymen, "Epithalamium in Matthaeum Herbam Mediolanensem et Margaritam Costabilem Ferrariensem" (*Nászdal a milánoi Mattheus Herba és Ferrarai Margarita Costabilis lakodalmára*) /A Wedding Song for the Marriage of Matthew Herba from Milan and Margaret Costabilis of Ferrara/ (307), Pannonius continues to dwell on man's identity-giving role in relation to woman. He compliments the newly-weds and declares them equal in nobility of lineage and character: "*mert oly egyenlő a kettő, erénnyel is ékes a kettő, /Mátkához vőlegény, ifjúhoz illik a lány*" /because the two are so alike, also with virtue they are blessed/. For the bride a suitable bridegroom, for the boy a fitting girl/. (307) Both are descendants of ancient, noble families from different cities. At the same time the poet reminds us, the bride is sweet and virtuous because her father, Bertrandus Costabilis, is a wise, fair, and energetic man of a great and noble family. How can the daughter be any different?

"Epithalamium in Liberam Guarinam et Salomonem Sacratum" (*Nászének Libera Guarina és Salomon De Sacrato esküvőjére*) /Wedding Song for Guarina Libera and Solomon de Sacrato/ (311) celebrates the wedding of Guarino's daughter Libera and her father's most judicious choice of a husband for her. Although the bridegroom is somewhat older than thirty, he's at the perfect age of wisdom, temperance and manly strength. As for the bride, her name Libera symbolizes her positive attributes, among them modesty and virtue. She is not unlike a goddess in her beauteous appearance and form, and all this Pannonius reiterates, she owes to her father Guarino: "*S még ha erényei nem lennének is: apja Guarino;/ily kitünő ember lánya, ez éppen elég*" /And even if she did not possess such virtue: her father is Guarino; being such an eminent man's daughter, is more than enough/. (313)

Pannonius's longest epithalamium commends the marriage of Jacopo Balbo and Paula Barbara. Interspersed between the praises of Paula's father and her husband are Pannonius's impressions of what makes a perfect wife. First of all, her teacher is her own mother who advises the bride on how she should run her household: faithful to her husband, kind to the servants and gentle with her family (414). The bridegroom we are told, is truly lucky for having found such a wife, who in her entire being reflects the vigorous intellect of her father and the graceful modesty of her mother. She is a goddess in the vein of Pallas Athena and Diana. In the moment of initial submission to her husband, she enters the marriage chamber tearfully (as she should) and ritualistically accompanied by her mother, who guides her into the waiting, loving arms of her new husband.

> Ekkor a nászasszony bekiséri a többi anyával
> nászágyához a síró lányt — mert sírnia illik, —
> hol mátkája, szerelmes karjaival megölelve,
> végre bevégzi a rég óhajtott éjszaka teljét.

> /At such time the mother-in-law, along with the other
> mothers, escorts/ the weeping girl to her marriage
> bed — because it is proper that she weep — / where
> her husband embraces her with loving arms,/
> and finally fulfills the long-awaited night's purpose./ (419)

Thus the bride, perhaps lamenting the bygone days of childish innocence or fearfully anticipating an unknown future, enters the state of matrimony in an age-old tradition, in which she is to seek and find her fulfillment and identity as companion to a man.

While Pannonius's understanding of woman and love in the epigrams and the epithalamia focuses on her role of mistress and wife, and on love as ignoble and noble, his approach in the third set of poems, the elegies, approximates a beatification of woman as mother, and maternal love as the epitome of a disinterested, all encompassing *caritas*. [24] Instead of the mistress-sex object of the erotic verses and the somewhat more idealized, yet restrained and dutiful wife-companion of the wedding hymns, the images of woman as mother, particularly those of his own mother, Borbála Vitéz, embody what in the poet's mature mind is perfected womanhood, devoid of any physicality and egotism. The changes that transpired in Pannonius's perspective on woman and love seem to mirror the poet's own mental and emotional develop- ment. His adolescent desires are described in his poetry in conjunction with images of women and situations that satisfied those hedonistic necessities. Later as the lust of youth diminished midst the myriad of political and personal problems, the poet envisioned a woman-companion, capable of sharing and meeting his spiritual needs as well. Finally the evolution of his own *Weltanschauung* led him to embrace the idealism of neo-Platonism in which woman was elevated to an unparalleled level of perfection. [25] She appears in Pannonius's final poetic phase as an intermediary and intercessor between the Supreme Good and man, a stellar figure, who has replaced her passionate gaze with the ethereal light of paradise.

The image of woman as mother is first encountered in the elegy, "De Morte Andreolae, Nicolai V. Pontificis Romani et Philippi Cardinalis Bononiensis Matris" (*Andreolának, V. Miklós római pápa és Fülöp bolognai kardinális anyjának halálára*) / On the Death of Andreola, the mother of Pope Nicholas V and Cardinal Philip of Bologna/ (273), and reaches its most profound conception in the encomium dedicated to his mother. In the former Pannonius praises the mother of Pope Nicholas V and Cardinal Philip of Bologna for having blessed the Christian world with two such eminent and important figures. In the introductory segment, the poet utilizes the popular medieval interpretation of death as the equalizer, for whom neither wealth nor poverty, neither youth nor old age, neither beauty nor homeliness, neither power nor humble rank, neither virtue nor vice is an obstruction in carrying out its fateful task.

> Mert ugyanúgy nem néz senkit meg semmit a Párka,
> > ősi nemesség, rang: megveti ő ezeket.
> Nem kíméli a vént, és nem kíméli az ifjút,
> > s a gyönyörű arctól sem veszi vissza kezét.
> Nincs oly erény, mely a biztos sírtól megmenekíthet,
> > kincsnek halmaira sem hederít a halál.
> Nem torpan meg a zsarnok díszes göncei láttán,
> > sem fejedelmek, sem hercegek anyja előtt.

> /Because in the same way Parca does not look at
> anyone or anything, ancient nobility, rank: she ignores these.
> > She does not spare the old, nor does she spare the young,
> nor does she withdraw her hand from the beauteous face.
> > There is no such virtue, that can save one from the
> inevitable grave, nor does death heed hordes of treasure.
> > She is not deterred by the sight of the pompous
> tyrant's garb, nor by mothers of emperors and princes./ (273) [26]

In the second part of the eulogy Pannonius lists Andreola's virtues, outstanding among them her wisdom, decency, and Christian faith. Her whole being shone with spotless modesty, the poet tells us. Still, he interjects, although her character was impeccable, her earthly fame is attributable to the fact that she bore such illustrious sons: *"Ám ha erényeit ismerték is szerte a földön, /fénylővé mégis két fia tette nevét"* /Although her virtues were recognized here on earth/her two sons gave her fame/ (273). Next he addresses the mourners and bids them to provide her with a rose-fragrance filled, ritualistic funeral, befitting of a saint. In sharp contrast, the next lines reveal the ugly countenance of death, wherein the poet speaks to the worms, admonishing them to spare her innards from the ravages of their teeth. He begs those who visit her grave to tread softly near her tomb, to kneel down and quietly send a kiss while whispering words of consolation and homage:

> Üdv neked, áldott öl, ki a roppant oszlopot adtad,
>   melyre a teljes föld terhe reánehezül!
> Üdv, ragyogó Hold, tiszta szülője a fényteli Napnak,
>   mely mindent, ami van, égi sugárba borít!
> Üdv, pompás asszony, kinek egyik sarja a legfőbb
>   főhatalom-viselő, s tiszteli mind a világ.

> /Hail, blessed womb, who gave forth the enormous pillar,
>   upon which rests the weight of the entire world!
> Hail, shining Moon, pure mother of the glittering Sun,
>   which envelops all that is with heavenly light!
> Hail, regal woman, whose one off-spring is mighty
>   and powerful, and respected by the whole world./ (275)

With the use of an anaphora, he creates a lyrical, prayerful chant that focuses on her role as creator of two important and powerful rulers. Her eternal fame is assured, the poet consoles us, and is not entombed with her body, his words echoing the Renaissance ideal of fame victorious over death. Thus Andreola too conquers death and is worthy of apotheosis by virtue of her two sons.

> Méhedből, Áldott, ama Szentatya jött a világra,
>   akinek érdeme a tengerig, égig elér.
> Adja a hit meg a jog, hogy majd templomba kerülhess,
>   új istennővel nőjön a mennyei kar!

/From your womb, oh Blessed One, the Holy
   Father came into the world, whose merits
   extend to the oceans and the heavens.
Let faith and justice decree that you may
   be deified, that the heavenly host
   increase its numbers with another goddess./ (277)

"Threnos De Morte Barbarae Matris" (*Siratóének Anyjának, Borbálának halálára*) /A Lamentation on the Death of His Mother Barbara/ (335) represents in Hungarian literature an eternal monument to the love relationship between a mother and her child, and the first poem to immortalize a poet's mother. Two rhetorical questions set the sorrowful tone of the poem and express the lack of any consolation for the poet's grief: "*Mért jajgassak? Friss gyászomra akadhat-e gyógyir?*" /Why should I lament? Is there a balm for my fresh wound?/ (335) Immediately Pannonius announces the death of his mother, "*Ó, de hisz édesanyám halt meg, a könnyem övé,*" /Oh, my mother has died, my tears are hers/ (335) and situates this grave event in time and space. December 10, the poet reveals will always be a day of mourning as well as a special day for him. Nature too partakes of his sorrow; she appears somber and grey beneath the shadow of death. He vents his anger and frustration by cursing the stars believed to determine the fates of men. [27]

Csillag-had, rátok nyilván helyesebb haragudnom:
   sorsot szabni elénk vagytok az ég tetején.
Egyformán úrkodtok az életen és a halálon,
   vagytok az alsóbb lét dolgainak gyökere.

/Starry way, I should rather be angry at you:
   You who tailor the fates of men from your heavenly home.
Equally you lord over both life and death,
   You are the source of all that men do./ (337/

Pannonius's suffering is so great that not even time can assuage the pain. In order to fully express the magnitude of his anguish, and in support of his idealization of the mother-son relationship, the poet cites a series of mythological and historical figures through whom the nurturer-child bond is glorified. Furthermore, the fact that his mother died at an older age does not take away

one iota from his sorrow, as some might think. Rather the poet
asserts, the grief of parting never loses its edge.

In the following verses Pannonius nostalgically recounts his
life with his mother from the moment of his conception until her
death, indicating her influence on him, noting her special love
for him (she had two other sons), and ascribing to her all that he
has achieved. He lovingly paints a series of maternal portraits,
captured moments that they shared and experienced: her labor,
his birth, the nursing of her infant, her loving touch, her
guidance, the poet learning to walk, his first words, his schooling
and education, his sojourn in Italy, her longing for him, his
political successes, her presence as an aging woman in his palace,
her daily labors, her striving to always please her son and make
him happy even at the hour of her death.

> Ám te anyám voltál még most is, e szörnyeteg órán,
>   édes a sír, mondtad, hisz fiad élve marad.
> Már-már fátylasodó szemmel fürkészted az arcom,
>   s hülő szád folyton súgta-motyogta nevem.

> But you still remained my mother even then,
>   during that terrible hour,
>   the grave is sweet, you said, since your son remains alive.
> Your increasingly veiled gaze searched my face,
>   and your cooled lips continued
>   to whisper-murmur my name./ (341)

He promises her a Christian burial of pomp and circumstance,
with a funeral procession followed by a Requiem Mass, in which
he will be the main celebrant. Every detail of the funeral rite is
carefully planned by the poet-son to fully honor one who has led
such an exemplary life.

> Bűntelen éltél, példásan végezted a dolgod:
>   szolgáltál embert, s félted az Égi Atyát.
> Végig hű voltál urad emlékéhez, a sírig,
>   nem kellett új nász özvegyülésed után.

> /You lived without sin, you carried out your duties
>   in exemplary fashion:
>   you served man, and feared the Heavenly Father.

> You were faithful to the end, to your husband's
>   memory, to the grave,
>   Once widowed you did not seek a new marriage./ (341)

Even death is good, the poet opines, for one who has led such a good life. Consequently, the final stanza of the elegy apotheosizes his mother:

> És most, szent anya, égi lakó, áldjon meg az Isten,
>   s engemet, itt maradót élni segítsen imád.

> /And now, holy mother, heavenly dweller, may God bless you,
>   and me, may your prayers help the one
>   who remains behind./ (343)

In her beatified state, his mother's all-embracing love will continue to intercede for him in heaven until they meet again on the judgment day. Pannonius ends the eulogy with a note of acceptance and with the hope that he and his mother will be blissfully reunited throughout eternity.

Briefly, we have seen that the two elegies in question that portray woman as mother either deify or sanctify her after death. For the poet, woman as mother is viewed as self-abnegating, guiding her sons to fame and success, unaware that her own laurels rest precisely on that accomplishment. In death, she is an angelic vision, worthy of adoration and continually vigilant regarding the well-being of her child.

In conclusion, in his evolutionary and kaleidoscopic presentation of woman and love, Pannonius utilizes much of the classical tradition that he absorbed under the tutelage of Guarino Veronese, as well as his own, sometime painful experiences. For the humanist poet Pannonius, the woman, whether mistress, wife, or mother, incorporates his image of love that also carried with it traces of his self-image, a sort of shadow of the shadow Narcissus saw below him in the pool. In the long run, love leads the poet Pannonius back into the self. [28] Indeed, the aforementioned synthesis of learned literary convention and individual life experience, of image upon image, lends Pannonius's poems on woman and love, a traditionally learned yet authentic and original voice. Likewise, the tension created between the emotion of the life experience and the logic and discipline inherent in the poetic form give his poems an added lyrical dynamism.

Nevertheless, the feminine and love images that populate Pannonius's verse offer us a glimpse of the ambivalence with which a fifteenth-century cosmopolitan Humanist perceived woman, on the one hand from an Epicurean posture as a sensual pleasure-seeking creature, on the other from the neo-Platonic stance as an ideal and reflection of the Supreme Good. Lastly, Pannonius, steeped in the learning of the classics, employs much of that tradition in the formulation of what in the final outcome is a male-centered philosophy that relegates woman to a secondary role, measuring her worth in relation to man and locking her into subservience, subject to the whims of man's changing self.

Notes

1. See Tibor Klaniczay, ed., *Magyar irodalom története* /*The History of Hungarian Literature*/ (Budapest: Akadémiai Kiadó, 1964), and Antal Szerb, *Magyar irodalom történet* /*History of Hungarian Literature*/ (Budapest: Magvető Könyvkiadó, 1972), among others that recognize Janus Pannonius (real name János Csezmiczei) as Hungary's first great lyric poet and creator of neo-Latin poetry in Hungary. A commemorative essay in the monthly *Új Idő* /New Time/, III, 2 (Cleveland, November, 1984), 10, points out his importance in bridging the gap between a cultured Europe and a then so-called barbaric Hungary.

2. For a list of critical works consult Albert Tezla, *Hungarian Authors: A Bibiographical Handbook* (Cambridge: Harvard University Press, 1970), 235-236, and the aforementioned literary histories. Ever since Count Samuel Teleki collected and published Pannonius's works in 1784, a number of critics, outstanding among them, István Hegedüs, Joseph Huszti and Rabán Gerézdi have produced biographies and evaluations of his political and literary career, especially the influence of the Italian Humanist movement on his poetry.

3. A brief but complete synopsis of his political career is found in Klaniczay, *A magyar*, 226-228, which along with Rabán Gerézdi's introduction, "Janus Pannonius (1434-1472)," in *Janus Pannonius válogatott versei* /*Selected Poetry of Janus Pannonius*/ (Budapest: Szépirodalmi Könyvkiadó, 1953), 5-30, examines his literary career based on the three periods of his poetic creativity: Ferrara (1447-1454), Padua (1454-1458), and Hungary (1458-1472). The summary found in *Janus Pannonius munkái latinul és magyarul* /*The Works of Janus Pannonius in Latin and in Hungarian*/ (Budapest: Tankönyvkiadó, 1972), 577, lists the offices he held during his lifetime: Provost at Titel, Coadjutor of John Vitéz and Royal-Councellor, Bishop of Nagyvárad, Head Chancellor of Queen Catherine, Ban of Slavonia.

4. Caius Valerius Catullus was one of the greatest Roman poets whose work was known to Pannonius. His name and work are mentioned in a letter from Pannonius addressed to Marcus Aurelius. See Janus Pannonius, *Beszédek, levelek* /*Speeches, Correspondence*/, introduction and notes by Gábor Szigethy (Budapest: Magvető Könyvkiadó, 1983), 32. The central principle of Renaissance literary creation was *imitatio*. For a discussion of this important aspect of Pannonius's poetry, see Fred J.

Nichols, *An Anthology of Neo-Latin Poetry* (New Haven and London: Yale University Press, 1979), 14-15, as well as the above-mentioned essay in *Új Idő*. The latter makes a special point of explaining the concept of *imitatio* as an aspect of the poet's aspiration to be an "earthly god," in the sense of being able to create new worlds with words as primal matter. *Imitatio* was a poetic technique which required a certain talent and mastery of the elements of classical verse including constant practice and the desire to surpass the original model.

5. See Martial, *Selected Epigrams*, translated by Rolphe Humphries, introduction and notes by Palmer Bovie (Bloomington: Indiana University Press, 1963), 16-18. For Catullus it became a poetic aim to defeat expectation. See Gordon Williams, *Tradition and Originality in Roman Poetry* (Oxford: The Clarendon Press, 1968), 784.

6. Pannonius himself describes the perfect epigram in his poem, "Ad Polycarpum" (Polycarpushoz) /To Polycarpus/: "*Könnyű ihletement sem táplálhatja akármi: / Adj méltó anyagot, úgy születik meg a vers./ Épp ez a klasszikus élces epigrammáknak a titka: Csíp és csattan a vers, hogyha a tárgya csípős...*" /Everything cannot nourish my light style: / Give me a deserving subject, then the poem is born./ This exactly is the classical witty epigram's secret: The verse is pointed and stings, if its subject is fitting...! Cf. *Janus Pannonius munkái*, 241. All translations from Hungarian to English are my own.

7. As the poet, Győző Csorba, so well expresses in his introduction to Janus Pannonius's collected works, "...Janus aligha nevezhető elefántcsonttorony-költőnek. Mohón, szinte telhetetlenül kereste, firtatta, kommentálta az élményeket, tapasztalatokat...Közéleti költő a szó legtisztább értelmében." /...Janus can hardly be called a poet of the ivory tower. Eagerly, even insatiably, he searched, he inquired, he commented on his adventures and experiences...He is a poet of the everyday in every sense of the word./ Cf. *Janus Pannonius munkái*, 10.

8. An example of this is Pannonius's epigram entitled, "Conqueritur, Quod se Socii ad Lupanar Seduxissent" (Panaszkodik hogy társai bordélyházba csalták), *Janus Pannonius munkái*, 95. Also see a discussion of this aspect of the epigram in Williams, *Tradition*, 126-127.

9. Williams, *Tradition*, 553.

10. *Ibid.* "Martial proclaims that he will mince no words on sex, advises the reluctant reader to skip the offensive parts, cites the precedent of such great lyric craftsmen as Catullus..," Martial, *Selected Epigrams*, 19. Besides Martial, Antonio Beccadelli, author of *Hermaphroditus* (1426) is also seen by Klaniczay as having influenced Pannonius's sometimes obscene phraseology. *A magyar irodalom*, 231.

11. In 1447, Pannonius traveled to Guarino de Verona's academy in Ferrara, Italy, where he was to spend eight years studying Latin and Greek with the end result of his adopting the Humanistic ideals of his classical predecessors both in his political life and literary output. See Klaniczay, *A magyar irodalom*, 226.

12. All of the textual quotes are taken from *Janus Pannonius munkái*, 68-69. Henceforth I shall use the original Latin titles giving the Hungarian and English translations. Each direct quote from the text will be followed by its page number in parentheses.

13. Pannonius reveals in the first line of the poem that Agnes is married: "*Ágnes, add nekem is mit emberednek*" /Agnes, give to me what you give your husband/. (69) It was customary for the classical authors as well as for the troubadours of the Middle Ages to compose poems to married women. The true name of the woman was never revealed, thus Agnes is probably a fictitious name. Other elements of courtly love are present in the poem, e.g., the antithetical effects of love, especially the pain and pleasure of infatuation, the emphasis on a woman's eyes, the corruptive as well as

virtuous effects of physical desire. Of course much of the courtly tradition can be traced back to Ovid's *Ars amatoria*, a work which Pannonius must have known quite well. Catullus also disguised the real name of his mistress. He used "Lesbia" in the poems for Clodia. See Williams, *Tradition*, 528. Otis H. Green discusses pertinent aspects of courtly love in *The Literary Mind of Medieval and Renaissance Spain* (Lexington: The University of Kentucky Press, 1970), where he states that the potentiality of desire is the greatest when directed towards an almost unattainable object. Marital relations lower the potential of desire, thus troubadour love poetry was rarely directed to the wife or sweetheart.

14. *Janus Pannonius munkái*, 71. Like the name Agnes, Magdalene is probably fictitious.

15. For a discussion of the go-between and her business of persuading respectable girls to become mistresses of men, see Williams, *Tradition*, 542-543.

16. Catullus used the striking image of the tree covered with ivy to symbolize the relationship between a man and a woman. See G. Karl Galinsky, *Perspectives of Roman Poetry* (Austin: University of Texas Press, 1974), 24.

17. Catullus's dictum was to shock the reader with the unexpected. See Note 5.

18. Nichols, *An Anthology*, 9.

19. Two epigrams about women written in Hungary deviate from the earlier epigrammatic norm. The one entitled "De Catharina Regina Hungariae," (Katalin magyar királynéról) /About Catherine, Queen of Hungary/ (202) speaks of the change in identity that the young Catherine had to undergo by leaving her Czech homeland to become queen of Hungary. Pannonius compares her rebirth as queen to the conversion of St. Paul. It is not surprising that Pannonius wrote only one poem in honor of the queen for whom he was chancellor since she died at a young age. The second epigram describes Pannonius's relationship with his mother, Borbála Vitéz, who died in 1463. Entitled "Epitaphium Barbarae Matris Suae" (Anyjának Barbarának sírfelirata) /An Epitaph for his Mother, Barbara/ (207), the poem is written in the Greek tradition of an epitaph-epigram and idealizes the unselfish love of a mother for her child. Whereas the earlier poetry viewed woman in a sexual role, these lines introduce a theme which will be fully developed by the poet in his long panegyric to his mother-woman as intercessor between God and man.

20. *Janus Pannonius munkái*, 578.

21. Galinsky, *Perspectives*, 24.

22. For other interpretations of a woman's life in Latin love poetry, see the essay "The Woman's Role in Latin Love Poetry" by Georg Luck in Galinsky, *Perspectives*, 20.

23. For another example of poetry in the service of politics and diplomacy, see Marianna D. Birnbaum, "Janus Pannonius, Bartolomeo Melzi, and the Sforzas," *Renaissance Quarterly*, XXX, (1977), 1-7.

24. A mother's love is almost divine, benevolent, and providential in Pannonius's eyes. It approximates God's love for man in its total self-abnegation. Even after death a mother continues to intercede for her son.

25. For a study of neo-Platonism and its influence on Pannonius, see Klaniczay, *A magyar irodalom*, 227.

26. The dance of death, in which no one can refuse her invitation, is a popular metaphor of medieval literature. See for example, "La danza de la muerte" in Spanish literature.

27. In Pannonius's day, the humanists, especially the neo-Platonists held that the stars determined the lives of men. See *Janus Pannonius munkái*, 547.

28. This is true about Renaissance poetry in general and especially Latin poetry. See Nichols, *An Anthology*, 3.

L. S. Domonkos:

6 / THE HUNGARIAN ROYAL CHAN-CERY, 1458-1490: WAS IT A CENTER OF HUMANISM?

During the course of the fifteenth century the influence of the Italian Renaissance was felt with increasing intensity in the countries of East Central Europe, among them Hungary. The relative proximity of the two countries, the political ties which go back to the Angevins in the previous century, and above all, the large number of Hungárian students who frequented Italian universities, aided this cultural diffusion.

The second half of the fifteenth century, and particularly the reign of Matthias Corvinus (1458-1490)[1], represents the hightide of Italo-Hungarian relations. King Matthias not only showed a strong personal interest in promoting the ideas of the Renaissance in his homeland, but also encouraged others to follow his example.[2] The result of this policy was twofold: First, and most important, was the rise of a royal court which tried to emulate the princely courts of Italy[3]; and second, a number of ecclesiastical dignitaries, often Italian educated, attempted to make their episcopal sees into havens of the new culture.

Matthias became an avid patron of the Renaissance and tried to make his royal residences at Buda and Visegrád into outposts of the New Learning. In order to accomplish his purpose, he invited Italian scholars and artisans to his capital, expanded his palace in the new architectural style, and built one of the most magnificent book collections North of the Alps, the *Bibliotheca Corviniana*.[4] His marriage with the Neapolitan princess Beatrice of Aragon in 1476 served further to increase the Italian influence in Hungary.[5] When Italian scholars were invited to grace the king's court, some, such as Galeotto Marzio and the historian Antonio Bonfini accepted, while Marsilio Ficino politely declined.

Several of the leading ecclesiastics in Hungary attempted to make their diocesan seats into centers of learning. Encouraged by the example of the royal court, or in many cases by personal exposure to the Italian intellectual climate during their student days, many of the high-ranking churchmen undertook the creation of small-scale Renaissance centers. They collected books and art objects, undertook construction projects, invited or corresponded with Italian Humanists and surrounded themselves with devotees of the New Learning. [6]

In evaluating the Hungarian Renaissance, a number of factors become apparent. While the Renaissance was never a mass movement, and even in Italy did not penetrate far down the social scale, in fifteenth-century Hungary it remained an imported foreign trend. Its effect was enjoyed and felt by the king, his court and a few educated ecclesiastics. It is not until the sixteenth century that a more thorough fusion of Italian Humanism and of the native cultural tradition took place. With a few exceptions, such as the famous poet Janus Pannonius, [7] who made positive contributions to the New Learning, most educated Hungarians were enthusiastic recipients rather than active contributors to the Renaissance.

For a number of reasons the Renaissance did not find a fertile base in Hungary. Because of certain socio-economic factors, Hungary failed to develop a strong and viable middle class, and urbanization did not keep up with the level of Western Europe. [8] The lack of a well-defined class of merchants, bankers and professionals was an obvious hindrance to the promotion of new intellectual currents. The void was partially filled by ecclesiastics, many of them from the ranks of the petty nobility, who played a most important role in the cultural life of the country. [9]

Hungary also failed to develop its universities into centers of Humanistic culture. While in the neighboring Austria and Poland the universities of Vienna and Cracow played an active role as Humanistic centers in the late fifteenth and early sixteenth centuries, [10] Hungary did not keep pace with this trend. The University of Pozsony and the *Studium* of Buda never developed into major Renaissance centers. In fact, after a brief initial flowering, both declined in importance,[11] and most Hungarian students continued to seek university training abroad.

A number of Hungarian scholars have, through the years, assumed that the Royal chancery was a Humanistic center[12] sharing with the royal court and episcopal sees the function of promoting the New Learning. This view needs to be modified, for a closer examination of the history of the Royal Chancery[13] during the reign of Matthias Corvinus leads to a revision of the previous interpretations.

An examination of the structure of government in Hungary during the second half of the fifteenth century reveals that the king had at his side only one major administrative body, the Royal Council.

According to recent studies, the Royal Council under Matthias had about 60 members, made up of major magnates of the realm (barons), the bishops (10-12) and officials who held administrative positions in the Chancery. Because of its size, the Royal Council was not present on a permanent basis at the court and usually met prior to or after the general meeting of the Estates of the Realm or Diet. Matthias also relied on a Personal Council, made up of 5-20 individuals, usually at least half of them ecclesiastics, who were either at the royal court permanently or on some special mission and thus were more easily accessible.[14] In this Personal Council, as well as in the larger Royal Council, the officials of the Chancery took an increasingly active role, and it developed into something far more than a mere office which issued charters.

Several decades before the Hunyadi period, the Royal Chancery of Hungary was divided into two departments, each with a very definite orientation. The *cancellaria major* became the office which issued charters regulating external and internal affairs, while the *cancellaria minor* developed into an office which dealt with judicial matters. The *cancellaria major* eventually lost the *"major"* designation, and simply became "the Chancery."[15]

During the reign of Matthias, the members of the Chancery often were part of the Royal Council, while Royal Council members were also high officials of the Chancery.

Therefore, there was an obviously close relationship between the Council and Chancery.

The major offices of the Chancery were: 1. The High Chancellor (*summus cancellarius*), 2. The Privy Chancellor (*secretarius cancellarius*), 3. The Vice-Chancellor (*vice cancellarius*), 4. The Secretary (*secretarius*). [16]

Examination of Chancery records for the years from 1458 to 1490 reveals four major periods of history during the reign of Matthias. The first of these periods, from 1458 to 1464, is characterized by consolidation of power and corresponds to the time from the election of Matthias to his coronation. The High Chancellor was the aged, pro-Habsburg, Cardinal Dénes Szécsi (1458-1464), [17] while the Privy Chancellorship was filled by two loyal Hunyadi supporters, Albert Vetési (1458-59), [18] followed by Nicolaus Bodó (1459-1461). Bodó advanced into this position from the Vice-Chancellorship, which then remained vacant until 1464. [18a] In the position of *secretarius*, we find an interesting figure, Georgius Polycarpus (Kosztolá-nyi), who held the position for four years (1458-1462). A noted Humanist and one of the few laymen connected with the Renaissance in Hungary, Polycarpus was employed extensively in diplomatic affairs by Matthias. [19] The only person whose tenure of office was not terminated by Matthias in 1464, was Johannes Beckensloer, who succeeded Polycarpus in the position of Secretary in 1462, and held it until 1466. (See Chart).

The second major period in the Chancery is from 1464 to 1471. The coronation of Matthias and the death of Cardinal Szécsi inaugurated this phase which ended with the tragic events of 1471, when a plot to unseat Matthias failed. This resulted in the falling from royal grace of a number of important figures who were implicated in the plot, among whom was the great Johannes Vitéz, the "Father of Hungarian Humanism."

Let us examine in more detail this most important period in the history of the Chancery. With the death of Cardinal Szécsi in 1464, Matthias had entrusted the High and Privy Chancellorships to two brilliant men, Stephanus Várdai, Archbishop of Kalocsa, and Johannes Vitéz, Archbishop of Esztergom, the two highest-ranking ecclesiastics of the realm.

Várdai had studied the *artes* at Vienna and had received his legal education in Italy where he attended the universities of Ferrara and Padua. [20] He received his doctorate in 1450, and upon returning to Hungary was employed in the Chancery of Ladislaus V. Although well-educated and from all indications a brilliant man, Várdai was not an active patron of the New Learning. Except for a few letters from his student days in Italy, he left no literary legacy which might identify him as a Humanist. [21] His ability as an administrator seems to have been greatly valued by the king who entrusted him with the domestic operations of the Chancery, while his colleague, Johannes Vitéz devoted his attention to foreign policy. Várdai was amply rewarded by Matthias for his services. After years of pressure and negotiations in Rome, the king was able to secure a cardinal's hat for him from the Pope. [22] Unfortunately, Várdai died in early 1471, and for a brief period Vitéz occupied the posts of both the High and Privy Chancellorship.

In Archbishop Vitéz, we have one of the most outstanding figures of the Hungarian Renaissance; and his position as Privy Chancellor, and later High Chancellor, marks a very important period in the history of the Chancery.

Born around 1408, and educated at the University of Vienna, [23] Vitéz entered the service of Sigismund (1387-1437) and rose in the Chancery. Pier Paolo Vergerio, who resided in Buda at this time, had considerable influence on his stylistic development. [24] A strong supporter of János Hunyadi, Vitéz was made Bishop of Várad and was instrumental in the election of Matthias Corvinus, the son of Hunyadi, as king of Hungary in 1458. As Bishop of Várad, and later Archbishop of Esztergom (1465-1472), he was one of the most active promoters of the Renaissance in Hungary and probably influenced the young Matthias in this direction. Vitéz was an avid book collector and bibliophile [25] who corresponded with a number of important scholars, gathered Humanists in his episcopal and arch-episcopal court and was the moving spirit behind the newly founded University of Pozsony. [26] His brilliant career ended in tragedy when he and his nephew, the poet Janus Pannonius, Bishop of Pécs, set themselves at the head of a rebellion against Matthias.

The main reasons for their discontent seem to have been the increasing centralizing tendencies of the king, his disregard for ecclesiastical privileges and immunities, and most importantly, the neglect of the Turkish menace. Matthias, who was deeply involved in the political affairs of Bohemia and Austria, displeased many of his subjects by his unkept promises to lead a major campaign against the Ottomans. In 1471, Vitéz and Pannonius plotted to depose Matthias and invited a Polish prince to the throne. The plot failed. [27] Vitéz had to bear the humiliation of imprisonment, and although he was nominally forgiven by the king and released, he died a broken and disgraced man. Pannonius attempted flight to his beloved Italy, but his weak health could not bear the strain and he died near Zagreb at the age of 38.

The historian, Bishop Vilmos Fraknói, whose research during the late 19th and early 20th century is still valuable, saw these years as the most brilliant phase of the Chancery. He viewed Vitéz's Chancellorship as the period when a true humanist directed the Chancery and when the correspondence of this important office, especially in external affairs, showed the most definite traces of the Humanistic, Ciceronian style. [28] In his analysis of the letters of Matthias, Fraknói maintained that many of the epistles can be attributed to Vitéz, and a large number to his brilliant nephew, Janus Pannonius. [29] In the years before 1468, when Pannonius was at the royal court for long periods of time, his style is definitely evident in diplomatic correspondence. By virtue of his place on the Royal Council—he was Treasurer for a time—and at his uncle's important office, he had an opportunity to exert this stylistic influence. [30] Later he spent less time at the royal court, and his influence was obviously diminished. With the fall of Vitéz and Pannonius from power after the plot of 1471, the Chancery was no longer openly Humanistic in its orientation, although a number of its officials personally showed great interest in the New Learning.

The reform of 1464 also restored the position of Vice-Chancellor and during the next seven years three men held that office, among them Georgius Handó (1466-68), who played an important role in later years. The other two men were Lucas Apáti (1464-66), and Gabriel de Matucsina (1468-1471). At this time, the office of Secretary was still filled by Johannes Beckensloer (1462-66), and later it went to a *familiaris* of Vitéz, Stephanus Bajoni (1467-69), who had received his doctorate in law from Bologna. [31] He was followed by Ladislaus Karai (1469-1471). (See chart).

THE ROYAL CHANCELLERY
1458-1490

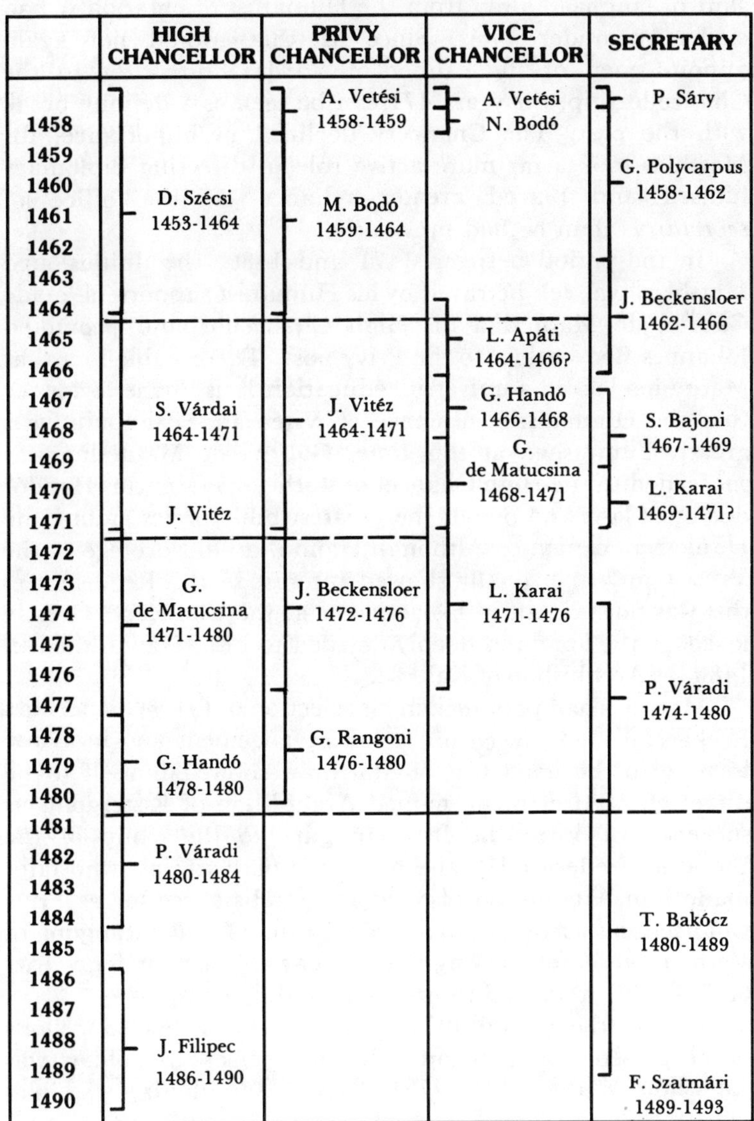

	HIGH CHANCELLOR	PRIVY CHANCELLOR	VICE CHANCELLOR	SECRETARY
1458		A. Vetési 1458-1459	A. Vetési / N. Bodó	P. Sáry
1459				G. Polycarpus 1458-1462
1460	D. Szécsi 1453-1464	M. Bodó 1459-1464		
1461				
1462				
1463				J. Beckensloer 1462-1466
1464				
1465			L. Apáti 1464-1466?	
1466				
1467	S. Várdai 1464-1471	J. Vitéz 1464-1471	G. Handó 1466-1468	S. Bajoni 1467-1469
1468			G. de Matucsina 1468-1471	
1469				L. Karai 1469-1471?
1470				
1471	J. Vitéz			
1472				
1473	G. de Matucsina 1471-1480	J. Beckensloer 1472-1476	L. Karai 1471-1476	
1474				
1475				
1476				
1477				P. Váradi 1474-1480
1478		G. Rangoni 1476-1480		
1479	G. Handó 1478-1480			
1480				
1481				
1482	P. Váradi 1480-1484			
1483				
1484				T. Bakócz 1480-1489
1485				
1486				
1487				
1488	J. Filipec 1486-1490			
1489				F. Szatmári 1489-1493
1490				

Based on Chart V of György Bónis, *A jogtudó értelmiség a Mohács előtti Magyarországon* (Budapest, 1971).

The so-called "Vitéz Plot" of 1471, brought a serious disruption in the Chancery and the next decade witnessed a shift of emphasis away from the Humanist orientation it had evidenced under Vitéz. Since Matthias would not again appoint men of the caliber of Várdai and Vitéz to the Chancellorship, the year 1471 can be seen as a definite break with the past. The Chancery declined in importance, for Matthias took a far more active role in directing diplomacy himself and placed greater reliance on the office of *secretarius* than he had previously.

In the period between 1471 and 1480, the disillusioned Matthias, who felt betrayed by his Humanist supporters, made Gabriel de Matucsina his High Chancellor and promoted Johannes Beckensloer to the Privy post. The notable fact that Matucsina lacked a university education [32] is further evidence that the Humanistic influence of Vitéz and Pannonius was greatly diminished at this time. Gabriel de Matucsina was succeeded in the High Chancellor's office by Georgius Handó, doctor of laws and one of the greatest bibliophiles among the Hungarian clergy. [33] Although Handó, an old protegé of the Vitéz family, personally showed interest in the Renaissance, this was not evident in his activities at the Chancery. Greatly loved by the king and deeply devoted to him, Handó died in 1480, as Archbishop of Kalocsa.

Matthias had poor luck in his selection of Privy Chancellors. Beckensloer, who owed his rapid advancement and immense fortune to the good will of Matthias, showed himself to be ungrateful. After being named Archbishop of Esztergom, as successor of Vitéz, he fled Hungary to the camp of the Emperor Frederick III, the bitter foe of Matthias, who later made him Archbishop of Salzburg. [34] His successor as Privy Chancellor was the Italian Franciscan, Gabriel Rangoni of Verona, who after serving the Hungarian king for four years (1476-1480), returned to his homeland. [35]

During the period 1471 to 1480, the Vice-Chancellor's office passed into oblivion. The last person to hold it was Ladislaus Karai (1471-1476), Provost of Óbuda, who had moved up from the position of *secretarius*. It was during his Vice-Chancellorship that Karai took steps to establish the first printing press in Buda and printed the *Chronica Hungarorum* in 1473. [36]

The position of Secretary seems to have remained unfilled for three years until Matthias appointed Petrus Váradi in 1474. This remarkable man, who appears again in another connection, was Secretary until 1480. (See chart). Váradi should not be confused with the Archbishop of Kalocsa Stephanus Várdai, who died in 1471.

The final phase of development in the Chancery occurred during the last decade of Matthias' reign (1480-1490). In 1480, the death of Handó and the departure of Gabriel Rangoni left both the High and the Privy Chancellorship vacant. Matthias turned his attention again to a Humanist ecclesiastic, the young Petrus Váradi, whose advance was meteoric. [37] With the death of Handó, he became Archbishop of Kalocsa and left his position as *secretarius* to become both Privy and High Chancellor. The two offices were now merged and remained in this fashion until the end of Matthias's reign. Although a man of importance, Váradi was not able to exert the same influence on the king as Vitéz had in the late 1460's. Matthias continued to direct much of the diplomatic correspondence himself, and the Humanistic style of Váradi, which is very apparent in a collection of his private letters, is not evident in the Chancery. Although an ardent Humanist was now Chancellor, the Chancery itself did not reflect his cultural orientation. [38]

Váradi's career as Chancellor ended in tragedy. An outspoken, almost rash young man, the Archbishop soon found himself in dispute with Matthias, who tolerated no contradictions. He also alienated Queen Beatrix, who still had great influence over her husband. In August of 1484, the Chancellor was arrested and taken prisoner to a castle where he remained until the king's death. [39] Matthias, whose luck with Chancellors was obviously not the best, left the office vacant for two years before turning to Bishop Johannes Filipec, a Moravian by birth, to become his Privy Chancellor. Matthias, however, came to rely increasingly on himself in matters of policy and on the advice of the clever, cultured, and unscrupulous secretary of the Chancery, Thomas Bakócz de Erdőd (1480-1489). Italian educated, this brilliant young man rose steadily in power and influence. His role as patron of the arts, as well as his political and ecclesiastical importance falls mainly into the period after the death of Matthias. [40]

It is a curious fact that during the second third of Mathias's reign the significance of the Royal Chancery declined. After 1471, the High and Privy Chancellors were no longer powerful forces in the kingdom. The year 1476, marked the end of the office of Vice-Chancellor, while the High and Privy positions were either combined or eliminated after 1480. The king did not share his power with the Chancellors as he had prior to the Vitéz plot, and it seems that Matthias was taking to heart the advice of the Italian, Callimachus Experiense, when he completely subordinated the Chancery to his power: "Do not utilize your Chancellors and beware of them. . .," said Callimachus in his warning to kings. [41]

Certain conclusions can be drawn from an examination of the Chancery of Matthias Corvinus. As far as the Humanistic orientation of the Chancery is concerned, we must conclude that with the exception of the Vitéz period, the Chancery did not really reflect the new spirit of learning. Although a number of men who were active supporters and patrons of the New Learning held positions in the Chancery, their thinking is not reflected in the operation of that body. Therefore, it is safe to say that while a number of individuals rose to important Chancery positions (especially men who were Italian-educated and showed themselves in other ways to be very receptive to the ideas of the Renaissance), the Chancery never became a center of Humanism in the way the royal court, or some of the episcopal courts did.

To talk of the "Humanist Chancery" of Matthias is therefore not correct. There were Humanists in the Chancery, but this did not make the institution itself a center of Humanism.

The direct involvement of the king in the affairs of the Chancery after 1471 had, in effect, a negative result. Although he continued to employ Italian educated and Humanistically-oriented men in the Chancery, there was no doubt that the king himself was the dominant element in the operations of the Chancery.

Another very evident trend can be seen in the decline of the Chancery as a whole. During the last few years of Matthias's reign, the Chancellor's position was greatly weakened and the king came to rely most heavily on the services of the *secretarius*. In view of Matthias's increasingly absolutist tendencies during the second half of his reign, this is not surprising.

An examination of the list of Chancery officials during this period reveals a definite upward mobility, from lower offices to the higher. It was not uncommon for the Secretary to rise to the office of Vice Chancellor or even High and Privy Chancellor. (See chart.)

And finally, in looking ahead to the period between the death of Matthias (1490) and the battle of Mohács (1526), we find that the Chancery will again play a far more important role in the development of cultural life in Hungary. This is particularly true of the secretaries of the Chancery, whose number will multiply to about seven by 1526.[42] During this otherwise rather bleak and tragic period of Hungarian history the Chancery will again become one of the centers of cultural life, and the seeds of Humanism planted by Vitéz and Janus Pannonius will blossom forth.

Notes

1. The last detailed study devoted to the life of Matthias Corvinus is now outdated: Vilmos Fraknói, *Mátyás király élete* /The Life of King Matthias/ (Budapest, 1890). Also published in German under the title: *Matthias Corvinus*, (Freiburg in Br., 1891). A more recent popular study is by Katalin Kisfaludy, *Matthias Rex* (Budapest, 1983).

2. On the question of the Renaissance in Hungary see: Tibor Kardos, *A magyarországi humanizmus kora* /The Age of Humanism in Hungary/ (Budapest, 1955), pp. 150-201; by the same author, "Mátyás király és a humanizmus" /King Matthias and Humanism/, *Mátyás király emlékkönyv* /King Matthias Memorial Volume/, ed. Imre Lukinich, 2 vols. (Budapest, 1940), II, pp. 11-105.

3. Jolán Balogh, *Adatok Milánó és Magyarország kulturális kapcsolatainak történetéhez* /Contribution to the History of Cultural Relations between Milan and Hungary/ (Budapest, 1928); also: "Néhány adat Firenze és Magyarország kulturális kapcsolatainak történetéhez a renaissance korban" /Some Data on the History of Cultural Relations between Florence and Hungary/, *Archaeologiai Értesítő*, 40 (1923-1926), 189-209; "Újabb adatok Firenze és Magyarország kulturális kapcsolatainak történetéhez" /More Recent Data on the History of Cultural Relations between Florence and Hungary/, *Archaeologiai Értesítő*, 43 (1929), 273-280.

4. The best studies on the library of Matthias are by Csaba Csapodi, *The Corvinian Library, History and Stock* (Budapest, 1973), pp. 17-95, and by the same author *Bibliotheca Corviniana; The Library of King Matthias Corvinus of Hungary* (Budapest, 1969), pp. 11-78; also Ilona Berkovits, *A magyarországi Corvinák* /Corvin Codices in Hungary/ (Budapest, 1962), pp. 7-110.

5. On the cultural influence of the queen see: Albert Berzeviczy, *Beatrix királyné 1457-1508* /Queen Beatrix/ (Budapest, 1908), pp. 287-317.

6. Jolán Balogh, "I mecenati ungheresi del primo Rinascimento," *Acta Historiae Artium*, 13 (1967), 205-212; also by the same author: *A művészet Mátyás király udvarában* /Art in the Court of King Matthias/ (Budapest, 1966), I, pp. 697-700. Also see my study: "Ecclesiastical Patrons as a Factor in the Hungarian Renaissance," *New Review of East-European History* 14 (1974), 100-116.

7. Tibor Klaniczay, "A magyar irodalom reneszánsz korszaka" /The Renaissance Epoch of Hungarian Literature/, *Reneszánsz és barokk: Tanulmányok a régi magyar irodalomról* /Renaissance and Baroque: Studies in Old Hungarian Literature/ (Budapest, 1961), pp. 9; 19-23. On the life of Pannonius see: József Huszti, *Janus Pannonius* (Pécs, 1931); Rabán Gerézdi, "Janus Pannonius" and "Egy költői hírnév története" /The Story of a Poetic Reputation), *Janus Pannoniustól Balassi Bálintig* (Budapest, 1968), pp. 7-67; and Marianna D. Birnbaum, *Janus Pannonius: Poet and Politician* (Zagreb: Jugoslavenska Akademija Znanosti i Umejetnosti, 1981).

8. The problems of urbanization and economic development have been treated in a number of studies in recent years, especially: Jenő Szűcs, *Városok és kézművesség a XV. századi Magyarországon* /Cities and Artisans in 15th-Century Hungary/ (Budapest, 1955), pp. 172-179; also by the same author: "Das Stadtwesen in Ungarn im 15-17 Jh.," *La Renaissance et la Reformation en Pologne et en Hongrie, 1450-1650* (Budapest, 1963), pp. 117-119. Also see: Vera Bácskai, *Magyar mezővárosok a XV. században* /Hungarian Manorial Towns in the 15th Century/ (Budapest, 1965), pp. 20-21, 30-43; István Szabó, "La répartition de la population de Hongrie entre les bourgades et les villages dans les années 1449-1526." *Études Historiques* (Budapest, 1960), I, pp. 359-385. On social and economic development see: László Makkai, "Die Hauptzüge der wirtschaftlich-sozialen Entwicklung Ungarns im 15-17 Jh.," *Ren. Ref. en Pol. et Hong.*, pp. 33-38; Cf. Erik Fügedi, "Die Aussenhandel Ungarns am Anfang des 16 Jahrhunderts," *Der Aussenhandel Ostmitteleuropas 1450-1650* (Köln-Wien, 1971), pp. 56-79. The best study on agrarian development is by: Zsigmond Pál Pach, *Nyugat-európai és magyarországi agrárfejlődés a XV-XVII. században* /Western European and Hungarian Agrarian Development in the XV-XVII Centuries/ (Budapest, 1963), pp. 45-95; and its German version, *Die ungarische Agrarentwicklung im XV-XVII. Jahrhundert* (Budapest, 1964).

9. On the social origins of the Hungarian upper clergy see the study of Erik Fügedi, "Hungarian Bishops in the Fifteenth Century: Some Statistical Observations," *Acta Historica* 11(1965), 375-391; also by the same author: *A 15. századi magyar arisztokrácia mobilitása* /The Social Mobility of Hungarian Aristocracy in the 15th century/ (Budapest, 1970), pp. 91-94.

10. Casimir Morawski, *Histoire de l'Université de Cracovie: Moyen Age et Renaissance* (Paris-Cracow, 1900-1905), II, pp. 220-236. The best recent study on the subject is by Professor Paul Knoll, whose article entitled: "Polish Humanism and the University of Cracow in the Fifteenth Century" I was privileged to read in typescript. Professor Knoll's excellent study treats the penetration of Humanism at the University of Cracow, and summarizes the most recent scholarship on the question.

On Vienna the classic study is: Josef v. Aschbach, *Die Wiener Universität und ihre Humanisten* (Wien, 1877), p. 41 ff. Also see: Karl Grossmann, "Die Frühzeit des Humanismus in Wien bis zu Celtis Berufung 1497," *Jahrbuch für Landesgeschichte Niederösterreich*, 22 (1929), 313-358.

11. See my study: "The Problems of Hungarian University Foundations in the Middle Ages," in *Society in Change: Studies in Honor of Béla K. Király*, ed. S. B. Várdy and A. H. Várdy, (New York and Boulder: East European Monographs, Columbia University Press, 1983), 371-390; and Ferenc Somogyi, "The Medieval

University of Pécs," in *Louis the Great, King of Hungary and Poland,* eds. S. B. Várdy, G. Grossschmid, and L. S. Domonkos (New York and Boulder: East European Monographs, Columbia University Press, 1986), 221-236.

12. Kardos, *A Magyarországi humanizmus,* pp. 117-119, 122, 167. Also see the study of György Bónis, *A jogtudó értelmiség a Mohács előtti Magyarországon* /The Legally Educated Intelligentia in Hungary before the Battle of Mohács/ (Budapest, 1971), pp. 219-244.

13. On the structure of the chancery see: Bónis, pp. 149-174; Loránd Szilágyi, *A magyar királyi kancellária szerepe az államkormányzatban, 1458-1526* /The role of the Royal Chancery in the Government of the Realm, 1458-1526/ (Budapest, 1930), 6-24; also see: György Bónis, "Einflüsse des romischen Rechts in Ungarn," *Jus Romanorum Medii Aevi,* V (Milan, 1964), 44 ff.

14. This information comes mainly from the study of András Kubinyi on the organization of the Chancery during the Hunyadi period. Dr. Kubinyi presented his paper at the Institute of Literary Studies of the Hungarian Academy, Budapest, in the winter of 1971.

15. Szilágyi, p. 6.

16. *Ibid,* pp. 6-24.

17. Archbishop Szécsi was educated at the Universities of Vienna and Bologna. See: Károly Schrauf, *Magyarországi tanulók a bécsi egyetemen* /Students from Hungary at the University of Vienna/ (Budapest, 1892), p. 59 and note 2. He entered the University on Oct. 13, 1424. Later he attended the University of Bologna and received his degree in law: Endre Veress, *Matricula et acta Hungarorum in universitatibus Italiae studentium* (Budapest, 1942), pp. 36-37. He became bishop of Nyitra, and in 1440 Archbishop of Esztergom.

18. Vetési studied in Vienna (Schrauf, p. 54), where he was inscribed in October of 1422. He later became *Magister Artium* and lectured on Boethius and Aristotle: Vilmos Fraknói, *Magyarországi tanárok és tanulók a bécsi egyetemen* /Teachers and Students from Hungary at the University of Vienna/ (Budapest,1874), pp. 25, 45. He received his legal training in Italy and received his doctorate from Padua (Veress, p. 9), and later became Bishop of Nyitra (1458), and Veszprém (1458-1486). Vetési was used extensively by Matthias in the diplomatic service: Vilmos Fraknói, *Mátyás király magyar diplomatái* /The Hungarian Diplomats of King Matthias/ (Budapest, 1898), pp. 32-51.

18a. A "Dominus Nicolaus Bodó" was inscribed in the faculty of law at the University of Vienna in 1435. Cf. Schrauf, pp. 135. There is no indication where he received his bachelor degree,nor is there information of the completion of his legal studies.

19. János Horváth, *Az irodalmi műveltség megoszlása: Magyar Humanizmus* /The Diffusion of Literary Culture: Hungarian Humanism/ (Budapest, 1944), pp. 167-168. Polycarpus was a student of Guarino at Ferrara at the time Janus Pannonius studied there. Cf. Sándor V. Kovács, *Magyar humanisták levelei, XV-XVI.század* /The Letters of Hungarian Humanists of the 15th and 16th Centuries/ (Budapest, 1971), pp. 413-414. Matthias Corvinus used him extensively in diplomacy and he represented the king at a number of important conferences. (Fraknói, *Mátyás magyar diplomatái,* pp. 4-16). Kosztolányi received rich benefices in Hungary and after 1468. lived mainly in Rome. He was employed at the Curia, married the daughter of the Greek Humanist Georgius Trapezunt and died in Rome in 1489: Cf. Flórián Bánfi, "Egy magyar diplomata sírja Romában" /The Tomb of a Hungarian Diplomat in Rome/, *Századok,* 65(1931), 104-109.

20. Várdai was inscribed at the University of Vienna in April of 1446. Cf. Schrauf,

p. 98.From there he migrated to Ferrara and in August of 1450, received his doctorate from the University of Padua. Cf. Veress, p. 9.

21. Pál Lukács, "Várdai István ferrarai diák levelei" /The letters of S. Várdai as a Student in Ferrara/, *Történelmi Szemle*, 14 (1929), 124-136.

22. Vilmos Fraknói, *Mátyás király levelei* /Letters of King Matthias/ (Budapest, 1893), I, pp. 55-56. The Pope sent him the red hat, but Gabriel Rangoni, the papal emissary, could not deliver it to Várdai before the latter's death. See August Theiner, *Vetera monumenta historica Hungariam sacram illustrantia* (Rome, 1860), II, pp. 419-422.

23. The best study on Archbishop Vitéz is still: Vilmos Fraknói, *Vitéz János esztergomi érsek élete* /The Life of Johannes Vitéz, Archbishop of Esztergom/ (Budapest, 1879). Also see: Leslie S. Domonkos, "János Vitéz, the Father of Hungarian Humanism, (1408-1472)," *The New Hungarian Quarterly*, 20(1979), 142-150.

24. On the university education of Vitéz see: Schrauf, p. 78; Kardos, *Humanizmus*, p. 106. Also see: Veress, pp. 39-41, who feels that Vitéz studied at Bologna. His evidence is not convincing.

25. The most recent research of Klára Csapodi-Gárdonyi, resulted in the positive identification of at least 36 codices which belonged to Vitéz. See: *Die Bibliothek des Johannes Vitéz* /Studia Humanitatis/ (Budapest, 1984), p. 73.

26. He was so closely identified with the University that the Acts of the Faculty of the University of Vienna call the University of Pozsony "his university" (*Act. Fac. Theol.* Lib. II, fol. 55 verso), Microfilm at the Medieval Institute, University of Notre Dame. My sincere thanks go to Dr. A. L. Gabriel for permission to use the facilities of the Institute, his constant kindness and encouragement.

27. Tibor Kardos, "János Pannonius bukása" /The Fall of Janus Pannonius/, *Pannonia* (1935), 115-138; Fraknói, *Vitéz élete*, 203-224. For a more detailed study of the centralizing policies of Matthias see: Lajos Elekes, *Rendiség és központosítás a feudális államokban* /Estates and Centralization in Feudal States/ (Budapest, 1962), pp. 63-81.

28. Fraknói, *Mátyás király levelei*, II, pp. XX-XXI. A number of manuscripts containing letters and speeches of Vitéz are known. The Vienna manuscript was published in the eighteenth century: Johannes Georgius Schwandtner, *Scriptores rerum Hungaricarum* (Vienna, 1756), II, pp. 1-105. The most recent critical edition is by Iván Boronkai, *Johannes Vitéz de Zredna: Opera quae supersunt* /Bibliotheca Scriptorum Medii Recentisque Aevorum/ (Budapest, 1980).

29. Fraknói, *Mátyás király levelei*, pp. XXIV-XXV.

30. *Ibid*, XXV. Also see: Tibor Kardos, "Stílustanulmányok Mátyás király kancelláriájából" /Stylistic Studies from the Chancery of King Matthias/, *Közlemények a pécsi Erzsébet Tudományegyetem könyvtárából*, 22 (1933), 1-24.

31. Apáti was a provost of the cathedral chapter of Eger and also *doctor decretorum*. Cf. Bónis, p. 225 and n. 37; Veress, pp. 51-52. He served also as a diplomat. Cf. Fraknói, *Mátyás király diplomatái*, pp. 86-87.

32. Bónis, p. 226; Szilágyi, p. 11, 21, 96.

33. Vespasiano da Bisticci, *Lives of Illustrious Men of the XVth Century* /Renaissance Princes, Popes, and Prelates/, trans. by W. George and E. Waters (New York, 1963), pp. 197-201. Also see: Veress, pp. 358-359. Handó was also employed extensively in the diplomatic service of the king. Cf. Fraknói, *Mátyás diplomatái*, pp. 16-32.

34. Fraknói, *Vitéz élete*, pp. 243-244. Bónis, pp. 223-224.

35. Szilágyi, *Kancellária*, pp. 22-31. On the diplomatic activity of Rangoni see:

Otakar Odložilik, *The Hussite King: Bohemia in European Affairs, 1440-1471* (New Brunswick, NJ: Rutgers University Press, 1965), pp. 194-196, 199-202. Cf. Frederick G. Heymann, *George of Bohemia; King of Heretics.* (Princeton: Princeton University Press, 1965), pp. 376, 418, 467, 489, 525.

36. Vilmos Fraknói, *Karai László budai prépost, a könyvnyomtatás meghonosítója Magyarországon* /Ladislaus Karai, Founder of Printing in Hungary/ (Budapest, 1898), pp. 1-17; on the printing press of Buda see: József Fitz, *Hess András, a budai ősnyomdász* /Andreas Hess, the First Printer in Buda/ (Budapest, 1932), pp. 12-42; by the same author: *A magyar nyomdászat, könyvkiadás és kereskedelem története: A Mohácsi vész előtt* /The History of Hungarian Printing, Editing, and Bookselling: Before the Battle of Mohács/ I. (Budapest, 1959), pp. 96-102; 116-125; Pál Gulyás, *A könyvnyomtatás Magyarországon a XV. és XVI. században* /Printing in Hungary during the 15th and 16th centuries/ (Budapest, 1929. pp. 17-24. The most important product of the press established by Karai was the *Chronica Hungarorum* printed in 1473. Also see the study of Vilmos Fraknói, "A budai krónika" in the facsimile edition of the *Chronica Hungarorum* (Budapest, 1900), pp. 7-34, and the most recent study by Erzsébet Soltész in the Preface of the newest facsimile edition: *Chronica Hungarorum* (Budapest, 1972).

37. Rabán Gerézdi, "A levélíró Váradi Péter" /The Letter Writer Petrus Váradi/, *Janus Pannoniustól Balassi Bálintig* (Budapest, 1968), 81. The best study on Váradi is by Vilmos Fraknói, "Váradi Péter kalocsai érsek élete" /The Life of Petrus Váradi, Archbishop of Kalocsa/, *Századok*, (1883), 489-514; 729-749; 825-843. Also see: Veress, pp. 48-51.

38. The letters were first printed in the 18th century: Carolus Wagner, *Petrus de Warda: Epistolae* (Pozsony-Kassa, 1776). Translated and edited recently: V. Kovács, pp. 284-406; also by the same author: "Váradi Péter ismeretlen levelei" /Unknown Letters of Petrus Váradi/, *Irodalomtörténeti közlemények*, 74 (1979), 63-66.

39. Antonio Bonfini, *Rerum Ungaricarum decades*, edit. I. Fógel, B. Iványi, L. Juhász, /Bibliotheca Scriptorum Medii Recentisque Aevorum/ (Leipzig, 1936), III, pp. 124-125; Gerézdi, pp. 100-103.

40. Concerning the career of Thomas Bakócz, see the study of: Vilmos Fraknói, *Erdődi Bakócz Tamás élete* /The Life of Thomas Bakócz of Erdőd/ (Budapest, 1889). Bakócz had attended the University of Bologna, where he was rector, received his doctorate at Ferrara: Veress, p. 47. He had an extensive library: Hoffmann, *Bibliofilek*, pp. 177-182. On the splendid marble chapel he built, see: Jolán Balogh, *Az esztergomi Bakócz kápolna* /The Bakócz Chapel of Esztergom/ (Budapest, 1955), pp. 7-12, 33-43. Also see: Csaba Csapodi, "Bakócz Tamás, a humanista" /Thomas Bakócz, the Humanist/, *Irodalomtörténeti közlemények*, 87 (1983), 59-66.

41. Tibor Kardos, *Callimachus Experiense: Tanulmány Mátyás király államrezonjáról* /Studies about King Matthias's Raison d'État/ /Minerva könyvtár, 36/ (Budapest, 1931), p. 68; cf., Bónis, p. 230.

42. Bónis, pp. 309-332; Horváth, pp. 180-233.

Astrik L. Gabriel:

7 / MARCUS MARK DE KÉMES: HUNGARIAN MASTER AT THE UNIVERSITY OF PARIS, ca. 1521-1523

In the early years of my academic career, I disserted on several instances on Hungarian students and masters at the medieval University of Paris from the earliest times to the end of the fifteenth century.[1] Later on, I devoted several studies to a single, outstanding Hungarian master in humanist Paris, Blasius de Várda, a confidant of the Bishop of Győr, a reputed scholar who studied as a student, functioned as editor, and held several offices as Master at the University of Paris between 1514-1522.[2]

Hungarians in the English-German Nation at the University of Paris

Recently, while working in the Archives of the University of Paris at the Sorbonne, it was my good fortune to discover an important group of Hungarian subjects studying and teaching at humanist Paris from 1495 to circa 1525. They were all members of the English-German Nation which comprised the foreign students and masters coming from the British Isles (English, Scottish and Irish subjects) forming the *Provincia Scotorum*; from the Holy Roman Empire, Scandinavian countries, Central Europe, Bohemia, Hungary, Poland, grouped in the *Provincia Altorum*; and subjects from the Low Countries of Europe: Holland and the neighboring Northern German dioceses assembled into the *Provincia Bassorum*.[3]

113

The English-German Nation was part of the Faculty of Arts in the University of Paris, along with the French, Picard and Norman Nations.

The Proctor of the Nation

The governing officer of the Nation, as a geographical unit, was the proctor or *procurator*. He was elected by the masters of Arts of the Nation. He represented his Nation at the meetings of the Faculty of Arts and assisted at the reunion of the General Assembly of the entire University in the company of the Deans of the "Sacred Faculty of Theology" and the "Advice-giving Faculty of Law," and the "Salubrious Faculty of Medicine." The proctor had to report verbally on the topics discussed at the meetings of the Faculty of Arts and that of the University. He had to inscribe it into the so-called *Liber procuratorum* together with the agenda of the meetings of his own Nation. He usually signed it with his signature, *signum manuale*.

Diocese of Pécs

The Hungarian scholar whose academic career and activities at the University of Paris I chose to describe here is Marcus Mark de Kémes. He came from the ancient diocese of Pécs (Fünfkirchen, Quinqueecclesiensis). The charter of foundation of the bishopric of Pécs was given in 1009 in the presence of the papal legate Azo.[4] The first bishop was the French Bonipert[5] who was acquainted with and corresponded with Fulbert of Chartes. The latter complimented Bonipert as someone blessed with deep learning by the Holy Ghost, *multa sapientia illustravit, ad docendum populum suum*.[6]

The magnificent Romanesque style cathedral of Pécs was built in the architectural tradition of the venerable Dome of Worms and of the Cathedral of Bamberg.

The diocese of Pécs counted the greatest number of Hungarian students who went abroad to study at the universities of Christendom. Just to name a few: in 1269, Jacobus, Archdeacon of Pécs was in Bologna; in 1346, Joannes, Provost of Pécs, Doctor in Canon Law, in an otherwise unidentified university.[7]

Hungarians from the Diocese of Pécs at Foreign Universities

The earliest university of Hungary was founded in 1367,[8] established not long after the University of Cracow (1364) and that of Vienna (1365). Pécs was selected for political and geographical reasons. The Hungarian South played an important role in Italo-Hungarian cultural relations.

After the foundation of the University of Pécs, the diocese of Quinqueecclesiae (i.e Pécs) saw many of its clerics—secular and religious—going to foreign schools. In the fourteenth century, Vienna welcomed ca. 15, Prague ca. 5 clerics from Hungary. During the fifteenth century, ca. 60 students studied at Vienna from Pécs, ca. 63 at Cracow, and ca. 14 at Bologna. Peruggia welcomed ca. 11, Siena ca. 4, Padua-Rome, ca. 3 clerics from the "Diocesis Quinqueecclesiensis." [9]

The intellectual stimulation of the City of Pécs, where the humanist poet Janus Pannonius was once bishop (died 1472), was very much alive during the reign of the renaissance bishop George Szatmáry (1505-1523), the ordinarius of Marcus Mark.[10]

Place of Origin of Marcus Mark of the Ormánság

Marcus Mark, the Hungarian proctor of the English-German Nation in 1523, came from Kémes,[11] a small village in the diocese of Pécs. It neighbored that of Páprád in a picturesque part of the Comitat of Baranya in its southwestern corner called Ormánság. Both villages, Kémes and Páprád, belonged to the parish church of Vajszló in the ecclesiastical deanery of Németi, not far from the castle of Siklós, where the future Emperor Sigismund, King of Hungary, was imprisoned in 1401.

The Ormánság[12] was, and in some way still is, a lovely territory where medieval tradition, ancient Hungarian proverbs, and colorful costumes were and, with older people, are still preserved in all their beauty and splendor. Upon the death of a beloved, the women of Ormánság were dressed all in white, wearing the *bikla*, a large pleated white skirt. When going to burials in olden times, the women of Ormánság looked like as many *Reine Blanche en deuil*, Queen of France in mourning attire.

To get to Paris from this small place of Kémes, even in the jet age of today, would be a considerable accomplishment.

Arrival in Paris

Marcus Mark de Kémes arrived in Paris during unfortunate times when a ravaging plague was taking its victims in and around the year of 1522. Many people died between 1521-1523, among them ca. five masters of the English-German Nation.

Departure of Master Blasius de Várda
from Paris in August 1522

In 1522, the probable year of arrival of Marcus Mark in Paris, even the senior Hungarian master, Blasius de Várda, was ready to leave the University. The latter had served the Nation between 1516 and 1522, five times as proctor and was elected treasurer (receptor) of the Nation for the period of September 20, 1521, to August 12, 1522.

While holding the office of treasurer, Blasius was entrusted for the 1521-1522 academic year with the office of the "reformator," a dignity usually reserved only for menbers of higher Faculties of Theology, Law and Medicine. Blasius obtained the office by dispensation.

The "reformators" elected from the four Nations—French, Picard, Norman, and English-German—had to visit the colleges of the University, examine the courses of study, oversee the state of discipline and make any reforms—hence, the name of "reformator"—which they deemed necessary. [13]

Blasius de Várda was forced to leave the French capital, partly because of the plague, and partially, because his country, Hungary, was invaded by the Ottoman Turks. In August 1522, he bid an emotional farewell to all the fellow masters of the English-German Nation, and handed over the official documents, books and ready cash to the dean of the Nation, Gaspardus Pistoris, [14] the oldest member of the Nation. [15]

Before departing for Pannonia, Blasius de Várda wished all the masters of the Nation, "cheerful mind, long life, and happy end:"

> Omnibus magistris, presentibus et futuris,
> animam hilarem, vitam longam, finemque
> beatam exoptans. [16]

Academic Career of Marcus Mark de Kémes

Marcus Mark fortunately survived the plague and was admitted to the *examen*, Lenten disputations, academic performances, necessary to obtain his degree of Bachelor of Arts. As with every student, Marcus Mark was also "taxed" according to his financial conditions. He must have been a well-to-do student because he paid a very high sum of 10 Paris sol. "bursa." [17]

A *bursa* was a "unit" of calculation of payment. It was based upon the weekly expenses a student paid out for food and lodging. This was a very democratic method of defraying tuition; the student had to pay to masters, rectors, beadles, etc. so many "bursa"-s, all in variable amounts. The treasurer (receptor) had to multiply the sum of the "bursa." If a student had to pay the beadles 2 "bursa"-s, then a poor student with a "bursa" taxable to 4 Paris sol., paid only 8 sol., but Marcus Mark, "taxed" to 10 Paris sol., had to pay 20 Paris sol. Quite a difference. Therefore, the *bursa* was taxed for the poor in lower, for the rich in higher, amounts. The average *bursa* was 4 sol., only the richest students paid 10-12 Paris sol. The very rich and only very few paid 16 solidus. [18]

Marcus Mark obtained his Bachelor of Arts degree in the Spring of 1523, during the "fifth" proctorship of the Dutch, Franciscus Osmanus (Ossmanus) from Alkmaar. He was ranked fourth among nine bachelors. Usually someone had to wait one year to obtain his important degree of *licentiatus* in Arts, and start as *incipiens* to demonstrate his teaching abilities in order to become Master of Arts. However, Marcus Mark and the other bachelors promoted together with him obtained both their degrees of *licentiatus* and that of *incipiens* (i.e., Master of Arts) the very same year.

The *licentiati* were ranked according to the excellence of their performance. In the list of the proctor Franciscus Ossmanus, in the *Liber procuratorum*, Marcus Mark was placed first among the seven *licentiati* (1 from Whitehall, 1 from Trier, 3 from Constance, 1 from Lausanne) [19] and first among the five *incipientes*. [20]

According to the records of the *Liber receptorum*, which were always better kept and more carefully written because of the finances involved, the receptor Guillelmus Manderston, diocese of Saint-Andrews, Scotland, licentiatus in Medicine, listed Marcus Mark also as first among eight *licentiati* (among them 1 from Whitehall, 1 from Trier, 3 from Constance, 1 from Lausanne, and 1 from Cologne). [21]

Marcus Mark, Proctor

The Hungarian Marcus Mark was promoted together in all his three degrees, namely, Bachelor of Arts, *licentiatus* and Master of Arts, with Melchior Volmarius, diocese of Constance, the future teacher of Calvin and Theodore Beza, later professor at the Universities of Paris (where he was Royal Reader in Greek, 1529), Orléans, Bourges and Tübingen. For Marcus Mark to rank first before Melchior Volmarius (died 1561), placed only second, was a distinction in itself. When Marcus Mark was promoted Master of Arts, there were 12 masters in the English-German Nation present in Paris.[22]

Brilliant as he was, Marcus Mark, very soon after obtaining his degree of Master of Arts, was selected proctor on April 7, 1523, during the receptorship of Guillelmus Manderston, who functioned from September 20, 1522, to September 19, 1523. [23] Marcus Mark was also re-elected, i.e., "continued," in the office as proctor. [24]

On the flyleaf of the Book of Proctors (*Liber procuratorum* or *Conclusiones*), (today kept in the Archives of the Sorbonne), he jotted down with his own hand while testing his pen (*probatio calami*):

Marcus Mark de Kémes, Hungarus ex Altorum
Provincia. Procurator Anno Domini 1523.

He affixed his *signum manuale* after it, still in a simpler form than the one applied later in the same Book of Proctors.[25]

Marcus Mark succeeded the proctor Franciscus Ossmanus, who completed his records on Wednesday, April 7, 1523, at 1 o'clock after midnight. The patriotic Alkmaarian painted the arms of his native place Alkmaar in the Book of Proctors showing a fortified city gate. Below it he added his *signum manuale*, designed in the shape of a heart which is shown pierced by two crossed arrows depicted above it.[26]

*The Records of Marcus Mark de Kémes
in the Book of Proctors*

The records of Marcus Mark as proctor are actually written on four pages: Sorbonne, Register 15(16), folios 38 recto-40 verso. He reported eight meetings and employed his special signature, *signum manuale*, six times leaving two reports without signature. His records were written in cursive hand with pearl letters much compressed and hard to read.

His *signum manuale* was quite complicated and reveals his efforts to make it such that few people would have the patience to imitate it. It was designed as a large letter "U" decorated with three loops, and a small triangle. The frame was crossed over several times with small lines, in the middle the word *Mkesius* was written, accompanied with two "r"-s written above to give the reading *Markesius*. He employed another sign adding to the first one, consisting of a capital "M" with one of the two descendens of "M" ending in an "N," the other in an uncial-looking "A." All this is followed by a capital "I" between two periods (Plate No. I).

Marcus Mark de Kémes held the office of the proctor of the English-German Nation from April 7, 1523, until June 6, 1523. He reported eight meetings. The first was dated on April 7, 1523, where he announced his own election to the dignity of proctor in the convent of Mathurins.[27]

The second report was written on April 8, 1523,[28] the third on April 21, 1523,[29] informing the Nation about the various business discussed at the meetings of the University held on these two days. The fourth report gave an account of the April 24, 1523, reunion of the University of Paris: *celeberrima Academia Parisiensis*. Here the appointment of a bailiff by the King to act as royal conservator of University privileges—replacing the Provost of Paris—was discussed. The University of Paris had two kinds of *conservatores*: apostolic or papal, and the royal one, both officially "defenders" of the scholarly privileges of the University.

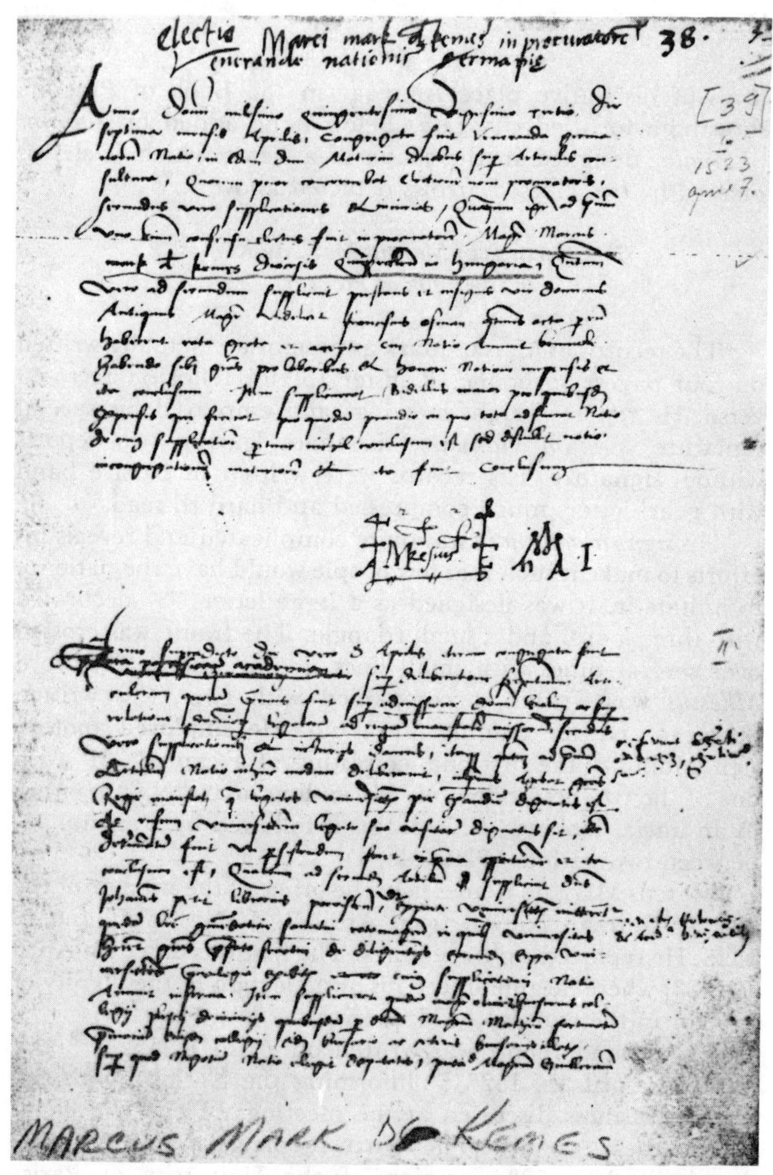

The first page of Records of Marcus Mark de Kémes in the
Liber procuratorum of the English-German Nation at the
University of Paris.
(Paris, Sorbonne, Archives, Reg. 15(16), folio 38 recto.)

The meeting of April 24, 1524, was a follow-up to that of April 22, 1523, when decision was made to bow before the will of the King Francois Ier and accept the nomination of Jean de la Barré to the office of the bailiff. [30] The April 26, 1523 meeting was that of the entire University as related here in Marcus Mark's fifth report. [31]

In his sixth report Marcus Mark summed up the various business discussed at the May 5, 1523, meeting of the Nation, among others that he himself was asked to "continue" in his office as proctor. [32] The seventh report was dated on May 14, 1523, with no mention of the locality and no signature of Marcus Mark de Kémes. [33]

The eighth entry was written on May 16, 1523, without indication where the meeting took place and with no signature at the end. [34] Marcus Mark here reported, putting his seal on certain letters of scolarity, for Grovilinius Grubilinius?/ Simonis, from the diocese of Cologne, who was promoted a bachelor four years earlier on February 23, 1519. Marcus Mark also listed Grovilinius Simonis as *licentiatus* and *incipiens* with 10 Paris solidus *bursa*. [35]

The brilliant Master of Arts, honored proctor of the English-German Nation, closed the reports of his proctorial office with an ironical but classical proverb appended after his *signum manuale*: "Optimum est aliena insania frui:" (It is best to profit from the folly of others). He did not identify or name the author of the saying. [36] The quotation is from Plinius the Younger, proof of Marcus Mark's classical learning and humanistic education.

Leaving Paris

In the *procuratoria* he was followed by a Scot, Gualterus Abercrom/b/i elected proctor on June 6, 1523. [37]

No information is available on the date of departure of Marcus Mark de Kémes from Paris. The pressure of the invasion of the Turks into Hungary was increasing. From the middle of 1523, we find no Hungarian subjects in Paris until the years after the tragic battle of Mohács on August 29, 1526. [38] This was a dark day in the history of Hungary. After one and one-half centuries of courageous defense against the Turks, the country succumbed and was annihilated at Mohács.

No bishops or *Studia* of higher learning were able to send scholars for a while to the faraway *Lutetia Parisiorum.* *

Notes

1. Astrik L. Gabriel, "La vie des étudiants hongrois dans le Paris du moyen âge," *Nouvelle Revue de Hongroie*, 62(1940), 29-34, 185-193; *idem*, "Magyar diákok és tanárok a középkori Párizsban," /With résumé in French: La vie à Paris des étudiants hongrois au Moyen Age/, *Archivum Philologicum*, 62(1938), 182-207; *idem*, "Alexandre de Hongrie, Maître-régent à l'Université de Paris (vers 1300)," *Revue d'Histoire Comparée*, N.s., 1(1943), 505-514; *idem*, Magyarországi Sándor Mester a középkori Sorbonne tanára," /With résumé in French: Alexandre de Hongrie, Maître-régent à la Sorbonne médiévale/, *Archivum Philologicum*, 64(1941), 22-40; *idem*, "Magyar vélemény egy középkori párisi dispután," /Participation of a Hungarian master at an academic disputation in medieval Paris/, in *A jászóvári Premontrei Kanonokrend gödöllői Szent Norbert Gimnáziumának 1942-1943 Évkönyve* /Yearbook of Szent Norbert Preparatory School of the Premonstratensian Canons of Jászóvár at Gödöllő/ (Pécs, 1943; reprint, Pécs, 1943), pp. 14 and 4 plates; *idem*, "Egy XIII. századi magyar klerikus párizsi egyetemi szentbeszéd-gyüjteménye," /With résumé in French: Le recueil de sermons d'un Hongrois, étudiant à l'Université de Paris au XIIe siècle/, *Archivum Philologicum*, 67(1943), 164-195; and *idem*, "Martin de Bereck, Receptor, Proctor and Rector at the University of Paris (1423-1432)," in Astrik L. Gabriel, *Garlandia. Studies in the History of the Mediaeval University* (Notre Dame, Ind.-Frankfurt am Main: J. Knecht, 1969), 125-134.

2. Astrik L. Gabriel, *Blaise de Várda, humaniste Hongrois à Paris*, Ostmitteleuropäische Bibliothek, no. 35 (Budapest: E. Stemmer, 1941); and *idem*, "The Academic Career of Blasius de Várda, Hungarian Humanist at the University of Paris," *Manuscripta*, 29(1976), 218-243.

3. Gray Cowan Boyce, *The English-German Nation in the University of Paris during the Middle Ages* (Bruges: Saint Catherine Press, 1927), 28-29; Madeleine Toulouse, *La Nation Anglaise-Allemande de l'Université de Paris des origines a la fin du XVe siècle* (Paris: Sirey, 1939), 22-23; and Pearl Kibre, *The Nations in the Mediaeval Universities* (Cambridge, Mass.: Medieval Academy of America, 1948), 19.

4. Josephus Koller, *Historia Episcopatus Quinqueecclesiarum* (Posonii /Pozsony/: J. M. Landerer, 1782), 3; and Egyed Hermann, *A Katolikus Egyház története Magyarországon 1914-ig*, /History of the Catholic Church in Hungary till 1914/ (München: Aurora Könyvek, 1973), 26.

5. Koller, Hist. *Episcopatus Quinqueecclesiarum*, 1-84. József Holub, "Bonipertus," in *Janus Pannonius Múzeum. Évkönyv 1959* (Pécs, 1959), 97-100.

6. Loren C. MacKinney, *Bishop Fulbert and Education at the School of Chartres* (Notre Dame, Ind.: The Mediaeval Institute, University of Notre Dame, 1957), 27. The text is in *Patrologia Latina*, Tomus 141, col. 189, Epist. I.

7. Andreas Veress, *Matricula et Acta Hungarorum in Universitatibus Italiae Studentium 1221-1864* (Budapest: Academia Scintiarum Hungarica, 1941), 10, 395.

8. Andor Csizmadia, *L'Université de Pécs au Moyen Age* (Budapest: Tankönyvkiadó, 1965); *idem*, ed., *Jubileumi Tanulmányok a Pécsi Egyetem történetéből*, /Studies Regarding the 600-Year History of the University of Pécs/ (Pécs: Univ. of Pécs, 1967); and Asztrik L. Gabriel, *The Mediaeval Universities of Pécs and Pozsony*.

Commemoration of the 500th and 600th Anniversary of their foundation: *1367-1467-1967* (Notre Dame, Ind.-Frankfurt am Main: Mediaeval Institute-J. Knecht, 1969).

9. Based upon Veress, *Matricula et Acta Hungarorum*; Karl Schrauf, *Die Matrikel der ungarischen Nation an der Wiener Universität 1453-1630* (Wien: Adolf Holzhausen, 1902); /Jac. Ferd. Miller/, *Regestrum Bursae Cracoviensis Hungarorum* (Budae: Typis Regiae Universitatis Hungaricae, 1821); B. Ulanowski and A. Chmiel, eds., *Album Studiosorum Universitatis Cracoviensis 1400-1606* (Cracow: Universitatis Jagellonica, 1887-1892), Tom. I-II; and Henryk Barycz, *Conclusiones Universitatis Cracoviensis ab anno 1441 ad annum 1589* (Krakow: Polska Akademja, 1933).

10. C. Eubel, *Hierarchia Catholica* (Münster, 1923), Vol. III, p. 280 and notes.

11. H. Mayerhofer, *Oesterreich-ungarisches Orst-Lexikon* (Wien, 1896), p. 319; *idem, Schematismus Quinqueecclesiensis* (Pécs, 1885), p. 32; and T. Ortvay, 319; *Georgraphia ecclesiastica Hungariae* (Budapest, 1891), Pars altera, p. 238, no. 42.

12. Géza Kiss and Kálmán Keresztes, *Ormánysági Szótár.* /Dictionary of Ormányság/ (Budapest: Akadémiai Kiadó, 1952), xxv-xlii.

13. Gabriel, "Academic Career of Blasius de Várda," 224-225; 233-237.

14. Gaspardus Pistoris from the diocese of Constance must have been around 70 years old at this time. He became Bachelor of Arts in 1471, *licentiatus* and Master of Arts in 1473: Astrik L. Gabriel and Gray C. Boyce, *Liber receptorum Nationis Anglicanae (Alemanniae) in Universitate Parisiensi*. Auctarium Chartularii Universitatis Parisiensis (Parisiis: Marcellus Didier, 1964), Tomus VI, col. 488, no. 12.

15. Paris, Sorbonne, Archives, Reg. 91(85), fol. 208 verso: "Et sic receptor. facto suo compoto, munimentis et pecuniis nacionis in manibus domini decani magistri videlicet Gaspardi Pistoris relictis, tum ob pestem que tunc in urbe Parisiensi grassabatur, tum vero quia Hungaria patria ejusdem receptoris ab infidelibus depopulata et pro parte occupata fuit, in patriam redire coactus fuit."

16. Reg. 91(85), fol. 208 verso.

17. "D. Marcus de Marck /sic/ diocesis Quinqueecclesiensis, cujus bursa valet 10 sol. par.:" Reg. 15(16), folio 35 recto.

18. See my chapter IX on *De bursarum natura et earum solutione* and chapter XV on *De statu economico et sociali Baccalareorum Nationis,* in Auct. VI, pp. xxxviii-xxxix; and xlix-li.

19. Under "Nomina licenciatorum" he was listed by the procurator exactly the same way as he was on the rostrum of the bachelors of Arts, except his name was spelled Mark: Reg. 15(16), folio 35 verso. There were really eight *licentiati,* not seven; Franciscus Ossmanus for some reason omitted one *licentiatus* from Cologne.

20. "Nomina incipientium: D. Marcus de Mark, diocesis Quinque Ecclesiensis, cujus bursa valet 10 sol. par.:" *Ibid.,* folio 35 verso.

21. "A *licentiatis*: Dominus Marcus Mark de Kemis, diocesis Quinque Ecclesiarum cujus bursa valet 10 sol par.,... 2 lb. 19 sol. par.:" Reg. 91(85), folio 214 recto.

22. Twelve masters received 12 sol. par. distributions from the receptor Guillelmus Manderston on March 25, 1523, feast of the Annunciation of the Blessed Virgin: *Ibid.,* folio 215.

23. *Ibid.,* folios 209 recto-217 verso.

24. The receptor, Guillelmus Manderston, listed payment made to three proctors, among them Marcus Mark de Kémes under the heading: "Procuratorum jura: Magistro Francisco Osmano, electo et continuato...viij sol. par. Magistro Marco Mark de Kémes electo et continuato...viij sol. par. Magistro Galtero Abercromio, electo et continuato...viij sol. par.:" *Ibid.,* folio 216 recto-verso. This is confirmed by the *Liber procuratorum*: Reg. 15(16), folio 38 recto: "Electio Marci Mark de Kémes in procuratorem Venerande Nationis Germanie."

25. Reg. 15(16), folio 1 recto.

26. Ossmanus wrote above his *signum manuale* and coat of arms the following text: "Sic procuratorio huic muneri, quando non sine labore quintum nunc fungi, finem ut animamque imponimus, posteris prosperiora optantes: Septime Idus Aprilis Paschatis, feria 4a, post mediam noctem, Hora prima. MDxxiij:" *Ibid.*, folio 36 verso.

27. The first report, without including the heading and the *signum manuale*, is written in 15 lines. In the first part he recalls his own election as proctor:

"Anno Domini millesimo quingentesimo vigesimo tertio, die septima mensis Aprilis, congregata fuit veneranda Germanorum Natio in edem divi Maturini, duobus super articulis consultura:

"Quorum prior concernebat electionem novi procuratoris; secundus vero supplicaciones et injurias."

"Quamquam igitur ad primum, uno omnium consensu electus fuit in procuratorem magister Marcus Mark de Kémes, diocesis Quinqueecclesiensis in Hungaria. Quantum vero ad secundum supplicuit prestans et insignis vir dominus antiquus magister videlicet Franciscus Osman quatinus acta per eum haberent rata, grata et accepta." Reg. 15(16), folio 38 recto.

28. Consists of 22 lines, followed by his *signum manuale*. *Ibid.*, folios 38(39) recto and verso, with marginal notes.

29. Written in nine lines followed by the *signum manuale* of Marcus Mark de Kémes is a report on the meeting of the university: *Ibid.*, folio 38(39) verso.

30. On the background of acceptance of the Bailiff as conservator of royal privileges of the University, see "Institutio Baillivi Conservatoris," Cesaris Egassius Bulaeus, *Historia Universitatis Parisiensis*, (Paris; 1673; Minerva Reprint, Frankfurt-am-Main, 1966), Vol. VI, pp. 153-154. The fourth report of Marcus Mark de Kémes, containing 19 lines, is written on Reg. 15(16), folios 38(39) verso-40 recto of the *Liber receptorum*.

31. *Ibid.*, folio 40 recto: Four lines followed by *signum manuale*.

32. This report contains his re-election as proctor and is introduced with the heading: "Continuatio Marci Mark de Kémes...Continuatus est Marcus Mark de Kémes in officio predicto usque ad mensem," written in 14 lines but without his *signum manuale*: *Ibid.*, folio 40 recto.

33. Report of five lines regarding the accreditation of messengers, persons who with the approval of the University against payment acted as "messengers" between the subjects of the Nation, and their parents, dioceses or bishops: Reg. 15(16), folio 40 recto.

34. Not a real report but rather a short notice of eight lines: *Ibid.*, folio 40 verso.

35. *Ibid.*, folio 40 verso.

36. *Ibid.*, folio 40 verso, quotation taken from Plinius the Younger, *Historia naturalis*, Bk. 18, 6, 31. H. Rackham, *Pliny Natural History with an English Translation*, (Cambridge, MA-London, 1950), pp. 208 (Latin), 209 (English). E. Margalits, *Florilegium proverbiorum Universae Latinitatis* (Budapest, 1895), p. 253.

37. Reg. 15(16), folio 41 recto.

38. L. Domonkos, "The Battle of Mohács as a Cultural Watershed," *From Hunyadi to Rákóczi. War and Society in Late Medieval and Early Modern Hungary*, eds. J. M. Bak and B. K. Király, (New York: Brooklyn College Press, 1982), pp. 203-224.

* Research for writing this article was facilitated by a travel grant from Mr. Wallace V. Bedolfe, President, United Casualty Co. Toronto, Ont. Canada.

Gilbert E. Mihályi, O. Praem.:

8 / THE INSTITUTION OF LICENTIATUS: HUNGARIAN EXPERIMENT WITH THE LAITY'S PARTICIPATION IN MINISTRY DURING THE SIXTEENTH AND SEVENTEENTH CENTURIES

Since the ever-growing number of "priestless parishes" is a world-wide phenomenon, servicing the ministry has become one of the burning issues of contemporary Catholicism. As a result, one of the priorities of the Church is to raise the number of participants in the ministry to meet the indispensable pastoral needs.

In response to the needs of "priestless parishes," the Catholic Church in Hungary offered a "first" in the form of the Institution of Licentiatus in the sixteenth and seventeenth centuries. This sharing of laity in ministry in Hungary centuries ago is not just a historical curiosity. It was an initiative that did not vanish without any trace in the vicissitudes of time, but became a worthwhile practice which survived and was accepted by the Vatican Council II. Since that time the problem of ministry exploded and constitutes today one of the most agitated and divisive issues in the Church.

It is this Hungarian experiment that this essay undertakes to study. First, the historical setting will be described; then the unique experiment itself will be discussed, and finally, the significance of the Hungarian Institution of Licentiatus will be assessed in the light of conciliar and post-conciliar developments.

I. THE HISTORICAL BACKGROUND

To appreciate the Institution of Licentiatus better, it must be examined in its historical context. Therefore, before discussing this Hungarian experiment, it is necessary to characterize the religious situation in sixteenth and seventeenth-century Hungary. There were two factors that determined the spiritual situation of the country: the Turkish domination and the Protestant Reformation.

The Turkish Conquest and Domination in Hungary

In their design to capture Europe, the Ottoman Turks, after having developed into a formidable military power, conquered a great part of the Balkans in the fourteenth century. Even Constantinople fell into their hands in 1453, but they were halted in their advance at Nándorfehérvár (Belgrade) in 1456 by János Hunyadi, the great Hungarian military strategist. This was, however, just a temporary setback for the horsemen of Asia, who continued beating at the gates of the Northern Balkans. In a decisive battle at Mohács (in Southern Hungary) in 1526, Hungary was defeated. King Louis II, almost all the Catholic bishops, and much of the Hungarian nobility perished on the battlefield. As a result, the country lay open to the enemy's whims.[1] At the peak of Turkish power, about two-thirds of Hungary was dominated by the Turks, a control that lasted for 150 years. The Western and Northern parts formed the kingdom of Hungary under the Habsburgs, while the independent Transylvanian princedom functioned in the Eastern region.

The Protestant Reformation

The political-military conquest of Hungary was augmented by yet another event, the Protestant Reformation.

There were many factors responsible for that challenge to Catholicism, which were further aggravated by the rather aggressive, consistent, and erudite work of most of the preachers of the new faith. Their persistence enabled them to win over not only many priests and members of religious orders, but also the great majority of the population who became refugees in their own country and who were spiritually abandoned by their defecting priests.

Being "aggressive" is not meant here in a physical sense. It was rather a kind of tactic adopted in promoting the religious revolution. Many preachers of the new faith resorted even to deception by celebrating Catholic Mass at the beginning. By doing so, they were more acceptable to the people who did not want to abandon the Catholic Church, nor the sacramental life. This is evident from the protocols of the canonical visitations of the diocese of Veszprém. It says, among others, that the faithful of the village of Tarány, who had converted to Protestantism, still made their Easter confession to a Catholic priest in the neighboring village in 1713. [2]

As a result of all this, the Protestant Reformation was spreading rapidly, without any real difficulty. But if this was true, what did all this mean for life in Hungary?

The Religious Disintegration

The Turkish domination and the Protestant Reformation in Hungary left their profound impact on the political, military, social, cultural, and religious life for a long time. The effect of these two important historical events on the religious life of the population was especially far-reaching.

First, there was a demographic dislocation resulting from the flight of the inhabitants from the invading Turkish forces, which disrupted and in most cases destroyed the regular parish structure. The almost total breakdown of the Church organization was completed by the lack of ecclesial communication: namely, the bishops lived in the royal territory and so they just could not fulfill their pastoral responsibilities from a distance. It meant a real life threat for them to cross over the border because they were regarded as spies. That these bishops appointed vicars did not really change the tragic situation substantially. Those bishops whose dioceses were located along the Turkish-Hungarian frontier (such as Vác, for example) found themselves in an advantageous situation because they could at least establish some kind of communication with their faithful. [3]

The Holy See did want the bishops to go back to their dioceses. But when the Congregation of the Propagation of the

Faith commissioned the Apostolic Nuncio at the imperial court in Vienna to ask the emperor to require his bishops to visit and to take care of their flocks, the latter protested, citing the dangers of such an undertaking and also their poverty, which stood in the way to carry out the order. [4] The Council of Trent also obligated the bishops to reside within their diocese, but Hungarian prelates, referring to the dangerous situation, did not comply with this request.

The number of the Catholic faithful decreased alarmingly. Miklós Telegdy, Bishop of Pécs wrote to the Pope in 1680 that there was a real likelihood that in time "not even the name of the Catholic faith will survive in Hungary." [5] Bishop Faustus Verancsics of Csanád estimated about the same time that Catholics constitute only about one-thousandth of the entire population. [6]

The number of priests dropped to a crisis point. It should be noted here that the problem was not the shortage of priests, but rather the virtual non-existence of priests. Whole regions remained without spiritual leaders, and in many cases, the people in need of solace were drawn to accept the ministers of the new faith as their leaders. Thus "priestless parishes" became a reality in the religious life of Hungary. For instance, the city of Kecskemét, in the middle of the Great Plains, had no priests at all, beginning with the mid-seventeenth century. In 1644 the faithful wrote to Primate Archbishop Lippay that following the death of their pastor they have not seen a priest for almost a whole year, and that there were really no priests around in their region covering an area of ten to twelve "miles" radius (i.e. 52 to 63 U.S. miles). [7]

It is obvious that the recruitment and education of the clergy became almost impossible under these conditions. Thus, even the prospect for an improvement in the religious situation appeared very remote. The Pope placed the whole area occupied by the Turks—from Buda to Constantinople— under the jurisdiction of the Bishop of Belgrade. This provision, however, did not change the pastoral situation, since their safe movement was not guaranteed, and the bishop and the priests did not speak Hungarian. However, the Hungarian Jesuit missionaries, who could penetrate into the Turkish zone, accomplished much, and their presence meant a great deal for the priestless Catholics of the region. [8]

While the Turks did not persecute the Christians, they did not make life easy for them either. For example, taking care of the church buildings presented a great problem. It was hard to get repair permits from the authorities, so the faithful were often forced to worship at the parish house or in private homes. [9] From a letter of Archbishop George Szelepcsényi it is known that priests and licentiati were often in grave physical danger. [10] They were subjected to vexations and at times to imprisonment. Some of them were even executed, while others were set free if their parishioners paid the ransom. During the constant fights between Catholics and Protestants, the latter turned to the Turks for help. When the Archabbot of Pannonhalma wanted to send a priest or licentiatus to the neighboring village to re-Catholicize the population, the Protestants denounced him to the occupying authorities, charging that he aimed at dispersing the people so that they would not be able to pay taxes. At hearing this, the Turks used threats against the Archabbot. [11]

All in all, in sixteenth and seventeenth century Hungary, the Church found herself in a situation of extreme emergency, which was the direct result of the general religious disintegration.

II. THE INSTITUTION OF LICENTIATUS

It is in this period of grave religious ordeal in Hungary's history that the Institution of Licentiatus came into being. The next part of this study will explore what this institution was really like, what purpose it served, and how it fulfilled the expectations of the Church.

The Meaning of Licentiatus

Licentiatus was actually a kind of ministry program which authorized lay people to do certain pastoral work in order to alleviate the harmful effects of the general absence of priests in Turkish-occupied Hungary that had been further devastated by the Protestant Reformation.

Within this context the term "ministry" generally refers to ecclesial service in which the one who ministers, serves, and helps others in many different ways brings the faithful closer to

Jesus. The performance of certain types of "pastoral work" also qualifies as ministry. Pastoral work can be priestly and non-priestly, sacramental and non-sacramental service. Here it refers to a non-priestly and mostly non-sacramental ministry: "mostly" because the ministry in question also has some sacramental functions.

This ministry was carried out by "lay people" who in Church parlance denote Christians who—in the framework of traditional ecclesiology—were supervised by priests who received their commission to minister through the sacrament of ordination.[12] The Institution of Licentiatus gave a share in certain ecclesial ministry to the lay people. It was this lay character of the Hungarian experiment that made it a unique kind of undertaking in the sixteenth and seventeenth centuries. Licentiati were in no way designed to replace priests. They were not priestly laymen nor lay priests. In accordance with this, the Turks called them "half-priests," and Cardinal Pázmány named them "catechists," while the people liked to address them as "Sir Licentiatus."[13] Most of them came from the ranks of teachers, because they could read, and so their preparation did not require a long time. Later, Protestant preachers, re-converted to Catholicism, also received admission to the ranks of the licentiati.

These lay people were authorized to perform certain types of pastoral work. The Church authorities formally designated and appointed them to carry out specific pastoral work to serve the needs of the faithful. Those chosen or those who volunteered for such service underwent preparation and had to take an examination. A license was then given to them which empowered them to share in the ecclesial ministry. It is from this license or permission that both the institution itself and the lay ministers take their name. It must be added that this license was periodically renewed, a provision which was intended to motivate the lay ministers to self-study.

The Purpose of Licentiatus

The establishment of the Licentiatus aimed at alleviating the harmful effects of the general absence of priests in Hungary. The institution, therefore, became a practical answer to the spiritual emergency situation caused by the Turkish conquest and the spread of Protestantism. Evidently, the Hungarian Catholic Church did whatever it could, even in this limited form, to carry out its ministry. To keep alive the ecclesial community was a matter of survival for Hungarian Catholicism.

At this point, the question of rationale for this unprecedented and unheard of ministry program should be discussed. More specifically: What kind of justification, beyond the survival proposition, was given for the participation of the laity in the ministry in Hungary? Was there a search for theological reasoning for this pastoral innovation?

From the data of our research we can conclude that there were no attempts to find a theological basis for the Institution of Licentiatus. There were probably three reasons for this: the lack of time, the low level of priestly training, and the lack of theological tools.

In the era of religious disintegration, there was no time for scholarly work. There were very few priests and religious teachers who ministered to the people, and their workloads prevented them from engaging in theological research.

The training of priests, especially of those who were destined to be the pastors in the provinces, was in no way adequate. It must be noted that these were the times prior to the Council of Trent (1545-1563). Only those priests who were chosen to be teachers of theology, or diocesan officials received a thorough education by being sent to universities such as Vienna or Krakow.[14] Priest-candidates, bound to work among the people, lived with the pastors, and by helping them in performing the daily duties, they learned their craft. What they had to prove mostly was their knowledge of reading and chanting. Writing was not explicitly required. The requirements for priesthood in the fifteenth and in the beginning of the sixteenth century may be classified into four categories: administration of the Sacraments, the preservation of the Eucharist, the celebration of the Mass, and the administration of the parish.[15] Thus their "on the job" training was more practical than doctrinal. Consequently, they were wholly unprepared to undertake any high-level theological study or debate.

Given the above circumstances, it is understandable that the Hungarian priesthood of that period failed to develop any kind of theological explanation for the Institution of Licentiatus. The argument they advanced was existential: the Hungarian Church could not stand idle amidst the most trying religious situation, and was obliged to provide some kind of practical pastoral service to meet the most fundamental and necessary spiritual needs of the faithful. There was no model to follow. Yet they responded to the challenge with innovation, creativity, and ingenuity.

Functions

It was said that the Licentiatus was a kind of ministry to perform "certain pastoral work." That phrase refers to the functions the lay ministers performed. The duties they were licensed to carry out were rather extensive. Since the Sunday worship is the central act of the ecclesial community, the main task of a licentiatus was to gather the people into the church or in another proper building, to lead the prayers and songs, read the readings, preach the sermon, and distribute the Holy Communion if the Eucharist was available. In addition, he taught catechism, visited the sick, and buried the dead. These were non-priestly, non-sacramental activities. But the lay minister was also licensed to baptize, and in many places, to perform marriages. Thus, his vocation included even a sacramental function.

At this time of ongoing polemics between the "old" and the "new" faith, the lay ministers were often challenged to engage in religious disputes. However, they were explicitly forbidden to be involved in them. Their preparation was simply not adequate for such an exercise that demanded special skills. [16]

The proclamation of the Word of God and teaching of the catechism received the primary attention in the lay minister's pastoral work. [17] This responded to the needs of that epoch, since the Protestant preachers passionately attacked the Catholic doctrine and the institution of the Church. But since the training of the licentiati was not adequate to the task, they were simply asked to read the sermons. To help them in this important duty, collections of sermons were made available to them. Cardinal Péter Pázmány, for example, wrote and

published his sermons for Sundays and feast days, with the
intention of providing the lay ministers with good source
material. Catechism was taught from the Dutch Jesuit Peter
Canisius's *Summary of Christian Doctrine*, which was translated into Hungarian.[18] This work presented the Catholic faith
in an apologetic manner, as required by the needs of the times.
However, it must be noted that these teaching-aid materials
were published in Royal Hungary, and their delivery to those
under Turkish occupation was not an easy task.

While the exact date of the establishment of Licentiatus is
not known, there is a sure point of departure to ascertain when
this institution was already in operation. It was Cardinal
Pázmány who gave official commission to the Licentiatus on
April 2, 1628 at the provincial Synod of Pozsony (Pressburg,
Bratislava).[19] But different historical documents strongly
indicate that these lay ministers were working among the
people already at the end of the sixteenth century.[20] Following
the expulsion of the Turks from Hungary in the late
seventeenth century, however, the Licentiatus simply faded
away without any official edict.

The renumeration of the licentiati varied from place to
place. They lived in the rectory or in any other place of
residence provided by the parishioners. They were paid either
in money or in kind, such as grain, potatoes, corn, and
wine—the produce being collected at harvest time.[21]

Rome's Position toward the Hungarian Lay Ministry

The Holy See's reaction toward this Hungarian pastoral
innovation was of great consequence to the functioning of the
Institution of Licentiatus. Soon after the Congregation for the
Propagation of Faith was established in 1622, the Hungarian
Church was placed under its jurisdiction. Thus Rome's
position toward the Institution of Licentiatus can be found in
its communications with the Congregation.

János Sávai, a recent scholar, researched the archives of the
Propagation of Faith to find out what Rome's verdict was on
this Hungarian experiment. According to his findings, it is
evident that the Holy See was rather well-informed about the
tragic situation in Hungary. This information came partially
from the Papal Nuncio in Vienna, and partially from the

correspondences of the missionaries and visitors sent by Rome to the lands under Turkish occupation. Through the constant threat of grave physical danger, the Propagation of Faith came to know the poverty and material misery of the Church and of the faithful, who apparently even "lacked bread." But what was equally important, the Catholics were also hungering after the Word of God and the Sacraments, and there was no one to satisfy their spiritual needs. Thus Rome was well aware of the basic problem confronting the Church of Hungary: the absence of priests and bishops.

From these same communications the Holy See also learned about the existence and the activities of the lay ministers. The information about them that reached Rome was mixed. Some praised the work of the licentiati and pointed out their usefulness, while others criticized the institution and liked to dwell on the abuses the lay ministers allegedly committed. However, for a long time the Holy See remained silent about the Hungarian experiment. When the problem of marriage performed by the lay ministers came before the Congregation, it became indignant and began an investigation as to whether the Council of Trent's decree regarding marriage celebration had been promulgated in Hungary. Another problem that disturbed the Congregation was the acceptance of Protestant preachers who converted to Catholicism, and then became licentiati. The Propagation of Faith, however, never issued an order regarding these matters.

Based on the above information, Sávai came to the conclusion that Rome neither approved nor disapproved the lay ministry in Hungary. Rather, the Holy See simply tolerated it as an unavoidable by-product of the unprecedented spiritual emergency in Turkish-occupied Hungary.

Evaluation

In the evaluation of the Institution of Licentiatus, it must be pointed out that the Hungarian practice had its negative as well as positive aspects. The poor preparation of the lay ministers must be regarded as the greatest deficiency of the whole system. Cardinal Pázmány wrote to Pope Urban VII in 1632 that "the licentiati are very poorly trained."[22] But because of "the absence of priests," he tolerated them.[23] In this spirit he wrote to the Apostolic Nuncio in Vienna in 1628: "I feel I am between fire and water.... To dissolve the Licentiatus would mean to open the door to Calvinist preachers.... I know the work of the Licentiatus involves many dangers. Between the two wrongs, I have to choose the lesser one."[24]

Beyond the poor preparation, the lay ministers often abused their office: they heard confessions, celebrated Mass at Easter, distributed Communion with non-consecrated hosts,[25] or they became negligent and did not preach. Some of them even abandoned themselves to a loose life. For that, they were reprimanded, and in some cases, their license was revoked.

In spite of all this, the Institution of Licentiatus proved to be a very positive phenomenon. The laity's sharing in the ministry was a revolutionary, pioneering, and daring Hungarian initiative, showing the vitality of the Church under extreme pressure. That the Church was still alive when the country was liberated from Turkish domination after 150 years, was to a great degree attributed to the work of the lay ministers.

III. THE HUNGARIAN EXPERIMENT AS A CHURCH PRACTICE

The Hungarian Institution of Licentiatus has much more than just a local or temporary value. Its historical significance can only be properly appreciated if it is considered in the light of subsequent developments. In this regard, Vatican Council II and the new Code of Canon Law of 1983 represent significant milestones. It is therefore important to examine their contribution to the laity's sharing in ministry.

The Second Vatican Council

Prior to Vatican II, when the hierarchical notion of the Church prevailed, ministry was the exclusive prerogative of the priests. But in the last decades, patristical, biblical, and liturgical studies, and the renewal movements effected a profound shift in ecclesiology: A more biblical and theological vision of the Church emerged. In the Second Vatican Council's Dogmatic Constitution—without abandoning its juridical-hierarchical nature—the renewed Church identified herself as a People of God.

In this recaptured self-vision, the place and role of the laity in the Church was necessarily clarified. This involved the following three insights: First, the fundamental equality of all Christians; second, the common vocation of all baptized persons in carrying out the mission of the Church; and third, the common priesthood of all who are baptized. As the Dogmatic Constitution of the Church states: "The faithful are by baptism made one body with Christ and are established among the People of God. They are, in their own way, made sharers in the priestly, prophetic, and kingly functions of Christ."[26]

It is this renewed ecclesiology that was not available to the Hungarian Church in the sixteenth and seventeenth centuries. Their rationale of the laity's sharing in ministry was "the absence of priests," as discussed above. The Second Vatican Council, on the other hand, though conscious of the shortage of priests (as attested to, among others, by such documents as the Decree on the Apostolate of Lay People), has put the lay ministry on a permanent, theological foundation. As a result of this, the ecclesial ministry became open to the laity. First of all, the ordained ministry of deacon, which was regarded before as a stage in preparation for priesthood, was made available to married laity as a self-standing order. Then, the laity was commissioned to read the Scriptures during the Mass, distribute Communion, teach catechism, visit the sick and bury the dead—all of which they were asked to do in Hungary during the Turkish occupation and Protestant Reformation.

The New Code of Canon Law

The Code of Canon Law of 1983 represents another significant point in the development of the laity's sharing in ministry. The old Code was revised in the spirit of the Second Vatican Council. Consequently, the new Code incorporates all of the conciliar teachings concerning the participation of the Christians in ministry. But the revised Code goes behind the conciliar stipulation: It opens up to the laity parish and diocesan administrative roles, and expands their liturgical and sacramental functions. From now on, lay ministers may proclaim the Word of God when other ministers are lacking, may confirm solemn baptism, and in certain circumstances may also act as official witnesses to marriages. [27]

Canon 1248, paragraph 2, also makes provisions for "priestless Sundays." [28] Thus, the Hungarian crisis repeats itself on a world-wide scale. According to Suzanne Elsesser's study, for example, Italy has 3,237, Spain 8,543, France 20,851, and North America 777 priestless parishes.[29] To meet this challenge, the above-mentioned Canon, adopting the Hungarian practice, recommends to the faithful to take part in a Sunday service conducted by a lay minister who preaches and distributes Communion.

In conclusion, it is clear that the Hungarian experiment of many centuries ago has now become a regular Church practice. Did the Institution of Licentiatus serve as a model for this development? It cannot be answered with absolute certainty, but that experiment must undoubtedly have survived in the memory of the Church. According to Yves Congar, [30] the seventeenth-century Hungarian Institution of Licentiatus was not unknown to the Fathers of the Second Vatican Council. As such, this formerly purely Hungarian experimentation has now become recognized as an integral part of the life of the Church in the late twentieth century.

Although the lay ministry is now widely accepted, the earlier Hungarian experience with the Institution of Licentiatus tells us that such solutions can never become the only solution to the "priestless Sunday" crisis of world-wide proportions. This is very much in line with the teaching of Vatican II, which forcefully asserted that the Eucharist is one of the constituting elements of the Church community. Therefore, the non-Eucharistic Sunday cannot be accepted as a regular mode of celebrating the Lord's day. It is the right of the faithful to have priests, and it is a matter of Rome's responsibility and creativity to make priests available to the People of God. [31]

Notes

1. One of the best Hungarian works on this epoch is by Bálint Hóman and Gyula Szekfű, *Magyar Történet* /Hungarian History/, 5 vols. (Budapest: Királyi Magyar Egyetemi Nyomda, 1935-1936), II, 595-611; III, 1-574.

2. János Sávai, *La Partecipazione dei laici al lavoro pastorale in Ungheria nei secoli XVI-XVII* (Roma: Tipografia F. Albanese, 1982), p. 26.

3. Hermann Egyed, *A Katolikus Egyház története Magyarországon 1914-ig*. /History of the Catholic Church in Hungary till 1914/ (München: Aurora Könyvek, 1973), p. 290.

4. Sávai, *La partecipazione*, p. 105.

5. Hermann, *A Katolikus Egyház*, p. 219.

6. *Ibid.*

7. *Ibid.*, p. 290.

8. László Szilas, S. J., "Inventar der die Jesuiten-mission im Türkischen Ungarn betreffenden Dokumente im Band AUSTR. 20 des Römischen Archivs der Gesellschaft Jesu," in *Südosteuropa unter dem Halbmond; Prof. Georg Stadtmüller zum 65. Geburtstag gewidmet* (München: Dr. Rudolf Tröfenik, 1975), pp. 255-267.

9. Hermann, *A Katolikus Egyház*, p. 292.

10. Sávai, *La partecipazione, p. 98.*

11. *Ibid.*

12. For a fuller explanation of the points raised here see the groundbreaking work of Yves Congar, *Lay people in the Church* (Westminster, MD: Newman, 1965).

13. Sávai, *La partecipazione*, p. 50.

14. *Ibid.*, pp. 160-164.

15. *Ibid.*, p. 151.

16. *Ibid.*, p. 99.

17. Ibid.

18. *Ibid.*, pp. 86-94.

19. *Ibid.*, p. 52.

20. *Ibid.*, p. 51.

21. Hermann, *A Katolikus Egyház, p. 256.*

22. Sávai, *La partecipazione*, p. 53.

23. *Ibid.*

24. *Ibid.*

25. Hermann, *A Katolikus Egyház* p. 291.

26. *The Documents of Vatican II*, ed. Walter M. Abbott, S. J., (New York: The America Press, 1966), p. 57.

27. Bradley K. Arturi, "The laity and the new Code of Canon Law," *Homiletic and Pastoral Review* (July 1984), pp. 16-21.

28. Bertram Griffin, "The Parish and Lay Ministry," *Chicago Studies*, XXIII (1984), p. 56.

29. Suzanne E. Elsesser, "Priestless Parishes: A Look at How They Are Being Staffed," *Quarterly Professional Development Publication* (June 1983) p. 2.

30. Sávai, *La partecipazione*, p. 140.

31. Mihályi Gilbert, "A vasárnap megszentelése pap nélkül" (The Celebration of Sunday Without Priests), *Szolgálat*, No. 59, p. 23.

Lél F. Somogyi:

9 / PRINCE FERENC RÁKÓCZI AND THE HUNGARIAN HISTORICAL MISSION

Prince Ferenc Rákóczi II became a legend on the day he died over 250 years ago on April 8, 1735. To the Hungarian people, the events of his life assumed almost legendary qualities. This phenomenon can only be explained by trying to understand Rákóczi and his belief in the "Hungarian historical mission" and the latter's significance for the nation.

Recently, Hungarians around the world have recalled the 250th anniversary of Rákóczi's death (1735), and also noted the 80th anniversary of the homecoming of his remains from Turkey (1906). These anniversaries provide us with a timely opportunity to examine the life and accomplishments of this great Hungarian. Also, since the situation of many thousands of Hungarians today parallels the fate of Rákóczi and his associates, his life and deeds may provide us with some useful insights into the beliefs and deeds of those many thousands who felt compelled to leave their native land in the course of the past several decades. And this leads us to the main question of this essay, namely: did Ferenc Rákóczi II, who is considered to have been "one of the greatest, most worthy, most unselfish, and most sacrificing individuals in Hungarian history," [1] act on the basis of the principles he professed concerning the so-called Hungarian historical mission?

While many philosophers of history would doubt this, according to some of its proponents, the "Hungarian historical mission" is one of the most ancient inheritances of the Hungarian people, which presumes and believes in the special destiny of this nation. Allegedly this belief in and consciousness

139

of a special destiny can already be detected in the legends of the Huns concerning the so-called "Sword of God" and the "special powers" it endowed Attila to lead his people. It can be found in the dream of Emese, grandmother of the conquering Árpád, who saw herself as the procreator of a whole nation that flowed forth from her womb. And it is also evident in many other aspects of Hungarian history where it is accepted by the Magyars and their leaders as a definition of their nationhood.

When examined in light of this consciousness of the Hungarian historical mission, many events in Hungarian history take on new meaning. Hungary's dedication to the defense of Christendom, for example, can be said to have been the conscious fulfillment of the ancient Hungarian historical mission. The battles of King St. Ladislas against the Cumans in the late 11th century; the Holy Crusade of King Andrew II in 1218; King Béla IV's death and life struggle against the Mongols at Mohi in 1241; King Louis the Great's defeat of the Ottoman Turks in 1377; the victory of the great Christian crusader, János Hunyadi, against the same enemy at Nándorfehérvár (Belgrade, 1456), which resulted in the proclamation of the Angelus (tolling of church bells at noon time) by Pope Calixtus III; the disaster of Mohács in 1526 and its consequences, including the century and a half of Turkish occupation; all attest to the strength that the Hungarians drew from the concept of their national mission.

It was this same consciousness that transformed the Croatian nobleman, Count Nicolaus Zrínyi (1508-1566), into one of Hungary's great war lords (*főkapitány*) and hero of the fortress of Szigetvár (1566); and it was likewise this consciousness that inspired his great grandson of the same name to write the heroic epic, *The Peril of Sziget /Szigeti veszedelem/* (1664), which is one of the earliest and most brilliant embodiment and expression of this consciousness of the Hungarian national mission. [2]

* * * * *

Ferenc Rákóczi II was the grandson of Count Péter Zrínyi (1621-1671), the younger brother of the author of *The Peril of Sziget*, who was beheaded for his membership in the anti-Habsburg conspiracy led by Palatine Nicolaus Wesselényi.

Rákóczi's father of the same name—Ferenc Rákóczi I—was an elected prince of Transylvania who also participated in the Wesselényi Conspiracy; while his mother was Ilona Zrínyi—Péter Zrinyi's daughter—who later became the wife of Count Imre Thököly (1657-1705), the *kuruc* (anti-Habsburg) "King" of Northeastern Hungary under Turkish rule.[3]

In the course of their long history in the Carpathian Basin the Hungarians were often forced to fight both the East and the West, depending on the source of the danger that imperiled their country. In the late 17th and early 18th centuries the danger from the East subsided, while the pressure from the West increased. At this time the source of this danger was primarily the Habsburg-ruled Holy Roman Empire which since the Peace of Karlovice in 1699 had treated Hungary like a conquered territory and heaped a whole series of oppressive measures upon its population. According to Gyula Szekfű, Hungary's most distinguished 20th-century historian, "the Hungarian nation has never been in greater depravity since Árpád,"[4] the 9th-century conqueror and founder of the Hungarian state. For this very reason—as expressed by Ferenc Somogyi—"the nation never expected as much and with such unanimity from anyone...as it did from Ferenc Rákóczi II," when the latter launched his War of Liberation.[5]

In light of Prince Rákóczi's family traditions, it should not have come as a surprise to anyone that he refused to accept Habsburg absolutism and issued his call for a national uprising. Drawn up on May 12, 1703 at Brezna in Poland, he dispatched this call with a red silk flag that was first raised by the peasants of northeastern Hungary (i.e., those of Tarpa, Vár, and Beregszász).

His struggle—which was intertwined with general European affairs through the War of Spanish Succession—ended eight years later with the compromise Peace of Szatmár on April 29, 1711. The reasons for this lack of victory were many, although a number of prominent Hungarian historians claim that "the fate of the Hungarian uprising was decided on the Western battlefields,"[6] and that Rákóczi was defeated "not by /the Habsburg General János/ Pálffy, but by developments in world politics and by the ravages of the Europe-wide Black Plague."[7] (Allegedly, in the period of the Rákóczi Uprising the Black Plague caused 410,000 deaths in Hungary and

Transylvania, while at the same time "only" 80,000 died in combat.) [8]

* * * * *

Recent writings published by Hungarian historians and publicists deal very little with Rákóczi's emigré life. [9] They simply observe that he could not accept the terms of the Treaty of Szatmár because he did not trust Vienna. These authors also state that the exiled prince could never accept the idea that King Louis XIV of France would abandon him after all the promises he had made. In actuality, however, King Louis always looked out only for French interests, and readily discarded allies he could no longer use. This is what also happened to Rákóczi.

As has been true during the eight years of his struggle against the Habsburgs, Rákóczi clung tenaciously to his belief in his nation's historical mission as understood by him, and also persisted in his demands for Hungary's national and international rights. In this tenaciousness he was undoubtedly inspired by some of the unforgettable events in his life. The first of these took place at the very beginning of the War of Independence in 1703 when he marched across the Carpathians from Poland to Hungary to unfurl the flag of liberation "with God, for country and freedom." In the course of this march, thousands of peasants and others greeted him, literally praying at his feet as though he were a prophet sent by God. They knelt down, and weeping, kissed the hoofmarks of his horse as he passed through. The other event occurred at the end of October 1710 on his ride from the fortress of Sárospatak to the city of Ungvár. At that time Rákóczi met many carriages filled with ladies, nobles, and army officers who were fleeing from the pillages of the Habsburg imperial armies in the Hungarian Lowlands /*Alföld*/. As they passed Rákóczi, they reached out to him weeping and encouraged him to press on with his struggle, pledging their eternal loyalty and allegiance. [10]

It is very likely that the images on the commemorative medallions struck at that time re-enforced the memory of these events and experiences in Rákóczi's mind during his exile. These medallions depict a Catholic priest, a Calvinist minister, and a Lutheran preacher joining forces against religious and national oppression with the Latin phrase "concurrunt ut alant." [11] In this manner Rákóczi also added the struggle for religious freedom to his national goals and commitments.

These images and views must have been in Rákóczi's mind when he tried to delay the acceptance of the Peace of Szatmár in 1711. At that time he was still hoping for Russian assistance as promised by Prince Yakov Dolgoruky; he questioned the sincerity of the Imperial Commissioner, Count János Pálffy, and the latter's loyalty to the cause of Hungary; and after the capitulation of the kuruc armies on the field of Nagymajtény, he refused to accept the imperial pardon that was extended to him. Rather, he decided to leave for Poland, where he planned to continue his efforts to convince the leaders of Europe to support the Hungarian cause.

In the years following the failure of the War of Liberation, Rákóczi tried to persuade various European governments to take up the cause of his homeland. Thus, in 1712 he attempted to win the good will of England. Unfortunately, however, due to the strenuous objections by the Habsburg Court, Rákóczi was denied an audience by Queen Anne.

Unwilling to give up, Rákóczi once more turned to France for support. In a memorandum to the "Sun King" dated April 27, 1713, he appealed for continued support. King Louis did receive Prince Rákóczi and his associates at an audience, but did nothing on Hungary's behalf. The Peace Treaties of Utrecht (1713) and Rastatt (1714) were signed without so much as a mention of Hungarian and Transylvanian interests.

Adding insult to injury, in 1715 the Habsburg-controlled Hungarian Diet proclaimed Prince Rákóczi and his associates "enemies of the fatherland, traitors, and subverters of true freedom." [12] All this hurt Rákóczi deeply. It depressed the exiled Prince to the point of questioning himself and his purpose in life. By this time he had sacrificed his whole fortune, lost his wife and two sons, and now his enemies were also trying to destroy his reputation. Yet, none of this destroyed his deep-seated belief in the mission of his nation.

When realizing that his selflessness and dedication had brought him nothing but misery, Rákóczi set about to change the direction of his life. At the end of 1715, after the death of King Louis XIV, he entered into the Monastery of the Camaldulian Order (*Congregatio Camalduliansis*) in Glosbois,

France. He hoped that here he could forget about some of his trials, serve God, and recognize God's purpose for the remaining portion of his life.

Yet, not even in the monastery was he able to sever his ties with various centers of power in Europe. In the spring of 1717, he met with Tsar Peter the Great of Russia, who was in France at that time. He constantly pondered the possibility of organizing a new uprising in Hungary. At the beginning he had used the War of Spanish Succession to his advantage. Now he again thought of exploiting the ongoing European conflicts for a new try at ousting Habsburg power from Hungary. Thus, he devised a scheme in conjunction with the Austro-Turkish War of that time. But this scheme also failed, for the Turks soon began peace negotiations with Vienna. By the time Rákóczi arrived in Turkey on December 12, 1717 and met Grand Vizier Chalil and Sultan Ahmet III on January 4, 1718, the situation had changed completely. Chalil's successor Damat Ibrahim Pasha who was a strong advocate of peace was also able to push the Sultan in that direction. Thus, on July 21, 1718 Turkey and Austria signed the Treaty of Passarowitz and ended Rákóczi's hopes for a renewal of his struggle against the Habsburgs. [13]

Emperor Charles VI (King Charles III in Hungary) demanded that Rákóczi be turned over to him, but the Turkish Sultan refused this request. He moved the Hungarian Prince and his associates to Rodostó (Rhaidestos or modern Tekirdağ). Not one to give up easily, Rákóczi planned to return to France, but he was prevented from doing so by the Prince Regent, the Duke of Orleans. After this rebuttal, he asked to be admitted to the now Bourbon-controlled Spain, but he never even received an answer to this request. Thus, he remained in Turkey. The Turks treated him with respect and honor, periodically consulted him on European affairs, but they were neither willing nor able to help him achieve his goal.

In spite of this, Rákóczi continued to seek ways to return to Western Europe. He monitored closely the international scene and also kept track of political conditions in Hungary. In search of the goal to liberate his native land, he prepared plan after plan. None of them proved to be realistic, however. All Rákóczi could do—as recorded by his friend and personal secretary, Kelemen Mikes (1590-1761)—was "to hope, and to hope...until we die." [14]

Notwithstanding Turkish hospitality, Rákóczi did not wish to resign himself to a permanent exile in Turkey. Thus, in 1729 he made an effort to move to Poland. King Augustus II of Poland (1697-1733) was open to the idea, and even King Frederick William of Prussia (1713-1740) supported his request. The Habsburg Court, however, intervened to block this attempt. Vienna feared that Rákóczi was still too dangerous. According to Prince Eugene of Savoy, the spokesman for the Habsburgs, "it was not the lack of desire, but only the lack of power" [15] that prevented the exiled Hungarian Prince from causing new difficulties and uprisings in Hungary.

Although by that time Rákóczi had little hope left, in 1734 he again sent his representative to Sultan Mahmut I with the request that the Porte make arrangements for him to return to France. The Sultan's answer was short and negative: "At the moment the Porte does not recommend that you leave here." [16]

This refusal finally obliged Rákóczi to resign himself to end his days in Turkey.

This acceptance of the inevitability of his permanent exile in Turkey coincided with Rákóczi's failing health and the realization that the end was near. Toward the end of March 1735 he came down with high fever, and on April 8th of that year, on Good Friday, he died. He had lived 59 years and 12 days. Honoring his last will, his heart was sent to the Monastery of the Camaldulian Order in Glosbois, while his remains were interred at the Jesuit Church in Constantinople. He was buried next to his mother, Ilona Zrínyi, with her skull enclosed in his coffin. [17]

* * * * *

There is no reliable source of information when the news of Rákóczi's death reached Hungary, but we know that it was received with much grief, and that reverence for his name and deeds never abated in the land of his birth. True, in the period following the Peace of Szatmár (i.e. after 1711) a spirit of resignation had spread across the country. Yet, the Hungarian people never ceased to regard Rákóczi as the true embodiment of the Hungarian historical mission; and for this very reason immortalized him in various forms of folklore.

Prince Ferenc Rákóczi II had served as a source of inspiration for many songs of the underground. Composers whose identities are lost in the haze of history had put the words of the disappointed Hungarians and their complaints into the mouth of the great exiled leader through such compositions as Rákóczi's "farewell song" /búcsúdala/, "supplication" /könyörgése/, "lamentation" /kesergője/ and "song" /nótája/. We know that the "farewell song" was already in existence by 1711, while the others were all born in that year of defeat. In these songs that were sung by ordinary people throughout the country the memory of the lost struggle for liberty had lived on unabated, and so did the memory of Prince Rákóczi who appears to have spoken to his people through the creative spirit of these anonymous poets. [18]

Rákóczi himself left a substantial body of written work that later became the source for much of what is known today about that period. Each of these works dealt directly or indirectly with Hungary, in recent and more remote history, and with the historical mission best represented by Prince Rákóczi himself. The most important of these are his French language *Memoires* on the War of Independence, the most recent version of which is the bi-lingual edition published in 1978 by the Hungarian Academy; [19] and his Latin prayer book entitled *Officium Rákóczianum*, which first appeared in 1726, and then in dozens of editions both in the original Latin and in Hungarian translation. [20] These and other works inspired much respect and adulation for the "exiled prince" /bujdosó fejedelem/ in Hungary, as did the various popular songs (i.e., *kuruc* lyrics) that came to be connected with his name. Among the great composers who wrote significant pieces based on these songs are the Hungarian Ferenc Erkel and Franz Liszt, and the French Hector Berlioz. [21]

* * * * *

One of Rákóczi's great achievements was the introduction of religious and social harmony into Hungarian society. Under his leadership, for the first time in the country's history, Catholics and Protestants fought together for the common goal; and this came in wake of the wave of persecutions that landed scores of Protestant ministers on Venetian galleys as slaves in the late 17th century.[22]

Similarly, under Rákóczi's leadership, Hungarian peasants and nobles fought shoulder to shoulder for the same goals at a time when the display of such social solidarity was still most unusual.

Prince Rákóczi was a pioneer in many other areas as well. While Act VIII of the year 1715 was the first law to establish a permanent Hungarian army, Rákóczi in effect had already created such an army in the period between 1703 and 1711. And he made this army work by studying the performance of King Matthias Corvinus's (1458-1490) famed Black Army, and by implementing some of the ideas of the great poet-general, Count Nicolas Zrínyi (1620-1664) who also dreamt and wrote about such a national army.[23]

Rákóczi's influence also extended beyond the frontiers of Hungary. In 1712, at his request, King Louis XIV of France appointed Count László Bercsényi, the son of one of his *kuruc* generals, a captain in his guard regiment. This same Bercsényi later became the founder of the French light cavalry and recruited many *kuruc* refugees into the French hussar regiments.[24]

From the point of view of general European politics, even more significant was the fact that by tying down large Habsburg imperial armies, Rákóczi was also able to influence the outcome of the War of Spanish Succession. Without Rákóczi's War of Independence, the Treaties of Utrecht and Rastatt would undoubtedly have been different and less favorable to France.[25]

At the same time, however, without the Rákóczi Uprising, the fate of Hungary would also have been different. The compromise Peace of Szatmár certainly compelled Emperor Chárles to temper his absolutistic aspirations in Hungary, as well as to share his powers with the Hungarian nobility.

While Prince Rákóczi's popularity in Hungary remained unshaken even after his death, yet it increased significantly after the discovery and publication of Kelemen Mikes's *Turkish Letters /Törökországi levelek/* in 1794.[26] Having been Rákóczi's friend and confidant throughout his exile, and having outlived his master by three decades, Mikes's letters contain many intimate pieces of information about the life, mind, and personality of the great exile that place him into a most favorable light. This already well established popularity continued to increase throughout the 19th and early 20th centuries, largely through the writings of such patriotic historians as Mihály Horváth (1809-1878) and Kálmán Thaly (1839-1909). As a matter of fact, the latter historian devoted the better part of his career to studying Rákóczi's life and struggles for the liberation of Hungary. [27]

On October 7, 1889, Kálmán Thaly was able to exhume and examine Prince Rákóczi's grave in Constantinople. At the same time he also undertook a campaign to repatriate his remains to Hungary. It took Thaly seventeen years to achieve this goal. One of the final steps in this campaign was Emperor Francis Joseph's proclamation of April 18, 1904, which reflected the Habsburgs' willingness to reconcile themselves with some of Hungary's past anti-Habsburg heroes and then gave the final permission for his repatriation: "Of the outstanding figures of Hungarian history only the remains of Ferenc Rákóczi II are still resting in foreign soil, and repatriating his remains is the oft-expressed sentiment of the Hungarian public. Praise be to the eternal care of God that those misunderstandings and disagreements that have placed severe burdens upon our predecessors for long centuries are today only memories of past historical periods. The mutual trust between the King and the Nation, and the re-establishment of constitutional peace and the introduction of peaceful rule have laid the basis for cooperative agreements between the Throne and the People of this nation. We can remember without bitterness the cloudy period that is now behind us, and together the King and the Nation can now look forward with forgiveness and recall the memories of those individuals under whose leadership we have come to where we are today in our progress. Accordingly, I direct that discussions be held and action be taken in the case of the repatriation of the remains of Ferenc Rákóczi II to Hungary." [28]

Two years later, on October 20, 1906, the Hungarian Parliament revoked the much-resented Act XLIX of 1715 that branded Rákóczi and his associates traitors and the enemies of Hungary. In the very same month Rákóczi's remains were brought back to the country of his birth and then laid to eternal rest in the Gothic Cathedral of the City of Kassa.[29] It is a strange irony of fate that only twelve years after these events, in 1918, Rákóczi's remains were once again on "foreign soil," since Kassa, along with much of the Northern Hungarian Highlands, was ceded to the newly created state of Czechoslovakia.

Prince Ferenc Rákóczi II still lies in "foreign soil" today, but his spirit shines just as brightly as ever in the past. This is true for all nationalities in the region, but it is especially true for the many millions of Hungarians living beyond their native frontiers throughout the world. Rákóczi's commitment to freedom and religious-social-national equality, and his self-sacrificing dedication to the Hungarian historical mission remains unique even today, and serves as an example to all Hungarians, but particularly to those who regard themselves as political exiles. To them, Prince Rákóczi is the very personification of Hungary's incessant quest for national independence and personal freedom.

Notes

1. Ferenc Somogyi, *Küldetés: A magyarság története* /Mission: History of the Hungarian People/, 2d ed. (Cleveland: Kárpát Publishing Co., 1973), p. 554.

2. Zrínyi's *Szigeti veszedelem* /The Peril of Sziget/ has appeared in numerous Hungarian editions, and it was also translated into English, French, German, Italian, Russian, as well as Croatian and Bulgarian. Zrínyi's most recent major literary biography is by Tibor Klaniczay, *Zrínyi Miklós* (Budapest: Akadémiai Kiadó, 1954).

3. The anti-Habsburg conspiracy led by the Palatine Count Ferenc Wesselényi, which included some of the highest magnates of Hungary, was betrayed in 1667, and most of the conspirators—except Rákóczi's father—were executed. This was soon followed by the *kuruc* crusade against the Habsburgs led by Ferenc Rákóczi's foster father, Count Imre Thököly, who subsequently was proclaimed the "king" of Upper Hungary by the Turkish sultan. The *kuruc* wars have been treated in hundreds of volumes. One of the best and most recent work is by Béla Köpeczi, "*Magyarország a kereszténység ellensége*": *A Tkököly-felkelés az európai közvéleményben* /"Hungary, the Enemy of Christianity": The Thököly Uprising in European Public Opinion/ (Budapest: Akadémiai Kiadó, 1976). For its German version see Béla Köpeczi, *Staatsräson und christliche Solidaritat. Die ungarischen Aufstände und Europa in der zweiten Hälfte des 17. Jahrhunderts* (Budapest: Akadémiai Kiadó, 1983).

4. Bálint Hóman and Gyula Szekfü, *Magyar történet* /Hungarian History/, 2d.

ed., 5 vols. (Budapest: Királyi Magyar Egyetemi Nyomda, 1935-1936), IV, p. 241.

5. Somogyi, *Küldetés*, p. 418. The most significant complaints against the Habsburgs following the expulsion of the Turks included: 1. The establishment of a "Neoacquisition Commission" that granted estates on the liberated areas to foreign favorites; 2. the settlement of foreigners en masse in the reconquered areas; 3. the steady decline of the quality of life for the Hungarian population through over-taxation and the degradation caused by Habsburg mercenaries. Cf. *ibid.*, pp. 415-416.

6. Ferenc Eckhart, *Magyarország története* /A History of Hungary/ (Budapest: Káldor Könyvkiadó, 1933; reprinted: Buenos Aires: Délamerikai Magyarság, 1955), p. 189.

7. Somogyi, *Küldetés*, pp. 423-424. For the description of the epidemic see György Moldova's romance, *Negyven prédikátor* /Forty Preachers/ (Budapest: Magvető Könyvkiadó, 1983), pp. 305-308.

8. Cited by Somogyi, *Küldetés*, p. 424.

9. The most thorough treatment of Rákóczi's life in exile is still Gyula Szekfű's *A száműzött Rákóczi, 1715-35* /The Exiled Rákóczi, 1715-35/ (Budapest: A Magyar Tudományos Akadémia, 1913). Some of the significant recent works include: Béla Köpeczi and Ágnes R. Várkonyi, *II. Rákóczi Ferenc*, 2d ed. (Budapest: Magyar Történelmi Társulat, 1976); István Sinkovics and Vilmos Gyenes, eds., *Rákóczi-tanulmányok* /Rákóczi Studies/ (Budapest: ELTE Bölcsésztudományi Kar, 1978); Kálmán Benda, ed., *Európa és a Rákóczi-szabadságharc* /Europe and the Rákóczi War of Liberation/ (Budapest: Akadémiai Kiadó, 1980); and Béla K. Király and János Bak, eds., *From Hunyadi to Rákóczi. War and Society in Late Medieval and Early Modern Hungary* (New York: Social Sciences Monographs, Columbia University Press, 1982), pp. 315-513.

10. Hóman and Szekfű, *Magyar történet*, IV, p. 297; and Mihály Horváth, *Magyarország történelme* /History of Hungary/, 2d ed., 8 vols. (Pest-Budapest: Franklin-Társulat, 1871-1873), VI, p. 573-574.

11. Horváth, *Magyarország történelme*, VII, p. 5, n. 1. See also Lajos Huszár, "A kuruckor érmészete" /Numismatics of the Kuruc Period/, in *Rákóczi Emlékkönyv* /Rákóczi Memorial Volume/, ed. Imre Lukinich, 2 vols. (Budapest: Franklin-Társulat, 1935), I, pp. 389-412.

12. Act XLIX of 1715. Cf. Miklós Asztalos, *II. Rákóczi Ferenc és kora* /Ferenc Rákóczi II and His Age/ (Budapest: Dante Könyvkiadó, 1934), p. 437.

13. Concerning Rákóczi's dealings with Russia and Turkey see especially the relevant studies by Artamanov, Benda, Gökbilgin, Nyikiforov, and Váradi-Sternberg, in Benda, ed., *Európa és a Rákóczi-szabadságharc*. See also Asztalos, *II. Rákóczi Ferenc és kora*, pp. 393-483.

14. Quoted by Horváth, *Magyarország történelme*, VII, p. 185. For the most recent edition of these letters see: Mikes Kelemen: *Törökországi levelek* /Letters from Turkey/, ed. Lajos Hopp (Budapest: Akadémia Kiadó 1966).

15. Eugene of Savoy's letter dated December 7, 1729, as quoted in Horváth, *Magyarország történelme*, VII, p. 181.

16. *Ibid.*, p. 186

17. *Ibid.*, p. 187.

18. Ferenc Somogyi, *Magyar nyelv és irodalom 1825-ig* /Hungarian Language and Literature to 1825/ (Cleveland: Kárpát Könyvkiadó, 1975), p. 133.

19. *II. Rákóczi Ferenc fejedelem emlékiratai a magyarországi háborúról, 1703-tól annak végéig* /Memoires of Prince Ferenc Rákóczi II about the War in Hungary from 1703 until its End/, eds. Béla Köpeczi, *et al.* (Budapest: Akadémiai

Kiadó, 1978). This is an annotated bilingual edition containing the original French version and its Hungarian translation by István Vas.

20. Rákóczi's *Officium Rakoczianum* was first published in Latin at Nagyszombat in 1726, and in Hungarian at Buda in 1746.

21. *Révai Nagy Lexikona* /Révai's Great Encyclopedia/, 21 vols. (Budapest: Révai Testvérek, 1910-1935), III, p. 170.

22. See especially *A magyarországi gályarab prédikátorok emlékezete* /The Memory of the Galley Slave Preachers from Hungary/, ed. László Makkai (Budapest: Magyar Helikon, 1976).

23. Cf. *Zrínyi Miklós haditudományi munkái* /Nicholas Zrínyi's Works on Military Strategy/ (Budapest: Zrínyi Kiadó, 1957). On Matthias Corvinus's "Black Army" see Gyula Rázsó, "The Mercenary Army of King Matthias Corvinus," in Király and Bak, eds., *From Hunyadi to Rákóczi*, pp. 125-140.

24. By 1758 Count László /Ladislas/ Bercsényi (1689-1778) rose to the rank of the Marshal of France. Cf. *Gróf Berchényi László, Franciaország marsallja* /Count Ladislas Berchényi, the Marshal of France/ (Budapest, 1925).

25. Some aspects of this question are treated in the above-cited works: Benda, ed., *Európa és a Rákóczi-szabadságharc*; and Király and Bak, eds., *From Hunyadi to Rákóczi*, pp. 433-492. See also Imre Bánkuti, *A szatmári béke* /The Peace of Szatmár/ (Budapest: Akadémiai Kiadó, 1981).

26. See note 14, above. For an excellent recent collection of relevant documents, see *Rákóczi tükör. Naplók, jelentések, emlékiratok a szabadságharcról* /Rákóczi Mirror. Diaries, Reports, Memoires about the War of Independence/, eds. Béla Köpeczi and Ágnes R. Várkonyi, 2 vols. (Budapest: Szépirodalmi Könyvkiadó, 1973).

27. On these two historians see Steven Béla Várdy, *Modern Hungarian Historiography* (New York: East European Monographs, Columbia University Press, 1976), pp. 35-37, 43-46; and *idem*, *Clio's Art in Hungary and in Hungarian-America* (New York: East European Monographs, Columbia University Press, 1985), pp. 11-22, 28. On Thaly's role specifically see Ágnes R. Várkonyi, *Thaly Kálmán történetírása* /Kálmán Thaly's Historical Writings/ (Budapest: Akadémiai Kiadó, 1961).

28. Quoted in *Révai Nagy Lexikona*, XVI, p. 52.

29. *Ibid.*

III.

FROM ROMANTICISM TO THE
AGE OF REFORM

Thomas Szendrey:

10 / MIHÁLY VÖRÖSMARTY AND THE DEVELOPMENT OF ROMAN-TICISM IN HUNGARY

The renewal of Hungarian intellectual, cultural, and literary life coupled with the movement for linguistic reform provides both the background and the constitutive elements of the development of Hungarian Pre-Romanticism and Romanticism.[1] These literary and cultural movements were accompanied by a great upsurge of interest in the past, motivated mostly by a desire to use the glories of that past to promote the emergence and development of nationalism. One of the leading figures in this movement, indeed the individual in whom it reached its apex, was undoubtedly Mihály Vörösmarty. However, the movement of Romantic nationalism and linguistic reform did not begin with him nor was it limited to the experiences of Hungarians. For this reason it is necessary to place both the movement and its manifestations, indeed the writer himself, into a broader setting.

The far-reaching concern with the defense and reform of the Hungarian language was given obvious impetus by the administrative machinations of the Emperor Joseph II. However, the concern with linguistic reform was to be found in the activities of an earlier generation as well, especially the work of two very distinct, but equally great literary organizers and writers, György Bessenyei and Ferenc Kazinczy.[2] Nonetheless, the gradual eastward movement of ideas, which reached Bessenyei in Vienna earlier than Kazinczy in eastern Hungary, occasioned by the renewal of German literature, especially the activities of Klopstock and Goethe, and shaped by thinkers identified with the French Enlightenment, had a demonstrable impact on Hungarian literary and cultural life. Before the impact could be exercised, however, it was necessary not only to assimilate these influences, but to provide a language suited to the expression of these new ideas. At first a small circle discovered these problems, and with the gradual extension of Romantic influences, the concern with linguistic renewal was extended to a greater number of individuals. Soon this renewal brought into being a literature, and some of the greatest Hungarian writers of the late eighteenth and early nineteenth centuries made their appearance. The first of these was Mihály Csokonai Vitéz, to be followed by Sándor Kisfaludy, then Ferenc Kölcsey and Dániel Berzsenyi, and finally one of the greatest geniuses in the literary use of the Hungarian language, Mihály Vörösmarty. In their lyrics, the Hungarian language has indeed grown to a stature seldom equalled earlier. Berzsenyi and Kölcsey provided poetic expression to the values of the Hungarian cultural and spiritual heritage, and Vörösmarty called to life the ancient mythological content of the Hungarian psyche, the release of which was hastened by the romantic impulse. [3] Vörösmarty thus combined an obvious linguistic talent and power with the elemental force of past glories to create some of the masterworks of Hungarian Romantic poetry in both the narrative and lyric forms.

It should be noted that the efficacy of expression brought about by this linguistic reform was at first limited to poetry. It had hardly any effect on scholarly writing, and was felt in prose only in the late 1830's and early 1840's, specifically in the works of Miklós Jósika, Zsigmond Kemény, and József Eötvös. In specific reference to scholarly writing, this renewed language had an impact on historical scholarship, especially in the romantically inspired historiography of Mihály Horváth and the somewhat more somber, but still effective prose of László Szalay. In the realm of philosophy, however, these renewal efforts proved to be minimal. The German style and influence, in numerous instances even the words, were borrowed and incorporated into the Hungarian language. This German influence remained paramount, although a depth of philosophical speculation, mostly unorganized and not systematic, was also to be found in the poetry and other

writings of Dániel Berzsenyi, Ferenc Kölcsey, and especially
Mihály Vörösmarty. The obvious value of this philosophizing
notwithstanding, it nonetheless remained a literary phenomenon, even if ultimately it did become a component
part of Hungarian intellectual life.

The literary movement which provided the setting for
all this varied activity was, of course, Romanticism, whose
Hungarian variant was also comprised of a Pre-Romantic
phase. The latter included the activities and writings of
András Dugonics, Benedek Virág, Gábor Dayka, Pál Ányos,
and to a certain extent even Dániel Berzsenyi, all of whom
were more spontaneous in their approach than the classicists.
Their search for themes extended to the post-rational manifestations of life, and their activities provided the inspiration for the Kisfaludy and Vörösmarty generation. This Pre-
Romantic phase was not so evident in Western Europe, and
in all probability Pre-Romanticism is a term that is better
suited to describe some of the reactions to the Enlightenment among the peoples of East Central Europe generally.

It should be pointed out that the great literary movements extended beyond the frontiers of individual European
states, and this was as true of Romanticism as any other
such movement. However, equally important as the common
features were the national variations of such movements. [4]
Therefore, a few observations about Romanticism in general and its Hungarian variant specifically, should place
Mihály Vörösmarty and his oeuvre both into the Hungarian
setting (where he is well known), as well as into the broader
European and world perspective (where he is little known).

* * *

Romanticism as a philosophical and literary movement
was essentially a reaction against classicist themes and overly
rationalistic attitudes. The Romantic impulse was concerned
not so much with the formal aspects of art, as with the role
of the emotions in the ordering of artistic experience, since
for the artist of the Romantic persuasion perfection (which
was a virtue of classicism, at least in terms of striving for it)
was not attainable. Thus the Romantic consistently longed
or pined for something and was invariably searching for another world. The dream and the story were considered as

the means of reaching this other world, and the romantic artist or writer was forever obsessed with the passage of time and impending death. These concerns were by no means missing from the often dream-like longings of Vörösmarty's lyrical and narrative poetry. The Romantic artist or writer thus stood facing the chasm between eternity and death. This undoubtedly was the origin of that sense of pathos so evident in many of the products of Romantic literature. Once again, this characteristic was present in the works of Vörösmarty.

Another of the fundamental differences between Classicism and Romanticism can be seen in the subjects of literature. For the romantically inclined writer, nature, the past, and the people were more significant than, for example, Greco-Roman antiquity. Romantic writers, and once again Vörösmarty is an excellent example, were much more concerned with the heroic ancient period of their nation's history, or at least with the chivalric Middle Ages. For the Classicist orientation, general human characteristics and values independent of time and place were considered more significant. The Romantic artists, and this was especially true for East Central European and specifically Hungarian writers, were more concerned with history. Nor did all of these considerations fail to have an effect on form. The writers of the Romantic period loosened the rules regarding literary forms, and tended to favor those that allowed more room for the imagination, including the ballad, the folk-song, and the reflective lyric.

As the climax of Romanticism in Hungarian literature coincided in time with the Hungarian Reform Period (1825-1848), it established a close link between socio-political reform and literature, and thus between reformers and writers. Indeed, being a writer often predestined one for a political career, or at the very least it gave a political dimension to artistic creativity. Simply put, the symbiosis of political and social reform and literary effort reacted positively to focus attention on the problems facing the Hungarian people at this time. Virtually all of the outstanding writers of the era were influenced by the interaction of politics and literature, and some played significant roles in the transformation of Hungary from a feudal to a modern state. The dominant literary figures of that period (e.g. Károly Kisfaludy, József Bajza, Ferenc Toldy, and Mihály Vörösmarty) fulfilled not only cultural and literary roles in the life of the country, but were often also inspirers of political and social change. [5]

Thus, Hungarian Romanticism viewed from a more general and broader European perspective, certainly projected the image of a people in search of a past, and as a contemporary Hungarian poet and essayist expressed it: "The great spring of the small nations is approaching. With a painful pride they look back to their ancient past; the springboard of their combative nationalism is this romanticized past." [6] After 1825, the pace of political and intellectual life in Hungary quickened, due in no small measure to the efforts of these young poets and writers, supported by a sense of history derived mostly from an emergent German historicism. This influence can be traced back to the writings of Herder, whose rather negative comments about the future of the Hungarian nation elicited a response destined to disprove Herder's assertions. Hungarians turned to their past, and their greatest poets, among them Mihály Vörösmarty, wrote numerous poems and dramas about their gloriously conceived past so as to provide inspiration for the future.

* * *

That age of national revival, characterized in historical accounts as the Era of Reform (1825-1848), was only the culmination of the period of renewal which had been brewing beneath the surface of everyday political, social, and cultural life for the fifty years before 1825. Indeed, the appearance of Vörösmarty's *Zalán futása* (The Flight of Zalán) may be construed as the event which crystallized the Era of Reform into a much more visible movement with an avowed historical sentiment.

The quickening pace of cultural and intellectual influences from Western and Central Europe (mostly French and German, with a smattering of English elements) were mediated mostly through the activities of the Hungarian Royal Guard in Vienna, especially through the efforts and writings of György Bessenyei. [7] Together with the ever-increasing study of Hungarian history and literature within the homeland, these influences were ultimately responsible for the cultural and national revival characterized as the

Era of Reform above, a period that could just as well be identified as the Era of Hungarian Romanticism. That era, of course, was preceded by what has been characterized as its Pre-Romantic transitional stage.[8] This term may sound strange to those whose acquaintance with the transition of literary eras has been limited mostly to the Western European (specifically French and English) patterns, which generally assumed that there was a transition of a more direct character from Enlightenment to Romanticism. Depending upon the sophistication and philosophical acumen of the writer, this change was invariably understood either in a schematic or multi-faceted manner. Notwithstanding the level of sophistication and understanding, however, this model of cultural and literary change can hardly be applied to any part of East Central Europe, nor to the understanding of the literary and cultural heritage of these peoples.[9] A changed attitude toward history was an integral part of the Enlightenment era of European civilization, which change was brought about by the Pre-Romantics and Romantics through their understanding of an attitude toward the past.

One of the most obvious and meaningful features of the Romantic movement of thought, expression, and sentiment in East Central Europe (including Hungary) was a deeply felt renewed interest in history and the consequent use of historical imagery in most literary works. To understand this dimension, so significant and actually central to the literary activity of Vörösmarty, requires an analysis of the development of intellectual life in Hungary during the era before Vörösmarty's birth and growth to maturity. This account must deal with the nature of historical thought and the attitude toward the past, because much of the historical allegory and imagery in Vörösmarty's work was an outgrowth of that historical yearning which developed in late eighteenth and early nineteenth-century Hungary.

There developed an impasse in Hungarian historical thought in the last quarter of the eighteenth and the early years of the nineteenth century—the impasse of Enlightenment and Romanticism—in an atmosphere still heavily charged with the ideals of a Baroque civilization.[10] In opposition to that Baroque concept of the world and life there developed various movements of thought and expression.

The tradition of scholarship, building upon an enviable heritage, continued to develop during these years. It made its greatest achievements in the field of history, which was a special area of concern for eighteenth-century Hungarian scholarship. In this field the works of M. Bél, I. Katona, G. Pray, and others were not to be equalled until this intellectual impasse was broken by the events leading up to the Revolution of 1848. During the years of this impasse, but especially during the two decades following the Congress of Vienna, the formerly high level of Hungarian scholarship was caught in the double vise of political involvement and romantic illusions. This is best exemplified by the somewhat dubious historical scholarship, but by no means limited influence, of István Horvát.[11] It should be emphasized that Horvát exercised a tremendous impact through his writings and lectures on most of the leading young Romantics, including young Vörösmarty, whose early writings reflect the type of historical enthusiasm found in Horvát's works.[12] The impact of this political involvement and romantic illusionism was further augmented by the use of historical imagery and allegory, indeed also the preponderance of historical themes, in virtually all types and genres of literature. These concerns were evident in the works of such Pre-Romantics as András Dugonics and Benedek Virág, as well as in the historical dramas and epics of such Romantics as József Katona, Gergely Czuczor, and Vörösmarty.

Given the broad range of expression and its diverse character, it is difficult to classify the historical thought and imagery of this era as either enlightened or romantic. The complex attitudes and ideas, not to mention the sentiments, of virtually all scholars, writers, thinkers, and others concerned with cultural affairs and issues, were hopelessly and constantly intermixed. Furthermore, in a period of national awakening, the past was glorified often beyond the range of even the romanticized truth. It was this mostly unrealistic glorification of the past which formed one of the common denominators of a large part of intellectual, cultural, and literary activity in Hungary between 1770 and 1840. Hence, it should be evident that the Enlightenment, because of the obvious admixture of nationalistic sentiment tending toward Romanticism, differed from the general patterns prevailing in Western Europe. It is, after all quite useless to speak of the Enlightenment as a concept applicable in the same manner to all of Europe. Rather, one should deal with the impact of ideas usually regarded as characteristic of the Enlightenment upon any particular nation or group of individuals.

The impact of the Enlightenment on Hungary was twofold during this period. One of these was characterized by a positive evaluation of the attitudes and mental climate of that era, best represented by individuals such as Ferenc Kazinczy, György Bessenyei, and Ádám Pálóczi Horváth among others, who were deeply influenced by the French Enlightenment, especially by the works and ideas of Voltaire. The other was marked by revolutionary sentiment, and it was influenced primarily by the second-generation Enlightenment intellectuals, [13] represented on the Hungarian scene by Ignác Martinovics and his circle. The impasse between the ideas of these two groups was dissolved partially in the life and literary and linguistic career of Ferenc Kazinczy, and partially in the attitudes of the generation of Romantics (including some of the Pre-Romantics) who were interested in the fostering and promotion of nationalism based upon historical impulses. They built upon some of the ideas of the Enlightenment and upon the idealization of the folk elements in Hungarian culture, which they coupled with a concern for the life and conditions of the peasant and with their recognition of the need for social and political reform. In a limited sense they also built upon the heritage of the revolutionary ideals of the Martinovics group and the young Kazinczy. Thus, the attitudes and ideals of the Enlightenment in Hungarian thought were rapidly, but almost imperceptibly transmuted into Pre-Romanticism, represented by the writings of the already mentioned Dugonics, Czuczor, Virág, Kisfaludy, and Vörösmarty, as well as by the activities of Ferenc Kazinczy, Dániel Berzsenyi, József Bajza, Ferenc Toldy, József Teleki, Mihály Horváth, and many others. [14]

This development of ideas and related attitudes greatly influenced the course of Hungarian historical thought and literary expression. The eminent Hungarian Marxist philosopher and literary critic, György Lukács, also commented, in more general terms, about this particular connection between Enlightenment and Romanticism:

> ...We must get rid of that romantic, reactionary legend, that the era of the Enlightenment did not have any feeling for history, that historical feeling was discovered by the opponents of the French Revolution, such as Burke, DeMaistre, and others. In order to declare this a legend it is sufficient to point to the outstanding historiographical accomplishments of Voltaire, Gibbon, etc. [15]

Actually, Lukács is expressing a half-truth, and for two reasons. First of all, feeling or empathy for the past as a living, creative and pulsating force is by no means the same as an interest in history. To put it differently, "historiographical accomplishments" are not the same as a "feeling for history," for the simple reason that one is an academic or scholarly concern, while the other is a sentimental and existential attitude. One need not be a scholar to have a feeling for history (e.g. Vörösmarty, the poet and writer), and scholarship does not always provide one with a feel for the past, not even historical scholarship. In the Hungarian situation at this time the distinction Lukács makes is not so easily made, because one must take into account the force or sentiment of nationalism, which in those days pervaded both enlightened and romantic attitudes. Bessenyei and many of his followers and contemporaries were interested in the Hungarian past for much the same reasons, although not necessarily with the same motivations, as the historians Benedek Virág, István Horvát, Ignác Fessler, and the Romantic writers generally. This interest was essentially functional, namely to use the past as a means of building the future. Only their methods differed. Some were literary figures with an interest in history, whereas others were historians with a literary and philosophical orientation. The symbiosis of the two was not always advantageous for literature, and it was generally less beneficial for the study of history. The relative advantage or disadvantage in each case depended upon the attitudes and concerns of the scholar or writer considered. Needless to say, these comments are in no sense to denigrate good writing in historical scholarship, nor effective historical imagery and analogy in literary works.

Before a discussion of György Bessenyei and his role in

the shaping of modern Hungarian literary life, of which he is considered the first significant figure, it would be illuminating to make certain observations about the general characteristic of intellectual life after 1790 and historical thought in the 1790-1830 period. This can prove useful because at the turn of that century linguistic scholarship and literary expression were more widespread and offered greater opportunities to compensate for past errors and shortcomings than the study of history. Literary works tended to use an obviously romantic historical imagery which promoted a sense of the past. Linguistic reform emphasized the use of the Hungarian language as a vehicle for communication in a modern sense. Historical scholarship, on the other hand, was characterized by the use of the Latin language (which isolated it from the national language movement) and by the collection of documents. But the use of the archaic Latin and the critical study of historical sources were not suited to inspire a movement of romantic nationalism which conceived of the past in a romanticized manner. The activities of Bessenyei thus serve as an excellent example of this situation. He and his circle had a profound influence not only on literary life, but also on historical scholarship in general. Bessenyei's plans for an academy and Kazinczy's wide-ranging activities testify to the influence these individuals exercised. Their influence was certainly more extensive and effective than that of historians such as Pray and Katona, especially because the former wrote in Hungarian and not in Latin.

The involvement of Joseph II in Hungarian affairs only accelerated the national movement and acted as a catalyst in the promotion of a broader and more extensive interest in history. During that era, interest in history and the past was coupled with the very existence of the nation. It became a widespread and valuable activity to praise the glories of the past in such a way as to elicit very pointed political goals out of this past for the present. This was done in both scholarly and literary works, with the predominant and more outspoken voice being that of the latter. This political dimension of the study of history was soon augmented by an interest in the past more for its own sake, or at least for less immediate political purposes. The final years of the eighteenth century, for example, witnessed some of the following developments: The discovery of the *Gesta* of Anonymus, praise of the Hunyadis in various literary and historical works,[16] the linguistic works of Sajnovics, the epigrams of Ádám Pálóczi Horváth, the writings of Gvadányi, the novels and dramas of Dugonics, and a number of other similar occurrences.[17] Bessenyei very aptly pointed out the meaning of this development when he stated that one can get closer to the hearts of men through literature than through any other means, and that people even appreciate knowledge and scholarship better through literature.[18] Needless to say, he was deeply influenced by the Enlightenment conception of history, especially as represented by Voltaire and other French thinkers and writers. The following brief statement drawn from one of Bessenyei's historical works entitled *Róma viselt dolgai* (The Deeds of Rome), published in 1801, illustrates this situation:

> Do you know that philosophy, statistics, politics and even the laws of nature are related as brothers to history? How can you write of man's activities, without these impinging on your reason? Why do you write history if you only want to tell a story? One must write about events in such a way that by reading it one can philosophize about man and his world: so that our activities in obtaining knowledge of the mistakes of the past may correct our fate.[19]

However, it was not only this Enlightenment philosophy, later transmuted into Romanticism in the service of national consciousness building, which served to turn the attention of ever larger number of Hungarians to their past. They were also influenced by the emphasis on the role of great historical personalities, whose deeds were eulogized in both literary and historical works. An especially good example of this was Bessenyei's portrayal of the members of the Hunyadi family (John Hunyadi, and his son King Matthias Corvinus), although the princely general and poet, Count Miklós Zrínyi was also widely recalled. These individuals represented the quintessence of Hungarian gallantry and statesmanship, and hence appeared as particularly germane examples in the difficult position of the Hungarian state and its people in the late eighteenth and early nineteenth centuries. The most obvious literary use of such heroic figures is to be found in the epics and dramas of Vörösmarty, especially *Zalán futása* (The Flight of Zalán), which was a portrayal of Árpád, the leader of the Magyars during the era of the conquest of the homeland in the late ninth century. (It should be pointed out that Vörösmarty made use of previous romanticized versions of the story of Árpád from diverse sources.)

A widespread interest was also occasioned by the rather complex and often misty question of the origins of the Magyars. Especially significant in this connection was the scholarly and literary activity of András Dugonics, who attempted to recreate a lost world and all of its particularities for the purpose of awakening and fostering national sentiment. This interest in the proto-history of the Magyars was one of the peculiarities of Hungarian Pre-Romantic thought and Dugonics was perhaps the best exponent of this tendency. As one scholar who worked out this theory of Hungarian Pre-Romanticism noted: "In him the Pre-Romantic past conception and the specifically Hungarian dedication to the past come to a synthesis; this is the significance of Dugonics." [20] His works in which this specific concern can be found include the following: *Etelka*, 1788; *Jolánka*, 1804; and *A magyarok uradalmaik* (The Rule of Magyars), 1806-1808. Further observations concerning him by the literary historian Antal Szerb are instructive in delineating the impact of all these concerns on Hungarian writers of a later era, certainly including Vörösmarty. He writes: "The Árpád-era cavaliers of Dugonics are from that same odd nation as Klopstock's Germans and MacPherson's Celts; from that Pre-Romantic pre-historic nation, which is not related to any existing nation, but only to the ideal Stoic Latins, the people of Plutarch, that still rule over the fantasy of those educated in the classics. And yet, every single past-conception of the European nations grew out of this prehistoric nation conception." [21] This statement refers to the foundations of historical development that subsequently came to form the roots of Hungarian Romanticism. During the early nineteenth century the historical interest was quite evident, but it was counterbalanced by an emphasis on the classical roots, especially the works of Horace and Vergil, coupled with a pervasive and normative image of classical civilization. This concern, for example, was quite evident in Kazinczy. However, the Romantic generation, and especially Vörösmarty, while still products of a classical education and also influenced by classical models, no longer conceived of this as normative and began to move away from classical models toward ones based more upon the national past, coupled with an interest in mostly mythological folk elements. What all of these writers had in common though, was an obvious desire to make use of the past to awaken and foster national sentiment. Thus goes the line of development from Dugonics to Vörösmarty. These concerns can be found in *Etelka* by Dugonics who wrote his intentions as follows: "I write this book of mine in Hungarian because with it I want to feed Hungarian hearts. Etelka, a rare Hungarian young lady, would not have sounded as sweet and effective in a foreign language. I brought the virgin out of the province of oblivion, the ancient darkness, so that the world of today may see, wonder at, and follow her." [22] Having thus stated his intentions, which were obviously consistent with the characterization of Pre-Romanticism, and having stated the importance of the national language, Dugonics then goes on to reveal something of his own state of mind at the time of the writing of this work. These concerns are also worth quoting:

> As to what pertains to my heart, I show thoroughly in my work. I can say from the outset: I am a true Hungarian and I love my homeland above all. That I was born here I am never ashamed of. Would God give that my country should not have to be ashamed of my upbringing. I am the type who could be happy at the happiness of my sweet homeland, be afraid of its oppression and terrified if it is in danger. I am the type, who for the preservation of my homeland, would struggle with my body and soul to the best of my ability. [23]

Thus, Dugonics turned not only against the feudalism of the court and the Habsburgs, by seeking the beauty of free life in the past, but he turned also against the Enlightenment attitudes of some of his contemporaries, and became one of the leading opponents of the cultural and centralizing policies of Joseph II. He found the emotional force for his opposition in the Hungarian past and thus tended to romanticize that past to make it even more effective as a form of opposition. In that sense he helped to develop an attitude toward history that found fulfillment in the Romantic historians of the nineteenth century, and especially in the historically grounded literary epics and dramas of Vörösmarty and his contemporaries. It should be added that the writings of Dugonics formed the reading material for that generation which comprised the parents of Vörösmarty's generation. By no means are youth immune from the influences of that generation which gave it birth and schooled it, even if the new generation turns against the older one.

The distinction between Enlightenment motivation and national Romanticism was obscured in the work of all of these individuals. This became very evident when the Romantic writers and poets followed in the footsteps of literary minded historians. Poets such as Mihály Csokonai Vitéz, Ferenc Kölcsey, and Mihály Vörösmarty were influenced by these trends and they accepted and indeed combined the historical interest of their forebears with their more explicit Romantic terminology, form, and attitude. Their activity also found a counterpart in scholarship, including the works of János Engel Keresztély (a transitional figure writing in German), Ignác Fessler (probably the most original scholar), and István Horvát. Although often naively chauvinistic, the latter exercised a profound influence on his students and followers, among them Ferenc Toldy, József Eötvös, and Mihály Vörösmarty.

These changes in post-1790 Hungary, lasting until approximately 1830, were characterized by the fostering of Romantic illusions and ideals, and also by the conflict that centered on the issues connected with linguistic change and reform. Latin scholarship wanted to become Hungarian, but in the process it underwent many transient difficulties. In attempting to turn itself into a nationally inspired scholarship it could not rid itself of its literary bent. It thus produced a literature-oriented national historical school, characterized by a historical consciousness with Romantic underpinnings.

While such romantic motivations may be acceptable, and in some instances even desirable, in literary endeavors, they were manifestly detrimental to the writing of history, even though the historical imagery of literary works may have been enough to fix some pictures of the past in the popular mind. For this very reason the level of historical scholarship (but by no means the level of historically inspired literary efforts) declined precipitously. Those scholars whose works and activities represented a continuity, but by no means an improvement, with the past lived and worked mostly outside this romanticized situation in Hungary. Engel and Fessler were the best examples of this situation. There is a divergence of opinion as to the value and significance of the Enlightenment for Hungarian intellectual and cultural life generally and historical studies specifically, as there is also a controversy centered on the impact of Romanticism on Hungarian historical scholarship. Louis Lékai, in his study of the historical scholarship of the 1790-1830 period, contended that for fifty years no one continued, on the same high level, the work of Pray and Katona. He further asserted that the positive values of the Enlightenment view of history remained outside the already laggard state of Hungarian historiography. [24] In his view, Edward Gibbon was the ideal of many of the Hungarian Enlightenment figures, which also holds true for such advocates of the Pre-Romantic and Romantic orientation as János Engel Keresztély and Ézsaiás Budai. His point may be well taken in reference to methodological concerns, but it is certainly questionable in terms of historical attitude and fundamental philosophical concerns about the nature of history and change. What remains certain, however, is that Hungarian scholarship did not produce any truly great historians in the period between 1790 and 1830, at least not one who wrote in Hungarian in Hungary. Nevertheless, it produced some of the most outstanding literary figures of any generation, and did so with a readily identifiable Romantic orientation coupled with an unusual historical interest.

Any number of reasons can be offered to explain this situation. There was, for example, much difficulty with the censorship, but it is not enough to mention such negative factors only. Perhaps a more suitable explanation would be to say that the 1790-1830 period was identical with the birth and early development of modern national consciousness in Hungary, and scholarship and literature were caught up in its throes. Scholars were more concerned with fostering a love for the past than with promoting new orientations in either historical method or new approaches and attitudes in the study of the past. Nor was this a time when the critical spirit was alive. The Romantic attitude was fostered in the education of Hungarian youth of that time, and those individuals who were destined to comprise the intellectually and politically active elements of the population in the 1820's, 1830's, and 1840's received their education during this period. Their consciousness was formed by the Romantic attitudes of contemporary scholars and writers, and also by their teachers and pastors.

Hence the narrowing horizons of national Romanticism in scholarship, but certainly not in art or literature (where they contributed to the *Vormärz* spirit and produced an intense national cultural and literary revival), exercised a negative impact at least through the turn of the century. The historical imagery and analogy of this literature, however, has continued to exercise a constant and pervasive impact on the consciousness of the Hungarian public irrespective of other, often also significant, developments. In this Vörösmarty and other writers had not only a dominant role, but the images they popularized have continued to inform Hungarian national consciousness for a long time.

* * *

The literary life of Hungary in the late eighteenth and early nineteenth centuries had no clearly defined focal point, nor did it possess an independent critical spirit based upon distinctive Hungarian models. Undoubtedly, the Hungarian writers of this period had learned the principles of Romanticism mostly, but by no means exclusively, from German sources. But this borrowing was counter-balanced by a desire to create an independent literature. This was one of the motivations of Károly Kisfaludy in establishing *Auróra*, a literary almanach, which while imitating Viennese literary life in its forms and inspiration, was to be filled with Hungarian content. The *Auróra* played a key role in the institutionalization of Hungarian literary life in the early years of the nineteenth century. Established in the fall of 1821 (although the first volume bears the date 1822), it was edited by Károly Kisfaludy until 1832. It contributed substantially to making the rapidly developing city of Pest the center of Hungarian literary life. Furthermore, it provided not only inspiration and a publishing outlet for young writers, but also a central source of financial and moral support for writers who were to exercise a shaping influence on Hungarian literary life in the 1830's and 1840's. These included József Bajza, Gergely Czuczor, Ferenc Kölcsey, Károly Kisfaludy, as well as Mihály Vörösmarty. *Auróra* also served as a forum for the development of Hungarian literary criticism. Many of the debates between this Romantic generation and the dominant spokesman of the more Classicist orientation, Ferenc Kazinczy, were conducted on its pages. [25] In addition to this, some of the most significant literary products of the Romantic generation appeared first in *Auróra* including two poems which have served respectively as the Hungarian national anthem, "Himnusz" by Ferenc Kölcsey, and as a national summons, "Szózat" by Mihály Vörösmarty. The increasing popularity and influence of *Auróra* was also evidenced by its widespread circulation (more than 1,000 by the early 1830's) and respected status in Hungarian literary life. After Kisfaludy's death in 1832 József Bajza edited it until 1837, at which time its role was taken over by the journal *Athenaeum* under the editorship of Bajza, Toldy, and Vörösmarty.

Vörösmarty, even after his acknowledged success as an epic poet, occasioned by the tremendous reception accorded *Zalán futása* (The Flight of Zalán), still felt most at home in the company of Károly Kisfaludy and the so-called Auróra Circle, composed of Vörösmarty, Bajza, Toldy, György Zádor, and Mihály Helmeczy. It was at their periodic gatherings that the elements of a distinctive Hungarian Romanticism emerged. The Circle also encouraged, by mutual support and criticism, the literary and scholarly activity of each of its members. Quite often the members of the Circle wrote for the almanach itself, not uncommonly under the pressure of a deadline, and then critically discussed these works. For example, Vörösmarty's epic *Eger*, based upon József Teleki's historical sketch, was written under the pressure of a deadline. Sometimes the members of the Circle suggested topics to each other. Vörösmarty's historical romance in verse, *Cserhalom*, for example, was derived from a suggestion offered by Kisfaludy. Mutual criticism was also one of the concerns of the group. Thus Vörösmarty's drama *Salamon király* (King Salamon) was revised on the basis of Kisfaludy's critique, as was a subsequent lecture on the nature of historical drama delivered to the group. Not only such literary concerns, but also the issues centering on linguistic reform occupied their time. Toldy and Helmeczy were the dominant figures in this opposition to the formulation of the more complicated and improbable neologisms that were sought for linguistic inspiration rather than for the rhytmic structure of folk songs and popular speech patterns. This concern, consistent with the Romantic idealization of folk elements, had a generally positive influence on the language and the development of a distinctive Hungarian prosody. Examples of this development were folk-inspired genre pictures, such as "Gábor diák" (*The Student Gábor*) and "Laboda" by Vörösmarty.

There was also a pervasive interest in the theory of literary forms, and the *Auróra* generation, concerned as it was with form in addition to language, tended to neglect the classical models. The members of this generation attempted instead to synthesize the forms of contemporary European literatures with the Hungarian spirit, and to do so in a quite nationalistic manner, with an obvious emphasis (most evident in Vörösmarty) on distinctive Hungarian elements. Vörösmarty was not particularly concerned with the theory of literature, except in drama. While influenced by a wide and extensive reading of Hungarian and general European literature of earlier eras and of his own time, he was undoubtedly the most original writer of the Circle that gathered around this almanach. Bajza possessed the most theoretical mind and most rapid wit, while Toldy was its best literary historian who also maintained the most extensive contacts with other literary movements both in Hungary and the German speaking world. It was Toldy who introduced the Circle to the available collection of Serbian folk songs, which then were translated in part by Bajza and influenced Vörösmarty to use this form in some of his poems. Toldy's studies made available to Vörösmarty the extant works of Szendrei Anonymous (sixteenth century writer of ballads and romances), on the basis of which Vörösmarty wrote his much praised ballad "Szilágyi és Hajmási" (Szilágyi and Hajmási).

All of these activities of the Circle had a tremendous impact on Vörösmarty and also on the development of an independent and mature Hungarian literature. This literature became conversant with foreign currents and was capable of assimilating those. It was also moving toward the formulation of a distinct set of principles shaping an emerging literary criticism, that were perceived of as necessary consequences of these tremendous literary developments in so short a time. [26]

While the Auróra Circle certainly had a shaping influence on Hungarian literary life, it nonetheless still imitated, especially in the works of Kisfaludy himself, some of the themes and literary forms of German literature emanating from Vienna. In some sense, therefore, Kisfaludy represented the last stage of the attempt to create Hungarian literature in the form and shape of the writings of András Dugonics. The new generation, however, especially the poets Ferenc Kölcsey and Mihály Vörösmarty, represented a nationally inspired Romanticism that was no longer tied to the Classicist spirit or form. Zádor (Stettner) and Toldy were among the first to recognize the Romantic elements in the work of these poets, especially the epics of Vörösmarty. But on account of the rapid development of this kind of poetic expression the critics still used the canons of criticism applicable more to German literature than to these new Hungarian developments. Hungarian criticism, at the time of the initial appearance of Kölcsey and Vörösmarty, could not find the proper measure to judge and evaluate their works. Thus, much of the critical writing was confused, or as in the case of Kazinczy, it was consistent, but measured according to Classicist standards. Nor were other critics and poets better informed. The poet Dániel Berzsenyi confounded Classical and Romantic themes in his theory of literature and critical writings. Younger critics, however, were better acquainted with the theory, derived mostly from German sources, but attempted to apply this to Hungarian literature without allowance for the particularities of Hungarian literary developments and the conditions of their homeland. This situation, however, could not be sustained and soon Hungarian criticism, having learned more thoroughly the German and other European writings on Romanticism, made use of this knowledge and attempted to apply it to Hungarian poetic expression. Significant in this development was the work of József Teleki, specifically a lengthy study in the 1818 issue of *Tudományos Gyűjtemény* (Scholarly Collection) entitled "A régi és új költés különbségeiről" (On the Differences between Old and New Poetry). [27] Based upon an extensive study of European Romantic literature, Teleki isolated some of the elements of the Romantic trend in Hungarian poetry. This scholarly activity was continued and extended in subsequent years by Pál Szemere, Ferenc Kölcsey, György Zádor, and Ferenc Toldy, among others. However, the applicability of the Romantic theory, mainly within the context of the historical development of Hungarian literature, was first demonstrated compellingly by László Szalay in some of his early critical works. The future historian (since Szalay eventually made his major contribution in that field) wrote as follows in 1833: "Among our poets, Sándor Kisfaludy and Vörösmarty are those who write epic poetry with the greatest originality and national sentiment. Both of them started from the impulse of Romanticism, but with the difference that they Magyarized this Romanticism and Romanticized the Magyars." [28] These new developments in the critical understanding of the Romantic writers opened up new vistas for their influence.

The activities of the Auróra Circle were by no means limited to literature. Its membership exercised both direct and indirect political and social impact, and their activities certainly helped to shape the cultural milieu. The Auróra Circle represented the future generation and the new literature. Its members wished to express not only universal truths. with the newly developed literary language (in which process they also played a role), but also truths with a national content as well. Their activities brought renewed life to Hungarian culture and eventually helped to call into existence a whole series of cultural intstitutions in the service of Hungarian culture, such as the Academy of Sciences, the Kisfaludy Society, and the National Theater. In each of these cultural organizations, one or more of the leading members of the Aüróra Circle were involved in some way.

The Autóra Circle was always closely related to and supportive of the reform activities of István Széchenyi. When he proposed that a new reform organ be established, it was Károly Kisfaludy who organized the editorial work for the paper *Jelenkor* (Present Age), and only his untimely death in 1832 led to the appointment of another individual as editor. Furthermore, when some of the conservative magnates attacked Széchenyi's reform tract *Hitel* (Credit), it was Bajza and his friends who spared no effort on behalf of Széchenyi. Indeed, one might even state that the entire Era of Reform elicited political reform activities from most of the writers active at that time, and these writers were more than willing to contribute their talents to promoting these reform ideals in almost any manner possible.

In spite of these rather obvious and widespread political involvements, the members of the Auróra Circle strived hard to raise the quality of Hungarian literature. Indeed, Kisfaludy once rejected even a poem that Vörösmarty had sent to the almanach for publication. Some of these efforts included serious literary debates, rejection of manuscripts, attacks upon those whom the members of the Circle perceived as opposing the extension of Romantic ideals as understood by the leading members of the Circle, (including attacks against Kazinczy), and linguistic and literary struggles with Gábor Döbrentei and others. Bajza even launched an attack on István Horvát's historical illusions, in spite of the fact that Horvát had greatly influenced some members of the Auróra Circle during their student days.

The Circle was actively involved in promoting the appreciation of the national past through bringing into being the national epic. Ever since the efforts of Csokonai in the waning years of the eighteenth century the writing of a national epic had occupied the minds of Hungarian poets. Kisfaludy encouraged both Vörösmarty and Gergely Czuczor to write such an epic, and the nation was soon to celebrate Vörösmarty's *Zalán futása* (The Flight of Zalán) as the long awaited national epic.

The Auróra Circle certainly played a significant role in the promotion of literature and the service of national goals.

Furthermore, it provided Vörösmarty, the greatest writer associated with the Circle, an opportunity to extend his talent and influence. Undoubtedly, Vörösmarty best expressed the aspirations of his age, [29] even if the external features of his life were by no means as significant as his thoughts, feelings, and writings.

Notes

1. The term Pre-Romanticism is used on the basis of the writings of Antal Szerb, "Magyar preromantika" /Hungarian Pre-Romanticism/, in *Gondolatok a könyvtárban* /Thoughts in the Library/ (Budapest: Révai, 1946), 373-454.

2. Concerning Bessenyei and Kazinczy, see especially József Waldapfel, *Magyar irodalom a felvilágosodás korában* /Hungarian Literature in the Enlightenment Era/, (Budapest: Akadémiai Kiadó, 1963); and László Négyesy, *Kazinczy pályája* /Kazinczy's Career/ (Budapest: Magyar Tudományos Akadémia, 1931).

3. Mihály Ferdinandy, *Mi magyarok* /We Hungarians/ (Budapest: Rózsavölgyi, 1941), 416-417.

4. René Wellek and Austin Warren, *Theory of Literature*, 3rd ed., (New York: Harcourt Brace Jovanich, c. 1977), 51.

5. This is well described by Gyula Farkas, *A fiatal Magyarország kora* /The Era of Young Hungary/ (Budapest: Magyar Szemle Társaság, 1932); and Dezső Tóth, *Vörösmarty Mihály* (Budapest: Akadémiai Kiadó, 1974), who consistently relates the life of Vörösmarty to its social and political setting, but one dominated by Marxist socio-political categories. The first major biography of Vörösmarty, Pál Gyulai, *Vörösmarty életrajza* /A Biography of Vörösmarty/ (Budapest: Franklin Társulat, 1890), does not neglect the significance of his literary activity for Hungarian political and social developments. See also D. Merwyn Jones, *Five Hungarian Writers* (Oxford: The Clarendon Press, 1966), 103-159.

6. László Cs. Szabó, *Egy nép és a költészete* /A People and Their Poetry/, reprint from *Új Látóhatár* (Münich, 1972), 18.

7. Concerning Bessenyei see also László Vajthó, *Bessenyei* (Budapest, Dante, 1947).

8. Concerning Pre-Romanticism, in addition to the article cited in note 1, consult also Antal Szerb, *Gondolatok a könyvtárban*, 455-550.

9. Wellek and Austin, *Theory of Literature*, 118-123.

10. Gyula Kornis, *A magyar művelődés eszményei* /The Ideals of Hungarian Cultural Development/, 2 vols. (Budapest: Királyi Magyar Egyetemi Nyomda, 1927), I, 365-407.

11. Concerning István Horvát see Thomas Szendrey, "Horvát Istvántól Horváth Mihályig: A romantikus történetírás kezdete és fejlődése Magyarországon" /From István Horvát to Mihály Horváth: The Origins and Development of Romantic Historiography in Hungary/, in *A XVI. Magyar Találkozó Krónikája* /The Proceedings of the 16th Hungarian Congress/, eds. Ferenc Somogyi and János Nádas (Cleveland: Árpád Könyvkiadó, 1977), 219-226.

12. Pál Gyulai, *Vörösmarty életrajza*, 115-119.

13. By second generation intellectuals I mean the popularizers of Enlightenment philosophy, as opposed to the more original thinkers. The generational approach, albeit differently, was also used by Peter Gay, *The Enlightenment: An Interpretation. The Rise of Modern Paganism* (New York: Knopf, 1966), 16-18.

14. On these points consult Frigyes Brisits, "Az öreg Kazinczy és a fiatal Vörösmarty" /The Old Kazinczy and the Young Vörösmarty/, *Katolikus Szemle*, vol. 47 (1933), 401-420; and also Margit Szekrényessy, *Romantika a német és magyar nyelvfilozófia tükrében* /Romanticism in the Mirror of German and Hungarian Philosophies of Language/ (Budapest: Minerva Társaság, 1937), 73-96.

15. György Lukács, *A történelmi regény* /The Historical Novel/ (Budapest, Szikra, 1947), 6.

16. Márta Mezei, *Történetszemlélet a magyar felvilágosodás irodalmában* /Historical Points of View in the Literature of the Hungarian Enlightenment/ (Budapest: Akadémia Kiadó, 1958), 21-24.

17. *Ibid.*, 12, 17, 42-46.

18. László Vajthó, ed., *Bessenyei György válogatott írásai* /The Selected Writings of György Bessenyei/ (Budapest: Magyar Helikon, 1961), 37, 67.

19. Cited in Sándor Eckhardt, "Bessenyei és a francia gondolat" /Bessenyei and French Thought/, *Egyetemes Philológiai Közlöny*, vol. 43 (1921), 201.

20. Antal Szerb, "Magyar preromantika", *Minerva*, vol. 8 (1939), 59.

21. *Ibid.*, 62.

22. Preface to Etelka as given in Ágnes Kenyeres, ed., *A kegyes olvasóhoz* /To the Dear Reader/ (Budapest: Gondolat, 1964), 152-153.

23. *Ibid.*, 153-154.

24. Louis Lékai, "Historiography in Hungary, 1790-1848," *Journal of Central European Affairs*, vol. 14 (1954), 14. See also Steven Béla Várdy, *Modern Hungarian Historiography* (New York: East European Monographs, Columbia University Press, 1976), 23-33.

25. Frigyes Brisits, "Az öreg Kazinczy és a fiatal Vörösmarty," 410-420; and Loránt Czigány, *The Oxford History of Hungarian Literature*, (Oxford: The Clarendon Press, 1984), 120-141.

26. Pál Gyulai, *Vörösmarty életrajza*, 119-130. Concerning the development of literary criticism, István Fenyő, *Az irodalom respublikájáért, 1817-1830* /For the Republic of Literature, 1817-1830/ (Budapest: Akadémiai Kiadó, 1976), 325-401.

27. Gyula Farkas, *A magyar romantika* /Hungarian Romanticism/ (Budapest: Magyar Tudományos Akadémia, 1930), 282.

28. *Ibid.*, 289.

29. Zsolt Beöthy, *A magyar irodalom története* /The History of Hungarian Literature/, 2 vols. (Budapest: Athenaeum, 1900), II, 31.

Steven Béla Várdy:

11 / BARON JOSEPH EÖTVÖS'S POLITICAL ESSAYS IN THE CAUSE OF REFORM DURING THE 1840s

The nineteenth century was a century of great men. The ideas of Liberty, Equality, and Fraternity and the coeval ideologies of Liberalism and Nationalism that emerged from the turmoils of the great French Revolution, have proven to be the procreators of great personalities. Under normal circumstances most of these men may have remained hidden on the level of blissful mediocrity and anonymity, but under the influence of these brazenly new ideas and ideologies they outdid themselves and became shapers of human history.

Naturally, the above statement holds true much more for the representatives of great and powerful states, than for the sons of small nations or insignificant nationalities. However great and gifted, the spokesmen of small nations can never really have as much role in the shaping of human history, as those who had the fortune to be born the sons of powerful nations. Within certain limits, however, even the former can influence human history; and this is amply demonstrated by the lives and achievements of some of Hungary's great — although in European and universal terms — relatively unknown 19th-century statesmen.

Undoubtedly, the best known among these in Europe and in America is Lajos /Louis/ Kossuth (1802-1894), but of at least equal importance were Count István /Stephen/ Széchenyi (1791-1860) and Ferenc /Francis/ Deák (1804-1876).[1] And right behind them in significance were such others as Count Gyula /Julius/ Andrássy (1823-1890)[2] and the subject of this essay, Baron József /Joseph/ Eötvös (1813-1871).[3]

Although not as well known as Kossuth and Széchenyi, or even Deák and Andrássy, the contemporary role of Eötvös was hardly less significant. It was not so much his lack of comparable contributions, but rather his lack of assertive personality that left him to some degree behind his well-known contemporaries. At the same time, however, he did offer something that none of the other enumerated or unenumerated Hungarian statesmen had to offer to such a degree as Eötvös, namely a high degree of compassion that manifested itself in fighting for various causes that were not really popular even among many of the liberal political reformers of those days. The most conspicuous of these causes was the question of Jewish emancipation. But we can also mention his struggle for a humanitarian solution to the pressing national minority question, and his injection of powerful humanitarian considerations even into such relatively popular causes as serf emancipation, economic and social modernization, and the transformation of Hungary into a modern parliamentary and democratic state.

In addition to his well-known humanitarian liberalism, Eötvös was also known for his pragmatism in dealing with critical national issues. Although a devoted Hungarian nationalist himself, he always moderated his national emotions by the ever-present humanitarian considerations as well as by a significant amount of realism. The latter is most evident in his views and policies concerning Hungary's relationship to Austria, i.e. Hungary's position within the Habsburg Empire. Thus, it was his conviction that Hungary's total independence from Austria was unrealistic that made him break with the Hungarian Revolution in the fall of 1848, and also pushed him later toward working for the restructuring of the Austrian Empire in a way that would satisfy the Magyars sufficiently to make them want to stay within the confines of the reorganized empire.

In addition to humanitarianism and pragmatism, a third and final consideration in Eötvös's political views was his desire to protect Hungary and the Magyars from such much more powerful neighbors as the Russians and the Germans, as well as from the seemingly significant force of Pan-Slavism. In face of these forces and realities, the only way he could envisage the future and security of his nation was within the confines of a larger political configuration, such as the Austrian Empire, that could serve as an ever-present bulwark against these threefold dangers. This was also an important consideration for his struggle to retain the unity of the Empire; and to do so by satisfying as many of its component nationalities as possible. In the late 1860s he thought he had achieved this goal, partially through the Austro-Hungarian Compromise of 1867, and partially through the Law of Nationalities and the Hungaro-Croatian Compromise of 1868.[4] Had Eötvös and his powerful liberal allies—such as Deák and Andrássy—been able to transmit the edifice they have created into the hands of similarly inspired and gifted political leaders, they may even have achieved their goals. But as it turned out, the "worthy fathers" were succeeded by "much less worthy sons" who squandered the achievements of their elders on the altar of intolerance and incompetence. And this holds true not only for the Hungarians, but also for most of the other nationalities of the Austrian Empire, or rather of Austria-Hungary that took its place in 1867. Pragmatism, humanitarianism, and liberalism gave way to emotionalism, intolerance and pseudo-liberalism, and this change of attitude ultimately brought their edifice down to a crushing end.

II

After a period of youthful experimentation with Romantic poetry, local politics, and West European travels, in 1839 Eötvös joined the Hungarian Diet as a hereditary member of the Upper House, and remained there as an active proponent of liberal reforms right up the the Revolution of 1848. His activities as a member of the Diet, however, were not limited to pressing for progressive legislation. During the same period he also sought to advance the cause of reform through his writings, which in that critical decade of Hungarian history (i.e., the *Vormärz*) took the form of three momentous novels (*The Carthusian*, 1839-1841; *The Village Notary*, 1845; and *Hungary in 1814*, 1847), a politically significant social drama (*Long Live Equality*, 1841), and a half a dozen political essays (*Opinions Concerning Penal Reform*, **1838**; *Poverty in Ireland*, 1940; *The Emancipation of the Jews*, **1840**; *People of the Orient and the Pesti Hirlap*, **1841**; *Prison Reform*, **1842**; and *Reform*, **1846**).[5]

The purpose of this study is to discuss briefly three of these essays that concentrate on three specific problems in contemporary Hungary's feudal society, namely serf emancipation, prison reform, and Jewish emancipation. This naturally leaves a number of significant problems untouched, including such critical issues as the national minority question and the reconstruction of the Habsburg Empire. The reason for this omission is that, while fully aware of these problems, Eötvös did not really deal with them at length until the post-revolutionary period, when he did so in a number of significant political essays, including his monumental *The Influence of the Dominant Ideas of the 19th Century upon the State* (2 vols., 1851-1854). Others included: *On the Equality of the Nationalities in Austria,* 1850; *The Guarantees of the Power and Unity of Austria,* 1859; *The Special Position of Hungary from the Point of View of German Unity,* 1860; *A Reply to Baron Gábor Kemény,* 1860; and *The Nationality Question,* 1865.[6]

Serf Emancipation

The transformation of feudal Hungary into modern Hungary, and the emancipation of the exploited peasant masses from serfdom was an issue that was close to Eötvös's heart, partly because of his political convictions, and partially because of his compassion for the downtrodden. This is evident from his youthful poetry, such as "The Castle and the Hut" (1837) where he related the tragic love affair of a young count and a beautiful peasant girl.[7] And this theme also cropped up constantly in many of his other writings during the 1830s. But not until 1840 did he devote a whole essay to this question, when he published his *Poverty in Ireland.* In this essay he examined the misery caused by the lack of social reform in the Land of the Irish, who in those days were suffering under a rather unenlightened English rule. While motivated partially by compassion for the exploited Irish masses, Eötvös was at least as moved by the parallels he perceived between the Irish and the Hungarian historical experiences and social conditions. Eötvös wanted his nation to learn from the experiences of the Irish, and preferably avoid the latter's pitfalls that soon led to the greatest famine and mass starvation in that nation's history and to the great Irish emigration to America.

In examining the history of these two nations, Eötvös saw a number of parallels between their historical experiences, including their political and economic dependence upon their dominant partners (i.e. England and Austria). In both instances there were these formally autonomous states whose identity and freedom of action had been lost within the confines of larger empires. Both of these states were forced to play the role of economic colonies for their dominant partners, and in this relationship the Irish and the Hungarian peasants were exploited not only by their native lords, but also by their "alien" landowning classes that had been planted on top of them by their ruling partners. In the case of Ireland, the fruits of this unequal partnership were reaped by the absentee Protestant (i.e. English or Anglicized) landowners, while in Hungary these same fruits were harvested by the largely unassimilated or de-Magyarized pro-Habsburg aristocracy— such as Eötvös's own forbears.

In this essay Eötvös also dealt with the question of industrialization as a possible cure for some of Ireland's—and therefore Hungary's—social and economic ills. But in light of Britain's numerous unfavorable experiences during the early phase of the Industrial Revolution (e.g. the pauperization and extreme exploitation of the urban masses), Eötvös doubted that industrialization alone could bring about the desired cure. In general agreement with Simonde de Simondi (1773-1842) and to a lesser degree with Karl Marx (1818-1883), he assumed that unregulated industrialization would simply result in another increasingly polarized society within urban surroundings. In other words, the problems of the countryside would simply be transferred to the cities, and thus the role of the oppressive landowners would merely be assumed by the unscrupulous industrialists and entrepreneurs. The rich would get richer, and the poor would get poorer. (viz. Marx's "Law of Increasing Misery.") This, in turn, would pose the threat of a violent revolution, a threat which in Eötvös's view could only lead to more destructiveness and which should be avoided at all cost.

So what was the answer? To Eötvös the answer was clear: Thorough social and economic reform. This was to be a well-thought-out and comprehensive reform that would result in terminating all forms of servitude, in a more equitable distribution of goods, and in the general equalization of society. This, in turn, would end the growing demand and threat of a revolution. In his view, the very threat of revolution should move every thinking man to promote the cause of social reform and social conciliation.

Penal Reform

Eötvös's appeal for serf emancipation and general social reform—which he treated much more extensively and dramatically in two of his great social novels of the mid-1840s, *The Village Notary* and *Hungary in 1514*—was paralleled by his search for penal reform. This included the revision of Hungary's antiquated criminal code and the humanization of its archaic penitentiary system.

The question of penal reform was first broached in Hungary in 1830 by the literary scholar Ferenc Toldy (1805-1875) who, learning about some reform attempts in Western Europe, called attention to the unusually primitive and inhuman conditions in Hungary's prisons. [8] Toldy's essay was soon followed by the publication of Sándor Bölöni Farkas's *Journey in North America*, which, among others, also gave a detailed account of recent American experimentations with prison reform, and referred to Hungary's prisons as "dunghills of evil and corruption." [9] He pointed out that in Hungary prisons are filled with "such wretched members of human society...who have threatened it with moral corruption," and there, "amidst boredom and inaction, they further indoctrinate each other into the ways of evil at the expense of the state..., /and while suffering/ physical tortures, they come to despise the vengeful laws and the society that have humiliated and excommunicated them.../and then/ dream of taking revenge on their persecutors."

Following the publication of Bölöni Farkas's book, public indignation in Hungary rose to high pitch. Demands for penal reform increased, and because the national Diet refused to deal with this question immediately, many of the counties decided to act on their own. One of them, Borsod County, went so far as to establish its own Commission and Penal

Reform. One of the prominent members of this Commission
was the young Joseph Eötvös who was already known for his
humanitarian views and reform zeal; and one of the results of
the Commission's deliberations was Eötvös's personal report
entitled *Opinions Concerning Penal Reform* (1838). In this
report he argued convincingly that the primary aim of modern
penal institutions should be not to punish, but to reform and
to reshape the criminal, so as to make him into a useful
member of human society.

In arguing for improved prison conditions, Eötvös
conceded the right of society to protect itself from criminals by temporarily excluding them from full-fledged membership in that society. Yet, he asserted that society does
not have the right to mistreat these unfortunate outcasts, nor
to subject the less evil among them to the likelihood of further
corruption by mingling them with incorrigible criminals.

In light of these activities and demands, one of the initial
acts of the Diet of 1839-1840 was to establish its own Committee
on Penal Reform, where Eötvös was once more a prominent
member. Here he worked with such other noted Hungarian
intellectuals and reformers as Ferenc Deák, Ferenc Pulszky,
and Lord Chief Justice Count György Mailáth.

The Dietary Committee was still in session when Eötvös
joined forces with his good friend and prominent legal scholar,
Móric Lukács, and then went ahead to publish his views on this
question in a bulky essay entitled *Prison Reform* (1842). Based
on the thorough examination of all relevant Western sources,
this work proved to be so comprehensive that it remained the
standard Magyar language study on this problem right up to
the end of the 19th century. Eötvös authored the section on
penal reform, while Lukács treated the question of the reform
of the criminal code. The depth of Eötvös's examination is
indicated by the fact that his earlier essay of some thirty-odd
pages was expanded here to over three-hundred pages, even
though the basic thrust of both studies remained the same. But
because of this expansion he was able to devote more attention
to the humanitarian aspect of this question.

Jewish Emancipation

Simultaneously with his appeal for serf emancipation and

penal reform—where he could count on the support of a sizable segment of Hungary's population, and even leading classes—Eötvös also began to champion a cause that was far from popular in contemporary Europe, including Hungary: the emancipation of the Jews. [10]

Although this may seem incredible today, many of Eötvös's contemporaries regarded both the serfs and the Jews unfit for emancipation. The view that the latter were really inferior beings was widespread, as was the belief that they were innately base and immoral. Many of the opponents of emancipation capitalized on this belief and tried to make it into a scientific creed. Eötvös was very adamant in rejecting these arguments. He pointed out that baseness and immorality are not innate to human beings. Insofar as these do exist within a subculture, they are undoubtedly the products of poverty, exploitation, and centuries of oppression. He was convinced that if one treats human beings as if they were beasts of burden, in time they are bound to act as beasts. "Or are we to believe," asked he, "that millennia of oppression can make a people moral?" [11]

As best as we can tell, Jews have lived in Hungary ever since the Magyar conquest of the 9th century. Their lot was never enviable, but through much of this period it was at least tolerable. In 1753 they were saddled with the so-called "Toleration Tax," which used to be rather customary throughout Christian Europe for many centuries. Joseph II's enlightened reforms improved their position somewhat, but in the early 19th century the general antipathy against them increased once more. And this was all the worse as this growing dislike of the "Children of Moses" coincided with the spread of liberalism in Hungary and with the hope of significant social reforms.

Although undoubtedly strange, this odd contradiction was the direct result of the beginnings of a large-scale immigration of the uneducated and poverty-stricken Galician Jews into Hungary. This rapid and unchecked influx of a culturally, linguistically, and religiously alien group caused much resentment among the native population. But when many of the newcomers also began to assume control over such sectors of the Hungarian economy as grain, wine, and wool trade, this resentment soon turned into outright antipathy. This feeling of dislike began with the country's middle social classes, the burghers and the lower nobility, but eventually it also spread to the peasants. The already exploited peasant serfs now found themselves increasingly indebted to the local Jewish innkeepers and grain merchants, who usually doubled as village moneylenders. Thus, the villagers soon began to blame much of their economic plight on the newcomers.

The Hungarian Reform Diet of 1825-1827 did raise the question of Jewish emancipation, but in light of the spreading anti-Jewish sentiment there was little hope for quick reforms in this area. The belief that the emancipation of the Jews would endanger the moral well-being of the country's Christian population was very widespread and many anti-Jewish propagandists took advantage of it to speak up against extending full civil and political rights to the Jews. The situation was so unfriendly and hopeless that only very few prominent personalities were willing to risk their popularity to speak up for the Jewish cause. And there was only one among them who was willing to stand up for the total and unconditional emancipation of the Jews: the young Joseph Eötvös.

Eötvös's interest in Jewish emancipation stemmed largely from his deep humanitarian convictions and in his unfaltering faith in the basic goodness of man. At the same time, however, he was undoubtedly also influenced by at least one of his recorded childhood experiences concerning discrimination that made him speak up for everyone who suffered such fate.

The turningpoint in Eötvös's life in this connection was the year 1840, when he spoke up twice for the extension of civil and political rights to the Jews. He did so, first in a speech to the Upper House of the Hungarian Diet, and then in a powerful essay entitled *The Emancipation of the Jews*. In both instances he followed his usual approach of first appealing to the emotions of his audience, and then following it up with an appeal to their reason. Eötvös, therefore, began by portraying the Jews as the innocent victims of many centuries of oppression, whose situation was and is on the brink of hopelessness: "The Jews are alone /among the people of Europe/ for whom the Middle Ages do not wish to pass; alone for whom no one feels any kinship; alone among the oppressed whose sufferings find no sympathy /and/ whose woes elicit no response." [12] In his view, a Jew was "a hundred times more miserable than he who had lost his public respect through his own evil deeds." Why? Because, as opposed to a criminal, who is able to repay his debt to society, a Jew "can never hope to improve. The sins he was born with will never be forgiven by the cruel and heartless world. He may follow the path of virtue, he may travel the road of honesty, he may remain in poverty, but he will never cease to be a Jew." [13]

Later Eötvös expanded upon these views in his novel *The Village Notary*, where he made the wandering Jewish peddler, Jancsi Üveges, into the prototype of the demoralized and amoralized Jews of Eastern Europe. And he shaped Jancsi's story in such a way that at the end of his life even this seemingly immoral Jew was turned into a sensitive human being who was moved by the same human fears, emotions, and anxieties as anyone else: "I never had much joy in this world," Jancsi confessed to the Reverend Vándory. "A poor Jew like me loses very little when he loses his life.... Perhaps after I am gone, they will leave me in peace." And then when Vándory characterized Christianity as the religion of love, Jancsi exclaimed with an irony: "Religion of love? Why don't you ask us Jews about our experiences /with this religion of love/? Had I known more Christians like you Dear Reverend..., I may even have relinquished my faith. /But/ how base would I have to be to desert my faith now, after having done no other good in life, except remaining faithful to it?" [14] And thus—in Eötvös's rendering—the poor, abused, and miserable wretch still triumphed at the end, and thereby proved what Eötvös wanted him to prove: the ultimate goodness of man.

Eötvös's emotional appeal for Jewish emancipation was followed by his appeal to reason and rationality. He methodically refuted all emotional accusations against them, among them the belief that they are morally corrupt, that they constitute an unassimilable alien minority in the country, and that their emancipation would endanger the fabric of Christian society.

Eötvös regarded all of these allegations as stemming from age-old prejudices and ignorance. But even if some of these problems were present, he viewed them as being the results of the millennial oppression of the Jews in Christian society. He could not accept the allegation that immorality was a peculiarly Jewish characteristic, and that Christianity *per se* could make anyone moral.

He similarly dispensed with the claim that the Jews constitute an alien body within a nation. In his view, Jewish separateness was due less to Jewish reluctance to merge with the Christians, than to the latter's unwillingness to accept the former on an equal basis. And then, with reference to Hungary, he asked: "After all, what was there in our nation's past that should have engendered their sympathy, or should have made them love this country?" [15] He was convinced, however, that should the Jews be able to share in the benefits of Hungarian citizenship, they would undoubtedly develop growing loyalties to their newly found nationality and would become Magyar patriots. The Age of Dualism, with its multitude of great Jewish-Hungarian intellectuals, scholars, and scientists—the majority of whom became good Magyar patriots—proved Eötvös to have been correct. [16]

Eötvös similarly disposed of the argument that Jewish emancipation would endanger Christianity. "It is an old custom," he wrote, "to connect the most evil of causes with the most sacred one. Therefore, I am not amazed at all that the proponents of /Jewish/ oppression—like the criminals in the past—seek security before the altar." [17] In his view, this was not Christianity, but the denial of the most important aspect of Christian teaching: love of one's neighbor.

He also pointed out that many of the opponents of Jewish emancipation were really fearful of Jewish economic competition, and were simply trying to hide their real interests and goals behind the facade of moral concerns. "Who would not sacrifice everything, even his most cherished principles in the defense of his own economic well-being? ....Woe be to him who undertakes reforms in the name of justice, and not in the name of usefulness." [18] And precisely because Eötvös recognized the significance of the economic aspects of this question, he also pointed out that the economic orientation of the Jews—both in Hungary and in Europe in general—was primarily the result of long-standing discrimination against them. In the Hungarian case, with the nobility unwilling to engage in gainful occupations, the burghers remaining a small and economically conservative class, and the peasantry lingering in servitude and ignorance, the ever-widening field of economic/business activities was left wide open for those who had the knowledge and the desire to enter it. These were mostly the incoming Jews, who moved quickly into the vacuum and soon established important holds over various segments of the nation's economy. Yet Eötvös was also convinced that "if through their emancipation, new paths were to be opened up for.../the Jews/, then their purely commercial spirit would diminish." [19] And here he was once more right. Following emancipation, the Jews began to move into the intellectual and creative worlds in ever-increasing numbers, and they became some of Hungary's top writers, poets, historians, musicians, artists, and scientists in the five decades between emancipation and the end of the Austro-Hungarian Empire (1868-1918).

Although Eötvös was sufficiently realistic not to expect immediate results, he still ended his essay on Jewish emancipation on a positive note: "Society cannot be unjust to anyone without repercussions," said he. And to bolster his spirit and the spirit of his supporters he concluded: "One who fights.../prejudice/ with truth is invincible." [20]

It did take some time, but Eötvös's struggle for Jewish emancipation did end in victory. Moreover, following the somewhat belated and ill-conceived emancipation effort by the Hungarian revolutionary government in 1849, ultimately it was Eötvös himself who made the dream into reality. He did this in 1868 in his capacity as Dualist Hungary's first Minister for Religion and Public Education.

Conclusion

If the 19th century was a century of great men, Baron Joseph Eötvös was undoubtedly one of them. His greatest achievements came in the decades following the Hungarian Revolution of 1848, when calm and pragmatic minds were needed to deal with the magnitude of Hungary's defeat, and respected men were needed to lift the nation out of the depth of its despair. But Eötvös's contributions were also significant in the decade before the Revolution, when he emerged as one of the most sophisticated and most humane proponents of social and political reform in Hungary. And while the most influential instruments of his reform ideals in those pre-revolutionary years were undoubtedly his great social novels which were read and wept over by many tens of thousands, the foundations of his reform goals and reform activities were really laid down in his political essays in the very early part of the 1840s. These essays — three of which we have discussed — had placed Eötvös on the map of contemporary Hungary as one of the listened-to champions of reform, and they also sketched the basic outlines of his social and political creed which were to make this most humane intellectual into one of the most admired 19th-century Hungarian statesmen and political thinkers.

Notes

1. Concerning these prominent statesmen see the following works: István Deák, *Lawful Revolution: Louis Kossuth and the Hungarians, 1848-1849* (New York: Columbia University Press, 1979); George Bárány, *Stephen Széchenyi and the Awakening of Hungarian Nationalism, 1791-1941* (Princeton: Princeton University Press, 1968); and Béla K. Király, *Ferenc Deák* (Boston: Twayne Publishers, 1975).

2. See János Decsy, *Prime Minister Gyula Andrássy's Influence on Habsburg, Foreign Policy during the Franco-German War of 1870-1871* (New York: East European Monographs, Columbia University Press, 1979).

3. Concerning Eötvös and his views I have relied primarily on my own long-standing research. See especially my two major monographs: *Baron Joseph Eötvös: A Literary Biography* (New York: East Europeam Monographs, Columbia University Press, 1987), and *Baron Joseph Eötvös: The Political Profile of a Liberal Hungarian Statesman and Thinker* (Bloomington: Ph.D. Dissertation, Indiana University, 1966). For additional information and interpretation see also Paul Bódy, *Joseph Eötvös and the Modernization of Hungary, 1840-1870* (Philadelphia: The American Philosophical Society, 1972; reprinted in East European Monographs, Columbia University Press, 1986).

4. The Austro-Hungarian Compromise of 1867 and the national minority problems that preceded and followed it have been the subjects of many essays, monographs, and polemical works during the past two decades. For various views by the historians of many nations see especially the studies in the *Austrian History Yearbook* (1965-present). For a most recent and detailed Hungarian assessment of this question — as viewed from Budapest — consult the sixth volume of the proposed ten-volume history of Hungary under the sponsorship of the Institute of History of the Hungarian Academy of Sciences, which is still in the process of publication: *Magyarország története, 1848-1890* /History of Hungary, 1848-1890/, ed. Endre Kovács and László Katus (Budapest: Akadémiai Kiadó, 1979), 1760 pp.

5. The original titles of the enumerated works are: *A karthauzi*, 2 vols., Pest,

1842; *A falu jegyzője*, 3 vols., Pest, 1845; *Magyarország 1514-ben*, 3 vols., Pest, 1847; *Éljen az egyenlőség*, Pest, 1841; *Vélemény a fogházjavítás ügyében ns. Borsod vármegye ebbeli küldöttségéhez*, Pest, 1838, *Szegénység Irlandban*, Pest, 1840; *A zsidók emancipációja*, Pest, 1840; *Kelet Népe és Pesti Hírlap*, Pest, 1841; *Fogházjavítás*, Pest, 1842; and *Reform*, Leipzig, 1846.

6. The original titles of these works, written in Hungarian, German or in both languages, are: *A XIX. század uralkodó eszméinek befolyása az álladalomra*. 2 vols., Vienna-Pest, 1851-1854; *Über die Gleichberechtigung der Nationalitäten in Österreich*, Leipzig, 1850; *Die Garantien der Macht und Einheit Österreichs*, Leipzig, 1859; *Die Sonderstellung Ungarns vom Standpunkte der Einheit Deutschlands*, Leipzig, 1860; *Felelet báró Kemény Gábor néhány szavára*, Pest, 1860; *A nemzetiségi kérdés*, Pest, 1865.

7. "A vár és a kunyhó," in *Báró Eötvös Jószef összes munkái* /The Complete Works of Baron Joseph Eötvös/, ed. Géza Voinovich, 20 vols. (Budapest, 1901-1903), vol. 18, pp. 3-5; hereafter cited as *Works*.

8. Ferencz Toldy, "Könyvismertetés" /Book Review/, *Tudományos Gyüjtemény*, vol. 12, no. 2 (Pest, 1830), pp. 102-109.

9. Sándor Bölöni Farkas, *Utazás Észak-Amerikában* (Kolozsvár, 1834). For an English version of this work, with an excellent historical introduction, see Sándor Bölöni Farkas, *Journey in North America 1831*, translated and edited by Árpád Kadarkay (Santa Barbara: ABC Clio, 1978). There is also a second recent translation, which is more complete, but it lacks the in-depth historical introduction of the former: *Journey in North America by Alexander Bölöni Farkas (Kolozsvár, 1834)*, translated and edited by Theodore Schoenman and Helen Benedek Schoenman (Philadelphia: The American Philosophical Society, 1977).

10. For a detailed treatment of this question see Steven Bála Várdy, "The Origins of Jewish Emancipation in Hungary: The Role of Baron Joseph Eötvös," *Ungarn-Jahrbuch*, vol. 7 (1976), pp. 137-166. Reprinted as *Duquesne University Studies in History*, no. 6 (Pittsburgh: Duquesne University, Department of History, 1979).

11. Quoted from his essay on Jewish emancipation, *Works*, IX, p. 16.

12. *Ibid*., p. 14.

13. *Works*, XII, p. 110.

14. All quotations are from Eötvös's novel, *The Village Notary*, in *Works*, III, pp. 367-368.

15. *Works*, XII, p. 128.

16. Concerning this question see William O. McCagg, *Jewish Nobles and Geniuses in Modern Hungary* (New York: East European Monographs, Columbia University Press, 1972; reprinted 1986); the relevant sections of vols. 6 and 7 of the above-mentioned multivolumed *Magyarország története*, which cover the period between 1848 and 1918; and Steven Béla Várdy, "The 'Mystery of the Hungarian

Talent'," in *The World and I* (Washington, DC), vol. II, no. 4 (April 1987), pp. 498-513.

17. *Works*, XII, p. 146.

18. *Ibid.*, p. 149.

19. *Works*, IX, p. 17.

20. *Works*, XII, pp. 155, 157.

Edsel Walter Stroup:

12 / HUNGARY'S TAX SYSTEM AND THE ISSUE OF TAX REFORM IN THE 1840s

In the 1840s, Hungary was in the throes of a powerful reform movement led by nobles. In the other states of Central and Eastern Europe in the nineteenth century, modernization was usually promoted by their monarchs, often against the wishes of their privileged classes. In Hungary, the situation was reversed. Influential individuals in the Hungarian titled aristocracy and groups of untitled nobles on the local level advocated fundamental change, while it was the Habsburg dynasty which displayed a distinct preference for the preservation of the *status quo*. Beginning in 1830, the Habsburg court, councillors, and bureaucracy in Vienna were forced to take note of the increasing restiveness in Hungary. "Vienna," as these entities may be collectively termed, responded with a typical blend of procrastination and non-essential concession. But, despite setbacks, the Hungarians' demand for substantial reform returned with increasing insistence until it eventually touched on virtually all aspects of society. Perhaps no area of concern was of more fundamental importance, both to the Hungarian reformers and to the Habsburgs themselves, than that of taxation.

Hungary's reformers in the 1840s knew that their country's tax system was inadequate to meet the needs of a modern state. Hungarian roads were in habitually poor repair. [1] One of the best informed contemporaries of the period reported that "the bad condition of our country's roads" was widely regarded as "the major obstacle to Hungarian commerce;" and he thought the problem should be addressed by the central Hungarian Government with national funding. [2] Hence, knowledgeable observers were aware that the country desperately needed a good national transport network if it were to accelerate its already perceptible and even strong economic development. But the tax system was so constituted that it did not produce enough revenue to finance large-scale improvements. As a result, Hungary (in 1845) exported only 277,627 short tons (4.45 percent) of its total grain production of 6,237,056.7 short tons (56.6 million hectoliters). [3] In 1845, most of this grain, as with all other major Hungarian exports, went onto the Austrian market. [4] Hungary did have some good roads leading across the mountains down to its Adriatic Port of Fiume, but the cost of mountain transport raised the price of export grain to a prohibitive degree. As a consequence, our contemporary observed that Hungary's "ocean commerce is in its infancy." [5] Both he and the great reform leader, Ferenc Deák, ardently advocated the construction of a railroad down to Fiume. [6] But the country's tax system could not produce the funds, and private capital was hardly forthcoming. It should also be noted in passing that the customs system unilaterally ordained by the Habsburgs constituted another significant obstacle to Hungarian export out of Fiume. Our astute contemporary took due note of this, both in the statistics which he provided, [7] and in his tactful statement, which had to pass an unpredictable Habsburg censorship. Foreign ships, he stated, were scarcely likely to call at the Hungarian Port of Fiume to purchase Hungarian goods, when the Monarchy's high protective tariffs virtually prohibited them from landing their own cargoes. [8]

Hungary's inadequate tax system also had an adverse effect on the country's economic life in another fundamental area. This area was even more important than transport and export, since it was the bedrock for both of them—i.e., the area of agriculture. Hungary's tax system, as the reformers were well aware, could not produce or secure the large sums necessary to compensate the nobility for its loss of land and services as proposed in diverse plans for peasant liberation. All these plans (in contrast to the situation, for example, in Ireland) envisaged the establishment of the peasant as a freehold landowner, and, as most peasants did not have the funds for this, the whole gigantic project would have to fall on the state in some fashion. [9]

Lastly, in the long-term view, Hungary's antiquated tax system was an integral part of her poor reputation abroad, which was to prove an increasing hindrance in attracting small or large scale foreign investment in the country—whether private or government-brokered. "In the opinion of the French, we are on the same level as the Kalmuks," a disappointed agent-friend reported to Lajos Kossuth in the 1840s. [10]

But Hungary, even with all these deficiencies, was actually a potentially rich country whose natural abundance compared quite favorably with its Central and East European neighbors. Hungarian agricultural production and the consequent well-being of Hungary's inhabitants also compared rather well with their counterparts in most of the non-Hungarian or Hereditary Lands of the Habsburg Monarchy—though it would be difficult to find a true Austrian to concur. Nevertheless, official Austrian statistics for 1845 and 1846 support this impression. Hungary, with admittedly almost one-half the land area of the total Monarchy (124,516 English square miles out of 257,861), but with only slightly in excess of one-half of the population of the Hereditary Lands (14,409,108 inhabitants to 22,541,439 in "Austria"), [11] had virtually as much land under production in all categories of use as in all the rest of the Monarchy combined, including Lombardy-Venetia (45,568,569 *hold* in Hungary versus 46,172,542 *hold* in "Austria"); and Hungary produced 57.31 percent of the Monarchy's wheat in 1845, with very respectable proportional production figures in most other crops as well. [12] Again, in the realm of taxation, which is our concern here, it is even possible to state that Hungary was, in the aggregate, a lightly taxed country in the 1840s when its large area, its natural wealth, and its growing population are taken into consideration.

However, the defects inherent in the Hungarian tax

system were monumental. As the Hungarian reformers sensed, if these deficiencies were left uncorrected, they would inflict incalculable damage on the country's nascent economic development. In the first place, during any given year in the 1840s, about 60 to 70 percent of all Hungarian revenues consisted of indirect taxes, which fell automatically under "Vienna's" jurisdiction. The Habsburg-held Crown, in effect, collected and expended those revenues at its own discretion. No proviso was attached or consent required by any Hungarian representative institution. In theory, the operation of the central Hungarian Treasury in Vienna was constitutionally independent of all Austrian authority. However, in practice, the constitutional independence of this Hungarian institution had long since been rendered ineffectual and subject to Austrian supervision. [13]

Direct taxes did, indeed, account for the remaining 30 percent or so of Hungary's public revenues, and their authorization did require an affirmative vote of the Hungarian Diet. However, under normal conditions, the monies raised by direct taxation were not substantial enough to give the Hungarian Diet any lasting influence over the formulation of "Vienna's" policies. The Crown usually carried on its affairs with scant regard for Hungarian wishes or recalcitrance. The King even frequently ignored the Hungarian Law XIII of 1791 which required him to convoke the Hungarian Diet triennially, or "earlier should the public welfare" make it desirable. [14]

The Habsburg monarchs were obviously able to act in such a manner because they collected such a large proportion of Hungary's public revenues automatically. But they could also afford to act independently of Hungarian wishes because their bureaucracy unilaterally assessed and collected substantial amounts of taxation from the Hereditary Lands of the Habsburg Monarchy. [15] These Lands were even more acquiescent in such matters than Hungary itself. As we have seen, they only just exceeded the Kingdom of Hungary in area. But they had, by far, a larger population, which was thicker on the ground in some places than Hungary's, [16] and their respective economies were comparatively more diversified. [17]

As a consequence of all this, the Hungarian Diet's opportunities to extract concessions from the Crown were quite limited. According to a traditional pattern of long standing, the Hungarians were able to mount financial clout in Vienna only in times of crises, such as war, or threat of war. In sum, during the 1840s, the Hungarian reformers' chance of securing the Crown's sanction for legislation introducing fundamental change appeared rather slim.

However, the Hungarian reformers did have a considerable amount of public discontent to work with at home. They could point out that Hungary was unjustifiably poor in public monies under its prevailing tax system. Not even all of the roughly 30 percent of the country's public revenue, which was raised by direct taxation with periodic Dietal assent, was actually expended for any direct benefit in Hungary itself. Out of this direct taxation, approximately one-half (the *contributio* or War Tax) disappeared into the centralized military budget for the defense of the total Monarchy. Only the remaining half of Hungary's direct taxation (the so-called House Tax) was spent for domestic purposes. In sum, of all the public revenue raised in Hungary in the 1840s only about 15 percent was spent to produce any visible benefit in the country itself.

The dissatisfaction and frustration of the Hungarian reformers with this remarkable tax system is all the more understandable when it is examined in detail. Our contemporary, the statistician, Elek Fényes, provides the following annual average of Hungarian public revenue for the years 1843, 1844, and 1845: [18]

	Source	*forints*
1.	Crown and Treasury Estates	3,895,019
2.	Salt tax	10,092,725
3.	Mines' Revenues	952,986
4.	Custom Revenues (1/30th)	5,380,975
5.	Post	184,391
6.	Lottery	513,000
7.	Pawn Shops	72,795
8.	Extraordinary Revenues	1,089,063

9.	War Tax	4,395,244
10.	House Tax	5,453,121
11.	Recruiting Tax	75,000
12.	Royal Cities' Census	18,041
13.	The Sixteen Szepes Towns	18,231
14.	Assistance for the Maintenance of Fortifications (from the Church)	68,000
15.	Income from the Military Borders	2,053,774
	Total	34,262,365

As indicated in the preceding paragraphs, with the exceptions of the direct War Tax and House Tax, all the sources of Hungarian public revenues consisted of indirect, fixed royal impositions based on fees, usage, or consumption. Combined, these automatic indirect taxes came to 24,414,000 forints or 71.25 percent of the national budget. The Hungarian Diet did indeed have control over the remaining balance of the revenues, and it periodically negotiated the amount of the War Tax (and the number of recruits) with the Crown. But it is illustrative of the situation that the King's indirect tax on salt alone yielded twice the sum authorized by the delegates at the Diet to the Crown and to the counties for domestic purposes in direct taxes.

In other words, Hungary's direct House Tax was the country's sole source of revenues for domestic purposes. In the mid-1840s, it yielded 5,453,121 forints annually, or just 15.91 percent of all national revenues. This was a modest sum with which to pay all the public officials, and to maintain all the public roads, bridges, waterways, and municipal buildings in the country. Moreover, as we shall see presently, there were great local variations in the assessment of the House Tax. In round figures, the assessment fell as follows: 3,069,415 forints was paid by the counties, 2,185,466 by the Royal Free Cities, and 198,240 by the Royal Free Districts. [19]

But if the House Tax produced inadequate sums to cover the increased need for domestic spending in the country, it had nonetheless become a mounting burden for much of the taxpaying populace, given the inequitable nature of Hungary's tax system. In earlier eras, direct domestic taxation constituted a very modest proportion of all the taxes and feudal dues rendered by the taxed populace. [20] In the early nineteenth century, however, the increasing need for domestic improvements drove the House Tax up sharply in comparison to the War Tax. In some places, such as in Hatvan in Heves County as late as 1846, this generalization did not hold true. [21] On the whole, however, the House Tax rose dramatically. In Pest County in the center of the country, the process started quite early. In 1725, Pest County's House Tax was only 5,651 forints. But in 1740 it rose to 12,000 forints, in 1790 to 91,000, and in the first three decades of the nineteenth century it just about equalled the War Tax. [22] The situation was quite similar in many other counties. [23] In extreme cases, the House Tax was double that of the War Tax. In 1817, for example, the *oppidum* (*mezőváros*) of Miskolc in Borsod County was assessed 4,308 forints for the War Tax and 9,316 for the House Tax. Borsod County as a whole paid 66,336 and 143,438 respectively. [24] It is more than mildly ironic that the Borsod County delegates in the Hungarian Diet stoutly resisted increasing the monies sent to the Habsburgs for military purposes, ostensibly in the interest of the "poor taxed people" ("*misera contribuens plebs*" - a stock phrase of long standing), yet these same delegates authorized large increases in the domestic House Tax without protest.

However, the increased House Taxes still constituted such a small percentage of the nation's total revenues under the prevailing tax structure that they failed to meet all but the most elementary needs of a growing population. Hungary's local governmental expenditures were even helped by the fact that the nobles' patrimonial courts still shouldered a good deal of the primary administrative and judicial functions (such as probate and civil and criminal lawsuits of the first instance) which normally fell on government in a modern state. [25] But even under these circumstances, Hungary's local officials found that the income derived from the domestic House Tax was barely adequate to carry out their traditional functions, and to preserve the existing material infrastructure.

In point of fact, the nation's House Taxes were mostly expended on personnel and transport costs, which left very little for material improvements. As of 1845, Hungary's fifty-two counties annually expended their 3,069,415 forints in House Taxes as follows: officials' salaries, 645,250 forints; salaries of officials' assistants (*hajdúk*), 463,213 forints; officials' transportation, 297,673 forints; maintenance of prisoners in jail, 218,900 forints; roads and bridges, 204,136 forints; assistants' clothing and arms, 168,368 forints; miscellaneous expenses, 115,129 forints; buildings, 101,677 forints; payment of debts, 89,320 forints; uncollectible debts written-off, 73,168 forints; writing materials, 69,147 forints; orphanages, 6,214 forints; repairs, 5,890 forints; stables, 3,642 forints; and the *deperdita*, 607,688 forints. [26]

The *deperdita* was a very special tax. It was peculiar to Hungary alone, and accounted for no less than 19.79 percent of the Hungarian counties' House Tax in 1843-1845. It was, in effect, a rather hidden assessment within the country's domestic taxation, which helped pay for the maintenance of the Habsburg Imperial Army regiments garrisoned in Hungary or passing through the country. Very simply, the county governments purchased food, fodder, and occasional lodging and transport for the regiments at current market prices. The county officials kept a strict account of their deliveries to the military, and argued successfully in the national Diet that the Viennese central authorities should credit these expenditures against Hungary's War Tax. However, "Vienna" persisted (with a short interruption during the reign of Joseph II) in giving credit only according to artificially low prices established in a *regulamentum* signed by Maria Theresa in 1751. The difference between the 1751 prices and the current market value of the goods (the *deperdita*) was then assessed by the county officials as part of the House Tax.

Consequently, the *deperdita* was actually an imperial rather than a royal tax, and Hungary's "poor taxed people" even contributed to the defense of the total Monarchy under the heading of their domestic taxes. As we have seen, as of 1845, the taxpayers in Hungary's fifty-two counties paid a healthy annual 607,688 forints in *deperdita* tax, which was almost exactly double the amount they paid for the maintenance of all the counties' public roads, bridges, and buildings. Beyond contributing to the security of the total Monarchy, the Hungarian taxpayers obtained no direct benefit for their *deperdita* monies other than having a security force available for the protection of life and property in the event of domestic disturbances which local authorities could not quell. In point of fact, such disturbances had been all too frequent through the 1820s, [27] and Habsburg troops were occasionally deployed to overawe the very peasants whose *deperdita* tax helped maintain them. And the Habsburgs added a nice touch to the whole convenient arrangement by habitually keeping a disproportionate number of regiments stationed in Hungary to the point foreigners were astonished at the Hungarians' patience in maintaining so large an army. Finally, *ex ungue leonem*. The Vienna Government was even known to store the grain purchased by the Hungarian counties for the maintenance of the regiments garrisoned in the country; then, at the opportune moment, the Viennese authorities transported the grain into the Hereditary Lands (paying no tariff at the border as the state would not tax itself), and sold it on the open market in Vienna for a considerable profit to Habsburg coffers. Hence, the *deperdita* was a uniquely abusive and uncontrolled tax, susceptible to corruption at every level of its imposition. Yet it remained in effect until 1848. [28]

The Hungarian reformers repeatedly expressed their exasperation with all such inequities — and they were myriad — in their country's tax system. [29] They complained about non-essentials as well as fundamentals. They protested that, in the country as a whole, the House Tax was too often spent foolishly on such items as expensive braiding on the uniforms of the *hajdúk*, who functioned as guards, police, messengers, and servants to the county officials. [30] The reformers advocated, in effect, that Hungary's ancient system of taxation acquire a modern sense of utilitarianism. They saw clearly that Hungary's need for internal improvements had far outstripped the ability of the country to pay for them under the existing tax system. It is certain that under the pre-1848 revenue structure, no surplus existed to finance innovative projects.

Hungary's inadequate amount of direct taxation was also assessed inequitably from several points of view. The Royal Free Cities, as we shall see below, were a rather bizarre world unto themselves in tax matters. In the counties, direct taxes were imposed exclusively on the possessions and productivity of "full peasants" with recorded urbarial lots. Subject peasants with less than one-eighth of a recorded urbarial lot or with no recorded urbarial land at all (known legally and socially as *zsellérek*) were exempt from state taxation. Ostensibly, this arrangement contained a measure of justice, since state taxes were designed to fall on the landed urbarial peasants, who were supposedly those in the peasant hierarchy best able to pay them. In practice, however, the system was gravely distorted and inequitable. Over many generations, sizable numbers of peasants had under-reported the value of their possessions, and had succeeded in minimizing or concealing the real area of their urbarial lands, thereby escaping the brunt of state taxation; in some instances, whole communities of urbarial peasants had themselves recorded in the county records as tax-exempt *zsellérek* working the lord's immediate estate under contractual agreement. [31] But even if one considers only those urbarial peasants who were listed in the county records as such, one finds that taxes were assessed unevenly on them also due to the lack of uniformity in the counties' tax schedules.

In the case of the War Tax, as stated earlier, the amount to be paid by Hungary as a whole toward the defense of the total Monarchy was established by negotiation between the Crown and the Hungarian Diet. A Dietal commission then determined the share of this burden to be paid by each county, city, and district in the country. However, the Dietal commission was guided in its allocation by tax assessment tables prepared and maintained by each jurisdiction's officials based on their locality's revenue-producing capacity.

Hence, the assessment of direct taxation was kept under the firm control of local officials in each of the country's jurisdictions. This was especially true of the country's fifty-two counties whose exclusively noble officials were elected by and responsible to the nobles resident therein. Experience had bred a deep distrust of the Habsburgs among these county nobles, and they not only kept a tight control over direct taxation, but repeatedly refused to grant "Vienna" a tax on the soil itself. Most notably, the Hungarian Law VIII of 1741 reiterated the tax-exempt status of the Hungarian nobles in their persons and possessions (i.e. their land), which, by definition, included their subject peasants' urbarial lands as well. This was the reason taxes were theoretically levied on the productivity of urbarial lots rather than on the lots themselves. Law VIII specified *ne onus publicum fundo quoquo modo inhaereat,* [32] and it certainly preserved the well-being of the nobles. But, to a degree and in a left-handed fashion, it sometimes helped the subject peasant as well. It historically provided him a latitude and variety of loopholes to escape what otherwise might have been a much more rigorous and onerous tax regime. Also, as the Law barred "Vienna's" direct taxation of Hungarian land, it gave the nobles some financial bargaining power vis-à-vis the dynasty. Hence, it preserved a vestige of real power to reinforce Hungary's *de jure* sovereignty. The dynasty, as we have seen, circumvented the situation by relying on indirect taxes.

In all events, the legal prohibition against the direct taxation of Hungarian land eliminated at one stroke the principal objective standard upon which tax tables might be based. This fact rendered the local tax tables all the more important, and susceptible to subterfuge if the local officials so desired. As Béla Grünwald remarks, in the absence of any objective standard or legal regulation, the discretionary power of Hungarian local officials over the assessment of the War Tax was enormous and "arbitrary." [33]

In point of fact, however, Hungary's local officials prepared the tax tables in an extremely detailed and even conscientious manner. They used calculating units of venerable origin known as the *nádor's portae* for geographic jurisdictions and the *dicae* for individuals. [34] The original intention of the noble officials was to assess the tax fairly on those subject to it, and this had logically required them to take into account the widely varying quality of ploughland, pasture, and livestock in diverse regions of the country. However, the resulting tax system was one which, by its very nature, required a regular updating of the tables. Perhaps

predictably, over the generations many anomalies had crept
into the tables—some undoubtedly, due to honest mistakes
and others quite likely by intentional oversight. After 1848, it
was discovered that both the extent of the peasants' urbarial
lots and many other types of land in peasant possession were
unrecorded in the tax tables. [35] This meant that a good
proportion of the peasants' production escaped state taxation, and that some peasants were paying more taxes and
others less, although they had virtually the same amount of
land under cultivation. Moreover, this under-registration
of the peasants' urbarial holdings carried through from the
War Tax to the House Tax since the same tax tables were
used to assess both forms of direct taxation.

Elek Fényes had a good sense of the various inequities
which abounded in the county tax tables of the 1840s. He notes
that some jurisdictions were taxed heavily while others got
off lightly. The Croatian counties and the Hungarian Littoral,
due to the poor quality of their agricultural land, were assessed at 135.6/8 *portae* compared to Inner Hungary's
6,210.3/8. [36] This appeared reasonable, but closer investigation indicated that the disparity was probably overly disproportionate in Croatia's favor. However, even Inner Hungary's rich counties which were comparable in area and natural wealth quite often assessed their urbarial peasants very
differently. Tolna County and Borsod County, for example,
were virtually equivalent in every respect in 1845. Each was
about 1378 English square miles in area. Tolna had 197,381
inhabitants and Borsod 199,135. Tolna had 711,070 *hold*
under cultivation followed closely by Borsod with 698,875. [37]
But, Tolna paid 89,696 forints in War Tax and 79,030 in
House Tax for a total burden in direct taxes of 168,726 forints,
while Borsod County paid 58,366 and 68,699 respectively
for a total of 127,065 forints in direct taxes. This was a 25
percent overall difference in favor of Borsod County, and
many of the comparative sums in the individual categories
of the assessment tables were even more disproportionately
in favor of the Borsod peasants. [38]

The tax tables in the country's Royal Free Cities were
also inequitable. This was largely a reflection of the cities'
unfortunate and basically unhealthy evolution over the

centuries, which requires special explanation. The royal charters which established these cities remained silent on the subject of their internal organization and governance. [39] Rather quickly, those among their largely German inhabitants, who possessed immovable property, reserved the rights of full citizenship, or burgher status, to themselves. Their descendants perpetuated and expanded this exclusive and even anti-national *Weltanschauung*. Some Royal Free Cities passed ordinances prohibiting Hungarians and other nationalities from holding public office or from acquiring burgher status altogether. [40] Certain cities had refused sanctuary to people fleeing the Turkish onslaught with the result that many peasants had preferred to settle in communities under the protection of noble landlords. [41] Conflicts between the Royal Free Cities' councils and resident Hungarian nobles over submission to municipal ordinances remained bitter until at least the end of the eighteenth century. Such conflicts were often settled in the nobles' favor, and, in many instances, the burghers tended to assimilate into the nobility rather than the reverse. [42]

The Hungarian nobles repaid the exclusiveness of the Royal Free Cities in similar coin. The nobles used their power in the Hungarian Diet to restrict the Royal Free Cities' representation in that body, and to prevent the issuance of new royal charters to other towns. [43] In choosing county seats, the nobles often ignored the Royal Free Cities in favor of less pretentious towns, and thereby denied the worthy burghers such economic activity as was generated by local government. The nobles sought, rather unsuccessfully, to bring the Royal Free Cities as corporate entities under the jurisdiction of county courts in cases where a burgher committed a crime within municipal boundaries against a noble or one of his servants. [44] Most importantly, the nobles nullified the Royal Free Cities' influence in national politics after 1687. The Royal Free Cities could continue to send delegates to the national Diet, but they were restricted to one collective vote. The cities responded by returning delegates who participated in the debates, but refused on principle to exercise their single vote until the upheaval of 1848. [45]

At the dawn of the nineteenth century, this whole unhappy situation was partially redeemed by the fact that Hungary's Royal Free Cities were experiencing their first real economic boom since the time of the Anjou Kings.[46] In reality, the cities were in the process of emerging from the economic disruption and realignment visited upon the country's economy by decades of Ottoman rule. However, the Hungarian cities were still not strong enough to exercise the social and economic influence of urban centers in Western Europe. In 1800, Hungary's fifty Royal Free Cities collectively mustered only 400,000 inhabitants, or 1/19th of the Kingdom's total population.[47] In other words, Hungary's unique historical development placed the issue of reform squarely in noble rather than burgher hands. It can certainly be argued that the burghers' hidebound outlook and guild monopolies worked more against than in favor of reform.

As can be inferred from the foregoing, the internal structure of Hungary's Royal Free Cities remained unchanged in the early nineteenth century. In all the cities, the burghers made up a mere fraction of the population. But they monopolized all political rights and most of the property. In Buda, in 1828, only 1,052 individuals enjoyed burgher status out of 11,411 inhabitants. In Debrecen, there were 1,228 burghers out of 11,986 residents. In Székesfehérvár, the figures were 930 to 1228.[48]

The Royal Free Cities' tax system reflected their undemocratic political structure quite accurately. In the mid-1840s, nationally, the well-off burghers paid only 25 percent of the fifty Royal Free Cities' collective House Tax. The urban populace at large paid the remaining 75 percent in the form of fees, tolls, and licenses levied upon it.[49] The Royal Free Cities, in these years, did contribute a healthy 2,185,466 forints out of the country's total annual House Tax of 5,453,121 forints. But this was still a relatively light tax in view of the Royal Free Cities' dramatically expanding commerce and manufacture.

The Hungarian reformers were aware of the inequities of the Royal Free Cities' tax structure, and cognizant of their increasing prosperity. The reformers wished to democratize the political and fiscal structure of these cities, and to integrate them in a comprehensive national tax reform.

But the reformers were faced, on one hand, with the obstinate self-interest of the burghers, and, on the other, with an acrimonious heritage of conflict between the cities and the nobles. Many nobles found it difficult to view the Royal Free Cities with anything but suspicion. They saw these ancient royal bastions as legally privileged enclaves, populated by a mixed bag of foreigners, whose first loyalty was to their own self-interest, and their second to "Vienna."

However, the most glaring inequity in all of Hungary's pre-1848 tax system was the continued immunity of the Hungarian nobles from any type of taxation on their persons or on their possessions. The inequity was especially striking because the nobles held almost 70 percent of the country's arable land in their own immediate (*allodial*) estates.[50] In round figures, these tax-exempt allodial properties came to roughly 32,000,000 *hold*.[51] This impressive statistic is, however, tempered by the fact that only 11,910,901 *hold* was actually cultivated as ploughland,[52] and much of this was in the hands of peasants (who, of course, paid no state taxes) under contractual agreement. Nevertheless, such an enormous national percentage of tax exempt arable land under the control of about 5 percent of the population (or 20 percent of the adult male heads of families) was an incalculable detriment to the future development of the country. This point was argued forcefully by at least one reformer.

Baron József Eötvös (using Elek Fényes' earlier 1842 statistics) wrote in 1846 that out of Inner Hungary's population of 11,184,288 inhabitants, 544,372 individuals, or about one in twenty, enjoyed noble status. "If we ask," he wrote, "what differentiates" the nobles from the non-nobles in Hungary, one answer could be found in the simple statement:

> All constitutional rights belong to the first class, and
> all obligations arising from the maintenance of
> public welfare pertain to the second. [53]

Eötvös also took pains to point out the harm visited upon Hungary by the fact that the nobles held such a large proportion of the country's arable land in their immediate estates on a tax exempt basis. It followed that virtually all of the

country's public necessities were derived from the productivity
of the subject peasants' urbarial lands. He wrote sarcastically:

> From the viewpoint of Natural Law, perhaps no
> one will be found to defend the nobility's tax im-
> munity, but if only someone in the middle of nine-
> teenth century would find it an unnatural situation
> when a country which covers 4,285 square miles
> /90,842 English square miles, since Eötvös, using
> Fényes 1842 figures for Inner Hungary's area, gave
> his figures in German Geographic square miles, one
> of which equals 21.2 English square miles/ only
> includes one-fourth of that to cover its necessities,
> that is to say, it hardly uses more than 1,000 square
> miles. This statement would not be any more
> reasonable than if someone were to announce that
> in all the Germanies, which cover 11,532 square
> miles, all necessities of every sort were to be covered
> by the 3,348 square miles of Prussia's German
> holdings.... [54]

Eötvös' arguments in favor of tax reform, together with
those of many other reformers, did, as shall be shown
presently, have a telling effect on noble opinion in Hungary.
However, it should be mentioned at this point, that the
nobles traditionally gave voluntary subsidies to the Crown. To
some degree, even these were wrung out of the taxpaying people, but they were usually expended on some project beneficial
to the nation. For example, on September 25, 1830, the newly
crowned King Ferdinand V of Hungary /Ferdinand I, as
Emperor of Austria/ directed that one-half of the 50,000
gold pieces presented to him by the Hungarian nobles be
used to relieve peasant distress in northern Hungary; the
other half of the sum was turned over to the Hungarian
Academy of Sciences. [55] Nor should the sacrifice which the
imposition of these subsidies caused, at least among the poorer
nobles, be discounted. [56]

However, the Hungarian nobles' traditional justification
for their tax exempt status on the grounds they paid for the
country's defense in their own blood was essentially outdated
in the eighteenth century by the creation of standing armies. [57]

This truth was only emphasized when the ill-prepared and badly armed Hungarian nobles broke before Napoleon's seasoned troops at Győr in 1807. [58] Yet, in the 1840s the Hungarian nobles still exercised the legal power to designate peasant recruits for the Hungarian regiments in the Habsburg army; this was certainly a necessary and useful *modus operandi*, and one which was fully in accord with national evolution and tradition, but its underlying principle was no longer just.

By the 1840s, the only possible justification for the Hungarian nobles (non-domestic) tax immunity was political, and lay in the peculiar nature of Hungary's relationship with the Habsburg dynasty. The astute English observer, John Paget, had no difficulty in understanding the situation in the mid-1830s. He wrote that he condemned the right of one class to enjoy the privilege of tax immunity at the expense of the rest of society. He especially condemned the failure of the nobles to pay the domestic House Tax. [59] Yet he also stated that the more progressive Hungarian nobles had:

> Some show of reason on their side when they declared that they will only yield up the privilege on obtaining a direct influence on the expenditure of revenue; in other words, a budget and a responsible ministry. [60]

In reality, by the 1840s the reforming nobles had managed to convince large and growing numbers of Hungarian nobles that the loss of their ancient right of tax immunity was an inevitable, and perhaps even a desirable necessity. In 1847 Elek Fényes reflected the temper of the times very well when he repeated what had become a standard phrase of the reformers:

> Our ancient explicit laws (Law LXIV of 1486, reinforced by Law LXVIII of 1659) direct every noble, be he lay lord, cleric, or whoever, to pay his share of those expenditures ordained by the country. [61]

In sum, Hungary's tax system still retained, as the reformers repeatedly stated, all the outmoded social inequities of earlier centuries. Equally important, the growing might of a modern Absolute State had succeeded in diverting the bulk of the country's revenues into the hands of an unresponsive and non-national Crown. The problem was not simply that the tax system abounded in anomalies and social inequities, but that so little of the revenue derived from it was spent for any direct benefit in Hungary.

In addition, compounding the fact that most Hungarian revenues went into the maw of a foreign bureaucracy was the further detriment that these revenues were collected and administered inefficiently. John Paget encountered widespread smuggling and a general evasion of the salt tax in Eastern Hungary. And he also discovered a notable lack of management and productivity on the Crown and Treasury Estates. Petty corruption and a disregard for the peasants' interests was common among these estate administrators. And the Viennese bureaucracy, to which they were responsible, actually viewed with suspicion and penalized any honest initiative on their part. [62] One certainly cannot discount the benefits which accrued to these delinquent officials or to those who evaded taxes. It is clear, however, that generations of tax evasion at all levels of Hungarian society fostered attitudes which would be injurious to the country should a more equitable and national tax system ever be enacted.

The Hungarian reformers, intent on modernizing their country with the creation of an efficient transport network and the eventual liberation of the peasantry, recognized that an indispensable first step toward these ends was the complete reformation of the existing tax system. And foremost on their tax reform agenda was the initial and crucial measure of inducing the nobility at large to relinquish its age-old right of tax immunity. The reformers' task in this regard was far from easy. Yet, the contemporary, Mihály Horváth, stated that no single book in Hungarian history could be compared to Count István Széchenyi's 1830 *Hitel* /Credit/ in the amount of controversy which it occasioned. [63] In it, Széchenyi had not presumed to instruct his fellow nobles on tax reform, nor, indeed, on any other specific measure to relieve Hungary's ills. But his brutal diagnosis of the country's condition had clearly wounded the Hungarian nobles' national pride in an unprecedented manner. His initial effort was soon followed by many others, and, as the incredulity which had met this first call for reform quickly melted away, the reformers made undeniable progress on the tax issue.

By the 1840s, due to the reformers' incessant effort, the concept of universal taxation was probably accepted, at least in theory, by a majority of the more influential nobles on the county level. Unfortunately, this statement is not suscept-ible to actual proof, since noble opinion on this as well as other reform issues was mercurial. It is certain, however, that the ranks of the Hungarian nobles who favored tax reform included conservatives who were outside the shifting Liberal coalition *per se*. [64] The situation, indeed, warrants a review, since it touches a wellspring of historic change.

In the early 1840s, the nobles of Csongrád County in central Hungary, were among the first to vote taxes on them-selves for domestic purposes. [65] In 1841, Borsod County, with a population of 30,000 nobles, saw its assembly vote enthusiastically in favor of universal taxation after hearing speeches by László Pálóczy and Bertalan Szemere explain-ing the necessity and justice of the measure. [66] In February, 1842, following months of vacillation, the nobles of Szatmár County definitively adopted the twelve "Szatmár County Points," the sixth of which was a resolution calling for the taxation of nobles throughout the country. The resolution advocated, "the revival and expansion of Mátyás' /Matthias Corvinus'/ Law of 1486 regarding the taxation of prelates, titled lords, and nobles." [67] In March, 1842, a meeting of the Bihar County assembly completely reversed its originally hostile attitude toward universal taxation following a mas-terful speech by Ödön Beőthy, a liberal noble. [68] An eminent conservative, Count Emil Dessewffy, announced in his book, *Alföldi levelek (1839-1840) és néhány toldalék (1841)* /Let-ters from the Lowlands (1839-1840) and a Few Additions (1841)/, published in 1842, that a national transport network for commerce should be funded by a system of indirect taxes applied to everyone without distinction. Furthermore, he concluded that the expenses of the Hungarian Government should be financed by a universal system of direct taxation to which it was only rational and just that the nobility be subject. [69] In a similar vein, in late 1844, several prominent nobles in Zala County, including the great Ferenc Deák, voluntarily added their names to the list of county taxpayers. [70] In 1847, Count Emil Dessewffy stated in the Upper House of the Hungarian Diet, just prior to its Christmas recess, that the nobles in almost every Hungarian county had for several years contributed large sums for county purposes. In Pozsony County, for example, the new county assembly hall had been paid for exclusively by a rate which the nobles voted on themselves. [71] In sum, the record on the tax issue reflects a good measure of credit on the Hungarian nobles. In Mihály Horváth's words: [72]

> Where the common nobility was not led down a false path by temptations, and where the question was decided by the more clearheaded part of the nobility, it can be said that everywhere the question of universal taxation for domestic purposes was accepted.

Nevertheless, such a fundamental issue involving material interests hardly proceeded toward victory in an orderly and amicable manner. It would be naive to believe that the Hungarian nobles of this era marched in patriotic lockstep toward the goal of reducing their own incomes. Moreover, the Habsburg Court and councillors, as Horváth's account makes clear, did everything in their power to impede the progressive movement in Hungary. "Vienna," never anxious to authorize reforms in Hungary in advance of the non-Hungarian Lands of the Monarchy, quite correctly sensed that the diminution of its own political power lay just beneath the surface of the Hungarian reform movement. Consequently, the Court used its extensive network of paid informants and agents of influence to obstruct, or at least divert, the Hungarian reformers. [73] The Court stirred up the disconsolate poor nobility, and enlisted the services of place-seekers in the Conservative Party to forestall or reverse the favorable decisions being taken in the counties on the question of universal taxation. In Szatmár County, the nobles'

initial 1841 endorsement of the progressive "Twelve Points"
was temporarily reversed due to the efforts of Bálint Uray,
who "could be called an adherent of the Court, rather than
of the Conservative Party." [74] In Fehér County, an especially
vehement opposition to reform was incited by Count Ödön
Zichy whom the Court later rewarded with appointment to
a government post. [75] The Court played on the natural
fears of the poor nobles faced with the loss of their tax immunity. They were plied with bribes and induced to stamp
about crucial sessions of the county assemblies shouting:
"we shall not be taxed." [76] It is well to remember, however,
that no one bribes where he can command, and these very
incidents of corruption are testimony to a vigorous, if class-
based, democracy in early nineteenth-century Hungary.

But the Court's tactics led to numerous political brawls
and not a few homicides which Mihály Horváth correctly
termed "scandalous." [77] As an example, when Zala County
held its elections for Dietal Delegates on April 4, 1843, in
Zalaegerszeg (a town of 3,944 souls), about 6,000 of the
county's 26,915 nobles [78] were present. Due to the large
crowd, the election speeches and the actual voting were held
in an open air assembly. Ferenc Deák described the scene
in a letter to Lajos Kossuth which he wrote from Zalaegerszeg
on that very day. "The entire intelligentsia," he declared,
"with very few exceptions" was in favor of a universal
tax. [79] The same was true, he stated, of the twenty to twenty-
four nobles who addressed the issue in their public speeches.
He even told Kossuth that a hundred more speakers could have
been produced to advocate tax reform.

There was, however, one exception among the speakers,
a county magistrate named György Forintos, who had appointed himself spokesman for the poor nobles. He must have
done his work well. As Deák described, the assembled nobles
listened to the pro-tax speakers quietly enough. But at the
conclusion of the meeting, in Deák's words, "the middling
nobles" defeated noble taxation with "one shout." [80] Deák
observed that the visible leaders of the opposition to tax reform
at the Zala County Assembly were György Forintos and one
other county official, as well as two officials who had lost
their offices. But as to "who the invisible ones were, God
only knows...." [81]

Deák, as well as other liberal spokesmen at the sessions of the assembly, had endured "numerous threats and injurious words." In Deák's case, however, the threats were carried out. Upon the dissolution of the assembly, a group of anti-tax nobles burnt down his home, and murdered one of his servants who attempted to stop the arson. Even before this, however, (as he stated in his letter to Kossuth) he had decided "for many reasons" to refuse election as one of Zala County's two Dietal Delegates. He urged Kossuth to "say as little as possible about me" in the event Zala's case was discussed in the newspapers. [82] He even rejected a subsequent second election to serve as Zala County's delegate, much to the ire of many liberals who had spent a good deal of money on his candidacy. [83] No one, then or since, has ever adequately explained Deák's mysterious decision. As a result of it, the liberal reformers were deprived of his incomparable leadership at the 1843-1844 Diet.

In April of 1843, it appeared as if "Vienna" had once again defused the Hungarian reform movement. This was especially the case in regard to the tax issue. In Mihály Horváth's words:

> The suicidal work was successful in a majority of the counties. The nobles' participation in domestic taxation was included in /the instructions of/ only nineteen of the country's fifty-two counties. [84]

At the opening of the Hungarian Diet on May 14, 1843, the liberal reformers were well aware that only a minority of Hungary's counties had issued positive instructions to their delegates on the tax question. But they were still hopeful that they might reverse the situation, even though they faced formidable odds. The historian, Ignác Acsády characterizes the prevailing mood:

> The Government now once again looked on the progressive pioneers with cold antipathy, and a majority in the Upper House supported its objective with servility, all of which caused a loud outcry, not only in the Lower House, and in the country at large, but also on the part of individual Magnates

> /in the Upper House/, who were castigated /in
> that House/ with a merciless rebuke....There were
> increasingly intense discussions on the preparation
> of questions, among them, on the obligation of
> the nobles to pay taxes....[85]

Lacking the votes to launch a fight on the floor of the Lower House, the reformers skillfully obtained the consent of both Houses for the appointment of a committee to investigate the question of how the country's public expenses could be met. The reformers then argued their case in committee so successfully that both Houses soon announced in favor of universal taxation in principle. Each House even "loudly proclaimed" that the nobles' tax immunity was "unjust."[86]

Following this auspicious beginning, the "Finance Committee," as everyone came to call it, reported, by a vote of twenty-nine to nineteen, in favor of a universal land tax to be assessed on noble and non-noble land holdings equally. Subsequently, on the day the Upper House formally voted to accept the committee's recommendation, Count István Széchenyi made his appearance on the floor of that body in formal dress to celebrate the inauguration of a new era.[87] He certainly viewed the decision as a national rather than a personal triumph. Yet he could take just pride in the result since he had worked tirelessly toward this end after the publication of *Hitel* in 1830. He had specifically called for universal taxation as early as 1833 in his book, *Stadium* (points VII and VIII),[88] and he had presented a proposal for a classless *"két garas"* (two cents) land tax in the very year the Diet was convoked.[89]

Next, the Diet's Finance Committee defeated by only fifteen votes a proposal that Hungary's first universal land tax replace the House Tax. In the ensuing debate, the liberal reformers argued that if the new universal land tax were imposed on top of the existing tax structure, it would constitute a crushing burden for many of the country's peasants.

Again, the liberal reformers were successful. The Delegates of the Lower House adopted their view almost unanimously. With only two counties' dissenting (Bács and Turócz), the

Lower House voted that Hungary's nobles should pay three-quarters, and those traditionally subject to taxation only one-quarter of the new land tax. This schedule was to last "only until the mutual bearing of burdens goes into effect completely." [90] The Diet clearly intended the new universal land tax as a first step in replacing the country's entire antiquated tax system with a modern schedule which would be blind to all the old social inequities and anomalies. At this point, all that appeared to remain was for the Finance Committee to work out the details of Hungary's first modern tax, and to report its recommendation to the whole Diet.

In the interim Széchenyi resolved to maintain support for the Diet's historic decision in the country at large. He left the Dietal city of Pozsony at the end of August, 1844, to speak in the assembly hall of Hungary's "leading county." He urged the nobles of Pest County to appoint their own finance committee, and to charge it with reporting its estimate of the amount of money which should be raised by the new tax. The Pest County Assembly followed Széchenyi's suggestion. It eventually settled on an annual minimum of 3,000,000 forints, if the new tax were to produce any appreciable benefit for the nation "in its present circumstances." [91] This Pest County resolution was then sent in the form of a circular letter to Hungary's other counties, and it evoked a great affirmative response. A majority of the counties sent supplementary instructions to their Dietal Delegates in Pozsony telling them to support the Pest County position.

This groundswell of positive opinion throughout the country had its effect, and the national Diet responded accordingly. The Lower House decided upon an annual imposition of 2,585,000 forints. It also decided that the noble landowners were to bear 75 percent of this sum, and that the remaining 25 percent was to be supplied by the urbarial peasants, the inhabitants of the Royal Free Districts, and the property owners of the Royal Free Cities. The authorization was for four years, with the resultant 10,340,000 forints to be spent on major public projects such as roads, waterways, and railroad construction. This was admittedly a modest beginning. But the Lower House looked on it as provisional "until the next Diet," [92] which would effect a complete renovation of the country's tax structure. The essential point was that the first crucial step had been taken toward noble taxation and the creation of a modern tax system.

At this juncture, with the Upper House on record as favoring universal taxation in principle, hardly anyone could have anticipated that the Magnates would reject the Lower House appropriation. One of the two Békés County Delegates reported back to his county assembly:

> There is scarcely anything left to decide, already everyone is figuring out the portion of the tax which will fall on him; our spirits leapt for joy within all of us; we saw the disintegration of a multitude of prejudices, the solution to complex ideas which had seemed (during the elections in the counties) to require the sacrifice of bloodshed, indeed, which had appeared to conceal within them our own demise; we believe that an irreversible step has been taken, and that, in a short time, Hungary's swamps should be drained, railroads should be running alongside our now bottomless roads, our waterways should bear ships laden with commerce; and, at last, having seen excellent foundations laid down for the melding together of Hungary's fragmented life, we should see our hopes and concepts take wing. [93]

These widely held expectations were completely shattered during the last weeks of the Diet. This was accomplished by a group of Magnates in the Upper House, who, as everyone realized, acted under the guidance and instruction of the King's councillors in Vienna. These Magnates, using the pretext that the nobles must be introduced to paying taxes gradually, persuaded the Upper House to recommend a reduction in the Lower House appropriation from 10,340,000 to 3,000,000 forints. the liberal reformers in the Lower House, led by Ödön Beöthy and others, quickly rallied the delegates against this intrusive tactic. [94] With the delegates of only five counties dissenting, the Lower House took the position that giving way on the amount of the appropriation would be disastrous. In the first place, it would establish a dangerous constitutional precedent. In the second place, the reduced amount would "completely disappear into the many categories of need" without producing any noticeable benefit.[95] The Government's adherents could then claim in the next Diet that universal taxation did not work. A leading liberal, Gábor Klauzál, presented the Lower House's position forcefully:

> There is no example among constitutional nations in which the Lower House's financial recommendations in respect to the amount are obstructed by the Upper House; and this is natural because the Government's men have the preponderant might in the Upper House; and to allow them the freedom to determine the amount of appropriations is the same as placing these in the hands of the Government.... If a million forints /the annual appropriation under the Magnates' proposal/ were to disappear without any outstanding result, we would be giving the Magnates ammunition to tell the perplexed poorer nobles: "See fellow countrymen, our position is correct; a million forints simply vanished in the hands of the middling nobles...." Therefore, we are not taking success home; soon enough, the result shall be a conviction taking root among the common people against the great injustice of bearing excessive burdens....[96]

During the last days of the Diet, neither House would give way on a matter of constitutional principle. Széchenyi worked frenetically to effect a compromise. He urged the Lower House to retreat for the sake of salvaging the Magnates' acceptance of universal taxation, and, along with it, the concept of a national treasury made responsible to the Diet, at least in matters of domestic taxation.[97] However, Széchenyi's last efforts at mediation failed at a Dietal session held on November 10, 1844. The Archduke Karl, acting for King Ferdinand V, personally conducted the formal dissolution of the Hungarian Diet three days later.[98]

"And thus," wrote Mihály Horváth, "the mutual bearing of burdens, which had been won in principle with so much difficulty, had to await the future once again."[99] A keenly disappointed Széchenyi expressed real bitterness over the actions of his peers in the Upper House on the tax issue. In a letter to his close friend, Baron Miklós Wesselényi, he stated:

> Never have Hungarians committed a greater crime than when the best of our blood threw away the victory which was in their hands. [100]

Hence, the Hungarian reformers came away from the Diet of 1843-1844 feeling disappointed and frustrated. [101] Not only had their tax initiative suffered defeat, but a series of other progressive proposals as well. They had failed in their objects of creating large-scale credit institutions, and of enacting legislation to facilitate the subject peasant's ability to redeem his land and services. [102] They had achieved an important symbolic victory in obtaining the Crown's sanction for Laws IV and V of 1844. The former specified that "any native born non-noble" could conduct his business affairs freely and acquire full ownership of noble properties. The latter stated that "any non-noble inhabitant of the country or its Attached Parts, either native born or naturalized," could be elected or appointed to any public office.[103] However, the immediate practical effect of this legislation was negligible. As Baron Eötvös wrote in 1846, "the situation of non-noble classes has not been changed very much by Laws 4 and 5 of the last Diet." [104] Above all, however, the reformers came back to the fact that a great opportunity to modernize the country had been lost with their defeat on the tax issue.

The reformers' defeat on the tax front certainly could not be attributed to a lack of effort on their part to win the nobility at large over to their viewpoint. The reformers used every argument and medium at their disposal to win public support for the measure. They especially appealed to the Hungarian nobles' national pride by constantly reiterating that legislative control of taxation and public expenditure was indispensable to such modern countries as England, France, and America. [105] These persuasive efforts were, in point of fact, largely successful. In the mid-1840s, virtually everyone in Hungarian public life at least paid lip service to the necessity for tax reform.

However, perhaps Hungary's liberal reformers did lack

the necessary dash of radicalism to realize their goal in the struggle over taxation. Moderation was actually a liberal attribute at the 1843-1844 Diet. Hungary's great reform figures—including Kossuth, so often viewed as a radical in Vienna and in Hungary itself—generally eschewed an attitude of *fiat justitia ruat caelum*. Their loyalty to the dynasty was more than professed, and they feared rather than incited *ultima ratio regum*.

And if the Hungarian liberal reformers were essentially moderate men, the Hungarian nobility at large can be charged with both a tendency to retain its priviliges, and with an innate conservatism—assuming the last is, indeed, an intrinsic fault. It is true that, throughout this era, the Hungarian nobility as a class exhibited a predilection to debate reform issues in a lively fashion, but was extremely cautious when actually putting reforms into effect.

Nevertheless, as this account has described, the record indicates that the Hungarian nobles in the 1840s did mount the political courage, unity, and will, both on the local and national levels, to begin to disestablish their own privileges. They did, indeed, take the first step to install a modern tax system designed to benefit the entire country. The principal reason for the failure of this initiative at the 1843-1844 Diet appears to have been "Vienna's" obstruction. Contemporaries believed that the Upper House played out its destructive role with no little parliamentary adroitness solely at the instigation of the Crown. The Habsburgs clearly viewed Hungary's growing movement to take control of its own finances as anathema.

In other words, the initial success and ultimate defeat of tax reform at the Hungarian Diet of 1843-1844 signified more than a clash of economic class interest. The debate over tax reform at this Diet went beyond a consideration of such important and pressing matters as noble taxation, schedules, appropriations, and plans to improve the country's transport system or to finance peasant liberation. The struggle over tax reform in the 1843-1844 Diet actually revealed the fundamental political issue of the era. Was Hungary to be governed by a near-absolute monarch and his dutiful bureaucracy? Or was the country to inaugurate a representative and responsible parliamentary form of government which would devote more of the nation's resources to its own benefit? The latter development may have appeared to be an impossibility to many in 1844, but in 1867, Hungary accomplished the feat while remaining—by its own Laws— loyal to the Monarchy as a whole.

In sum, at the Hungarian Diet of 1843-1844, it was "Vienna's" bedrock refusal to relinquish its cardinal power of *de facto* control over the assessment and expenditure of most Hungarian revenues which foreshadowed the final strain and ultimate break between Crown and nation at the end of 1848. A modicum of sincere cooperation from the Crown on the Hungarian tax issue in 1844 might conceivably have avoided much of the dislocation and suffering visited upon Hungary in 1848-1849. Unfortunately for all concerned, the central policy-making councils in Vienna in 1844 were notably lacking in any disposition to accommodate necessary change. The Archduke Ludwig, Prince Clemens Metternich, and Count Francis Anton Kolowrat-Liebsteinsky simply continued perpetuating the policy of immobility perfected by the late monarch, Francis I (II). [106] In the words of Ignác Acsády:

> The Court was naturally not opposed to /Hungarian/ noble taxation, for this would have considerably increased its revenues, which up to now, it had spent without conditions. But, on the other hand, it flatly refused that which the Diet absolutely stipulated, that is, that the Diet should receive a regular report on financial affairs, and that Hungarian public revenues should be placed under the control of the legislature. It was on this reef that universal taxation in any form was to suffer shipwreck. [107]

Hence, "Vienna's" primary motivation in opposing tax reform in Hungary sprang from an almost instinctive concern to maintain its absolute political power, and to thereby preserve, according to its light, the stability and unity of the total Monarchy. There was, however, an allied fear to which not even all Hungarian reformers (Széchenyi was a prime example) [108] were totally immune. A truly modern system of universal taxation, with corresponding political rights for those who were taxed, was an unknown quantity in Hungary, just as it was in most of central and eastern Europe. It constituted another step toward a more popular form of government, the fear of which, if exaggerated, was quite real to the many intelligent people throughout Europe who held it.

On the other side of the coin, there were those who held fast (despite the experiences of the great French Revolution) to the faith that the masses possessed some ability to participate in government. In the Hungarian context, such believers repeatedly referred to the desirability of tax reform on social as well as material grounds. Their faith in the potent symbolic value of universal taxation, and in the extension of equal political rights in general, approached the sacred. The copious writings and statements of Hungary's liberal reformers repeatedly refer to a system of universal taxation and to the extension of mutual rights as a means of drawing the nation's disparate classes together. Ferenc Deák told his fellow delegates in the Hungarian Diet on May 20, 1835, that it was high time they granted landownership to the people, and thereby "draw them at least a little bit closer to us." [109] Lajos Kossuth thought that the whole Hungarian people would be raised up as a nation if privileges were converted into freedoms, and "the bearing of public burdens should become a common obligation." [110] Bertalan Szemere announced in the Hungarian Diet on November 29, 1847, that the enactment of general taxation was the first letter of all reform, and that "the day the common bearing of burdens is announced and put into effect shall be the day Hungary is founded for a second time." [111]

Subsequently, as Interior Minister in Hungary's first truly modern Government, Szemere was in large measure actually responsible for realizing what he had so ardently advocated. Yet his faith in the efficacy of reform remained intact, if somewhat tempered. He acted in the spirit exemplified by Hungary's first responsible Prime Minister, Count Lajos Batthyány, who wrote on March 23, 1848, that, with the sanction of the liberation laws, "the last traces of what has caused jealousy, inequality, and anger among the inhabitants of the country shall dissolve." [112] On April 19, 1848, Szemere directed an official circular letter to all Hungary's local government authorities which began:

> Our Constitution has been built on a completely new basis and out of completely new elements by the 1848 Laws. The feudal order has been exchanged for popular representation, privileges have been replaced by law, the differences between the classes have been replaced by equality, arbitrariness has been replaced by responsibility, and this fundamental reformation is already making itself felt in our social relationships. [113]

In regard to the introduction of general taxation, Szemere instructed the local authorities to keep "a watchful eye" on the nobles to see they did not resist it. It was these authorities' "duty and glory to make the noble class friendly toward this new order of law."[114] The authorities were to convince the nobles at large that "when the nobility participates in bearing the mutual burdens, the general wealth shall increase, and the noble himself shall profit as well."[115] Szemere also ordered the local authorities to "explain clearly" to the common people that their debts were abolished only in regard to urbarial obligations, and that all their other obligations, especially the payment of taxes, were still valid and binding. It was even the authorities' "duty" to make sure the peasant paid all his debts "promptly," since he could not improve himself if he remained in arrears. [116]

Perhaps it is best to close at this point and on this practical note, since the prospects for the peaceful development of tax reform in Hungary were soon subordinated to the demands placed on the Hungarian Government by a devastating war. But the Hungarian reformers' real faith in the symbolic social efficacy of tax reform was probably not altogether misplaced or naive. The always astute and brilliant contemporary, Mihály Horváth, captured, in a phrase, the Hungarian reformers' optimism about the inauguration of general taxation as a legal principle. He stated that the Hungarian Reform Party wanted mutual taxation, not simply out of a desire for justice toward the traditionally taxed common people, but even more:

> As the most powerful instrument with which to meld our nation's distinct classes together in interests, to equalize them in their rights and burdens; in a word, as a step toward the principle of democracy.[117]

Notes

1. The problem was a major one. See, for example, a quote from an article in an 1842 issue of *Magyar Gazda* in Gyula Mérei, *Mezőgazdaság és agrártársadalom Magyarországon 1790-1848* /Agriculture and Agricultural Society in Hungary, 1790-1848/ (Budapest: László Kenyeres, 1948), p. 33.

2. Elek Fényes, *Magyarország leirása* /Hungary's Description/, 2 parts in one vol. (Pest: Beimel, 1847), I, 102.

3. More specifically, in 1845, Hungary (without Transylvania and the Military Borders) exported 148,649.25 short tons of wheat, 58,149 of rye, 48,321.72 of oats, and 22,507 of barley. Corn and buckwheat exports are not given. The short tons (1=2000 lbs.) have been derived from the original mázsa (1 = 123.48 lbs.), and to derive hectoliters from short tons, one must multiply by 9.09. For the original figures, see *ibid.*, pp. 51, 95-96.

4. *Ibid.*, p. 94.

5. *Ibid.*, p. 97.

6. *Ibid.*, p. 98; Manó Kónyi, ed., *Deák Ferencz beszédei* /Ferencz Deák's Speeches/, 6 vols. (Budapest: Franklin-Társulat, 1882-1898), I, 529-530.

7. Fényes, *Magyarország leírása*, I, 99.

8. *Ibid.*, p. 92.

9. For example, Lajos Kossuth, in a letter to Baron Miklós Wesselényi on May 27, 1846, proposed a plan for peasant liberation which he soon made public. He set the landlord's compensation at four hundred forints per urbarial *telek* (subject peasant lot), and he estimated the minimum sum necessary for the whole country at 120 million forints. He thought that one-half of this sum could be paid to the landlords immediately by the state on the basis of a loan secured with tax-backing. He suggested that the other half of the sum be paid by the former subject peasants themselves on a ten to twelve year schedule. Kossuth stated that universal taxation was necessary if the state were to be able to carry out such a large scale financial operation. Cf. Ignác Acsády, *A magyar jobbágyság története* /The History of Hungarian Serfdom/, 2d. ed. (Budapest: Imre Faust, 1944), pp. 516-517. See also a wide-ranging discussion of the problem by an intelligent conservative. Among other things, he compares the Hungarian situation with the use of the state treasury to effect peasant liberation in 1836 in the Kingdom of Württemberg. Cf. Gróf Emil Dessewffy, *Alföldi levelek (1839-1840) és néhány toldalék (1841)* /Letters from

the Lowland: (1839-1840) and a Few Additions (1841)/ (Budapest: Magyar Királyi Egyetem, 1842), pp. 61-75. Acsády notes that all the Hungarian plans for peasant liberation reject the notion of turning the peasant into a tenant farmer as in Ireland or Northern Italy. The Hungarian reformers wanted to make the formerly subject peasant the full legal owner of his land. *A magyar jobbágyság*, p. 518.

10. István Deák, *The Lawful Revolution: Louis Kossuth and the Hungarians 1848-1849* (New York: Columbia University Press, 1979), p. 48.

11. Austria, k.k. Direktion der administrativen Statistik, *Tafeln zur Statistik der österreichischen Monarchie für die Jahre 1845 and 1846*, Erster Teil (Vienna: Aus der kaiserlich-königlichen Hof- und Staatsdruckerei, 1850), Tables 1-4; also, *Tafeln zur Statistik der österreichischen Monarchie für die Jahre 1845 und 1846*, Zweiter Teil (Vienna: Aus der kaiserlich- und königlichen Hof- und Staatsdruckerei, 1851), b. *Statistische Übersicht von Ungarn für das Jahre 1845.* Table 27.

12. "Hungary" as used here includes Croatia-Slavonia, Transylvania, and the Military Borders, *Tafeln zur Statistik der österreichischen Monarchie*, Zweiter Teil, Table 1 (subsection on "Grains," as well as other subsections on livestock, tobacco, etc.) and table 30.

13. Béla K. Király, *Hungary in the Late Eighteenth Century: The Decline of Enlightened Despotism* (New York: Columbia University Press, 1969), pp. 99-102; István Nagy, *A magyar kamara 1686-1848* /The Hungarian Treasury, 1686-1848/ (Budapest: Akadémiai Kiadó, 1971), pp. 346-353.

14. Charles d'Eszláry. *Histoire des institutions publiques hongroises*, 3. vols. (Paris: Librairie Marcel Rivière et Cie, 1959-1965), II, 143.

15. C. A. Macartney, *The Habsburg Empire 1790-1918* (New York: Macmillan, 1969), pp. 28 and n. 4, 29, 203.

16. In 1846, Inner Hungary had 3,736,080 inhabitants living in communities above 2000 in population, and 7,263,920 in communities below 2000. In most of the Hereditary Lands the proportions were actually about the same. But there were exceptions. In Lower Austria the figures were 552,623 and 94,776 respectively; in Lombardy 1,283,432 to 1,387,401; in Venetia 1,753,797 to 521,403. Cf. *Tafeln zur Statistik der österreichischen Monarchie für die Jahre 1845 und 1846*, Erster Teil (Vienna: 1850), Table 2, p. 29.

17. Macartney, *Habsburg Empire*, pp. 43-44, 274-275.

18. Fényes, *Magyarország leirása*, 1, 161-162.

19. *Ibid.*, pp. 159-160.

20. Béla Grünwald, *A régi Magyarország 1711-1825* /Hungary of Old, 1711-1825/, 3d ed. (Budapest: Franklin-Társulat, 1910), pp. 215-216, 242.

21. A quarter-lot subject peasant family in Hatvan paid only 2.60 forints in House Tax per annum, while it expended the equivalent of 3.12 forints on medicine, 4.16 forints for the maintenance of the priest and church, 2.34 forints in school fees, and no less than 44.75 forints at local fairs, in the local pub, and for pipes and tobacco. Cf. F. Le Play, *Les ouvriers de l'orient et leurs essaims de la méditerrannée: populations, soumises à la tradition, dont le bien-être se conserve sour trois influences dominantes: le décalogue éternel, la famille patriarcale et les productions spontanées du sol, Vol. II: Les ouvriers européens*, 6 vols.; 2d ed. (Tour: Alfred Mame et fils, 1855-1878), II, pp. 292-293.

22. Grünwald, *A régi Magyarország*, p. 242.

23. Bálint Hóman and Gyula Szekfű, *Magyar történet* /Hungarian History/, 5 vols., 7th ed. (Budapest: Királyi Magyar Egyetemi Nyomda, 1941-1943), V, 254.

24. *Ibid.*, p. 237.

25. The greatest number of civil cases in the large patrimonial court maintain-

ed by the Károlyi family dealt with indebtedness, and second came probate. The greatest number of criminal cases, by far, involved theft, most usually of livestock. Cases dealing with murder, assault and battery, adultery or perjury were rare. Cf. Ágnes Kovács, "A földesúri joghatóság érvényesülésének néhány kérdése a Csongrád-vásárhelyi uradalomban a 18-19. sz. fordulóján" /A Few Questions Concerning the Application of Seignorial Jurisdictional Privileges in a Latifundium in Csongrád-Vásárhely at the Turn of the 18th-19th Centuries/, in *Mezővárosok* /Oppida/, vol. II of *Paraszti társadalom és műveltség a 18-20. században* /Peasant Society and Culture in the 18th-20th Centuries/, 4 vols. (Budapest: Magyar Néprajzi Társulat, 1974), p. 60.

26. Fényes, *Magyarország leirása*, I, 159n.

27. Mérei, *Mezőgazdaság és agrártársadalom Magyarországon*, pp. 144-145. In the 1820s, the number of domestic disturbances in Hungary's rural communities decreased markedly. This was so because, in the agricultural depression occasioned by the end of the Napoleonic Wars, the conflicts between landlords and peasants over labor and land lessened. Cf. János Varga, *A jobbágyi földbirtoklás típusai és problémái 1767-1849* /The Types and Problems of Serf Land-ownership, 1767-1849/ (Budapest: Akadémiai Kiadó, 1967), pp. 27-28. Also, Hungary's traditional system of compulsory agricultural labor (*robot*) was very inefficient, and one suspects that even unscrupulous landlords who had extracted *robot* illegally found that the practice did not increase their production for a commercial market significantly.

28. For information on the *deperdita*, see Fényes, *Magyarország leirása*, I, 159-160, n.; Grünwald, *A régi Magyarország*, p. 243; d'Eszlary, *Histoire des institutions publiques hongroises*, III, 168; Király, *Hungary in the Late Eighteenth Century*, p. 104; Henry Marczali, *Hungary in the Eighteenth Century* (New York: The New York Times, 1971), pp. 137-138; Erik Molnár, ed., *Magyarország története*, 2 vols., 3d ed. (Budapest: Gondolat Könyvkiadó, 1971), I, 432; Mérei, *Mezőgazdaság és agrártársadalom*, pp. 148-149.

29. See, for example, Baron József Eötvös' devastating critique of Hungary's tax system. Cf. his *Reform*, 2d ed. (Pest: Mór Ráth, 1868), pp. 75-106; and *Deák Ferencz beszédei*, I, 392.

30. Hóman and Szekfű, *Magyar történet*, V, 254.

31. Varga, *A jobbágyi földbirtoklás típusai és problémái*, pp. 14, 16-17, 25-27; Mérei, *Mezőgazdaság és agrártársadalom*, p. 150; István Szabó, *Tanulmányok a magyar parasztság történetéből* /Studies Concerning the History of Peasantry/ (Budapest: László Kenyeres, 1948), pp. 375-376.

32. Hóman and Szekfű, *Magyar történet*, IV, 359.

33. Grünwald, *A régi Magyarország*, p. 244; see also, Mérei, *Mezőgazdaság és agrártársadalom*, pp. 150-151.

34. The *portae* were originally gates to peasant farmyards. Cf. *Ibid.*, pp. 234-235.

35. János Varga estimates that at the time of the 1848 liberation, the Hungarian peasants had 1,871,000 *hold* (2,006,647.5 English acres) of hidden urbarial ploughland, which was 15.29 percent of the total 12,233,000 *hold* (13,119,892 acres) of the urbarial ploughland in their possession. Cf. his *A jobbágyfelszabadítás kivívása 1848-ban* /The Struggle for Serf Emancipation in 1848/ (Budapest: Akadémiai Kiadó, 1971), p. 342. See also his *A jobbágyi földbirtoklás típusai és problémái*, pp. 20-21, 31, 35-36. In addition, although it is virtually impossible to determine the amount, the Hungarian peasants had possession of portions of the landlords' immediate estates under various contractual agreements. Cf. Szabó, *Tanulmányok*, pp. 334.

36. Fényes, *Magyarország leirása*, I, 158.

37. *Ibid.*, II, 42, 47, 242, 246.

38. *Ibid.*, I, 158.

39. d'Eszlary, *Histoire des institutions publiques hongroises*, I, 271-280.

40. *Ibid.*, II, 249.

41. *Ibid.*, II, 249; III, 308.

42. Hóman and Szekfű, *Magyar történet*, V, 243.

43. d'Eszlary, *Histoire des institutions publiques hongroises*, II, 251; III, 217-218.

44. Hóman and Szekfű, *Magyar történet*, III, 556-557.

45. *Ibid.*, V, 556.

46. d'Eszlary, *Histoire des institutions publiques hongroises*, II, 248.

47. Hóman and Szekfű, *Magyar történet*, V, 242.

48. *Ibid.*

49. Fényes, *Magyarország leirása*, I, 159-160.

50. György Spira, *A magyar forradalom 1848-1849-ben* /The Hungarian Revolution in 1848-1849/ (Budapest: Gondolat, 1959), p. 137; Gyula Mérei and György Spira, eds., *Magyarország története 1790-1848: A feudalizmusról a kapitalizmusra való átmenet korszaka* /The History of Hungary 1790-1848: The Period of the Transition from Feudalism to Capitalism/ (Budapest: Tankönyvkiadó, 1961), p. 411.

51. Acsády, *A magyar jobbágyság*, p. 535.

52. Specifically, 9,406,219 *hold* in grain-producing ploughland, and 2,504,682 *hold* planted in fodder crops; the nobles also had 980,853 *hold* in vineyards; these estimates are for Hungary without the Partium, Transylvania, and the Military Borders. Cf. Fényes, *Magyarország leirása*, I, 6-7, 161, n.

53. Eötvös, *Reform*, p. 6.

54. *Ibid.*, p. 79.

55. Mihály Horváth, *Huszonöt év Magyarország történelméből 1823-1848* /Twenty-Five Years from Hungary's History, 1823-1848/, 3 vols., 3 ed. (Budapest: Mór Ráth, 1886), I, 238.

56. John Paget, *Hungary and Transylvania with Remarks on their Condition, Social, Political and Economical*, 2 vols., New London Edition (Philadelphia: Lea and Blanchard, 1850), II, 263.

57. The Hungarian Law VIII of 1715 authorized the funding for Hungarian regiments in the Imperial Habsburg Army. It also emphasized the Hungarian nobility's traditional obligation to arm itself at its own expense and take the field under the command of the King for the defense of the country. However, the nobility's participation in military exercises remained theoretical until the Napoleonic Wars, when it did take the field on four occasions - 1797, 1800, 1805 and 1809. Cf. d'Eszlary, *Histoire des institutions publiques hongroises*, III, 155-156, 174-175.

58. *Ibid.*, p. 176.

59. Paget, *Hungary and Transylvania*, I, 324.

60. *Ibid.*, pp. 242-243.

61. Fényes, *Magyarország leirása*, I, 159; see also Eötvös, *Reform*, pp. 85-96.

62. Paget, *Hungary and Transylvania*, II, 57-59, 171-172, 217-218.

63. Horváth, *Huszonöt év*, I, 213.

64. *Ibid.*, II, 345.

65. Hóman and Szekfű, *Magyar történet*, V, 322.

66. Horváth, *Huszonöt év*, III, 346-347.

67. *Ibid.*, II, 330.

68. *Ibid.*, p. 349.

69. Dessewffy, *Alföldi levelek*, pp. 219-243, especially pp. 228-233.

70. Béla K. Király, *Ferenc Deák*, (Boston: Twayne, 1975), p. 105.

71. Edsel Walter Stroup, *Hungary in Early 1848: The Constitutional Struggle against Absolutism in Contemporary Eyes* /State University of New York College at Buffalo's Program in East European and Slavic Studies Publication, Number 11/ (Buffalo, New York-Atlanta, Georgia: Hungarian Cultural Foundation, 1977), p. 54 and ns. 1, 2.

72. Horváth, *Huszonöt év*, II, 348-349.

73. It is true, however, that the Secret Police were less onerous in Hungary than in the Austrian Lands. Cf. Macartney, *Habsburg Empire*, pp. 163-165, 210-211, 296.

74. Horváth, *Huszonöt év*, II, 348.

75. *Ibid.*

76. *Ibid.*, p. 349.

77. *Ibid.*, p. 347.

78. Fényes, *Magyarország leírása*, II, 85, 89.

79. *Deák Ferencz beszédei*, II, 485.

80. *Ibid.*

81. *Ibid.*

82. *Ibid.*, p. 486.

83. Király, *Ferenc Deák*, p. 95.

84. Horváth, *Huszonöt év*, II, 350.

85. Acsády, *A magyar jobbágyság*, p. 510.

86. Horváth, *Huszonöt év*, II, 444.

87. *Ibid.*

88. Gyula Szekfű, ed., *A mai Széchenyi. Eredeti szövegek Széchenyi István munkáiból* /Today's Széchenyi. Original Sections of István Széchenyi's Works/ (n.p.: A Magyar Kulturális Egyesületek Szövetsége, 1935), p. 243.

89. *Ibid.*, p. 348; Horváth, *Huszonöt év*, II, 352, 353.

90. Horváth, *Huszonöt év*, II, 344.

91. *Ibid.*, p. 445.

92. *Ibid.*

93. *Ibid.*, pp. 445-446.

94. Hóman and Szekfű, *Magyar történet*, V, 331.

95. Horváth, *Huszonöt év*, II, 446.

96. *Ibid.*, p. 447.

97. *Ibid.*

98. *Ibid.*, p. 460.

99. *Ibid.*, p. 447.

100. Hóman and Szekfű, *Magyar történet*, V, 331.

101. Acsády, *A magyar jobbágyság*, p. 511.

102. Horváth, *Huszonöt év*, II, 266.

103. Acsády, *A magyar jobbágyság*, p. 511.

104. Eötvös, *Reform*, p. 8.

105. Horváth, *Huszonöt év*, II, 341-343.

106. Macartney, *Habsburg Empire*, pp. 235-239.

107. Acsády, *A magyar jobbágyság*, p. 510.

108. George Barany, *Stephen Széchenyi and the Awakening of Hungarian Nationalism, 1791-1841* (Princeton, New Jersey: Princeton University Press, 1968), pp. 131-133., 174, 240, 402, 460.

109. Acsády, *A magyar jobbágyság*, p. 499.

110. *Ibid.*, p. 507.

111. *Ibid.*, p. 530.

112. Győző Ember, ed., *Iratok az 1848-i magyarországi parasztmozgalmak történetéhez* /Documents Concerning the History of Hungarian Peasant Movements/ (Budapest: Közoktatásügyi Kiadóvállalat, 1951), p. 252.

113. *Ibid.*, p. 253.

114. *Ibid.*, p. 254.

115. *Ibid.*

116. *Ibid.*, p. 255.

117. Horváth, *Huszonöt év*, II, 443.

IV.

FROM TRIANON TO WORLD WAR II

Sándor Szilassy:

13 / HUNGARY'S ROAD TO TRIANON

The Treaty of Trianon. [1] signed on June 4, 1920, was more punitive than most treaties which follow lost wars. It separated over 3,000,000 ethnic Hungarians from the mother country together with 71.4 per cent of her territory and 61 percent of the total population. Trianon also forced Hungary to officially recognize the Successor States, which were established on the ruins of the Austro-Hungarian Monarchy.

According to the data of Oscar Jászi, in round numbers 5,500,000 people were liberated and 4,500,000 became irredentists as the result of the treaty. [2] Jászi's figures are rather conservative, since he had not considered those who, for the sake of jockying for positions in non-Magyar areas of Hungary, started to call themselves Romanian, Slovak or South Slav well before the end of World War I, although their mother tongue was Hungarian.

The wishes of the population regarding ethnic and territorial affiliation could have been best determined by plebiscite, to be held in overwhelmingly Hungarian or ethnically mixed areas, but this was opposed by the Successor States, and the Allies in Paris relied on the *fait accompli* resulting from the military occupation of the territories in question.

In attempting to analyze the reasons for the severe provisions of the peace treaty, first of all the geographic location of the country should be mentioned. It resulted in many historical catastrophies. For over ten centuries the fertile basin surrounded by the Carpathian mountains was known as Hungary. It proved to be one of the major crossroads of Europe. One enemy invasion followed another, the most destructive of which were the Mongol invasion in 1241 and the

Turkish occupation of approximately two-thirds of the country, which lasted from 1526 to 1699.

It has been estimated that before the Turkish invasion about 80 percent of the country's population had been Hungarian. Four centuries later, according to the 1910 census report, the majority was non-Magyar, if we consider Croatia too, which was an autonomous part of Hungary for eight centuries.

Without the Croatians, in round numbers 54% declared themselves Hungarian, 15% Romanian, 10% Slovak, 10% German, 2.5% Ruthenian, and 2.5% Serbian. The leaders of the nationalities frequently referred to the fact that in 1869 only 45% of the population was Hungarian; accordingly, almost 10% of the ethnic groups were absorbed by Magyarization in four decades.

During this period the number of Hungarians increased from 6 to 10 million. The Romanian population had grown by half a million, the Germans and Slovaks each by 100,000, and the number of Ruthenians decreased from 469,000 to 464,000. This decline, however, was not only the result of the Magyarization process (voluntary or otherwise), but also of the mass emigration, which hit the Germans, Slovaks, and the Ruthenians especially hard. Thus, in the four decades before World War I, 20.2% of the Slovaks, 11.6% of the Ruthenians, and 11.5% of the Germans emigrated to America, and did so almost exclusively for economic reasons. [3]

In assessing this population change, one also has to take into consideration the fact that in 1910 five per cent of Hungary's population were Jews (i.e. 900,000), and that an overwhelming majority of these have by this time become conscious Hungarians.

It is almost evident that the absorption of the nationalities was the direct result of compulsory education, opportunism, political developments following the Austro-Hungarian Compromise of 1867, urbanization, and administrative pressure. The frequently undemocratic handling of the ethnic question was also an outgrowth of the anti-Habsburg revolt of 1848-49, during which the imperial government attempted to use the nationalities against the revolutionary regime.

Historical wounds heal slowly and upset the balance of public opinion. The idea of national unity, prevalent throughout the entire continent, also was in the way of ethnic equality.

Baron József Eötvös drafted a bill jointly with Ferenc Deák — the father of the Austro-Hungarian Compromise of 1867 — which regulated the status of the nationalities. It was passed by Parliament in 1868. The law granted far-reaching rights to all national minorities, but it was not consistently implemented. Rampant and intolerant nationalism on the part of the most militant organizations of the nationalities was another obstacle.

For such reasons, the theoretically liberal Hungarian governments which followed each other in short sequence after 1867 were generally opposed to universal franchise and secret vote. Prime Minister Count István Tisza declared in the upper house of Parliament on January 14, 1910: "I cannot imagine any universal suffrage which would not lead the nation to destruction". In June, 1917, he criticized the franchise proposal of the new Prime Minister (Count Móric Esterházy), declaring the 24-year age limit "too low" and opposing the extension of voting rights to those who received the Charles-Cross for meritorious service in the war. Again, he equated the franchise with endangering of the existence of the Hungarian nation. [4]

In 1910 only seven per cent of the adult population were eligible for voting in Hungary. [5] The lack of suffrage based on proportional representation alienated even otherwise pro-Hungarian ethnic leaders.

Croat historians deem that Hungarians and Croatians coexisted quite peacefully until the Hungarian Diet (Parliament) in 1844 changed the language of deliberations from Latin to Hungarian, which representatives of the ethnic districts did not speak. [6] This resulted in a chain reaction among the nationalities, who began to demand similar linguistic privileges and autonomy. Because of the sharpening differences between Hungarians and their national minorities, Russia could pose as a defender of Slavs in Austria-Hungary. Pan-Slavism, on the other hand, increased the dependence of the Vienna government on Germany, even though it was well known that Berlin also had far-reaching plans in East Central Europe.

Some episodes of post-revolutionary Hungarian history

prove that well before 1918 the political situation was ready for a major explosion. Magyar-Croat relations had worsened since the romantic, nationalistic Illyrian Movement headed by Ludevit Gaj received official assistance from Vienna. (Gaj claimed that the Croatians were direct descendants of the ancient Illyrians of the time of the Roman Empire.) During the 1848-49 revolution, Croatian troops under Baron Joseph Jellǎsić entered Hungary to overthrow the revolutionary regime. The Zagreb provincial assembly disassociated Croatia from Hungary in 1861, recognizing only the common ruler. The Romanians were even more active in their demands for recognition. Their representatives delivered a memorandum to Vienna in 1892, listing complaints about Magyarization and oppression. Later Romanian youth leaders, replying to a proclamation of Hungarian students, openly declared in their "Replica" that they would rather live in a Romanian state. Those sentenced to prison terms in the so-called "memorandum and replica trials" (1894) later were granted amnesty, but the criminal procedures turned an influential segment of international public opinion against Hungary. Some of the leading intellectuals and politicians of Europe, including Tolstoy and Clemenceau, sharply criticized Hungarian policies. Menotti Garibaldi, whose father — Giuseppe Garibaldi — had supported the Hungarian fight for freedom in the mid-19th century, also lodged a protest against "the oppression of three million fraternal Romanians in Transylvania." [7] Professor R. W. Seton-Watson personally observed the elections in Hungary and became convinced that the Hungarians oppressed their nationalities. [8] In a letter that he wrote to Oscar Jászi on November 20, 1919, the influential Scottish historian remarked that he remained the enemy of the Hungarian oligarchy "which no less is responsible for the war than Berlin itself." [9]

Anti-Hungarian sentiments in Western Europe had another source: the backwardness of social conditions in Hungary. Socialism had begun to take root at the end of the 19th century. It had won over a segment of the bureaucracy and many of the industrial workers in Budapest and other cities. Trade unions were banned in rural areas, where the only safety valve for easing poverty and social tension was emigration to America. Between 1871 and 1914 about 1.7

million Hungarian citizens settled in the United States, of whom perhaps 650,000 were Hungarians (i.e. Magyars). According to the census of 1920, almost 500,000 Americans declared Magyar as their native tongue. [10]   Prior to World War I, instead of a more favorable distribution of national income, the issues of civil versus church marriage and divorce, and parliamentary obstruction to the funding of the needs of the generally unpopular Austro-Hungarian Army occupied the lawmakers in Budapest. (Many Hungarians had been opposed to the language of command, which was German.) The Catholic Church, one of the biggest landowners of the country, paid scant attention to the 1891 *Rerum Novarum* encyclical of Pope Leo XIII, which attempted to analyze and heal social and economic ills. About half of the cultivable land was in the hands of large landowners.

After nearly eight decades, it is easy to say that Austrian and Hungarian statesmen should have avoided a war even at the price of great sacrifices. The dualist system was a product of the acute crisis of the Habsburg Empire, which created many problems by solving others. It had established a more or less stable governmental organization, provided protection against Russian and German expansionist policies, and secured the framework for industrial and agricultural development through a considerable degree of economic autarchy. On the other hand, the peaceful decades of the rule of Francis Joseph were the seedbed in which the nationalities developed their intelligentsia, which increased old grievances and began to undermine the traditional political order. The structure of the Habsburg Empire was loosening and a war—just or unjust— could only accelerate the process.

The July 7, 1914 minutes of the Council of Ministers for Common Affairs prove that Hungarian Prime Minister Count István Tisza had serious reservations about the wisdom of sending an ultimatum to the Serbs, [11]   who were in a state of emotional frenzy over the annexation of Bosnia-Herzegovina. At the July 19 meeting it was Tisza again who foresaw the problem of war guilt. Upon his suggestion the government of the Dual Monarchy decided that no war for conquest was intended. Tisza's big mistake was that he did not protest publicly and finally acceded to the issuance of the ultimatum. It should be noted, that in an atmosphere of nationalistic fervor even the Social Democrats (led by Ernő Garami) sided with the dynasty.

Few countries had suffered more than Hungary during the World War. The losses of the country in the first months of the war were numerically larger than those of any other participant except Russia. Only the Serbs lost proportionately more men than Hungary did between 1914 and 1918. [12] The trenches at the front stank of blood and corpses, while at home the population was starving, especially in the cities. After America joined the Anglo-French war efforts, pessimism increased in Budapest. Many leading politicians believed that the Central Powers had lost the war, and therefore the long-postponed social reforms could not be delayed any longer. According to the assessment of Count Albert Apponyi, who was Prime Minister Tisza's political rival, "amidst the sharpening social crisis. . .Count István Tisza did not recognize the importance of universal franchise, therefore he had to quit." Also in Apponyi's view "the reason of revolutions is not reform activity, but the postponement of reforms." [13] The German General Staff took over in Berlin in March, 1918, but was unable to reverse the course of events. By that time international agreements had already secured the territorial demands of Serbia and Romania. The Pittsburgh Pact, signed by Thomas G. Masaryk and other emigré leaders, brought the Czechs and Slovaks under one political roof. The Romanians sided with France, England and Italy in 1916, by signing a secret treaty, [14] which delimited the postwar boundaries of Greater Romania. President Wilson, in the tenth of his fourteen points, held out the prospect for autonomous development for the national minorities of Austria-Hungary, but was won over to Czech, Romanian, and Serbian aspirations when the collapse of the Dual Monarchy became imminent. The bright promise of just peace, self-determination, and the plebiscite, in which most Hungarians blindly trusted, gradually faded away.

On June 20, 1918, Prime Minister Wekerle dealt in the Hungarian Parliament with the intervention of the gendarmerie in the machine factory of the State Railroads, which ended "with death and many injuries," and stated that the evidence available to him proved that "it was an organized workers' movement, which unfortunately extended to the capital city, and even beyond." [15]   Discontent was obviously growing in the country. Yet not even the largest and best organized political organization of the country, the Social Democratic Party, could air the workers' grievances in the Parliament, since it did not have a single representative there.

King Charles (whose title in Austria was Emperor) made a last attempt for separate peace by sending Prince Louis Windischgraetz to Switzerland. He negotiated there with representatives of France, Great Britain, and the United States. Five days later a diplomatic note was handed to him declaring that "the peoples of the hitherto Austro-Hungarian Monarchy have resolved the dissolution of the Danubian State," [16]   therefore the three powers were not in a position to continue negotiations. Burian, the Foreign Minister of Austria-Hungary, was succeeded by Count Gyula Andrássy, who dismantled the most important creation of his father, the alliance with Germany. It was too late. After Prague and Vienna, on October 25 a National Council was also formed in Budapest. Its president, the liberal-leftist antiwar activist, Count Michael Károlyi, took over as Prime Minister six days later. His five-year struggle against German orientation as well as for universal franchise, and his close connections with the dominant leftist forces predestined him for leadership. Károlyi believed that the new European order would be built on Wilsonian ideas. His government attracted dilettante politicians and idealistic dreamers like a magnet. King Charles relieved Károlyi of his oath, and on November 13 he renounced "all participation in state affairs." [17]   This opened the way to a People's Republic, with Károlyi as its provisional President.

The new Hungarian head of state had outlined his political philosophy earlier in a speech at Cegléd in January, 1917. In his view "in the future...only those will be considered civilized nations that will relinquish selfish aims, find a way to general disarmament and have the strength and courage to fight for peace." [18]   Oscar Jászi, the Minister of Nationality Affairs, wanted to transform Hungary into an "Eastern Switzerland" using Kossuth's "Danubian confederation" as a model, whose principal aims were: "wide autonomy, freedom of thought and association, and fraternity of free people." [19]   Kossuth also had urged alliance and cooperation between Hungarians, Romanians, and Serbs. [20]

As it turned out, however, it was too late for reconciliation between Magyars and their nationalities. The undeniable sincerity of Károlyi and Jászi were not considered satisfactory guarantees for the Slavic and Romanian leaders, whose goals at that time far exceeded autonomy and free development within Hungary.

The organization of the diplomatic service proved to be slow and inefficient. The new Hungarian Minister to Switzerland was Róza Bédi-Schwimmer, a feminist leader. She made a number of serious mistakes, including quoting from a secret, coded telegram to newspapermen. She was soon replaced by the experienced Baron Gyula Szilassy, who made the Hungarian Legation at Bern into an important listening post for the new Hungarian government. [21]

The five-month rule of the Károlyi regime did not solve burning problems at home either. There was unemployment and starvation in the cities. In contrast to a 300 to 1,000 per cent increase in the prices of consumer goods, the workers' wages rose only by 100-120 per cent. Before the war, a factory worker could buy one kilogram (2.2 pounds) of meat with one hour's wage; in the first months of 1919, he had to work 10 to 12 hours for it. [22]   The promised land reform did not materialize. Károlyi distributed part of his vast holdings among the peasants, but the rest of the aristocracy, the clergy, and other big landowners did not follow his example. Members of the former ruling class formed counter-revolutionary organizations. Elections were promised, but not held. Extremism, primarily communist agitation increased. Károlyi was unable or unwilling to curb the propaganda spread by the *Vörös Újság* (Red News), the organ of the Communist Party of Hungary, which was founded on November 24 1918 by former Russian prisoner of war, Béla Kun, and his collaborators. When four policemen were killed as the result of a demonstration at the editorial offices of the Social Democratic Party newspaper, Kun and others were imprisoned. They soon emerged as heroes, however, after the liberal press reported that they were badly beaten by police officers.

Following the demobilization of the army, the defenseless country was attacked from the north, east, and south by Czechs, Romanians, and Serbs. On November 13, 1918, the day on which an armistice agreement was signed by Károlyi with General Franchet d'Esperay in Belgrade, news was received in Budapest about the appearance of Czech troops in Northern Hungary. Emil Štodola, the Prague government's envoy to Hungary, explained that those were irregulars and they would soon be withdrawn. He asked the Hungarian military authorities not to shoot at the regular troops that would chase the guerillas away. Of course, both the irregulars and the regulars continued their advance. Štodola's diversionary tactics made it possible for the Czechs to occupy additional Hungarian territories without resistance. [23] Károlyi complained to the Peace Conference, but did not get any satisfaction. Only the Italians showed some sympathy, which probably stemmed more from anti-Yugoslav than from pro-Hungarian sympathies.

In early January, 1919, an American political mission, headed by Archibald C. Coolidge, a Harvard history professor, arrived in Vienna to study the fast changing Central European situation. After spending some days in Austria, Coolidge traveled to Budapest, where he was warmly received. His report of January 19 to the American Peace Commission referred to Hungarian informants and stated that "Hungary forms a natural geographic and economic unity to a greater extent than any other state in Europe except Great Britain." Coolidge recognized that the country's river system and food-producing and industrial areas complemented each other, and therefore "Hungary needed a treatment as a whole." [24]

This was one of the few friendly gestures of the Allies toward the Károlyi regime. [25] Colonels Miles and Causey examined the problem of national boundaries, but were expelled by the Serbs and thus did not accomplish anything constructive. The Peace Conference turned a deaf ear to their recommendation for the termination of the blockade. Democratic Hungary was not invited to Paris. Representatives of the neighboring states, on the other hand, had many opportunities to outline and explain their territorial aims. Eduard Beneš, the Czechoslovak emissary, stated on February 19, 1919, before the Supreme Council that—with the help of the Allies he and his associates organized "three armies in the field" that fought not for territory, but "for the same principles as the Allied Nations." [26] His oratory against "a medieval dynasty backed by bureaucracy, militarism, the Roman Catholic Church, and, to some extent, by high finance" [27] could have been just as popular in Budapest as it probably was in Prague. It was also effective, all the more so as the Hungarians—in contrast to many other Habsburg nationalities—did not set up organizations in Allied countries to gain sympathy for the country's independence and official recognition of national aspirations. It is also true that Károlyi rose to political power too late, and that he had inherited the liabilities of the former regime.

Hungary was in a desperate position when Lieutenant Colonel Vyx, the plenipotentiary of the Paris Peace Conference in Hungary, demanded the evacuation of a large part of Central Hungary for the invading Romanians (March 20, 1919). By that time "disorder, anarchy, counter-revolutionary diversion had reached their peak," [28] according to Böhm, the Hungarian Minister of Defense. Károlyi immediately convened the Council of Ministers and declared that the coalition government could not be maintained, because the bourgeois parties had lost their popular support. In his opinion only the Social Democratic Party was in a position to organize a strong army against the invaders. "Western orientation and policies built on Wilsonian principles are definitely over. We need a new orientation which will secure for us the sympathy of the (Socialist) International." This view was expressed by Károlyi in an article published in the July 25, 1919 issue of the Social Democratic *Arbeiter Zeitung* in Vienna. The Council of Ministers unanimously decided that the government would resign and Károlyi would continue as President. He would then name a Social Democratic cabinet, which would refuse the demands of the Peace Conference.

The Ministers apparently were not familiar with some new developments. The Soldiers' Council, upon the suggestion of Chairman József Pogány, decided that the armed forces would support the communists. The soldiers confiscated the ministers' automobiles and the garrisons in Budapest came under communist control. In the Workers' Council, Sándor Garbai announced the formation of a Soviet (Council) government. A newspaperman, Pál Kéri, visited Károlyi later that night and asked him to reassess his position and resign." [29] An American observer vividly described the situation that had arisen:

In February, 1919, the Peace Conference announced preliminary boundaries for Hungary which gave Slovakia, Serbia and Rumania chunks of undoubtedly Hungarian population and denuded her of industrial and agricultural areas vital to her national existence. This at once gave impulse to communist agitation and greatly weakened the Károlyi regime. Károlyi apparently got the notion if the country went Bolshevik it would frighten the Peace Conference. [30]

The circumstances of the establishment of the proletarian dictatorship are still not entirely clear, but it can be stated as a fact that on March 21, 1919 the power slipped to the Soviets, whose leader, Béla Kun, sought Russian help immediately. Lenin was eager to support his Hungarian comrades, but his hands were tied. Precisely at this time Admiral Kolchak's troops launched a powerful offensive against the Red Army, while in April war broke out between Russia and Poland. A government telegram sent to the *Leipziger Volkszeitung* by the new Hungarian regime stated that the communists in Budapest were not afraid of Allied military intervention, because if that would happen "the proletariat of the whole world would line up behind Hungary." [31] Although it soon became obvious that the time was not ripe for a global socialist revolution, the Sovietization of Central Europe was a not too distant possibility. Internal unrest increased in the Successor States, as well as in Austria and Germany. Marshal Foch presented a plan at the March 27 meeting of the Council of Four in Paris, which set as a goal "the organization of a barrier against Bolshevism." He did not advocate offensive action, only some sort of a demarcation line behind which the Allies could proceed to clean up the region. Foch insisted that Vienna should be occupied to ensure the lines of communication with Poland and Romania since five days before the meeting a communist government was established in Hungary.

President Wilson and British Prime Minister Lloyd George opposed any intervention. The only way to take action against Bolshevism, said Wilson, was to eliminate its causes. Finally, the Allies—upon learning about Károlyi's resignation and the establishment of Béla Kun's communist regime—sent General J. C. Smuts to Budapest. General Smuts arrived in the

Hungarian capital on April 4 and immediately invited the People's Commissars to his train. The Hungarian regime was represented by President Garbai, the nominal head of the Soviet state, by Commissars Kun and Kunfi, and by the Vienna envoy of the Soviets, Elek Bolgár. During the negotiations Smuts emphasized that he had brought with him the last proposals of the victorious states that "wanted to live in peace with Hungary and secure the appropriate internal development of the country." [32]

The Hungarian standpoint was very similar to that expressed by A. A. Joffe, the head of the Soviet Russian delegation at the Brest-Litovsk peace conference in December, 1917: peace without annexations and indemnities and the right of self-determination for all nationalities. As Kun said later, Hungary was simply "too weak to negotiate," and therefore the proposal of the Allies was not unreasonable under the circumstances. Smuts suggested the drawing of a new demarcation line between the Hungarian and Romanian armies five to thirteen miles east of the line demanded by the Vyx ultimatum, and the establishment of a wide neutral zone which was supposed to be occupied by English, French, Italian and possibly American troops. The Vyx ultimatum of March 20, 1919 had assigned a number of purely Hungarian cities (such as Debrecen, Hódmezővásárhely, Szeged, Makó and Orosháza) to the Romanians. The new proposal would have returned them to Hungary. Smuts solemnly declared that the new demarcation line would not influence the determination of the final boundaries of Hungary, promised the termination of the Allied blockade, and indicated that the Hungarian Soviet government would be invited to the Peace Conference. He finally suggested a meeting with representatives of other nations of the former Dual Monarchy. The position of Kun was strengthened by this visit, which he believed was a "de facto" recognition of the new regime by the Allies, and an expression of willingness on the part of the Peace Conference to seriously negotiate with him. Kun's final offer was considered excessive and was refused by Smuts, who then left for Prague the very next day. The Hungarian Soviet government had to look for new alternatives.

On April 6 Tibor Számuelly, Vice-Commissar for Defense, ordered the organization of front-line propaganda, hoping that the Czech and Romanian troops would not oppose a proletarian army. The "spreading of communist ideology and the call for rebellion against their own imperialists," [33] however, did not prove to be successful, although some Romanian soldiers turned against their commanders, and near the city of Makó, Serbian troops threw away their weapons and gave up plans for the occupation of an important bridge. [34] On the other hand, the new Budapest government organized a combat-worthy army, virtually overnight. At the beginning of the Romanian military intervention, the forces of the Hungarian Soviet Republic consisted of undisciplined, politically oriented units, most of which were organized by the Károlyi government. Kun and his associates dissolved the Soldiers' Council right after the takeover, without regard for the important role which it had played in the overthrow of the People's Republic. Political commissars were appointed, and Revolutionary Military Courts were established. Workers' battalions and international brigades were sent to the front daily.

Until the end of April, seven Romanian divisions, more than 50,000 soldiers, fought against numerically weaker Red Army units. On April 20 the invaders reached Nagyvárad (Oradea Mare) and three days later occupied Debrecen. Newly formed regiments were sent to the eastern front from Budapest and other industrial cities, and on May 3 the Hungarian Red Army dispersed the Romanians at Szolnok and stopped their advance at the Tisza river. At the same time the Czech offensive also came to a standstill. On May 10 a Hungarian counterattack drove the enemy behind the Ipoly river and consolidated the position of the Red Army in northern Hungary. Later in June, the Czech troops had to be withdrawn 40 to 100 miles as the result of a Hungarian offensive.

Among the changes that characterized the home rule of the communist regime was the nationalization of industrial enterprises and mines employing more than 20 workers. Foreign commerce, apartment buildings and large stores, as well as farms bigger than 100 cadestral yokes (about 57 hectares) were also taken over by the state. As a result of the sudden and radical reorganization of the economy, chaos and restlessness developed. Popular reforms, such as the introduction of eight-hour work days, free medical services, lower rents and wage increases could not pacify the country, despite the prophetic fanaticism and enthusiasm of the leaders.

The communists did not distribute the farmland to peasants—as Károlyi had promised—but nationalized it and set the starving urban population against the government by confiscations, red tape, arrests, and executions. Terrorist groups traveled around in armored trains, executing many counterrevolutionaries together with innocent people, denounced by their enemies. The majority of the production commissioners who sat in the offices of former managers were ignorant and ineffective. The loyalty of the socialists in the Soviet government was wavering. One of the Commissars, Péter Ágoston, told an American visitor (Professor Brown) on April 24 that he and some of his comrades intended to send Kun to Switzerland, which would have provided an opportunity for the formation of a moderate government. In the late hours of May 1, following a mass demonstration, non-Bolshevik members of the Governing Council and trade union leaders suggested the transfer of power to a more representative Directorium.

Béla Kun reviewed the proposal at the May 2 meeting of the Governing Council, admitting that the fighting ability of the troops was equal to zero, although he did not consider the situation entirely hopeless. On the same day two employees of the Hungarian Soviet legation in Vienna broke into the room of envoy Elek Bolgár, who was in Budapest. They found 135 million Hungarian crowns, 98,000 Swiss francs, and 333,000 French francs, which were destined to support foreign revolutionary movements. The larger part of the money reached the counterrevolutionary government in Szeged, which functioned there with the tacit approval of the French army of occupation.

In the meantime, decrees issued by the Soviet government socialized private libraries, works of art, jewelry, pianos, Oriental rugs, bicycles, microscopes, and stamp collections. Private bathrooms were to be made available to members of assigned proletarian families on Saturday nights. The general confusion was characterized by a statement which denied rumors that women would be made common property of men. ("Die Frauen nicht communisieren wird. . .") [35] Clemenceau sent one telegram after another, demanding the evacuation of reoccupied former Hungarian territories, promising the stabilization of front lines. Finally the Soviet government ordered the retreat of the troops from the northern front. It demoralized the soldiers as well as the commanders, many of whom had joined the Red Army for patriotic reasons.

On June 24, cadets of the national Ludovika Military Academy in Budapest organized an armed uprising and marched against government buildings under the command of some of their officers. Simultaneously Danube river gunboats opened fire on the Hungaria Hotel, the headquarters of the Soviet-Hungarian leaders and their families. Riots also started in Transdanubian towns and villages, proving that the counterrevolutionaries were centrally organized and directed. The result of the June uprisings threw cold water on many hesitant socialists who took positions in the new government. In July, Vilmos Böhm, the former Commander-in-Chief of the Red Army, was appointed Minister Plenipotentiary to Austria. He was hesitant at first to represent the Soviet government abroad, apparently because of a mandate to negotiate with the Allies was among his instructions. But his socialist friends, Kunfi, Garbai and Weltner, convinced him that he might be able to save the regime, and that his mission was not that of a gravedigger.

On July 23, Allied representatives presented to Böhm a memorandum. It demanded the expulsion of Kun's communist government, the organization of a new government representing all social classes, and the end of political persecution. In return for this, the Allies promised to terminate the blockade. On July 31 the military situation became critical. The Romanian Army started a concentrated attack along the entire frontline. At night one of the Romanian divisions stood one mile from Szolnok, a key city at the Tisza river. Other units occupied Tokaj and Tarcal in the northeast.

Colonel Julier, the non-communist Chief-of-Staff of the Hungarian Red Army sent a report to War Commissar Landler, in which he described the position of the Hungarian forces as "hopeless". [36]   As Béla Kun told the members of the central Revolutionary Worker-Soldier Council on May 2, the Hungarian Red Army. was transformed into "a fleeing, cowardly, running throng." [37]   Finally, after a meeting of the

500-member Workers' Council, which served as the parliament of the Soviet regime, Commissar Zoltán Rónai concluded
that the dictatorship of the proletariat, by the will of the
majority of the proletarians has fallen. "Clearly and frankly:
we are talking about a lost military campaign." [38]

General dissatisfaction with the government increased
further in Budapest as well as in the countryside. The farmers
were unwilling to sell their products for the new "white"
banknotes (so called because one side of the bills was
left blank); they practically starved out the cities. Kun's
proclamation, issued on July 31 to the proletariat of the world,
was a last frantic effort to reverse the situation. He complained
in it about the starvation of Hungarians which was the result of
the Allied blockade, and stated that Balkan hordes were
released against his people in the name of high cultural ideas.
Just as in the case of the June 15 proclamation of the
Hungarian communist leaders to the French proletariat for
help "against the international counterrevolution of Versailles," this final call was also unsuccessful, The expected world
proletarian solidarity did not materialize. The only result was
the protest of a socialist conference in Lucerne against Allied
policies.

Béla Kun and his associates arrived by special train to
Vienna on August 2, after the Austrian socialist government
gave them political asylum upon the request of Böhm. On the
way to the railroad station in Budapest anticommunist crowds
assembled, rocks and curses flew and someone shot Commissar
Landler's daughter, who was seated with her father in an
automobile. The fall of the Hungarian Soviet government was
final; the way was open to Gyula Peidl and his social
democratic associates, who were asked by the Workers'
Council to take over.

The chances of the Peidl government were not very
promising, mainly because it included four former commissars
who suddenly transformed themselves into social democrats.
The first meeting of the new Council of Ministers started on
August 2 with the abolition of the Soviet Republic and the
re-establishment of the People's Republic. Peidl and his
colleagues dissolved the revolutionary courts, confirmed the
traditional judiciary system, and set free all political prisoners
and hostages. On the same day the Prime Minister sent a

telegram to István Nagyatádi-Szabó, the leader of the centrist Smallholders' Party, inviting him — together with Catholic prelate Sándor Giesswein, a founder of the Christian Socialist movement in Hungary — to accept portfolios in his government. As a result of such steps, Colonel Romanelli, the chairman of the Interallied Military Mission, promised the termination of the blockade. Good news came from the front line, too. The Hungarian Army — still called Red Army — gained an unexpected victory on August 2, and reoccupied Szolnok from the Romanians. Peidl and Interior Minister Peyer ordered the capture of the escaping exponents of the communist system. [39]

All of these steps were meaningless in the opinion of the fast growing anticommunist organizations. Leaders of some conservative groups, which included royalists (i.e. those faithful to the Habsburgs), army officers, farmers and landowners wanted revenge and the complete restoration of traditional legality, with Archduke Joseph Habsburg at the helm. Archduke Joseph had praised Károlyi's People's Republic in 1918 and was among the first to take the required oath, but this was no longer an obstacle. Emissaries of the royalist right, led by István Friedrich, a machine manufacturer, visited the hesitant Archduke on his estate and took him to Budapest on August 4. This happened on the very day the Romanian Army had occupied Budapest, despite Allied warnings.

At that stage everyone wanted change, not only the members of the former ruling class. The behavior of an increasing segment of the population was just as ominous. Several state and city employees insulted the ministers of the trade union government, some of whom were afraid to enter their offices. Some units of the Red Army deserted to Miklós (Nicholas) Horthy, the Minister of Defense of the rival Szeged government. Ever-present opportunists, who just days before supported the Soviet government, now attacked Peidl who courageously resisted the communist measures when others were ducking.

The deposal of the Peidl government was originally scheduled for August 5. One of the reasons for the feverish haste was a telegram sent by Vilmos Böhm to Peidl from Vienna. It stated that "the agreement with the Entente is ready. If you will include four bourgeois and two peasants in your government, we will continue to be in charge." [40] From the content of this telegram and the conferences that were taking place between Peidl and middle class politicians, the Friedrich group drew the conclusion that a coalition government was in the making and they could probably not get Romanian help for its removal if they don't act swiftly.

The plan of the coup d'état was discussed with Colonel Romanelli, who opposed it. General Vasilescu, the Chief-of-Staff of the Romanian army approved the plan, but threatened with armed intervention if the conspirators would not grab the power at once and confusion would result. On August 6, the police and some army units were already controlled by the conspirators. In the afternoon, they arrested Interior Minister Peyer and learned from him that the Council of Ministers was holding a meeting in the Sándor Palace, the Prime Minister's residence. Accompanied by policemen and army officers, an emissary of Friedrich, András Csilléry, entered the conference room with a walking stick in his hand and demanded the resignation of the government in the name of the "United Revolutionary Parties." He informed Peidl that the cabinet would be arrested if he disobeyed the order. Peidl mildly protested, but following a short debate that took place in the absence of the conspirators, the government decided to yield to force and resigned. [41]

As the result of the successful *Putsch*, Archduke Joseph became Regent. He in turn appointed István Friedrich the new Prime Minister. Friedrich's political career was quite eventful and controversial. In 1914 he accompanied Károlyi to America and in 1918 became Deputy Minister of Defense in the first Károlyi cabinet. In Károlyi's opinion Friedrich was an "uncontrollable demagogue." He was the one who on the eve of the October, 1918 populist revolution urged the excited crowd to storm the palace of Archduke Joseph, the King's plenipotentiary, so as to force Károlyi's nomination. Then, Friedrich was an "extreme leftist" and a republican, but one year later he became the leader of the royalist counter-revolution.

Following the coup d'état, Archduke Joseph and Friedrich hurriedly called on General Gorton, Admiral Troubridge, and Colonel Romanelli of the Interallied Military Mission and reported to them that they have taken over the government. Now the Paris Peace Conference was confronted with three problems: "The looting by the Romanian army, the return of the Habsburgs, and food supply." [42]   The "Big Four" asked the Romanians on August 7 "if they intended to defy the Allies," [43]   but the invaders were unwilling to comply with the demand to withdraw. Bucharest was encouraged by French army leaders, whose support meant more than the official warnings. The Romanian Army did not evacuate Budapest; rather extended the occupation zone to Transdanubia. Munro of the British Food Commission and a Swiss Captain, Brunier, who represented the International Red Cross, visited a number of towns occupied by the Romanians and issued a statement on their findings. It listed murders, floggings, imprisonments without trial, theft of personal property under the name of requisition, and the killing of hundreds of Hungarian prisoners of war. On August 25, American Marine Corps soldier Hargraves was arrested by a Romanian patrol for unknown reasons and the Romanians opened fire on a British Danube warship, which returned the fire and wounded a Romanian enlisted man.

The Peace Conference was infuriated. A telegram sent by the Supreme Council to the Romanian government on August 14 called attention to "the directions forwarded on three occasions by the Conference to the Mission of Allied Generals and communicated to Budapest." [44]   Among these instructions were the disarmament of Hungarian troops, maintenance of order with a minimum of foreign troops, supplying Hungary with provisions, abstention from all interference in internal affairs, and the allowing of free expression of the national will. The Supreme Council insisted that "no definite recovery of war material, railroad material, agricultural supplies or stock, etc. may take place at the present time." [45] The Romanians paid scant attention to the views of the Peace Conference. As Viscount Bryce explained in the House of Lords in London on December 16, their behavior was still "anything but creditable," and it "called for the attention of the Allied Powers, who were obliged to remonstrate with them on the way they were behaving." [46]

Meanwhile Friedrich attempted to consolidate his control. According to the minutes of a meeting of the Interallied

Military Mission in Budapest, "there was a possibility of the
Entente's accepting Friedrich's government," [47] which probably included the recognition of the regency. Consequently, the
Friedrich cabinet made preparations for a long term in office.
These included the issuance of several decrees, the first of
which returned to landowners all estates nationalized by the
Soviets. The ardour of Friedrich was dampened only by one
obstacle: the National Army, organized by Admiral Horthy [48] in Szeged, which grew into a formidable force. The
Romanians did not allow Friedrich to establish an army, which
put him at a disadvantage vis-à-vis Horthy. The leaders of the
Allied Missions explained to him that they were not in a
position to provide a military contingent which could protect
the new regime.

Friedrich had to look for support elsewhere. Gusztáv Gratz,
the new Hungarian envoy in Vienna, visited Chancellor
Renner in October and asked him to endorse the idea of a
Polish-Hungarian-Austrian block that was originally proposed
by the Polish government. The plan proved abortive, and
Friedrich realized that there was only one road open: he
recommended the confirmation of Horthy's appointment as
Commander-in-Chief. The so-called "Szeged-government"
that was reorganized by Dezső Pattantyus-Ábrahám on July
12, included some liberals. Those considered extreme rightists
by the Allies, such as Horthy and Captain Gyula Gömbös were
left out, although the Admiral retained his position as
Commander-in-Chief. The French showed more willingness to
negotiate with the new Szeged government; Horthy's recruiting
attempts were hindered less often. The anticommunist
Serbian government was the only one that accredited a
diplomatic representative of the Szeged government. This
came after a trip to Belgrade by Horthy and Count Teleki of
the Vienna-based Anti-Bolshevik Committee. The goodwill of
the Serbs was important, because the National Army had to
cross Serbian occupied territory to reach Western Hungary,
and this would have been impossible without the approval of
Prime Minister Protić's government.

Horthy realized that he could lean on the power of
bayonets and requested Prime Minister Pattantyus-Ábrahám
to make his command independent of the Ministry of War. His
troops were soon marching to the unoccupied sector of

Western Hungary, not paying any attention to the order of the Interallied Military Mission, which demanded the withdrawal of the troops to Szeged. Horthy himself left Szeged by plane, leaving the French military authorities in the belief that he was going to drop a return order over his troops. Instead of doing so, he landed near Siófok, at Lake Balaton. Two days later the vanguard of his army arrived there and continued the march northward. The National Army now controlled a sizeable part of Hungary, and Horthy was in a position to initiate negotiations with the Allies. [49]

The leaders of the Peace Conference changed their mind upon Czech pressure and forced Archduke Joseph to resign the Regency on August 23, 1919. On that day an emissary of the Peace Conference, Sir George Clerk, arrived in Hungary with the aim of promoting the formation of a democratic regime that would be acceptable to the Allies. The negotiations took place in Clerk's apartment in Budapest. On November 5, Horthy met there with Vilmos Vázsonyi, the leader of the National Democratic Citizens' Party, István Nagyatádi-Szabó of the Smallholders' Party, Ernő Garami of the Social Democratic Party, and Márton Lovászy of the National Party. Horthy denied that the occupation of the capital city by the National Army would result in military dictatorship and officially declared that he stood on the basis of civil rights, adding that his army would eradicate every form of Bolshevism. His statement soothed the doubts of Clerk and the party leaders, who all knew that resentments and revenge-seeking sentiments erupted into violence in many areas of the country. Bands of army officers handed out punishment indiscriminately to those who in their opinion had been associated with the Kun and Károlyi regimes.

In August and September, 1919, hundreds of suspected communists were hanged or otherwise executed without trial. [50] The foreign echo of the murders was very unfavorable and Horthy wanted to stop illegal actions, but it was not easy to force the jinni back into the bottle. The fury of the officers frequently turned against Jewish radicals who had formed "almost the whole of Károlyi's intellectual General Staff and nearly all Béla Kun's Commissaries, including the most notorious perpetrators of the Red Terror which had preceded the White; although, even so, many of the most violent White Terrorists would have denied that they were attacking Jews as such." [51]   The elimination of Bolshevism was their admitted goal. To endow the apprearance of legality, concentration camps were organized for politically dangerous elements. An editorial in the November 19, 1919 issue of the liberal daily *Az Est* (Evening) pointed out that the return to productive labor and "establishing peace with ourselves and the whole world" was the solution. In order to end illegal actions, a decree was published in the official *Budapest Gazette* on June 19, 1920 which dissolved special military organizations.

Horthy's entry in Budapest at the head of his troops on November 19, 1919 meant the return of the traditionalist forces. In his reply to the speech of the Mayor of the City of Budapest, Horthy criticized the capital which "has disowned her thousand years of tradition, dragged the Holy Crown in the dust and clothed herself in red rags." [52]   He could have mentioned the senseless and disastrous war among the causes of Hungarian problems, but he remained silent about it. After thirty-two years in uniform he could not go that far, but declared that he was ready to forgive Budapest "if she would return to the service of the Fatherland." [53]   Those politicians who had sensitive ears understood that Horthy was in charge, and gathered around the new source of power.

Friedrich was regarded in Allied circles a representative of feudal interests. His government was never recognized by them, and therefore he had to go. On November 23, Károly Huszár took over the premiership. But similarly to Friedrich, Huszár also lacked Horthy's confidence, largely because of his erratic behavior at the end of the war, when he occasionally cooperated with Károlyi in the parliament. From Horthy's point of view, however, Friedrich was more dangerous, because his unlimited ambitions stood in the way of the Supreme Commander, who wanted to secure power for himself, at least temporarily.

Huszár was a teacher by profession, without any practical experience in policy-making and public administration, but he was acceptable to the Allies. The new multi-party government represented a broad spectrum of political opinions. Independent royalist Count László Somssich became the Minister of Foreign Affairs, and Friedrich received the defense portfolio which was insignificant, because the army accepted orders from Horthy only. On December 19, the leaders of the Social Democratic Party instructed Károly Peyer, the Minister of Labor, and Ferenc Miákits, Deputy Minister of Commerce to resign because of the commando actions, but then changed their minds two days later "in view of the foreign political situation." [54] Finally, after several political trials, electoral irregularities, and the destruction of the Party's printing presses, both men left the cabinet on January 15, 1920.

On December 2, 1919 Huszár received an invitation to the Peace Conference, and on January 25-27, 1920 elections were held for membership in the National Assembly. Elections, however, took place only in Western and Central Hungary (i.e. in Transdanubia and in the area located between the Danube and Tisza rivers) from which the Romanian troops were withdrawn. Nagyatádi-Szabó's Smallholders' Party received 79 seats, the Party of Christian National Unity 75, the Democratic Party 6. Four Independents were also elected. The Smallholders' Party was anti-Habsburg, while the Christian National Unity Party represented a pro-Habsburg and clerical ideology. It was evident, that sooner or later the two major parties, that were of almost equal strength, would have to fight it out.

Horthy himself created the impression during conversations with supporters of the dethroned ruler, Charles, that his restoration to power would be difficult if not impossible. In a letter sent to the king in the spring of 1920, Horthy asked for "patience, and above all, confidence." [55] It is, of course, understandable that the majority of Hungarians who lived in poverty after the war, and were confused by ever-changing extremist political propaganda, could not care less about Habsburg restoration or the future form of state. Politically charged constitutional questions left most people cold. On the other hand, it was evident that the victorious Allies were against Habsburg restoration. The Paris Peace Conference considered the Habsburg question on February 2, 1920. In a note that the Allied and Associated Powers sent to the Hungarian Peace Delegation, they denied the rumors which "made them appear to recognize and help the return of the Habsburg dynasty to the Hungarian throne." [56] The Allies were convinced that the restoration of a dynasty, "which represented the oppression of foreign nationalities in the view of its subjects," would not be compatible with the ideas for which the war was allegedly fought, i.e., the liberation of the oppressed people. The note emphasized that a Habsburg restoration would "neither be recognized nor tolerated," [57] and the Allies would not consider it an internal affair of Hungary.

Meanwhile the mushrooming Hungarian nationalist organizations worked hard to convince the nation that a head of state had to be elected before the conclusion of the peace treaty. The Chief of the Intelligence Section of the National Army instructed political officers to spread the news that "there was a man who had the ability to lead the country and that was Miklós Horthy." [58] Telegrams from mass meetings demanded Horthy's election. The office of the Commander-in-Chief had to be informed about the drafting and discussion of a bill which was supposed to fill the gap in the supreme national leadership. The National Assembly started the debate of the bill on February 26 and after only a few days, on March 1, it was ready to elect a Regent. Admiral Horthy received 131 votes out of 141 cast. Liberal Count Apponyi got 7 votes. Archduke Joseph was not even considered, because of the opposition by the Allies and the Successor States.

During the election, the Parliament building was surrounded by commandos. Some of Apponyi's supporters were not allowed to enter the building. One Government Minister, Baron F. Korányi, was also stopped at the door. [59] It is undeniable that the 131 votes represented the absolute majority of the (at that time) 160-member Assembly. The voting was secret. Still, the presence of the military was a serious legal defect. As a parliamentary committee report stated, "when the Regent arrived to the Parliament a large number of soldiers wearing service insignia and equipped with weapons, some with hand grenades, invaded the building without permission. Many of the soldiers showed up in the great hall, before the oath was taken. During the oath they blocked the entrance doors and did not let the members of the Assembly enter from the corridors. Armed guards and sentries also could be seen in other parts of the Parliament building. The said armed gathering prevented the National Assembly to exercise its duties freely." [60] This was a clear and courageous statement, but the conclusion was compromising: "In view of the fact that the Speaker of the House issued a firm declaration and enforced the authority of the National Assembly, it is recommended that the grievance be considered void." [61]   The Assembly had surrendered to the military, and Horthy had no serious rivals. Only the problems of the peace treaty, and the eventual return of King Charles remained unsettled.

Most Hungarians felt that further resistance would only prolong the period of uncertainty, especially in light of the fact that Germany had already signed the peace treaty at Versailles on June 28, 1919, and that Austria had also signed the Treaty of Neuilly three months later. Of course, it was generally believed that the territorial demands of neighboring countries were negotiable, and that the new frontiers would be drawn following plebiscites. Former Prime Minister Friedrich was one of those who opposed the peace negotiations, believing that the newly formed neighboring states would rapidly crumble and fall apart. Therefore, all Hungary had to do was to wait patiently and assume for a while the role of an international outcast. Regent Horthy and Premier Huszár wanted to conclude the peace treaty for different reasons. Horthy wished to strengthen his rule and create political stability. Huszár, on the other hand, was convinced that the treaty was inevitable and Hungarians could not be kept in doubt any longer.

On January 16, 1920 the Allies presented the peace conditions to the Hungarian delegation. The Peace Conference had approved the text of the treaty on February 26, 1919, but it was delivered to the Hungarians only one year later because of the revolutionary turmoil in the country. The peace makers in Paris accepted the view that the principle of self-determination called for the separation of all non-Magyars from Hungary, amended only by considerations for geographic, economic, and transportation problems. [62]   They also disregarded the circumstances among which some of the claims originated. The Pittsburgh resolution of May 30, 1918, by which the American Slovaks expressed their approval of the union of Czechs and Slovaks in a single state, was passed by the "delegates" of three emigré organizations: the Czech National Federation, the Alliance of Czech Catholics and the Slovak League. Thereby, American citizens made the decision in the name of European ethnic groups.

The reply of the Huszár government was delivered on February 10. It denied that the Slovaks, Romanians, Ruthenians and other nationalities intended to join the Czechs, the Regat Romanians, or the Serbs in common states. It also disputed the claims that these nationalities constituted a majority in all areas destined to be detached, and asked for plebiscites in those regions. As could be expected, the Hungarian proposal was rejected on May 6 and the draft of the treaty was declared final. [63]   Prime Minister Huszár did not want to take the responsibility for the consequences of the treaty and resigned on March 14. [64]   Sándor Simonyi-Semadám, the Deputy Speaker of the National Assembly, became the new Prime Minister on March 15.

Count Albert Apponyi was the leader of the Hungarian peace delegation. He delivered a speech before the Peace Conference listing statistical, geopolitical, and economic data in three languages, but no one supported him, not even Lloyd George, who in his January 5, 1918 statement denied that the breakup of Austria-Hungary was among the British war aims. [65]   President Wilson's sublime ideas about "justice and equality of right," about the nations of the world being entitled "not only to free pathways upon the sea but also to assured and unmolested access to those pathways," and that "the freedom of the seas is the sine qua non of peace" [66]   were completely forgotten. The Peace Conference did not pay any attention to another Wilsonian promise "not to. . .impair or rearrange the Austro-Hungarian Empire." [67] As it turned out, Germany's territorial losses were not even comparable to those suffered by Hungary, although that country also had sizeable national and linguistic minorities.

On June 4, 1920 the Hungarian peace treaty was signed. [68] Of the 325,000 sq. km. which comprised the area of historical Hungary, only 92,963 sq. km. was left. Romania received 103.000 sq. km., Czechoslovakia 61,633 sq. km., while Yugoslavia incorporated 63,092 km. of former Hungarian territory. Smaller chunks were given to Austria, Italy, and Poland. Of the 9,945,000 persons of Magyar tongue, [69] more than 3,000,000 found themselves under alien political roof.

A British expert of Hungarian affairs stated that "it was not genuine self-determination that was applied at all, but a sort of national determinism which assumed that all peoples in

Hungary of the same kindred stock as their neighbours ought to be transferred; their wishes were taken for granted. Thus the Ruthenes of the northeast were attached to Czecho-slovakia, although they were neither Czechs nor Slovaks, simply because they were not Magyars." [70]

Hungary lost all of her gold, silver, mercury, copper and salt mines, almost one-half of her coal fields, and all but one of her iron mines. More than four-fifths of its forests were also taken over by the Successor States. Following the peace treaty, the formerly largely self-sufficient country had to import most raw materials for the industrial enterprises which grew considerably during the war years and provided livelihood for 25% of the people.

Budapest—designed for pre-Trianon Hungary—became a hydrocephalic capital city. Industrial, cultural, and human resources were all concentrated there after the loss of most of the hinterland. The treaty did not pay attention to interrelationship between areas supplementing each other. It split railroad lines, cities and villages.

Trianon included provisions which were hardly justifiable by any consideration. Prohibiting the production of heavy artillery, tanks and military planes, it also banned the manufacturing of civilian aircraft and limited the armed forces to 35,000 professional mercenaries. Among the categories of indemnification, the expenses stemming from the crushing of the Hungarian Soviet Republic came first. [71] Thereby the Allies repeated the method used against the Károlyi regime, not paying attention to the changing political atmosphere and making the new government responsible for the actions of both the imperial and the communist regimes.

Enemy occupation of Hungarian territories forced more than 400,000 Hungarians to escape. Many of them settled in Budapest and other cities, living in railroad cars and slums. It was the result of such circumstances that "there began in Europe a great and exciting drama: the fight for the revision of the Versailles Peace. It was one of the greatest and most dramatic struggles in the political history of Europe. It ended in a new tragedy, vast and destructive: the second World War," as Eduard Beneš wrote in his *Memoirs*. [72] Beneš also emphasized that the struggle for revision "was a normal development" in a certain sense, because after every war the defeated party tries to wipe out its defeat," either by political or diplomatic means, or by a new war." [73]   But it was not only the defeated who turned against the victors. Some of the "liberated" nationalities also indicated that they were dissatisfied with the new order. Nationalism became a dominant force among Slovaks, Macedonians, Croatians and others, who after the war attacked their new masters, seeking total independence.

The treaty was clearly punitive. [74]   Data in percentages show how difficult it was even to attempt reconstruction. Hungary could keep only 28.6 per cent of her former territory. 31.3 per cent was given to Romania, 19.6 per cent to Yugoslavia, 18.9 per cent to Czechoslovakia and 1.2 per cent to Austria. France, the dominant continental power decided to rely on the Successor States in East Central Europe and did not worry about Hungary's fate. It should be added, that plenary sessions of the Peace Conference were unimportant in decision-making. The Council of Four, consisting of Clemenceau, Lloyd George, Wilson and Orlando (later Nitti) made the awards, frequently under French pressure.

Responsibility for the Treaty of Trianon has haunted Hungarian politicians and other public figures ever since 1920. The social democratic daily *Népszava* (People's Voice) said in an editorial on June 21, 1928: "A forgery of historical facts is going on. The regime would like to shift the odium for the destruction, collapse and dissection of Hungary to those men and parties who attempted to save what could be saved from the ruined country. . .Shameless falsifiers shout from certain political circles that the war could have been won if October (of 1918) would not have come..." Although the representatives of the Horthy regime signed the treaty under coercion, it cannot be denied that Károlyi and Kun fought for a while for the territorial integrity of Hungary, risking their political existence rather than giving in. Károlyi's pacifism and the internationalist attitudes of the Hungarian Soviet Republic cannot wash away the fact that they also represented Hungarian irredenta long before Admiral Horthy consolidated his power. Many Hungarians clutched at the straw of Russian orientation, together with Károlyi and Kun, when the Russian Red Army advanced in Poland. It turned out later, that their hopes were unfounded.

The antipathy toward Hungary in Paris can be traced back, at least partially, to the bloody rule of Kun and his associates. But there were other reasons too. Some of these went back to the dualist period, while others came later, such as the forced removal of Peidl's "Trade Union Government," and the widely publicized White Terror, all of which had tragic consequences for Hungary's internal politics, as well as for its foreign affairs. They made impossible any kind of sincere cooperation between Social Democrats and the conservative forces, and alienated many decent politicians who disliked unlawful methods and foreign interference.

It was, of course, quite impossible to tame and transform the Hungarian Soviet regime into People's Republic, since both political systems had been overthrown earlier and were not supported by the people. Yet it is also true, that the nation needed a peaceful transitionary period during which passions could be calmed and the spirit of reconciliation could be nurtured. After four centuries of Habsburg rule, the majority of the nation was watching the royalist counterrevolutionary takeover with mixed feelings.

The coup d'état by Friedrich against the Peidl government was also a blow to Hungarian hopes in the international arena. In Paris the representatives of the Successor States could now frighten the delegates of the Peace Conference with the possibility of a Habsburg restoration in Hungary.[75] Beneš stated that "the Magyars did not admit their defeat. They remained imperialist in spirit... There were strong objections to the course of negotiating with any Hungarian Party."[76] Habsburg restoration in any part of the former Dual Monarchy could have meant reunification, which was highly undesirable for the governments of those countries which gained or regained independence.

It belongs to the propaganda myths that Hungary signed the peace treaty only after the delivery of the May 20, 1920 letter of French Prime Minister Millerand, which held out the prospect of the eventual revision in the name of the Peace Conference. All that Millerand promised was that if the special committees charged with the marking of the new frontiers would find these unjust for ethnic or economic reasons, they would ask the League of Nations for intervention.[77] Since according to the League's Covenant unanimous decision was mandatory in such cases (and the opposition of even one of the Successor States would have made such a decision impossible), the letter was mere window dressing.

In addition, Article 10 of the Covenant guaranteed the territorial integrity of all members, proving that the preservation of the European *status quo*, as established in 1919-1920, was the chief goal of those who drafted it.

Some Hungarian politicians also had great expectations regarding Article 19 of the Covenant. This made possible the revision of those international agreements which were not applicable any more in a given situation or if they endangered world peace. As it turned out later, the revision of peace treaties was the least of the League's cares, even in the crisis atmosphere of the late thirties. The victorious Great Powers simply wanted to rearrange European boundaries according to the new power relations.

The frontier-establishing committees suggested the return of only 37,000 acres alongside the Yugoslav, Romanian, Czechoslovak, and Austrian borders. Later another 18,000 acres were regained by Hungary as the result of the Sopron plebiscite, [78] which seemed to prove that Apponyi was right when he claimed that Hungary would have gotten back a considerable proportion of occupied areas had the population been given the right to express its feelings through plebiscites. In light of this, the Hungarian government could have refused the signing of the peace treaty, upon the instruction of Horthy. But Horthy did not even threaten such a step. The Simonyi-Semadám cabinet resigned on June 26, after submitting the treaty to Parliament. Count István Bethlen attempted to form a new cabinet, but returned his assignment on July 14. Finally Count Pál Teleki became the new Prime Minister on July 19. Horthy stayed on, seeking political consolidation.

The question arises, what could have happened if Hungary would not have signed the treaty? Not having the gift of prophecy, we can only assume that the territorial debate in Paris would have continued and after a while a compromise agreement could be signed—as in the case of Turkey. The Czechs, Romanians, and Serbs had incorporated more territory than they expected realistically. They knew that the Pittsburgh Agreement of May 30, and the Resolutions of Gyulafehérvár (Alba Iulia) of December 1, 1918 (which proclaimed the union of Transylvania with Romania) did not represent the consensus of the local population. As such, they would probably have reconciled themselves to the return of at least the border regions with Hungarian ethnic majority.

Regent Horthy was well aware that in case of his resignation no basic changes would result in Hungary. It would simply mean that someone else would take up residence in the Royal Palace in Budapest, upon the pressure of the Allies, who were not enthusiastic about Francis Joseph's former Aide-de-Camp anyway.

It is evident, that in the course of 1918-1920 many political activists had displayed good will, but also political incompetence, much of which may be the result of Hungary's long-standing dependence on Austria. Louis Kossuth, the leader of the 1848-49 uprising in Hungary, wisely pointed out in a letter which he wrote to Francis Deák prior to the Compromise of 1867 that the abandonment of the two most important national rights, the control of foreign affairs and the army, was extremely dangerous for the future of Hungary. This was proven, among others, in the fall of 1918, when—upon the suggestion of Prime Minister Wekerle—Emperor-King Charles gave his consent to the transfer of Hungarian troops from Tirol to the defense of Hungary's frontiers. The so-called Austro-Hungarian military command simply sabotaged this order and thereby made it impossible for the Hungarians to defend their frontiers effectively against Successor States. [79] Kossuth had foreseen that the German Empire would drag with her Austria (and therefore Hungary) into a major war. He had also predicted that at the approaching European /armed/ conflict Hungary will be a target of "hostile ambitions." [80]

The White Terror, which followed the Red Terror, turned many influential people against Hungary, especially among the liberal intellectuals of Western Europe. Count Apponyi was well aware of anti-Hungarian sentiments. In a letter, written from Paris to Prime Minister Simonyi-Semadám, he asked for the restraining of counterrevolutionary excesses "by all applicable means," otherwise the Hungarian delegation would not be able to fulfill its mission.

We can lay down as a fact that the confusion following the World War only completed a process which began much earlier. Trianon's conditions were unjust and cruel, but they were the direct results of the lost war, and of the centuries-old dependence on Austria. The lack of a Hungarian diplomatic corps which could have represented the country in the international arena after the collapse of Austria-Hungary, the increasing ethnic consciousness of the nationalities, and the shortsightedness which characterized the internal affairs of post-1867 Hungary all contributed to Hungary's debacle and to the injustices of Trianon.

Still, it is evident that "the Trianon peace treaty did not mean the democratic solution of the nationality problem. It healed old wounds by inflicting new ones, and did not put an end to the hostility and animosity that existed between the peoples of the Danube Valley, but increased them among new conditions." [81]   One solution would be the territorial revision of the Trianon peace treaty (based on internationally controlled, fair plebiscites in ethnically mixed areas) that could eliminate the danger of a new explosion in East Central Europe, which had already served as the storm-center of two world wars. [82]   An other alternative would be the establishment of a just and equitable democratic confederation of the Danube Valley, which could perhaps lessen the national antagonisms in the former lands of the Austro-Hungarian Empire.

Notes

1. Representatives of the Allied and Associated Powers signed the peace treaty in Versailles' Grand Trianon Palace, hence it is called commonly the Treaty of Trianon.

2. Oszkár Jászi, *Magyar kálvária, magyar feltámadás* /Hungarian Calvary, Hungarian Resurrection/, (Munich: Auróra Könyvek, 1969), p. 170.

3. See S. B. Várdy, *The Hungarian Americans* (Boston: Twayne Publishers, 1985), pp. 18-19, statistics on p. 21. See also Julianna Puskás, *From Hungary to the United States, 1880-1914* (Budapest: Akadémiai Kiadó, 1982), pp. 15-44; and S. B. Várdy, "The Great Economic Immigration from Hungary, 1880-1920," in S. B. Várdy and A. H. Várdy, eds., *Society in Change; Studies in Honor of Béla K. Király* (New York: East European Monographs, Columbia University Press, 1983), pp. 189-216.

4. Antal Balla, ed., *A magyar országgyűlés története, 1867-1927* /History of the Hungarian Parliament, 1867-1927/, (Budapest: Légrády, 1927), p. 342.

5. Ödön Málnási, *A magyar nemzet őszinte története* /The Frank History of the Hungarian Nation/, (Munich: Mikes Kelemen Kör, 1959), p. 131.

6. According to Public Law XXX of 1868, which defined the relations of Hungary to Croatia-Slavonia, "the deputies of Croatia-Slavonia...may use Croatian

also in the Common Parliament and in the Delegation." (Sects. 56-59.) C. M. Knatchbull-Hugessen, *The Political Evolution of the Hungarian Nation* (New York: Arno Press, 1971.), II, p. 240. This solution did not satisfy the Croat delegates, many of whom did not understand the essence of the discussions which were conducted in Hungarian.

7. B. Hóman and G. Szekfű, *Magyar történet* /Hungarian History/, (Budapest: Egyetemi Nyomda, 1936), V, p. 581.

8. His son indicated that in 1910 R. W. Seton-Watson witnessed the parliamentary election in Szakolka. Béla Király, *et al.*, eds., *War and Society in East Central Europe* (New York: Columbia University Press, 1982), VI, p. 4. During the war Seton-Watson was named Head of the Research Department of the British Foreign Office. According to O. Jászi, he was a convinced supporter of the Habsburg Monarchy until World War I. Columbia University Archives, *Jászi Collection*.

9. *Ibid.*

10. S. B. Várdy, *The Hungarian Americans*, pp. 20-21, 28.

11. S. Szilassy, *Revolutionary Hungary, 1918-1921* (Astor Park, FL: Danubian Press, 1971), p. 13. Also Dominic G. Kosáry, *A History of Hungary* (New York: Arno Press, 1971), pp. 350-351.

12. Mihály Károlyi, *Egy egész világ ellen* /Against the Whole World/, (Budapest: Gondolat, 1965), p. 135.

13. Count A. Apponyi's June 8, 1917 remark in Parliament. A. Balla, ed., *A magyar országgyűlés története*, p. 384.

14. The August 17, 1916 Treaty allowed Romania to annex approximately 15,000 square kilometers more that the territory given to her by the Trianon peace treaty. President Wilson told Romanian Prime Minister Bratianu in February, 1919 that the U. S. did not recognize secret treaties. Wilson's opposition to "secret covenants entered into in the interest of particular governments" was included in his Jan. 8, 1918 address to the joint session of Congress, "The Romanian government was unsatisfied:. . .'if Roumania should now have her occupied territory returned without occupying Transylvania there is no necessity to stay in the war any further. . .'R. S. Baker, *Woodrow Wilson; Life and Letters* (New York: Greenwood Press, 1968), VII, p. 456, Note 2. Lloyd George at the February 1, 1919 meeting of the Supreme Council questioned the validity of Romanian claims in regard to Transylvania. F. Deák, *Hungary at the Paris Peace Conference; The Diplomatic History of the Treaty of Trianon* (New York: H. Fertig, 1972), Doc. 6. p. 380.

15. Answer to Mihály Károlyi's question in the Hungarian Parliament. Hoover Institution, TS, *Hungary*, A2, Box 2.

16. Lajos Windischgraetz, *My Adventures and Misadventures* (London: Barrie and Rockliff, 1965), p. 110.

17. Francis Deák, *Hungary at the Paris Peace Conference*, p. 11.

18. *Az Est* /Evening/ Sept. 18, 1917. Quoted in *Hungary, Külügyminisztérium, Doc. 1.* Hoover Institution, Hungarian Collection.

19. B. Hóman and G. Szekfű *Magyar történet*, V. p. 455.

20. Oscar Jászi, *Revolution and Counter-Revolution in Hungary* (New York: H. Fertig, 1969), p. 3.

21. Julius Szilassy, *Der Untergang der Donau-Monarchie* (Berlin: Verlag Neues Vaterland, 1921), pp. 330-331.

22. Vilmos Böhm, *A munkások és a termelés* /The Workers and Production/ (Budapest: Népszava Könyvkereskedés, 1919), p. 13.

23. Wilhelm Böhm, *Im Kreuzfeuer zweier Revolutionen* (Munich: Verlag für Kulturpolitik, 1924), p. 109. The author was Minister of Defense in the Károlyi

(Berinkey) government, later Commander-in-Chief of the Hungarian Red Army.

24. F. Deák, *Hungary at the Paris Peace Conference*, Doc. 3, p. 362.

25. In December, 1918 A. E. Taylor, an associate of Herbert Hoover, arrived to Budapest to survey the food situation. His commission, which included four other Americans, two Frenchmen and an Englishman, "took Károlyi to task because the Hungarian government had taken no steps to arrest communist leaders." Peter Pastor, *Hungary between Wilson and Lenin; the Hungarian Revolution of 1918-1919 and the Big Three* (New York: East European Monographs, Columbia University Press, 1976), p. 98.

26. F. Deák, *Hungary at the Paris Peace Conference*, Doc. 7, p. 389.

27. *Ibid.*

28. W. Böhm, *Im Kreuzfeuer zweier Revolutionen*, p. 266.

29. D. Berinkey, the Prime Minister of the People's Republic, stated in court that he saw the original abdication document, signed by Károlyi. His widow declared in a letter to the editor of *Századok* that her husband returned the draft to his secretary, remarking: "I will not sign this." Cf. *Századok*, Vol. C, No. 6 (1966), p. 1264.

30. Herbert Hoover, *Memoirs* (New York: Macmillan, 1951), I, p. 398.

31. Hoover Institution, TS, Hungary, A2, Box 1.

32. Smuts especially wanted to "fix an armistice line between the Hungarians and Romanians, yet the real idea /was/ to see whether Béla Kun was worth using as a vehicle for getting in touch with Moscow." F. S. Crawford, *Jan Smuts; A Biography* (New York: Doubleday, 1943), pp. 156-157.

33. *Magyar hadügyi népbiztosság* /Commissariat of Defense/, Nos. 331/151 and 332/151. Hoover Institution, Hungary, XII.

34. Government telegram, addressed to the *Leipziger Volkszeitung*, dated April 15, 1919. Hoover Institution, TS, *Hungary*, A2, Box 1.

35. Government telegram, addressed to the *Leipziger Volkszeitung*, dated April 19, 1919. Hoover Institution, TS, *Hungary*, A2, Box 1.

36. Tibor Hetes, ed., *A magyarországi forradalmak krónikája, 1918-1919* /Chronicles of the 1918-1919 Revolutions in Hungary/ (Budapest: Kossuth, 1969), p. 362.

37. *Ibid*, p. 262.

38. Elek Karsai, *A budai Sándor Palotában történt* /It Happened in the Sándor Palace in Buda/ (Budapest: Táncsics, 1963), p. 8.

39. *Ibid*, p. 17.

40. Hoover Institution, *Hungary*, XII, Appendix, p. 1.

41. *August 6, 1919 Council of Ministers Minutes*. Hoover Institution, Hungary, XII, Suppl. 1, pp. 1-4.

42. Herbert Hoover, *Memoirs*, I, p. 401.

43. *American Commission to Negotiate Peace, Paris, 1918-1919*, Cases 181,9202 to 181,9220. RG M820, National Archives, Washington, D.C.

44. Hoover Institution, *Hungary*, XII, Appendix, p. 1.

45. *American Commission to Negotiate Peace, Paris, 1918-1919*, Cases 181,9202 to 181,9220. RG M820, National Archives, Washington, D.C.

46. *The Hungarian Question in the British Parliament* (London: Grant Richards, 1933), p. 12.

47. *American Commission to Negotiate Peace, Paris, 1918-1919*. Cases 181,9201 to 181,9202. RG M820, National Archives, Washington, D.C.

48. His last rank was Vice-Admiral in the Austro-Hungarian Navy.

49. Two years earlier, near the end of the war, the fifty years old Horthy was promoted over the head of many of his comrades to the rank of Commander-of-the-

Fleet by Emperor Charles. According to the 1917 edition of the *Almanach für die k. und k. Kriegsmarine*, Horthy was 24th in line among 46 *Linienschiffskapitäne*. Charles apparently wanted to reward the loyalty and faithful service of the former Aide-de-Camp to Francis Joseph, hoping that determined leadership might save his Navy from disintegration.

50. Elek Karsai and Ervin Pamlényi, *A fehér terror* /The White Terror/ (Budapest: Művelt Nép, 1951), p. 28.

51. C. A. Macartney, *October Fifteenth: History of Modern Hungary, 1929-1945*, 2nd ed. (Edinburgh University Press, 1961), I, pp. 28-29. Horthy acknowledged "the frequent outbursts against Communists and Jews" in his *Memoirs*, and remarked that these were "regrettable." The Allies finally sent U. S. Army Colonel Yates to Budapest in October to reorganize the police and the gendarmerie.

52. Miklós Horthy, *Emlékirataim* /Memoirs/, 2nd ed. (Toronto: Vörösváry-Weller, 1974), p. 118.

53. *Ibid*.

54. E. Karsai, *A budai Sándor Palotában történt*, p. 35.

55. *IV. Károly visszatérési kísérletei* /The Return Attempts of King Charles IV/ (Budapest: Magyar Királyi Minisztérium, n.d.), p. 7.

56. *Ibid*, Supplement 2, p. 65.

57. F. Deák, *Hungary at the Paris Peace Conference*, Doc. 45, p. 550.

58. M. Kozma's instructions to propaganda officers, dated Dec. 1, 1919. E. Karsai, *A budai Sándor Palotában történt*, pp. 38-39.

59. As stated by an eyewitness, police and army officers formed a ring around the Parliament building, and after 9 a.m. groups larger than three persons were dissolved. László Frank, *Cafe Atlantis* (Budapest: Gondolat, 1963., p. 35.

60. S. Szilassy, *Revolutionary Hungary, 1918-1921*, p. 71.

61. *Ibid*, pp. 71-72.

62. Hungary "did not altogether deny the 'right of self-determination,' but she protested very warmly against the conclusions drawn from it. She admitted as valid only the decision taken by the *Sobor* (Diet) of Croatia-Slavonia. . .and maintained stoutly that the nationalities never really wished to separate from her at all." C. A. Macartney, *Hungary and Her Successors; The Treaty of Trianon and its Consequencies* (London: Oxford University Press, 1968), p. 5. In M. Károlyi's opinion the aim of the "impossible" peace conditions was "the maximum /economic/ exploitation of the defeated countries." Letter to Pál Szende, dated Lazne Schlag and Prague, Feb. 21-27, 1920. Columbia Univ. Archives, *Jászi Collection*.

63. Secret negotiations took place between Hungary and France simultaneously with the peace negotiations in 1920, when Hungarian military assistance was deemed necessary in the Russo-Polish war. These negotiations were conducted by Ambassador Paleologue, then Secretary-General of the French Ministry of Foreign Affairs, and Dr. K. Halmos, a Hungarian lawyer-businessman, but members of the Hungarian peace delegation and other diplomats were also involved. The negotiations ended in failure. F. Deák, *Hungary at the Paris Peace Conference*, pp. 253-338.

64. Huszár resigned repeatedly, according to the *Documents of the National Assembly*, authenticated edition (Budapest: Pesti Könyvnyomda, 1920), I. The relationship between Horthy and Huszár became very cool after the intrusion of officers to the Parliament building and the murder of two social democratic newspapermen on February 17.

65. H. W. V. Temperley, ed., *A History of the Peace Conference of Paris* (London: Oxford University Press, 1920), I, p. 190.

66. August Heckscher, ed., *The Politics of Woodrow Wilson: Selections from his*

Speeches and Writings (Freeport, N.Y.: Books for Libraries Press, 1956), p. 266. At the July 1, 1919 meeting of the Commission of the International Regime of Ports, Waterways and Railways Manley O. Hudson, the U.S. representative, stated that the Allies were making Hungary into "an enclaved State," and that by so doing "they incurred a heavy responsibility." Upon Hudson's suggestion the question of Hungary's access to the Black and Adriatic Seas was referred to the Supreme Council. RG 59, *State Department Records,* National Archives, Washington D.C. On May 14, upon the recommendation of Lloyd George, it was agreed that a clause should be inserted in the Treaty providing for access of Austria and Hungary to the sea, but no action was taken on it.

67. *The Messages and Papers of Woodrow Wilson* (New York: The Review of Reviews Corp., 1924), I, p. 447.

68. Parliamentary ratification took place on Nov. 13, 1920.

69. 1910 census.

70. C. A. Macartney, *Hungary and Her Successors,* p. 206.

71. According to Article 183, the priority of the charges was: "a. the cost of the armies of occupation, as defined under Article 181, during the Armistice; b. the cost of any armies of occupation, as defined under Article 181, after the coming into force of the present Treaty." Reparation and other payments came next in order. The amount to be paid for reparations was unspecified by the treaty.

72. *Memoirs of Dr. Eduard Beneš: From Munich to New War and New Victory* (Boston: Houghton-Mifflin, 1954), p. 1.

73. *Ibid,* p. 2.

74. During the Belgrade negotiations with Károlyi, General Franchet d'Esperay apparently expressed official French opinion by saying that "Hungarians marched with the Germans and will be punished with them." Michael Károlyi, *Faith Without Illusion* (New York: Dutton, 1957), p. 134.

75. "A cry arose from. . .Eastern Europe to Paris, 'The Habsburgs are coming back.' " Herbert Hoover, *The Ordeal of Woodrow Wilson* (New York: Dutton, 1957), p. 134.

76. The behavior of Beneš was characterized by misleading tactics throughout the peace negotiations. At the February 5, 1919 meeting, at which President Wilson presided, Beneš stated that "Slovakia had at one time formed part of the Czecho-Slovak State. It had been overrun by the Magyars at the beginning of the 10th century." He added that taking over the region claimed by him, the Czecho-Slovak State "would be including some 350,000 Magyars." F. Deák, *Hungary at the Paris Peace Conference,* p. 392. The truth is, that Slovakia as an organized country with defined boundaries, or a Czecho-Slovak State had never existed, and even according to the Czechoslovak census of 1921, there were 761,030 Hungarians living within the Czechoslovak Republic.

77. "An on-the-spot inquiry will perhaps reveal the necessity of altering certain parts of the boundary line, provided for in the Treaty. . ." In his May 6, 1920 letter Millerand also declared that "a state of affairs, even when millenial, is not meant to exist when it has been recognized as contrary to justice." F. Deák, *Hungary at the Paris Peace Conference,* p. 552.

78. On December 14-15, 1921, 15,334 people voted for Hungary and 8,227 for Austria. E. Karsai, *A budai Sándor Palotában történt,* p. 536.

79. A. Balla, ed., *A magyar országgyűlés története,* p. 403.

80. *Ibid,* p. 78.

81. Erik Molnár, ed., *Magyarország története* /The history of Hungary/. (Budapest: Gondolat, 1967), II, p. 375.

82. The 1947 Paris Peace Treaty essentially reconfirmed the territorial provisions of Trianon, with some minor additional territorial losses to Czechoslovakia. For a massive recent work on the roots and consequences of the Treaty of Trianon by nearly three dozen American and European scholars, see Béla K. Király, Peter Pastor, and Ivan Sanders, eds., *War and Society in East Central Europe*, Vol. VI. *Essays on World War I; Total War and Peacemaking. A Case Study of Trianon* (New York: Social Sciences Monographs, Columbia University Press, 1982), 678 pp.

B. A. Rektor:

14 / THE HUNGARIAN GENDARM- ERIE: ITS TRAGIC ROLE IN WORLD WAR II

I. THE FRENCH POLICE SYSTEM

The purpose of this study is to discuss the rise and development of the Hungarian Gendarmerie, its role in interwar Hungary, its involvement in the affairs of World War II, and its dilemma in facing the problems created by the collapse of Regent Horthy's Old Order in the fall of 1944. In order to achieve this goal, however, it is desirable to summarize briefly the history of this organization.

Similarly to all such paramilitary police forces, the roots of the Hungarian Gendarmerie can be traced back to the French Revolution, and more specifically to the laws of 1791 (June 6th and June 20th). Based on the traditions of the *Marechaussee*,[1] in that year the modern French *Gendarmerie* was born. Its members were selected from the ranks of the French Army, who then were organized along military lines into *escadrons*, each of which had mounted and foot *gendarmes*.

This paramilitary French police force survived the fall of Napoleon, and in the course of its development it came to serve as a model for similar forces in dozens of other countries. These include The Catholic Netherlands /Belgium/ (1795), Luxembourg (1798), Prussia /Germany/ (1806), Piedmont /Italy/ (1814), Papal States /Vatican/ (1816), Russia (1826), Spain (1829), Greece (1833), Austria (1849), San Marino (1874), Switzerland (1876), Hungary (1881), as well as such other countries created, reconstructed, or resurrected in wake of World War I as Bulgaria, Czechoslovakia, Poland, Romania, Yugoslavia (all around 1920), and Cyprus (1960).[2]

Before World War II, twenty-one European and fourteen non-European countries had such French-type paramilitary law enforcement agencies. Including among the latter was Canada with its famed Canadian Mounted Police. A number of these forces have since been dissolved and abolished, including the Royal Hungarian Gendarmerie, which in 1945 had to relinquish its place to a Soviet-type "people's police."

II. THE ROYAL HUNGARIAN GENDARMERIE

The defeat of the Hungarian War of Independence in 1849 by the Habsburg imperial forces aided by Russia was followed by a period of absolutism and by the establishment and introduction of the Austrian Gendarmerie into the defeated country.

Following the Compromise of 1867 and the creation of Austria-Hungary, the Austrian Gendarmerie regiments in the Kingdom of Hungary—except in Transylvania—were dissolved. The Transylvania Gendarmerie survived in that eastern province of Hungary until 1876, when Emperor Francis Joseph—who was also king of Hungary—relinquished its control to the Hungarian Parliament. The Hungarian authorities promptly changed the name and language of this organization to Hungarian, and then five years later (Act III of 1881) extended it to the whole country. This is how the Royal Hungarian Gendarmerie /*Magyar Királyi Csendőrség*/ was born. [3]

The primary driving force behind the establishment of this paramilitary organization was the fact that the old type of decentralized county police force—which was similar to the sheriff's office in the United States—was unable to keep law and order in the provinces. The comprehensive Bill for the proposed organization was prepared by Louis Schatz and Lajos Jékelfalussy—the former of whom had been a lieutenant-colonel in the Austrian Gendarmerie. Once mandated by the Hungarian Parliament, the new organization was placed under the command of Ferenc Török, the former chief of the Tranyslvanian Gendarmerie, who was now put in charge of recruitment, training, and of generally putting the new organization on track. [4]

According to the Law of 1881, the country was divided into six districts, each of which was commanded by a gendarme colonel or lieutenant-colonel. Each district command, in turn, was divided into two or three "wings," each of which covered two or three counties. Under the wing commandants were two or three squadrons, each having fourteen to eighteen gendarme posts.

In 1925, wings were renamed sections and squadrons were renamed wings. This organizational structure then remained essentially unchanged right up to the end of World War II, although in the period between 1939 and 1941—when certain largely Hungarian-inhabited territories were returned to Hungary—the number of districts were increased to ten.

Throughout this period, the real law enforcement units in the country's rural regions were the gendarme posts, whose members patrolled their assigned territories day and night.[5] In the cities the law enforcement was handled by the city police, which subsequently became a national police force /*államrendőrség*/. Act X of 1882, however, authorized the Minister of Interior to enter into contract with cities that wished to replace their own police with the gendarme forces. It is to the credit of the Hungarian Gendarmerie that by 1906 sixteen cities have opted to do so. The success of this organization, however, is also evident from the fact that by 1904 a separate gendarme section was established within the Ministry of Interior, which then was placed under the command of Colonel Pál Kosztka.

III. PEACE, WAR, REVOLUTIONS

In addition to regular police duties in the provinces, in the period before World War I the Hungarian Gendarmerie also became entangled in a number of events and operations that shaped its public image—be it negative or positive. The former were usually connected with attempts to control violent workers' strikes and to keep order during political demonstrations,[6] while the latter included successful operations to stem cholera-epidemics and to rescue the victims of major floods and fires. While the latter operations earned much praise and many decorations to the members of the Gendarmerie (575 between 1908 and 1918), the former blackened their name before certain segments of the Hungarian public.[7]

Starting with 1894, members of the Hungarian Gendarmerie were also being increasingly used for military police duties. These obligations grew considerably during World War I, when Hungarian gendarme units were charged with keeping order among the troops and were also entrusted with policing some of the occupied territories in Serbia, Italy, and Russia. As a consequence of these additional obligations, the country suffered increasingly from a shortage of trained gendarmes. This was particularly true toward the end of the war, when most of Hungary's main cities lacked the necessary police force to keep order in the growingly unstable situation that soon led to a series of revolutions.[8]

The first of these revolutions was connected with the name of Count Michael Károlyi, whose short regime (October 1918-March 1919) turned out to be simply a transition between the monarchy of Emperor Charles I (1916-1918) and Béla Kun's Hungarian Soviet Republic (March-August 1919), the latter of which represented the second of these revolutions.[9] While during Károlyi's tenure in office the Hungarian Gendarmerie remained intact and continued to perform its duties, during Kun's equally short, but violent rule, it was replaced by the Red Guard and many of its members suffered persecution. According to one fairly reliable report, of the 590 persons who fell victim to Kun's so-called "Red Terror," twenty-seven came from the ranks of the Gendarmerie.[10]

The White Terror that followed the Red Terror reversed the situation completely and took revenge on those whom it blamed for all the real and alleged atrocities committed by the Hungarian Bolsheviks. It was particularly harsh on self-proclaimed or alleged communists and on Jews, the latter of whom were very heavily represented in the leadership of the Hungarian Soviet Republic. The instruments of this White revenge were mostly the numerous freebooting battalions composed of ex-soldiers under the command of such self-appointed leaders as Pál Prónay, Iván Héjjas, and Gyula Ostenburg. The latter were motivated both by their unleashed nationalistic anger against Hungary's territorial mutilation, as well as by their conviction that the Hungarian Bolsheviks and the Jews were somehow behind all of the country's misfortunes. These "White" battalions went far beyond all permissible limits in their retributions, and thereby they actually aided

Hungary's enemies in their effort to undermine the country's credibility. This was all the more wrong and undeserving, as "a great part of the assimilated /Hungarian/ Jewry" who fell victim to the terror, had "preserved its loyalty to the country." [11]

While relatively few members of the Hungarian Gendarmerie were actually involved in these operations, as all leaders of these detachments called their units "Gendarme Reserve Battalions," the prestige of the Hungarian Gendarmerie was also badly hurt.

IV. INTERWAR YEARS IN MUTILATED HUNGARY

The year 1920 saw both the signing of the Treaty of Trianon (June 4th) which reduced Hungary to a small fraction of its former self, as well as the rise and consolidation of Admiral Nicholas Horthy's counterrevolutionary regime that placed its stamp on the small country and its society for the next two and a half decades.

Although Admiral Horthy and the "White Army" that placed him into power were likewise motivated by anti-communism and Hungarian nationalism, they also stood for law and order. For this reason, under Horthy's leadership, both the communists and the anticommunist freebooters were rooted out. Order was restored to the now much reduced country, but at the same time Horthy also made sure that the conservative social order—which Hungary's greatest contemporary historian, Szekfű, appropriately labeled "Neo-Baroque"—would also survive. [12]

In this atmosphere of "Restoration," the Hungarian Gendarmerie once again regained its respected place in society. At the same time, however, it was also made by Admiral Horthy into one of the staunchest and most reliable upholders of the re-established conservative socio-political order. Yet, post-Trianon changes in Hungary's size and infrastructure demanded that the resurrected Gendarmerie also be adjusted to these new realities. In line with these demands, Act VII of 1922 subordinated the Corps solely to the authority of the Ministry of Interior.

Starting with the late 1920s, the Hungarian Gendarmerie was also subjected to increased modernization, which, however, was thwarted by the country's general poverty and the negative impact of the world depression. Even so, some steps were taken in this direction. Thus, in 1929 special traffic control units were set up to patrol the highway between Budapest and Hungary's western frontiers. These units were equipped with motorcycles with sidecars and were also obliged to give first aid to injured persons on the highways. After several years of successful experience with these units, in 1935 the traffic gendarme service was expanded to the whole country.

In 1930 four investigation units were also established, each with two or three officers and eight to ten enlisted men. Their chief duties were to support local gendarme posts with laboratory work and in solving major crimes. Later every gendarme district received it own investigation unit.

During the 1930s shortwave radio network was also introduced into the gendarme system. Direct communication was established between the Ministry of Interior and all gendarme districts' headquarters, although initially the individual gendarme posts had only receiving stations.

In 1940 and 1942, respectively, separate railroad and water gendarme units were also set up. Of the former there were several units, all of which were located at main railroad junctions, but with headquarters in Budapest. Of the latter, there was only one, which was headquartered at Siófok on Lake Balaton. [13]

The years 1938-1940, which saw the outbreak of World War II, also witnessed a partial realization of Hungary's revisionist dreams. In wake of the two so-called "Vienna Awards" Hungary regained some of her mostly Hungarian-inhabited territories lost after World War I. The First Vienna Award of November 2, 1938 returned to her a narrow strip of southern territory from Czechoslovakia, while the Second Vienna Award of August 30, 1940 transferred Northern Transylvania from Romania. In the meanwhile, following Hitler's dismemberment of Czechoslovakia and the creation of Msgr. Tiso's Slovak puppet state under German tutelage, Hungary also initiated a successful military operation to recover Carpatho-Ruthenia in former Northeastern Hungary (March 15, 1939). Moreover, in April 1941, after the German attack against Yugoslavia, Hungary likewise began military operations in the

Bachka /Bácska/ or Vojvodina region of North-Central Yugoslavia, again with the intention of recovering some of her territories lost after World War I. [14]

Naturally, all of these territorial acquisitions and border revisions required the active involvement of military forces, including the Hungarian Gendarmerie, which marched alongside the Hungarian Army. The returning Hungarian military and police forces were received with joy and acclamation by the Hungarian-speaking population. This feeling of euphoria, however, could not conceal the displeasure of the non-Hungarians, nor the fact that these re-acquisitions also implied additional duties and obligations to the Hungarian authorities. After all, the regained territories had to be administered, and their administrative operations had to be synthesized with Hungary's own administrative and judicial systems.

One of the first problems encountered by the Hungarian Gendarmerie following these border revisions was the lack of adequate manpower. The leadership of the corps was forced to establish several new gendarme districts (Kassa/Kosice, Kolozsvár/Kluj, and Marosvásárhely/Tirgu Mures) and transfer one from Pozsony /Bratislava/ to Szombathely. In order to man the new territories, it was compelled to withdraw officers and men from the existing ones. [15] Moreover, to fill some of the vacancies in the re-acquired lands, the Corps also accepted volunteers from those regions, all the more so as these new enlistees also spoke the language of the non-Hungarian local population.

The relationship between the Hungarian Gendarmerie and the local non-Hungarians was not always friendly, but that was usually the result of the lack of open-mindedness on the one side, and the unconcealed display of hostile intentions on the other. At the same time there were those who went out of their way to further the friendship and to enhance the co-operation of the various nationalities in those multinational regions. One of these was Major Arpád Zámbory, who upon entering Western Bachka at the head of two-hundred Hungarian gendarmes, urged his men to respect every citizen and to handle all of them fairly and equally: "We have to win the confidence of the local population for the Hungarian state regardless of religion, race, or nationality. We have to treat everyone with tolerance, forgiveness, and understanding.... Contacts have to be established, especially with members of the older generation who are familiar with the institution of the Hungarian Gendarmerie from the period before World War I." [16]

V. THE TRAGIC YEARS OF WORLD WAR II

On June 26, 1941, five days after Germany's attack against the Soviet Union, the northeastern Hungarian cities of Kassa, Munkács, and Rahó were bombed by unknown assailants. The aggressor planes were not identified and scholars are still in disagreement as to their identities. Yet, it was this unprovoked attack that landed Hungary in the war. [17]

Although a number of the civilian ministers of the Hungarian Government opposed military retaliation, supported by Hungary's staunchly pro-German ambassador in Berlin (Döme Sztójay), the generals ultimately won out. Convinced or presuming that the attackers were Russians, on June 27, 1941 Regent Horthy declared war against the Soviet Union, and did so without the prior approval of the Hungarian Parliament. Naturally, this decision was influenced first of all by the fear that by failing to join Germany, Hungary would again lose the territories regained from Romania which now proved to be a staunch ally of Germany.

The declaration of war was a fateful step indeed. It landed Hungary squarely in the midst of a world conflict where she had no place to be, and from which she was unable to extricate herself. Moreover, it also made it unavoidable for her to suffer the consequences — including the loss of all territories she had regained in the years immediately preceding the war.

The declaration of war was immediately followed by an invasion into Soviet territory, first by a relatively small contingent called the "Carpathian Group" /*Kárpát-csoport*/, and then after more ample preparation by the Hungarian Second Army. Outmanned and outgunned, and really unprepared for such a world conflict, the Second Army was totally destroyed in the great battles at the Don River in January 1942. [18] After that defeat, the various Hungarian army units participated only as occupying forces in the Ukraine, and Hungary began a long, arduous, and largely unsuccessful effort to distance itself from Germany and ultimately to get out of the war with the least possible of losses.

In contrast to regular military units, the Hungarian Gendarmerie never fought on Soviet territory as an individual Corps. Some of its smaller units were subordinated to the headquarters of the higher commands where they served in accordance with the "Service Regulations of the Field Gendarmerie. "In addition to the "Military Gendarmes" who were assigned to them and whose numbers were very small, every larger army unit organized from its own manpower "Regimental Gendarmes."

The latter's duties were prescribed for them by their army commandants, who also had the authority to use them for military police duties. The other non-professional army units in this category were the "Gendarme Service Battalions" who served behind the battlefields. They were composed mostly of older reserve soldiers who guarded railroad lines, depots, and, in case of emergency, also served as military police officers.[19]

A. The Massacre of Újvidék /Novi Sad/

Six months after the reoccupation of Bachka, the royalist *Chetniks* and the communist *Partisans* undertook a series of saboteur actions against Hungarian authorities. More and more harvested wheat and hemp were set on fire, and an increasing number of farmsteads were burned down. They also blew up railroad lines and bridges, and at times attacked and killed small military and gendarme units. Tito's Partisans were particularly in the forefront of these activities.

When in January 1942 the Partisans broke up a border guard gendarme unit near a farm in the vicinity of the town of Zsablya, the Army ordered three battalions under the command of Colonel László Deák to search the area for the guerillas. Soon after, when the news came that the Partisans have all melted into the City of Újvidék /Novi Sad/, a similar search was ordered in that city. To carry out this "search mission," the regional military commander Lieutenant-General Ferenc Feketehalmy-Czeydner ordered most of the locally available military, gendarme, and police forces into that city. All suspected persons were screened by a committee headed by Brigadier-General József Grassy, aided by Colonel

László Deák. Those who were condemned to death—largely because they were not from the area and were unable to explain their presence at Újvidék—were taken to the Danube and then executed by a firing squad under the command of Lieutenant Gusztáv Korompay. Most of them were shoved into the river through a hole cut into the ice. There were also those who were not even given the chance to confront the "screening committee," but were taken directly by their captors to the Danube to be executed.

No one knows the exact number of the victims. Estimates range from a low of 1,300 (Regent Horthy) to the high of 3,340 (communist author Buzási). Whatever their number, it was way too high and hardly justifiable on the basis of local conditions and considerations.

Following this search, which turned out to be a "search and destroy mission," the Hungarian Chief-of-Staff accepted the report of the military commander, but the uproar in Hungarian political and intellectual circles was so great that the government was obliged to set up a Military Tribunal to deal with those responsible for this massacre. This Tribunal—composed of Major-Generals J. Kiss, I. Náday, and J. Németh, and Colonel J. Babos—sentenced four military and one gendarme officer to death, and twenty lower ranking officers (among them eleven gendarmes) to imprisonment ranging from five to fifteen years. The latter were held responsible for sabotaging their supervisory duties. The Hungarian Parliament also voted an annual compensation of twelve million *pengős* for the surviving family members of the victims.[20]

The meting out of justice, however, had to wait until after the war. With the exception of the lower ranked officers, all of those primarily responsible for this massacre escaped to Germany, where they immediately joined the SS and received German protection. They returned to their country only after Hungary's German occupation on March 19, 1944, when they came as "conquerors." Following World War II, they were all extradited to Yugoslvaia, where they were executed along with other war criminals.

The heavy presence of gendarme officers among those implicated in this massacre hurt the Corps's reputation considerably; and this was to haunt them for many years even after the war.

B. Attempts to Leave the War

The Massacre of Újvidék was one of the factors in the fall of the Bárdossy-Government and the rise of Nicholas Kállay to the prime ministership (March 9, 1942). As soon as it was feasable without undue danger, Kállay contacted the Western Allies through Istanbul (L. Veress) and Stockholm (A. Ullein-Reviczky) with the hope of engineering Hungary's exodus from the war, while at the same time avoiding both a German and a Soviet occupation. In Kállay's own words: "Our official representative in Istanbul was our consul general Desiderius (Dezső) Ujváry. (László) Veres /who had been dispatched by Kállay/ was specially attached to Ujváry for the purpose of his mission. On August 17, 1943, these two informed Mr. Sterndale Bennett, the British minister, representing the Allies, of Hungary's readiness to surrender to the Allies...if Anglo-American troops reached the frontiers of Hungary." [21]

Another diplomat who was entrusted by Kállay to negotiate with the Allies was György Bessenyey, Hungarian minister at Bern, who contacted American delegates Royal Taylor and Allen W. Hulles. As recalled by Kállay, the Allies suggested that "when Italy changed sides...Hungary should /also/ jump out." [22] But as at that moment the British and American troops were five-hundred miles from Hungary's frontiers, Hungary "could not undertake to commit a suicide that would have benefited no one." [23]

In the United States, Archduke Otto von Habsburg—who had several personal meetings with President Roosevelt—and Tibor Eckhardt—the personal representative of Regent Horthy—were working hard to prepare Hungary's eventual Anglo-American occupation. Unfortunately, their efforts came to naught.[24]

In the meanwhile, things were also moving along on the home front, particulary in wake of Hungary's German occupation in March of 1944. Regent Horthy, who still retained some semblance of power, was personally involved in a number of the efforts to free the country from Germany's powerhold. As an example, in September 1944, he dispatched General István Náday and the English Colonel Charles Telfer Howie—who, after his escape from the German POW camp, was harbored in Hungary—to Italy and authorized them to ask the commander of British Army there to send Anglo-American occupation troops to Western Hungary. According to this plan, the reliable units of the Hungarian Gendarmerie were to prepare the ground for this occupation, and then they were to cooperate with the Western occupying forces to the fullest extent.

Sir Henry Maitland Wilson, the British commander of the Allied Armies on the Mediterranean front, and General Mark Wayne Clark, commander of the 5th American Army in Italy, both supported this initiative, as both of them favored the Allied invasion through the Balkans proposed by Sir Winston Churchill. In Italy, they prepared the ground by selecting Hungarian speaking officers from the ranks of the American troops for deployment in Hungary. Their uniforms bore a badge with the Hungarian coat-of-arms and the inscription: "Hungary-Magyarország." This whole plan, however, collapsed because of President Roosevelt's opposition, who favored "Operation Anvil," i.e. the invasion of Southern France. [25]

After realizing that his hopes for an Allied landing in Hungary have failed, and after being directed to do so by the Allies, Horthy sent an armistice delegation to Moscow that was headed by Lieutenant-General Gábor Faragho, the Superintendent of the Hungarian Gendarmerie. Based on these negotiations, on October 15th, 1944, he proclaimed Hungary's withdrawal from the war. Unfortunately, this attempt at extricating the country from the war failed; partially because it was not well prepared, and partially because a sizeable percentage of the strongly anticommunist Hungarian officer corps was unwilling to give up its alliance with Germany for a similar arrangement with Soviet Russia. [26]

In order to thwart this Hungarian effort to switch alliances, the Germans kidnapped Horthy's only remaining son, forced him to resign the regency, took him into "protective custody," and placed Ferenc Szálasi, the head of the Hungarian Arrow Cross /Nazi/ Party into power. As a result, Hungary continued to fight on the German side up to the bitter end, and she was accordingly punished much more than Germany's other allies who have contributed more to the war effort, but who had the sense to leave the sinking ship before Hungary did.

C. *German Occupation and the Deportation of the Jews*

On March 15, 1944, Hitler invited Regent Horthy for a meeting at Klessheim, near Salzburg, where they were to discuss the withdrawal of the remnants of the Hungarian Army from Soviet territories. In spite of Prime Minister Kállay's opposition, on the 17th of that month Horthy left in company of Chief-of-Staff General Ferenc Szombathelyi, Foreign Minister Jenő Ghyczy, and Defense Minister Lajos Csatay, and on the 18th he was told of Hungary's impending occupation. Although Horthy protested, on March 19th eleven German divisions passed into Hungary, and thus the Hungarian Government's freedom to act became very limited. Moreover, only three days after occupation, the Regent was forced to name a new government under the prime ministership of the openly Germanophile former ambassador to Berlin, General Döme Sztójay.[27]

With the occupying forces came large *Waffen-SS* and *Gestapo* units, who soon established contacts with their Hungarian sympathizers and extended their control over much of the country. One of the most prominent and notorious of the Gestapo leaders was SS Lieutenant-Colonel Adolf Eichmann, commandant of the *Judendezernat*, in charge of the "de-Jewification" of Hungary. On the very next day after occupation, Eichmann assembled the leaders of the Hungarian Jewry and proclaimed his sole authority over them. He also stated that he would protect them if they would fulfill his wishes. He asked discipline and work, for which he promised them regular wages. Morever—so he said—once the war was brought to a successful completion, all restrictions on them would cease.

As is well known, these promises were never fulfilled. As early as April of that year, the Germans ordered the collection into concentration camps all Hungarian citizens in the rural areas who were classified as Jews, and by June all similarly classified Budapest residents were also obliged to move into ghettoes. This was soon followed by their deportation and ultimately by their liquidation in various German death camps. Only a minority of the Budapest Jews were able to save themselves, partially by hiding among daring and caring Christian friends, and partially through various methods of misindentification. As stated by one of the top authorities of this question, "by June 20, 1944, 427,000 Jews, that is about half of the Hungarian Jewish population, had to suffer the terrible order of deportation." [28]

All of these collection and deportation procedures were carried out by Hungarian authorities—more specifically by the Hungarian Gendarmerie and by various local police forces—at the orders of and under the supervision of the German occupying forces. Often the Germans filmed segments of these deportation procedures. But on such occasions they usually withdrew into the background, downplaying their own role in these affairs, and making certain to record the presence and actions of the Hungarian auxiliary forces. Their goal was to project to the neutral European states the alleged brutality of the Hungarians as opposed to their own alleged humanity. But these films rarely show the fact that a good number of those Hungarians, including gendarmes and policemen, were there only because they had no choice, and because they were ordered to be there by the German occupying forces. [29]

But going beyond this, there are also examples of various gendarme units defying and sabotaging German orders for Jewish deportations. Such was the case on July 8, 1944, when Regent Horthy attempted to put an end to the mass transfer of Hungarian Jews to Germany. After informing the German occupying authorities that Hungarian "military and gendarme units had been brought into the capital, which—in case of necessity—will take up arms against German deportation attempts," he ordered a gendarme unit to stop and to return an already departed train. They did so near the city of Hatvan, and then returned the 1,500 Jewish deportees to their camp. There were also numerous examples of Hungarian gendarme and police units saving Jewish political prisoners on the streets of Budapest and preventing them from being taken out of Hungary. Moreover, gendarme units also guarded the International Ghetto in Budapest against planned Nazi atrocities. [30]

The enumeration of these facts and explanations is not an attempt to lessen the responsibility of those who participated willingly in actions against the Jews and other political prisoners, nor even of those who were unwilling, if timid and obedient tools in the hands of the administrators of an evil empire. It is simply an attempt to put things into the right perspective, and to point out the incorrectness of the wholesale condemnation of the Hungarian Gendarmerie—as it happened in 1945.

D. Final Struggles and Disbandment

Following Romania's successful switch to the side of the Allies on August 23, 1944, the attacking Soviet troops rapidly reached Hungary's southeastern frontiers. In addition to a few scattered army units, only a few quickly assembled and lightly equipped gendarme units were available to defend Hungary's territory. The latter were led by Lieutenant-Colonel Pál Fekete and Captain Tibor Szelevényi, who, along with most of their men, were among the first Hungarian gendarmes to perish fighting Soviet forces on Hungarian soil.

Hereafter, gendarme units were used on a regular basis and in ever increasing numbers in the hopeless, if protracted struggle against Soviet occupation. They participated in large numbers in the defense of the Northeastern Carpathians, in the battles around the city of Nagyvárad /Oradea/, at the siege of Budapest, and finally in the final battles around Lake Balaton in Western Hungary. According to official estimates, in the course of these encounters, the Corps lost about fifty percent of its officers and men, whose mostly unmarked graves are scattered all over the country and even beyond.

For Hungary the war ended on April 4, 1945, when the last piece of Hungarian territory was occupied by the Soviet Army. Those who feared the new Soviet masters and the new communist system they were about to install escaped to Austria and to Germany. Some of these later returned to Hungary, but others—accepting the classification of **Displaced Persons** or **DPs**—emigrated to various other parts of the world.

As could be expected, the Treaty of Paris of 1946 once more deprived Hungary of all the territories regained before World War II. But more than this, Hungary lost some additional lands to Czechoslovakia and was also forced to pay huge reparations to Soviet Russia.

On December 21-22, 1944, while the war was still on and the Soviet Army was preparing for its protracted siege of Budapest, a Provisional Hungarian National Assembly was called into session in Debrecen. After appointing the Provisional National Government headed by General Béla Miklós de Dálnok /Dálnoki Miklós/ and after dealing with other matters, it also authorized one of the new ministers, General Gábor Faragho—the last Superintendent of the Hungarian Gendarmerie who was in charge of Horthy's peace mission to Moscow in early October 1944—to establish a new centralized law enforcement agency for the country. While, in light of the rapid communist takeover of police matters in Hungary, Faragho had little chance to implement this plan, three months later he was one of those who was forced to accept Decree No. 1960: 1945 (March 1945), which disbanded the Hungarian Gendarmerie once and for all, and accused its members of collective responsibility for the overt and inhuman acts connected with the last phase of the war.

With this decree, the surviving members of the Hungarian Gendarmerie who chose to remain at home were collectively placed outside the law of the land. They lost their jobs, pensions, as well as their right to gain employment in public service jobs. Unless they were able to prove to the "Special Screening Committee for Ex-Gendarmes" that they have personally participated in the anti-German underground movement, that they have disregarded the country's laws during Hungary's German occupation, and that during that period they gave active help to anti-fascist and communist organizations, they had no chance of being cleared of collective responsibility. As these conditions were totally unrealistic, very few of them were cleared. [31]

VI. SHARE FOR THE RESPONSIBILITY IN THE ATROCITIES

One cannot end this study without examining the role of the Hungarian Gendarmerie in the events of World War II and attempting to assess its share of responsibility in the atrocities of those years. The sources available to us, however, are limited and tainted with considerable personal bias. Undoubtedly, sometimes in the future, when more official documents will be available to the researchers, scholars will have to re-examine these events and the role of the Gendarmerie therein. Already at this time, however, we can call attention to a number of factors which have to be taken into consideration in the current and all future assessments about this institutions.

One of the first things to be remembered is the fact that, having been a national police force, all courts, public prosecutors, county and district administrators had the authority to call upon the Gendarmerie in their efforts of executing or upholding the country's laws. In many instances, young and inexperienced honorary district clerks may have issued orders to the local gendarme units to break workers' strikes or to dissolve political gatherings. And the gendarmes were obliged to execute these orders without question as to their validity or the reasons behind them.

These problems also emerged in conjunction with executing orders concerning the collection of overdue taxes or private debts, which always produced resentment. The local population only saw the actions of uniformed gendarmes, and seldom recalled that these actions were the result of orders issued by civil administrators. As a result, they turned their anger and resentment against the executors of these orders, and not against those who have formulated and issued them.

A. Responsibility for the Massacre at Újvidék /Novi Sad/

To conduct a search of a territory is the mission of a competent police or gendarme force. This appears to have been acknowledged in 1942 also by the military authorities in the Bachka region, for when the search for the Yugoslav Partisans was being prepared, Brigadier-General Grassy asked Assistant Police Chief József Tallián of Újvidék and Gendarme Lieutenant-Colonel Lajos Gaál to prepare the search plan. Their plans, however, were not taken into consideration when the Ministers of Defense and Interior ordered a search of Újvidék and its vicinity. Three high ranking military officers— Generals Feketehalmy-Czeydner and Grassy, and Colonel Deák—took charge of the affair. They had no experience in such urban search missions, and they mixed together army, gendarme, and police units without determining their specific duties and responsibilities. When the military leadership ordered revenge action against the Partisans. most army personnel carried out the orders without question. Gendarme officers, however, — who were afraid of the reaction of military tribunals—often sabotaged the unlawful orders of the generals.

In restrospect it is reasonable to assert that the bloodshed could have been avoided under the following circumstances: 1. If the Ministers of Defense and Interior had authorized police and gendarme units to conduct the search mission by themselves and the role of the military would have been limited to blockading the city; 2. if the superintendent or the district commandant of the Gendarmerie or their deputies had supervised the execution of the search; 3. and if, in the course of the search, the highest ranking gendarme officer (a lieutenant-colonel) would have had the courage to refuse cooperation with the Army and report the events to the Minister of Interior.

In wake of the political aproar following these massacres, Minister of Defense Lajos Csatay was obliged to re-examine his departmental order concerning the search mission at Újvidék (ll5. 645, eln. 20-943). But after having done so, he relegated this incident to the category of public safety service, where the gendarme officer is the specialist, and where he has to follow his own professional advice. [32] But this ministerial order failed to explain how a gendarme captain or lieutenant-colonel could follow gendarme search regulations in face of the contradictory orders of higher ranking army officers without facing the charge of insubordination.

Had gendarmes and policemen been authorized to execute the search mission at Újvidék without the involvement of the military, no massacre would have taken place. Consequently, "the responsibility for this shameful affair...(lies) with local army commanders, who not only over-reacted to guerilla harrassments, but apparently wished to make 'example' of the case as a deterrent to the recurrent guerilla activities." [33]

B. *Responsibility for the Deportations of the Jews*

The deportation of the Hungarian Jews and the collection and confiscation of their property was carried out by Hungarian governmental bureaucracy under the pressure and direct orders of the occupying German forces. All this happened with the knowledge—if not with the approval—of

Regent Horthy, the Council of Ministers, members of the Parliament, central and local administrators, and the country's whole population. The execution of the various "Jewish Laws" was carried out—at the orders of the relevant ministries—by various units of the Army, Gendarmerie, and police forces, by railroad and other transporation workers, and by innumerable central, county, and city administrators. They all were instruments of the vicious German political and military machine headed by Adolf Eichmann that took control over Hungary in the spring of 1944, and that was bent on eliminating all Hungarian citizens who were classified as Jews. Therefore, to put the blame on a single institution—the Hungarian Gendarmerie—that by its very nature had always been only the executor of bureaucratic orders, is both unfair and unwarranted.

The sharing of responsibility for these events had been recognized also by an authority of the question of the Hungarian Holocaust, Randolph L. Braham:

> It appears that considerable blame falls on those who might be called onlookers—the Allies..., the International Red Cross..., the Vatican..., the local Christian population and church authorities... To a lesser extent blame must also be shared by the Hungarian and world Jewish leaders... Ultimate responsibility, however, must be borne almost exclusively by the Germans and their Hungarian accomplices....[34]

In light of the above, the obvious question we have to pose is: Can a whole institution become an "accomplice" to an evil deed, or should guilt be limited to such members of those institutions who have ordered that deed to be committed? The obvious answer to this question is that evil deeds are always ordered by individuals and not by institutions.

This should also have been held true for the Hungarian Gendarmerie. The fact, however, is that in and after 1945 the whole Gendarmerie Corps was indicted and condemned in Hungary; and this was done without regard to the views and actions of its individual members. And what is even more shameful, the Provisional National Government that was responsible for the March 1945 law that disbanded and branded the Hungarian Gendarmerie Corps was headed by a three-star general of the former Royal Hungarian Army, Béla Miklós de Dálnok, and had as one of its members another general, the former Superintendent of the Hungarian Gendarmerie, Gábor Faragho.

This application of collective guilt violated all aspects of Western legality, and it also went against the grain of the United Nations Resolution on Human Rights of 1948, which states: "No one shall be held guilty of any penal offense on account of any act or omission which did not constitute a penal offense, under national or international law, *at the time it was committed.*" [35]

VI. EPILOGUE

The gendarme type of law enforcement system is a universally accepted institution in Europe, and a good number of European and non-European countries still have their own gendarmeries. Until the end of World War II, the Hungarian Gendarmerie, founded in 1881, was also one of these functioning forces, and it occupied a rather respected place among them. During the war it became involved in a number of deplorable incidents which were largely within the competence of various civil and military authorities, and later of the German occupying forces. As a result it was blamed for events and results which were beyond its control, but which blackened its good name, at least in the eyes of the uninformed. This is both unfair and deplorable, which only time and objective historical scholarship can erase. Our hope is that with this study we have contributed something toward this goal.

Notes

1. *Notes et Etudés Documentaires. La Gendarmerie Nationale* (Paris: Secretariat General du Government, 1970), pp. 7-20; and *La Gendarmerie Nationale* (Paris: La Tour du Guet, n.d.), pp. 48-68.

2. On the gendarme organizations of these diverse countries see the folowing works: Harold K. Becker, *Police Systems of Europe* (Springfield, IL: Charles C. Thomas, 1973), pp. 94-97, 156-157; James Cramer, *The World's Police* (London:

Cassel Company, Ltd., 1964), pp. 304-306, 308-314, 348-349, 362-363, 369-370; Department of the Army, *US Army Area Handbook for West Germany*, 2d ed. (Washington, DC: U. S. Government Printing Office, 1964), p. 603; *L'arma dei carabinieri 1914-1968* (Roma: Edizione Fuori Commercio, 1969), pp. 13-22; Direction General de la Guardia Civil, *La Guardia Civil* (Madrid: Taller-Escuele de Artes Graficos, 1963), pp. 13-20; Franz Neubauer, *Die Gendarmerie in Österreich, 1849-1924*(Graz: Steiermarkische Landesdruckerei, n. d.), pp. 35-40, 64; Foreign Area Studies, *US Army Area Handbook for Cyprus* (Washington, DC: U. S. Government Printing Office, 1964), pp. 380-385; P. S. Squire, *The Third Department* (Cambridge: Cambridge University Press, 1968), pp. 39-54, 78-94; Peter Deriabin, *Watchdogs of Terror* (New Rochelle, NY: Arlington House, 1972), pp. 122-131; and Béla Rektor, *A Magyar Királyi Csendőrség oknyomozó története* /The History of the Royal Hungarian Gendarmerie/ (Cleveland, OH: Árpád Könyvkiadó Vállalat, 1980), pp. 23-397.

3. Lóránd Preszly, *A csendőrség úttörői* /The Pioneers of the Gendarmerie (Budapest: Budapesti Hírlap, 1926), pp. 35-37.

4. *Ibid.*, pp. 31-32.

5. M. Kir. Belügyminiszter, *Utasítás a M. Kir. Csendőrség számára* /Directives for the Hung. Roy. Gendarmerie/ (Budapest, 1881), pp. 8-10. Concerning the specific structure and duties of the Hungarian Gendarmerie, and the conditions of service during the interwar years, see M. Kir. Belügyminiszter, *Szervezeti és szolgálati utasítás a M. Kir. Csendőrség számára* /Organizational and Service Regulations for the Roy. Hung. Gendarmerie/ (Budapest: Stádium, 1941).

6. As an example of such strike-breaking, see the description of the affairs at the town of Élesd, "Élesd, 1904. április 24," in *Élet és Tudomány* /Life and Science/ (May 1, 1904), pp. 819-821.

7. *A M. Kir. Csendőrség zsebkönyve, 1909* /Handbook of the Roy. Hung. Gendarmerie for 1909/ (Budapest: Franklin-Társulat, 1909), pp. 186-204.

8. *A M. Kir. Csendőrség zsebkönyve, 1905* /Handbook of the Roy. Hung. Gendarmerie for 1905/ (Budapest: Franklin-Társulat, 1905), pp. 224-240; and *A M. Kir. Belügyminiszter 1916. évi 33.333 V-a sz. körrendelete. A munkára kiadott hadifoglyok tekintetében szükséges államrendészeti, közbiztonsági teendőkről* (Roy. Hung. Minister of Interior's Circular No. 33.333 V-a of the Year 1916 on the Necessary Maintenance of Law and Public Safety in Connection with the Working of War Prisoners/ (Budapest, 1916). Cf. Rektor, *Csendőrség*, pp. 142-143.

9. For some contemporary or eyewitness accounts of the Bolshevik rule in Hungary, see: László Szabó, *A bolsevizmus Magyarországon* /Bolshevism in Hungary/ (Budapest: Athenaeum Irodalmi és Nyomdai Rt., 1919), p. 6; József Breit, *A magyarországi 1918/19. évi forradalmi mozgalmak és a vörösháború története* /History of the Revolutionary Movements and of the War of the Reds in Hungary in the Years 1918-19/ (Budapest: Grill Károly Könyvkiadó, 1929), p. 28; Gramma J. Cesurat, *Borzalmas vallomások, hiteles rendőri adatok* /Terrible Confessions, Official Police Data/ (n.p., n.d.), pp. 12-24; and Tiborné Szamuely, Jolán Szilágyi, *Emlékeim* /Memoires/ (Budapest: Zrínyi Katonai Kiadó, 1966), p. 115. The last mentioned was the wife of one of the top Bolshevik leaders.

10. Albert Váry, *A vörös uralom áldozatai Magyarországon* /Victims of the Red Regime in Hungary/ (Vác: Az Országos Fegyintézet Nyomdája, n.d.), pp. 1-55.

11. Dominic G. Kosáry and Steven Béla Várdy, *History of the Hungarian Nation* (Astor Park, FL: Danubian Press, Inc., 1969), p. 212. See also: "The White Terror in Hungary," in *Report of the British Joint Labour Delegation to Hungary* (London, May 1920), pp. 1-26; and József Pogány, *A fehér terror Magyarországon* /White Terror in Hungary/ (Vienna, 1920).

12. Gyula Szekfű, *Három nemzedék és ami utána következik* /Three Generations and What Comes After/ (Budapest: Királyi Magyar Egyetemi Nyomda, 1934), pp. 385-505.

13. On these post-Trianon developments concerning the Hungarian Gendarmerie, see Rektor, *Csendőrség*, pp. 164-297. See also Károly Kövendy, *Magyar Királyi Csendőrség* /Hungarian Royal Gendarmerie/ (Toronto: MKCSBK Hungarian Veterans, Sovereign Press, 1973); idem, *Harcunk. A M. Kir. fegyveres erők képekben, 1920-1945* /Our Struggle. The Hung. Roy. Armed Forces in Pictures, 1920-1945/ (Toronto: MKCSBK Hungarian Veterans, Sovereign Press, 1975); and Ervin Hollós, *Rendőrség, Csendőrség, VKF 2*/Police, Gendarmerie, Secret Police/ (Budapest: Kossuth Könyvkiadó, 1971). The last of these works presents us with a Marxist interpretation of these developments.

14. Elek Karsai, *Országgyarapítás - országvesztés* /Territorial Gains-Territorial Losses/ (Budapest: Kossuth Könyvkiadó, 1961), pp. 105-106.

15. Rektor, *Csendőrség*, pp. 217-218.

16. Árpád Zámbory, *"Délbácska csendőri megszállása"* /The Occupation of Southern Bachka by the Gendarmerie/ (Unpublished manuscript, Grossgmain, Germany, 1950).

17. Concerning the bombing of Kassa and nearby cities, see Julian Borsányi, *Das Rätsel des Bombenangriffs auf Kaschau, 26 Juni 1941* (Munich: Ungarisches Institut, 1978); and the related studies by Thomas Sakmyster, Francis S. Wagner, and N. F. Dreisziger in a special issue of the *Hungarian Studies Review*, X/1-2 (1983), 53-97.

18. On the fate of the Hungarian armed forces in Russia during World War II, see Ferenc Adonyi, *A magyar katona a második világháborúban, 1941-1945* /The Hungarian Soldier in the Second World War/ (Klagenfurt: Ferdinand Kleinmayer, 1954); Miklós Horváth, *A 2. Magyar Hadsereg megsemmisülése a Donnál* /The Annihilation of the Second Hungarian Army at the Don/ (Budapest: Zrínyi Kiadó, 1959); Lajos Dálnoki-Veress, ed. *Magyarország honvédelme a II. világháború előtt és alatt, 1920-1945* /Hungary's Defenses before and during World War II, 1920-1945/, 3 vols. (Munich: Danubia Druckerei, 1970-1973); and István Nemeskürthy, *Requiem egy hadseregért* /Requiem for an Army/ (Budapest: Magvető Könyvkiadó, 1972).

19. M. Kir. Honvédelmi Minisztérium, *Tábori rendészeti szolgálat* /Service Regulations for Military Police/ (Budapest: Stádium, 1942), pp. 6-7.

20. Concerning the Massacre of Újvidék, see János Buzási, *Az újvidéki razzia* /The Search of Újvidék/ (Budapest: Kossuth Könyvkiadó, 1963), pp. 29-30, 53; Dezső Sally, *Szigorúan bizalmas. Fekete könyv, 1939-1944* /Strictly Confidential. Black Book, 1939-1944/ (Budapest: Anonymus, 1945), p. 673; and Stephen D. Kertesz, *Diplomacy in a Whirlpool. Hungary between Nazi Germany and Soviet Russia* (Notre Dame, IN: University of Notre Dame Press, 1953), p. 57.

21. Nicholas Kállay, *Hungarian Premier* (New York: Columbia University Press, 1954), pp. 373.

22. *Ibid.*, p. 387.

23. *Ibid.*

24. Sándor Szilassy, "Az amerikai magyarság a második világháborúban" /Hungarian Americans in World War II/, in *Új Látóhatár* /New Horizons/, 30/1-2 (June 15, 1979), pp. 138-143; and Steven Béla Várdy, *The Hungarian-Americans* (Boston: Twayne Publishers, 1975), pp. 109-112.

25. Károly Vígh, *Ugrás a sötétbe* /Jumping into Darkness/ (Budapest: Akadémiai Kiadó, 1979), pp. 48-51.

26. Lajos Dálnoki-Veress, ed., *Magyarország honvédelme*, III, pp. 119-130.

27. Miklós Horthy, *Emlékirataim* /Memoires/ (Buenos Aires, 1953), pp. 250-257.

28. Jenő Lévai, *Fekete könyv* /Black Book/ (Budapest: Officina, 1946), 93-95; and *idem, Eichmann in Hungary* (Budapest: Pannonia Press, 1961), pp. 107, 114.

29. Lévai, *Fekete könyv*, p. 193.

30. *Ibid.*, pp. 187, 205, 207, 256,

31. Rektor, *Csendőrség*, pp. 298-305.

32. Decree No. 115.645/eln. 20-942, by the Minister of Defense, Lajos Csatay. Cf. Rektor, *Csendőrség*, pp. 475-478.

33. Kosáry and Várdy, *History of the Hungarian Nation*, pp. 351-352.

34. Randolph L. Braham, *The Politics of Genocide*, 2 vols. (New York: Columbia University Press, 1981), pp. xxv-xxvi.

35. William J. Bosh, *Judgment at Nuremberg* (Chapel Hill, NC: The University of North Carolina Press, 1970), p. 46.

Botond R. Clementis-Záhony:

15 / BÁRDOSSY RECONSIDERED: HUNGARY'S ENTRANCE INTO WORLD WAR II

Because a nation cannot create new constellations to surround itself, it has to perceive clearly the objective situation into which history and fate have placed it. It has to be able to analyze each element of the total condition, differentiating between objectives that are possible and objectives that are impossible to reach. Better said, it has to know the difference between real and imagined dangers.

The above is a constant struggle with both openly evolving and hidden forces. In this struggle to recognize the correct path, to step onto that path at the right moment, to live within the given means and to use the correct tools — that is politics.

The true value of a given political decision is determined by correct timing. The same decision executed in a different time frame is not the same decision. Its value, its importance is lost if circumstances force the decision. That is, in a true sense of the word, we cannot even speak of a decision, rather only of accommodation — or better said — a bowing before the power of facts.

Life does not stop and wait for the hesitant individual searching how he should utilize the advantages of a given constellation. This is what the French call *facteur temps* and what is one of THE essential elements of practical politics.

LÁSZLÓ BÁRDOSSY in
Magyar politika a mohácsi vész után
/Hungarian Politics after the Battle of Mohács/ (1943).

Writing in the April 1947 issue of the *Journal of Central European Affairs,* in an article entitled "Two Teleki Letters," Richard V. Burks produced the following, rather revealing footnote:

László de Bárdossy, the Minister of Foreign Affairs. He succeeded Csáky on the latter's death on January 27 /1941/. Bárdossy's activities during this crisis /the 1941 Simović Putsch, followed by the German attack on Yugoslavia through Hungary and Teleki's suicide/, as presented in this letter, *contrast sharply* with the pro-Nazi positions he later adopted. [1]

It is worthwhile to remember that this remark by Burks was written in 1947, hence only one year after Bárdossy's 1946 execution. To my knowledge, this was the first instance when Bárdossy's stylized image as a "war criminal" was questioned in the West.

My purpose, in light of the above, is to show that this stylized image can, through existing documentation, be repeatedly questioned. It is, however, not my intention to write revisionist history, but simply to add new pieces — long forgotten — to the mosaic, and thus give new depth to Bárdossy's rather complex personality. Hence, this essay can also be labelled bibliographic, depending heavily, though not exclusively, on Western sources.

But let us turn to the substance of these letters, specifically to the second letter that Burks presents. It was written to Baron Gábor Apor, Hungarian Minister to the Holy See, himself of strong anti-German orientation. [2] The date of the letter is even more important. It was written on April 2, 1941, hence on the last known full day of Teleki's life, before his suicide on the night of April 2/3. Burks calls the letter Teleki's "epistle."

Two quotations from this letter are essential. The first states:

> This Yugo affair drew us into the most terrible situation. H. /Hitler/ sent a message through that Nazi Sztójay to the K. /*Kormányzó*, i.e. Regent Horthy/ asking whether we wanted to realize our southern claims, plus the sea, plus whatever else we wanted. The K. became very enthusiastic at once, and not less but more so, after he slept on it. He wanted to write that he was body and soul with them and would go along. It cost Bárdossy and me immense efforts to delete the dangerous passages from this letter, and leave the doors open. Finally, after two

days the situation improved somewhat, because he
came to realize that we would lose our honor before the world if we would attack the Yugoslavs.[3]

Later in the same letter he states:

But my struggle is difficult! Bárdossy is helping
me very well /i.e., greatly/.[4]

C. A. Macartney, in his seminal *October Fifteenth* substan-
tiates the above. He further states that in a letter written to his
son in February of that year, Teleki coupled Bárdossy with
Keresztes-Fischer and Bánffy as the only ministers in his
cabinet whom he could trust. [5]

But there is another part of this Teleki-to-Apor letter
which bears heavily in Bárdossy's favor. In this part Teleki
defines very clearly the decisions of the Defense Council of
the previous night, April 1. Here the specific conditions,
jointly agreed upon by Horthy, Teleki, Werth (the Chief
of Staff) and Bárdossy for the movement of Hungarian armed
forces into the *Délvidék*, i.e. Southern Hungary, after 1919
the Voivodina section of Yugoslavia:

1. We will not budge until the Germans reach
beyond Zagreb, when the Croations will probably
switch over.
2. We will not march further than the former
/Hungarian/ frontier and will guard that area
between two German armies, that is to say up to the
Danube and the Drave. We will not enter Croatian
territory at all.
3. We will concentrate smaller forces only,
lest the Germans get an appetite and take them
to the Balkans.
4. The Regent will retain supreme command
to avoid subordination.

Further on, he adds:

The situation is very difficult because if we resist
they /the Germans/ will roll over us first, and
worse, if we do not enter the Bácska, the Germans

will make themselves at home there. Should they
not be beaten back /preempted/, they will set up
a German state from the Bácska-Bánát-Hunyad-
vár, the Saxon country, and perhaps Baranya and
Tolna. [6]

The above decision refers to an even earlier Ministerial
Council held March 28, where, among others, the future move
into the *Délvidék* and its justification were developed by Teleki
and Bárdossy. [7] The conditions for the *Honvéd*'s /i.e.Hun-
garian Army's/ move into the *Délvidék* were set down at
this meeting as follows:

1. If Yugoslavia disintegrates as a state, i.e., if
the Croats proclaim their independence.

2. If the security of the Magyar minority in the
Voivodina (*Délvidék*) is endangered by Serb military action.

3. If a vacuum is created in the Voivodina in
consequence of the German military action. [8]

Now let us look at the actual diplomatic circular sent
out by Bárdossy to all the embassies on April 10, hence,
after Teleki's suicide, explaining the reasons for Hungary's
move into the *Délvidék*.

The German move /against Yugoslavia/ is proceeding at an extremely rapid pace, and is going
to result by all indications in a rapid withdrawal
of all Yugoslav military forces deployed in the
northern part of the country. With such withdrawal a vacuum is created in the former Hungarian territories /*Délvidék*/, in which the fate
of the large Hungarian population will become
uncertain. Under such circumstances we almost
certainly will have to defend the fate of this population from anarchic conditions. Therefore, in
the above situation we can count on having to move
our military forces into the Voivodina, Bánát and
Baranya... Once we move, I ask your Excellency
to do your best to clarify to those in authority that
our action, which is our duty, is aimed *solely* at

securing the safety of the Hungarian population of
the *Délvidék*, and is not aimed at Yugoslavia.[9]

The reasoning of this circular is clearly based on the previous two decisions made *jointly* by Teleki and Bárdossy.
Hence Bárdossy was not in any sense changing policy when
the *Honvéd* troops moved into the *Délvidék*; rather he was
carrying out Teleki's policy based on the preconditions that
they *jointly* agreed upon.

Yet, the People's Court, intent on proving Bárdossy's
"war guilt," argued that Bárdossy pursued a policy that
Teleki rejected and then condemned with his suicide. This,
on the basis of the above material, is untrue. The reasons
for Teleki's suicide lay clearly elsewhere.

Taking into consideration what has been said above, let
us now look at Bárdossy's defense at his trial and his view of
Teleki's real motives for suicide.

Starting off with the statement: "Legends are being formed
about Paul Teleki," Bárdossy goes on to state that it is
simply ridiculous to imagine that the same person who since
1919 had been the heart and soul of Hungarian revisionism,
would, under the favorable conditions of 1941, pass up the
chance to regain those territories for which he had fought
for twenty years.[10] "Hence, for Paul Teleki it was absolutely
imperative *to act* when certain conditions had arisen."[11]

He then refers back to the Horthy letter, mentioned by
Burks, of which Teleki had stated to Apor: "It cost Bárdossy
and me immense efforts to delete the dangerous passages
from this letter." On the basis of the above, Bárdossy logically continues:

> The prosecution itself has determined—although,
> it's true, only superficially—that the Regent notified
> Hitler on March 28, that Hungary would assert its
> revisionist rights to the *Délvidék*. This letter of the
> Regent was handed to Hitler by the Hungarian
> Ambassador in Berlin on March 28.

> Hence it is an undeniable fact that Hungary's
> decision to actualize its demands was finalized by
> the official notification of a foreign power /Ger-

many/ as of March 28. It is simply incomprehensible that this decision would have come about without the approval of the responsible prime minister, who in fact was not only the Regent's prime minister, but also his friend.[12]

On the basis of the above we can actually push back the date of mutual agreement on the *Délvidék*-policy by Bárdossy and Teleki to March 28. It also becomes clear that the Ministerial Council's initial decision defining the conditions for the move into the *Délvidék* took place specifically on March 28, in order to define and *limit* the effects of Horthy's letter of the same date. On this definition and limitation, the Apor letter unquestionably proves that Teleki and Bárdossy worked closely together.

In referring to the April 1st Defense Council at his trial, Bárdossy very simply asked why no member of the People's Court tried to find Teleki's personal notes and handwritten proposals for this meeting. "The justification for the guilty verdict, without using the obvious evidence, makes for judgements which are in total contradiction with the facts." [13]

And how does the prosecution do this? "By purposefully mystifying and confusing the complex interconnection—yet separation—between the question of our participation in the German attack on Yugoslavia, and the question of our legitimate territorial demands being realized under specific conditions." [14] Apparently, the People's Court refused to recognize this distinction. Moreover, asserted Bárdossy, the prosecution acted "as if Paul Teleki—who really did not want to partake in Germany's war [15]—would also have opposed the retaking of the territories that had historically always belonged to Hungary. The truth was that it was exactly Teleki who first proposed the retaking. I remember that there was no one in the cabinet who wanted to get involved unconditionally in the German war. But all the ministers found it their inescapable duty that the half-million Hungarians of the *Délvidék* be liberated, that they be returned into the body of the Hungarian state." [16]

The paradox in the above situation was quite clear and had to be resolved. A decision had to be made. Teleki resolved it by making it into a moral question and then projecting it unto the national and international arena. This he did via his suicide. Bárdossy in turn carried out the actual policy jointly agreed upon. Both were heroic acts, but of course the person alive had to take the responsibility. Bárdossy never shrank from this responsibility.

One cannot resist a Krasinskian observation on this "Undivine Comedy," based, however, on very real facts: Teleki's and Bárdossy's acts must be viewed as complementary. I am in no way suggesting this as rationally planned; rather, we come to understand this from Ullein-Revicky's description of the last tragic moments of these two men together. He describes how on April 2nd he saw the two men at the foreign office at about 9 P.M. Both were silent. Teleki was pacing about the room, his head sunk, his hands in his pockets. Barcza's telegram — indicating Britain's declaration of war in case Hungary joined the attack under any pretext — was lying on the desk. After a while Teleki said in a low voice, "I have done what I could. I can do no more." [17] Aladár Szegedy-Maszák, head of the Political Division of the Ministry for Foreign Affairs, in a memorandum written in June or July of 1943 and passed on to the British in Stockholm, defined the whole question in the following manner:

> Paul Teleki grasped the full weight of both the moral and political conflicts in the situation and of the tragic contradiction present in the dual responsibilities i.e., both to revision and to staying out of the war. It was for this reason that he voluntarily chose death, that is, via his sacrifice to document Hungarian politics' bitter dilemma.... But beyond this symbolic meaning, Paul Teleki's act also produced results in practical politics. The Hungarian troops only entered Bácska, that had been detached in 1919, when Yugoslavia's collapse was certain, when Croatia had already proclaimed its secession from Yugoslavia, and when the only question remaining was how to prevent Bácska's occupation by German troops, as has been and still is the case with Bánát.[18]

These "results in practical politics"—as *Szegedy-Maszák*

calls them — also alluded to in Teleki's posthumous letter to Horthy (as quoted by Bárczy, "Perhaps by my voluntary death I may render a service to my nation")[19] were the responsibilities that Bárdossy had to shoulder and follow through.

In fact, Teleki succeeded in defining to the Allied Powers Hungary's dilemma. This is reflected in Churchill's comments on Teleki in his *The Grand Alliance*:

> His suicide was a sacrifice to absolve himself and his people from guilt in the *German* attack upon Yugoslavia.[20]

This dilemma is also reflected in his above-cited letter to Apor, where Teleki declared: "It cost Bárdossy and me *immense efforts...to leave the doors open.*"

Let us now proceed to our second problem, i.e. Bárdossy's attitude toward Hungary's entry into the war. It is important to concentrate on Hungary's declaration of war against the Soviet Union, and not on her declaration against the United States, nor on Britain's declaration of war on Hungary. The reasons for this will become clear later. Here again, emphasis will be on deepening the Bárdossy portrait.

That Bárdossy initially resisted entering the war on Germany's side, and that he fought aggressively against the General Staff's wish to have Hungary join Germany in the Soviet campaign, has been well documented and need not be underlined again.[21] On three different occasions he refused to give in to Chief-of-Staff General Werth's pressures. N.F. Dreisziger goes a step further, however, when he deals with Bárdossy's June 24 irritation with the Germans for receiving from them contradictory signals as to whether they wanted Hungary in the war against the Soviet Union or not. Soon after the German attack on Russia, the German High Command's representative in Hungary, General Kurt Himer, delivered to Bárdossy a message, via General Werth, to the effect that if Hungary wanted to participate in the campaign against Russia, she would have to join voluntarily.[22] Dreisziger, describing the government's response, writes:

> The Hungarian premier's response to the German demand deserves special attention.... Bárdossy stated to the German ambassador that the matter of Hungary's participation was up to the civilian government to decide. If Germany desired Hungary's assistance, she would have to request it through regular diplomatic channels.... It is doubtful Bárdossy could really expect Hitler to beg for Hungary's assistance, especially when all of Germany's other "friends" offered their help voluntarily. Bárdossy's motives were probably different. In telling the Germans that Hungary's government would consider the question of participation in the war if Germany asked for this officially, the premier probably wanted to avoid his country's involvement in the war, without having to admit openly that Hungary did not want to participate.[23]

The above quotation leads to the examination of Bárdossy's style in dealing with German pressure. This question becomes even more important as we examine the events of June 26, the day of the mysterious Kassa bombing and Hungary's entry into World War II.

Again Ullein-Reviczky's description is in order, on whom N.F. Dreisziger, M. Fenyő and C.A. Macartney all relied extensively. His opus, *Guerre Allemande, Paix Russe*, is often quoted, yet it is puzzling that precisely his description of Bárdossy's reaction to the Kassa bombing has been neglected *ad nauseam*.[24] Ullein-Reviczky relates that initially Bárdossy ordered the news, received via the General Staff, that Soviet aircraft had attacked Kassa suppressed. The reason was that Bárdossy suspected German mischief behind the bombing, although he had no information to that effect. The bombing, however, had unnerved him. Furthermore, he was under pressure from Regent Horthy for immediate reprisals. Concluding that the Germans had already made up their minds to bring Hungary into the war, that the Hungarian generals whom up to now he had vehemently resisted were on the German side, and that the Regent, whose behavior he clearly interpreted as being similar to his behavior in the Yugoslav crisis, was under the influence of the generals, Bárdossy completely reversed his earlier policy. There had been no way out other than war, Bárdossy told Ullein-Reviczky. If the Germans were willing to go to such extremes to have their way, resistance was useless, and Hungary better accept the inevitable and join the war at once. [25]

The real puzzle in the above is the *reversal* of his earlier decision and the *speed* of this reversal. It is a fact that within an hour and a half of the attack, and less than an hour since he ordered Ullein-Reviczky to suppress the general's communiqué identifying the attackers as Russians (suspecting all along that they were in fact Germans), Bárdossy made the decision to put the blame on Russia. Ullein-Reviczky, in this connection also relates that Bárdossy told him that it took him only five minutes to reach this decision; and that, while another person might have taken longer, the results would have been the same. [26]

The emphasis in this description seems *not* to be on the substance of the why's of the decision, but rather, on the dynamics of decision-making and on making it as fast as possible.

There are two additional observations regarding Bárdossy's reactions to the Kassa bombing which should be brought up here — both of them being basically new observations.

One involves the Krudy question, which has been discussed extensively by Julian Borsányi, Joseph Ormay and N.F. Dreisziger. In his post-war "revelations," however, Krudy mentioned a second officer present at the Kassa airfield observing the bombing of that city. This officer was Jenő Chirke, who later recalled this event as follows:

> Around midnight of the 26th of June, a military chauffeur came to my house with a message that Prime Minister Bárdossy wanted to talk to me on the phone. I arrived at the post office, where a telephone connection was made. It was hard to understand each other. I'm not sure whether I was speaking with the prime minister or with one of his secretaries. To the question who bombed Kassa, the Russians or the Germans, I could only answer that the planes were not of German make.[27]

The above interview confirms that Bárdossy had doubts as to who bombed Kassa, even after his decision had been made.

The second observation is based on Bárdossy's defense speech of November 3, 1945:

> If by any chance the hitherto unproven theory that the bombing of Kassa was instigated by German hands were somehow proven correct, beyond any doubt this would be the best proof of Hungary's predetermined course in 1941. For if the Germans would not shirk from the use of such drastic methods, then it is also possible to hypothesize that they would not have shrunk from the use of even more extreme methods later. [28]

And a little later he continues:

> The majority of Hungarian public opinion was quite clear on the fact that Hungary, by the sheer fact of its geopolitical location *could not* remain outside of the life and death conflict of its two immediate great power neighbors....Therefore, in the interest of its own self-defense, it had to take sides with one or the other. [29]

The interesting element in the above two quotations is that they are worded in a way as to be applicable to *either* the USSR or Germany as being the nation that bombed Kassa. That exactly was the core problem of the Prime Minister. Bárdossy had concrete proof that paralleled with the Kassa bombing, Soviet aircraft had attacked at Rahó.[30] These aircraft were definitely identified as Soviet. Furthermore, and this was even more important to Bárdossy as a diplomat, he also had to consider Vishinsky's statement to the Hungarian Minister to Moscow, Kristóffy, at the time of Yugoslavia's collapse and Hungary's reconquest of the *Délvidék*. Vishinsky at that time warned:

> It is not difficult to realize what would be Hungary's position if it would itself get into difficulties and would be torn to pieces by her neighbors, since

it is known that there are national minorities in
Hungary too. [31]

The above information was reaffirmed to Bárdossy in
a news communiqué published in the beginning of April,
1941 in Moscow. Both of these statements referred to Hungarian *Kárpátalja* (Sub-Carpathia), an area with a large
Ruthenian population speaking a language very similar to
Russian. *Kárpátalja* was also where Rahó, the place of the
identified Russian attack, was located. In 1945 the Soviet
Union — for the first time in Russian history — annexed
this territory, confirming Bárdossy's 1941 suspicion, that
as in the case of Romania with Northern Bukovina, the
Soviets were bent on using the Ukrainian question to expand
their borders westward, *even* into areas that historically had
never belonged to them. Movement into these areas was a
logical continuation of Soviet westward movement into
Europe from Finland and the Baltic States in the north,
through Eastern Poland in the center, to Bessarabia in the
south.

On the basis of the above, Bárdossy stated:

> It was both logical and fair to conclude that by this
> act, i.e., the attack of the Soviet air force upon
> Hungarian territory, the Soviet government was in
> effect already considering and treating Hungary
> as an enemy state. [32]

Bárdossy had to conclude that Hungary's territorial
integrity was threatened by both Germany and the Soviet
Union. And here one again arrives at the *categorical
imperative* of having to make decisions, of having to act because incidents have happened (i.e. the two attacks) that
demand attention and need solution. A decision had to be
made and the responsibility had to be assumed, even though
no one knew for certain as to who was the responsible party.

No one has described this situation better than the writer
Lajos Zilahy, who, questioning Bárdossy as to his motivation in
declaring a state of war, received the following answer:

"We could do nothing else; we had to indulge in a blind-
flight." [33] Actually, at closer observation, the problems
were rather similar to the problems Teleki had to

face — including Horthy's immense pressure "for immediate reprisals" — at the time of the Yugoslav crisis. Of
course, the solution could not be the same. Furthermore,
as the letter to Apor clearly indicates, Bárdossy, perhaps
more than anyone else, suffered through all of Teleki's decision-making, from March 28, 1941 on, when he tried to minimize Horthy's reactions to the Simović Putsch and the subsequent German offers, all the way to that tragic night on
the 2nd of April at the Foreign Ministry.

Within the given context, Bárdossy had to maneu-
ver, as weaker states always tend to do when faced
with great power pressure. He had to make prompt choices
between Nazi Germany and Soviet Russia. Not a very pleas-
ant choice, one might add.

He joined the war against the Soviet Union — in
this case conceding to German pressure — since the Soviets
were in retreat at this time along the whole eastern front.
But there was also a balance in the Soviet direction,
though this was not immediately clear. In the crusade
against Communism, a crusade which incidentally
Hungary could not but ideologically support due to her
experiences with Communism in 1919, Bárdossy vehemently insisted on sending only the minimum number of
military forces to Russia. [34]

There is even a stronger proof of this minimalization of
forces to be deployed in Russia. In a letter on August 26,
1941 to the Regent, Bárdossy stated that he was dissatisfied
with Chief-of-Staff Werth, because he was constantly pres-
suring for the total mobilization of Hungary's war and military capacities to be used on the eastern front. He requested the removal of Werth from that position.[35] Surely if
there is a "constant" in the Bárdossy Werth relationship, it was the perpetual disagreement and friction that
culminated in Werth's dismissal. Werth's removal was in
turn followed by the appointment of Ferenc Szombathelyi
as Chief-of-Staff, a general whose philosophy of "minimum
participation" closely coincided with Bárdossy's views on
this question. [36]

But if all the above is viewed by the critical reader as a
sign of weakness, it is important to examine the following
two observations. In his memoirs, the German diplomat

Hans Kroll, stationed with von Papen in Ankara, related the following:

> ...as the news of the beginning of the German-Soviet war came in, State Secretary Numan called me at six in the morning to express his satisfaction /with the above situation/. I quote him verbatim: "Our sympathies are totally on your side, and we hope that you will destroy these bandits to the core..." Germany could undoubtedly count after the beginning of the Russian campaign on the sympathy and the moral support of both the Turkish government and the Turkish people. [37]

The above, strong words were proclaimed by a neutral government expressing its heartfelt opinion about the Russian campaign. It is not at all surprising that anticommunist Hungary, threatened as it undoubtedly was by Soviet pressure, would harbor similar feelings. Or for that matter Regent Horthy. This observation, however, should be combined by again emphasizing Bárdossy's sense of caution. Very similar to the Polish Jozef Beck's policy of "balance" between Nazi Germany and Soviet Russia, Bárdossy was in fact also aiming — as Beck did in the 1934-1939 period of the German-Polish Nonaggression Pact — at a policy of "balance." [38] By giving minimal concession to the Germans, whose strength in turn protected Hungary against the Soviet Union (German strength hence was used by Hungary), Hungarian sovereignty was maintained. This in turn gave Hungary the ability to develop "reassurances" towards the Western powers.

And here again we must correct impressions. Andor Gellért, in a two-part article entitled "The Stockholm Scene: Additions to the History of Hungary's Secret Diplomacy," states:

> Nicholaus Kállay and Antal Ullein-Reviczky claim that the so-called "second line" /i.e., of secret negotiators/ was established by them with the objective of maintaining systematic contact with the Allied Powers, and with the long-range goal of conducting secret negotiations for a withdrawal of Hungary into neutrality. It would be much more precise,

however, to state that it was Paul Teleki who brought this organization into being and that László Bárdossy also knew of its existence. [39]

Later on he continues:

The members of this circle consisted of intimate friends, selected former pupils, leaders of the youth movements, and finally members of the Revisionist League and of the Institute of Governmental Studies. [40]

Gellért then goes on to state that it was really his mission to Stockholm in September 1942 that initiated the "diplomacy of detachment" from Germany. [41]

The above is repeated, in an obviously contradictory manner by the best diplomatic historian of present-day Hungary, Gyula Juhász, in a work entitled *Hungarian Foreign Policy - 1919-1945*. On page 282 of this work he states: "The first try at secret diplomacy occurred in the summer of 1942 via Andor Gellért, former representative of the Revisionist League in Berlin." Then on page 283 he states:

...and finally there were the possibilities via the Ambassador to Lisbon, Wodianer,...with close connections to the London Polish Government-in-Exile. Colonel *Kowalski*, representative of the Polish Government-in-Exile had the assignment to maintain contact with the Home Army and held a number of meetings with Wodianer ever since 1941. For it is important to know that one of the lines of communications between the Government-in-Exile and the Polish Resistance ran through Hungary. As a matter of fact, with the settling in Hungary of a large group of Polish refugees in 1939, a secret group of the Polish Resistance operated out of Hungary. [42]

I wish to make two points here. First, that the Colonel's name was not *Kowalski*, but *Kowalewski*: and second, that there is an obvious contradiction between statements on pages 282 and 283 of this volume. The latter proves conclusively that Hungary's secret diplomacy began in 1941 in Lisbon, and not in 1942 in Stockholm. In 1941 Bárdossy was prime minister, for Kállay assumed that position only in the summer of 1942. One wonders if the above confusion stems from a lack of knowledge of the Lisbon negotiations, or purposely to get around Bárdossy's role.

In her book, *Crusader in the Secret War*, the Countess of Listowel, in what is essentially a biography of Colonel Kowalewski, posits the following:

> As he /Kowalewski/ had met Bárdossy in Bucharest /Bárdossy had been Hungarian Ambassador when Kowalewski was Polish Military Attaché/, he (K) wrote him (B) a personal letter and asked Wodianer to forward it. Bárdossy answered immediately and instructed Wodianer to transmit his thanks to Colonel Nart /alias of Kowalewski/. Wodianer invited Peter (K) and solemnly informed him of the contents of Premier Bárdossy's telegram. [43]

And what was Kowalewski's mission in Lisbon? Listowel describes it as follows:

> Nart (K) set himself to disintegrate the Axis by lurking the minor Axis partners over to the allied side. He believed that in the satellite countries a few could be convinced that Germany would not win the war; therefore, it was in their interest to break away from the Germans in good time... Of course, Nart (K) needed diplomatic channels to establish direct contact with such would-be conspirators. [44]

Finally, let us clarify the other end of Kowalewski's line:

> Peter was confident that Sikorski would understand his plan and Sikorski meant the Polish Government- /in-Exile/.... His reports were so persuasive that Sikorski visualized what he had in mind and sent word that he was to go ahead, but be discreet.... [45]

The above material prepares us for András Tamás's in-depth clarifications. We have already identified in connection with Andor Gellért, a "second line diplomacy" as "a system of secret negotiators, having the objective of maintaining systematic contacts with the Allied Powers, with the long-run objective of conducting secret negotiations for a withdrawal of Hungary into neutrality, brought into being by Paul Teleki with the knowledge of László Bárdossy, and basically consisting of members of the Institute of Governmental Studies and the League of Revision."

Tamás had been born in Targoviste, Moldavia, of so-called "Csángó" stock. These so-called "lost Hungarians" of Moldavia, cut off for centuries from their people, learned to fight for their rights at a very early age. Tamás had spent a number of years in Romanian prisons. Moving to Hungary and graduating from the University of Budapest, he was also active in the "Populist Literary Society," a cover for intelligence work against Romania, but later expanded to cover all of the Balkans. The society in turn was fused with the Revisionist League. In 1927 he was assigned as representative of the Revisionist League to the League of Nations in Geneva. In 1938 he was sent to Rome to organize the Mediterranean Society, with the purpose of propagating Hungary's belonging to the Italian sphere of influence so as to be able to counter German pressure on Hungary. His most important assignment, however, came about in August 1939, when reacting to German anti-Hungarian manipulations in Carpatho-Ruthenia, Tamás was sent first to that province and then to Warsaw to cooperate with the Ukrainian section of the Polish General Staff in countering German propaganda and political pressure in the area. [46]

By September 1939, the war had broken out, at which time, to quote Tamás:

> We immediately put into operation the machinery which became the core of /the already mentioned/ Polish Resistance in Hungary, headed by Press Attache Zbigniew Kosciuszko and Colonel Jan Bem, Military Attaché. [47]

It should also be mentioned here that after the collapse of Poland, Kowalewski, on his way from Romania to France, had also stopped and visited Bem in Budapest. [48]

With the above Polish connections in hand, the Revisionist League discharged András Tamás in September 1941 to Lisbon. His assignment was to follow up on the already initiated Wodianer-Kowalewski contacts, which might just as well be called the Bárdossy-Sikorski secret contacts. Access to Sikorski implied, of course, indirect access to Churchill. Hence Bárdossy, through Tamás, was the first utilizer of "second line diplomacy."

Tamás elaborates on the Listowel information in the following in-depth manner:

> In October 1940 Wodianer began developing the so-called "Polish channel," i.e., when he made contact with Polish Colonel Jan Kowalewski, representative of Sikorski, who in the chronicles of the secret service was called Peter Nart, and in the Hungarian secret service Uncle John. He was a very dear and old friend of Bárdossy. They had known each other already in Bucharest where Bárdossy had served as Hungarian Ambassador, Kowalewski as /Polish/ military attaché....

> He (K) knew that from the point of view of secret service, the Hungarians were of value. Because of this, he suggested to Wodianer that in order to open a door /for Hungary/ to London, Horthy and his government should give some kind of a signal that they do not believe in a German victory. This signal by itself would already be a great step forward....

> In order to make the contact official, Kowalewski received authorization from Sikorski, that in his own name he should write a letter to Bárdossy, and have Wodianer deliver the letter via official channels.... If Bárdossy accepts it, the secret channel to the Hungarian diplomats will be opened. Wodianer accepted the letter, forwarded it to Bárdossy and received an answer to be given to Kowalewski. [49]

He concludes:

> At this point I find it absolutely essential to pinpoint for posterity the fact that the first successful contact

of Hungary to the West was the accomplishment of Ambassador Wodianer and that this first step was taken by László Bárdossy when he wrote his letter to Kowalewski. [50]

As to the concrete results of this "opening to the West," three areas can be pinpointed, namely, the diplomatic, the military, and the secret service.

Undoubtedly the most important was the diplomatic. In the councils of the London-organized Inter-Allied Conference, chaired by the Polish Foreign Minister Edward Raczynski (but also in the British press), Hungarian views were systematically represented by the Polish Government-in-Exile. [51]

Certain contacts in the military area have already been mentioned. But perhaps it should be pointed out that already in 1939, with the collapse of Poland, it was the Hungarian military attaché in Warsaw (continuing in Warsaw), who became the intermediary between the newly formed resistance under the command of General Tokarzewski and the Polish Government-in-Exile. Stefan Korbonski states:

> In mid-October 1939, Tokarzewski forwarded through the intermediary of a Hungarian military attaché a report addressed to the Commander-in-Chief, whose name, however he did not specify.... The Hungarian attaché saw to it that the report reached Marshal Rydz-Smigly who was at that time interned in Romania and who formally speaking, continued to be the Commander-in-Chief until General Wladislaw Sikorski's appointment in November 7, 1939. [52]

All this, Orlowski tells us, took place during the term and with the agreement of Chief-of-Staff Werth. [53] During the same period over 30,000 Polish troops transited through Hungary to join the Polish Army in the West. These troops in turn became the core of the Polish "Anders Army," commanded by General Wladislaw Anders and stationed in the Middle East. Of the mission of this army Anders wrote:

I once again raised with Sikorski the question of the regrouping of our land forces in the Middle East, as I still considered that the future offensive of the Allies would have to be carried out from the south, across Italy and the Balkans, and that our troops would be used only in the latter. [54]

By late 1942, through the trusted agent Andrew Frey, Chief of the General Staff Szombathelyi was conveying the following message to the Poles:

Hungary did not intend to oppose Polish (or Anglo-American) troops if they reached the Hungarian frontier and advanced into the country. Furthermore, Hungary was in principle prepared to take positive action against the Germans if it proved possible to work out in advance a practical plan for cooperation between the armies concerned. [55]

Clearly, Szombathelyi's and Anders' strategy presumed a "southern strategy," by the Allies.

George Kennan, joining all the above threads, summarized Hungarian policy to the State Department on September 21, 1943 in the following manner:

The Hungarians have for a long time now cooperated and consulted with the Poles. I believe their wish to withdraw their troops /in Russia/ to the line of the Carpathians has been carried out with the knowledge and agreement of the Poles. This plan undoubtedly is connected to the hope that the British Middle Eastern Command attached Polish Army /Anders Army/ will eventually reach the Hungarian border, and with the assistance of Hungarian forces will descend on the other side of the Carpathians. [56]

Finally, we should summarize the secret service contacts that came about as a result of Bárdossy's policy. As of 1939, both the MIR and Section D of British Military Intelligence had parties in Hungary assisting with the exit of members of the Polish armed forces.[57] After his arrival in Lisbon,

Tamás maintained his contacts with the Polish Intelligence, and it was due to his and Wodianer's efforts that the "Hungarian diplomatic bag was placed at the service of the Allies since 1941," transmitting material between the Polish Government-in-Exile, through Hungary, to Poland and the Resistance. [58]

In June 1942—hence after Bárdossy's dismissal—Tamás became the contact between the Revisionist League and SIS/SOE "Continental Action" represented first in Lisbon by Sigismund Zawadowski, later to be replaced by Colonel Kowalewski. As the representative of the Revisionist League in Lisbon, he became SIS/SOE's channel to the Hungarian Resistance Movement inside Hungary. These lines lead to Endre Bajcsy-Zsilinszky — a member of the Directorate of the Revisionists League, whose Smallholders Party became the core of this resistance. [59]

I find no better way to conclude this study than to agree with Tamás:

> He /Bárdossy/ was the only head of government who completely and totally served Hungariandom precisely by following up on our contracted responsibilities toward the Germans, but at the same time never forgetting that Hungary also has to secure itself towards the West. In such a grandly conceived policy, all personal categories disappear and become immaterial. [60]

Teleki's quotation is again and finally apropos: "It cost Bárdossy and me immense efforts...to leave the doors open."

Notes

1. Richard V. Burks, "Two Teleki Letters," *Journal of Central European Affairs*, VII, 1 (April 1947), 72, n. 12.

2. Tibor Talpassy, *Betöltötte hivatását* /He Fulfilled His Mission/ (Budapest: Magvető Könyvkiadó, 1975), 292; Mario D. Fenyo, *Hitler, Horthy and Hungary* (New Haven and London: Yale University Press, 1972), 63 n. 25.

3. Burks, "Two Teleki," 71-72.

4. *Ibid.*, 72.

5. C. A. Macartney, *October Fifteenth - A History of Hungary: 1929-1945*, 2 vols. (New York: Frederick A. Praeger, 1956), I, 486. See also I, 466 n. 2. and I, 468 n. 1.

6. Burks, "Two Teleki," 71.

7. Macartney, *October Fifteenth*, I, 476.

8. *Ibid.*

9. L. Zsigmond, *et. al.*, eds. *Magyarország és a második világháború* /Hungary and the Second World War/, 3rd ed. (Budapest: Kossuth, 1966), 306-307.

10. L. Tilkovszky, *Pál Teleki: A Biographical Sketch* (Budapest: Akadémiai Kiadó, 1974), 25-65.

11. László Bárdossy, *A nemzet védelmében: Utolsó beszédei* /In Defense of the Nation: Last Speeches/ (Switzerland: Duna, 1976), 95.

12. *Ibid.*, 94.

13. *Ibid.*

14. *Ibid.*, 95.

15. *Ibid.* See also John Pelényi, "The Secret Plan for a Hungarian Government in the West at the Outbreak of World War II," *Journal of Modern History*, XXXVI, 2 (June 1964), 170-177.

16. Bárdossy, *A nemzet*, 96.

17. Antal Ullein-Reviczky, *Guerre Allemande, Paix Russe* (Neuchatel: Histoire et Societé d'Ajourd hui, 1947), 92-93; Tilkovszky, *Pál Teleki*, 63.

18. Gyula Juhász ed., *Magyar-brit titkos tárgyalások 1943-ban* /Hungarian-British Secret Negotiations in 1943/ (Budapest: Kossuth, 1978), 196-197.

19. Macartney, *October Fifteenth*, I, 488-489. It is my intention to use the Bárczy memoir version of this letter as taken over by Macartney, *October Fifteenth*, I, 488 n. 4. I am of course aware of Tilkovszky's and Ránki's interpretation of Teleki's suicide. Tilkovszky, *Pál Teleki*, 65; and György Ránki, ed. *Magyarország története: 1918-1919 — 1919-1945* /The History of Hungary 1918-1919 — 1919-1945/, 10 vols. (Budapest: Akadémiai Kiadó, 1976), VIII, 1038-1043. As Teleki was a deeply religious person, I cannot see how Marxist class conflict categories can be applied to his decision and mental processes. I much prefer Prince Primate Cardinal Serédi's explanation of this riddle: "Whether killed, forced into suicide, or sensing suicide as the only constructive alternative, Teleki had in any and every case suffered violence." The above quotation, as well as Teleki's final message ("Perhaps my voluntary death may render a service to my nation.") can be found in: András Zakár, ed., *Teleki Pál halála* /Pál Teleki's Death/ (Vienna: Edition Eola, 1983), 54, 41-49. Teleki's final message—written on a piece of paper, separate from his posthumous letter—had been seen by at least three persons, Bárczy, Zsindely, and the pathologist Dr. Bakay.

20. Winston Churchill, *The Grand Alliance* (Boston: Houghton Mifflin Company, 1950), 168.

21. C. A. Macartney, "Hungary's Declaration of War on the USSR in 1941," in A. O. Sarkinissan, ed. *Studies in Diplomatic History and Historiography* (London: Longmans, 1961), 156-165; and M. Szinai and L. Szűcs, eds. *Horthy Miklós titkos iratai* /Secret Papers of Nicholas Horthy/, 2d ed. (Budapest: Kossuth, 1963), 300-306.

22. Macartney, *October Fifteenth*, II, 24-25; György Ránki, *Emlékiratok és valóság Magyarország második világháborús szerepéről* /Memoirs and Reality concerning the Role of Hungary in World War II/ (Budapest: Kossuth, 1964), 141-146.

23. N. F. Dreisziger, "The Kassa Bombing: The Riddle of Adam Krudy," *Hungarian Studies Review*, X, 1-2 (1983), 81-82.

24. Ullein-Reviczky, *Guerre*, 106-108.

25. *Ibid.*; see also Macartney, *October Fifteenth*, 28, n. 6.

26. Ullein-Reviczky, *Guerre*, 108.

27. Written statement by Jenő Chirke to Joseph Ormay editor of *Magyar Szárnyak* /Hungarian Wings/ publication of the Hungarian Aero Museum, Oshawa, Ontario, Canada. Dr. Ormay kindly gave me a copy. It will be published as part of a joint book by Julian Borsányi and Joseph Ormay. The substance of the statement is also in Dreisziger, "The Kassa Bombing," 91.

28. Bárdossy, *A nemzet*, 53.

29. *Ibid.*, 53.

30. Borsányi Julian, "Az 1941-es hadüzenet 'causus belli'-je," /The 1941 Declaration of War's "Causus Belli"/, *Hadak Útján*, XXIII, 279 (October, 1971), 12-13.

31. James E. McSherry, *Stalin, Hitler and Europe: 1939-1941*, 2 vols. (Cleveland: The World Publishing Co., 1970), II, 213; Péter Gosztonyi, "A magyar hadbalépés története" /The History of Hungary's Entry into World War II/, *Irodalmi Újság*, XXXII, 5-6 (May-June, 1981), 3; and Grigore Gafencu, *Prelude to the Russian Campaign* (London: Fredrick Muller Ltd., 1945), 153.

32. Bárdossy, *A nemzet*, 80. Bárdossy's elaboration of the Sub-Carpathian question is contained in: Ferenc Ábrahám and Endre Kussinczky, eds., *Ítél a történelem: A Bárdossy per* /History Judges: The Bárdossy Trial/, 2 vols. (Budapest: Híradó Könyvtár, 1945), II, 22-24. See also András Hóry, *Még egy barázdát sem* /Not Even a Furrow/ (Vienna, 1967), 34; and McSherry, *Stalin*, 120-124.

33. István Benedek, "Éjszakai beszélgetés Zilahy Lajossal," /A Night Conversation with Lajos Zilahy/, *Új Látóhatár*, II, 4 (July-Aug. 1959), 250. Bárdossy defined the two attacks to the People's Court as "being of dual nature." See Ábrahám and Kussinszky, *Ítél*, 9.

34. Szinai, *Horthy*, 301-304; Ábrahám and Kussinszky, *Ítél*, 24.

35. *Ibid.*, see also Péter Gosztonyi, *Szombathelyi Ferenc visszaemlékezései* /Memoirs of Ferenc Szombathelyi/, (Washington, DC: Occidental Press, 1980), 10-12.

36. *Ibid.*, see also Péter Gosztonyi, "Magyarország a második világháborúban" /Hungary in World War II/, *Katolikus Szemle*, XXXIV, 3 (1982), 219-222.

37. Hans Kroll, *Lebenserinnerungen eines Botschafters* (Köln: Kiepenheur und Witsch, 1967), 122-123.

38. Grigore Gafencu, *Last Days of Europe* (New Haven: Yale University Press, 1948), 26-53; 214-217.

39. Gellért Andor, "A stockholmi színtér, 1942-1944," /The Stockholm Scene: 1942-1944/, *Új Látóhatár*, XXV, 5 (1974, Oct. 25), 365-366; see also Fenyo, *Hitler*, 114-115.

40. *Ibid.*, see also 366, ns. 7 and 8.

41. *Ibid.*, 366.

42. Gyula Juhász, *Magyarország külpolitikája, 1919-1945* /Hungary's Foreign Policy, 1919-1945/ (Budapest: Kossuth, 1975), 282-283.

43. The Countess of Listowel, *Crusader in the Secret War* (London: Christopher Johnson, 1952), 94.

44. *Ibid.*, 105.

45. *Ibid.*, 106.

46. András Tamás, *Délkeleteurópa a diplomáciai törekvések sodrában 1939 és 1944 között* /Southeastern Europe in the Currents of Diplomacy between 1939 and 1944/ (Montréal: Északi Fény, 1961). This information is dispersed on pp. 1-59.

A short biography of this author was given to me by his son. For more on Tamás see: Watson Kirkconnell, "A Canadian Meets the Magyars," *The Canadian-American Review of Hungarian Studies*, I, 1 (Spring-Fall, 1974), 10.

47. Tamás, *Délkelet*, 59.

48. Listowel, *Crusader*, 61.

49. Tamás, *Délkelet*, 63-64.

50. *Ibid.*, 65.

51. Count Edward Raczynski, *In Allied London* (London: Wiedenfeld and Nicolson, 1962), 123; 358-59; see also Fenyo, *Hitler*, 117.

52. Stefan Korbonski, *The Polish Underground State*, (New York: East European Quarterly, 1978), 21, 102.

53. Leo Orlowski, "Budapesti emlékeim" /Memories of Budapest/, *Nyugati Magyarság*, V, 5 (Sept.-Oct. 1953), 457.

54. Lt. General W. Anders, *An Army in Exile*, (London: McMillan and Co. Ltd., 1949), 148. For Szombathelyi's view on this question see Ránki, ed., *Magyarország*, VIII, 1086-87.

55. Nicholas Kállay, *Hungarian Premier* (New York: Columbia University Press 1954), 370; Ránki, ed., *Magyarország VIII*, 1086-87.

56. Juhász, *Magyar-Brit*, 254.

57. M. R. D. Foot, *Resistance* (New York: McGraw Hill Book Company, nd.), 199.

58. Anthony Cave Brown, ed., *The Secret War Report of the OSS* (New York: Berkley Publishing Corporation, 1976), 161. See also Fenyo, *Horthy-Hitler*, 131 n. 1, and 117 n. 31. Fenyo is not clear on Tamás' identity. On 131 he identifies him as Ernő Tamás of the Revisionists League, on 117 he correctly identifies him as András Tamás, courier for the Polish Underground.

59. Tamás, *Délkelet*, 96-97. Tamás' activities by July 1942 involved both the secret service and the diplomatic area. For further information on his post-1942 activities see Listowel, *Crusader*, 171-199. A detailed description of these activities is to be found in his unpublished manuscript, "January 1, 1943 — March 19, 1944." I wish to thank his son, Paul Tamás, for the right to use this manuscript.

60. *Ibid.*, 66.

V.

NATIONAL MINORITIES IN HUNGARY AND IN THE SURROUNDING STATES

Julius Varsányi: *

16 / REGIONALISM IN PRACTICE: THE ETHNOPROTECTIVE ROLE OF THE SEMI-AUTONOMOUS COUNTY SYSTEM OF HISTORIC HUNGARY**

There is always a rather characteristic flavour, an almost fatal individualism when a people on its way to nationhood lays down the basic norms of its own life. These norms which arise from deep down in the collective consciousness of the people, while tradition-forming at the cultural level, are, at the same time, the building blocks of the first, yet primitive, communal institutions.

It is in this way, then, that ethnicity leaves its indelible, history-forming mark on the framework of emerging early statehood. Its imprint remains on the national psyche long after its *raison d'être* is changed or even completely disappears.

This incipient process, creating what perhaps could

---

*Deceased

** The writer wishes to thank Professor David St. L. Kelly for reading part of this manuscript, Mrs. Ruth Lucke for stylistic recommendations, and the National Széchényi Library of Budapest for making available some of the relevant source material through interlibrary loan. The first version of this study apeared in the *Revue de Droit International de Sciences, Diplomatiques et Politiques* (Geneve), 63/1 (January-March 1985), pp. 57-91.

tentatively be called institutional stratification, after establishing time honoured forms of early statecraft, often has certain side effects which later turn out to be significant in a constitutional sense. Especially significant are those proto-institutions or early organizational forms adapted by a people at a time of drastic change in its lifestyle. The task of solving crucial questions of ethnobiological importance as also the need for security at the time of temporary imbalance in the body politic caused by transition from one cultural and socio-economic stage of ethno-national existence to the other, faced the leaders of the second wave of the Magyar conquest of the Carpathian Basin towards the conclusion of the 9th century. [1] This was the historical background from which in a hundred years' time the beginnings of a specific administrative solution emerged, which, by its vitality, feasibility and permanence became the most important governmental institution in the Carpathian Basin under Hungarian rule: the county system.

At this time, the shattered remains of the once mighty Avar empire, a medley of semi-independent small peoples under mostly Bulgarian leadership, formed the bulk of the population to the South and West of the arch of the Carpathian Mountains, to the North and East of which small Slavic peoples were settled by the Avars all along East Central Europe from Silesia to the Balkans.[1a] As archeology has revealed, the middle of the arch formed by the Carpathians was inhabited by the dominant components of the Avar Empire. [2] Among them were what the distinguished archaeologist Gyula László calls the "Proto-Magyars" or Late Avars, who settled there in the 7th century. [3] Professor László also points out that after the disintegration of Avar power, around 800 A.D., the formation of small Slavic ethnic islands within the Carpathian Basin also began. There is ample proof, he warns, that the descendants of the "Late Avars" or "Early-Magyars" lived to see the second Hungarian conquest of the Carpathian area by Árpád and his Magyars toward the end of the 9th century. The great number of archaeological finds, especially cemeteries all over the Carpathian Basin, but mainly in its middle and western parts, suggests the existence of a significant number of these "early" Hungarians at that time. [4]

This view is supported by evidence of the predominantly Hungarian names of geographical sites (rivers, towns, baulks between strips of land, etc.) in areas where these widespread archaeological finds are situated. This, in turn, gives substance to the view that the Slavic, mainly Bulgaro-Slavic, population of that age was thinner than earlier estimated in most parts of the inner Carpathian region. A number of 12th to 14th century documents prove this. [5] The fact that the Slavic migration of the 6th and 7th centuries was mainly established over East Central Europe under the politico-military leadership of Turkish speaking [6] Eurasian horsemen who settled the Slavs in a peripheric position around the inner parts of their empire also supports that conclusion. [7] Historiography and linguistics alike conclude that the centre of the Carpathian Basin, the great Plain and its smaller continuation to the Northwest, the eastern part of Pannonia and the middle of Transylvania were at the time of the Hungarian conquest or soon after, practically free from other than Hungarian or related ethnic population. [8] Wide tracts of the area, on the other hand, were virtually uninhabited. [9] So it is plausible, even widely accepted, that most of these unconnected Slavic settlements were peacefully absorbed and assimilated by the Hungarian population by the end of the 12th century [10] There is no trace of forced assimilation anywhere. [11] Certainly, the conquering Magyars of the 9th century did not find any nation on this territory with the slightest claim for "historical right". The reason was simply that no power before the Hungarians was able to take permanent roots here because of the area's geopolitical location.

The only substantial exception to this general ethnic situation was the northern part of the Carpathian Basin, especially its western half. Here were settled the ancestors of the Slovaks, the only component of the basin's thin population not assimilated. These people of Moravo-Slav origin were living alongside of the Northwestern Carpathians mainly in the valleys of the Morva, Vág, and Garam. These Western Slovaks, however, appear to have been ethnically somewhat different from the inhabitants of the eastern part of the Sub-Carpathian territory. Their origin has been described in the following terms: "... in addition to Magyars, Germans, Moravo-Slavs, Poles and Russians penetrated the forests at the foot of the Tatra, the Present Central and Eastern Slovakia, the Zólyom Forest (*Silva de Zolium*) and the Szepes Forest (*Silva de Scepus*). [12] All these contributed to the formation of Central and Eastern Slovakia's linguistic and ethnic picture. To quote the Czech historian Chaloupecky "early history does not distinguish a Slovak nation as an original ethnic unit...Not until the 13th century do the Slovak dialects, the youngest of all Slav idioms, begin to develop from a Slav mixture...." [13] It could be added that the "Slovak" name itself is hardly more than 200 years old. Thus, it was not an organized, developed and stable state which was found here by the conquering second wave of Hungarians in the 9th century, but a rather thin population devoid of centripetal force. Even the anthropological type of the Slovaks shows considerable variations owing to the absorption of a great number of Hungarians, Germans, Vlachs and Poles, as pointed out by a 19th century student of the region's history. [14]

Nevertheless, at the time of the second Hungarian conquest of the Carpathian Basin there lived a sizeable, if not necessarily compact, contiguous and connected ethnic community in what became Upper Hungary and was later called Slovakia. This community developed and preserved its cultural and biological heritage up to the present day; in the past within the realm of St. Stephen's Crown, and more recently as part of Czechoslovakia. This unique fact, the preservation and even expansive development of an ethnic community within the sphere of the exclusive governing power of a racially different state such as the medieval Kingdom of Hungary proved to be, must have had a number of reasons, some of which perhaps have not been fully evaluated as yet. Among the acknowledged and traceable reasons should be mentioned the relative geographical segregation of the mountain area; the friendly and peaceful relationship between the majority and minority including frequent intermarriages all which lasted well into the 19th century; the fact that the Catholic clergy in Hungary contained a disproportionately high Slovak element, especially in its top echelons, and last but not least the ancient trend discernible in the statecraft of conquering nomadic horsemen towards building friendly and cooperative foreign ethnic units into a quasi-federal empire. [15]

Built-in factors of contemporary geopolitical importance

tend to produce new structural components when a people decides to settle down permanently as Árpád's Magyars did finally in 896 A.D. Among these structural components, the county system, as developed in medieval Hungary, seems to have been the linchpin in the evolution of a semi-autonomous regional administrative state system, of which one side effect was the preservation, biologically and linguistically, of compactly settled ethnic units, especially those of Slovak origin.

Arnold Toynbee once observed that among the three post-Christian ideologies: nationalism, communism and individualism, nationalism has proved itself to be the most potent. When nationalism collides with either communism or individualism nationalism invariably wins. [16]   A logical consequence of this would be that administrative units ought to be organized on the national or ethnic principle instead of the territorial one, with its arbitrary borders drawn as the result of historical accidents. This latter structure is based on the unitary, mainly centralistic, French-type state, which proved itself to be totally inadequate for the needs of the multinational East Central European area.

It appears that by some fortuitous interplay of historic necessities, ethnic strivings and geopolitical facts that stage had been set around the turn of the millennium for the establishment of a unique and beneficial early administrative structure in the Carpathian Basin, which created the basis of a genuine survival of ethnic minority populations in historic Hungary.

1.

Origin and Development of the County System in the
Carpathian Basin and its Historic Significance

For a West European it would be a surprise to learn that one of Europe's oldest, if not the oldest administrative regional system was born in that part of the Carpathian Basin which used to be the historic Kingdom of Hungary. Although the area belongs and has always belonged to Central Europe it is stubbornly misnamed, especially since the second world war, as "East Europe". It would be hard to determine whether this misnomer is the result of a subconscious urge to write off the area on the part of some politicians and political writers, or that of sheer ignorance of elementary geographical facts.

Notwithstanding such present-day fallacies certain historical facts remain clear. The foremost among them is the notion that a developing new politico-administrative system's emergence in the Carpathian Basin became discernible soon after the second or main conquest of the area by Arpád's Magyars in 896 A.D. The settlement of the vast area was facilitated by the comparatively thin spread of population, with huge pockets of uninhabited tracts on the one hand, and the ethnic affinity of part of this population with the conquering Magyars on the other.[17]

The settlement itself, whose completion took probably some decades, was twofold in its character. The land became either tribal or regal territory. The former was the land taken up by one or other of the seven conquering tribes composing the tribal federation and had the character of land community with tribal customary law as the traditional source of justice and tribal rule. The regal territory, on the other hand, was composed of the possessions of the leading Megyer tribe from which the Árpád dynasty originated, together with all the rest of the land not subjected to tribal settlement. This was the larger part of the area. According to some estimates it constituted about two thirds of the country's total territory.[18] This part of the territory became the substratum on which the specific Hungarian county system grew up, beginning with the organization of these royal lands into *domains*, mainly for the sake of easier management, but possibly also with the political intent of keeping the old tribal units away from each other.[19] Under the rule of King St. Stephen (1000-1038) this new division was consolidated with each of the domains having appointed heads called *ispán*, who within the borders (*mesgye*) for the domains were the king's representatives. The Hungarian name of these domains or counties *"megye"* is thus derived from the concept of the border. The population of the domain-county was endowed with various rights and duties. The more prominent ones, the so called *várjobbágyok* or castle serfs, were the ispán's helpers. From their ranks was appointed the county judge, the *comes curialis*, as well as the commander of the force.

This was the simple structure of the royal county, that is an organ of *central power*, at that time the king's *quasi private* possession. This was to be transformed into an organ of local self-government and an institution of a considerable degree of constitutional freedom. The transformation was neither quick, nor smooth. But its effects could be sensed throughout the country's constitutional history, almost to the turn of the last century. Not the least important among these was *its silent psychological effect on the general shaping of conditions leading toward the biological and cultural consolidation of historic Hungary's ethnic minorities or nationalities.*

* * *

It is important to examine briefly those parts of the country which were occupied by the tribes constituting the tribal federation of Árpád's forces. Here it was not the law of St. Stephen, which was that of the royal domain-counties, that is to say the actual governing rule, but ancient Hungarian customary law which was applied by the elders of the clan. Controversial decisions, however, could be appealed to the king. The tribe was bound to join the royal forces if war happened to occur within the borders of the country. But there was little agreement, if any, on the ambit of private law.

With the establishment of St. Stephen's county system the development of the inner life of the tribes took a different turn. The first change was their geographical division according to the confines of the nearest county, of which their lands slowly became part. Although the county heads had no jurisdiction over them, nor over their lands, still the presence of a royal organizational unit nearby had its integrating effect at least in a territorial sense. And the county, although still a royal domain, was at the same time an early administrative organ as well. This latter role of the county was felt at an early stage in two ways which widely concerned tribal interests: the periodic replacement or exchanges of gold and silver coins from the royal mint with new ones, and the collection of the tithe for the church.

It was inevitable that in line with the increase in central power and the radiance of the royal court the authority of the county heads also grew, and it was natural that those serving the court were the first to share the land donations and became a kind of office-holder aristocracy. These developments were, of course, not without effect on the ancient tribal organization, which, as a consequence of the continuous divisions and subdivisions of the huge tribal lands had already became weaker. It was the beginning of a slow disintegration of the tribal organization. The tribal heads, with shrinking possessions and powers, envied not merely the enrichment of the royal office-bearers, but especially the circumstance that their possessions, unlike tribal possessions which were owned by the community, were fully at their disposal. This led, as early as the 12th century, at the time of power struggles of rival royal candidates, to the entry of tribal leaders into these struggles and their subsequently being rewarded in some cases with personal possessions. The full development of this new aristocracy based on land possession caused the final disappearance of the ancient institutions and the emergence of new organizational and constitutional forms. As few of the rulers felt strong enough to resist this bend, in the course of one century the once huge royal domain-counties melted into scraps.[20]

This trend was, however, sharply against the interests of the office-bearers of the counties, whatever their rank or occupation, as their personal freedom and property rights were protected by their bond to one of the counties. They felt they had been let down when sometimes even the king turned against the integrity of the county. So they assumed an intensely protective attitude toward their unit, defending its possessions, and by now traditional rights, against anybody, at times even against the king.

This was the time when, owing to the constant need to protect acquired rights, a new legal principle was born, which in the course of the following centuries, became the most important and unique precept of the Hungarian Constitution, the doctrine of the Holy Crown of Hungary.[21]   The gist of this fundamental and truly history-shaping principle was that, not the king, but the Crown was the repository and source of all state power. Consequently, the dominion-counties were not strictly the king's possessions, but common lands of the country. The view gathered strength that the destiny of the people living on these lands could not solely depend on the king's whims; on the contrary, they were entitled to the public freedoms of the country. As a result of these ideas, a rapprochement between the different grades and occupational categories of county office-bearers took place.

This trend was interrupted by the Mongol invasion of Hungary (1241-43) which devastated large areas of the country, killing or dispersing the population, shaking the legal order of the country in its foundations. The Mongols' departure rendered the royal donation of country lands even more easy, which, in turn, brought the dispossessed county people closer together in defense of their means of existence. This was the first sign of the *emergence of a new social class*.

All this happened at a time when the ancient tribal organization was also undergoing radical changes. While some of its prominent members had left the tribal organization already, the possessions and prestige of the rest were disappearing. They became the *köznemesség* or lesser nobility with fading awareness of even their blood kinship, and with the common tillage of the tribal land as their only remaining bond. As their old way of life fell apart their right to property and their personal freedom became uncertain. The amount of litigation grew, and the rules of the ancient customary law were no longer adequate for their settlement. So they had to turn to the king and his law. The increase in the number of such cases in the king's court made it impossible for the king to attend in person. So he delegated this power. [22]

When the more prominent members left the tribal units in order to settle on their own, often uninhabited lands, donated possessions, including their slaves went with them, and by virtue of an ancient legal principle—became free. Thereby they became direct subjects of the king under his local representative, the *ispán*. The economic consequence of this was a further deterioration in the tribal land system, and a weakening of the lesser nobility. The result was the gradual extension of the royal county's competence over them also. All this resulted in the slow disappearance of the dividing line between the territories of the nobility and those of the counties. And this was so not only in territorial respect, but also in regard to possessions, prestige, rights, and duties. In the meantime a parallel trend became discernible: the oligarchic aspiration of the enriched landed aristocracy.

At this critical time the lesser nobility began to demand access to the management of the royal county, and because of their distance from the central government, they began *to elect* their judges to dispense justice. Another step toward county self-government was the election of the panel of judges with jurisdiction in property right questions and other disputes.

The royal court which had thus voluntarily depleted itself of most of its possessions in the hope of satisfying the oligarchs now felt threatened by them and was inclined to support the lesser nobility's self-government strivings, the more so because they were by now in charge of the county administration. Installations and other important legal acts were not carried out by emissaries of the court, but were entrusted to one of the members of the local lesser nobility. The royal commands were not addressed to the *ispán* anymore, but to the community of the county, which also reported back directly.

In the early part of the second half of the 13th century the institution of *judex servorum regis* or *szolgabíró* emerged as permanent judges of the king's servants, i.e. the lesser nobility. Their emergence signifies the victory of the self-government idea in that particular county, for they performed the duties of an administration and the function of administering justice from then on. Their independence was based on elections, and initially submission to their judgements was voluntary.

The county assemblies were open to the nobility and to the free peasants who were equal members of the county. [23] Only later in the 14th century, at the time of the Angevins, when the principle of the *una eademque nobilitas* began to take shape, did the concept of the royal county change to become that of a community of nobility and, as a parallel phenomenon, an early form of municipal self-government. [24]

Commencing in the 13th century, and gathering strength in the Angevin era (1308-1395), the autonomy of the city communities opened a new chapter in this development. Based on royal *privilegia*, these cities were granted rights of management of their domestic affairs and exemption from the general and judicial jurisdiction of the county to which they territorially belonged. [25]   Entrenched within the security of this autonomy the material and cultural development of these city municipalities was granted. The more so because it was only in exceptional cases that they took sides in the frequent struggles between the central power and the counties concerning constitutional issues. And, as the citizens of these municipalities were usually descendants of foreign migrants, mostly German and Italian, at times French or Flemish, the flourishing of these communities provided the first historical evidence of the most important side-effect of the constitutional struggle, i.e. its effect upon the country's ethnic minorities it indirectly facilitated their biological and cultural survival and development.

In general terms, up to this point, the development of the municipal system can be summed up thus while, during the 11th to 13th centuries, the kings had the upper hand in social affairs, in the 14th-15th centuries the community of the nobility became *primary factors* in the constitutional government of the country. These communities' possession of regional political power was not received by royal grant, but as a continuation of ancient freedoms and customs in new form.[26]

The overriding importance of this circumstance became evident in the period of Turkish occupation of nearly half of Hungary after the battle of Mohács in 1526. The subsequent 167 years, until the Turks were driven out of Hungary, witnessed a terrible loss of life, property and cultural goods, not only in the Turkish occupied parts of the country but in the Northwestern regions as well. In those areas where the Habsburg kings ruled, the situation was only slightly better. The quarrels of king and counter-king and their mutual adherents, Turkish and Tartar raids and the invasions of greedy mercenaries rendered it almost impossible to carry out royal commands and to uphold respect for the legal order. A certain feeling of belonging together and a very restricted exercise of the most elementary administration was all that was left. In this atmosphere of protracted disaster the counties situated in the unoccupied parts of the country tried to use their constitutional right to refuse the payment of taxes not passed by legislation. However feeble they may have been during this difficult period—as an observer of their history put it—the counties were the "split sovereign part of the nation." [27]

As it could be expected the brunt of these immense difficulties was born by those tilling the land, and this peasant population, if not exclusively, was overwhelmingly Hungarian at the turn of the 15th and 16th centuries.

The terrible Turkish devastations were followed by migrations of German, Vlach, Serb and to a lesser extent Slovak settlers into these regions, upsetting the previous Hungarian numerical supremacy in these parts of the realm. [28]

This process of slow but incessant change of ethnic proportions, different in various parts of the country, confronted the leaders of the counties with a Janus-faced problem: trying a) to uphold a semi-autonomous, constitutionally established regional state *vis-à-vis* the central power, while b) leaning, in certain parts of the country, on a population which was no longer purely Magyar.

In order to cope with this situation on a permanent basis a policy of nondiscrimination was applied. In addition to the long established practice of admitting persons of foreign ethnic origin in considerable numbers to the nobility, the non-Magyar peasant population was never hindered in the use of their native language, customs or religion, and their material opportunities were in no respect worse than those of their Hungarian counterparts.

The living proof for this was Rákóczi's War of Independence against the Habsburgs (1704-1711) when, apart from Hungarians, Ruthenes, Slovaks, Germans and even Vlachs were fighting together in his army *"pro patria et libertate"* against the House of Austria. Transylvania, during the Turkish occupation of the mother country, had become a semi-independent Hungarian principality whose politico-legal situation was similar in a certain degree to that of Finland today. It was always renowned for its religious, ethnic and political tolerance.

In other words, the price for maintaining constant alertness and, at times, a struggle for constitutional freedom against the centralizing trends emanating unwaveringly from Vienna had to be an attitude of benevolent nondiscrimination against ethnic minorities. This secured not merely their biological survival, but also that of their language and customs. At times and in certain parts of historic Hungary, this resulted directly in the expansion of ethnic minorities at the cost of Hungarian settlements, as will be shown in the following chapters.

The 1711 Peace of Szatmár brought to an end the freedom fights of the Rákoczi era and confirmed the authority of the royal executive power, mainly by its determined efforts to bring the counties to heel. Thus the initiatives for the general regulation of legal and constitutional practice beginning with the 18th century can be regarded as a turning point in the centuries-old rivalry.[29] The most important among these initiatives was the establishment of the *royal regent council* (*helytartótanács*) as a separate central governing authority with the task of guiding and unifying the county administration.[30] With this, the direct dependence of the counties from the Diet[31] was substituted with their subordination to this new governing authority. The advantage of this development was the discontinuation of the practice of "so many counties, so many legal customs." The new system thus increased the efficiency of the county administration. Not even this comparatively quiet period of the expansion to almost all modern spheres of administrative competence[32] was used by the counties with significant minority populations to harass them or impose any kind of restrictions upon them.

After these few decades of comparative peace a constitutional struggle erupted during the reign of Joseph II (1780-1790), the Reformer. His centralist strivings, fed by enlightened absolutism, clashed with the counties' rights to autonomy which were still safeguarded by the constitution. The clash, occasionally resulting in actual fighting, took the form mainly of passive resistance triggering the suspension of municipal jurisdiction. The administrative functions were to be carried out by officials appointed by the Court in Vienna and the official language was to become German instead of Hungarian and Latin.

On his deathbed, however, Joseph II withdrew most of his decrees, and in a very short time the *status quo ante* was restored. The counties were able to exercise their normal administrative functions again. One result of the lessons learned in this period was that legislation was passed whereby the Hungarian language partially supplanted Latin[33] in official matters and the teaching of it began on a general, although not exclusive, level. [34] *Tis, at a time when, in all West European countries, the language of the dominant majority,* without regard to their ethnic minorities, *had already been exclusively used in all ambits of national life for many centuries.*

The next changes in the county system were heralded by the events of 1848. In accordance with the general trend of democratisation of all aspects of public life, the counties had to adopt a few reforms. The principle of popular representation and the establishment of responsible government after long, semi-autocratic rule from Vienna were only of a temporary nature, and their logical adaptation to and by the county administration had hardly commenced [35] when the Russian intervention in the fighting in 1849 tipped the scale in Austria's favor. Eighteen years of autocratic rule were to follow before in 1867 the Austro-Hungarian Compromise restored freedom and reinstated most aspects of former county autonomy. [36] From this time until the end of World War I a gradual but steady restriction of the county administration's sphere of competence can be seen. This was already apparent in the 1870 legislation, [37] and even more so in the municipal legislation of 1886 which took away the sustance of county autonomy in all but name.

As adroitly pointed out by a turn-of-the-century historian of the county system, its Latin name, *comitatus*, means an institution which manifests itself in meeting or assembly. [38] It was the interaction of specific Hungarian ethnic traits, tradition and ancient customary law, among other things, that shaped the administrative law concept of the county system. Its unique strivings for autonomy, with which, in a rather short and rudimentary form we had been acquainted on the preceding pages, provided the spiritual background on the common denominator of "meeting", or, using a more recent concept, consensus, for a long constitutional struggle, usually against foreign rulers, for a measure of autonomy.

Although there are certain similarities to regional administrative solutions in other parts of Europe, these similarities are more or less superficial and lacking in substance. The Carolingian *Gaugrafschaften*, the Slav *oblast*, the French *département*, the English *counties* not only lacked constitutional legal aspects and significance, but usually any degree of autonomy as well. If not always expressly feudal in character, they were at least transmission agents of a central power.

Nevertheless, an institution, particularly one that is over 900 years old, must have received its constant, life-giving nourishment from somewhere. If it was not from the central power of the country, then it must have been from the local or regional community. Without such support the resistance to the often unconstitutional, coercive measures emanating from the central power would have been impossible. And this support was usually granted not only by the thin layer of nobility running the administration, but, in critical stages of the nation's history, by the broad masses of peasants and serfs, whether of Magyar ethnic background or belonging to one of the minorities of historic Hungary. And if their trust was so readily forthcoming for the counties' struggle that, until the ripening of the Pan-Slavic agitation towards the middle of the last century, their cooperation with the Hungarian cause was sincere, even in wartime, then their treatment as minorities could not have been so bad. The evaluation of some details of the relationship between Hungary and the Slovaks, an important former minority, will be attempted in the following chapters.

2

County Autonomy and the Ethnic Minorities

The main stages in the development of the county system in historic Hungary suggest that a double transformation must have taken place. First, the royal domain-counties took over the administrative and organizational duties on a regional basis, gradually absorbing the initially self-governing tribal lands. Secondly, these counties, led by local and created nobility, in protecting their regional powers and jurisdiction by necessity became the defenders of country-wide political independence, and of whatever constitutional, regional self-government could be attained later for the whole country when the centre of power—political and military—was located beyond the confines of the country.

At this juncture the obvious question arises: if the counties were not entirely and exclusively the organs of central power,

and even for long periods and different reasons have had to
oppose it, then what was their power base? This foothold must
have been firm enough to withstand the tempest of centuries.
At the risk of stating the obvious: it could only have been their
own regional population, because *tertium non datur*. But the
"obviousness" of this statement becomes less flagrant when we
recall that substantial changes had taken place in the ethnic
composition of Hungary, beginning with the Turkish occupation of two-thirds of the land and the devastation—human and
material—that followed in the 16th century.

We must remember that the population of the land (not
including the associated country of Croatia) was almost purely
Magyar during the Middle Ages, except for the Slovaks in its
northern and northwestern parts, and some sporadic Vlach
settlements in the western and southern mountains of
Transylvania, whose first documented presence is noted there
from the 13th century. Between this time and the 1870-1880
censuses, when the first territorially detailed ethnic data were
obtained, the situation changed dramatically. According to
these censuses, the mother tongue of less than 50% of the
population in 36 of the then 64 counties of historic Hungary
was Hungarian, and of these 36 counties there were 12 in
which the percentage of inhabitants whose mother tongue was
Hungarian was less than 10%. [39]

This dramatic change within about three centuries could
be divided into two phases. The first phase was the Turkish
occupation of the central and southern parts of the country,
which lasted from the Battle of Mohács in 1526 to the
liberation of Buda in 1686, and the subsequent retreat of the
Turks and fragments of the Balkan peoples whom the Turks
settled in Hungary. This latter retreat was only partial. The
second phase was between 1686 and the middle of 19th
century, when the new policy, directed from Vienna, opened
the way for resettlement of the depopulated areas. Apart from
some organized German migration, the settling of Serbs,
Slovaks, Ruthenes, and a continuation of the centuries-old
Rumanian migration from the Balkans into Transylvania and
adjoining parts of Hungary proper (which commenced in the
13th century), was relentlessly pursued. [40]   Magyars came
back from the North also in considerable numbers, but were
not numerous enough to re-establish their former predominance.

How did the county system fit into this changing historic and ethnic situation? In considering this we must turn first of all to the ethnogenesis of the Turk-dominated, nomadic horsemen-peoples in the early Middle Ages, such as the Huns, Avars, Petchenegs and the Magyars. By building up loose confederation-like state structures based on the power of a leading ethnic group and led by a powerful personality, they dominated the huge Eurasian territory from the Chinese Wall to the Carpathians. Mighty empires were built, which disappeared as fast as the cohesive force of the leading people or a charismatic personality in charge of it vanished. [41] The constituent parts of these empires, the peoples, were always allowed to maintain their traditions, their ethnic characteristics and, last but not least, their language. This, as M. Ferdinandy points out, is in sharp contrast to the behaviour of the Romans, where conquest was always equivalent to Romanisation. [42]

There was always a great deal of flexibility in the relationship of these ancient Eurasian horsemen-peoples towards their conquered or voluntarily allied subject peoples. The reason is probably to be found in their basic attitude to the concept of land. While, for the permanently settled, early medieval peoples of Western Europe, land was the basis of political entity, for the pastoral-horsemen nations the peoples of their quasi-deflative empires were the sources of power. [43]

This latter traditional attitude or undercurrent of political thinking became a permanent nature of Hungarian statecraft, and was hardly altered by the transforming influence of conversion to Christianity either. Although, as Szekfű emphasizes, the earlier view that ethnic or national differences were unknown in the Middle Ages cannot be maintained; these differences could not be reconciled with the ideal of the universal Christian State, [44] and so lay dormant.

The direct result of this traditional attitude, inherited from the Eurasian horsemen-peoples, was that wherever the security of the dominant majority was not at risk the cultural identity of a subjected people was not interfered with. In an interethnic sense, therefore, the Hungarians were never inclined toward oppression: that was simply not necessary or desirable from the point of view of political or military efficiency. This traditional policy, or mental attitude, was the basis for their relationship not only with a people like the Slovaks, or the fragments of other small peoples found in the Carpathian Basin in the 9th century, but even with those migrants who settled in the wake of the Turkish devastations, and whose descendants are today the dominant majority in two thirds of dismembered historic Hungary. There could hardly be a better proof of the validity of the degree of ethnic tolerance shown by the Hungarian people.

The ethnic and linguistic tolerance of the medieval Hungarian state became the behavioral background and canon for the transactions and procedure of the county system, which functioned so well without the need of many statutory provisions. This was one side of the coin.

The other was the quality of those who were running the affairs, the administration and representation of the county. Everywhere in Western Europe, until the French Revolution, it was the role and privilege of the nobility to meddle in differing degrees with the central power in the administration of regional affairs. In East Central Europe, west from the Carpathians, this stage lasted well beyond the middle of the 19th century. East of the Carpathians, as it is well known, it lasted much longer.

Thus the Hungarian nobility managed the county system. And here comes the *punctum saliens*; this nobility was not only completely devoid of racial prejudice, but, by inclusion of immigrants into the nation concept under the Holy Crown doctrine, a constitutional possibility existed and was used abundantly for foreigners to become members of the lesser nobility and even of the aristocracy of the country.

This possibility was used even more frequently by upward-striving members of the ethnic minorities. Among the best known family names belonging to higher and lesser nobility before World War I in nine counties in what was then Upper Hungary, the percentage of non-Hungarian names varied between 4 and 43%, [45] as a random test shows. Nevertheless, this nobility of ethnically mixed origin turned out to be a staunch pillar of the state throughout many critical periods of the country's history. This devotion to public affairs was, of course, not entirely altruistic, as most of the land, with the exception of the regal (later state-owned) territories and land possessions of the Church, belonged to them until 1848.

Still it meant that the regional administration was within their sphere of authority, and by means of the counties' right to send delegates to the Diets, their influence did not end at the confines of their respective counties. The nobility thus defended both the constitution of the country and the basis of their own powers. The adversary in this struggle was always the centre of the state power: the king, the court and the chancellery. This was especially so after the royal power moved from Buda to Vienna in the late 16th century.

Resistance, both peaceful and violent (e.g. the freedom fights of Francis Rákóczi) was the answer, which was as good as unknown at the beginning of Habsburg rule in Hungary. The nobility rallied round the county, and the *universitas nobilium* established itself as their official organ from the 17th century, especially after Joseph II's rationalist and enlightened absolutist rule. [46]   Even during his reign a country-wide systematic resistance commenced mainly against his decrees concerning wartime deliveries and material services.

The transition from such 18th-century performances of *vis ineriae* to the linguistic reform legislation of late 18th and early 19th centuries, whereby Hungarian became the official language in place of Latin, was comparatively smooth. [47] Nothing could throw a clearer light upon the still basically unspoiled relationship between majority and the ethnic minorities of that time (the 1820's) than the fact that only the delegates of some counties of Upper Hungary raised a claim for twelve years deferment of the bill until the schools had had time to teach the language uniformly to the new generation in their territory. [48] These delegates were the descendants of Hungarian or, in several cases, Hungaro-Slovak families which usually spoke both languages.

The county administration's most important relationship, however, was with the population of its own region, which, irrespective of ethnic differences not only paid the state taxes, but also provided the funds of the *cassa domestica*, the coffers of the administration. This meant paying the Diet delegates' expenses which, because the early 19th century increase in Diet sittings was a heavy burden for the serfs and peasants alone to bear. An astounding example, as Szekfű points out, was the case of Borsod county, where, in 1817, the domestic tax amounted to 143,438 florins while the state tax was only 66,336. [49]

Thus, the increase in the counties' sphere of jurisdiction resulted in increased burdens for their own population without regard to ethnic affiliation. This gave a strong impetus to the reform movement of the 1840's, led mainly by Széchenyi and Kossuth, the various aspects of which were first formulated in resolutions at county meetings and submitted to the Diet. Because considerable number of the nobility belonged to ethnic minorities, the situation was not without dangers for the unity and integrity of the country.

Indeed, as could be expected, cumulative concomitants of this nation-wide reform movement were the nascent strivings of the minorities after recognition. The Slovaks, Croatians and Serbs reached the transient age between emotional and cultural nationalism, while broad masses of the non-urban Rumanians were mainly at the emotional stage. It turned out to be a tragic situation. From now on a strong Hungarian drive for democratization and independence had to fight a two-front war, with forces of the Habsburg imperial establishment on the one hand, and with some, but not all, of the self-appointed advocates of the ethnic minories on the other. The result was emotional trauma in the body politic of the nation. [50]

In the opinion of some leading historians of this age there was no causal connection between the Hungarian reform movement in the first half of the 19th century, and the turning of increasing ethnic nationalism against it, and against the Hungarian state-idea altogether. According to this view they are parallel phenomena, still separate national movements, which, being part of the process of European nationalism, turned against each other, obeying inherent politico-historical laws. [51]

Thus, the changeover of the Diet's language from Latin to Hungarian around 1840 was used by some groups of ethnic minorities as a basis of complaint, in spite of the fact that at the beginning of the 19th century the languages of most of them were in want of finalized alphabet, uniform spelling and unified grammatical rules. The Hungarian literary language at this time, owing to late 18th and early 19th century semantic reforms was already in a rather developed stage. [52]

Such considerations, however, could hardly satisfy the few intellectuals among the leadership of the ethnic minorities of historic Hungary, and hostile articles in newspapers abroad, and especially the political pamphlet literature attacking the change, increased. The adoption of this process in the modernization of county administration, such as the change of language of the discussions in county meetings, the drawing up of minutes, etc., were used by the self-appointed representatives of the nationalities for propaganda purposes. One wonders whether it has ever occurred to those mainly Pan-Slavistic propagandists of the time, that, apart from Hungary, there would hardly be another country in Europe where in the 1840s the majority's language needed legislative action for its use in the semi-autonomous ambits of regional administration.

It appears that until about 1848 no coherent policy even existed in Hungary toward the ethnic minorities. It was thus left to those counties to deal with the manifold problems of everyday life, whose population used to be partially non-Hungarian. Understandably there was no uniformity, and conscious or planned suppression was impossible.

Towards the middle of this socially and nationally fermenting 19th century, the 1848-49 Hungarian War of Independence against Austria gave, for a brief period, some chance for the inhabitants of the Carpathian Basin to express their feelings. The majority of the Slovaks, the Ruthenes and the Germans—free from dreams of national separatism—sided with the Hungarians. In the revolutionary Hungarian Army, the *Honvéd*, there were an estimated number of 40,000 Slovaks [53] alone. Some of their intellectuals,(i.e. Štur, Hudan, Hodža) meanwhile tried to popularize Austro-Slavism at first and later Slovak separatism with varying success. [54] The Rumanians of Transylvania and the Serbs of Southern Hungary, however, were behaving differently. In the hope of a union with their co-nationals beyond the border, they rejected any meaningful compromise and fought guerilla war against the Hungarian Army. In spite of this, in the subsequent period of absolutist rule emanating from Vienna, their strivings were thwarted.

This was an early proof that, in the cultural nationalism of some of the ethnic minorities in the Carpathian Basin, the dormant striving for power was always present. In 1848, after shedding the cultural mask, it openly demanded exclusive politico-territorial predominance." [54a]

During the period between the defeat of the freedom fighters in 1849 by the combined Austrian and Russian armies, and the Austro-Hungarian Compromise of 1867, the administrative work of the counties was suspended.

The architect of the 1867 Compromise, Francis Deák, emphasized that the counties were not federative parts of the whole state, and consequently could not possess separate or contrary rights to the state. It was the 1867 legislation which reunited the many small county units, at the same time separated the judicial and administrative branches, [55] and regulated the election of delegates to the new parliament. This meant that in the last quarter of the 19th century the representatives from ethnically mixed regions were, during the whole dualistic period, i.e. until the end of World War I, selected by means of the same, unwritten but proven rules as for centuries before. The ethnic background of the candidate or office-bearer was completely irrelevant as long as he accepted the supranational principle of St. Stephen's Crown.

The Dual Monarchy in its true sense lasted about half a century. [56] Increasing restlessness could be observed, however, on the part of the minorities in both Austria and Hungary, despite a sincere attempt by the new government to arrive at a mutually acceptable solution by legislative means. The result of this was the *Law on National Minorities*, [57] which was the most advanced and most humanitarian legislation on this topic in Europe at that time. Its main architect, Joseph Eötvös, even though he foresaw that the ethnic principle, derived from the existence of a linguistically different community, could destroy many historic countries of Europe, still attempted to prevent this development by granting equal rights to all without regard to national origin. This legislatively confirmed non-discrimination principle was a unique step in 19th-century Europe which was not yet ripe for such tolerance. Nevertheless, the Act introduced the use of minority languages in the lower and middle levels of administration and courts, and maintained the exclusivity of Hungarian language only in the higher spheres of state practice.

Unfortunately, the main ethnic minorities were not satisfied even with this. The Slovaks wanted to transform their linguistic territory in Upper Hungary into an exclusively Slav district [58] with self-government. The Rumanians wanted the autonomy of Transylvania, and the Serbs insisted on the creation of a Serb *vojvodina* in South Hungary. It became clear that the goal of these minorities was not the achievement of more human and political rights, but the dismemberment of historic Hungary and the establishment of their own administrative structures, with much more exclusivity than that which the *Law on National Minorities* was prepared to allow to Hungarians themselves. It is little wonder, therefore, that this Law, which by mutual acceptance could have altered the course of history in East Central Europe, but which was not accepted by the leading politicians of the minorities, was not enforced either. In the higher echelons of government the Hungarian language remained in use, while in local administration in ethnic regions everything remained as it was before 1848, i.e. the population and the officials tried to understand each other in the counties where the ethnic minorities were more numerous. Although the language of court procedure was Hungarian, that of the local and county administration in ethnic regions was the ethnic language or the Hungarian. The old spirit of the ethnically indifferent and, more importantly, minority protective county was still to be felt well into the turn of the century.

The half century between the Austro-Hungarian Compromise of 1867 and the end of World War I was the first time that beyond, but not contrary to, the supraethnic principle and practice of St. Stephen's state idea, a contemporary Hungarian nationality policy slowly evolved. Its main scope was the spreading of the Hungarian language and culture mainly by educational and administrative means. However welcome, assimilation was happening mainly on middle class level, and was not only voluntary but was most willingly carried out usually by assimilated new Hungarians, as an observer of this historical period noted.[58a]

For the sake of historical justice it is to be pointed out, that there was never any pressure of economic nature involved, and the broad masses of ethnic minorities were treated the same way as the corresponding true-born Hungarian classes. Freedom on personal and religious level, use of one's own language was always secured, and the high ethical standard of the judiciary was never in doubt. Although assimilation in a much harsher and more effective way was the rule, at this time, in

most European countries and America, this fifty-year period's
pent up charges were used against Hungary during and after
World War I in order to prepare and carry through its dismemberment with its tragic consequences for the whole
Danubian area.

3

*Expanding Slovak-Language Borderline in Upper Hungary
till the Dismemberment of Historic Hungary in 1919*

In the previous chapters, a description of the substance and
historic role of one of the Continent's most unique administrative system, the Hungarian county, had been attempted, with
references to the positive effects of its limited, yet substantial
regional autonomy upon the development of ethnic minorities
in Hungary. A description of the origin and growth of the
various minorities in historic Hungary would require much
wider research and greater length than the clarification of our
theme and the limits of this paper allow. Most of the
nationalities there, the Germans, Serbs, Ruthenes and
Rumanians, migrated there after the second and final
conquest of the Carpathian basin by Árpád's Magyars, and
they were related to neighbouring peoples. Almost the only
considerable exception were the Slovaks, settled in part of
former Upper Hungary, or today's Slovakia: for this reason
they are more suitable for continuous observation and the
drawing of some long-term conclusions.

While the presence of the Slovaks in the northwestern part
of the Carpathian Basin in the 9th century is beyond dispute,
they merely appear to have been the last occupants of this
region before the arrival of the Magyars. [59] In other words,
they are hardly more autochtonous inhabitants of that part of
the Carpathian region than the Hungarians themselves.
Especially if the results of the late archeological discoveries are
taken into consideration, which ascribe a high degree of
probability to the Avar-Hungarian close affinity, if not
sameness, and explain the settlement of Slav tribes around the
mainland, occupied mainly by the Avars. [60]

At the end of the 9th century, when Árpád's people
arrived, a coexistence, lasting over one thousand years,

commenced between the Hungarians and the Slovaks. At the end of this period the area in which the Slovak language was spoken surpassed its original limits. This fact, documented by linguistic and archeological research and discoveries, [61] is itself the best indicator of the substantially good relations which existed between the two peoples and of the national tolerance of the then dominant Magyars.

The comparative scarcity of similar historical developments warrants a quick glance at some of the scholarly attempts to explain this phenomenon. Most scholars agree that the late Middle Ages witnessed the swift assimilation of the ethnically kindred peoples — Turks, Petchenegs, Cumans Jazygs — by the Magyars. In Szekfü's estimate (as pointed out above), the Magyars constituted 85-87% of the country's population at that time. Apart from the spirit of ethnic and linguistic tolerance, the traditional and state-building force of which was stressed above (p. 339), the Admonitions of Hungary's first Christian king, St. Stephen, to his son lays great weight on the benevolent treatment of migrants. In the chapter entitled *De detentione extermorum et de nutrimento hospitum* he suggests that "... a country of one language and one morality is weak and fragile. Therefore, I exhort thee, my son, to accept them with benevolence and hold them in esteem, in order that they may prefer staying with thee rather than elsewhere." The authority, social as well as quasi-legal, of the *Admonitions* was so great and lasting that, when centuries later the collection of Hungary's laws, the *Corpus Juris Hungarici*, was compiled (printed in 1517), it was based on the *Admonitions*.

The history of this precept, however, shows that, while the charismatic Hungarian kingdom in the 11th and 12th centuries "attempted a conscious assimilation of the racially foreign elements. . .the fuedal kingdom dropped this policy. . ./and/ endeavoured to condense the nationalities, combined them into juridical entities and did not deny *privileges* even to the smallest nationality settlement." [62]

The legal sources of these privileges were royal decrees regulating the rights and duties of particular ethnic groups in medieval Hungary. Some of them had significant human rights contents beside their administrative legal value, [63] a rather novel phenomenon in that age. Their main feature, nevertheless, was the widely differing extent of autonomy or grade of self-government enjoyed by the various recipients, which grades were determined mainly by geopolitical considerations.

In this respect the case of the Slovaks was an individual one, described by an observer as follows: "It is a noteworthy fact that among the non-Magyar peoples of medieval Hungary the Slovaks had no autonomy of any kind. Nor do we possess any indication that they ever claimed autonomy. This may be explained by the fact that the bulk of the Slovak people, the earliest associates of the Magyars, already belonged to the country when the *administrative organization* instituted by St. Stephen was established. The Slovaks fitted into this from the beginning and consequently in their case there was no need for opportunity to apply the new forms of organization introduced in the various territories of nationalities who had immigrated at a later date." [64]

This "administrative organization" was, of course, that of the county, the management of which, in the areas with a Slovak majority, became the task of the Slovak nobility as an integral part of the nation, i.e. the *Populus Sacrae Coronae*, members of the nation under the Holy Crown of Hungary. Although the semi-autonomous status of the various counties differed as a result of historical and geopolitical causes, that of the counties in the Slovak-inhabited regions was among the wider, more liberal, ones. [65]

The complete and steady fitting of the Slovaks into the county system, their considerable number in the ranks of the local nobility, and consequently in the running of its administration in the Slovak-inhabited areas, offers an excellent point of departure for sizing up the original ethnic-linguistic situation of the territory concerned and its later development.

Historical research into settlements and the related literature is one of the most specialized branches of the science of history, and the best approach to a valid assessment of the initial ethnic position appears to be reliance on those monographs concerning the area which, because of their strict scientific methodology, are considered to be dependable. Such are, among others, the works of E. Mályusz, [66] I. Kniezsa, [67] E. Fügedi [68] and A. Petrov. [69] These scholars have ascertained the early ethnic situation in the region under scrutiny by examining early medieval documentary evidence, usually on a village to village, town to town detailed pattern. Most important in this respect are the names of localities and persons, geographical names, archeological discoveries, results of linguistic research and, from the 13th century on, fairly abundant documentary material, especially tax conscriptions, the so called *urbarium*. In the following brief assessment of the general ethnic situation, the conclusions reached by above mentioned settlement-historians will be set out.

For the sake of easier oversight, Kniezsa proposed the taking of two centres of territorial assessment in the area of the then Upper Hungary Nyitra (Nitra) in the West, and Kassa (Košice) in the East, with their surrounding regions as bases for evaluation. Without being a definitive, all-embracing history, his survey seeks to capture the essence of the region's general state in ethnic terms during several centuries when—most of the time—the decisive support of direct statistical data was not available. Accordingly, the ethnic history of the region can be summed up as follows.

In the 10th to 12th centuries, the areas around both Nyitra and Kassa had an overwhelmingly Hungarian character, while in Árva, Liptó, Turóc and Zólyom areas an overwhelmingly Slovak population was settled. The Slovaks were mainly in the mountains, while the Hungarians were moving northwards, following the river valleys and settling down mostly along these. Towards Poland and especially Bohemia, the ancient system of *gyepüelve*, which was a strip of land beyond the march land, surrounded the populated areas. The function of this arrangement was to defend the country with a ring of uninhabited and impenetrable marches. This by itself excluded any significant territorial contiguity between the Moravians and the Slovak population of the area.

In the Nyitra region,[70] the compact Hungarian settlement reached up to Appony, and in the Kassa region up to the middle of Sáros county. This position remained more or less unchanged until well into the 16th-17th centuries as the sources on family names in these localities clearly show. This balance was upset by the Turkish wars which, about this time, involved the lower part of Hungary as well. The Hungarian population to the south of Nyitra was eliminated in the years between

1650-1685 by Turkish assaults and intermittent occupations. The Hungarians living in the Kassa region were also decimated, if not completely destroyed, in the second half of the 17th and first half of the 18th centuries.

After the defeat of Francis Rákóczi II's struggle for independence in 1711 — the bulk of whose armies were recruited from adherents to the Reformed Church (Calvinists) — "the Magyar peasantry, which had taken sides with the Reformation, was driven away in particular from the Western Highlands, being everywhere replaced by Slovak settlers imported for the purpose." [71] Part of the Hungarian population of the lower regions fled to the higher, mainly Slovak-inhabited mountain regions of the northern counties of Túróc, Trencsén, Liptó, etc. After the expulsion of the Turks, these Hungarians together with some Slovaks were settled in the devastated, formerly Hungarian areas. It was at this time that the Hungarian population of the northernmost Sáros county lost contact with the Hungarian-speaking areas further to the south. It was absorbed by the Slovaks in the second half of the 18th century. The subsequent waves of Reformation and Counter-Reformation descending upon Catholic and Protestant Hungarians, one at a time, also contributed to the southward movement of the Slovak language border.

The new ethnic settlement pattern is mirrored in the *Lexicon Universorum Regni Hungariae Locorum Populosorum* of the year 1773. This locality register indicates the predominant language in every locality as "*principaliter in eodem viget lingua*" [72] and reveals that the Hungarian speaking area is interrupted by now at Nyitra and at Kassa by an isthmus-shaped Slovak-speaking area.

The Slovak ethnic expansion of the last two centuries is acknowledged by Czechoslovak sources also. "It is certain that during the 150 years previous to 1921 the Slovak-Hungarian language frontier in spite of every political pressure changed rather in favor of the Slovaks. Out of the 319 villages of the language frontier 73 changed nationality and out of them 49 became Slovak." [73] In other words, under Hungarian government, 67% of these 73 villages were Slovakised, and only 33% became mainly Hungarian.

This view, however, is contested by other experts. One of these, L. Jócsik, after a thorough research of the Surány area's

56 villages comprising some 3000 sq. kilometres, writes: ". . .in this territory there is not a single case of Magyarization but 55 cases of Slovakization; and only in a single case do we find the ratios of nationalities unchanged." [74] The population of Nyitra and Kassa regions situated close to the slowly changing linguistic border, consisted of Hungarians as well as Slovaks from the mid-18th century on. According to some expert views, the reason for this was the uncertain national identity of the population. The same person, professing at one time to be Hungarian and at some other time to be Slovak, was less induced to be endogen in his or her marrying terms.

That, apart from periodically changing political bends, might also have been the reason for the fact that between the two world wars according to subsequent censuses the same locality sometimes had a Hungarian, and at other times a Slovak majority. Nevertheless, this could not completely explain the striking inconsistencies and contradictions of the Czechoslovak statistical data. There were many villages, points out Kniezsa, [75] where three subsequent Czechoslovak censuses, in 1919, 1921 and 1930, showed three entirely different and contradictory results. Referring to the results of the 1938 Hungarian census, taken in the area reunited with Hungary by the Vienna Award of the same year, Kniezsa emphasizes that its data generally do not show much change from the ethnic situation registered in the 1773 Lexicon. [76] If they do, they are in the Slovaks' favor.

The Slovak ethnic and linguistic expansion from its rather narrow, regional beginnings in the 10th to 12th century to its present size of approx. four million, was steady and relentless, absorbing in the process a considerable number from other nationalities. Among these were quite a number of Hungarians also who, for one millennium were regarded as the dominant majority of the population, and as such were still conveniently accused of imperialism or suppression whenever dubious foreign aspirations for power or territory in the Carpathian Basin were to be justified.

It is significant, however, and for the Hungarian-Slovak coexistence characteristic, that the first serious stirrings against the long centuries of harmonious relationship were felt only in the first half of the last century. The interesting and little publicized fact was that the Slovak people of the time were not playing any signicant part in the "Czechoslovak" efforts started and maintained by Jan Kollár, František Palacky and P. J. Šafařik. Furthermore, the Slovak leaders, almost without exception, belonged to the Lutheran minority among the mainly Catholic Slovaks and were facing the bulk of their own people almost as strangers. This was also reinforced by the fact that, in a socio-economic sense, there was little difference in the treatment of Hungarian and of Slovak peasants by the then quasi-feudal government in Vienna. Consequently, there were few conflicting interests between them. These facts rendered the Slovak movement of the 1840s rootless. Ludwig von Gogalák points out that the number of nationally-conscious Slovaks in Jan Kollár's time (first half of the 19th century) was hardly more than about 200 leaders and about 1000 followers. [77]

The Slovak-centered movement of Ludovit Štur, J. M. Hurban and M.M. Hodža soon followed, breaking completely with this Czechoslovak oriented activity. Stur, the leader, wanted a constitutionally not quite clear separation of the Slovak inhabited areas. For him, "nation" was more a constitutional legal concept than a popular one. Instead of conceiving of a politically effective national idea, he promoted the ideal of the "people" and its spiritual purity. As a student of his work calls attention to the fact: he had little understanding of the realities of political life. [78]

Confronting these two rival movements, most of the Catholic majority of the Slovaks stood loyal to the multiethnic ideology of St. Stephen's *Hungaria*. The movement, led by the philologist A. Bernolák, while working on the purity of the Slovak language, freeing it from Czech influences, regarded the Slovaks as part of the Hungarian nation without giving up their individual, popular character. The expression Hungaro-Slovak, in counterdistinction to Czechoslovak, was coined by the Bernolák movement in the early years of the 19th century. [79]

The closing decades of the 19th century witnessed two significant events in favor of the Czechoslovak oriented groups. One of these was T. G. Masaryk's passionate criticism from 1885 of Štur's ideology of Slovak romanticism, as well as his criticism of the Magyarophil trend of Bernolák somewhat later. His new Czechoslovakism was, however, not linguistically

but sociologically based. The other event was the establishment in 1896 of the "Československa Jednota" (Czechoslovak
unity) in Prague. Its scope was to regain the Slovaks culturally,
linguistically, nationally and, if possible, politically for the
Czech orientation. Most of the news items and articles
published about Upper Hungary in European newspapers in
this time were supplied by this organization, contributing
thereby substantially to the establishment of the Czech state in
1919.

Opposing the groups of Czechoslovak, Austroslav and/or
Pan-Slav orientation (Kollár, Palacky, Šafařik), and the
self-centered Young Slovaks (Štur, Hurban, Hodža) was the
North-Hungarian nobility, a dominant class built up by
centuries of Hungarian-Slovak symbiosis. This bilingual and,
until the middle of the 19th century, mostly Slovak speaking
nobility held to the old Hungarian state-idea and the
constitution based on the Estates. At the same time, owing to
its almost exclusive role in county administration, the
influence of these nobles on the long-term development of the
population was considerable. Consequently, its influence, not
only through smooth coexistence, but also in the steady
expansion of the Slovak language frontier, was also to the
detriment of the Hungarian one. Thus, when as a result of the
Hungarian Reform Movement of the early 1800s and the
subsequent 1848-49 freedom fight against the Habsburg
Empire, these nobles sided with the new liberal-democratic
Hungarian regime of Louis Kossuth and gave up their
privileges and power bases, they began to lose contact with the
bulk of the Slovaks.

This was the time when the traditional Hun-Avar-Magyar
principles or *tenets* of ancient-type federalism between
associated peoples should have been formulated *in new,
contemporary constitutional terms*, particularly because,
subconsciously, they had been applied in practice towards
ethnic minorities throughout many centuries by the medieval
Hungarian state. It would certainly have been easier to create
a feasible and suitable federal image for the relationship with
the Slovaks than in relationship with any other ethnic minority
in historic Hungary, not only because of their early presence in
the country, but also because of the special socio-political and
administrative situation in the counties with a Slovak majority.

Mutual acceptance and a common development of this idea as part of the Reform Movement of the 1840s could have led to a different outcome, not only to the 1848-49 freedom fight, but also to development in East Central Europe generally. For the proof of this, it is enough to turn a few pages of history and read Louis Kossuth's "Address to the People of the United States of America." [80] He expressed his faith in the "idea of a federation which would weld Hungarians and the other smaller neighbouring nations into a union, to secure the nationality and independence of each and freedom for all." The "Address" also contained a rather specific methodical insight: "If I were asked why I am a friend of the *county system*, I would answer: Because I see the idea of *federation* also approachable in the inner organization of my country by planning the county system on a democratic basis." [81]

Tragically for all East Central Europe, Kossuth's federalist dream, based on his unique insight into the regional-integrative force of the county system of historic Hungary, was never put into practice. The freedom fight of the Hungarians was defeated by the combined forces of Austria and Czarist Russia in 1849, and long years of authoritarian repression followed.

Finally, after the Austro-Hungarian Compromise of 1867 had established a new constitutional relationship between the Hungarian nation and the Habsburg dynasty, and also between the two countries, the counties, losing much of their pivotal character, more and more became centrally-directed organs of the Ministry of the Interior. By this time their secondary role, probably unintended but never challenged, had achieved its purpose: the efficient protection and preservation of historic Hungary's ethnic minorities.

* * *

Although a description of the ethno-pathologically important and benevolent role of the county system in the Hungarian-Slovak relationship has been attempted in this paper, the picture would not be complete without recalling the main events in this relationship after the cession of Upper Hungary dictated by the Treaty of Trianon in 1920. An area of 61,633 sq. km. was ceded to the newly established Czechoslovakia, with a Slovak population of 1,702,000, and

1,874,000 persons of other nationalities, among them 651,000 Hungarians. Most of these last were living in a zone contiguous with the present border.

The lack of enthusiasm of the Slovak peasant population for this change, most of which were at the turn of the century still loyal to the Hungarian state-idea, was such that, as a distinguished historian of the area pointed out: without Western, mainly French, pressure the establishment of Czechoslovakia would not have been possible. [81a] This was the real reason behind Beneš' desperate efforts to prevent the holding of plebiscite in Upper Hungary, as promised in the Wilsonian Points. Western politicians, nonetheless, recognized Czechoslovakia even before its establishment. The annexation of territories of pure Hungarian ethnic character was meant to be a wedge preventing reconciliation between the two peoples.

After World War II, the so-called Hungarian-Slovak Population Exchange took place in 1947-48. Initially 53,000 Hungarian residents of Slovakia were exchanged for 60,000 Slovaks living in Hungary. Soon after a further 39,000 Hungarians were expelled from Slovakia. These 92,000 persons repatriated or expelled to Hungary represented 11.9% of the 774,055 Hungarians who were then permanent residents of Slovakia. The latter figure is the result of the combined figures of the Hungarian and Slovak national censuses taken in 1938. [82]

These expulsions, and what was then called "re-Slovakization" were mostly carried out by the "bourgeois-democrat" regime of the most fateful, hate monger in East Central European history: Eduard Beneš. The following passage offers an explanation: "Before the Paris Peace Conference, when the Beneš regime returned to power, the situation was that the compact Hungarian language territory adhering to the mother country in the southern part of Slovakia was either to be disconnected or to be wiped out. It appeared to be an anachronism on the map since every one of the adhering national minorities in Eastern Europe (except the Hungarian minorities and the Albanians in Kosovo) have been reunited with their respective mother country. . .or eliminated by expatriation. Since, under the Moscow Agreement, concluded during that war, the Czechoslovak politicians successfully removed the danger that Hungarian territories would be taken from Czechoslovakia, the other alternative had to be to wipe the Hungarian character of the respective areas." [83] This was the complete deprivation of civil rights of Hungarians in Slovakia, 1945-48. [83a]

Compared with the blind chauvinism of the Benes regime, the Communist takeover of Czechoslovakia in 1948 certainly represented some relief on ethnic minority terms. In 1949-50 the Hungarian language schools, which were closed between 1945-48, were opened again. But it was only in December 1963 that the Central Committee of the Czechoslovak Communist Party disapproved of the deprivations of civil rights, of the "re-Slovakization" and expulsions. And even this belated condemnation was kept secret: the public was not informed about this significant event. Nonetheless, there, as in most other East Central European countries today, nationalism is again getting the upper hand in practice, behind the Potemkin walls of Leninist minority policy principles.

The lesson to be learned was that the collapse of multinational Czechoslovakia in 1938 was the result of the centrifugal force of discontented minorities. However, this was denied by Beneš, who stubbornly maintained that the collapse was caused by the revolt of the national minorities, incited by Hitler against "humanist democracy." This view was somewhat reluctantly accepted by the Western Powers, and, for obvious political considerations, by the Soviet Union also. Nevertheless, Beneš' attempt to expel the Hungarians completely did not succeed. However, the complete lack of any United Nations regulation for the protection of minorities in the Charter was mainly due to his intrigues.

With that we arrive at the present. And the future?

A glance at the ethnographic map of East Central Europe suffices to make one realize that the area, with its mosaic of small and medium-sized peoples, ethnic and linguistic fragments, is simply not suitable for the establishment of centralised unitary states, with West European notions of sovereignty, but without the historical maturity to provide a just solution for inter-ethnic co-existence. The general situation of the area is further irritated by the resurgence of nationalism, especially in Rumania and, in a somewhat lesser extent, Slovakia. This is obviously contrary to the Marxist tenets of the present states and a serious hindrance to genuine supranational integration, which is the best hope for progress, stability, and cultural fulfillment in that area.

Apart from and beyond geopolitical considerations, one is inclined to search for more deeply ingrained psychological causes or national attitudes. One possible inquiry could be into collective reactions to basic forms of government. The West European (mainly common law) interpretation of the distinction between *imperium* (i.e. sovereignty and ownership coincidental) and *dominium* (i.e. sovereignty over something which could not in its nature be owned), as expressed by Grotius, [84] is different from the interpretation given to this distinction in most of the countries of East Central Europe. It was the conscious or unconscious striving of many rulers in this area to attain *imperium* over their subjects, which in many cases developed into absolutism over the centuries. The milder concept of *dominium*, more suitable for adaptation for human relations, was seldom utilized, particularly toward ethnic minorities.

In the course of the last millennium, East Central Europe was twice on the road to political and military integration. In the 14th and 15th centuries under Hungarian kings, and under the Habsburgs in the 18th and 19th centuries. The integrating process was interrupted in both cases by the interference of forces from outside of the area. In the first case it was the Turkish conquest; in the second it was French and British miscalculations which destabilized the area by creating artificial "successor" states, incapable of defending themselves against increasing pressures from the West and from the East.

Because of their central geopolitical situation, it was the historic burden of the Hungarians, and later also of the Austrian peoples, to be ground between two millstones for long periods of their history. The net result of two world wars has been that this has now become the destiny of all the small and medium-sized peoples of East Central Europe. The common destiny, however, would require common efforts for reconciliation. The elimination of covert, and even open, ethnocide efforts behind the "fraternal" mask should be only the first step.

The second should be the realization of the fact that all the ethnic minority problems of East Central Europe are basically interdependent and correlated, in spite of their regionally different character and intensity. The understanding, furthermore, that declarations of human rights and multilateral conventions of general character based on individual rights, and conceived of in the spirit of a faraway liberal-democracy are inadequate today in the atmosphere of totalitarian regimes, because of the numerous loopholes they offer for those in possession of power.

As far as the two peoples—Hungarians and Slovaks—are concerned, some historical, but artificially beclouded truths are to be rediscovered and elucidated again. Among these is the fact of a thousand years old co-existence resulting in Slovak ethnic consolidation and extension of their language border; the circumstance that the cession of Upper Hungary to become a part of Czechoslovakia was not supported by a plebiscite of the Slovak people, but was carried out by political agitators by means of transparent intrigues, obvious falsehoods and leaning on unquestioning French diplomatic and military support, resulted in the fatal destabilization of the whole East Central European area.

In spite of all the blunders and stupidities, committed by the leaders on both sides, there was no hatred, not even significant animosity between the two peoples. But only until the wake of World War II. Still the maintenance of tension and suspicion is definitely not in the interest of either, because their problems are correlated, if not common.

Some of the conditions for genuine integration of the region are: the restoration of ethnic frontiers as far as possible; the participation of peoples in the totality of their ethnic existence, and wherever clear-cut ethnic frontiers cannot be drawn; an attempt to ensure that the number of minorities remaining in the respective alien countries are kept as nearly equal, as possible. For the remaining compact minority settlements wide autonomy should be established, for the diffused minorities, as a more effective form of personal autonomy, the rules of the concurrent interstate jurisdiction [85] ought to be secured.

Habent sua fata libelli...

Notes

1. Ethnobiology can be defined as a discipline based on the recognition that cultural behaviour is innate, biologically determined in the race. See Scheidt, W., *Lebensgezetze der Kultur* (1929), *passim*.

1a. Stadtmüller, Georg, *Geschichte Südosteuropas* (1976), pp. 88-95.

2. Csallány, Dezső, *Archeolog. Denkmäler der Awarenzeit in Mitteleuropa* (1956), *passim*; by the same author, *Népvándorlás-honfoglaláskori bizánci kapcsolataink* (Our archeological connections at the time of migrations and conquest in Byzantium (1965), *passim*.

3. László, Gyula, (1) *Vértesszőlőstől Pusztaszerig* (1974) pp. 190 *et.seq.*, and (II) "Die Awaren und das Christentum im Donauraum und in östlichen Mitteleuropa," in *Annales Instituti Slavici* (1969-70) II, 1, 2, and see especially by the same author (III) "Kettős honfoglalás" (Double Conquest) in *Archeológiai Értesítő* (1970) vol. 97, pp. 161-187; regarding Slavic territorial expansion in the 7th century see Müllenhoff, K., *Deutsche Altertumskunde* (1887) vol. 2, pp. 103 *et seq.*

4. See map in László, *op. cit.* (I), p. 217.

5. See Mályusz, Elemér, *Turóc megye kialakulása* (The Formation of County Turóc) (1922) *passim*; Kniezsa, István, *Ungarns Völkerschaften im XI. Jahrhundert* (1938) p. 55.

6. Stadtmüller, *op. cit.* p. 88; see also Szekfű, Gyula, "A magyarság és kisebbségei a középkorban" (Hungarians and their minorities in the Middle Ages) in *Magyar Szemle* (1935) vol. 25, pp. 5-33.

7. For a thorough description of the Avar Empire see Fehér, M. J., *A nyugati avarok birodalma* (The Empire of the Western Avars) (1972); see also Stadtmüller, *op. cit.* pp. 95 *et seq.*

8. According to the estimate of Gyula Szekfű, the most prominent Hungarian historian between the two world wars, the Magyars and their racially kindred peoples constituted 85-87% of the country's population. See also Asztalos, Miklós, *A nemzetiségek története Magyarországon* (The History of the Nationalities in Hungary) (1934) p. 7; Tóth, József, "Hun-avar-magyar néptöredékek" (Hun-Avar-Magyar People-Fragments) in *Hungarian Past* (1982) vol. 9, pp. 23-51 at p. 47.

9. Flachbart, Ernest, *A History of Hungary's Nationalities* (1944) pp. 2 and 5; Zarek, Otto, *The History of Hungary* (1939), p. 49.

10. Flachbart, *op. cit.* pp. 2-3; Németh, Gyula, *A honfoglaló magyarság kialakulása* (The Evolution of the Conquering Magyars) (1930) *passim*; Mályusz, E., *Geschichte des ungarischen Volkstums von der Landnahme bis zum Ausgang des Mittelalters* (1940) *passim*; Asztalos, *op. cit.* pp. 17-28.

11. Mályusz, *op. cit.* p. 36.

12. Flachbart, *op. cit.* pp. 3-4.

13. *Ibid.*

14. Pelsőczi H. Gyula, *Magyarország s a tótok* (Hungary and the Slovaks) (1882).

15. Szekfű, *loc. cit.* pp. 8-9.

16. Toynbee, Arnold, *Change and Habit* (1966), p. 175.

17. See above p. 58; see also Asztalos, *op. cit.* pp. 7 *et seq.*

18. This included the uninhabited territories also. See Tagányi, Károly, "Megyei önkormányzatunk keletkezése" (Origins of Our County Self-Government) Inaugural lecture (1899), p. 3; See also Steier, Gyula, *A vármegyei közigazgatás múltja, jelene és jövője* (1908) *passim*; Tagányi, K., Réthy L. és Pokoly J. *Szolnok-*

Doboka vármegye monográfiája (Monography of Szolnok-Doboka County), (1901) *passim.*

19. Stadtmüller, *op. cit.* p. 156.

20. Tagányi, *loc. cit.* p. 7. Evaluation of this historic period was largely on this author's presentation.

21. See Endrey, Antal, *The Holy Crown of Hungary* (1977) *passim.*

22. The king delegated power to the *nádor*, who was the highest constitutional dignitary (secular) after the king until 1848.

23. Tagányi, *loc. cit.* p. 13.

24. Steiner, *op. cit.* p. 24.

25. See Varsányi, Julius, "The Beginning of an Ethnic Law of Human Rights in Medieval Hungarian Minority Statutes" in *Revue de Droit International de Sciences Diplomatiques et Politiques*, vol. 55, No. 4. (1977) pp. 241-250.

26. Steiner, *op. cit.* p. 28.

27. *Ibid.* p. 29.

28. Asztalos, *op. cit.* pp. 11 *et seq.*

29. Regulations of guardianship conditions in Law 68 of 1715; of customs and excise in Law 91 of 1715; of the election of county officials in Law 56 of 1723, among others.

30. Laws 97, 98, 101 and 102 of 1723.

31. *Országgyűlés* — could be translated as countrywide assembly, its origins reaching back to the 12th century, developing as assemblies or diets of temporal and church nobility and, finally, as parliament.

32. Financial, tax collector and accountancy personnel, guardianship authority, county archives, prosecutor's office, county physician and engineer, clerks and the "arms of the law" the *hajdú* personnel.

33. Law 16 of 1790; see also Asztalos, *op. cit.* pp. 27-29.

34. Law 7 of 1792.

35. The leading principle of Law 16 of 1848 was that the "county structure is to be set on the popular representation basis."

36. The so called "October Diploma" of 1860 restored already some powers of the former county administration. See Asztalos, *op. cit.* p. 54.

37. Law 42 of 1870.

38. Steiner, *op. cit.* p. 9.

39. Keleti, Károly, *A nemzetiségi viszonyok Magyarországban* (The Nationality Situation in Hungary) (1882) pp. 42-43.

40. Haraszti, Endre, *The Ethnic History of Transylvania* (1971) *passim*; Lőte, Louis L. (ed.) *Transylvania and the Theory of Daco-Roman-Rumanian Continuity* (1980) pp. 80 *et seq.*; Stadtmüller, *op. cit.* pp. 205 *et seq.*; Flachbart, *op. cit.* pp. 9 *et seq.*, 15 *et seq.*, 18 *et seq.*; Asztalos, *op. cit.* pp. 14-19; Gonda, Imre and Niederhauser, Emil, *A Habsburgok* (The Habsburgs) (1978) pp. 92 *et seq.*

41. Szekfű, *loc. cit.* pp. 7-9; Harmatta, J. "The Dissolution of the Hun Empire" in *Acta Archeologica Hungaricae* (1952) pp. 277-305; László, Gyula, "The Significance of the Hun Golden Bow. Contribution to the structure of the Hun Nomad Empire," in *ibid.* (1951) pp. 91-106; Ferdinandy, Michael, de, "Die nordeuropäischen Reitervölker und der Westen bis zum Mongolensturm," *Historia Mundi*, vol. 5 (1956), p. 175 at p. 176.

42. Ferdinandy, *loc. cit.* p. 177.

43. See Ecsedy, Hilda, "Tribe and Tribal Society in the 6th Century Turk Empire," in *Acta Orientalia Academica Scientiarum Hungaricae*, Tomae XXV (1972), pp. 245-262, at 247.

44. Szekfű, *loc. cit.* p. 9.

45. The counties: Trencsén 40%; Turóc 43%; Zólyom 36%; Liptó 37.5%; Bars 26%; Hont 4%; Nógrád 23%; Gömör 24% and Szepes 29%, in *Hadak Útján* /On Warpath/ vols. 32 (1980) No. 353 p. 19, vol. 33 (1981) Nos. 354, p. 19, 356, p. 17, 357, p. 19, 358, p. 17, 359, p. 18, vol. 34 (1982) Nos. 361, pp. 14 and 19, 364, p. 17; Regarding the great proportion of nobility of Slovak origin in Upper Hungary (today's Slovakia) see Gogolák, Ludwig von, *Beiträge zur Geschichte des slowakischen Volkes* (1969) vol. II, pp. 41-42.

46. 1780-1790. He suspended the jurisdiction of the counties for several years as a retribution, and even a new division of provinces was arranged for a while. See Gonda-Niederhauser, *op. cit.* p. 136.

47. Law 16 of 1790; Law 7 of 1792; Law 4 of 1805; Law 8 of 1808; Law 8 of 1830 and Law 3 of 1836.

48. Hóman, Bálint-Szekfű, Gyula, *Magyar történet* (1936) vol. 5, p. 197.

49. *Ibid.* p. 2/537.

50. See Gonda-Niederhauser, *op. cit.* pp. 169 *et seq.*

51. Hóman-Szekfű, *op. cit.* p. 349; For a contrary view see Asztalos, *op. cit.* pp. 43 *et seq.*

52. Professor Stadtmüller points out that among Slovenes, Slovaks and Rumanians written literature was first formed on the influence of the German Reformation. Stadtmüller, *op. cit.* p. 250; see also Gogolák, *op. cit.* pp. 55, 74.

53. Hóman-Szekfű, *op. cit.* p. 402; see also Gogolák, *op. cit.* pp. 245, 252 *et seq.*

54. For a thorough analysis of this group's ideological background see Gogolák, *op. cit.* vol. 2, p. 218 *et seq.* The almost unanimous common attitude of the broad masses of the Slovak people in favour of the Hungarian revolutionary army did not prevent these leaders, in their petition of 13.4.1849, lodged at the Imperial Ministry in Vienna, to request in "poetic-pathetic words" the introduction of Slovak as the language of administration and education in Upper Hungary, the removal of the Hungarian administrative personnel and the summoning of a Slovak regional assembly. *Ibid.* vol. 3, p. 11.

54a. For the linguistic proportions of the educational institutions in Upper Hungary some useful data are contained in Joseph Hain's statistical survey of this period. Out of the 61 high schools in Hungary, Slovak was the teaching language in 8, partly German — partly Slovak in 1, German-Slovak-Hungarian in 1, and Hungarian-Slovak in 1 also. In other words, entirely or partly Slovak language teaching was maintained in 11 high schools out of 61, which is 18%. This compares rather favourably with the percentage of the Slovaks in the total population, which at this time (early 1850s) and the following decade was 13.8% only. Joseph Hain, *Handbuch der Statistik des österreichischen Kaiserstaates* (1853) Wien, p. 669; and Lajos Thirring, "Magyarország népessége 1869-1949 között" (Hungary's population between 1869-1949), in Kovacsics, József, *Magyarország történeti demográfiája* (Historical Demography of Hungary) (1963).

55. Law 4 of 1869.

56. 1867-1918.

57. Law 44 of 1868. The final text was formulated by F. Deák and was regarded to be one of the most progressive of that time. and included the precept that every citizen of Hungary, without regard to his mother language, is a full member of the political nation and as such entitled to use in certain legally determined situations his own minority language. See also Asztalos, *op. cit.* pp. 65 *et seq.* For the history of pertinacious reconciliation efforts by a Hungarian parlamentarian, see: Kemény Gábor, G. "Mocsáry Lajos (1826-1916)," in *Létünk*, vol. 1973, no. 5.

58. In accordance with the decision of the 1861 Slovak ethnic meeting in Turócszentmárton.

58a. Gogolák, *op. cit.* vol. 3, p. 57.

59. Mályusz, *op. cit.* p. 18; Regarding the history of Slavic migrations see also Bretholz, B., *Geschichte Böhmens und Mährens bis zum Aussterben der Przemysliden* (1306) (1912) p. 28 *et seq.*

60. László, *op. cit.* (III) pp. 161-187; Baráth, Tibor, *The Early Hungarians* (1983) pp. 208 *et seq.* This distinguished historian even maintains that "Magyar speaking ethnic groups continuously poured into the Carpathian land, ever since neolithic times". Also by the same author *A magyar népek őstörténete* vols. I-III (1968-74) (The Ancient History of the Hungarian Speaking Peoples). A detailed bibliography is added to Hajdu, P.-Kristó, Gy.-Tas, A. *Bevezetés a magyar őstörténet kutatásának forrásaiba* (Introduction into the Sources of Hungarian Ancient History Research) (1976); See also works referred to in Note 2.

61. Kniezsa, *op. cit.* (I) and by the same author *Zur Geschichte der ungarisch-slowakischen ethnischen Grenze* (1941); Jócsik, Louis, *How the Magyars Figure on Czech and Slovak Ethnographical Maps* (1943).

62. Flachbart, *op. cit.* pp. 6-7. (Author' italics).

63. Varsányi, Julius, "The Beginnings of an Ethnic Law of Human Rights in Medieval Hungarian Minority Statutes," in *Revue de Droit International de Sciences Diplomatiques et Politiques* vol. 55 (1977) no. 4, pp. 241-250.

64. Flachbart, *op. cit.* p. 10 (Author's italics).

65. For evaluation of county autonomies in Upper Hungary see Gogolák, *op. cit.* p. 23.

66. Mályusz, *op. cit.*

67. Kniezsa, *op. cit.* (I) and (II).

68. *Nyitra megye betelepülése* (The Settlement of County Nyitra) (1938).

69. *Przispevky k Historické Demografii Slovenska v XVIII-XIX stoleti* (Contributions to the Historical Demography of Slovakia in the XVIII-XIX centuries) (1928).

70. According to Fügedi's documentation in the then 10 districts of Nyitra county the result of the analysis of serfs' names appearing in 13th to 15th century documents shows the following proportions: Hungarian names 40.1%, Slovak names 35.4%, German names 1.6%, of uncertain origin 22.3%. Fügedi, *op. cit.* pp. 28-57.

71. Jócsik, *op. cit.* p. 30; Körösy, József, *A Felvidék eltótosodása* (The Slovakization of Upper Hungary) (1898), p. 15 *et seq.*

72. The register, preserved by the Hungarian National Archives, was published in 1920 by the Hungarian delegation to the peace conference. As the *Lexicon* was not available at the time of the writing of this paper the related evaluations of Kniezsa, *op. cit.* pp. 67-68 are presented in the following paragraphs.

73. Häufler-Korcák-Král, *Zempis Československa* (The Czechoslovak Lands) (1960), p. 236.

74. Jócsik, *op. cit.* pp. 15-17; Körösy, *op. cit.* p. 15.

75. Kniezsa, *op. cit.* p. 68.

76. This was also the conclusion of the Russian scholar, A. Petrov, who undertook the writing of Slovakia's ethnic history, commissioned by the Czechoslovak government. His work was published by the Czechoslovak Academy of Sciences in 1924. Thus he could hardly be suspected of anti-Slovak propaganda.

77. Gogolák, *op. cit.* p. 67.

78. *Ibid.* p. 209.

79. *Ibid.* p. 216, and vol. 3, pp. 102-3.

80. Published in Washington, DC, by the newspapers *Union* on October 21, 1851, the *National Era* on October, 1851 and by the *New York Herald* on October 20, 1851.

81. Kardos Talbot, Béla, "From Kossuth's Unknown Federalist Papers," in *Studies for a New Central Europe* (1963) vol. 1, no. 1, pp. 60-71, at p. 61. (Author's italics.)

81a. Gogolák, *op. cit.* vol. 3, p. 147.

82. *Hungarians in Czechoslovakia*, Published by the Research Institute for Minority Studies on Hungarians Attached to Czechoslovakia and Carpatho-Ruthenia, Inc. (1959), p. 126.

83. *Ibid.* pp. 134-5; See also Janics, Kálmán, *Czechoslovak Policy and the Hungarian Minority, 1945-1948* (1982); Wojatsek, Charles, *From Trianon to the First Vienna Arbitral Award. The Hungarian Minority in the First Czechoslovak Republic, 1918-1938* (1981).

83a. The Czechoslovak Presidential Decree 1945/33, published on August 2, 1945, deprived the Hungarians living in Slovakia from their citizenship.

84. Grotius, Hugo, *De jure belli ac pacis libri tres*, Editio nova, Washington, Carnegie Institution, 1913-25, 2 vols., vol. II, chap. 3, s. 4.

85. Varsányi, Julius, *Border is Fate — a Study of Central European Diffused Ethnic Minorities* (1982) p. 128.

Hungarian – Slavonic area with Hungarian majority
Hungarian – Slavonic area with Slavonic majority
Hungarian area
Slavonic area
10 5 0   10   20   30   40   50
SCALE
ETHNOGRAPHICAL MAP OF UPPER HUNGARY
IN XI CENTURY
According to the study by ISTVAN KNIEZSA & L.GLASER

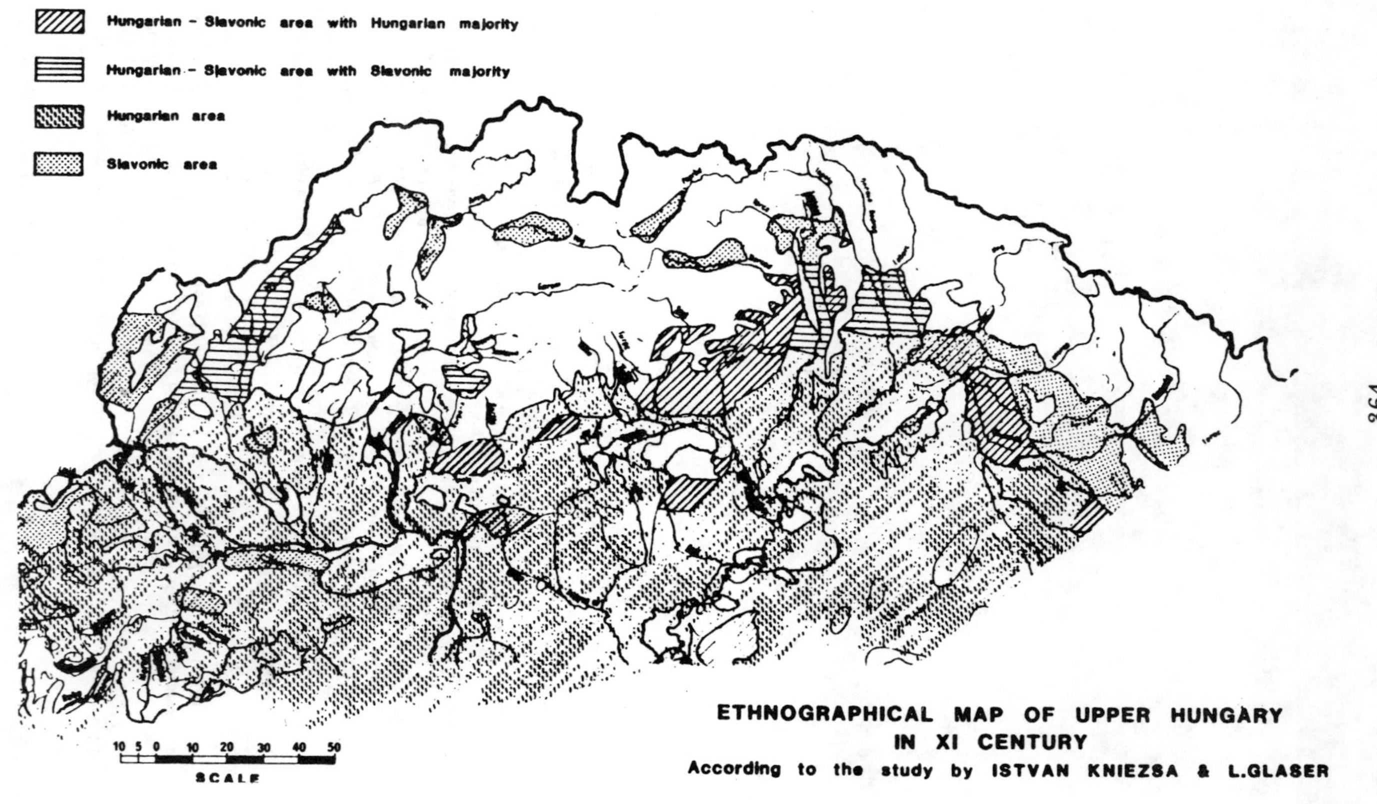

364

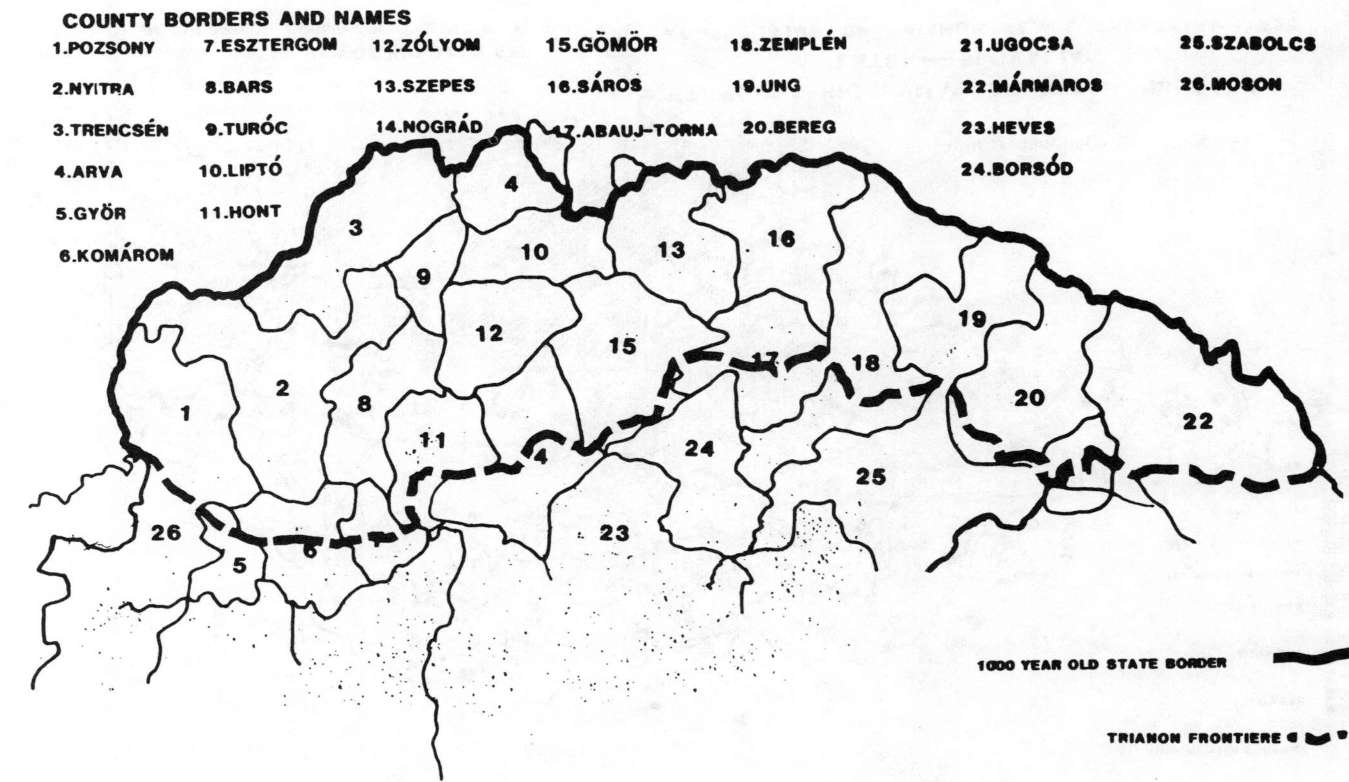

COUNTY BORDERS AND NAMES
1.POZSONY
2.NYITRA
3.TRENCSÉN
4.ARVA
5.GYÖR
6.KOMÁROM
7.ESZTERGOM
8.BARS
9.TURÓC
10.LIPTÓ
11.HONT
12.ZÓLYOM
13.SZEPES
14.NOGRÁD
15.GÖMÖR
16.SÁROS
17.ABAUJ-TORNA
18.ZEMPLÉN
19.UNG
20.BEREG
21.UGOCSA
22.MÁRMAROS
23.HEVES
24.BORSÓD
25.SZABOLCS
26.MOSON
1000 YEAR OLD STATE BORDER
TRIANON FRONTIERE

ETHNOGRAPHICAL MAP OF UPPER HUNGARY LATER — SLOVAKIA

AT THE TIME OF TRIANON PEACE TREATY IN 1920

Based on ETHNOGRAPHICAL MAP OF HUNGARY AND DENSITY OF POPULATION compiled by COUNT P.TELEKI

Francis S. Wagner:

17 / ETHNIC MINORITIES IN HUNGARY SINCE WORLD WAR II

The sense of belonging, of togetherness, just as the feeling of being different, are primordial instincts. This complex sentiment usually causes pride in one's ethnic origin as well as an unreasonable feeling of supremacy, often accompanied by xenophobia. The first great Czech chronicler, Cosmas (d. 1125), a canon of Prague, expressed his views of contemporary Germans with unprecedented hatred in his *Chronica Boemorum*. His attitude towards foreigners was negative, and it also reflected an early form of Czech and Slavic self-consciousness. The roots of such feelings became deeply embedded in the movements of the Renaissance, Reformation, the Counter-Reformation, and the Enlightenment. These phenomena can clearly be observed in the eighteenth-century evolution of the national consciousness of ethnic entities living together in a common state.

The Carpathian Basin and thus the Kingdom of Hungary was multinational, and increasingly so, ever since the Middle Ages. Already in the 12th and 13th centuries, a number of its cities had multiethnic populations mostly living in separate ethnic quarters, or ghettos. Geographical names of these cities and other communities well reflect their multiethnicity: Vicus Latinorum, Vicus Judeorum, Platea Slavorum, Windischgasse and similar place names point to the presence within one and the same community of Germans, Slavs, Hungarians, Romanians, Jews, etc. There were even statutory provisions to regulate the coexistence of various ethnic groups. Thus the palatine */nádor/* of the Kingdom of Hungary in 1612 issued an order prescribing that the municipal council of the city of Eperjes (Prešov) be elected alternately: one year by the German, the following year by the Hungarian and Slovak population, thereby ensuring that persons of different ethnic backgrounds rotated in their jobs and offices.[1] The same order set up a mixed nationality commission which supervised the procedures and practices of local guilds to ensure the acceptance of Hungarian and Slovak artisans into the membership of the guilds.

The Turkish rule for at least half a century after the Battle of Mohács in 1526 exerted a many-sided influence on the peoples of the Danube Basin. The ethnic map of the whole area was changed to a considerable degree through internal mobility and migration of peoples. The Turkish occupation very much hindered cultural development of the masses. The Ottoman Empire was in principle against the assimilation of the oppressed peoples, but because of the cultural passivity of those decades, the people relapsed into quite primitive economic, social and intellectual conditions. Since the Turkish rule did not affect all of the Danube Basin, after the liberation the area showed significant differences which were never before witnessed in the mentality of various ethnic groups. In addition, a significant gap developed between the life of the lower social classes of the occupied area and their Western counterparts, which conditions survived well into the twentieth century. The primitive socio-economic conditions which the Turkish rule created almost entirely blocked the early emergence of a native intelligentsia. Thus the period of national awakening started late, and the national consciousness of the ethnic minorities began to play its epoch-making role just before the middle of the nineteenth century. The feudal socio-economic structure and the Turkish Empire prevented mass movements of a nationalistic character, while the conglomerate state of the Habsburgs, through several centuries, witnessed only isolated local nationality conflicts. By the end of the eighteenth century, however, the once uniform economic conditions exhibited basic dissimilarities in the Austrian and Hungarian parts of the Habsburg lands. Henceforth, economic and cultural development, in accordance with the gradual growth of the forces of production, took place in specific and quite differing forms within certain provinces of the Empire. Differences in the standard of living of the nobility and of the serfs within Hungary were also enormous. Since about 90 percent of the nobility was of Hungarian (Magyar) descent, the differences in employment opportunities and social standing contributed to the perpetuation of national distinctions. The socio-economic conditions of changing feudalism helped reduce the so-called *Gens Hungarica*, which heretofore politically comprised all existing nations or ethnic entities within historic Hungary, to its natural and individual elements: the Hungarian and numerous non-Hungarian nations. This rapid process of disintegration was greatly stimulated by the French theory of nationality. This "one language—one nation state" concept generally corresponded to the interests of the great homogeneous national states of Western Europe. But the French revolutionary concept and its German practice tragically destroyed the very foundation of any future interethnic collaboration in the multinational states of the Danube Valley. Simultaneously, such concepts as *"Deutschungar"* and the short-lived *"böhmischer Landespatriotismus"* also lost their historic role as an aftermath of the French revolutionary ideas. Emperor Joseph II was captivated by the ideas of the French Enlightenment. In this spirit, in 1784, he issued his decree making German the official administrative language of Hungary, asserting that Latin was no longer suitable for official transactions and had to be supplanted by the German. The 1784 Germanization decree and the later centralization policy of the Imperial Court were primarily directed against the Hungarian nation, because Hungarians were politically more independent than any other non-German nation, and therefore, represented a greater menace to the implementation of the idea of *Gesamtmonarchie*. Chancellor Prince Kaunitz of Austria, as early as 1791, formulated the guiding principle of how to administer a multinational state: "The more apparent and well-considered the attempts at securing the unity of Hungary, Transylvania and the Illyrian nation, the more recommended and necessary is the principle of *divide et impera*." [2]

The language problem itself has remained a highly controversial issue up to the present. At first, all nations, especially the Hungarians, reacted vehemently against the Germanization decree, defending the constitutional rights of *lingua patria* (Latin) against *lingua monarchica* (German). But a few years later, all these nations began promoting their own national languages. Thus the possibility of a peaceful coexistence completely disappeared in the course of further occurrences. The movement of the Enlightenment, and the far-reaching effects of the American and French Revolutions, caused deep-seated socio-economic changes as well as the appearance of politico-cultural nationalism in its modern forms. All these developments created an entirely new framework for the sense of belonging and togetherness, which was the strictly ethnically-based nation-state. Peoples and nations living in Central and Eastern Europe, without exception, sooner or later tried to materialize the nation-state concept even at the expense of peaceful coexistence and with no regard to the region's historically multiethnic character. In addition to the nation-state idea, some theorists, and later on right-wing totalitarian regimes, interjected the principle of racial superiority, which made impossible any kind of cooperation among ethnic and national groups of the area. Another history-making factor was the close German-Hungarian collaboration which poisoned Hungarian-Slavic and, to a much lesser extent, Hungarian-Romanian relations.

During the centuries the Habsburg rule, the dynasty was unable to develop a uniform platform or an Austrian consciousness as a model for the heterogeneous population of the Empire. Therefore, the Germanization policy in the service of the principle of the *Gesamtmonarchie* proved to be unattainable for the divergent forces. Moreover, it was not Austria, but Prussia that incarnated the mission of Germanization, and the Habsburg Empire played only a subordinate role.

Austria could not entirely free itself of its medieval, feudal heritage and adopt the ideas of liberty and democracy, the main pillars of French nationhood. Instead, Austria slavishly imitated Prussian expansionism, without proper power base. The 1848-49 revolutionary events serve as an example. It was quite evident that all nationalities, and not only the Magyars, tried to reach a state of affairs which would have satisfied their nationalistic ambitions. For this reason, Prime Minister Bertalan Szemere later condemned Lajos Kossuth's extreme views relating to the nationality issues. As he stated: "In this regard it was a real disaster that he /Kossuth/ was at the head of the nation."[3] Later events, however, clearly demonstrated that, regardless of Kossuth's extreme views, minorities tended to develop their own national states in accord with the dynamic emotions of their national consciousness. This innate tendency wanted to create a national state. This attitude in itself explains the intense opposition of the minorities to Law No. 44 of 1868, and decades later to the Lex Apponyi (1907). Both of these laws were designed to help promote a Hungarian political nationhood that was to include all other ethnic groups. In the last analysis, the relevant nationality fights contributed to the collapse of the Habsburg Monarchy in 1918.

Because of this innate tendency of nationalism, the same mistakes were committed — between the world wars — by the Czechs when they created the illusion of a uniform Czechoslovak nation /*jednotný národ československý*/, as well as by the Serbs who used the phrase "Yugoslav nation /*jugoslovenski narod*/. Such irrealistic concepts helped to destroy both regimes on the threshold of World War II.

THE PEOPLE'S DEMOCRATIC PERSPECTIVE

For Equality against Discrimination

During the interwar period, the position of the German minority became gradually much better than that of the Slavic and Romanian ethnic groups. Within the framework of the *Volksbund*, Germans virtually constituted a *corpus separatum* in the country, and in most important political and cultural issues they were guided by the Third Reich authorities. The conclusion of World War II drastically changed the situation. Key to this change was the Article XIII of the July 1945 Potsdam Agreement in which the three major victorious Allies declared: "the transfer to Germany of German population, or elements thereof remaining in Poland, Czechoslovakia and Hungary, will have to be undertaken."[4]

The 1941 census figures show that on the territory of Hungary the number of people of German vernacular amounted to 477,057, while those of German ethnic origin to 303,419. In the spirit of the Potsdam Conference, around 250,000 Germans were expelled from Hungary into the Allied occupational zones of Germany. The transfer in most cases was based on the mere fact of German origin or speaking German as a mother tongue, and in many cases exclusively on German surnames. In 1948 the Hungarian government suspended this discriminative process of deportation and shortly thereafter acknowledged the principle of equality of all nationalities. Besides the international constellation, the genuine and fairly general anti-German feeling that existed in the ruling circles of Hungary in immediate post-war years also contributed to this inhumane solution of the German problem. Mátyás Rákosi, Zoltán Tildy, László Rajk, Ferenc Erdei, and Péter Veres, to mention just a few, were instrumental in carrying out the policy of collective responsibility.

Following the conclusion of World War II, Slovaks and Southern Slavs, more correctly their new leadership, fell under the influence of all-Slavic movements. The Belgrade-based All-Slavic Committee (*Všeslovanský výbor*) proclaimed Ján Kollár's age-old idea of Slavic reciprocity (*idea slovanskej vzájemnosti*). Slovaks and Southern Slavs conducted negotiations with the aim of forming a common platform of Slavic solidarity. For this purpose a special organization was founded: the Anti-Fascist Alliance of Slavs in Hungary /*Anti-Fašistický Blok Slovanov v Madărsku*/, with its well-edited weekly journal, *Sloboda*. This organization proved to be short-lived. Its demise came in June 1948, when Tito's Yugoslavia seceded from the Moscow-led bloc of people's democratic countries. As a consequence, the Budapest government started treating its Southern Slav subjects in a hostile manner. But since the middle of the fifties, the Hungarian government gradually rectified the situation and issued a host of regulations to improve the position of national minorities, first of all that of the Southern Slavs and the Germans.

Apart from the brief interval of prejudice directed against the Germans and the Southern Slavs, the country's nationality policy has manifested entirely different principles and practices, shaped almost exclusively by the directives of the

Communist Party. Already on November 30, 1944, the Hungarian Communist Party issued its guidelines, emphasizing among others the following: "We should put an end to the Hungarian imperialistic manomania, to the reactionary vision of Greater Hungary. Once and for all, we should put an end to those efforts which under the pretext of the leading role of the Hungarians tend toward the domination over other peoples living in the Danube Basin."[5] No people in Central and Eastern Europe has ever made such a conciliatory gesture in renouncing its historic claims in order to establish — though unsuccessfully — a foundation for fruitful interethnic cooperation.

The platform of the newly founded Hungarian Workers Party /*Magyar Dolgozók Pártja*/, agreed upon at the unity congress in June 1948, referred also to the nationality question: "For the nationalities living in the country, the Party — along with guaranteeing full civil rights for them — advocates free development of their progressive national culture and complete freedom for their political organization, as well as freedom of cultural exchange and contact with mother nations living in the neighboring countries."[6] After such preparatory measures, the Constitution of the Hungarian People's Republic, promulgated as Law No. XX of 1949, in its Pragraph 49 declares that: (1) all citizens of the Hungarian People's Republic are equal under law and enjoy equal rights; (2) any kind of disadvantageous discrimination of the citizens according to sex, denomination, or nationality is severely punished by law; (3) the Hungarian People's Republic guarantees for all of its citizens the opportunity of education in the mother tongue and the fostering of national culture.[7] The Constitution was augmented by a number of laws and decrees intended to regulate all important phases of the mechanism of the administration of justice for all minorities. Paragraph 183 of Law No. III of 1952 on civil procedure prescribes the compulsory use of an interpreter if the person(s) involved do not speak Hungarian. The same procedure is followed in criminal cases as ordered by Edict No. 8 of 1962. Law No. X of 1954 (point h of Paragraph 6) provides local councils with instructions "to enforce the rights of the nationalities." Paragraph 12 of Law No. IV of 1957, on the general rules of administrative procedures, makes it unmistakably clear that "the lack of the knowledge of the Hungarian language cannot be disadvantageous to anyone in public administration."

Though the minorities are scattered throughout the country, there still exist settlements in which they outnumber the Hungarians. The May 21, 1956, a decision by the Hungarian Workers Party prescribed that in these communities officials should be bilingual. On October 7, 1958, the Political Committee of the newly organized Hungarian Socialist Workers Party /*Magyar Szocialista Munkáspárt*/ passed a resolution of fundamental importance. It deals with political, educational and cultural work to be carried out in these minority communities. Accordingly, the only criterion for evaluating minority workers should be the fulfillment of their civic duties in the socialist construction of the country. The same resolution called upon all party organizations to perform their duties relative to the minority policy scrupulously: "The Central Committe is monitoring carefully the observance of nationality rights, and demands all Party organizations to overcome the lack of comprehension that is in evidence in some places. Party organizations should consistently be active in the application of the Marxist-Leninist principles in the nationality policy.... It is of basic significance to fight against any kind of nationalistic phenomena."

The 1961 Criminal Code enacted on December 22 provides for the protection of the equality of national minorities. Its implementation is taken very seriously. According to Paragraph 138 of the Criminal Code: "If someone causes serious physical or mental damage to a member of a national, ethnic, racial or religious group for simply belonging to these groups, it is a crime punishable from 2 to 8 years of imprisonment." [8]

Public Education

With the exception of the network of the German schools, and to a lesser extent of Slovak schools during World War II, the schools of the national minorities (Romanians, South Slavs) were neglected by the government. It was all the more so because a number of their schools were administered by the churches. Since 1949, following the nationalization of schools, education fell under government control. Measures were taken by Edict No. 15 of 1951 to introduce mother-tongue education all over the country. Its main provisions were adopted ten years later by the laws on the educational system and on compulsory education. [9]

According to these laws, the use of the mother tongue in public education already starts in the pre-school age. Law No. III of 1953 in its Paragraph 4 states that: "In those villages (cities) where the number of the population of non-Hungarian mother tongue justifies, nationality kindergartens should be established in line with the development of the kindergarten system." [10]

The most favorable resolution to protect and foster the cultural development of ethnic minorities was issued by the Presidential Council /*Elnöki Tanács*/ of the Hungarian People's Republic as Edict No. 13 of 1962. Its Paragraph 3 contains the following unique instruction: "In villages (cities) where at least fifteen parents of school-aged children so desire, it is of paramount importance that these national minority school-aged children a) receive their education in their mother tongue or b) can study their native tongue as a compulsory subject in the schools." [11]

Similarly to conditions in interwar Hungary, the regulation of the use of the native language remained the central issue of the national minority question. Based on this realization, the post-1945 years saw the rise of two types of minority schools: 1) in one of them teaching was in the native tongue, with the compulsory study of Hungarian; 2) while in the other one, instruction was in Hungarian, and the native (minority) language was taught as a compulsory subject. But since the sixties, this system, at the request of nationality parents and the national federations of minorities, has gradually changed to bilingual education, where natural sciences are taught in Hungarian, while the humanities are studied in the mother tongue. Moreover, teachers in both types of schools also make an effort to teach terminologies in both languages.

Statistical Survey [12]
of Nationality (Minority) Education in 1968/1969:

	Number	Teachers	Students
1. Kindergartens	42	50	1340
2. General schools:			
a/ Bilingual	23	156	1991
b/ With minority language as a compulsory subject	254	353	18,284
3. High schools (*gimnázium*)	7	52	717

3. German 3 in Baja, Pécs, Budapest; Slovak 2 in Budapest and Békéscsaba; Southern Slav in Budapest; Romanian in Gyula.
4. Total number of nationality teachers: 611
5. Number of student hostels: 7 with 1340 living accomodations. For Slovak students in Budapest, Békéscsaba, Szarvas, Sátoraljaújhely; for Southern Slavs in Budapest and Pécs; for Romanians in Gyula. (Germans live in Hungarian hostels.)
6. Between 1953 and 1968 about 1600 students received bilingual graduation certificates (*érettségi bizonyítvány*). The number of university students specializing in German, Slovak, Serbo-Croatian and Romanian languages was 261 in 1968/1969.

Training of nationality teachers is provided by special teachers colleges and the Loránd Eötvös University in Budapest. German kindergarten teachers are prepared at Sopron; Slovak, Serbo-Croatian, and Romanian at Szarvas. Elementary (general) school teachers obtain their diplomas in Budapest (Slovak), Baja (German and Southern Slav), and in Debrecen (Romanian). Language teachers for general schools graduate from colleges at Pécs (German and Southern Slav) and at Szeged (Slovak and Romanian). The Loránd Eötvös University qualifies all nationality teachers for high schools /*gimnáziums*/.

It is indeed a difficult task to provide minority schools with quality textbooks. Relevant difficulties are twofold: the number of textbook writers is extremely limited, and the production price — due to the small number of students — is fifty or sometimes one hundred times higher than the selling price. Despite these conditions the textbook publishing enterprise /*Tankönyvkiadó Vállalat*/ has been able to supply the required number of textbooks for minority schools. Recently things have turned for the better, since more and more textbooks have been imported from Czechoslovakia, the German Democratic Republic, Yugoslavia and Romania.

Revival of Cultural Heritage

The cultural life of the national minorities has generally been stagnant. Their centuries-old settlements were cut off from communication with their mother countries. Besides, the network of their settlements has never comprised a comprehensive whole. The overwhelming majority of ethnic minorities had settled in the countryside, and most of them continued to live there until the socialist construction of the country. In the last decades a number of these settlements were dispersed as a result of the ever-growing tide of urbanization which increased the trend towards the reduction of agricultural population. Furthermore, the large-scale urbanization (industrialization) process resulted in their younger generations' move from the villages into industrial centers with overwhelming Hungarian population, which is the surest and most natural way of Magyarization. Although the government has done everything possible to implement its clearly positive nationality policy, some insurmountable obstacles work against the improvement of the position of ethnic minorities. Foremost among them is the social mobility and migration, as already alluded to. Between 1960 and 1970, the portion of the total population living in towns with more than 20,000 inhabitants increased from 37.5% to 42.1%.[13] In the mid-seventies 38% of the 4.9 million wage earners worked in industry (building trades included), and only 23% of the labor force was employed in agriculture, 6.5% in transportation, 7.5% in trade, and the remainder in the tertiary sector.[14] The increase in the proportion of urban inhabitants is a steady process, and is expected to rise within the next few years to 70%.[15]

In addition to the above, there are also several other factors which impede the successful application of the government's policies. Among them is the fact that the Germans are afraid of expressing freely their national identity because a large number of them only years earlier were expelled from the country. The situation is different with the Slavs. Although they never faced the threat of expulsion, they are scattered all across Hungary. Moreover, in the past they had little or no possibility for the political or cultural expression of their Slavdom. As such, they generally lack national or ethnic consciousness, with the exception of the members of the Orthodox Church, and to a lesser extent of the members of the Slovak Lutheran Church. In spite of these shortcomings, a number of the minorities wish to participate in the political process at local as well as national level, and do so with the aid of their newly founded national organizations.

The nationality organizations have an important part in the fostering of the nationality cultures. The Democratic Association of the Southern Slavs in Hungary was established in 1945, the Democratic Association of Slovaks in Hungary in 1949, the Democratic Association of Romanians in Hungary in the same year, while the Democratic Association of German Workers in Hungary in 1955. All these nationwide organizations of minorities are closely connected with the Patriotic People's Front /*Hazafias Népfront*/ in their political and cultural activities: 30 German, 25 Slovak, 30 Southern Slav, and 7 Romanian cultural groups are active in disseminating folk culture. Their top cultural organization, the Central Nationality Ensemble /*Központi Nemzetiségi Együttes*/ unites the best German, Slavic, and Romanian amateur artists, and also makes successful tours of Eastern and Western European countries. Interstate cultural agreements between Hungary and its neighbors, as well as the German Democratic Republic, initiated the exchange of cultural goods and individuals. These exchange programs have naturally improved the cultural life of national minorities. Journals and calendars published in nationality languages also try to improve the situation. But their circulation is so small that they do not count much:

Journals Published in Nationality Languages [16]

Narodne Novine	Southern Slav	Weekly	3000 copies
Ľudové Noviny	Slovak	"	1200 copies
Neue Zeitung	German	"	4000 copies
Foaia Noastra	Romanian	Biweekly	950 copies

Calendars Published in Nationality Languages [17]

Narodni Kalendar	Southern Slav	4500 copies
Náš Kalendár	Slovak	3000 copies
Deutsche Kalendar	German	10,500 copies
Calendarul Nostru	Romanian	1400 copies

The already cited October 7, 1958 resolution of the Political Committee of the Hungarian Socialist Workers Party stressed emphatically the Party's responsibility "to nominate also minority workers in adequate numbers for election into the national assembly and local councils." Since ethnic groups do not live in compact, homogeneous communities, territorial solution had to be discounted as a basis of establishing the representation ratio of ethnic minorities in elective national and local legislative and administrative bodies. Minorities, however, are still well represented in the elective bodies of the Patriotic People's Front, agricultural cooperatives, as well as in other mass organizations.

The Gypsy Question

The Gypsy question is by far the most serious issue present-day Hungary is facing in interethnic relations. It is a cause of grave concern, all the more because many specialists do not put the issue into historical perspective and, therefore, make contradictory statements which cannot be truly applied. A great many people do not realize that in order to realistically evaluate nationality (racial) topics one has to go back to their roots. Since the end of the eighteenth century it has generally been agreed that the ancient home of the Gypsies was the Malabar Coast region in Southwest India from where they migrated between the 11th and 16th centuries and mingled with peoples of the Near East and

Northern Africa. Then, moving through the Balkan Peninsula, they emerged in Eastern and Central Europe. [18] The mingling with other peoples was not considerable so that this itinerant race has retained its distinct phenotype to the present.

For centuries there were very few sources availabale on Gypsy life. In the eighteenth century Maria Theresa and Joseph II tried to solve the Gypsy question in the spirit of the Enlightenment. Decrees issued considered Gypsies as antisocial (and not racial) elements and made efforts to put an end to their itinerant life. The aim was to settle them down, and treat them at the level of non-Gypsy serfs. But this experiment proved to be futile, partially because of the landowners' opposition to socializing the Gypsies. Up to the conclusion of World War II, Gypsies were treated as social outcasts, and they were also subjected to genocide by Nazi authorities.

There is no question that the post-1945 regimes in Central and Eastern Europe have treated the Gypsies in a positive, humane way, quite contrary to the policies of the previous governments. It is very much true that the socio-economic and cultural level of a part of the Gypsies has been elevated since 1945 (more precisely since 1961), and nowadays a considerable proportion of them hold permanent jobs with a rising work ethic. But it is equally true that, as a concomitant phenomenon, the nationality consciousness of the Gypsies has grown in Hungary and elsewhere in the Danube region, and that it is already exhibiting some of the symptoms of the American black separatist movements.

It is an undeniable fact that the Gypsies, similarly to other non-Magyar groups in Hungary, enjoy full civil rights as well as some of the guarantees enjoyed by the country's other ethnic entities. But the application of minority rights and guarantees is not complete. This is the result of the conceptual differences and uncertainties in the decades-old controversy surrounding the identity of the Gypsies.

A 1961 resolution of the Political Committee of the Hungarian Socialist Workers Party declared that there is no Gypsy nationality. According to this resolution the Gypsy question is really a social problem with economic and other implications; and it can be solved by means of education. In June

8, 1969, a national Conference on Gypsy Lore was arranged in Budapest by the Sociological and Ethnographical Group of the Society for Dissemination of Scientific Knowledge. [19] As was expected, one of the main themes of this important session of experts was the above-quoted Party resolution. The *Minutes* of the conference revealed that László Mándoki (Chief, Ethnographical Division, Janus Pannonius Museum, Pécs) deviated openly from the official Party line. His remarks prove that Mándoki is indeed a highly qualified expert on nationality issues. Among other things, he said at the Conference: "The Gypsies, who have lived in our country for centuries, should be considered a nationality without any preconcepts... All of us here assert that there is a Gypsy culture, /and that/ like every other nationality, the Gypsies also have their own indigenous culture. Mrs. Lajos Marosán expressed in her lecture the opinion that 'though culturally there are distinguishing signs, there is no sufficient basis to consider the Gypsies a nationality'. May I ask why? I know that according to the 1961 Party resolution we cannot regard them as a nationality, but since then our views may have changed. Not so long ago the Congresses of the Democratic Federations of Hungary's Nationalities took place. A cultural survey of nationalities is being conducted. It is indeed timely to address ourselves to the question whether the 220,000 Gypsies are entitled to the same rank and treatment as the seven or eight thousand Wend or Bunievac nationalities... Is it possible that the reason we are not considering the Gypsies as a nationality is because there is no Gypsy state in the world to represent them?" [20]

Because of the uncertainty of opinions concerning Gypsy identity, the enforcement of the relevant statutes is somewhat ambiguous. For example, in 1964, a governmental decree ordered the liquidation of Gypsy settlements which did not suit social requirements and called for the establishment of new but scattered settlements. But contrary to the letter and the spirit of this decree, Gypsies were resettled in segregated ghettos again. [21]

With a view of elucidating the confusion around the essential features of Gypsy identity, let us refer to some recently published substantial contributions. [22]

According to these studies, today there are two views relating to the identity of the Gypsies: the official view, which claims that the Gypsies constitute only a social category; and the scientific or scholarly view, which holds that the Gypsies are a racial/ethnic group, with at least three subdivisions in Hungary. The official view implicitly accepts some racial features, but without taking group (ethnic) relations into consideration. This definition overvalues the effect of social factors, while denying the existence of any form of ethnicity. This official version appears to disregard reality, namely the fact that within the Gypsy race there are three distinguishable ethnic groups in Hungary: 1/ Magyar Gypsies with Hungarian as their native language, 2/ Romanian Gypsies whose mother tongue is a dialect of the Romanian language, and 3/ the bilingual Wallachian (*Oláh*) Gypsies who, in addition to the Romany (Gypsy) language, can also speak Hungarian. These three groups also differ in cultural heritage, as well as occupation.[23] Fortunately, scholars of Gypsy culture and language have an acute power of observation. In many instances they are able to ascertain the correct interplay of racial, ethnic, and social elements, and thus come up with a realistic interpretation of Gypsydom in which none of these elements are predominant.[24]

Notwithstanding the confusion of ideas, applied politics has produced many favorable results. It is not an overstatement that since 1961 there has been much more progress in the life of the Gypsies than in the past several centuries. Let us compare some statistical figures. In the light of the 1971 survey of the Gypsy population conducted by the Sociological Research Institute of the Hungarian Academy of Sciences, only 30% of the able-bodied male adults had permanent jobs, 39% of the population over 14 years of age was illiterate, and 15% of school-aged children did not attend schools. During the school year of 1970/1971 altogether only 2,400 Gypsy children attended the eighth grade, while there were virtually none of them in Hungarian kindergartens. In the same year, 70% of the Gypsies lived in primitive ghettos. A decade later, however, most of these conditions have ameliorated: by the early 1980s, 85-90% of the male population had steady jobs, and 40-50% of the women also worked. They also made radical gains in the area of education, and currently over 96% (in some instances, 100%) of the school-aged Gypsy children attend schools. Moreover, nowadays only 20% of the Gypsies live in backward settlements.[25] To improve their socio-economic and cultural conditions, more and more Gypsies adapt themselves to the lifestyle of the majority nation. Out ot the 370,000 Gypsies living in the country, about forty to forty-five thousand were assimilated in the past decade.[26] This assimilated stratum is ashamed of and disavows its Gypsy origins. Although there has been a tremendous change in the positive direction, the country's Gypsies are without native leadership, and their participation in public life is negligible.

SOME CONCLUDING REMARKS

Despite the relatively low numerical strength of the minorities, Hungary laid down a set of guiding principles relating to human and nationality rights affecting the well-being of approximately 220,000 Germans, 110,000 Slovaks, 100,000 Southern Slavs, 25,000 Romanians, and 370,000 Gypsies. These figures do not represent a high percentage of the total population of eleven million. It is worth noting that even foreign experts of German and Slovak nationality have expressed a favorable opinion about the current state of affairs in Hungary. Among them is Wenzel Jaksch, a member of the German *Bundestag*, who, in his 1961 report on the fate of the German population groups in Eastern Europe and the Soviet Union had this to say: "In Hungary...since the events of October 1956, the German school system and the German language instruction have become more stable again. Contacts through visits from Austria and the Federal Republic /of Germany/ are relatively unhindered. The sending of parcels is given more generous treatment than in any of the other Eastern Bloc countries, and it is not forbidden to receive literature or donations for religious purposes. As a rule, Hungarian authorities make no difficulties about issuing personal documents for expelees living abroad."[27] The periodical *Slovensko*, a publication of the highly esteemed Slovak cultural organization *Matica Slovenská* of Martin, Czechoslovakia, also expressed similar positive views about conditions in Hungary: "In People's Democratic Hungary, the equipment for Slovak cultural work in many mixed villages is of better quality than those designed for the Hungarians." [28]

In contrast to the situation in Hungary, the national minority policies of the neighboring Czechoslovakia and Romania leave much to be desired. As evidenced by the recent flood of international publications, both countries violate flagrantly the internationally accepted norms of civil and minority rights, and sharply contradict the Marxist-Leninist solution of the national question. Some of these violations have actually been recognized, at least in Czechoslovakia. Thus, the Central Committee of the Communist Party of Czechoslovakia, in its December 1963 session, [29] deplored and condemned all the oppressive measures (deprivation of civil rights, dispersion, expulsion, and transfer of population, etc.) that had been used against the Hungarian minority in postwar years. But this was only a temporary phenomenon that ended in 1968, and never applied to Romania. Today, camouflaged with expressions of socialism, the oppression continues more than ever. The goal is total denationalization of the Hungarians. Apparently, the authorities in neither of these countries are able to appreciate that in lands of mixed nationalities, only a morally well-meaning policy can achieve the task of lasting coexistence. Instead of harboring outdated, chauvinistic designs or past political differences, the political regimes of the region should stress common interests and common cultural heritages.

The Hungarians are in a particularly difficult situation. There are two weighty factors that work against them, both of which are beyond the control of Hungary. These factors disadvantageously influence the relationship between the Hungarians and their neighboring ethnic groups at governmental levels. The first of these is the fact that the Hungarians are Finno-Ugric people, and as such they have no linguistic or ethnic relatives in the area. Secondly, they were the dominant people in the Carpathian Basin for a whole millennium, and are therefore resented by those whom they used to rule. In fact, the official circles of Czechoslovakia and Romania are engaged in covert retributions for every real or imagined injury that their nationality may have suffered at the hands of past Hungarian governments.

In reality, the history and fate of the people of the Danubian area are very intertwined, and are also filled with progressive traditions. These traditions also include great historical personalities, whose roles in interethnic relations were positive, and whose memories and achievements should be cherished and used accordingly. This is all the more desirable, as the nations of this region are really much closer to each other than they believe themselves to be. Moreover, their long common history displays not only antagonism, but also much cooperation and mutual sympathy. Thus, the already quoted Czech chronicler, Cosmas, wrote favorably about the Magyars in his *Chronica Boemorum*. In recent years, Czech and Slovak scholars discovered that the great 17th-century Czech thinker, Ján Amos Comenius (Komenský, 1592-1670) was partially of Hungarian descent, and that his work at the Reformed College of Sárospatak in Hungary (1660-1664) was of lasting value for all nations. Sándor Petőfi (1823-1849), the great Hungarian poet, happened to be the son of South Slavic and Slovak parents (Petrovics and Hrúz), while the great Slovak poet Hviezdoslav (1849-1921) was born into a noble Hungarian family (Országh). Likewise, Stefan Báthory, one of the most respected kings of Poland (1575-1586) was a Hungarian by birth. These and similar facts should be brought to the surface and emphasized to lessen the effects of conflicting political and national ideologies, and thereby create an atmosphere conducive to cooperation. The current Hungarian approach to the national minority question is much more in line with this ideal than its Romanian or Czechoslovak counterparts. It certainly attempts to correct past instances of discrimination, which can hardly be said for the Czechoslovak and the Romanian governments.

Notes

1. Kálmán Eperjessy, *Városaink múltja és jelene* /Past and Present of our Cities/ (Budapest: Műszaki Könyvkiadó, 1971), 88. See its review by Francis S. Wagner in the *Slavic Review*, XXXIII, 1 (March 1974), 169-170.

2. Francis S. Wagner, "Széchenyi and the Nationality Problem in the Habsburg Empire," *Journal of Central European Affairs*, XX, 3 (October 1960), 290.

3. *Szemere Bertalan miniszterelnök emlékiratai az 1848/49-i magyar kormányzat nemzetiségi politikájáról* /Prime Minister Bertalan Szemere's Memoirs

on the Nationality Policy of the Hungarian Government in 1848-49/ (Budapest: Cserépfalvi, 1941), 49.

4. For details see Stephen D. Kertesz, "The Expulsion of the Germans from Hungary: A Study in Postwar Diplomacy," *The Review of Politics*, XV, 2 (April 1953), 179-208; Matthias Annabring, "Das ungarlandische Deutschtum. Leidensweg einer südostdeutschen Volksgruppe," *Südost-Stimmen*, II, Sondernummer, (March 1952), 1-80; Lucius D. Clay, *Decision in Germany* (New York, 1950) describes the agreement concluded between the U.S. and Hungarian governments regulating the transfer procedure.

5. Anonymous, "The Position of Nationalities in the Hungarian People's Republic," in *25 Years of Hungarian Culture* (Budapest: Kossuth Könyvkiadó, 1970), 111.

6. *Ibid.*, and László Kővágó, "Népköztársaságunk nemzetiségi politikájáról," /On the Nationality Policy of the Hungarian People's Republic/, *Társadalmi Szemle*, XXIII, 11 (November 1968), 31. See also Anonymous, "Nemzetiségeink helyzetéről" /On the Situation of Our Nationalities/, *Népszabadság* (Budapest), vol. 26, no. 235, Oct. 6, 1968, 3.

7. "1949. évi XX. törvény — A Magyar Népköztársaság alkotmánya" /Law No. XX of 1949 — The Constitution of the Hungarian People's Republic/, in *Hatályos Jogszabályok Gyűjteménye, 1945-1968* /Collection of Statutory Provisions in Effect 1945-1968/ (Budapest: Közgazdasági és Jogi Könyvkiadó, 1969), I, 12.

8. "1961. évi V. törvény a Magyar Népköztársaság büntető törvénykönyvéről" /Law No. V of 1961 on the Criminal Code of the Hungarian People's Republic/, in *Hatályos Jogszabályok*, I, 134.

9. "1961. évi III. törvény a Magyar Népköztársaság oktatási rendszeréről" /Law No. III of 1961 on the Educational System of the Hungarian People's Republic/, in *Hatályos Jogszabályok*, I, 168; and "1962. évi 13. sz. törvényerejű rendelet a tankötelezettségről" /Edict No. 13 of 1962 on Compulsory Education/, in *Hatályos Jogszabályok*, IV.

10. *Hatályos Jogszabályok*, I, 71.

11. László Kővágó, "Népköztársaságunk," 34.

12. Anonymous, "The Position of Nationalities," 115; and L. Kővágó, "Népköztársaságunk," 35.

13. György Enyedi, *Hungary: An Economic Geography* (Boulder, Co: Westview Press, 1976), 235.

14. *Ibid.*, 41.

15. Márton Pécsi, ed., *Hungary: Geographical Studies* (Budapest: International Geographical Union, European Regional Conference, 1971), 236. See also Edith Lettrich's substantial treatise entitled *Urbanizálódás* /Urbanization/ (Budapest: Akadémiai Kiadó, 1965).

16. Anonymous, "The Position of Nationalities," 116.

17. *Ibid.*

18. Cf. Kamill Erdős's critical appraisal of Gypsy lore under the title "Cigánykutatók" /Gypsy Researchers/, in *A Gyulai Erkel Ferenc Múzeum Jubileumi Évkönyve* /Anniversary Yearbook of the Ferenc Erkel Museum in Gyula/ (Gyula, 1960), 85-88.

19. Tudományos Ismeretterjesztő Társulat. Szociológiai és Néprajzi Csoport, Budapest, *Jegyzőkönyv a TIT Szociológiai és Néprajzi Csoportjának cigánykutatással foglalkozó 1969. június 8-i konferenciájáról* /Minutes of the Conference on Gypsy Lore. Sponsored by the Sociological and Ethnographical Group of the Society for the Dissemination of Scientific Knowledge on June 8, 1961/ (Budapest, 1962), 115.

20. *Ibid*. 75.

21. Zsolt Csalog, "Etnikum? Faj? Réteg? Adalékok a 'cigányság' fogalmához" /Ethnic Group? Race? Stratum? Contributions to the Notion of the 'Gypsydom'/, *Világosság*, XIV, 1 (January 1973), 44.

22. László Siklós, "Cigányok a társadalom szorításában" /Gypsies in the Grip of Society/, in *Írószemmel* /As Seen by the Writers/, compiled by György Nemes (Budapest: Kossuth Könyvkiadó, 1973), 249-267; Zsolt Csalog, *Kilenc cigány* /Nine Gypsies/ (Budapest, 1976), 240; and István Tauber and Katalin Vég, "A cigányság bűnözésének néhány összefüggése" /Some Correlations in Gypsy Crime/, *Magyar Jog*, XXIX, 8 (August 1962), 692-701.

23. For more details see Zsolt Csalog, "Etnikum? Faj? Réteg?"

24. *Ibid.*, 40.

25. István Tauber and Katalin Vég, "A cigányság," 694. See also the No. 1016/1979 (VII. 12) resolution of the Council of Ministers on further goals in conjunction with the improvement of the position of the Gypsy population, in *Magyar Közlöny*, no. 47 (July 12, 1979), 633-634.

26. *Ibid.*, 694.

27. *Germany and Eastern Europe. Two Documents of the Third German Bundestag 1961.* (Bonn-Bruxelles-New York: Atlantic Forum, 1963), 50.

28. *Slovensko*, no. 1 (1984), 6.

29. Juraj Zvara, *Madărská menšina na Slovensku po roku 1945* /Hungarian Minority in Slovakia after 1945/ (Bratislava: Epocha, 1969), 75-76.

Edward Chaszar:

18 / THE HUNGARIAN MINORITY IN CZECHOSLOVAKIA: A STATUS REPORT

Introduction

This study will focus on the situation of the Hungarian minority in Czechoslovakia during the mid-1980s, and on the three main factors which influenced that situation. These were: (1) The question of the use of the Hungarian language of instruction in the Hungarian-inhabited parts of Slovakia, (2) the arrest of Miklós Duray, a spokesman for the Hungarian minority and leader of the movement to protect Hungarian schools in Slovakia, (3) the problem of the Gabčikovo-Nagymaros Hydroelectric Project on the Danube River, which has more of an indirect effect on the situation of the Hungarian minority.

Before discussing the three main factors, and some of the minor ones, which shaped the situation, it is advisable to look into the background of the Hungarian minority in Czechoslovakia.

Background to the Grievances of the Hungarian Minority in Czechoslovakia

The creation of Czechoslovakia at the end of World War I came about as a result of the peace treaties imposed by the victorious Allied and Associated Powers on the vanquished at Versailles, Saint Germain-en Laye, and Trianon. These dictated, non-negotiated peace treaties forced various national groups to live against their will in Czechoslovakia.

Among them were, according to the census of 1910, over one million Hungarians who, by the stroke of a pen, suddenly found themselves separated from their connationals and were transformed into a national minority.

British historian Alfred Cobban observed astutely in his book *National Self-Determination* (1945): "It was ironic that a settlement supposed to have been largely determined by the principle of nationality should have produced a state like Czechoslovakia, with minorities amounting to 34.7 percent of its population, quite apart from the question of the doubtful identity of nationality between Czechs and Slovaks."[1]

According to Charles Seymour, American delegate to the Paris Peace Conference, the boundaries of the successor states did not even "roughly" correspond with the ethnic or linguistic line. In short, national self-determination was granted to all, but denied to the Hungarians.

When the Hungarian Peace Delegation was handed the dictated terms of the treaty for signature, the chief of the delegation suggested that in accordance with the principle of self-determination the population affected by the treaty ought to be consulted through plebiscites. This, indeed, would have been entirely consistent with the Wilsonian idea of self-determination. The fear of plebiscites, however, prevailed among the victors, who were able to block all such efforts. The truth was revealed bluntly by André Tardieu (who was to become Prime Minister of France twice between the two world wars) in his book *La Paix*, in the following terms: "We had to choose between organizing plebiscites or creating Czechoslovakia."[2]

A great deal was alleged about the treatment of the nationalities in Hungary in the decades before World War I. However, compared to the situation prevalent in the old Austro-Hungarian Monarchy, the lot of the new national minorities was (and continues to be) miserable. "Is it not scandalous," exclaimed Sir Robert Gower, Member of the House of Commons in Britain some 15 years after the peace settlement, "that a European reconstruction, loudly hailed as one that was going to liberate the national minorities, should have resulted in their persecution, the severity of which is such that there is no parallel to it to be found in the ancient Kingdom of Hungary, where nationalities had been treated with infinitely more benevolence." [3]

The government of the newly-founded Czechoslovak Republic agreed to accept the guarantee of the rights of national minorities under the protection of the League of Nations, but the history of the First Czechoslovak Republic (1918-1938) abounds with examples of violations. These ran the gamut from discrimination in the acquisition of citizenship and discrimination in language rights, through the displacement of the Hungarian minority or the changing of the ethnic mix under the pretext of land reform, to inequalities in tax rates, censorship, and expulsion of Hungarian clergymen. [4]

In November, 1938, due to the shifting European balance of power, the border between Czechoslovakia and Hungary was redrawn as a result of an arbitral process mutually agreed on by the affected parties. Based on the ethnic principle, the Vienna Award of 1938 returned to Hungary some of its lost territory (12,103 square kilometers, or approximately 4,600 square miles) with a population of 1,030,000 inhabitants, over 80 percent of them Hungarians. However, the Award did not survive World War II; it was annulled by the Paris Peace Treaties of 1947. [5]

The government of the Second Czechoslovak Republic blamed the national minorities for the disintegration of the First Republic (1939), and decided to deal with them accordingly. On April 5, 1945, in Košice (Kassa, Kaschau) the head of the new republic, Eduard Beneš, proclaimed the program of the new government which contained an inhuman oppression and barbarous persecution of the non-Czech, non-Slovak and non-allied population of the partially restored republic. The destruction of the Hungarian population took various forms: expulsion, deportation, interment, people's courts procedures, revocation of citizenship, confiscation of property, condemnation to forced labor camps, placement of Hungarian businesses and farms under state management, and change of nationality by a process known as "reslovakization." [6]

The Communist takeover in February 1948 resulted in a temporary amelioration of the situation of the Hungarian minority in Czechoslovakia. In order to win the allegiance of the working masses, including the persecuted, demoralized, and totally disenchanted Hungarians, the nationalistic course of the Košice Program was abandoned in favor of "proletarian internationalism." The persecution of Hungarians and the deportation and expatriation measures were halted, and Hungarians were slowly granted the formal rights of a minority within the institutions of the monolithic state.

As an additional improvement, theoretically at least, the so-called Socialist Constitution of 1960, and again the Constitution of 1968 (which transformed Czechoslovakia into a federal republic of Czechs and Slovaks) recognized certain limited rights for minorities, but the implementation of these constitutional provisions through national legislation is either **nonexistent**, or falls short of expectations. Ethnic minorities, for example, do not have effective political representation as corporate groups, and therefore "they frequently feel themselves to be second-class citizens whose ethnic rights are entirely subject to the will of the dominant Czechs and Slovaks." [7]

The Problem of the Hungarian Schools in Slovakia

The right to use their own language in everyday life as well as in educating their children is considered as one of the fundamental rights of national, ethnic, and linguistic minorities. Consequently, when the Slovak government in 1978-1979 made an attempt to curtail the use of the Hungarian language in the public education system, a sharp reaction had set in among the Hungarian minority, including the founding of the Committee for the Defense of the Rights of the Hungarian Nationality in the Czechoslovak Socialist Republic.

In a *Statement*, submitted in May 1979 to the highest state and (Communist) party authorities of the Republic and its two constituent parts, the Committee listed unconstitutional discrimination in education in the following terms:

—Neglect in establishing Hungarian language nursery schools;

—Reduction in the number of Hungarian language primary and secondary schools;

—Reduction of the number of pupils by about 30% in Hungarian language primary schools in proportion to the number of children of school age;

— Experimental substitution of Slovak for Hungarian as the language of instruction;

—Unsatisfactory quality and level of Hungarian secondary education in technical schools and industrial vocational institutes;

—Abolition of the Hungarian Division of the College of Education of Nyitra, effectively ending teacher training for basic schools with Hungarian as the language of instruction;

—Low number of Hungarian students in the colleges and universities of the CSSR;

—Hindering of study and acquisition of academic degrees at the colleges and universities of the Hungarian People's Republic;

—A deepening educational chasm between the Hungarian minority and Slovak majority.[8]

The *Statement* pointed out that the measures and actions listed were violating Constitutional Law 100/1960, Chapter II, Article 19, Pragraph 2; Article 20, Paragraph 2; Article 24, Paragraph 3, and Article 25, as well as Constitutional Law 144/1968, Article 3, Paragraph 1/a. It then called for remedial action.

However, instead of contemplating remedial action, the Slovak government proposed a plan for schools in which the language of instruction was Hungarian. Under the plan, the language of instruction—with the exception of the subjects of Geography, History, and Hungarian Language—was to become Slovak, starting with the fifth grade and including high schools (vocational and academic). The plan would have changed the character of Hungarian schools completely.

As the *Statement*, and subsequent *memoranda* of the Committee, pointed out repeatedly, the plan was clearly unconstitutional. Article 25 of the 1960 Socialist Constitution reads: "The State shall ensure citizens of Hungarian, Ukrainian, and Polish nationality every opportunity and all means for education in their mother tongue and for their cultural development." Since 1968, Article 3/a of Constitutional Law 144/1968 assures the same right for all nationalities, including Germans.

In the end the plan was not implemented, not so much because of its unconstitutionality, rather, because of the widespread opposition to it, manifested in protests. Yet, at the same time, the Slovak authorities launched an investigation to uncover the members of the Committee for the Defense of the Rights of the Hungarian Minority, and in this connection they arrested and interrogated a number of Hungarian intellectuals. Ultimately one of these, the geologist Miklós Duray was accused with "incitement" and "subversion," and in 1983 he was put on trial. The outcome was unexpected: Due partly to the lack of convincing evidence, partly to international pressure—such as the presence of numerous foreign observers at the trial—the process was indefinitely suspended and Duray was set free. The charges, however, were not dropped.

One could guess already then that both the suspended plan and the suspended process would be resumed at a later time. The trial was suspended in February, 1983. The plan was taken up again in the fall of the same year, and Duray was re-arrested in May, 1984. The details are worth considering.

The question of the use of the Hungarian language as a language of instruction in the schools was to be taken care of within the new Law of Education which was to be passed by the Legislature (Slovak National Council) in the Slovak Socialist Republic. In order to avoid the charge of unconstitutionality, the article dealing with the language of instruction was rewritten several times, until finally it was submitted by the government (on the recommendation of the chief ideologist of the Central Committee of the Slovak Communist Party) to the Slovak National Council on November 25, 1983, with the following text:

Article 32a. The language of instruction

(1) The language of instruction is either Slovak or Czech; Czech is the language of instruction in schools (classes) indicated by the Ministry of Education.

(2) In schools or classes created for students of Hungarian, German, Polish, Ukrainian (Ruthenian) nationality, the language of instruction is that of the nationality.

(3) Inasmuch as in a school the language of instruction is not Slovak or Czech, it is mandatory to teach the Slovak or Czech language.

(4) In schools created pursuant to paragraph 2 and using a nationality language of instruction, the Ministry of Education may permit the teaching of certain subjects in Slovak or Czech, if this is proposed by the territorially competent National Committee in agreement with the parents of students attending these schools.

(5) The Ministry of Education may require in certain schools the teaching of specific subjects in a language other than the language of instruction of the school. [9]

Note, that the text was approved by the Council of Ministers; the next step to be taken was to get the approval of the Legislature.

Paragraph 4 as proposed was a contravention of the right of nationalities to use their language, disguised so as not to make it look unconstitutional by shifting the burden of the change in the language of instruction to the (terrified) parents "...if this is proposed by the territorially competent National Committee in agreement with the parents of students attending these schools." The National Committees referred to in the text are organs of state power and administration in the regions, districts, and localities.

Paragraph 5 went even further; it authorized the Ministry of Education to change the language of instruction without "consulting" the parents.

Under the circumstances it is understandable that the proposed bill encountered widespread resistance and protest. The protest was directed by the "Group to Defend the Hungarian Schools in Slovakia" /*Szlovákiai Magyar Iskolák Védelmi Csoportja*/, supposedly led by Miklós Duray. The Group is said to have issued a circular letter in some 600 copies, addressed to Hungarian teachers, parents, and members of CSEMADOK (the Cultural Organization of Hungarian Workers in Czechoslovakia), urging them to use their constitutional right of free speech and protest the passing of this unconstitutional Bill. Duray himself addressed a letter to President Gustav Husak, to the Slovak National Council, and the Slovak Government, expressing the same views and his opposition.[10]

As a result of the circular letter, an unprecedented wave of protest swept the Hungarian-inhabited parts of Slovakia. By the middle of March, 1984, approximately 10,000 signatures were collected, protesting the proposed action. Not surprisingly the Werstern European information media picked up the story in Bratislava, capital of Slovakia; newspaper articles and radio reports started to deal with the adverse situation. Public opinion in Hungary reacted adversely, putting pressure on government and party organs to abandon their policy of noninterference, and approach the appropriate authorities in Prague and Bratislava to alleviate the problem.[11]

An interesting offshoot of the entire case was the change—albeit temporary—in the role of CSEMADOK. Forced into a purely cultural role in the fall of 1968, as opposed to its former character of political representative organ of the Hungarian minority, the Association took a definitely political stand on the question of education in the Hungarian language and asserted its right to represent the interests of the Hungarians. A majority of the Central Committee of the Association (all of them communist party members) voted to protest the proposed Bill.

After repeated delays, the Bill was placed on the agenda of the Slovak National Council on its meeting of April 2, 1984. Surprisingly, the two paragraphs which were objectionable to the Hungarian minority (and would have affected other minorities as well) were omitted from the text passed by the Council. As a matter of fact, they were withdrawn by the Council of Ministers after an extraordinary meeting held on March 19, 1984. However, the Minister of Education, Juraj Buša, made it clear in a press conference on March 23 that the measures omitted from the text will be accomplished eventually through administrative and educational practices. This seems to indicate that the chapter concerning the use of the Hungarian language in education in Slovakia is far from being concluded. Moreover, the regime did not hesitate to indicate its displeasure with the attitude of the Hungarian minority; in retaliation and as a first step in a campaign of intimidation, Miklós Duray was arrested again on May 10, 1984, for "harming the interests of the State abroad," and for "spreading alarming news." [12]

The Case of Miklós Duray

Miklós Duray was born in 1945 of Hungarian parents in the town of Losonc, as it is called in Hungarian. Losonc is located in the central part of Southern Slovakia, the belt inhabited until recently by Hungarians, and it is referred to exclusively by its Slovak name, Lučenec. Young Duray obtained his high school diploma in the Hungarian "Gymnasium" of Fülek in the year 1962 and proceeded to the Comenius University in Bratislava to study applied geology. Interrupting his studies because of illness, he obtained a doctor's degree in natural science in 1977, and found employment with the state-owned Doprastav Bridge and Road Construction Company as a geologist. He is married to Susanna Szabó, also of Hungarian parentage in Slovakia.

As a student, Duray was a member of the Hungarian Youth Organization (MISZ) and, in the Presidium of the Central Committee of CSEMADOK, he was a leading figure in the efforts to establish democracy in the country during the period known as the "Prague Spring."

Since 1978 he has been active in the Committee to Protect the Rights of the Hungarian Minority in Czechoslovakia (CSMKJB). [13] In this capacity he has been repeatedly exposed to harrassment by the state security police. In January 1979 he petitioned the Slovak government concerning the question of Hungarian language schooling. In May 1979 he prepared a *Statement* or aide-memoir summarizing the grievances of the Hungarian minority. [14] In February 1980 the Committee published an analysis of the problems of the Hungarian minority in relation to the human rights provisions of the International Covenant of Civil and Political Rights and of the Helsinki Agreements. This was forwarded to all of the signatory governments of the Helsinki Final Act, and to international organizations. In addition to pointing out violations of international human rights instruments, the analysis again dealt with the unconstitutionality of various actions and measures affecting the Hungarian minority in Slovakia. In the summer of 1980 the Committee presented proposals for resolving internal minority problems to the Madrid Meeting of the Conference on Security and Cooperation in Europe.

According to the circular letter of Amnesty International, calling for urgent action on behalf of Miklós Duray, his office was searched on June 3, 1982, and so was his home; a number of documents were seized in both places. Duray then admitted that he was the author of the documents published in the name of the Committee. Afterwards he was frequently summoned to the police "and some 50 people were questioned as witnesses in connection with his case. On June 10, 1982, the investigating authorities proposed to the Procuracy that Miklós Duray be charged under Article 100 with 'incitement'.[15]

Subsequently, he was arrested on November 10, 1982. The charge was changed to that of "subversion," or more precisely, "hostile acts against the state" which, under Article 98 of the Czechoslovak penal code, carries a prison sentence of between three and ten years.[16]

Duray's trial started on January 31, 1983. On February 1, it was adjourned for ten days and continued on February 11, when it was adjourned again indefinitely. On February 22, 1983 Duray was released without a sentence, but the charges against him were not dropped. The adjournments and the release have been attributed to international pressure, which included the presence of several Western observers at the trial, the protests of many human rights organizations in different parts of the world, including the Czechoslovak human rights organization Charter 77, the presence of three well-known writers from Hungary, and the supposed behind-the-scene intervention of the Hungarian government.[17]

The European press followed the arrest, trial, and release of Duray with great interest; some reporters speculated on what would come next, and sought to interview him. His answer was predictable:

> On 22 February I was set free whereby it was stressed
> that nothing has changed in the legal situation of
> my case: thus, I continue to be indicted under para-
> graph 98/section 2, which means imprisonment for
> up to 10 years. And I don't know which day the in-
> definitely adjourned process against me will start
> anew.[18]

He also knew that the state attorney's office kept collect-
ing additional evidence against him. In fact, the type of evidence looked for was readily available: in 1983 two of Duray's
works were published in the United States. One of them
was a collection of literary essays, the other was an autobiographical account entitled *Kutyaszorító* (Choke Collar),[19]
discussing among others the unenviable situation of the
Hungarian minority in Czechoslovakia, and, therefore, fit to
be labeled as another instance of "spreading false news abroad
harmful to the interests of the State."

The rest of the story has already been discussed. The
introduction of a new Bill of Education in the fall of 1983
led to the creation of the Group to Defend the Hungarian
Schools in Slovakia, the publishing by Duray of the circular
letter calling for protest action, as well as the letter to President Husak and other party and state authorities, the successful wave of protest (and again a supposed intervention
by the Hungarian government), leading to the omission of
the discriminatory paragraphs from the Bill, but ending
in the arrest of Miklós Duray on May 10, 1984.

Duray's re-arrest immediately elicited considerable international attention. There followed a spate of protests,
appeals, expressions of concern by governments, nongovern-
mental organizations, individuals, and information media
in the United States and Europe, including Hungary, where
a "Duray Committee" was formed to mobilize public opinion, much to the dislike of the government, which—for
various reasons—until now did not pursue an open policy
of concern for the Hungarian minorities living outside its
borders.[20]

Among those protesting Duray's arrest and asking for
his release were a number of Czechoslovak intellectuals:
Ján Čarnogurský, a lawyer disbarred for having defended

a number of human rights activists; Milan Šimečka, philosopher and journalist, who was himself arrested earlier for
engaging in activities allegedly harming the interests of the
state; Miroslav Kusý, a member and spokesman of Charter
77, who lost his job at Comenius University when he, too,
was arrested for "subversive activities," and Jozef Jablonický.
In their letters to the Prime Minister of Slovakia or to the
First Secretary of the Slovak Communist Party, each of these
individuals defended Duray's right of freedom of expression;
one of them suggested that the problem of the minorities
be subjected to rational debate and solved on that basis;
and all condemned Duray's arrest, asserting that this action
hurt the interests of the state much more than did the activities of Duray.[21]

Despite all these protests and appeals Duray remained
in jail, held "incommunicado," and accused with "harming the interests of the state abroad," and "spreading alarmist
news" under Articles 112 and 119 of the Czechoslovak Penal
Code, which carry penalties up to three years and six months,
respectively. In addition, he was to face the charge of "subversion," carried over from his prior arrest.

According to one report, the decision to imprison Duray
again may have been motivated—in addition to official
vindictiveness—by broader domestic and foreign policy
considerations, namely a hardened attitude toward dissi-
dents at home and ideological differences in the Soviet Bloc. In
addition, it was interpreted as a clear signal of displeasure
to the Hungarian government. As the report says:

> Budapest keeps a watchful eye on the treatment of
> the Hungarian minority in Czechoslovakia and
> raises the issue regularly in high-level bilateral con-
> sultations. Slovak Prime Minister Čolotka was in
> Budapest at the end of June /1984/ at the invita-
> tion of Hungarian Deputy Prime Minister József
> Marjai. His visit was apparently routine, concern-
> ed mainly with matters of economic cooperation;
> but Duray's case could well have been on the
> agenda. The current harsh climate in Prague, how-
> ever, offers little hope that the Husak regime will
> respond as readily as last year to Hungarian inter-

cession on behalf of Miklós Duray or to international appeals from world renowned writers. [22]

Events later in 1984 seemed to confirm the correctness of the above assessment. Toward the end of November President Gustav Husak traveled to Budapest, supposedly to discuss economic matters, such as the disparity of the value of the two countries' currencies, which Czechoslovakia had long found disadvantageous, and matters related to the Danube hydroelectric project. Husak's presence was used by the Duray Committee in Budapest to stage a press conference and publicly demand Duray's release. Things must have turned sour for Husak also in his meeting with his Hungarian counterparts, for he hurriedly left Budapest after a few (some say four) hours. Then, on December 3, 1984, the German *Frankfurter Allgemeine Zeitung* reported that for the first time in its history the Hungarian Socialist Workers' Party (Communist Party) included among the guidelines of its forthcoming Congress the question of the treatment of the Hungarian minority in the neighboring countries. [23]

Meanwhile, Miklós Duray, afflicted with a liver ailment, continued in jail still in pre-trial arrest. His supporters, especially those who collaborated with him in the protest movement by handing out petition forms or even just signing them, are said to be subjected to various forms of pressure. "It is devilishly difficult to be Hungarian in language and in spirit in the very Slovak Bratislava," wrote the French daily, *Le Monde*, in November, 1984. [24]

"Tears for the Beautiful Danube"

The third factor influencing the situation of the Hungarian minority in Czechoslovakia, not so much directly as indirectly, is the proposed plan to dam or divert part of the Danube River for a hydroelectric project. The plan affects a 138-mile stretch, from Gabčikovo or Bős in Hungarian (near Bratislava) to Nagymaros in the scenic Danube-bend north of Budapest, Hungary. Some of the work has already begun in the Gabčikovo area, where the river itself forms part of the Czechoslovak-Hungarian border. As a result of the construction, the frontier will be shifted in some areas.

According to the plan, agreed upon by the two countries in 1977, two power plants are to be built: one at Gabčikovo, the other at Nagymaros. The estimated costs would run the equivalent of $1.12 billion for each of the two countries. When completed, the entire system would generate 3.6 kilowatt hours of electricity annually, saving nearly 10 million barrels of crude oil a year for the two countries. Originally planned to begin operations at the two places in 1986 and 1989, respectively, the start-up dates have been changed to 1990 and 1993, and very likely will have to be changed again.[25]

The trouble started when, in what was believed to be the biggest environmental protest in the Soviet Bloc, about 7,000 Hungarians signed a petition in the spring of 1984 against the project. The petition, whose signers included fifty prominent scientists, writers, artists, and other intellectuals, was addressed to the Hungarian Parliament and the Council of Ministers and called on them to drop the project because of a large number of adverse consequences, unanticipated at the time of the agreement.

According to studies performed by competent scientists, engineers, and ecologists individually or in teams (including some under the aegis of the Hungarian Academy of Sciences), the dam systems would cause serious damage to the drinking water supply, agriculture, the forests, as well as the network of human settlements in the counties affected. The petition itself claimed that the project would cause "irreparable damage to the landscape and natural environment" of two Danube regions, known as the Csallóköz or Ostrov Zitni (an area of fertile farmland inhabited mostly by Hungarians, but now situated on the Slovak side), and Szigetköz. What the petition did not mention, but Hungarians are painfully aware of, is that the reservoir ensuing from the dam project at Gabčikovo would result in the resettlement of Hungarians, thereby contributing to the efforts of Slovak nationalists to change the ethnic composition of the borderland areas.[26]

In a newspaper article, Hungarian biologist János Vargha, a chief critic of the project, contended that the amount of money Hungary would need to prevent or offset environmental damage was twice the amount to be invested in the construction.[27]

Apart from cheap electric power, the planners hope to prevent yearly flooding and to enlarge the channel so smaller seagoing ships can go upstream as far as Bratislava. That is "an old Slovakian dream," said one Hungarian, who asked to remain anonymous. Due to old, and now seemingly resurgent, national rivalries, bitter feelings simmer between Slovaks and Hungarians. The protest against the project had temporarily slowed down the construction, at least on the Hungarian side, although the government claims that this is due purely to economic reasons. On the Slovak side construction is not only proceeding on schedule, but it is being speeded up, thereby putting pressure on the Hungarians. All this contributes to the worsening of Hungarian-Slovak relations and affects indirectly the problem of the Hungarian minority in Czechoslovakia. In an atmosphere of suspicion and mistrust, accomodation and compromise have much less of a chance. [28]

Epilogue

On the 21st of January, 1985, Amnesty International again issued an "urgent action" call for the release of Miklós Duray. Letters of appeal and protest poured into the office of the Chief Procurator General in Prague and in Bratislava, demanding the release of Duray, and asking for information concerning his status. At the time of the "urgent action" call it was unknown whether Duray had been indicted or not, and whether his lawyer and his wife were permitted to visit him. The urgent action increased international pressure on the Czechoslovak authorities.

In the spring of 1985 Hungary's Minister of Education paid a visit to his counterpart in Slovakia, and later to that in Prague. According to the Hungarian Minister, Béla Köpeczi, interviewed in Prague, the discussions concerning questions of mutual interest proceeded in a "constructive atmosphere," and touched both cultural and educational matters, including the education of minorities in their mother tongue. It was decided to create a mixed working committee to determine "which subjects should be taught in what grades in the mother tongue or both languages, and by what methods best suited for the purpose." [29] It is safe to assume that in the course of these discussions the case of Duray was also discussed, and perhaps some decision reached. Proof of this seems to lie in the fact that members of the Budapest-based Duray Committee, when interceding later in the spring for Duray at the Central Committee of the Hungarian Socialist Workers' Party and demanding action through Party channels, were told to drop the case, because Duray was to be set free. [30]

Indeed, Duray was released on May 10, 1985 (and reinstated in his former job) under an amnesty order for certain categories of prisoners, passed by the government in celebration of the 40th Anniversary of ending World War II. The timing of Duray's release may have saved the Czechoslovak Government from the embarrassment of Western countries airing the case at the Conference on Human Rights of the signatories of the Helsinki Agreements, which just got underway in Ottawa, Canada, at that time. At any rate, the action taken removed one of the obstacles in the way of improving Hungarian-Czechoslovak relations.

The year 1985 also produced some developments concerning the Gabčikovo-Nagymaros Waterstep System. First came the environmentally influenced decision of the Austrian government not to engage in the building of a power-station on the Danube, at least for the time being. Next, it was announced that Hungary and Czechoslovakia had agreed on postponing the Gabčikovo-Nagymaros Project. This came as a surprise and was interpreted as a victory for the environmental protest movement in Hungary. [31] Unfortunately for the latter, the announcement proved to be premature, or rather, a "misinterpretation" of facts, according to the Czechoslovak side, and called for a clarification on the part of Hungary. The promised re-examination of the possible environmental effects of the waterstep system did not mean the abandonment of the project, merely its corresponding modification, explained György Lázár, Hungarian Prime Minister. [32]

During the middle of August, 1985, Hungary's participation in the project was again confirmed by the government. According to a Swiss report, this meant that "despite the great environmental danger, Hungary gave in to Czechoslovak pressure." [33] At the same time, however, it was noted that the Hungarian Press Agency MTI referred to a modification of the 1977 State Treaty between the two countries, including the time table for the construction. According to the new time table the power station at Gabčikovo will commence operations in 1990, the one at Nagymaros in 1995.[34] The fact remains that there is still no sign whatsoever that would indicate the beginning of the construction at Nagymaros, and the delay is still explained in purely economic terms, namely cost factors. All this seems to indicate that the Hungarian government would like to extricate itself somehow from the now unwanted project, if it could. Behind the verbal consent lurks factual resistance; disagreement over the project continues under the surface between the two countries.

Meanwhile, the problem of the use of the Hungarian language in Slovakia remains as yet unresolved and creates uncertainty for the battered minority. At the same time, the smoldering disagreement over the Danube project continues to exacerbate relations between the two countries and diminishes the ability of the Hungarian government to create goodwill and use its influence across the border.

By the end of the year 1985, Czechoslovak-Hungarian relations have shown only slight improvement, and the situation of the Hungarian minority in Slovakia continues to be unenviable.*

Notes

1. Alfred Cobban, *The Nation State and National Self-Determination* (London: Collins, 1969), p. 86.

2. Quoted in Yves de Daruvár, *The Tragic Fate of Hungary* (Munich: Edition Nemzetőr, 1974), p. 92.

3.Sir Robert Gower, *La Revision du Traité de Trianon* (Paris, 1937), p. 16, quoted by Daruvár, p. 111.

4. These violations are discussed in detail and documented in Charles Wojatsek, *From Trianon to the First Vienna Arbitral Award: The Hungarian Minority in the First Czechoslovak Republic, 1918-1938* (Montréal: Institute of Comparative Civilizations, 1981).

5. See Edward Chaszar, *Decision in Vienna: The Czechoslovak-Hungarian Border Dispute of 1938* (Astor, FL: Danubian Press, 1978).

6. The pertinent chapters of the Košice Program, and the discriminatory government decrees which helped to implement the anti-Hungarian measures, are attached to the *Supplement to the Memorandum of the National Committee of Hungarians from Czechoslovakia*, submitted to the Ottawa Meeting of Human Rights Experts of the Signatory Governments of the Final Act of the Conference on Security and Cooperation in Europe, dated February 15, 1985 (Portola Valley, CA: NCHC, 1985). For a comprehensive treatment of the subject see Kálmán Janics, *Czechoslovak Policy and the Hungarian Minority, 1945-1948* (New York: Social Science Monographs, Brooklyn College Press, Distributed by Columbia University Press, 1982).

7. David W. Paul, *Czechoslovakia: Profile of a Socialist Republic at the Crossroads of Europe* (Boulder, CO: Westview Press, 1981), p. 124. Paul explains that the present two-nation view was a matter of serious controversy in the First Republic, when the dominant assumption of the political elite was the existence of a single "Czechoslovak" nation. This idea was disputed hotly by the Slovak nationalists and an important faction in the Communist Party. "The grievances of the Slovak nationalists led them into collaboration with Hitler, and, as a result of the fratricidal conflict between Czechs and Slovaks, the Czechoslovak idea became discredited and was abandoned by the end of the Second World War." (p. 124) Today the Czechs and Slovaks are considered the constituent "nations," all others are merely "nationalities."

8. *Statement of the Committee for the Defense of the Rights of the Hungarian Nationality in the Czechoslovak Socialist Republic*, submitted to the Government of the Czechoslovak Socialist Republic, May 1979. The English text of the *Statement* may be found in the *Memorandum of the National Committee of Hungarians from Czechoslovakia* (Cleveland, OH: NCHC, 1980), submitted to the Signatory Governments of the Final Act of the Conference on Security and Cooperation in Europe, popularly known as the Helsinki Agreements, during the follow-up meeting in Madrid, in the fall of 1980.

9. For the original text in Slovak see Hungarian Human Rights Foundation, *In Defense of Hungarian Schools in Slovakia: Documents on the Struggle for Self-Protection of the Hungarian Minority in Czechoslovakia, November 1983 - August 1984* (New York: Hungarian Human Rights Foundation, 1984), p. 12. This remarkable publication contains documents in Hungarian, Slovak, English, and German languages, including some written by Miklós Duray himself.

10. Both the circular and Duray's letter are reproduced in the book cited, *In Defense of Hungarian Schools*, pp. 14-15, and pp. 16-17, respectively.

11. The *Neue Zürcher Zeitung* in Switzerland reported as early as September 16, 1983, the adverse situation of the Hungarian minority in Slovakia due to widespread and undisguised discrimination, in a lengthy article entitled "Bedrängte Magyaren-Minderheit in der Slowakei; Eine inoffizielle Dokumentation mit offiziellen Zahlen." The report was datelined in Bratislava. The *Frankfurter Allgemeine Zeitung* (Federal Republic of Germany) ran a story in its January 11, 1984, issue, under the title "Eine fast vergessene Minderheit." Other articles in the same vein were published by the *Zürichsee Zeitung* in Switzerland, "Schutzlose Minderheiten in der CSSR," May 24, 1985; and at the same time by the *Thungauer Zeitung*, also in Switzerland, "Prag plagt die Ungarn in der Slowakei," the title suggesting that the Federal Parliament authorized the legislation.

12. This was reported in *The New York Times*, May 22, 1984, based on the reports of the Associated Press, the Agence France Presse, and the Reuters Agency, of the same date.

13. Also referred to variously as Committee for the Defense of the Rights of the Hungarian Nationality, or Committee for the Legal Protection of the Hungarian Minority, or Committee for the Protection of the Rights of the Hungarian Minority.

14. See note No. 8, above.

15. Amnesty International circular letter dated London, 30 November 1982, No. US 273/82, *Legal Concern*, Czechoslovakia: Miklós Duray.

16. *Ibid*.

17. See the *Newsletter* of the International P.E.N. Club, Centre for Writers in Exile, American Branch, Fall 1984 issue, p. 2. Among those who publicly demanded that the Czechoslovak Government fulfill the provisions of the Helsinki Final Act in its treatment of Duray and the Hungarian minority were several United States Government and Congressional figures and the writers Irving Howe, Susan Sontag and Kurt Vonnegut.

18. The quotation is from an interview given by Duray to Anna Bojkovski and Georg Breitner of *Gegenstimmen* (Vienna, Austria), No. 12/4, Summer 1983, pp. 33-38, and translated into English by the Foreign Broadcast Information Service in its *East Europe Report*, No. 2240, dated December 9, 1983.

19. Miklós Duray's books are: *Tegnap alighanem bolondgombát etettek velünk* /Yesterday we were Probably Fed Poisonous Mushrooms/ (Chicago: Szivárvány, 1983); and *Kutyaszorító* /Choke Collar/ (New York: Püski, 1983).

20. A representative selection of news items, reports, letters of protest, telegrams, and the like, is found in the book cited before, *In Defense of Hungarian Schools in Slovakia*.

21. Copies of these letters in the Slovak original, and their English translation, were made available by the Czechoslovak National Council of America in Washington, DC. In its periodical *Update* the Council monitors the fate of arrested Charter 77 members, including Duray.

22. "Situation Report: Czechoslovakia." *Radio Free Europe Research* (Munich, Germany), 11 July 1984, p. 3.

23. "Budapest erhebt Minderheiten zum Parteitagsthema." *Frankfurter Allgemeine Zeitung*, 3 Dezember 1984, Nr. 273/49D. The passage referred to in the news item is item No. 7 in the *Guidelines* issued for the 13th Party Congress. See *A Magyar Szocialista Munkáspárt Központi Bizottságának irányelvei a Párt XIII. Kongresszusára* /Guidelines of the Central Committee of the Hungarian Socialist Workers' Party for the Party's 13th Congress/ (Budapest: MSZMP-KB, 1984), p. 9. The inclusion of this item in the *Guidelines* is considered by many as a rather surprising development. The question of the treatment of the Hungarian minority in the neighboring countries, especially in Rumania (where they are outright persecuted) has not been raised publicly before, so as to avoid charges of 'bourgeois nationalism" and "revisionism." Besides, under the concept of "proletarian internationalism" in the socialist countries there is not supposed to be discrimination or differential treatment based on grounds of nationality or ethnic origin; supposedly the question of minorities would resolve itself spontaneously, and disappear altogether. Item No. 7 suggests that a re-evaluation may be in progress in the higher cadres.

24. "Les Hongrois silencieux de Bratislava," in *Le Monde* (Paris), 4-5 November, 1984. Commenting on the educational and cultural affairs of the harrassed Hungarian minority, the article describes in vivid terms the situation and the fear these people have of speaking their mother tongue in public, the changing of place names to Slovak, and other measures of discrimination.

25. "Tears for the beautiful Danube," in *The Plain Dealer* (Cleveland), Sunday, July 15, 1984, p. 1 of Section AA. See also "Ungarn: Protestwelle gegen Stauwerk," in *Die Presse* (Wien), May 7, 1984.

26. "Tears...." The *Neue Zürcher Zeitung* of Switzerland, in a full-page article published on May 5/6, 1984, under the title "Kommt die Donau-Korrektion zwischen Bratislava und Budapest?" went into considerable detail concerning the expected adverse consequences of the project.

27. János Vargha, "Mindenáron? /At Every Price?/ *Heti Világgazdaság* /World Economy Weekly/, December 3, 1983. In Hungary there exists a large literature on the project.

28. A news item in the Slovak capital Bratislava confirmed the progress of the construction. See "Závăzok budovatel'ov" /Concerning Obligatory Construction/, in *Smena na Nedelu,* /Sunday Exchange/, May 25, 1984.

29. "Magyar-Csehszlovák kulturális tárgyalások" /Hungarian-Czechoslovak Cultural Discussions/, *Magyar Hírek* /Hungarian News/ (Budapest), June 22, 1985, p. 4.

30. Information received from the Hungarian Human Rights Foundation of New York.

31. "Neues Donauwerk in Ungarn aufgeschoben," *Die Presse* (Vienna), February 14, 1985, p. 1.

32. "Donau-Dissonanzen zwischen Ungarn und CSSR," *Tages Anzeiger* (Zürich), March 11, 1985.

33. "Budapest sagt Ja zum umstrittenen Donau-Stau," *Tages Anzeiger,* August 17-18, 1985.

34. "Definitive Teilnahme Ungarns an Donau-Ausbauprojekt," *Neue Zürcher Zeitung,* August 17-18, 1985.

* In 1988 Miklós Duray received permission from the Czechoslovak Government to visit the United States.

SOCIAL AND ECONOMIC DEVELOPMENTS IN TWENTIETH-CENTURY HUNGARY

Andor Csizmadia:*

19 / THE DEVELOPMENT OF SOCIAL POLITICS IN HUNGARY DURING THE INTERWAR ERA**

In its origins, social policies during the bourgeois era in Hungary were unduly restricted to the problem of the poor. Although insurance was made a part of the complex of social policies in the 1850s (which in Hungary commenced with the so-called insurance programs of the fraternal organization of the miners), it was extended to larger numbers and developed further only in the closing years of the nineteenth century. Act XIV of 1891 introduced compulsory medical insurance in industry.[1] This industrial medical insurance was, as a subsequent government itself admitted, quite primitive and unsuccessful, but at least it established the principle that medical insurance of the workers was the responsibility of the state. The situation was worse in the agricultural sector, even though the harvester strikes had forced the government to take action. Act II. of 1898, which was intended to regulate the legal relationship between employers and agricultural laborers, only decreed, in lieu of social insurance, that the employer was responsible for eight days of the laborer's medical care (article 33). Nor was the agricultural laborer law of the coalition government — the former opposition — any better (Act 1907:XLV). This did not provide for insurance either, but instead specified that if the permanently contracted family

---

*Deceased
**Translated by Thomas Szendrey

411

(including the wife and children under 12) became ill during the period of service, the landlord was responsible for medical treatment and supplies for a maximum term of 45 days, except if the sickness was the fault of the sick person. A small landholder could deduct one-half of these expenses from the wage of the laborer, a large landholder or the owner of an estate only 10%, but only if it was attributable to the medical expenses of wives and dependents. If the sickness came about as the result of fault or negligence on the part of the landlord, he was responsible for the whole amount (article 28). While the extent of social care in agriculture seemed embryonic, developments in industry—not without the influence of the developed social policies of Austria, the other partner in the Dual Monarchy—resulted in the establishment of the accident and sickness insurance of those employed in industry and commerce (Act 1907:XIX). This represented a major step in the hitherto neglected area of workers' insurance. [2]

These primitive social policies were replaced during the interwar years by some extension of social insurance, since the working classes had become acquainted with the more advanced, but not always implemented, social policies of the Hungarian Soviet Republic of 1919. [3]

On the basis of Acts 1927:XXI, and 1928:XL, the sickness and accident coverage of those employed in industry, commerce, mining, and foundries, as well as the social security of the old, disabled, widows and orphans, was developed into a system of social insurance. Not covered by these two statutes were the agricultural servants and laborers, as their social insurance had been regulated earlier by Act XX of 1900, and developed further by Acts 1902:XIV, 1912:VIII, and 1913:XX. The coverage provided by these insurance schemes, however, remained below subsistence levels.

In the year 1936 the National Agricultural Insurance Institute (Act 1936:XXXVI) was established, which, however, regulated primarily the compulsory old-age, disability, and life insurance of the stewards and farm managers. This was followed by Act 1938:XII, which dealt with the compulsory insurance of agricultural laborers and finally by Act 1939:XVI, which extended benefits to the widows of agricultural laborers. All of these insurance schemes—even taking into account their extension to more individuals—nonetheless suffered from the common failing that the payment of benefits commenced only later (those authorized by the 1928 statutes only in 1939), and even then the initial benefits were so minimal that these did not provide for the needs of the elderly. [4]

The solution to the social problem in Hungary, as in just about every other capitalist state, confronted the country's leadership with almost insurmountable problems. These were soon augmented by the great economic crisis of the 1930s and the accompanying unemployment in both industry and agriculture, as well as by the ever-increasing impoverishment of vast numbers of people.

Before the economic crisis, but after the end of the years of inflation, at the instigation of the then minister of social welfare and labor, a national sociopolitical congress met. (Among all the invited groups concerned with the problem of social politics, only the Council of Trade Unions did not send delegates.) This congress took into account virtually all the problems facing the country: education in social ethics and social policy matters, the sociopolitical training of public officials, the crisis of the middle class, the politics of population growth, the problem of the isolated farmstead, the establishment of the institute of social politics, the issue of workers housing and public nutrition programs, the factory committees and workers cooperatives, the achievement of social peace and coalition rights, the legal defense of workers rights and propaganda efforts for social policies, the issues related to the statistics of social policies, patronage, and finally charitable efforts and the issues of poverty. However, none of these issues were really discussed in depth and the participants were never able to get at the core of these matters. Morover, even if they could have done so, the necessary resources were simply not at their disposal. [5]

Social politics in the 1930s were generally limited to the reform of the poverty issues and even this was restricted to the level of administrative reforms. This was the case because until this time the care of the poor was the responsibility of the respective place of domicile. The determination of the place of domicile, however, was a complex matter, especially on account of certain provisions of the Treaty of Trianon, which attempted to determine the citizenship of the population living in the territories detached from Hungary on the basis of their place of domicile. In all certainty this was one of the most complex issues in certain cases. During his earlier years, the author of this study was an official charged with determining issues of domicile in the Hungarian city of Győr, where he ran across domicile cases which had commenced in 1910 with the admittance for treatment of an old beggar to the hospital in Pozsony where he soon died. The expenses of the hospital care were to be charged to the village of domicile. They were unable to make a determination in this case because the beggar had never obtained a domicile in his own right. His mother had been a household servant, who also could not obtain a domicile paper in her own right. In such cases it was necessary to go back as far as the grandparents. Even though the various legal entities corresponded with each other, it proved to be impossible to determine the proper place of domicile. In the meantime Pozsony—now known as Bratislava—had become the capital of Slovakia, the beggar had been dead for a long time and the onetime hospital bill had devalorized. There was no reason to increase the files any more. Thus, with the "proverbial stroke of the pen" it was placed *ad acta*, i.e. deactivated.

It was this difficulty which the authorities wished to resolve, namely that the responsibilities of the townships for the administration of the poor laws be taken care of in some simpler manner, without resorting to the determination of the place of domicile. This goal was served by the decree 1931:6000 of the prime minister, which stated that instead of the official place of domicile the actual place of residence had to assume responsibility. The place of residence was defined as the place where the individual seeking support had spent the most time during the five previous years.

The decree specified in detail the condition of poverty as well as the extent and means of public assistance. All of this proved to be only an amelioration of the conditions. It occurred to no one to make provisions for the townships and cities to have the necessary financial means for this. It should be pointed out that in the 1930s the assistance to the poor presented a serious problem for these civic entities. The economic crisis had reached its height at that time and the cities and towns—especially the industrial cities—consider- ed it their primary obligation to provide employment op- portunities for the large numbers of unemployed in order to reduce their direct assistance budgets. Ever since the early 1920s, Act 1922:I, paragraph 29, had made it possible to initiate other relief actions, for it empowered the minister of public welfare to permit the imposition of fees and pre- mium charges by municipalities and towns. On this basis the minister of the interior (who was the responsible suc- cessor of the minister of public welfare in these matters) decreed that during the economic crisis certain towns and cities may impose indigence premiums, the income of which was to be used for the organization of public works projects in those towns and cities. These so-called relief measures only amounted to temporary expedients in social welfare, and more effective social care was made possible only with the passing of the economic crisis and the beginnings of prosperity.

At the time of the world economic crisis—sensing the inability of the state and local organs—society hastened to take into its own hands the solution to the problem of widespread poverty. This movement of voluntary social organization led to the formulation of the so-called "Norm of Eger," in the city by that name. The establishment of these norms was one of the significant facets of the chari- table dimension of the Catholic Church and adhered to the activities of the Rev. Oszwald Oslay, Prior of the Fran- ciscan House in Eger. He was the initiator of that assistance movement which attempted to organize skillfully the Church's social-charitable activities so as to help the poor in such a way that they would constantly see only the supportive dimension of such help and thereby become receptive to the spiritual concerns and values of the Church. The public authorities agreed with this movement, since it was also within their interests to decrease social tension. Also, the organized social charitable effort took over a large part of the ever-increasing public burdens involved in caring for the poor.

Known throughout Europe were the so-called Elberfeld System, and the Strassburg and Frankfurt Systems, which attempted to obtain with the help of volunteer efforts the necessary means for the care of the poor. Within these systems, society itself was expected to take active part in the process of caring. The new system that originated in Eger had the expressed goals of ending begging, making better use of society's willingness to sacrifice through organized effort, providing more assistance to the poor by minimizing administrative expenses, guaranteeing a more human environment for those who needed help, making it possible for those reluctant to apply for assistance to be helped, and assuring social peace for the community by providing for the needs of the poor, at least on some minimal level. As a contemporary writer on social issues stated, it also provided for the spiritual care of the poor by placing love in the central position in their efforts at alleviating poverty.[6]

The provision of this Eger care was assured by a testamentary donation of a widow in Eger who deeded her house and 59 hectares of land to the Franciscans for the support of social welfare institutions. With this, the daily needs of five third-order Franciscan nuns—who considered social service as their life work—were provided for. This was further augmented by the income derived from their concession to sell religious articles at the local Franciscan monastery. The number of nuns engaged in this work grew to six by the end of 1927; at that time they moved into their own house and commenced their work.

By the end of 1927 the city officially became involved in the care of the poor. Under the chairmanship of the mayor, a so-called Commission on Poverty was established, which brought together all the relevant public (administrative, financial, educational) and social (cultural, religious, and charitable) organizations. The Commission charged with the care of the poor took care of the compilation of the survey of the poor and the collection of the financial means for this purpose. The Commission had only a single administrator, a law student, whose salary was paid by the city in order that the bulk of the collected money might be used for the purpose intended, specifically the care of the poor.

The Commission requested the merchants—who were being constantly visited by these beggars—to redeem their contributions to the beggars with a monthly donation. In return for this the merchants were to receive from the city a printed sign stating: "Begging is forbidden. The owner of this shop is making a monthly contribution for the support of the poor." Thus even the professional beggars were forced to report to the committee dealing with poverty and submit to the new rules.

After this the agitation for the new plan was conducted in the community. The city was divided into 24 districts and the populace was called upon by the social workers (the charitable ladies) with their collection lists in which the donations in the form of monthly offerings were duly noted.

The Commission held monthly meetings where the results and patterns of the collection activity were discussed. Some of the other issues dealt with were the care of the poor and related administrative matters. As a result of these efforts, beggars soon disappeared from the streets of Eger, and three months later the mayor was able to report to the city council the following achievements: 1. For the first time the city was enforcing the statute of 1905 concerning the elimination of begging, which for 23 years had only been a law on paper; 2. an office for the affairs of the poor had been established to which the poor could come with their complaints; and finally a call was issued to the citizens not to give in to beggars, but rather to give their donations to the charity ladies who would visit them on a regular monthly basis. In Eger at this time 44 ladies had volunteered for this task.

The actual care was provided by the district visitors who sought out the poor and prepared not only studies of living conditions, but actively participated in the care of the neglected sick and elderly. [7]

Putting aside for the moment the fact that even according to the Eger Norm it was not possible to solve completely the beggar problem in an industrial city—not even in Eger—there were many positive aspects to this volunteer social work. This was especially evident in the activities and methods of operation of the social workers who perceived their duties as a calling. Consequently, many other cities, especially medium-sized ones such as Eger, took over with greater or lesser success the Eger Norm in the years following.[8]

The partial success of the Eger Norm in the care of the poor induced the Ministry of Interior in 1936 to introduce this system of care as the "Hungarian Norm" in all cities, as well as in some smaller towns, but only with the consent of the chief county administrator in these towns. This was the intent of Decree No. 172.000:1936 of the Ministry of Interior. In the municipalities that introduced the Hungarian Norm, it was mandated that a permanent committee dealing with the poor be established under the leadership of the mayor or the chief magistrate of a town. It was also mandated that the representatives of the religious groups as well as the "suitable" charitable associations and institutions be invited to participate. In Budapest, under the direction of the district leaders, additional district committees for the care of the poor were established.

The task of these permanent committees was similar to that of the Eger Norm system. They compiled the list of those who were dependent on public assistance, prepared studies of living conditions, organized the collection of donations on the basis of the Eger Norm, and generally were supportive of these undertakings. Finally, the committees made proposals about the means of supporting those incapable of work (e.g. placement with institutions or with families) and the extent of support, based upon Articles 4-10 of the above-cited decree of the Minister of Interior.

The manner and method of utilizing public donations— whether in money or in kind—was to be determined by the mayor or chief magistrate of the town on the basis of the recommendations of the committees dealing with poverty issues. A separate register had to be kept about those incapable of working (the poor), and a separate one about those who were capable (the indigent). In addition to the personal data of those receiving support, these registers also recorded the nature of support, changes in marital status, employability, income, as well as changes in economic status. This decree of 1936 (Art. 14) also stated that when donations were received for the support of the poor incapable of working, no handling fees of any kind could be imposed. These donations had to be given to the poor as received.

The decree introducing the Hungarian Norm also forbade begging in those areas. Begging elsewhere was possible only on the basis of a permit. However, this permit could not be granted in cities, spas, or resorts, nor in localities where the Hungarian Norm had been introduced. According to the decree, "begging permits could be obtained only by Hungarian citizens who had reached the age of legal maturity, had not committed acts of immorality and public disorder, and had suffered such elemental calamity or personal injury through no fault of their own that they had become dependent on public support." (Art. 2, Par. 2). The permit was limited to the individual to whom it was issued and could not be transferred to anyone else. If, however, the permit holder was sick or could not engage in begging on account of his physical condition, it was mandated that the name of a relative be included on the permit who would then undertake the actual begging. This person, however, had to be a Hungarian citizen at least 18 years of age against whom there was no objection from a moral or public safety standpoint (Art. 14). The begging permit was issued by the chief administrative officer of a respective township, valid for that township only, and then only for a three-month period (Art. 3).

The Ministry of Interior was undoubtedly proud of the Hungarian Norm, which had been developed from the Eger Norm, because at an international social welfare congress held in London in 1936, the delegation of the ministry presented an extensive account of it and invited interested parties to visit Hungary and examine the Norm in action.

The Hungarian Norm had been introduced in most larger Hungarian cities by 1936. This did not mean that the beggars had everywhere disappeared from the streets, nor that those who had been beggars were everywhere provided for by the Hungarian public. The implementation of the Hungarian Norm, however, began a process that mobilized part of the population for social welfare activities.

An evaluation of the Hungarian Norm in a Hungarian setting was provided by the lecture of József Antall, Secretary of the Ministry of Interior, later a much respected organizer of Polish refugee affairs in Hungary, and then after World War II, the minister for recontruction. This took place at the National Sociopolitical Institute, where Antall stated that this concern had united the authorities, the religious groups, and various other segments of society in a common effort to solve the problem of poverty. In addition to the advantages of the Hungarian Norm, however, he also pointed out its non-satisfactory feature, including the method of collection. Antall was opposed to hiring money collectors, yet he pointed out that if the monthly collections were to be carried out by domestic servants—as has occurred on many occasions in the past—it would result in a decline of interest and good-will toward the whole undertaking. [9]

József Antall noted with appreciation the efforts of the religious sisters involved in the care of the poor, whose caring efforts provided the most support for the system. He noted with satisfaction that Decree No. 172.000:1936 of the Ministry of Interior had become a part of the public administrative structure and had been implemented in every city. In most cities the voluntary donations amounted to about one-fourth of one percent of the income of the donors.

Antall characterized the relationship of the Hungarian Norm and the charitable associations as follows: "The Norm does not wish to destroy the charitable associations, nor force them to follow other norms. It only wishes that they should work together; or if failing that, they should choose their beneficiaries from among those whose right to such support had been recognized by the city governments. They should also report the amount of the support for statistical purposes." [10]

*　*　*

After the introduction of the Hungarian Norm, the oppressive impact of the economic crisis ended and the government now had the means to introduce other sociopolitical policies. Thus, Act XIII of 1937 and Act XXXVIII of 1938 reconsidered and raised the family supplement payments of active public servants, while Act XXXVI of 1938 established a supplement for the education of the children of those working in industry and commerce, as well as for the children of workers in mines and foundries. At this time there emerged a certain collaboration in the organization of relief efforts between the government and the local autonomous bodies. Decree No. 198.000:1937 of the Minister of Interior tied together their respective functions and in order to advance institutional structuring decreed the establishment of County Public Welfare Funds. The goal of these Funds was to increase the financial base of public welfare and thus prevent the standard of living from falling below subsistence level, or where that had already occurred, to provide the necessary help. The County Public Welfare Fund was funded by a supplemental county tax of .25 to .5%, by occasional town or city subsidies, by voluntary donations, and by collections and governmental appropriations.[11] The relief efforts of the cities with their own municipal authority was supported from these same sources.

It was already mentioned that Act 1936:XXXVI had introduced compulsory old age insurance for stewards and farm managers, Act 1938:XXII established the foundations of old age insurance for those engaged in agricultural labor, and Act 1939:XVI guaranteed a minimal allowance of 60 *pengős* per month to all widows.

Even though it was not an issue of social insurance, but since it was a sociopolitical issue, it is important to take note of Act 1937:XXI, which, on the basis of the pertinent international accords, introduced the idea of the minimum wage in industry. At the same time, also on the basis of international accords, the law specified the maximum time of work. Finally, this law also numbered among its provisions the concept of paid vacations for industrial workers. It must be noted here that in terms of social benefits (family supplements, working hours, wages, paid vacations, etc.), public servants comprised a privileged category in Hungary.

Introduced not so much to modernize the care of the poor, but rather as a means to eliminate paid-in-kind relief work, the government established The National Foundation for Folk and Family Protection (*Országos Nép- és Család-védelmi Alap*) (Act 1940:XXIII) as a means of carrying out its social policies. It came to be known by its initials as *ONCsA*

In some respects, especially in terms of its impact on families, *ONCsA* achieved a measure of success. The minister speaking on behalf of this new policy argued that the government "has broken with that notion of absolute economic freedom" which wished to solve social problems with charitable assistance. The law promised "a comprehensive and planned, organically related, comprehensive socio-political" organization "which would provide for those who needed not only monetary assistance, but a permanent opportunity for a meaningful life and the assurance of a respectable livelihood." The promise in this form—certainly in part because of the coming of the war—could not become a reality. The National Folk and Family Defense Fund in its particular applications provided productive support to certain families, but this did not solve the economic problems everywhere.

The government—especially during the years of the Second World War, a gradually more crisis-ridden era for the ruling classes—assured quite significant sources of support for the National Folk and Family Defense Fund. Specifically the government offered 27% of the state fees collected and the total revenue of the folk and family defense supplementary tax which had replaced the relief tax. The minimum income from these sources could not have been less than 28 million *pengős* in 1940, 40 million in 1941, and 46 million in 1942. This amount would have increased from year to year because most of the support given from this Fund was in the form of loans. Moreover, with the exception of the amounts given to large families, which did not have to be repaid, the repaid loans would have been returned to the Fund.

ONCsA began to carry out extensive activity during the war years. In 1941 and 1942, more than 42 million *pengős* were provided for the building or purchase of homes. In the course of these two years 4,958 homes were built and another 1,916 started. [12] During this same period the public welfare cooperatives, which carried out the economic activity of the Fund, deeded 6,732 hectares of land to individuals and provided 14,832 hectares for leaseholding. The cooperatives also provided for use 2,053 horses, 9,964 heads of cattle, and 7,546 hogs. They also organized different kinds of household industries in horticulture, and established 220 handicraft cooperatives which employed 11,542 individuals. In 1942 *ONCsA* joined those organizations providing marriage loans, which could be paid back simply by having children. Finally, it also organized summer daycare centers.

If we also take into account the percentage of the population that needed support, it is not difficult to determine that even if *ONCsA* provided effective support for some large families, its short-lived activities can only be considered as the beginning of a new socio-political effort.[13] *ONCsA* operated with a rather large organizational structure and a large budget, which consumed some of those funds that could have been used for its charitable activities. Even though *ONCsA* was the most significant effort of the social policies of the interwar era, and its activities undoubtedly reduced the number of those still on the poverty rolls, its effots were unable to solve the poverty situation in Hungary.

* * *

Before dealing with the details of the foundation and activities of *ONCsA*, it is appropriate to summarize the development of the new social policies. We have already dealt with the formulation of Decree No. 198.000:1937 of the Ministry of the Interior which, breaking with simple relief efforts, attempted to develop a new direction with its public welfare orientation, for the present only on the level of the counties. They established public welfare committees in the counties, composed in part of members drawn from the municipal governments and in part of individuals active and competent in welfare work. They were appointed to these committees by the deputy county administrators. According to this decree the "public welfare executive administrator" would serve as the central county administrator for issues related to public welfare. At the same time, public welfare funds were also established in the counties, so that all income and expenses related to social concerns could be handled as a distinct entity. According to this decree, the public welfare administration could not expend its efforts merely by providing assistance or conducting charitable activities, but had to carry out an economically motivated public welfare program.

Subsequently, counties developed their own welfare administrative systems. For the administration of these activities they formulated a system of public welfare ordinances, which in turn assured the functioning of the economic structures and made possible the formation of the public welfare cooperative associations. These cooperative associations were mandated to establish various kinds of cottage industries and to engage in related economic activities, such as weaving, spinning, carving, bee-keeping, poultry and silkworm breeding, horticulture, viniculture, and others. Among the other tasks of the cooperatives were the encouragement of agricultural surplus production, support for the maximum utilization of industrial opportunities, and generally everything which augmented employment opportunities, created independent economic entities, and assured the growth of income opportunities. The cooperatives were also expected to organize courses of study for the acquirement and development of economic and industrial skills, provide scholarships to encourage participation in such activities, and also support artisans who lacked capital with interest-free loans.[14]

The county public welfare administrators prepared public welfare action plans, in which they included all of those possibilities that could advance the public welfare of the respective counties. Among the activities appearing in these action plans were efforts at increasing tourism, the revival of the folk arts movement, the development of cottage industries, hemp cultivation, wicker work, and the gathering of medicinal herbs. Also included were road construction, housing in the villages, shoe and clothing production, and the food service programs of the "Green Cross" public health organization. [15]

The year 1938 also witnessed extensive activity in the development of the public welfare administrative system. Decree No. 195,000:1938 of the Ministry of Interior stipulated that it would provide even to the lowest levels of the self-governing entities—the villages and the notarial districts—the necessary supporting personnel they needed, if these could be provided within the perceived needs and budgetary limitations. As stated by this decree, these personnel were "called upon to work cooperatively with those responsible for carrying out social welfare tasks in the villages and towns. In order to advance collaborative efforts, they were responsible to observe social trends and to master those legal, economic, and other fields of knowledge which enabled them to carry out their assigned tasks." Furthermore, the decree stated that "it will be the function of this support personnel in the villages and towns to expeditiously gather statistical information on local demographic patterns, economic conditions, and all related factors which were necessary for understanding and improving the social conditions of the populace."[16] The Minister of Interior at that time, Ferenc Keresztes-Fischer, born in Pécs, later functioned there as an attorney, and held the position of the county's Lord Lieutenant. He had come into contact there with Lajos Esztergár, one of the major exponents of social politics in interwar Hungary. Esztergár had formerly been the councillor for social affairs in Pécs. Later he became the mayor of that city, and then after the war, he briefly held the position of professor of administrative law. Esztergár had worked out the principles of social politics for the city of Pécs in an exemplary manner already before World War II, and his interests also extended to these issues on a national level as well. In these matters he was the advisor to Keresztes-Fischer for a number of years. The initiative in the social policies of that period—especially in the area of child and family protection, was connected primarily with the work of Lajos Esztergár and his colleagues.[17]

In addition to the village and township social service supportive personnel, in 1938 social councillors also appeared on the scene. At that time the Ministry of Interior proposed that in each county the government should appoint social affairs councillors "who are well informed about social conditions and are also familiar with the government's sociopolitical ideas." It was presumed that "as a consequence of their activities on the county level they could provide valuable information to the authorities."[18]

These social affairs councillors were undoubtedly chosen from among the most outstanding and best informed provincial social politicians, sociologists, sociographers, populist writers, and scholars in related disciplines. Thus, Ferenc Somogyi, a Professor of Law at the University of Pécs and a member of the Hungarian Parliament, became the social affairs councillor for Baranya county.[19]

The great experiment continued in 1939. After a conference at Pécs, the Minister of Interior announced a month long social affairs training workshop in Budapest. In its relevant decree (No. 640:1938)[20] the minister made references to the July 27, 1938 resolution of the council of ministers which decreed that the next (fourth) public administration training workshop would be devoted to social welfare concerns. The topic of the lectures would therefore be the administration of social welfare, including the work of the public authorities, offices, institutions, and other organs.

In accordance with the stated goals, the lectures and practical demonstrations informed the participants (mostly county and city officials who dealt with social affairs) about every aspect of social welfare administration. Thus, the lectures and demonstrations dealt with the following topics: the condition of the agricultural population, the industrial working class, those employed in private firms and households, the social care of public employees, institutions devoted to the welfare of students, the struggle against the high level of unemployment among the intelligentsia, the development of labor law, the so-called National Program of the Protection of Labor, the institutions of social insurance, the organization and institution of care for mothers and infants (the so-called "Green Cross" public health sercice), general issues of the welfare of children, guardianship, patronage, the courts dealing with minors, the institutions of public charity (public welfare funds), the care of the poor in cities and villages (including the status of the Hungarian Norm), and the work of institutions operating on the basis of public charters and fulfilling public tasks, i.e. the so-called "parastatalis" institutions such as the National Stefania Association, and the Hungarian Red Cross. In addition to the public bodies, careful attention was also paid to the nature and activities of the private institutions dealing with social care.

In general terms, the purpose of the workshop was to introduce "the new Hungarian social politics" and to foster a greater concern for social care by greater knowledge and also increase the social sentiment of the civil servants. As the minister himself acknowledged, "the success or failure of every social reform plan ultimately depends upon the work of the civil servants." In this case the organizers wished to follow with concern the relationship between the general organs of administration and the specialized agencies, on the one hand, and the social agencies, on the other; while also examining the extent to which these organs may make use of the social agencies. [21] One of the lectures was given by Professor Ferenc Somogyi, bearing the title: "The Turnover of Landed Estates and its Social Effects in Transdanubia." [22]

The following year the parliamentary debate of the bill dealing with folk and family protection, was presented to the Parliament by Ferenc Somogyi. The final bill reached the council of ministers only after lengthy discussions and ministerial rejections. Some of these problems stemmed from the Minister of Interior's earlier call for the establishment of a fund to support families with many children. As announced at the meeting of the council of ministers on August 17, 1938, support for this fund would come in part from an increased assessment upon childless adults, and in part from its rightful share of the inheritance of testators who were either childless or had only one child. Since the Prime Minister Pál Teleki supported the proposal, the council of ministers agreed to it in principle. He ordered, however, that the Minister of Interior, together with the Ministers of Finance and Justice, make the inheritance laws of other countries the object of their study. Only after the conclusion of this survey would the council of ministers be in a position to state its final position on these matters. [23]

A proposal concerning the establishment of a National Family Protection Fund was ready as early as the end of 1938. It proposed that this fund be established with income derived from the following sources: 1. the sum of inheritances passing legally to the national treasury; 2. amounts derived from a surcharge for family protection on legally specified fees for public services; 3. income from legally specified fines as determined by a court of law; 4. income derived from special ordinances for these purposes; 5. voluntary donations given for this purpose. The Minister of Interior, together with the Finance Minister, were to exercise control over this fund, and its use was to be specified yearly in the form of a bill submitted to parliament. [24]

Objections against this proposal were submitted first of all by the Ministers of Agriculture and Justice. The former attempted to extend his own authority over this fund, while the latter considered the increase in fees to be too high. [25]

Additional discussions were commenced in the council of ministers. First the Prime Minister and subsequently also Foreign Minister Csáky, and Minister of Culture and Religion Hóman were concerned with the size of the impositions and wished to see a reduction. [26] Keresztes-Fischer made certain concessions and thus the council of ministers at its meeting of June 14, 1940 agreed to the final form of the proposed bill and authorized the Minister of Interior to submit it to the Regent. [27] He did so on the very next day, and Regent Horthy approved it immediately (i.e. June 15, 1940), allowing the minister to place the bill for constitutional consideration before parliament. [28]

The Minister of Interior submitted the proposal to parliament already on June 19, 1940. In the governmental explanations it was pointed out that "in the development of any economic system a point is reached at a certain time when it becomes necessary to bring about such supportive and compensative acts which are suitable for the removal of its own extremes and anti-social manifestations." This is how it happened under early capitalism which preached unlimited freedom, "but also opened the way to an unlimited free competition, and at the same time exposed the hungering proletarian masses to the greatest squalor." This economic system searched for a solution in the universal extension of charitable assistance, and this expectation persists to our own day in many societies.

This type of charitable activity was also present in Hungary, where those who were temporarily endangered in their livelihood, were supported by poverty assistance or relief efforts. In the opinion of the Minister of Interior, however, these relief efforts, "even if upgraded, would not have been capable of solving the most serious social problems." It is a rather well-known fact that "relief efforts..., however well organized, are...nothing more than temporary solutions,

which are incapable of providing independent livelihood...
for those whose existence is endangered." [29] The Minister
of Interior, therefore, was right in his proposal to replace
the fragmented charitable efforts with comprehensive national solutions, represented by the activities of the proposed National Folk and Family Protection Fund.

The primary goal of the Fund was to be the protection
of the family. However, the support of the family was to be
manifested in all the activities of the state. Thus, the Fund
was to provide child support to all large peasant families who
were without such assistance. It was to be the task of the Fund
to place the state-sponsored child welfare program on new
foundations. Among its significant new initiatives were to
be the support of all state and municipal efforts that were
geared toward aiding such families in their entrepreneural
ventures. It also aimed to increase job opportunities and
to support changes in inheritance laws, particularly with
reference to the regional system of having only one child
in a family. It wished to start a propaganda campaign against
this tradition outside the formal educational system, while
also working to resolve the acute housing problem in the
country as a whole. Furthermore, it called for the establishment of a network of childrens' homes, public kitchens, and
boarding schools.

As stated earlier, the bill for this proposed Fund was
presented to the parliament by Ferenc Somogyi. In the course
of his speech Professor Somogyi—who by that time had written
a number of studies concerning family protection in Hungary— [30] pointed out that the principles of proper family
life were not always applied in Hungarian history. He illustrated this by a number of historical and sociological references, and then pointed out that popular opinion took note
of the sad consequences of this lack of family protection only
after the catastrophe of World War I. Somogyi then listed
some of the officially and privately organized manifestations on behalf of the Hungarian family, while also detail-
ing the struggle against the system of having only one child
in a family. He supplemented well-known facts with information based on archival research, and then asked that the
proposal be accepted.

Somogyi's presentation was followed by a wide-ranging and comprehensive debate. Even though the bill was opposed by the Arrow Cross (Nazi) delegation, and the Social Democrats expressed their lack of confidence in the government, the majority of the delegates still approved the proposal on July 5th. The bill was already before the Upper House on July 12th, where it was presented by Kálmán Papp, the prelate of the Sopron cathedral chapter. (After this he became Bishop of Győr.) Here too a comprehensive debate followed, but after a statement of the Minister of Interior, the bill was passed first in its general form and then in its particulars.

Act XXII of 1940 authorized the government to issue decrees concerning the establishment of the National Folk and Family Protection Fund. One of the decrees (7,000:1940 M.E.) established the National Social Affairs Board, which was built into the structure of the Ministry of Interior, which handled all social affairs. With the exception of responsibilities specifically reserved for the Minister of Interior, the National Social Affairs Board handled all social welfare affairs independently. At the head of the Board stood its administrative president—generally one of the under-secretaries of the ministry—and its functions were carried out by social affairs supervisors whose authority extended to a number of counties or cities. The first deputy of the administrative president of the Board was Ferenc Somogyi, the former social affairs supervisor of Baranya County, the City of Pécs, and of all of southern Transdanubia. In social welfare affairs the organizational structures of the counties and cities were accountable to the Board. In the counties there were everywhere public welfare executives, public welfare commissions for the conduct of financial affairs, and for the actual task of providing social services, there were also social workers, generally with a number of assistants.

Social services and the relevant financial and administrative work was aided by the cooperatives of the local social work volunteers. Among these, a special level was achieved by the so-called Organization of Tithers in the Transylvanian city of Kolozsvár, which was a well-functioning cooperative of the heads of prominent local families. It provided much assistance to the local social welfare office. At its head stood Lajos Puskás, a teacher and former scoutmaster, whose selfless social work was widely respected, not only in Kolozsvár, but throughout Transylvania. [31]

In the years 1941-1942, under the leadership of the National Social Affairs Board, a wide-ranging social welfare effort was conducted within the confines of the Folk and Family Defense Fund. The administrative president at that time, Under-Secretary Levente Kádár, issued a report which presented a detailed account, already cited in this study. It is important to note the Fund's significant organizational efforts to develop a nationwide social service training program. This training of the social workers had begun at Pécs in 1934 through the spirited efforts of Lajos Esztergár. This work was carried out by two university professors Ferenc Vasváry and Imre Dambrovszky, but under the direction of Esztergár and his major supporter in these efforts, Ferenc Somogyi. At the initiative of the National Social Welfare Board, a special social affairs course for social training was instituted in the academic year 1942-1943 at the Universities of Pécs, Szeged, Kolozsvár, and the József Nádor Technical University at Budapest. These programs offered high-level courses in social affairs for the students, lasting two academic years.

These sociopolitical efforts of interwar Hungary came to an end with the country's transformation into a socialist state after World War II. The socialist state follows a new direction for the solution of social problems. Nonetheless, Hungarian social politics, social thought, and social welfare activities during the latter part of the interwar period — especially the introduction of the Hungarian Norm and the resulting folk and family protection scheme—represent an edifying and in many respects productive chapter in the history of social welfare.

Notes

1. Act 1891:XIV permitted employees and their dependents not covered by insurance to join the ranks of the insured (par. 4.). Concerning this see Andor Csizmadia, *A szociális gondoskodás változásai Magyarországon* /Changes in Social Care in Hungary/ (Budapest, 1977), p. 64. The sections pertaining to Budapest were written by Mrs. András Csizmadia, dr. Erika Rothermel, assistant professor at the College of Public Administration.

2. Compare on this point Ernő Lőrincz, *A munkaviszonyok szabályozása Magyarországon a kapitalizmus kezdeteitől az első világháború végéig 1840-1918, különös tekintettel Erdélyre* /The Regulation of Working Conditions in Hungary from the Beginning of Capitalism to the End of the First World War, 1840-1918, with Special Emphasis on Transylvania/ (Budapest, 1973).

3. Concerning this consult Katalin Petrák and György Milei, eds., *A Magyar Tanácsköztársaság szociálpolitikája* /The Social Politics of the Hungarian Soviet Republic/ (Budapest, 1959).

4. Concerning these matters consult the publication of the Ministry of Justice, *A magyar szociális jogszabályok ismertetése* /A Review of Hungarian Statutes on Social Issues/ (Budapest, 1943).

5. Andor Balogh and Béla Kovrig, eds., *Társadalompolitikai feladataink:Az 1926. október 24-30-ig tartott közegészségügyi és társadalompolitikai értekezlet munkálatai* /Our Sociopolitical Tasks: The Proceedings of the Conference on Public Health and Sociopolitical Issues of October 24-30, 1926/ (Budapest, 1927), with the foreword of the president of the National Conference, Béla Földes.

6. Gusztáv Ladik, *Jóléti intézményeink* /Our Charitable Institutions/ (Budapest, 1940).

7. *Az egri szegénygondozás* /The Care of the Poor in Eger/ (Eger, 1928), published by the committee concerned with the care of the poor. In this work see especially Gusztáv Urbán, "Az egri szegénygondozás kifejlődésének története" /The Development of the Care of the Poor in Eger./ See also Archives of Heves County, Documents Concerning the City of Eger, Proceedings of the General Assembly: Resolution of the General Assembly, No. 1928:63.

8. Károly Pálos, *Szegénység, szegénygondozás* /Poverty and the Care of the Poor/ (Szombathely, 1934; 2nd revised edition, Újvidék, 1941). Kálmán Szathmáry, *A kecskeméti szegénygondozás. Az egri Magyar Norma kifejlődése és eredményei Kecskeméten* /The Care of the Poor in Kecskemét: The Development of the Eger Hungarian Norm and Its Accomplishments in Kecskemét/ (Kecskemét, 1935).

9. "Az 'Egri Norma' vagy újabban 'Magyar Norma' néven szereplő szegénygondozás ismertetése" /The Description of the Poor Care System known first as the "Eger Norm" and More Recently as the "Hungarian Norm"/, *Szociálpolitikai előadások* /Sociopolitical Lectures/, first series, vol. 2, (Budapest, 1938), pp. 551-567.

10. *Ibid.*, pp. 566-567.

11. Concerning their functioning see Ervin Pálos, *A vármegyei önkormányzatok társadalompolitikai feladatai* /Concerning the Functioning of the Sociopolitical Tasks of the Autonomous Counties/ (Eger, 1939).

12. Levente Kádár's report, *Nép- és családvédelem az 1940-42. évben* /Folk and Family Protection in the Years 1940-1942/ (Budapest, 1943), p. 137.

13. Concerning the development of folk and family protection and its connection with the issues of poverty see Ferenc Somogyi, "Ungarische Armen und Volkesfürsorge," *Donaueurope* (1941), pp. 387-394.

14. The Official Gazette of Tolna County, Oct. 14, 1937, no. 41, Acta 63 (16162 alisp. -1937).

15. Compare Gábor Mészáros, "Népélelmezés" /Public Food Program/, in Károly Mártonffy, ed., *A mai magyar szociálpolitika* /Hungarian Social Politics Today/ (Budapest, 1939), pp. 366-375.

16. A great role in the management of public service was held by the Minister of Interior Ferenc Keresztes-Fischer. He had been the Lord Lieutenant of Pécs and then Minister of Interior from 1931 to 1935. Following this, he became the president of the Central Corporation of Banking Companies, and then once again Minister of Interior, serving in that post from May 14, 1938 until March 22, 1944. He was arrested by the Gestapo on March 19, 1944, and then taken to Austria. He died there at Attersee on March 3, 1947.

17. The major work of Lajos Esztergár, *A szociálpolitika tételes jogi alapjai* /The Legal Foundations of the Statutory Provisions of Social Politics/ (Pécs, 1936).

18. National Archives, Budapest, K. 27. 1938, session of the council of ministers, Proceedings, no. 10, Aug. 17, 1938.

19. Ferenc Somogyi commenced his scholarly career as a legal historian and student of the eminent professor Zoltán Kérészy. His dissertation for the university lectureship was entitled: *Végrendelkezés nemesi magánjogunk szerint 1000-től 1715-ig* /Testamentary Disposition According to the Civil Law of Our Nobility from the Year 1000 to 1715/ (Pécs, 1937). In addition to legal scholarship, however, Somogyi soon became interested in social welfare issues which were being studied at the School of Law of the University of Pécs. He thus came into contact with Lajos Esztergár, one of the prime movers of welfare reform. Together they edited the proceeding of the conference on sociopolitics which they organized at Pécs in January 1939. Published under the title *A magyar szociálpolitika feladatai* /The Tasks of Hungarian Social Politics/, in the volume Esztergár mapped out the desired path of the new Hungarian social welfare policy, while Somogyi attempted to clarify the theoretical aspects of the solutions to existing social problems and to come up with solutions based on the comparative study of these issues. See the introductory study to this volume by the two editors.

20. National Archives, Budapest, K. 27. Proceedings of the council of ministers, July 27, 1938, no. 4.

21. The study aids for the workshop were collected and published in the same year by the organizer and spirited leader of the course, Károly Mártonffy, *A mai magyar szociálpolitika* /Hungarian Social Politics Today/ (Budapest, 1939).

22. Published in the above-cited volume, pp. 622-629.

23. National Archives, Budapest, K. 27., Proceedings of the council of ministers, August 17, 1938, no. 11.

24. National Archives, Budapest, K. 150., 2999, 1-10, 1940-I-b., p. 521.

25. National Archives, Budapest, 3136/1939. Eln. 2. FM official communication to the Ministry of the Interior with the documents numbered K. 150-2799-I-10-g-1940-I-b-521. In the same location is the official communication from the Minister of Justice, numbered T. 115/78.

26. National Archives, Budapest, K. 27, 1939. Proceedings of the council of ministers, November 24, 1939, no. 5; December 1, 1939, no. 2.

27. National Archives, Budapest, K. 27, 1940. Proceedings of the council of ministers, June 14, 1940, no. 20.

28. The original submission and Horthy's consent can be found in the Hungarian National Archives, Budapest, 524/1940, I-b. BM among the documents with the following base number: K 150-2799-I-10-g-1940-I-b-521.

29. The quote is from the justification for the bill, Session of Parliament 1939-1944, Papers of Parliament, vol. 4, p. 338.

30. Somogyi's relevant studies include: *Az ősiség intézménye és a hűbéri vagyonjog* /The Institution of Entailment and Feudal Property Rights/ (Pécs, 1931), and *Társadalompolitikai törvényalkotás Werbőczy után* /Social Legislation After the Age of Werbőczy/ (Kassa, 1944).

31. Puskás died in Kolozsvár in 1982. See his necrolog: "Halotti beszéd helyett—Puskás Lajos temetéséről" /In Place of a Memorial Speech — On the Occasion of the Death of Lajos Puskás/, *Új Ember* /The New Man/, May 2, 1982. Concerning the operation of Puskás's Tithing scheme, see his *Tizedesség és a kolozsvári tizedesek* /Tithing and the Tithing System at Kolozsvár/ (Kolozsvár, 1942); and Andor Csizmadia, "A kolozsvári tizedesek" /The Tithers of Kolozsvár/, *Nép- és családvédelem* /Folk and Family Protection/ (Budapest, 1942), pp. 298-306.

Sarolta B. Somogyi:

20 / SOCIAL WORK IN HUNGARY BETWEEN 1940 AND 1945

As defined by Walter A. Friedlander in his well-known work on social welfare, "social work is a professional service, based upon scientific knowledge and skill in human relations, which assists individuals, alone or in groups, to obtain social and personal satisfaction and independence." [1] Undoubtedly, the desire to make life livable is a most important part of any social service that is there to advance human welfare in an organized manner with the help of professionals called "social workers." The latter are really "community trouble-shooters. Through direct counseling, referral to other services, or policy-making and advocacy, they help individuals, families, and groups cope with their problems." [2] As such, social workers have to be well-educated persons who have drawn their knowledge for improving human conditions from a wide variety of disciplines, including sociology, psychology, psychiatry, economics, medicine, anthropology, biology, and even history, political science, education, and philosophy. [3]

In Hungary, this knowledge-base of social welfare was developed and expanded particularly in the period between l940 and l945, when the socio-political perspective was conducive to such developments. The overall objective of the new social welfare policy of those critical years of the period of World War II required that every Hungarian citizen should feel that there exists a mutual relationship of obligations and benefits between Hungarian society and all of its members, and that in case of need, society would be there to take care of all of its needy members. [4]

* * *

435

The origin of social welfare goes back to ancient times. We can find traces of it in the teachings and cultures of all major religions and civilizations. This is particularly true for Judaism and Christianity, where this practice reaches back to the Old Testament roots of these religions. As summarized by Friedlander: "The teachings of the prophets of Israel and of St. Paul, St. Augustine, St. Francis, and St. Thomas Aquinas in the Christian Church gave the recipient of alms dignity, whereas alms-giving ennobled the generous donor. The early Christians helped one another when facing poverty and persecution, but the medieval Church entrusted the administration of charity to the bishops, local priests, and the deacons." [5]

For centuries, it was the Church that took responsibility for providing charity. The first significant step toward organized lay public relief was the Poor Law of 1601 in England. [6] A concerted social welfare policy which had as its goal the orderly organization, co-ordination, and direction of all major aspects of society's functions, activities, and goals emerged only in most recent times, more specifically at the beginning of the 19th century, when it began to assume an increasingly important role in human society. [7]

The situation in Hungary was no different. The same pressures that forced other societies to adopt new ways of dealing with the problems faced by their members also acted upon Hungarian society. Industrialization, urbanization, technological changes, and the gradual reduction of the role and significance of agriculture created a new social environment and ended much of the family and communal social welfare system that had been associated with the traditional peasant way of life.

At the same time, this free economic (i.e., capitalistic) environment, which did not have mercy on traditions and recognized no restraints, also spawned widespread exploitation, misery, and poverty. In fact, it threatened with personal failure, spiritual defeat, and even extinction all of those who were unable to compete under the new circumstances. The resulting social incongruities were bound to lead to new social problems and protracted class conflicts. Thus, providing cure for these problems and smoothing out the glaring social and economic differences quickly became one of the highest priorities facing governments throughout the world.

These were the conditions that led to the development of organizations that were devoted to social assistance and welfare. At the same time new legal codes were formulated that were designed—along with the various economic reforms—to impose some controls on the unhampered power of the free economic system. It was hoped that by doing so, the negative or exploitive manifestations of this system could be limited, and thereby a more harmonious and liveable society would come into being. This search for harmony and satisfaction was also designed to prevent the rise of social unrest and thus ensure the continued existence and peace in human society.

* * *

In Hungary, the various governments began their social reform efforts immediately after the appearance of the symptoms of poverty and social unrest. As such, all social welfare laws passed during the first half of our century had their roots in the latter part of the 19th century. Unfortunately the world-wide economic dislocations—including mass emigration that hit Hungary very hard—prevented the implementation of lasting and comprehensive solutions during those early years.

There was some progress in the early 20th century, but the outbreak of World War I had put an end to all of these efforts. After World War I, the dismemberment of historic Greater Hungary only added to the existing social ills and tensions, and also imposed additional economic and social burdens on the mutilated country and its people. During the 1920s it became increasingly evident that the social problems confronting the nation could not be resolved through the unfocused attention and uncoordinated activities of a few scattered organizations.[8] It also became clear that the only way to achieve true success in the area of social welfare was to concentrate the attention and energies of the whole country upon this question.[9]

* * *

This awareness for the need of a general social welfare reform in Hungary was paralleled by the recognition of a number of specific social ills in the country, including the custom of artificially limiting the number of children per family to one through the use of illegal and dangerous abortion techniques. This practice was extremely widespread in Hungary, and it was undoubtedly a partial reflection of the general fear of bringing children into the world whom they could not support. But as this practice began during the country's Turkish occupation in the 16th and 17th centuries, another factor may have been the people's refusal to raise children under foreign domination. Although the Turkish occupation ended in the 1699, this practice continued right into the 20th century.

The first step to put an end to this phenomenon known as *egykézés* (having only one child) was taken by the Reformed minister Sándor Széles. He began a campaign against this practice in the fall of 1921. [10] This initiative was followed by several others, including that of Géza Antal, Bishop of the Transdanubian Region of the Hungarian Reformed Church, who on November 10, 1925 demanded that laws be passed to alleviate all conditions and root out all social preceptions that feed this phenomenon. Among others, he recommended the creation of a centralized agency to deal with this problem.

Based on these initiatives, the Hungarian Parliament entrusted the preparation of the needed laws and the planning of the proposed organization to the newly created Ministry of Welfare. [11] The necessary bill to start the whole process was prepared and introduced by János Láng, on the basis of which the Ministry of Welfare was instructed to develop appropriate laws to deal with the problem of *egykézés*. During the same period, based on an initiative coming from the County of Tolna, the country's legal authorities were also instructed to look into this problem and to take some action in so far as possible. [12]

The first bill addressing this question was introduced into the Hungarian Parliament on March 12, 1927, but the Lower House never took it under consideration, even though Hungarian public opinion and many of the county authorities were pressing for the passage of such a law. As a matter of fact, the Parliament failed to take serious action on this problem until the fall of 1938, [13] when it did so under the influence of Hungary's success in having regained from Czechoslovakia some former Hungarian territories lost in the Peace Treaty of Trianon in 1920. [14] At that time the Minister of Interior appointed special "social councelors" as advisors to the Lord

Lieutenants (*főispáns*) of each county. (The *főispáns* were the chief appointed political representatives of the government at the county level, while the Deputy Lord Lieutenants or *alispáns* were the chief administrative officers of the counties.)[15]

* * *

One of the major exponents of planned social reform in interwar Hungary was Lajos Esztergár, a noted legal scholar, who had worked out the principles of social politics for his native city of Pécs in an exemplary manner during the 1930s.[16] Esztergár's ideas were best implemented elsewhere by Antal Streicher, the Deputy Lord Lieutenant (*alispán*) of Szatmár County, whose practical application of these plans in that overpopulated northeastern county of Hungary lessened the problems of the agricultural workers considerably. Streicher's successful experiments in Szatmár County soon gave rise to the hope that their general application would solve many of the problems of the agricultural workers throughout Hungary.

With these successes behind them, the proponents of the bill on social assistance had now high hopes for their legislative proposal. Even so it took some time and effort, for the relevant Act XXIII of 1940 was not passed for another year and a half.[17]

Act XXIII of 1940 established the National Foundation for Folk and Family Protection (*Országos Nép- és Családvédelmi Alap*) known by its Hungarian acronym as *ONCsA*. It had the threefold charge of improving living conditions, lessening social polarization, and encouraging increased birthrate. All three of these goals were "to be achieved primarily through the support and advancement of the class of people who required economic, moral, and spiritual assistance from society." [18]

Act 1940:XXIII defined the National Foundation for Folk and Family Protection (*ONCsA*) as an institution whose specific goals were to include: 1. Providing organized support to families with many children; [19] 2. supporting the institutionalized protection of large families; 3. aiding the families of agricultural and industrial workers in buying or building homes, in relocating them in case of need, in improving their agricultural yield or starting them off in new business ventures, and in familiarizing them with the various existing social programs; 4. providing specific financial assistance to families or individuals who met certain criteria; and 5. making provisions for issues and situations that may have an impact on the achievement of these goals. [20] All of these goals were covered by the funding provisions of the Bill. [21]

The *ONCsA* established an independent central office called "National Social Welfare Superintendency" (*Országos Szociális Felügyelőség*) that was to oversee the implementation of these goals. This function provided the Superintendency control over ninety-five welfare cooperatives throughout the country whose organizational activities were now to be directed and coordinated from above. It also gave the Superintendency the right to coordinate the work of the social workers nationwide. It is not necessary here to deal with the problems and difficulties faced by the National Social Welfare Superintendency in implementing this law on social welfare. It is adequate to point out that — although under the direction of the Superintendency — the actual social work was performed by professional social workers. [22]

These social workers were assigned as aides to public servants and various local administrators throughout the country.[23] Because of their dual responsibilites as social workers and as consultants on social welfare matters, their official designation was not "social worker," but "social referee" (*szociális szakelőadó*). This fact made the Hungarian social workers and the work they performed almost unique among the nations of the modern world. For the sake of convenience, however, we shall continue to refer to them in this study simply as social workers.

In line with the requirements of Act 1940:XXIII, the Deputy Lord Lieutenant (*alispán*) of every county, the administrative officer (*főszolgabíró*) of every district (*járás*), and each mayor of a district-level municipality (*megyei város*), was assigned a social worker. [24] These individuals had responsibilites to oversee all social work in their respective regions, as well as to act as social referees to their administrative superiors.

Professional social workers were assigned in this manner so as to have support for their work by people of authority, who in turn were obliged to consult their social workers on all issues concerning social welfare. Naturally, the social worker assigned to the Deputy Lord Lieutenants had authority over social workers in charge of various districts or municipalities in their respective counties.

It is also important to note that each Deputy Lord Lieutenant had to appoint a separate welfare referee from among the officers of the county. [25] This referee was the same county officer who was assigned to provide administrative support to the social worker.

Every goal of the *ONCsA* was interpreted and recommended for action by the appropriate social worker, who took all the necessary steps to bring each issue before the decision-making authorities of the appropriate county, district, or city. The social worker was also involved in the process of implementation, and was personally responsible for maintaining contact with the families that were to receive assistance. [26] This responsibility and full involvement from the start to the finish made the role of a social worker very important.

One of the secrets of the success of this social welfare program during the period of World War II was the fact that social assistance was provided not in a formal, insensitive manner, but rather in a personal and affectionate way. In other words, the social worker was personally and intimately involved in the support-structure of this aid program, as well as in delivering this assistance to the needy families or individuals. [27]

Precisely because of the emotional and psychological implications of delivering social welfare, the National Foundation for Folk and Family Protection did not hire just anyone to perform social work. Prospective social workers had to fulfill certain specific requirements, such as displaying a sense of vocation, being people of ability and of impeccable morals, and qualifying themselves through specific courses of study. The applicants' fitness and dedication to vocation were determined by the appropriate authorities at the National Social Welfare Superintendency. Only then did hiring and assignment to specific jobs take place. [28]

Initially, the training of prospective social workers was provided by the Hungarian Red Cross. Later this obligation was assumed by the Catholic Order of the Sisters of Social Charity in the cities of Budapest and Kolozsvár; [29] and still later by Hungary's four universities in specially designed courses on social welfare, [30] as provided for by a special governmental decree. [31]

The university-level program required two years of study, and it was basically divided into three semesters of course work and one semester of on-the-job training. The former of this involved fifty-one concept-oriented course sessions and sixteen hours of seminar workshop; the latter was a twenty-four week internship in the course of which the trainees had to go through sixteen different types of work environments. This was followed by two separate comprehensive examinations that tested the students' socio-political knowledge both in theory and practice. [32]

This comprehensive and broadly based university-level program was required of all prospective social workers because the *ONCsA* demanded that its social workers be able to perform on a high level of competence in seven different areas. These included the following: 1. The identification of all large families and idividuals requiring social and economic assistance; 2. monitoring the conditions of these families and individuals; 3. organizing social support cells in the individual communities; 4. making recommendations of specific nature relative to the needs of large families; 5. supplying family care to these families; 6. forming and nurturing a spirit of social responsibility in the communtities; 7. and maintaining the records of these functions and reporting on the status of individual cases. [33]

At the focus of these functions and obligations was the need to support families with many children through specific recommendations and with actual financial, material, and moral help. Both of these required the social worker or referee to be skilled at observing, drawing conclusions, and making specific recommendations about the conditions in which the individual families lived.

The study of the surroundings was used to determine the specific nature, type, and extent of the family's needs for normal human existence. The recommendations based on these observations were very varied and diverse, the single most important and potentially the most costly of these being the recommendation concerning housing needs. Precisely because of the difficulty in implementing the goals concerning proper housing, the National Foundation for Folk and Family

Protection went to work to establish so-called "*ONCsA Communities*" throughout the country. [34]

In addition to proposing solutions concerning housing, the social worker could also recommend the financing of repairs or additions to existing houses, as well as supplying land and equipment for peasant and/or artisan families so as to make them economically independent. [35]

The social workers were also required to provide spiritual and moral support for needy families, to generate a mood or public opinion conducive to aiding such families, and to organize a local community effort to accommodate the needs of such families on a long term basis. These goals included close cooperation with churches, social clubs, and other local associations, so that some of the efforts of these organizations could also be redirected and focused on the long-term social welfare needs of families and individuals. [36]

To supplement all of the above measures, in 1942 a decree of the Ministry of Interior [37] directed the establishment of local committees in all counties to deal with the problem of family protection. Each town and village was also obliged to organize teams of volunteers to assist this work. That this decree was taken seriously is demonstrated by the fact that by the end of 1942 over two-thirds of all Hungarian municipalities and villages had such functioning teams (i.e., 4421 out of 6152 villages and 70 county-level municipalities). [38] Working very closely with the local social workers, these teams were successful in accomplishing some very significant social welfare reforms and in initiating a number of useful programs.

If the successes of the next two years are also taken into consideration, then we must conclude that the new social welfare policies introduced into Hungary at the beginning of World War II were indeed most successful, notwithstanding the brevity of the time available to its apostles and executors. Nor should we forget that much of this success depended on the competence and self-sacrificing dedication of the newly trained social workers, who had done much to move the country forward on its path of needed social reform. The structure, mode of operation, scope, and approach to the solution of social problems of their parent organization, the

ONCsA, was truly unique. For this reason, the achievements of these social workers stand alone in the annals of social work, and their performance can serve even today as an example to others throughout the world.

Notes

1. Walter A. Friedlander, *Introduction to Social Welfare*, 3rd ed. (Englewood-Cliffs, NJ: Prentice-Hall, 1968), p. 4.

2. U.S. Department of Labor, Bureau of Labor Statistics, *Occupational Outlook Handbook. 1984-1985* (Washington, DC: U.S. Government Printing Office, 1984), p. 88.

3. Friedlander, *Introduction*, p. 6.

4. Ferenc Somogyi, "A magyar szociálpolitika története" /The History of Hungarian Social Welfare Policy/, in *Szociális Magyarország* /Social Hungary/, ed. Ede v. Faragó (Budapest: Athenaeum, 1943), pp. 15-46, reference to p. 15.

5. Friedlander, *Introduction*, p. 10.

6. A. B. McPadden, "Social Work," in *New Catholic Encyclopedia* (San Francisco and Toronto, 1966), XIII, pp. 361-364.

7. Somogyi, "A magyar szociálpolitika," p. 15.

8. Ferenc Somogyi, "Szociális törekvések és eredmények Trianon után" /Social Aspirations and Accomplishments after Trianon/, in *Históriás Kalendárium* /Historical Calendar/ (Youngstown, OH: Katolikus Magyarok Vasárnapja, 1953), pp. 33-48, reference to p. 33; reprinted in the journal *Vagyunk* /We Exist/, vol. IX (1956), pp. 97-112, reference to p. 97.

9. *Ibid.*, p. 109.

10. The name of Rev. Sándor Széles's movement was *"Magyar Fajmentő Misszió"* /Mission for the Protection of Hungarian Ethnicity/.

11. The referee for the proposed law was Levente L. Kádár from the Ministry of Welfare, who later became Under Secretary of State for Internal Affairs, as well as the Executive President of the National Foundation for Folk and Family Protection.

12. The Transdanubian counties of Baranya and Somogy had already sent memoranda on this issue to the government as early as 1906.

13. October 11 and November 6-10, 1938, respectively.

14. Some former Hungarian territories were regained from Czechoslovakia on the basis of the First Vienna Award of October 5, 1938.

15. I am using the British terms "Lord Lieutenant" for *főispán* and "Deputy Lord Lieutenant" for *alispán*, as they reflect better the respective positions and powers of these officials than do the American terms "County Commissioner" and "Deputy County Commissioner." It is to be noted here that in 1938 Professor Ferenc Somogyi of the Royal Elizabeth University of Pécs was appointed the "Social Counselor" for the County of Baranya, which was one of the hotbeds of *egykézés*, i.e. the practice of having only one child per family. Later Professor Somogyi was named the Social Superintendent as well as Executive Vice President of the National Social Welfare Superintendency.

16. The Hungarian social welfare policy ended the earlier relief system. Cf. Somogyi, "Szociális törekvések," p. 110.

17. In the Lower House of the Hungarian Parliament the referee of this bill was Professor Ferenc Somogyi, who represented the City of Pécs.

18. Act XXIII of 1940.

19. The Hungarian welfare reform law (Act 1940:XXIII) uses the term "*sokgyermekes*" (with many children), which in this context refers to families with at least four or more children.

20. One of the goals of the law of 1940 was to aid families in becoming active participants in the nation's socio-political life, and in the activities of its various public institutions.

21. The income of the National Foundation for Folk and Family Protection (*ONCsA*) was derived from the following sources: 1. 27% of all national duties, the total of which was to amount to no less than 28 million *pengős* in 1940, 41 million *pengős* in 1941, and 46 million *pengős* for 1942 and beyond; 2. specific surtax for folk and family protection that was originally authorized by Paragraph 29, Act I of 1922, for relief purposes; 3. and all future donations and bequests to the Foundation. In 1942 and 1943, these combined sources provided a total of 120 million *pengős* to the Foundation. Cf. Somogyi, "Szociális törekvések," p. 111.

22. Ferenc Somogyi, ed., *Nép és családvédelem az 1940-1942. évben* /Folk and Family Protection in the Years 1940-1942/ (Budapest: Magyar Királyi Állami Nyomda, 1943), pp. 16-21.

23. Decree No. 1522: 1941 of the Ministry of Interior.

24. Paragraphs 7 and 8 of Decree No. 7000: 1940 of the Ministry of Culture and Education.

25. Decree No. 47: 1941 of the President of the National Social Welfare Superintendency.

26. Somogyi, *Nép- és családvédelem*, p 62.

27. *Ibid.*, p. 61.

28. *Ibid.*, p. 117.

29. *Ibid.*, p. 63.

30. *Ibid.*, p. 77.

31. Decree No. 4150: 1942 of the Ministry of Culture and Education.

32. Those enrolled in the social welfare program at Hungarian universities were generally full-time students, who in many cases already had university degrees, including some doctorates.

33. Somogyi, *Nép- és családvédelem*, p. 69.

34. *Ibid.*, pp. 136-153.

35. *Ibid.*, pp. 154-159.

36. *Ibid.*, pp. 95-109.

37. Decree No. 528.797: 1942 of the National Social Welfare Superintendency (*OSzF*).

38. Somogyi, *Nép- és családvédelem*, p. 125.

Michael Sozan: *

21 / THE PILLAR OF HUNGARIAN SOCIETY: THE "GOOD PEASANT"

Introduction

With the collectivization of agriculture in Eastern Europe during the 1950s and 1960s, rural society entered a new stage of social evolution. A widely shared diagnosis given by Marida Hollos and Béla Maday is that "collectivization...eliminated the use of private property as the criterion for social standing...and the values of rural society have undergone a tremendous upheaval."[1] Most scientific observers would also agree with Peter Bell that this "transformation has been one of the greatest examples in history of large scale social engineering (exceeded in magnitude only by that in the Soviet Union and China)."[2] Katherine Verdery asserted that "there are...unprecedented elements in the current situation: today's state is right in the villagers' midst as it never was before, and it has effectively decreed their disappearance altogether as qua peasants, through collectivization and the developement of industry."[3] A lone voice of dissent comes from British ethnographer, Chris Hann, who after years of observation, concluded that "there has yet been relatively little change in rural life styles."[4]

Of the innumerable ramifications of this "large scale social engineering," the most obvious and quantifiable result is in the area of agricultural output. Statistics indicate that today, collectivized agriculture produces more food than private farming has ever done.[5] Whether a free market private

------

*Deceased

farming system in Eastern Europe would exceed present-day production levels, and prove to be socially healthier than collective farming is another question. Collective farms in Hungary are now producing more than sufficient amount of food, and it appears that the gravest of the agrarian problems, such as rural unemployment, poverty, malnutrition, class differences, and other forms of social injustice, are remedied— at least for the time being. Of the many reasons for this success one may cite the New Economic Mechanism (NEM), through which more flexible marketing practices and incentives were introduced, but another cause of this relative prosperity, in my opinion, is the role of the ex-middle peasant in farm management. According to Hungarian sociologists and my own first-hand observations, the socialist sector capitalized on the work ethic and managerial talents of the ex-middle peasants. Sociological investigations revealed that the leadership of the communal farms is dominated by ex-middle or well-to-do peasants.[6] Hanák, for example, concluded in a national survey that "the economically more prosperous peasants had a much higher rate of success in becoming cooperative managers and technical experts than any other social strata." [7]

Considering their disproportionately high profile in socialist farm organizations, the middle peasant is well worth scientific inquiry, especially in light of the scarcity of information on this social stratum. The present paper will limit itself to a historical inquiry about the middle peasant of pre-World War II Hungary.

Who were the middle peasants? How did they form a social entity? What role did they play in village society prior to collectivization? Observers noted that these agriculturists— sometimes referred to as "proper"[8] or "good" [9] peasants, were the most dynamic segment of rural Hungary, and beyond the visible or artifactual achievements, they acted as the primary upholders of peasant culture. This stratum embraced many of the national characteristics that were perceived by both rural and urban intellectuals as desirable for historical and contemporary Hungary. Middle peasants were an agricultural stratum with an adequate amount of land and related agricultural wealth, to afford them economic independence; to generate income for the schooling of those children who did not want to continue their parents' profession; to maintain a harsh but respectable lifestyle, and a high profile in village affairs. They had a reputation for being self-reliant and entrepreneurial. Their family was synonymous with their unit of production and husbandry /*gazdálkodás*/. They drove themselves hard in unceasing competition for village prestige and power. The husbandman or *gazda* was a confident man, his wife a self-respecting, self-denying strict mother and a household boss, and the children well-behaved, hard workers by age ten. As a social stratum, the middle peasants class consciousness surpassed that of any other stratum, and exhibited a good deal of cohesion within village society.

Middle peasants excelled in the elaboration and exploitation of traditional peasant culture, while they showed skill in incorporating low-cost but rational innovations within their farming methods. Ruthless in their drive to maximize available natural and human resources, they embraced a puritanical if not stoic outlook on life. In their insistence on retaining and increasing the ancestral land, they earned the admiration and envy of the rest of society. In a troubled and socially stagnant society as Hungary was, the middle peasant was also called upon as a national revitalizer (viz., Dezső Szabó's novel, *Az elsodort falu* (*The Village that was Swept Away*). Political leaders began to coopt the middle peasant in the Independent Smallholders' Party which became the only oppositional party during the conservative years of the 1930s and 1940s. Following World War II this party captured the majority of votes and led the coalition government until the Soviets decided to dismantle all but the Communist Party.

A few words about interwar Hungary should precede my analysis. As a part of the defeated Austro-Hungarian Empire, losing three-fourths of its land, the country experienced grave economic displacement. Historians judged the nation economically to be somewhere between the Balkan and Western European nations, possibly on the level of Spain, Italy or Poland.[10] Its industrial output lagged well behind that of Western Europe, while its agriculture was stymied by anachronistic socioeconomic circumstances. Two of the most striking features included the disproportionate land ownership patterns (favoring the rich), and a severe shortage of capital funds. Fifty-four percent of the arable land was owned by only

1.7% of the landowners, and 75% of the holdings amounted
to only 10% of the arable land. The middle peasant, whose
arable land was between 11 and 28 hectares, comprised 4.5%
of the landowning class and held only 13.5% of the land.[11]
Although there are no statistical data on the agricultural
output of each stratum, contemporary eyewitnesses and
testimonies by peasants accredit the middle peasant a
disproportionately higher production level than either the
wealthy or the poor strata. This must be a remarkable
achievement in light of the fact that the middle peasant
employed a minimum amount of mechanization and wage
labor.

The Village of Aba: Environment and History

For the purpose of gaining special insight into the life of
the middle peasant, I selected a single village in Central
Hungary known for its "good" peasants. The village Aba
(population 4,026 in 1981), where I conducted anthropological fieldwork in 1983, is located 100 kms west of Budapest, and
29 kms south of Fejér County's seat, Székesfehérvár.[12] Its
immediate vicinity, referred to as the *Mezőföld* is flatland with
good to excellent soil. Geologically the *Mezőföld* is a part of the
Great Plain, the "breadbasket of Hungary". The area now
comprising the township of Aba (8,806 hectares), has been
settled by various people since the Neolithic Revolution (3000
B.C.). There were Celtic tribes, Romans, Etruscans, Longo-
bards and Avars prior to the arrival of the Hungarians in the
9th century.[13] Following the formation of the Hungarian
feudal state (11th century) kings encouraged semi-nomadic
herding people, such as the Pechenegs and the Cumans to
settle in this region. Since the area was in the immediate
vicinity of the capital, Székesfehérvár, the monarch drew on
these groups for political support against feudal lords.[14]

The *Mezőföld* was an ideal environment for the herdsmen:
swamplands alternated with grazing fields and hay meadows,
while the Sárviz River with its generous flow of water made the
region difficult to penetrate by outside forces. Tribal
sovereignty was insured for centuries. The Pechenegs and the
Cumans, retained their immense cattle, horse, and sheep
herds, and according to local tradition, they still practiced

shamanism two hundred years ago. Their sense of independence and pride survived to the present day. Many of the good peasants of Aba claim Pecheneg heritage.

Aba is first mentioned as a place and property /*possessio*/ in 1334 (over 650 years ago) when János, the son of Salamon sued János, the son of Lőrinc, for a certain amount of land, which included possessions of Guth, Athya and Aba. Such medieval documents indicate that a few of the titular owners of the village and township were of high noble rank. Especially important were some by the name of Abai, who played increasingly significant roles as kingsmen. Another family of high rank was the Aran, or Arany, which was first mentioned in a 1498 suit against István Szapolyai, Hungary's palatinate /*nádor*/. This family has burgeoned into more than a dozen distinct branches, which survived until the 20th century as wealthy and middle peasants. [15]

With the ascent of the Ottomans in Hungary, Aba fell to Turkish rule in 1543. During the 150-year long occupation, the rich landlords fled to the western and northern parts of Hungary, and the commoners relocated the village in an inaccessible area well inside the swampland. [16] When the Turks were finally driven out of Hungary in the late 17th century, Aba's landlords returned with additional "copossessors" (the Fördős, Fiáth, and Buús families). They began asserting themselves more vigorously than ever before, subjugating the population into the ranks of serfs and cotters. While some freemen could not escape feudal bondage, others were able to retain their rank as "lesser nobility." Among these so-called "seven-plum-tree-noblemen" were the descendants of the Pechenegs and Cumans, as well as the Magyar Arany families.

At the time of Hungary's first official census (1784-1787) the adult noblemen of Aba numbered 55, which indicates that there were more than 200 people in Aba of noble standing. [17] In a population of 1,100 they were of considerable political and economic significance. By 1828 the number of noble males increased to 109. [18] Most of them were Protestant and resided close to their church in the Öreg (old) Street—each family on its own estate. Six additional noble families resided on serf plots, but there were the above mentioned wealthy noblemen (Arany, Fiáth, Fördős, Buús) who owned two-thirds of the township. [19]

Judging from cadaster maps and last wills and testaments, the estate of a lesser nobleman was not much more prosperous than that of a well-to-do serf, and in some cases his standard of living fell short of that of his subservients. However, his minimal taxes and spatial and social mobility gave him advantages vis-à-vis the serfs and cotters. Radical changes did not take place until the Revolution of 1848, when the serfs and cotters (approximately 1,500 people in Aba) were liberated, becoming owners of the land they cultivated in lieu of corvèe. Henceforth the lesser nobility lost their titles and privileges and began to compete for the scarce resources with the liberated new peasants. Many of the lesser nobility became impoverished and were forced to leave their estates which were now being taken over by successful ex-serfs. The unity of the once homogeneous Öreg Street began to break down and toward the end of the 19th century economic compatibility superceded principles of patrilineal succession and inheritance. They numbered approximately 150 families (based on the 1930 census). At the outbreak of World War I, Öreg Street was a one km long lane of highly competitive middle peasants who, when marrying off their children, "looked for matching wealth and not for name." They prided themselves on being good peasants /*jó paraszt*/, a designation referring to being skillful peasants rather than virtuous or moral.

Another expression characterizing them was, "Jól forgatja magát" (literally: "he turns himself well"), meaning "he is an agile farmer and a skillful businessman." However, most people simply called them *gazda* (pl. *gazdák*). Let me now turn to the middle peasant's farming practices by examining his land, livestock, and labor force.

Land and Crops

The primary measure of any peasant was the size of the family's land. A good peasant's holdings had to exceed 11 hectares (henceforth *ha*). A person with 11 ha of land was said to be: "a' már jó gazda; neki má jó köll mennie" (he is already a good *gazda*, he must be doing well). Short of this land size, the good peasant's criterion was reached only if the soil was of especially good quality, or if the family specialized in some lucrative branch of agriculture.

Landholdings in Aba (1930, in ha) [20]

size of holding	number of holdings	stratum
28.5 - 57 ha	26	rich peasant estate owners, renters
5.7 - 28.5 "	137	middle peasant
0.57 - 5.7 "	212	smallholder
0 -0.57 "	3	poor peasant
Total:	378	

According to the above national census, 1,377 families, or 30% of the landowning strata, belonged to the middle peasant category in 1930. By 1941, their number dropped to 93, indicating the severity of the Great Depression. A serious loss of *gazdák* occurred in Öreg Street, where only thirty years before everyone was either a middle or a well-to-do peasant. Of the eighty families residing here, only 37 remained *gazdák* (three were rich peasants). They were stratified in the following manner:

The gazdák of the Öreg Street in 1941 [21]

size of holding in ha	number of holdings
over 50 ha	2
30 - 50 "	1
20 - 30 "	17
10 - 20 "	14
5 - 10 "	3
Total holdings	37

By and large the quality of the soil was good-to-excellent east of the village proper (where most of the villagers owned land), and it was poor-to-average west of it. According to elderly *gazdák*, the soil was best for grain production. This generally held belief, which of course was well founded, discouraged the peasant from raising livestock for the market. By contrast, the *gazdák* of the neighboring village, Sárkeresztúr, were famous for their cattle and hogs, but not for wheat and other grains. Aba's land was thus "meant for wheat and rye," and indeed, the village produced the "hardest (i.e., the highest in starch content) wheat in Transdanubia." (S.A., informant, voicing the consensus in Aba, and elsewhere in the region).

Land was part of the family's heirloom, and the basic asset or property of a given lineage. It was seldom sold or traded. The selling of but the smallest piece of land was tantamount to the betrayal of one's ancestors. Selling one's house or livestock was a much more acceptable alternantive than parting with one's plowlands or vineyards. When a *gazda*, in a moment of flamboyance and intoxication, bet half hectare of his land on cards and lost it, the entire village began to talk about it as a "national catastrophe." He was henceforth held to be a professional gambler, who "gambled away the entire wealth of his family." He was labeled thus even if he remained an outstanding producer and a good businessman.

In most parts of Hungary inheritance customs favored the partible ideology (heirs receiving equal portions of the family estate). In Aba the entire estate was passed down to the eldest son, whose obligations now included the support of his parents. Younger sons received a settlement from the successor. Daughters received dowries, which ideally included a trousseau of linen and clothing, a calf, and cash. "Bridal money" was collected from dance partners at the wedding —often amounting to more than half her monetary asset, which was supplemented by her mother's savings from eggs and dairy.

Young boys acquired a taste for the land and animals by following their fathers around during work, beginning at about age five or six. By age ten, the boys knew each of the family's plots and most of the furlongs of the township. A young adult male's physique was adapted to the rigors of farming, which included 16-18 hours of strenuous labor in the summer, the lifting of heavy loads (i.e., 80-100 kg sacks), and the handling of large, often unpredictable animals. A special feature of peasant life was the alternating harsh agricultural work season with the "lazy winter days"—for which the physique had to make difficult adjustments.

By the time they reached adulthood, men developed such a close attachment to the land, that some observers characterized this as a mystical relationship. The mystique of the land was expressed in numerous proverbs, legends, fables and religious rituals. This relationship was broken only after the time of collectivization (1959-69). Enyedi, in his conservative, but revealing work, calls our attention to the mass migration of peasants to the cities after World War II: "In addition to economic factors, rural-to-urban migration can be attributed to the agrarian policies of the 1950s, and to the psychological effects of the 1959-61 collectivization. This created upheaval...typical of the demographic movements of the 1950s in that almost half a million people moved to the city from the village, while between 1960 and 1974 the number of people taking up permanent residence in cities exceeded 3 million" (30% of Hungary's total population).[22] Between 1960 and 1968, 2,780 people, half of Aba's population, moved away from the village.[23] In 1949 half of Hungary's population was in agriculture; by 1976 this number fell to 19%.[24] Aba's agricultural wage earners dropped from 1,707 in 1949 to 400 in 1980.[25]

Prior to the war, the middle peasant's love for the land included all forms of physical contact with it, from plowing to harrowing, seeding, hoeing, and harvesting. Individuals, who otherwise demonstrated few emotions toward people and events, related to the anthropologist a range of feelings whose account would sound banal in a scientific analysis. There were also ex-peasants who were willing to talk about their sense of mastery over nature. "Every year I could see how wheat or corn grew, how the grainfields turned from green to yellow. All by the labor of my hands," remembered an elderly *gazda*. The daughter of a middle peasant recalled how her father referred to a piece of land as "greasy," another as being "black", or "granular." Peasants had a very rich vocabulary regarding the quality of the soil.

Soil improvement in Aba meant little more then the use of animal manure, which ideally was spread every four years. The more enterprising peasants (and all the wealthy landlords) experimented with chemicals after the turn or the century. This included a mixture of ammonia nitrate and potassium carbonate (called *mészamonsalétrom* in Hungarian, manufactured by the *Péti Nitrogénművek*). In addition to this chemical, a horse-drawn "hoe-plow" /*purháló eke*/ was also introduced for weeding corn and potatoes, easing the family's burden.

Significant strides were made during the interwar years in the cultivation of grains. Two highly productive wheat strains were introduced. Both were refined in Bánkút, which gave them the name "Bánkút wheat." The first of its variety, type B/1201 was brought to Aba by grain merchants, the second by Jenő Szőke, an agricultural expert leasing the 2,640 ha estate of the Count Zichy family.

The *gazdák* themselves succeeded in further improving their grains by gathering stalks of wheat growing wild along the roads and in fields. During long winter nights they threshed these by hand and sowed them the following fall. These "orphan grains" /*árvakelésű gabonák*/—having survived rough winters and other adverse conditions—were not only hardier than the domesticated ones, but had a higher starch content (with a specific gravity of 82-83).

Livestock

Since the middle peasants of Aba placed a high premium on grain production, few of them specialized in stock raising for the market—in contrast to neighboring villages (i.e. Soponya and Sárkeresztúr). Two-three families kept large herds, but the pastures were plowed under for grain production at a very rapid rate following World War I. While in 1863 Aba's pastures extended to 2,872 ha, by 1895 they shrank to 1,328 ha, and in 1940, to 1,087 ha. The vast majority of the pastures belonged to the large estates (the Zichy family and the Catholic Study Foundation). Only a fraction of them were in the possession of the peasants. In 1929 the village community possessed only 53 ha, which was further reduced to 50 ha by 1936. This may explain why a population of over 4,000 held—by Hungarian standards—relatively small number of animals.

Aba's Livestock in 1935 [26]

Cattle	1,563
Horses	764
Hogs	3,500
Sheep	1,058
Poultry	16,425
Rabbits	186

Aba's peasants thought of animals in utilitarian terms. They were used for consumption and as draft animals. Stagnating quantity, however, did not mean stagnating quality. Better dairy cows and leaner, so-called "English bacon" hogs were introduced, along with a more marketable horse, the Remonda, which was sold to the army.

A model *gazda's* barnyard housed two plow horses, 2-4 cows, 3-4 hogs (2-3 for slaughter), 30-40 chickens, some geese and ducks. By contrast, a wealthy peasant owned 4 horses (2 for the plow and 2 for the carriage), 2-4 oxen (for the plow), 8-10 cows, approximately 10 hogs, and a "yardful of poultry." A poor peasant, on the other hand, owned 1 horse and a cow, and slaughtered a pig every year. As elsewhere in Hungary, the middle peasant of Aba preferred horses to other draft animals. Not only were they faster than, say, oxen in covering the several km distance between the village and the fields, but they constituted a symbol of status. Short of a "horse cult," Aba's peasants groomed some very handsome and tall specimens. However, because of the govermment's frequent requests for hauling, peasants began to replace them with oxen after World War II.

Gender Roles

Men. Primary among the daily routines for men was animal care. Young and middle age adults rose at 4 a.m. in the agricultural season, and around 6 a.m. in winter. They fed and watered the animals at this time, and in the evening, cleaned the stables and sties, and helped out with milking.

Plowing, harrowing, fertilizing and sowing were the exclusive domain of males. Anything related to driving teams of animals (or handling large animals) was considered too taxing for females. There was much ambivalence about widows who took over these tasks. Some people had high regard for them, others viewed them as having lost their femininity. The most demanding agricultural activity, requiring the utmost in human energy (a minimum of 7,000 calories per adult male from sunrise to sunset), was harvesting. For the middle peasant, who mowed 6-7 hectares of wheat with a scythe, it required— besides a well-developed physique—the careful organization of a team, which usually included his wife and children, often supplemented by relatives and friends. Hiring professional harvesters would not have been worthwhile. The timing of the harvest (as well as haymaking) was of crucial importance, for the ripe grain had to be hauled home just in time for threshing. Harvesting took one or two weeks, depending on the amount of grain and the weather. Threshing was usually a 1-2 days operation in the barnyard. Besides the horse-drawn sowing machine, the thresher (always hired along with its owner) was the only form of mechanization.

In order of physical exertion, harvesting was followed by plowing, hoeing (together with women), hauling grain to the mill 20-30 kms away, and work in the vineyard. The last was one of the most time-consuming labors for peasants, and it interfered with all other—more productive—agricultural activities. The lightest tasks, such as husking corn by hand, repairing tools, harnesses, or weaving baskets were left for the winter days and long evenings. Boys were expected to carry a full workload after finishing school at age 12.

Women. Seldom did women wake after their husbands. Before milking the cows, they started the fire in the stove, placed the pigs' slop on it (or if they had a separate steamer, they prepared it in that). After milking, they fed the hogs and the poultry, and prepared breakfast for the family. By this time they had let out the cattle, horses, and hogs to join the herds which grazed in the village pastures. Then they followed the daily routine of dressing small children, cooking, cleaning the house, making the beds, baking bread once a week (at certain houses once every other week). In families where there was a daughter-in-law and a mother-in-law, the former did all the harder chores, the latter the cooking. Vegetable gardens were the exclusive domains of women, and there were small flower gardens in front of the house which required continuous care. In the spring women set brooding hens, ducks and geese on eggs. They also force-fed some geese and ducks. One of the more demanding jobs of women was the cooking and carrying of lunch to the fields, where the men worked. Among the non-routine tasks women performed were: canning tomatoes, apricots, and plums; storing potatoes, carrots, and onions in the cellar, and apples, grapes, and prunes in the attic; cooking laundry soap from suet and scraps; spinning hemp and flax for homespun linen. Until the early 1960s most households spun their own linen. Women also whitewashed the house at least once a year during Easter, at which time, and before Christmas, they did a thorough cleanup in the house.

Girls beginning at around 6 or 8 years of age helped out their mothers. Specifically, their jobs included the supervision of the poultry in the street or backyard; watering and weeding the vegetable gardens; going to the store; occasionally watching smaller children. By age 12-14 girls were "little mothers" (baby sitters), baked bread and cooked.

As in peasant society in general, Aba's middle peasants, too, had a very marked division of roles among the age groups and the gender roles, which did not overlap. They complemented each oher. Therefore: there were few areas of contention between the sexes and generations. It is obvious from the above enumeration that women performed a greater variety of roles than men. (Some, like marketing, were not mentioned because not all women performed them). Most were carried out in and around the house.

Prior to World War II women had almost no opportunities for employment either in or outside the village; therefore marriage for them was imperative. It was not before becoming a mother-in-law that a woman could gain any substantial decision-making power. At this time, however, almost all matters pertaining to the house were subject to, or fundamentally influenced by her. The true "home decisionmaker" was the eldest but not infirm woman, whose sphere of influence included children and grandchildren, their education, hygiene, clothes, spending money, and eventual spouses. Men rarely involved themselves in these matters. For example, they did not inquire about the next meal, or the type of clothes the children wore. Many—if not most of the husbands—gave their money to the women to keep, so that when they wanted to have a drink at the inn they had to ask for money from their women. Important decisions regarding economic matters (land, animals, investments, sales, etc.), were reached by the men of the house, although older women were often present and consulted during discussions. The men of Aba were not of the absolutist patriarchal type—typical of the Slavic family, or the type described by some ethnographers [27]—but their decision-making and veto powers were substantial. Fathers/husbands demanded compliance with their expectations. At times they were severe, stubborn and stern, even temperamental with their wives and children. They reversed decisions without warning or prior discussion, levied out punishment without regard to the gravity of infraction. In a word, middle peasant fathers were demanding and sometimes even unreasonable. However, their wives, mothers or in-laws could, singularly or in unison, place subtle pressure on them to "bring them to their senses." For example, BA was threatened by his in-laws with calling their eight-months-pregnant daughter home if he did not cease insisting on her working a full load. He eased up. Similarly, after relentless pressure from his mother, a father finally called out a doctor to his son with a congenital heart problem—which he had opposed for a year insisting "he was merely lazy and didn't feel like working."

With the approach of World War II, under increasing urban influence, important changes took place within the family's decision-making structure. Authority began to be decentralized within the extended family by men handing over more power to women, and the middle-aged men's willingness to share power with their elder children earlier than in the previous generation. This shift was necessitated by the differentiation of roles as a result of agricultural specialization and the concomitant "capitalization of agriculture."

Enculturation

Between the two world wars, almost all children were born in the village with the aid of a midwife or the local doctor. Since there was a physician and a professional midwife in Aba, medical innovations were fast replacing peasant healing or folk medicine. All complicated cases, which prior to World War II were doomed to death, were now rushed to the hospital 20 kms away in Székesfehérvár.

Babies were swaddled in a down swaddle up to six months. Swaddles were not as tight as those elsewhere east of Hungary: the arms, for example, were kept outside the swaddle, and the legs vere not bound. The generally held belief about the necessity of swaddling was that it supported the spine.

Infants were breastfed either by the mother or a midwife until 1-2 years of age or longer, since it was believed that nursing prevented pregnancy, and that children grew faster and healthier. By 7-8 month, gruel, mashed potatoes or beans, or breadcrust during teething were the baby's menu. Right after weaning milk was not considered important for the child; therefore, there was an unusually high number of children with rickets in the villages. Diapering consisted of "bundling the baby up" in rags. Early toilet training (under one year) was the rule rather then the exception, facilitated by the "unisex" flannel shirts worn by all children until five years of age. After this time simple clothes, skirts for girls and pants for boys, were worn by children. Unlike poor peasants' offspring, the children of middle peasants wore shoes to school and church, showing a marked status and economic difference between them and the lower strata, who could not afford them.

One of the signs of being a *gazda's* child was that parents and children sat together during meals. Another was the number of store-bought toys, including bicycles for boys, and still another, a promise that he or she could go to secondary school. Children picked for higher ecucation were treated very differently from the rest. They were allowed to rest more and work less; they were kept away from children of "undesirable" background and were discouraged from forming strong friendships. "Stay at home, don't wander all over the village," were the *gazda's* last words before leaving home.

Parent-child relationships were hierarchical.Children were continously reminded of their subserviance and exploitability. They were both blessing as well as burden, important as well as in the way. Middle peasants put them to work quickly, because work meant training for life. Very few *gazdák's* children had time to play during the week. Poor peasants' children, on the other hand spent much of their time roaming around the village after school in gangs. Punishment, rather than reward was the main principle of child rearing.

A hindrance to the formation of healthy personality was the different and often contradictory treatment of the child by parents, grandparents and relatives (i.e., godparents). Women were much more indulgent than men, grandparents more lenient than parents. Women used terms of endearment expressed in flowery, remarkably ornate idioms, or forms of diminutives and suffixes, while men usually did not even use children's names. There was—as in urban society too—a very strong gender differentiation from the moment of birth. By age 5-6 the sexes played separately, set apart in school and in church.

Among the greatest infractions of children were: a) neglecting one's duty, b) lying, c) stealing d) being disrespectful toward parents. All of these would be followed by physical punishment, the most common of which was a slap in the face. In severity, slapping was followed by lashing with a strap or belt, kneeling on dry corn for hours, meal skipping and hair pulling. They were so common that children were quite used to them and did not rebel. Punishment was followed by verbal lashings to humiliate children (i.e., "You, you thankless, sly little predator! Just wait, I'll show you! You'll never forget this day!") Parents expected children to ask for forgiveness and a promise of good behavior. Instilling fear was an important way of keeping youngsters in line. Children's relationships to fathers and grandfathers was defined by intimidation. Fathers were also well known for their frugality in words. "We learned what they were thinking and what they were about to say," remembered the daughter of a *gazda*. "Asking my father a question, or for an opinion seldom brought results," she continued.

Discouraged from forming friendships with other children, boys and girls adjusted to home life with various degrees of success. Their relationships were amiable with their mothers and grandparents and with their fathers they had good working relationships. By and large the *gazda's* children were well-disciplined, industrious and respectful when they entered first grade at age six. At this time their status suddenly improved, as if knowledge suddenly raised the child's value. But there was also a competition between the school (authorities) and the family for the child's attention and energy. The parents attempted to keep their children at home whenever they needed them. The school rooms were almost empty in the beginning of the agricultural season.

Prior to the 1920s there were three parochial schools in Aba, but with the closing of the Jewish school only two remained: the Calvinist and the Catholic schools. Each had six grades with three teachers. Following the sixth grade the child entered the "Repeater" /*ismétlő*/, a twice a week post-elementary school program up to age 15, which meant an additional three years of schooling. During the interwar years the Repeater's curriculum included the teaching of agricultural innovations (hybridization, grafting of fruit trees, etc.).

Following schooling there was a period of 3-4 years of intense parental supervision (especially for girls) coupled with a greater work load. Simultaneously with this heightened demand was a period of socialization outside the family. By age 16 the *gazda's* children belonged to organizations whose manifest functions included a strong sense of cooperation, comradery, leadership, and religious values. They staged folkplays, folkdances and learned folksongs, kept libraries, invited speakers, and organized festivals. A Protestant organization was the *Keresztyén Ifjúsági Egyesület* /Young People's Christian Association/ with a membership of about 90. The *Katolikus Országos Legény Egyesület* /National Association of Young Catholic Men/, with its counterpart, the *Katolikus Leányok Szövetsége* /Catholic Girls' Association/, had a combined membership of approximately 7,080. There were other youth associations, such as the *Cserkészet* /Boy Scouts/, and the *Levente* (a military association).

A *gazda's* daughter, 62 years old in 1983, evaluated the *Keresztyén Ifjúsági Egyesület* in the following way:

> **Its purpose was religious education and unity...we had a very lively and enthusiastic group with girls of all kinds of families, rich and poor alike...Our ways of looking at things broadened a good deal. We went there to become more than the rest of the peasants, and the KIE offered lots more than our parents could.**

Youth associations with their strong *esprit de corps*, helped to weaken social barriers between the classes, and village and the city. They emphasized Hungarian ethnic and national unity through the learning of the common cultural heritage. An additional theme was injustice of the Trianon Peace Treaty (1920), which trunkated St. Stephen's thousand year old kingdom, "Historic Hungary." Peasant youths in interwar Hungary were thus targeted for political purposes: to enter a "holy war" for the recapturing of its ancient borders.

Village Politics

The distribution of political power within village society was a function of historical and socioeconomic factors resulting in considerable variation across the country. In some communities, for example, the village government was made up of militant poor peasants, but in the majority of the Hungarian villages they were manipulated by the landed aristocracy or a handful of rich peasants. Interwar rural politics had not yet shed its feudal heritage. Yet, there were a number of local politico-administrative bodies wielded by middle peasants. There were many factors contributing to their power, one of which was high visibility through economic success, and another one, demographic strength. Aba was an example of both.

The major contenders of political power in Aba were the wealthy landlords, the middle peasants and the poor peasants. Left out of the competition were the 200-300 estate servants and twice as many seasonal laborers who could not, and the white collar stratum, which did not want a part in the political process. Aba's landlords in possession of 62% of the township were silent participants following World War I. [28] Although they retained their titles as *virilisták*, best translated as trustees, their direct involvement in village politics was negligible. As long as the town council abstained from curtailing their economic freedom, they remained neutral in most matters. The wealthiest family, the Zichys never attended council meetings either in person or through a representative.

The poor peasants and the landless masses attempted to organize a political block. During the brief proletarian dictatorship of 1919, they took over the local administration and threatened the wealthy landlords with the collectivization of their properties. But for the most part they ended up being fed by the landlords, who set up souplines for them and saved them from starvation. Following the demise of the proletarian rule, their leaders were easily neutralized by Admiral Horthy's "counterrevolutionary" government. All remaining leftist ideology was now restricted to the Social Democratic Party—organized by the poorer elements of the artisan stratum (cobblers, smiths, coopers, barbers, and taylors). This small circle of disgruntled ex-peasants exhausted its energies in the heated ideological exchanges of their club, the *Olvasókör* /Reading Circle/. The most they achieved was to place one or two of their members in the town council because of their village-wide popularity. Throughout these decades the politically conscious poor people were effectively surveilled by the *Csendőrség* /Gendarmerie/, which arrested a few of them for a brief period for the purpose of intimidation. By the onset of World War II Aba's left wing politicians faded into history.

In sharp contrast to these two extreme strata, the middle peasants not only succeeded in acquiring village leadership, they became synonymous with it. The mayor (*bíró* in Hungarian, literally "judge"), came from their rank. József Kasó, who served during all but a few of the interwar years, was a "good" peasant, who eventually owned 52 ha of land. He was a model of all *gazdák* because of his rational managerial talents, and his ability to "speak to people." He lived at the rich (southern) end of the Öreg Street. His tri-yearly re-election was virtually ensured because of his prestige, and what we would nowadays term immaculate public relations.

He was an articulate and persuasive man vigorously defending the village against the district and county in their efforts to squeeze ever-increasing taxes out of peasants. While he made no secret of his defense on behalf of the *jó gazdák* in opposition to the "lazy unemployed day-laborers," he secured funds from the village budget for the maintenance of the infirm and unfortunate families of the poorer segment. He was an active member of the *Abai Kölcsönös Népsegélyző Egylet* /People's Credit Association of Aba/, established by his good friend, the Protestant minister, László Kulifay.

Local ordinances, the budget, road and bridge maintenance, the upkeep of public facilities and houses, the physical and fire safety of the village, and the salaries of the servants of the village, were all in the hands of the mayor and the twenty-five councillors. The latter were also from the ranks of the middle peasants, most of them from Öreg Street. As it will be recalled, these *gazdák* were also Protestant; therefore, it goes without saying that the village council was a Protestant political organization, with a few "token Catholics" and occasionally a Jewish member. Yet, the council's composition was no cause of political alienation for either the poor or the wealthy stratum. For one thing, the poor peasants, instead of blaming the middle peasants for their own poverty, blamed themselves or "fate." In fact, the poor emulated the middle peasants for they too wanted to be *gazdák* who had tribulations resulting from the Great Depression. For another, the middle peasants succeeded in remaining in the political center—a sort of power broker between extreme elements—and insisted on representing the entire village community and its interests.

Formal political meetings were infrequent. Months went by before the council convened, and when it did, it was only for an hour or less. Issues had already been debated and resolved at another forum, the *Gazdakör* /Gazda-Circle/. This organization resembled a men's club providing the structure of informal political behavior in Hungarian village society. Its primary purpose was the improvement of husbandry, yet the *Gazdakör* functioned as a casino (without alcohol, gambling or women) where all village matters were discussed. While membership was open, two signatures by members were necessary for entry, vouching for the applicant's character, and that he "would abide by the rules." There were a few poor as well as rich peasants in it, but the vast majority were *gazdák*. They met on Sunday afternoons in a rented house (owned by Sándor Farkas, a poor peasant in Homok Street), where they bowled a few games, and socialized. Some were dissatisfied with the treatment they received by the notary /*jegyző*/, or the secretary at the *községháza* /townhall/, or complained about the accumulation of power by the notary. They may have started forming a block for his removal, while others made proposals for the modernization of the village through bringing in electricity or paving the roads. As in most associations, here too, membership was divided into conservative and liberal factions. By and large the *Gazdakör* championed conservative causes; its members usually voted for the *Magyar Élet Pártja* /Party of Hungarian Life/, the governmental party in power, which was, therefore, viewed by many as a "club for backward Protestant peasants." The fact remains that it gathered almost all the political elites of Aba's agricultural strata, for whom it meant many things from entertainment to education and politicking. The philosophy of the *Gazdakör* and its activities dovetailed with those of the church organizations and other clubs. Its officers often held positions in several organizations simultaneously. Like most peasant associations, the *Gazdakör* dissolved in 1945. The books of its modest but valuable peasant library were ordered to be burned in the street by plundering Russian soldiers.

Conclusions

There are reasons to believe that, as in the law of physics where "matter does not disappear in the universe," in the process of social transformation, such as brought about by the Soviet presence in East Central Europe, social classes or strata do not totally disappear either. Attempts by Communist regimes to rearrange social hierarchies fell far below expectations. Forced restratification removed the aristocrats and the lumpenproletariat from society, but it was unable to liquidate the pillar of the old rural society, the middle peasant. Although a large segment abandoned their homes in face of their "kulakization" and relentless persecution by the authorities during the 1950s and 60s, many remained behind to take over socialist agriculture and continue the production of food on both the public and the private farms. Their persistence can be understood only if we realize their ingrained values of work, maintenance of peasant lifestyles, ancestral homes and lands.

The present tract attempted to reconstruct the lifestyle and the social subsystem of the middle peasant in a single village, Aba. Rather than comparing Aba's *gazdák* to those of other villages or regions—a necessary and fruitful project begging to be undertaken—the present analysis restricted itself to a diachronical search for causality. Thus, instead of trying to answer the question of why the middle peasant was the most mobile and dynamic segment of interwar Hungary, rather than, say, the rich or the poor peasant, I tried to trace its origins to certain historical conditions. According to this explanation Aba's *gazdák*—by and large—descended from the ranks of the lesser nobility through the rather rough path of "denobilization," loss of rank-identity, and the gaining of a new identity. Missing from my analysis are considerations of many historical and economic conditions responsible for structuring feudal and post-feudal society; global and East European developments, and several other factors. For example, one could make a case for the success of the middle peasant by analyzing the agricultural market conditions of the post World War I era. In this respect it could be then pointed out that the entry of the United States, Canada, Argentina, and India in international grain-competition, with a dramatic reduction of prices, all but ruined the Central and East European peasant economies. In the ensuing struggle for scarce resources the middle peasant exhibited the best survival technique, as he was able to harness his family's energies most effectively. The *gazdák* drove their family and relatives hard (minimized their desires and needs) and clung rigidly to their wealth. While the poor and the wealthy peasants experienced downward mobility during the harsh interwar years, the middle peasants succeeded in insuring the continuity of their farming operations, as well as diverting some of their offsprings from village to urban professions. Trans-generational mobility for some *gazdák* now meant search for new lifestyles, learning a trade or entering professions that required higher education.

The middle peasant's social mobility was not accidental or due to some special sociocultural circumstance, as in the case of, for example, the Amish or the Hutterite in the United States. Religious beliefs had only general and indirect role in the formulation of their world view. Neither was the ready application of certain innovations the exclusive domain of this stratum. (There were many poor peasants who could also minimize needs and maximize production). The dynamics of this stratum ought to be seen in terms of their ability to maximize *all* available resources without investing in or employing new and expensive techniques, such as machines and modern transportation devices; their willingness to continue the lifestyle of their ancestors with minimal structural modification, their insistence on clinging to puritanical values (i.e., the work ethic, self-denial, willingness to endure pain and other forms of deprivation); their retention of class unity through forms of residential, marital, and political cohesion, and isolation from other social strata. These "themes" or value orientations were intricately woven together to form a complex whole, and one could not function without the other. Marital and family cohesion, which included endogamous practices, could not, for example, be maintained without the insistence on residential rule, or the retention of a certain estate size. Once the *gazda's* estate or family disintegrated, he could no longer claim the status of a middle peasant, and his chances for re-emergence became remote. By the time they reached adulthood, middle peasants knew the type of life that lay ahead of them. That life had been carefully rehearsed every day at home under the strict supervision of parents and grandparents. Roles were played out routinely, and infractions drew harsh punishment. Not scolding children was a form of reward. They learned to appreciate silence from their parents. Eventually young people came to view work as being intrinsically good. They frowned on idleness and could not understand why agricultural servants moved slowly on their employers' estate.

The elaborate and intricate nature of the pre-World War II peasant social system with the middle peasant's prominent position in it, was obvious to the postwar political leadership. The realization that peasant society could be dismantled if, and only if its **pillar**, the middle peasant was dislodged, was voiced by Lenin during the 1920s, and in Hungary, by the Rákosi regime during the 1950s. While in Soviet Russia the campaign for the liquidation of the middle peasant succeeded, the Hungarian experiment proved to be a failure.

Notes

1. Hollos and Maday, eds., *The New Hungarian Peasants*, p. 1.

2. Bell, *Peasants in*, p. 1.

3. Verdery, *Transylvanian Villagers*, p. 72.

4. Hann, *Tázlár*, p. 172.

5. Vágvölgyi, ed., *Falu a magyar*, pp. 11-40; *Hung. Stat. Pocketbook, 1971*.

6. Juhász, "Előtanulmány."

7. Hanák, "A falusi," p. 264.

8. The only thorough study devoted entirely to the investigation of the small-to-middle-peasant is by Fél and Hofer, *Proper Peasants*.

9. I adopted the term "good peasants" from the local usage in Aba. Although the term *jó paraszt* has several meanings (i.e., honest, reliable, true, or successful peasant), in Aba it denotes the middle peasant most commonly. As shall be seen in the text, there were several criteria for being a good peasant, including a certain amount of land, "proper" ancestry, as well as diligence.

10. Ránki, ed., *Magyarország története*, p. 770.

11. Berend and Szuhay, *A tőkés gazdaság*, p. 302.

12. For a good overview of the region's geography, see Kogutowicz, *Dunántúl* pp. 199-282. Other works of relevance are: Cholnoky, Princz, Teleki, *Magyar föld*; and Ádám-Marosi-Szilárd, *A Mezőföld*. I wish to express my appreciation to the American Council of Learned Societies and the International Research and Exchanges Board for the support of my research between February and August, 1983.

13. See Makkay, *Fejér megye*; and Gyimesi, "Kajtor."

14. The two most authoritative works dealing with the medieval period of the region are: Kállay, "Aba."; Károlyi, *Fejér vármegye*.

15. Village records of Aba, 1900-1981.

16. Geological surveys indicate that the present location of the village was indeed swampland during the Ottoman occupation, while the alleged earlier location yielded many medieval artifacts and some building foundations in the Arany tag (a furlong in the eastern section of the township). For a general view of the reoccupation of the region after the Ottoman occupation, see Farkas, "Nagy-birtokosok."

17. Móra, "Fejér megye," pp. 312-13.

18. "1828. évi nemesi összeírás."

19. "Jobbágytelken...1846."

20. Source: *1930. évi népszámlálás.*

21. Source: Sándor Arany, informant, resident of Öreg Street. I hereby wish to express my appreciation to all my informants of Aba, among whom special thanks are due for their rich and accurate accounts to: Eva Spitzer (Mrs. Mezey), Károly Gyímesi (Gräber), Katalin Bor (Tankáné), and Katalin Pákozdi.

22. Enyedi, *Falvaink*.

23. *Községi törzskönyv. Aba. 1980.*

24. Enyedi, *Falvaink*.

25. *Községi törzskönyv. Aba.*

26. These data include the large estates. Source: *Magyarország állatállománya*.

27. Morvay, *Asszonyok*.

28. See, Sozan, "Zsidók egy magyar faluban."

Bibliography

Ádám, László, Sándor Marosi and Jenő Szilárd, *A Mező-föld természeti földrajza* /The Natural Geography of Mező-föld/ (Budapest, 1959).

Bell, Peter D., *Peasants in Socialist Transition. Life in a Collectivized Hungarian Village* (Berkely, 1984).

Berend, Iván and Miklós Szuhay, *A tőkés gazdaság története Magyarországon, 1848-1944* /The History of Capitalist Economy in Hungary, 1848-1944/ (Budapest, 1973).

Cholnoky, Jenő, Gyula Prinz, and Pál Teleki, *Magyar földrajz* /Hungarian Geography/, 2 vols. (Vols. I and II. of *Magyar föld - magyar faj* — The Land and the People of Hungary) (Budapest, 1938).

Enyedi, György, *Falvaink sorsa* /The Fate of Our Villages/ (Budapest, 1980). "1828. évi nemesi összeírás. Aba" (Conscription of Aba's Nobility. 1828/ (MS in the Archives of Székesfehérvár).

1930. évi népszámlálás. II. Foglalkozási adatok /The Census of 1930. II. Occupational Data/ (Budapest, 1934).

Farkas, Gábor, "Nagybirtokosok Fejér megyében a török kiűzése után" (Landed Nobility in Fejér County After the Expulsion of the Turks/, in *Fejér megyei történeti évkönyv, 5.* /Historical Annals of Fejér County, 5/ (Székesfehérvár, 1971), pp. 171-176.

Fél, Edit and Tamás Hofer, *Proper Peasants* (Chicago, 1969).

Ferenczy, Endre, *A magyar föld népeinek története a honfoglalásig* /The History of the Peoples of Hungary Prior to the Hungarian Conquest/ (Budapest, 1958).

Gyimesi, Károly, "Kajtor településtörténete" /The History of Kajtor's Settlements/ (MS in István Király Múzeum, Székesfehérvár, 1979).

Hanák, Katalin, "A falusi lakosság nemzedékek közötti mobilitásának néhány vonása" /A Few Aspects of Rural Intergenerational Mobility/, in András Vágvölgyi, ed., *A falu a mai magyar társadalomban* /The Village within Contemporary Hungarian Society/ (Budapest, 1982), pp. 237-288.

Hann, C. M., *Tázlár: A Village in Hungary* (London, 1980).

Hollos, Marida and Bela C. Maday, eds., *New Hungarian Peasants; An East Central European Experiment with Collectivization* (New York, 1983).

Hungarian Statistical Pocketbook (Budapest, 1971).

"Jobbágytelken élő nemesek összeírása. 1846. Aba." (Conscription of Noblemen Occupying Serf-Plots. 1846. Aba./ (MS in the Archives of Székesfehérvár, Hungary).

Juhász, Pál, "Előtanulmány a falusi társadalom tagolódása és a mezőgazdasági szövetkezet című témában" /A Preliminary Study on Rural Stratification and the Agricultural Cooperatives/ (MS, Szövetkezeti Dokumentációs Könyvtár, Budapest).

Kállay, István, "Aba," in *Fejér Megyei Történeti Évkönyv, 13* /Historical Annals of Fejér County, 13/ (Székesfehérvár, 1979), pp. 7-40.

Károlyi, János, *Fejérvármegye története* /The History of Fejér County/, 5 vols. (Székesfehérvár, 1896-1904).

Községi törzskönyv. Aba. /Village Statistics of Aba/ (MS, Aba, 1980).

Magyarország állatállománya, gazdasági felszerelése, és gyümölcsfaállománya az 1935. évben /Hungary's Animal Stock, Farm Equipment, and Fruit Trees in the Year 1935/ (Budapest, 1937).

Makkay, János, *Fejér megye története* /The History of Fejér County/, vols. I/1, 3, 3, 5 (Székesfehérvár, 1970-1971).

Móra, Magda, "Fejér megye népessége II. József korában" /The Population of Fejér County in the Age of Joseph II/, in *Fejér Megyei Történeti Évkönyv, 5* /Historical Annals of Fejér County, 5/ (Székesfehérvár, 1971), pp. 303-323.

Morvay, Judit, *Asszonyok a nagycsaládban* /Women in the Extended Family/ (Budapest, 1957).

Ránki, György, ed., *Magyarország története, 1918-1919, 1919-1945* /The History of Hungary, 1918-1919, 1919-1945/ (Budapest, 1976).

Szabó, Dezső, *Az elsodort falu* /The Village that was Swept Away/ (Budapest, 1919).

Sozan, Michael, "Zsidók egy magyar faluban" /Jews in a Hungarian Village/, in *Új Látóhatár* /New Horizons/ (Munich), 35 (1984), pp. 45-60.

Tanka, János, "Aba krónikája" /The Chronicle of Aba/ (MS, Székesfehérvár, 1975).

Vágvölgyi, András, ed., *Falu a magyar társadalomban* /The Village in Hungarian Society/ (Budapest, 1982).

Verdery, Katherine, *Transylvanian Villages* (Berkeley, 1983).

Nicholas A. Vardy:

22 / HUNGARIAN FOREIGN TRADE UNDER THE NEW ECONOMIC MECHANISM, 1968-1980

Following the Second World War, Hungary adopted, with a few modifications, the traditional Soviet model of centralized planning. Throughout the 1950s and 1960s Hungary exhibited all the characteristics and problems of a traditional Centrally Planned Economy (CPE): strong, centralized control of the economy, rigid plan mechanism, incentive problems, and an emphasis on investment in heavy industry at the expense of consumption. The traditional Soviet model was also strongly autarchic and advocated a policy of trade aversion with regard to Western nations. Stalin had developed an ideological base for this when he declared the aim of a "socialist world market," independent of Western markets. In its extensive phase of development, Hungary achieved impressive rates of growth with this model: growth reached an almost 17 percent annual rate in the early 1950s, and averaged 6-7 percent until the late 1960s.[1]

In spite of its considerable achievements in its early period of industrialization, it soon became clear that Hungary's traditional CPE would have to be modified. The fact remained that Hungary was a small country with limited natural and human resources. An ideologically motivated attempt to isolate itself from Western markets was an unrealistic approach to economic policy; Western markets, technology, and natural resources inevitably came to play an important role in the economic development of this small nation. This need to integrate Hungary into Western trade flows was reflected in the reforms of the New Economic Mechanism

(NEM) introduced by Hungarian planners in 1968. Although NEM was labelled a comprehensive reform, and altered some of the most basic mechanisms and institutions of foreign trade, planners were still subject to several constraints consistent with the state's social policies. Trade liberalization in Hungary is still a difficult problem; foreign trade performance in the 1970s illustrates some of these problems. In fact, many of the NEM reforms were briefly abandoned in the early to mid-1970s. But NEM's principles were later reaffirmed and strengthened in the "reform of the reform" in 1980.[2]

This study will examine some of the constraints on reform, the institutional elements of Hungarian foreign trade, and Hungarian foreign trade policy and performance since the introduction of NEM until 1980.

The Background to Reform

Foreign trade in CPEs. The traditional CPE was systematically incompatible with market based foreign trade. Planning in a traditional CPE was based on the method of material balances: the ex ante determination of aggregate supplies and demands, and bringing both together in balance without relying on market forces. This method accounted for imports, but only in fixed amounts. Imports, along with current production and current stock were carefully balanced against intermediate and final demands for goods. Under such conditions, the flow of imports had to be stable and directly accounted for: their quantity and composition could not be subject to the vagaries of the world market. To avoid upsetting this balance, imports from the West were de-emphasized.

The domestic price structure served little more than an accounting function: it failed to reflect relative scarcities of goods, and proved inadequate for resource allocation. Firms were unable to make proper decisions concerning product mix. In the foreign trade sector, there was no real basis for determining comparative advantage. Gross output measures were the primary success indicators, failing to generate concern about product quality. Hungarian products were noncompetitive on world markets. Centralized decision—making blocked horizontal exchanges of information between export enterprises and domestic industries; this made coordination of product mix difficult. The irrational price structure also resulted in an inefficient allocation of investment to export industries. [3]

As a traditional CPE, pre-reform Hungary was suited for trade only within the Eastern Bloc or Council of Mutual Economic Assistance (CMEA or COMECON). Such trade was based on carefully balanced individual agreements with other Socialist countries in the CMEA. These intra-bloc agreements outlined all details of foreign trade including quantity and composition. With all exports and imports predetermined by individual branch ministries, this system offered the stability demanded by the method of material balances. Because of irrational price structures, the lack of purchasing power parity, and convertibility, trade was essentially conducted on a barter basis. [4] The notion of comparative advantage was nonexistent. Exports only served to pay for imports. The transferable ruble—essentially a unit of account—was established for CMEA trade.

Increasing Dependence on Foreign Trade. As foreign trade represents one of the best examples of decision-making under uncertainty, the CPE in its pure form was ill-suited for international trade based on world markets. Despite the structural rigidities of a traditional CPE, Hungary developed considerable ties to foreign trade. In 1959, foreign trade accounted for 25 percent of national income, and in 1967 this figure had reached 40 percent. By 1978, foreign trade accounted for 55 percent of national income or 45 percent of Gross Domestic Product (GDP). [5] Throughout the 1950s and 1960s the rate of growth in foreign trade exceeded the rate of growth in productivity and income. From the 1950s to the early 1970s, Hungary conducted about two-thirds of its trade with CMEA nations, and the rest with Western nations. [6] In spite of inherent inefficiencies, the institutional and political constraints under strict control planning, trade with the West became an important means of supporting industrialization and alleviating disturbances in the domestic economy. [7]

Industrialization was only the initial cause of an upward shift in import demand. Trade with the West was not only used to supplement deficiencies in high priority industrial sectors, but in lower priority sectors as well. After 1952, Hungary began to experience a sharp increase in its balance of payments deficit; an increasing amount of materials and goods were being obtained on less favorable terms. Imports had been gradually given an important role, and their curtailment would affect all sectors of the economy.[8] For example, energy imports which were unimportant in the early 1950s, by 1958 accounted for 20 percent of total energy consumption.[9]

Motivations for the expansion of trade. Hungary had several reasons for wishing to alter its institutional mechanisms and provide incentives for the expansion of this trade. In the early period of the development and throughout the 1960s Hungary had relied greatly on CMEA countries for obtaining necessary materials. As trade was not based on world prices reflecting Hungary's comparative advantage, its export composition was skewed. Once exposed to market conditions Hungary's structure of exports quickly changed. In 1970, two-thirds of Hungarian exports were agricultural; by the end of the 1970s the exports had declined to 40-50 percent.[10]

The lack of information provided by the price system not only prevented correct decisions about composition of exports, but also resulted in trade which was glaringly inefficient. Some of the systemic causes of these inefficiencies in CMEA trade have been outlined above. For an illustrative example: in the late 1960s Poland and Czechoslovakia agreed to produce tractor parts for each other's markets. But there was so much disagreement about the relative values of the parts to be traded that the two sides finally entered into a barter agreement in which 10 kg. of exports was exchanged for 10 kg. of "similar" imports. Under such conditions, it was impossible to assess gains and losses, and to conduct efficient foreign trade. If Hungary wished to conduct foreign trade on a rational basis, it would have to abandon the system which yielded such blatant inefficiencies.[11]

Hungary realized that both its domestic and export oriented industries stood to gain from increasing links to international trade. Introduction to national world market prices into its economy would improve efficiency across the board. In integrating themselves into Western trade Hungarian firms would be forced to become competitive on demanding Western markets, and thus improve the quality of their goods. Increased trade with the West, it was hoped, would give Hungary access to advanced technology which

CMEA countries were unable to provide under any conditions. The only great advantage to CMEA trade was its certainty, but even this was called into question when in 1975 the Soviet Union cut back on its supply of oil to Hungary as part of its effort to reduce its subsidization of Eastern European Economics.[12] In this case, too, Hungary was forced to rely on world markets to fill its supply gap.

In Hungary, more so than in other Eastern European countries, foreign trade considerations were prime movers in the direction of economic reform. Hungary's small domestic market and lack of natural resources demanded that it place a great emphasis on foreign trade. The political directive which laid the basis for the introduction of NEM attached great importance to international trade in its potential for reversing Hungary's declining productivity and growth.

This need was ably summarized by Brown and Licani in their analysis of Hungarian foreign trade in the mid-1970s: "Faster rate of economic growth require that /Hungary/ increase its participation in the international division of labor, and make more extensive use of its advantages...an organic link must be established between domestic and foreign markets.../reducing/...the overproduction of domestic products, eliminating the laxness resulting from overproduction. Foreign trade must be encouraged to play a role of speeding up specialization, and in the more rapid attainment of technological standards."[13]

It was against this background that Hungarian planners introduced the NEM in 1968.

General Aims. The purpose of NEM was to allow the economy to be directed by economic and not by administrative considerations.[14] NEM was to reduce the scope of central planning in the Hungarian economy. "Economic considerations" did not mean "pure market," rather, reformers wanted to stimulate market conditions through regulation. The government maintained, controlled, and implemented its economic policies through "economic regulators." It retained control over price, wage, tax, credit, and budgetary policy. The government also introduced a comprehensive price reform allowing for greater flexibility in price formation. Prices were to provide incentives for producers and consumers to make economically efficient decisions. Domestic prices were to be organically linked to foreign trade prices. Separate foreign trade multiplier were introduced for CMEA and Western markets to link domestic profits with overseas markets. But traditional subsidies on imports and exports were maintained.[15] Considerable independence was given to enterprises and their decision-making capacities. They could formulate their own plans, and control their implementation and operation. Gross output targets were eliminated; profits became primary success indicators. One year operational plans were abandoned in favor of five year plans based on aggregate sums. The government, however, retained its power to allocate major investments and to form new enterprises.

The reform sought to increase factor production through improved incentives, to increase the efficiency of the economy to improve foreign trade performance, and to alter the seller's market conditions in the Hungarian economy making it more responsive to consumer demand.[16] One scholar viewed the entire reform movement as a natural consequence of economic development in CPEs. After a period of massive extensive development, there is a natural tendency toward modification of extant institutional structures to provide for intensive development.

Constraints on Reform. In planning the reform, architects of NEM were subject to several constraints. Some were ideological. The reforms had to be consistent with the societal goals of the state. Some were environmental. There were limits to acceptable change given Hungary's previous commitments to CMEA countries, and the potential for dislocation in the economy with the imbalances inherent in a CPE. Some of these constraints were hard, while others grew softer with time. Nevertheless, the combination of these constraints put considerable limits on the feasible set of organizational solutions.

Full Employment. The maintenance of full employment in Hungary is the most basic and inflexible constraint on reforms. The guarantee of the "right to work" has always been touted as one of the fundamental advantages of socialism over capitalism. The rate of open, and even fractional unemployment permitted by the state is considerably lower than in Western nations. Dismissal of workers was not permissible, except in cases of gross misbehavior and incompetence.[17]

Adherence to this policy led the government to support numerous inefficient enterprises.[18] Enterprises were the beneficiaries of a massive subsidy system which allowed them to remain operational despite unprofitability, leading to market disequilibrium and a clear case of static inefficiency. The constraint on full-employment resulted in prices being set below equilibrium levels to assure profits to even the most inefficient enterprises.

Some of the reforms instituted in 1980 and beyond have made it easier for firms to go bankrupt and to dismiss their workers because of unprofitability. At first glance, this seems to challenge the constraint on full employment. This is, however, untrue. The ideological conviction of the "right to work" is very strong; even if he is fired, the worker will be guaranteed work elsewhere. Beyond ideological considerations, the labor shortage in Hungary assures employment to all those who seek it.

Price Stability. Through the early years of the reform, rapid increases in consumer prices were politically unacceptable. Memories of post war hyper-inflation were vivid; rapid price increases were seen as an admission of weakness on the part of the government.[19] This meant, at least in the early years of reform, a low rate of open inflation. Between 1968 and 1978 consumer prices rose only 2.8 percent.[20] But signs of repressed inflation were evident in shortages of goods and services. The state operated an extensive system of subsidies and taxes on goods and it intervened directly with these tools whenever it saw necessary.

The operation of this constraint was observable in Hungarian price policy in the years immediately following the sharp increases in raw material and oil prices in 1973. All that time, these price increases were not passed on to Hungarian consumers. Instead, the government tried unsuccessfully to isolate the Hungarian economy from world markets; the implications of this policy reverberated through Hungary throughout the 1970s and 1980s.

This constraint—which at one time was the most inflexible—is today one of the softest. The sharp price increases of 1976, 1980 and beyond have exposed Hungarian consumers to considerable price shocks; between 1979 and 1981 consumer prices rose by a previously unacceptable 7.5

percent.[21] On the other hand, many necessities are still offered below producer cost, reflecting the government's continued dedication to keeping the price of non-luxury goods low. In 1980, Hungarian subsidies of consumer goods still accounted to over 40 billion forints.[22]

Distribution of Income. This is a highly ideological constraint, and is in line with the societal policy of the state. In Hungary, as in other socialist countries, the government is expected to assure the social well-being of its population. For reasons stemming largely from Marxist ideology, the state wishes to avoid the concentration of wealth in the hands of the few. Economic reformers were thus constrained from undertaking any reforms which would significantly alter present income distribution statistics. Reconciling this constraint with need for material incentives to augment enterprise efficiency is one of the most challenging problems for Hungarian economic reformers. The ratio of the wealthiest 10 percent of households to the poorest 10 percent as measured in income (not total wealth) is about 4:1.[23]

Changes in Institutions, Bureaucracies, and Management. Hungarian planners were faced with an environmental constraint on rapid administrative, organizational, and managemental changes.[24] Although heralding considerable changes in the way in which enterprises were to be changed, the reform of 1968 called for little if any changes in institutional structure. Personnel changes were rare; in spite of the new demands of the post-reform era, all the previous directors and managers of economic policy were retained. The established bureaucracy had entrenched interests in the old system and yielded to change unwillingly. In fact, once the reform started to expose some of the inefficiencies of some firms, the leaders of these firms jumped to the forefront of a movement to roll back some of NEM's principles. They succeeded partially, when at the end of 1972, 50 of the largest firms were placed in a special category, exempting them from many NEM rules.[25]

Reformers also wished to maintain an appearance of political stability and consistent policy. Underlying the reluctance to inject new blood into management and administration, and promulgating substantial institutional reforms, was the fear of changing the status quo too quickly.

Hungarian officials were eying very carefully the invasion of Czechoslovakia in 1968 — along with the rapid abolishment of their recently introduced economic reforms. In fact, planners retained certain "brakes" in the reforms through which the government could still closely control the economy; the government reserved itself the right to intervene in all essential areas of the economy to maintain stability and ease the transition.[26]

CMEA obligations. A constraint planners faced specifically regarding foreign trade was the extent to which they could integrate themselves into Western markets without threatening Hungary's continued commitment to CMEA integration. CMEA agreements are fundamentally political and not economic: they are agreements between governments and not enterprises. Because Hungary's commitment to the CMEA was considerable, and because CMEA prices diverged significantly, planners were faced with problems of an economic type. In fulfilling CMEA obligations, Hungarian enterprises were constrained to sometimes far from optimal production mixes. To ensure the continued fulfillment of these obligations, some sort of direct control was necessary over these enterprises. Branch ministries which directed the flow of trade between Hungary and her CMEA partners inhibited decentralization and trade liberalization in two important ways: first, the measure of success was not a function of the sum of the profits of each industry; fulfillment of CMEA obligations was still a partial measure of success. This not only led to inefficiencies in product mix, but also set a barrier to the general atmosphere of profit maximization. Secondly, since only branch ministries accounted for profit, informational exchanges took place only within a rigid vertical structure. Changing economic conditions were thus difficult to integrate into the planning process.[27]

Foreign Trade Reforms Under NEM

Decentralization of Decision Making. Important changes in the decision making structure were implemented in foreign trade. Consistent with the tendency toward decentralization, administrative authority was redistributed from the

National Planning Office and branch ministries to the National Material and Price Office, the banking system, and the Ministries of Foreign Trade, Finance and Labor. [28] The Planning Office prepared the broad, indicative outlines for producers, and coordinated the elaborate system of economic regulators. The Materials and Price Office formulated and implemented government price policies. The Ministry of Foreign Trade worked in conjunction with other branch ministries to control economic regulations relating to foreign trade. It also conducted trade negotiations with other nations. [29]

The Hungarian National Bank acquired new prominence in the realm of foreign trade. It carried out payment, administered foreign exchange controls, and granted credit to export industries. The Hungarian Foreign Trade Bank Ltd. was the only other commercial bank authorized to conduct business in foreign exchange; its tasks, however, were limited to the scope of joint ventures between Hungarian and foreign firms. [30]

With the implementation of NEM, most foreign trade was conducted by so-called foreign trade enterprises (FTEs), firms who engaged solely in such activities. A large portion of the trade conducted by FTEs was conducted on behalf of other enterprises: less than 10 percent of trade conducted by FTEs was for their own account. FTEs were reimbursed on a commission basis and with the sharp increases in raw materials prices in 1973 many did quite well. So well, in fact, that the government imposed a tax on the "excess profits" of these enterprises. [31]

All export and import transactions by Hungarian firms required licenses distributed by the Ministry of Foreign Trade. Licensing ensured some direct control by the government over foreign trade. Not only did it provide assurance that only licensed firms would engage in foreign trade, but also allowed the government to guarantee the fulfillment of various bilateral agreements made among CMEA countries. It also allowed the government consciously to control the balance of trade to a large extent. [32] The majority of trade was conducted under so-called "global" licenses, which gave an enterprise the right to import and export goods from both Eastern and Western countries.

Allocation of a maximum amount of foreign exchange to enterprises was eliminated. Under the reform, firms with import licenses would be granted by the National Bank.[33]

Price Policy. Price policy had great implications for foreign trade, and rationalization of the price structure in the Hungarian economy was a central issue in NEM.

The administered price structure used with the method of material balances had to be abandoned; it had little to do with real world prices and was inconsistent with a policy of exposing the domestic economy to the world market. Traditional Marxian view holds that the value of a commodity is composed of the price of capital, current labor, and surplus value. This formulation and other Marxian alternatives did not relate relative scarcities and consumer demand to price formation; prices could not be used as a guide for resource allocation.[34]

Under the reform, prices were to be determined by the supply and demand of international markets. Relative prices of goods (except agriculture and retail trade) were to be determined by the world market, and linked to the domestic economy by arbitrary exchange rates.[35] In the realm of exports, this system had few drawbacks; prices were converted back to forints at the given exchange rates. In the realm of imports, the problem was more complex. Hungary imported from both socialist and non-socialist countries, and prices in the two regimes were substantially different. With this in mind, a system of dual-tiered exchange rates was established for converting both convertible and non-convertible currency export earnings into forints.

Working within the constraint of price stability, NEM planners introduced different categories for different imported goods. Their prices were permitted to move only in specific margins. The reform of 1968 abolished central price determination for 12 percent of agricultural goods, 28 percent of domestically produced materials and semi-finished products, 78 percent of industrial products, and 23 percent of consumer goods. Prices remained fixed or were subject to upper limits for 70 percent of goods in the first two categories, 20 percent in the third, and over 50 percent of the fourth. The remainder were allowed to fluctuate within certain limits.[36] These reforms went far in rationalizing the price system; they made prices reflect relative scarcities more accurately. Within two years, the scope of price determination was further reduced for material and semi-finished products. Nevertheless, some conditions remained which gave rise to disequilibrium conditions. Differences in rates of profit were recorded even between firms of the same industry. For those involved in exports, profitability was determined on the basis of international prices. [37]

The constraints on price stability, however, led to further distortions of world economic conditions. Originally, architects of NEM envisioned a consumer price level 6-10 percent higher than producer prices.[38] Although this difference was initially kept, the rapid surge in import prices in 1974 caused production prices to be actually 4 percent *higher*, on the average, than on the consumer level. Rates of exchange were not revalued, and under the constraints of price stability, goods had to be subsidized more and more heavily. In 1979, the average subsidy on food stuffs was 18.3 percent (up to 54 percent on milk), electricity 34 percent, home heating 31.5 percent, mass transit 141.2 percent. Sales taxes on luxury goods, at the same time rose to 40 percent. [39]

Exchange rates. The role of the exchange rate under NEM was outlined by the longtime head of the Materials and Price Office, Béla Csikós-Nagy in 1979. The exchange rate must: 1) maintain the stability of the domestic economy, by insuring the stability of domestic currency; 2) inform export enterprises about the relative values of foreign currencies; 3) bring exports and imports to an equilibrium in the balance of payments. [40]

NEM introduced a system of dual-tiered exchange rates which was to reconcile price differences between goods imported from or exported to CMEA and Western countries. This system had three aims: to rationalize the prices of imports and exports to assess the profitability of individual firms and to direct government trade policies through economic regulators with regard to Western trade. There were actually exchange rates; a commercial rate, used by enterprises for foreign trade transactions, and a tourist or non-commercial rate. Within the CMEA, the forint's value was calculated on the basis of the transferable ruble.[41] In 1968, the conversion rate was established at 40 forints for 1 transferable ruble, and 60 forints for 1 dollar. Both these rates were periodically revised to reflect the devaluation of the dollar. By 1980, the transferable ruble had declined to 28 forints and the dollar to 34 forints.[42] These rates were however, essentially arbitrary; they were not pure exchange rates in the traditional sense. Nevertheless, the establishment of an exchange rate based on rough purchasing power parity with other nations for a non-convertible currency like the forint was an important step.

The reason for separate commercial and non-commercial rates is understandable in light of Hungary's policy of mass subsidization of consumer goods. The government subsidized the same goods on which tourists spent money, such as food, restaurants, public transportation, and entertainment. Even with the lower tourist rate, in 1978 the government was subsidizing tourist consumption to the tune of 1.6 billion forints — over 1 percent of the national income.[43]

Convertibility. The first twelve years of the reform did not see the introduction of full convertibility of the forint. Beginning with the reform, any Hungarian firm with an export license could obtain currency from the National Bank. Convertible currency could not be obtained legally by a private citizen; significant amounts, however, were made available every four years for purposes of travel to the West. Western tourists, on the other hand, were free to convert their convertible currency into forints to purchase Hungarian goods.

A primary goal of Hungarian economic policy since the introduction of NEM has been to obtain external financial convertibility for the forint. Such a declaration would demand a Hungarian economy so strong that it could induce foreigners to hold its currency, and guarantee its immediate conversion to any Western convertible currency. Hungary would also have to offer attractive interest rates in relation to international financial markets. Financial convertibility, however, would not mean free access to convertible currency by Hungarian citizens travelling abroad.[44]

If Hungary were to succeed in obtaining convertibility for the forint, several advantages would accrue: it would improve Hungary's international prestige and credit worthiness; it would attract foreign capital on a more favorable basis; it would further rationalize the price structure, yielding other general benefits to the economy.[45]

Tariffs, Quotas, Subsidies. The introduction of NEM

signaled a reform in the system of tariffs on goods flowing into
Hungary. Tariffs serve as essential tools of foreign trade policy.
They can be used to grant concessions to countries in return
for similar favors, to regulate the quantity and composition of
imports, and to protect domestic industries from international
competition. Hungary divides the nations with whom it trades
into three categories: less developed countries (who are looked
on very favorably), those nations to whom Hungary has given
Most Favored Nation (MFN) status, and all others. [46] Tariffs
for countries with MFN status are about 30 percent.

Although clearly an exercise in trade liberalization, the
reform continued to limit the importation of certain goods.
Quotas served the dual purpose of limiting imports from
Western (convertible currency) countries, and in making sure
firms were living up to their CMEA obligations. [47] In 1968
items such as electrical energy, automobiles, foundry and
furnace coke, and consumer goods were all subject to import
quotas. [48] Conditions permitting, these quotas were to be
abolished in the near future.

Export subsidies were granted to individual enterprises in
relation to the number of dollars or rubles earned. They were
set individually for each enterprise and product. A single subsidy rate for each individual enterprise, was to encourage it to
choose export products based on relative prices. [49] A special
import turnover tax was also used to harmonize the prices of
raw materials from the three different sources—domestic,
CMEA, and Western countries. [50] An import price subsidy was
used to keep firms who manufacture goods with high priced
imported inputs working and profitable. [51] Temporary price
fluctuations of the world market were curtailed through a
so-called reserve fund for import price equalization. [52] Savings
for the fund were obtained in relation to given reference
prices. In times of price increases, losses were covered by this
same fund.

"Brakes" on the Reform. The New Economic Mechanism
gave a great deal of independence to enterprises with respect to
production, planning, and sales. Yet how much real
self-determination could be given to the firm, especially in the
foreign trade sector? Enterprises were free to establish their
own product mix based on perceived consumer demand, to
procure materials necessary for their production, and to sell

their output. The reform tried to create a direct relationship between the firm and the consumer, both in domestic and foreign trade sectors. Yet, it is evident that the reform did not result in the abandonment of all administrative control over foreign trade. The government retained strict control over prices, exchange rates, convertibility, tariffs, quotas, and subsidies. It is quite likely that a drastic reform in combination with a sudden release in administrative control would have greatly exacerbated the problems of adjustment. Pressure from domestic shortages, for example, could have increased imports to an unacceptable degree. Complete and sudden trade liberalization would have unavoidably challenged the constraints of societal policy in the implementation of the reforms.

This potential for instability ensured that foreign trade restrictions and instruments of state control were retained. Government intervention guaranteed that Hungarian enterprises which were not yet competitive on an international level would be protected. Controls could be used sparingly to increase gradually the pressure on certain enterprises to produce more efficiently. [53] Despite these "brakes" on complete liberalization, Hungarian foreign trade policy had come a long way from its bilateral orientation, and had moved toward multilateral trade where conditions of comparative advantage were considered.

Performance Under NEM

Early Performance and Response to the Price Shocks, 1968-75. The first six years of the reform bode well for Hungary. The architects of NEM were successful in reversing a declining growth rate. In the foreign trade sector, export performance in market economies improved markedly. The dollar value of exports in the period between 1968-73 rose at an annual rate of 24 percent; this compares with growth rates of between 14 percent and 18 percent for other CMEA countries. [54] Hungary's performance was only exceeded by Romania's 28 percent growth rate. Romania had significantly increased its oil exports during this period. Total trade with the West was in rough balance; convertible currency deficits were only two percent of Western imports. [55]

This encouraging performance was soon challenged by the external price shocks of 1973 and the 1974-75 recession which followed. There were two general responses to the worldwide disequilibrium in the early 1970s. [56] Outward oriented economies like Japan, responded to these shocks with a deflationary policy causing recession, but one that limited the deterioration in the balance of payments. Inward oriented economies like Hungary, tried to isolate themselves from the world market, and relied on foreign loans to maintain rates of economic growth. This demanded that the government increase its regulation of prices and other market activities.

Hungary was determined not to compromise its rate of growth in consumption and investment in response to external disturbances. Growth rates of Net Material Product averaged 6 percent between 1973 and 1975; there were similar increases in consumption. Net investment showed a rapid rise during this period — 34.2 percent in 1973 and 11.5 percent in 1978. [57] The goal of foreign trade policy was to insulate Hungarian producers and consumers from price increases and the effects of deteriorating terms of trade. Hungarian decision makers wanted to protect the economy from the adjustment costs that internalizing the new set of world market prices would have entailed.

To finance its increases in consumption and investment, Hungary increasingly turned to foreign borrowing. Hungary's indebtedness in convertible currencies more than doubled between 1973 and 1975. [58] It rose from 3.1 billion dollars in 1975 to 8.8 billion dollars in 1979. [59] Its debt service ratio of 42 percent in 1981 was exceeded only by Poland's. [60]

Meanwhile, Hungary's terms of trade had deteriorated significantly. In the first five years after the price shock, import prices jumped by 70 percent. Export prices, however, could not follow suit. They increased by only 30-40 percent. Terms of trade declined by 19 percent in the period between 1975 and 1980. [61]

About 65 percent of the increase in convertible currency deficit reflected deterioration in terms of trade. The remaining percentage represented an increased growth of imports, and a decline in export expansion. [62] Imports rose to maintain previous levels of domestic consumption; at the same time exports lagged because of their inferior quality and a reduction in export incentives.

A conscious effort to isolate producers and consumers from the world market made increased government regulation of firms' activities necessary. At this time, firms experienced a reduction in incentives to export. Special subsidies were withdrawn from those FTEs that seemed to be reaping "excess profits" from the sharp increases in the price of Western imports. [63] In some instances special taxes were placed on these firms; the government grew concerned about the equality in the distribution of income. At the same time, enterprises that were losing money in their production of exports (including the most inefficient ones) received additional subsidies to compensate for their losses, and to maintain their "competitiveness." [64] Import subsidies were also used extensively at this time to protect the consumer from rising world prices.

The widespread use of such subsidies meant that domestic prices were becoming increasingly isolated from world market prices. Their usefulness as signals for consumers and producers were significantly reduced. Through various taxes and subsidies, firm by firm, product by product differences were being gradually introduced. [65] The consequences of these policies were much more severe than planners had anticipated. Distortions between the world market and producer prices, as well as between producer and consumer prices, gave consumers little incentive to alter their patterns of consumption to reflect the changing scarcities in the world market. Despite the quadrupling of oil prices in 1973, Hungarian consumers had no incentives toward conservation: the domestic price of petroleum was only one-third of world market price in 1974. [66] Energy intensive patterns of production in manufacturing and agriculture were not altered. Ironically, the use of import subsidies in this period actually increased the demand of imported inputs by industries. Imports increased 25 percent between 1973 and 1975. [67]

At the same time, while extensive import and export subsidies offset change in world prices, no incentives were offered to alter the export structure of the Hungarian economy in response to changed conditions. [68] Between 1967 and 1973 Hungary's volume of exports grew at 11 percent per annum. By the period between 1973-76 this had declined to about 4.5 percent. [69]

Attempts at Adjustment, 1976-1979. As Hungarian exports were not bringing in adequate amounts of foreign exchange, and maintenance of high rates of growth and consumption and investment was dependent upon extensive foreign borrowing, it became clear that Hungary could not maintain its present policies. Borrowed funds had largely been used to subsidize consumption, and for costly, long-term investments. Thus, the Hungarian economy could not generate the necessary foreign exchange with its export industries, to service foreign loans, and to maintain rates of growth. Hungary finally succeeded in improving its balance of payments in 1976 with a decline in the rate of growth of aggregate expenditures. But in 1977 and 1978, demand expenditure once again exceeded output.[70] This led to an increase in imports and a decline in export expansion; consequently, Hungary's convertible currency debt continued to rise.

In an effort to bring domestic prices closer to world market prices, Hungary introduced major price increases in 1976. Export taxes were abolished and subsidies were reinstituted as incentives for expansion in the export sector. In addition, a special fund was established to provide financing for exports which would earn convertible currency. [71] The new incentives, however, were not enough to regain previous growth rates. Although exports had risen at an annual rate of 10 percent between 1968 and 1973, they rose by only 7 percent between 1973 and 1978. In contrast to the earlier years of the economic reform, during this period, Hungary could surpass only one of its neighbors, Czechoslovakia, in increases of the dollar value of exports in the 1970s. [72]

In 1979, the Hungarian government abruptly applied a stringent deflationary policy, and consumption rose by only 2.4 percent in 1979 and 1.4 percent in 1980. As a result, Hungary's deficit in convertible currency trade declined to .3 billion in 1979 and to almost nothing in 1980. [73]

The Reform of the Reform, 1980. On the first of November, 1979, the official gazette of the Hungarian People's Republic, *Magyar Közlöny* /Hungarian Gazette/, published 56 new regulations concerning economic policy which were to come into force in January 1st, 1980. [74]

This new set of reforms returned the economy to the course

NEM had set for it eleven years earlier. The new reforms gave highest priority to improving Hungary's trade balance; they signalled an acknowledgement that the policy of trying to isolate the economy from world market disturbances could not be maintained. To improve its economic position, decision makers introduced painful austerity measures, and in a direct reaffirmation of NEM, introduced measures to further improve the efficiency and export capability of domestic enterprises.

The new reform brought significant changes in Hungarian price policy, introducing competitive prices into the industrial sector. Béla Csikós-Nagy, president of the Materials and Price Office saw this as existing when "the input of natural resources is determined by the input price, and the final product price is determined by the export price in non-ruble forms." The reform applied to over 80 percent of industrial prices. [75]

Producer prices were also directly linked to consumer prices. Policy makers wanted to undo the policy blunders made after 1973, and to reaffirm the role prices were to play, as outlined in the 1968 reform. This resulted in major price increases in consumption goods. The price of necessities such as bread, meat, electricity, and heating all rose by up to 50 percent. Although these increases were substantial, only one item, bread, correlated to the producer's price. [76]

Linking domestic prices to world markets, it was hoped, would once more make profit a relevant success indicator. The production of exports and other goods thus could be made more efficient, and more responsive to consumer demand. Product quality, it was also hoped, would be brought up to par with Western goods, making them competitive on Western markets.

Competition from abroad and the use of realistic world-market prices were chosen as the motivating forces behind Hungary's second round of reforms. But reforms in the foreign trade sector also sought to improve the competitiveness of domestic industries by reducing **enterprise-specific** import and export subsidies, lowering tariff barriers, encouraging firms to engage in foreign trade directly, rather than through FTEs. [77] The reduction of import and export subsidies, for example, forced domestic firms to compete with foreign firms on a least cost basis.[78] Firms that would continue to be unprofitable at world prices, would either be merged with more profitable ones or go bankrupt. Exports were explicitly encouraged. A uniform subsidy rate was established to rebate the sales tax normally applied to consumer goods to be exported. Thus, producers could charge a higher price for goods produced for export than for those produced for domestic consumption.

Convertible currency trade was made more attractive to domestic producers when the forint was revalued upward 12.5 percent against the ruble.[79]

Obstacles to the Expansion of Trade. With the introduction of NEM in 1968, and its reaffirmation in 1980, planners decided to base Hungary's economic policy around the competitive and uncertain environment of world trade. But there remained some significant political, institutional, and attitudinal obstacles to integration into world markets.

World Conditions: In 1980, following the invasion of Afghanistan, U.S.-Soviet relations deteriorated to a great extent, spelling the end to the era of detente.[80] Although its economic policy diverged significantly, Hungary's foreign policy remained closely linked with that of the Soviet Union. Thus, as a nation in the Eastern Bloc, Hungary was subject to the same biases stemming from the West as the Soviet Union (e.g. Stricter COCOM list, etc.). Secondly, there was still a great uncertainty about world market prices for fuel and raw materials (to which Hungary had made itself increasingly vulnerable with the reforms of 1980). Such uncertainty may have forced Hungary to rely on more stable sources from its CMEA partners. Thirdly, the changing of relative world prices led to further deterioration in Hungary's terms of trade. This was especially burdensome at a time when export enterprises were expected to expand.

Obstacles Originating in the East: The Hungarian export industry was still manufacturing products which were non-competitive in the West. Although they were adequate (indeed, sometimes highly desirable) in the less-demanding CMEA markets, they were unable to compete in West European and American markets. Often their packaging was unattractive to Western customers. Hungarian companies were unable to offer to service the goods they sold. Hungary's shortage of convertible currency limited its ability to purchase Western technology with which it could improve its export industry. The range of goods available for trade was also limited by Hungary's obligations to its CMEA partners. This is a major obstacle to Hungary's ever becoming a country where comparative advantage is the prime consideration for trade. Western companies often complained about the lack of timely decisions on the part of Hungarian companies; the slowness of the Hungarian bureaucracy, even with its greater decentralization, often discouraged companies from trade.

Obstacles Originating from the West: Obstacles against the expansion of trade with Hungary stemming from the West are often politically motivated. Western nations, under the leadership of the United States, have a common embargo policy toward Eastern Bloc nations. By placing certain items on the so-called COCOM list, they prevent the exportation of high technology and strategically important goods to the Soviet Union and Eastern Europe. Some of the items on the list are of questionable strategic value. Even so, one businessman who ships wood-paneling to Hungary routinely has his goods stamped "prohibited."[81]

Although the United States granted MFN status to Hungary in 1978, this is subject to annual review. The uncertainty of its renewal inhibits Western companies from making long term commitments to Hungary. In addition, Hungary is still subject to assorted quotas and tariffs which discourage its entrance into Western markets. Western creditors are hesitant to finance sales to Hungary. Eastern Europe is still often viewed as a Communist monolith. Western consumers also exhibit a bias against goods from Eastern Europe.

Conclusion

In the foreign trade sector, Hungarian performance between 1968-80 has been mixed. Hungary's balance of trade has deteriorated through the decade of the seventies, and its convertible currency debt has increased substantially. These problems essentially stemmed from poor world economic conditions, the inefficiency of Hungarian domestic production, and the policy decision made in trying to insulate the

Hungarian economy from the effects of sharp increases in raw material prices. Hungary's performance is not indicative of the fundamental misdirection in the nature of the reforms themselves. With the introduction of the 1980 reform, Hungarian planners reaffirmed their commitment to establishing a competitive price structure, and integrating Hungary into Western trade flows. The incentive to do this has come within Hungary itself, as it has realized that it must adjust its own economy to the laws which govern the rest of international trade.

In view of the limitation imposed on it as a small, resource poor country, Hungary had to reform its traditional CPE with special reference to foreign trade. To a certain extent, it had succeeded; much has changed since the days when its foreign trade was reduced to bilateral agreements among CMEA countries. At least in its first five years of implementation, NEM pointed in the direction of a long term success. But in 1973, Hungarian planners made fateful decisions reflecting their unwillingness to expose Hungary to world market conditions, and the negative effects of this could be felt throughout the rest of the decade. Nevertheless, relative to other East Bloc nations, Hungary has shown a great willingness to implement significant reforms in its foreign trade sector. This spirit of reform and the willingness to change and improve—unless sidetracked by such other factors as heavy indebtedness to the West—bodes well for the long term prospects of Hungarian foreign trade.

Notes

1. Iván T. Berend and György Ránki, *Hungarian Economy in the 20th Century* (London, 1985), p. 254.

2. T. Vajna, "Problems and Trends in the Development of the New Economic Mechanism: A Balance Sheet for the 1970s," in *The Eastern Economics in the 1970s*, eds. A. Nove, H. Hohman, G. Siedenslicher (London: Butterworth, 1982), p. 207.

3. A Brown and J. Licari, "Hungary and Foreign Trade," in *Comparative Economic Systems: A Decision Making Approach*, eds. E. Neuberger and W. Duffy (Boston: Allan and Barron, 1976), p. 291.

4. F. Holzman, *Foreign Trade Behavior in Eastern Europe* (Princeton: Princeton University Press, 1973), p. 28.

5. Berend, Ránki, p. 276.

6. *Ibid.*, p. 279.

7. Brown, Licari, p. 291.

8. *Ibid.*, p. 292.

9. Berend, Ránki, p. 275.

10. *Ibid.*, p. 279.

11. P. Marer and J. M. Montias, "CMEA Integration: Theory and Practice," in *East European Economic Assessment*: *A Compendium of Papers Submitted to the Joint Economic Committee, Congress of the United States*, (Washington: U.S. Government Printing Office, 1981), p. 159.

12. Berend, Ránki, p. 282.

13. Brown, Licari, p. 296.

14. István Friss, "Tiz év gazdasági reform" /Ten years of Economic Reform/, *Valóság*, July 1978, p. 1.

15. M. Bornstein, "Price Formation Models and Price Policy in Hungary," in *The Socialist Price Mechanism*, ed. A. Aboucher (Durham, NC: Duke University Press, 1977), p. 63.

16. X. Rachet, "Is There a 'Hungarian' Mode of Planning?" in *Hungary*: *A Decade of Economic Reform*, eds. P. G. Hare, H. K. Radice and N. Swain (London: George Allan and Unwyn, 1981), p. 7.

17. David Granick, *Enterprise Guidance in Eastern Europe* (Princeton: Princeton University Press, 1975), p. 245.

18. Granick, p. 246

19. Granick, p. 251.

20. B. Csikós-Nagy, *A magyar árpolitika* /Hungarian Price Policy/ (Budapest: Kossuth Könyvkiadó, 1982), p. 41.

21. Csikós-Nagy, p. 41.

22. Vajna, p. 209.

23. Personal interview with György Szelényi, Research Fellow, Hungarian Institute for Financial Research, 27, February, 1985.

24. Granick, p. 253.

25. P. Marer, "Economic Reform in Hungary," in *Comparative Economic Systems*: *Models and Cases*, ed. M. Bornstein (Homewood, Illinois: Richard D. Irwin, Inc., 1985), p. 294.

26. B. Balassa, "A magyar gazdasági reform tiz év után" /The Hungarian Economic Reform After Ten Years/, *Valóság*, July 1978, p. 29.

27. M. Marrese, "The Hungarian Economy: Prospects for the 1980s," in *Economic Reform in Eastern Europe and Prospects for the 1980s* (New York: Pergamon Press, 1980), p. 199.

28. P. Marer, "The Mechanism and Performance of Hungarian Foreign Trade, 1966-1979," in *Hungary*: *A Decade of Economic Reform*, p. 162.

29. Marer, "Mechanism and Performance," p. 162.

30. *Ibid.*, p. 162.

31. *Ibid.*, p. 164.

32. *Ibid.*, p. 165.

33. *Ibid.*, p. 166.

34. *Ibid.*, p. 167.

35. *Ibid.*, p. 170.

36. B. Balassa, *The Hungarian Economic Reform, 1968-81* (Washington, DC.: World Bank, 1981), p. 7.

37. *Ibid.*, p. 8.

38. Marer, "Mechanism and Performance," p. 169.

39. Csikós-Nagy, p. 128.

40. Marer, "Mechanism and Performance," p. 174.
41. *Ibid.*, p. 170.
42. Csikós-Nagy, p. 144.
43. Marer, "Mechanism and Performance," p. 174.
44. P. Marer, "Exchange Rates and Convertibility in Hungary's New Economic Mechanism," in *East European Economic Assessment*, p. 542.
45. Marer, "Exchange Rates," p. 543.
46. Marer, "Mechanism and Performance," p. 177.
47. *Ibid.*, p. 165.
48. *Ibid.*, p. 167.
49. *Ibid.*, p. 178.
50. *Ibid.*
51. *Ibid.*
52. *Ibid.*, p. 179.
53. W. Lindner, "Hungary: Marching Forward," in *Reform in Soviet and East European Economies* (Toronto: Lexington Books, 1972), p. 82.
54. Balassa, *1968-81*, p. 12.
55. *Ibid.*, p. 13.
56. *Ibid.*
57. *Ibid.*
58. *Ibid.*, p. 14.
59. P. Marer, "East European Economies: Achievements, Problems, Prospects," in *Communism in Eastern Europe*, ed. T. Rakowska-Harmstone (Bloomington, Indiana: Indiana University Press, 1983), p. 313.
60. Marer, "East European Economies," p. 316.
61. Berend, Ránki, p. 282.
62. Balassa, *1968-81*, p. 15.
63. Marer, "Mechanism and Performance," p. 169.
64. Granick, p. 274.
65. Balassa, *1968-81*, p. 14.
66. *Ibid.*, p. 16.
67. *Ibid.*
68. *Ibid.* p. 15.
69. Balassa, "A magyar gazdasági reform," p. 28.
70. Balassa, *1968-81*, p. 19.
71. *Ibid.*, p. 20.
72. *Ibid.*
73. *Ibid.*
74. Vajna, p. 207.
75. *Ibid.*, p. 208.
76. Marer, "Mechanism and Performance," p. 197.
77. Marrese, p. 196.
78. *Ibid.*, p. 197.
79. *Ibid.*, p. 198.
80. *Ibid.*, p. 199.
81. John Grunwald, President, Webb Company of Edinburgh, Indiana. *Trade with Hungary*, lecture given at Indiana University, 23 February, 1985.

VII.

HUNGARIAN-AMERICAN LIFE, CULTURE, AND POLITICS

Ferenc Tar:

23 / ALEXANDER ASBÓTH: HUNGARIAN GENERAL IN THE AMERICAN CIVIL WAR*

In 1984 there was a small exhibit in Keszthely, Hungary, concerning Sándor /Alexander/ Asbóth, a native son of the city. Preparation for the exhibition presented an excellent opportunity to take a closer look at the life and accomplishments of this eminent man and outstanding personality.

Already at the beginning there appeared a number of contradictions in his biographical data. Based on the information provided by the *Hungarian Biographical Dictionary* /Magyar Életrajzi Lexikon/,[1] he was born in the city of Keszthely on December 11, 1811, and died in Buenos Aires on January 21, 1868. The twenty-one volume *Révai's Great Encyclopedia /Révai Nagy Lexikona/,*[2] however, sets the date of his death in 1870. Data do not correspond in connection with the date of his birth either. According to most authors who have written about him, Asbóth was born on December 18, 1811. Yet, Ede Lósy-Schmidt[3] and Tivadar Ács[4] mention 1812 as the year of Asbóth's birth.

Having considered all this, it was only natural to try to find the correct date of his birth in local parish archives where the newborn's date of birth must have been entered more than 170 years ago. His name did not appear among those born in 1811; neither was he mentioned in 1812. Finally, after perusing the 1810 Register of Births, it became clear

---

*Translated by Hajnal Fekete; translation revised by
S. B. and A. H. Várdy.

that Sándor Asbóth was born in Keszthely in the year 1810, on the 18th of December.

Sándor Asbóth came from a family of English origins. [5] They were ennobled in 1715 in Hungary, and then given the praenomen or title of nobility of "Nemeskéri." His great-great grandfather was Prince Imre Thököly's court chaplain, while his grandfather, János Gottfried Asbóth, was a Lutheran minister in Sopron. His son, János Asbóth was educated in Sopron, and then later at the University of Göttingen, after which he became a reputable agricultural expert.

After teaching in the Northern Hungarian cities of Lőcse and Késmárk, in 1801 János Asbóth was appointed professor at the Georgikon Agricultural Academy in Keszthely by Count György Festetics, the Academy's founder. Nothing proves the Count's satisfaction with the new professor better than the award he received already in February of 1802, for his "commendable teaching of botany...." [6] By 1811 János Asbóth was the director of the Agricultural Academy, and five years later Count Festetics commissioned him to organize the first so-called "Helikon Feast," which was a great honor, later bestowed only upon men of distinction.

Professor János Asbóth and his wife had three sons, the eldest of whom was Lajos Asbóth, who later replaced General Lajos Aulich as commander of the 2nd Corps in the Hungarian War of Independence in 1848-1849. After the Hungarian defeat of August 1849, General Asbóth was sentenced to death, but his sentence was later changed to life imprisonment. Then in 1857, he was granted amnesty and set free. But in 1861 he was again arrested for conspiracy and imprisoned in the Austrian fortress of Kufstein. A flaw in his character is a recent allegation that, having been broken in spirit during the many years of imprisonment, he became an informant for the Viennese regime, and revealed the details of a Hungarian political conspiracy to the authorities during the late 1850s. Having been released from Kufstein, he finally died on May 6, 1882. [7]

* * *

Sándor /Alexander/ Asbóth began his studies in his

home town of Keszthely, similarly to his older brother Lajos. Then he attended the North Hungarian Mining Academy of Selmecbánya, and in 1834 he received a degree in Engineering at the University of Pest (today Budapest).

In 1836 he went to work at the Provisionary Institute for Shipping. In 1844 he was appointed to the National General Office of Architecture /*Országos Főépítészeti Hivatal*/ in Temesvár [8] where he participated in the work instituted by Count Stephen Széchenyi to regulate Hungary's river system. Still later he also took part in the construction of the Chain Bridge over the Danube in Budapest.

The War Council of Temesvár refused to obey Louis Kossuth's order when the War of Independence broke out in 1848. For this reason Sándor Asbóth transferred his office to Nagybecskerek, and took up arms against the Imperial forces in Gen. György Klapka's Corps. From December 1848, he was a *honvéd* (home guard) engineering captain in Gen. Antal Vetter's headquarters. Then from May, 1849 onward he headed the War Department in Kossuth's Office with the rank of a major. While having this assignment, on July 16, 1849, he was promoted to the rank of a lieutenant colonel. [9]

In the course of the war he took part in the battles of Kápolna and Nagysalló and fought at the fortifications of Szenttamás. As opposed to the majority in the military leadership, he was not among Gen. Arthur Görgey's supporters, but remained faithful to Kossuth through thick and thin. He had met Kossuth in Debrecen in the spring of 1849 while he (Asbóth) was there as General Klapka's adjutant. [10] Asbóth was also there at Arad when the two rivals, Kossuth and Görgey, met just before the former's resignation as governor and flight to Turkey. Asbóth accompanied Kossuth into exile, but in doing so he could not forsee that like Kossuth, he too would never be able to return to his fatherland. [11]

The first stage of their exile in Turkey was Vidin, where Kossuth lived in the same house with Asbóth. As recalled by one of their fellow political exiles, "Kossuth was exceedingly fond of Asbóth. He esteemed and respected Asbóth, as the latter was a well-educated gentleman of flawless character and manly virtues who rightly deserved Kossuth's utmost friendship." [12]

Life for the refugees in the camp was miserable. Kossuth depicts the time of dire necessity as follows: "Here are with me Foreign Minister Count Kázmér Batthyány, Lieutenant Generals Mészáros, Dembinszky and Bem, Brigadier Generals Perczel, Guyon, Visinszky, Kmety and Stein, with many of the field garde officers, 3,400 soldiers, the Italian and Polish Legions, and also with a good number of civilians.... Many of the foot soldiers, civilians, and officers would like to return, but are not allowed to. They are doomed to perish here, deprived of money and everything. They are only given food and nothing else. The soldiers are mostly barefeet and without overcoats; and with the weather getting evermore severe, they are dying off like flies. They are given neither boots nor money, and yet they are not allowed to return home. To call this friendship is outrageous." [13]

We know from Gábor Egressy's diary that a concert was held "for the benefit of sick and unclothed *honvéds.*" Though the aid never materialized, the performance did take place in Asbóth's flat. "The works performed included a couple of solos and recitations, and folk songs by the whole choir accompanied by a guitar.... Asbóth recited Vörösmarthy's poem "Hontalan" /The Exile/, the last lines of which seemed to have the effect of a dagger on Kossuth's soul." [14]

After a promise of amnesty, about 3,000 of the 3,500 refugees left for Hungary on October 21, 1850. Most of them, however, came to be enlisted into the Imperial Army.

The ones who stayed, left Vidin at the end of the month for Shumla in Bulgaria, where they arrived nearly a month later. From there sixty of the most important exiles were moved to Kütahya in Asia Minor, where they were interred in February of 1850. While in Kütahya, they were quartered in barracks, which of course meant top security surveillance for them. During their stay in that city, Kossuth tried to keep the discipline among his followers, and also corresponded on this matter with Sándor Asbóth.

The camp in Kütahya was disbanded on September 1, 1851. [15] As recalled by one of the exiles: "At last the hour of liberty has struck. At the crack of dawn we were awakened by rub-a-dub and fanfare heralding the end of our long captivity. Obeying this merry call we hurried to put our baggages on pack-horses. Having the children and women installed in tetra-sledges, and having ourselves mounted on horses, we left Kütahya at seven in the morning. The country-side we traversed was quiet and deserted...." [16]

Similarly to all other refugees, on September 4, 1851, Asbóth also received a passport from the Turkish authori-ties. [17] Kossuth and his companions were taken aboard the American frigate "Mississippi." [18] The latter wanted to reach England via France, but while waiting in Marseilles the Hun-garians received Napoleon III's word prohibiting their transit. The Hungarian passengers aboard the "Mississippi" parted in Gibraltar. Kossuth and his company sailed to Southampton aboard the English steamship "Madrid," while the others, Asbóth among them, sailed to New York, where they landed on November 10, 1851.

* * *

Upon landing in the New World, the former engineer-ing Lieutenant Colonel of the Hungarian War of Independ-ence immediately sought employment. Armed with Kossuth's recommendation, who arrived there in the last month of that year, Asbóth found work at a canal construction in Syracuse, New York, and then somewhat later in the ore mines of the Rocky Mountains. Later on, entering into partnership with a certain contractor named Davis Baldwin, he set up the largest steel foundry in America. However, he could not make a success of it; his partner "made away with the firm's money." [19] Later Asbóth was appointed an engi-neer in New York City, and was the first to use bitumen asphalt for paving sidewalks. He prepared plans for the city planning commission for designing Central Park and for the reorganization of Manhattan and Washington Heights. His plans for Manhattan were "exhibited at the 1933 Chicago World Fair as an example of a thoughtful proposal that could foresee for centuries the many needs of the incredibly fast developing metropolis." [20] Upon having seen Central Park in New York, the globe-trotting János Kadosa was proud to note in his book: "On my second excursion I made my way towards Central Park. This beautiful and huge public gar-den was designed by a Hungarian long before the city could have dreamed about it. The city accepted the plans of Asbóth, *honvéd* General, one of the most eminent refugees of our ill-fated War of Independence in 1848-49.... He rambled all over the suburbs and surroundings of the city, preparing various designs prompted by his genius, which became much called-for, both by the city and by wealthy individuals. The realization of these plans was thrust upon him as well." [21]

The Hungarian emigrants who landed in New York in November 1851 brought word that they would soon be followed by Kossuth himself. The American authorities would not have been opposed to Kossuth's final settling down in the New World. The leader of the Hungarian exiles, however, had nothing more in mind than winning over the American public to the Hungarian cause and then returning to Europe.

On his arrival on December 5, 1851, Kossuth held his first speech on Staten Island: "I have not come to the United States to interfere in your domestic affairs. You are the supreme masters of your own fate. I came on behalf of my downtrodden but unbroken nation...to humbly ask the people, and not any party, of the United States to kindly support our cause." [22] During his more than six months' stay in America, Kossuth called on almost every major city. He was seeking not only moral but also financial help. First, voluntary donations were collected; later $1.00, $5.00, $10.00 and $100.00 notes were issued for the benefit of the "Hungarian Fund," bearing the dates "February 2" and "July 1, 1852." On the money raised 6,000 guns were bought, and two gun factories were set up. Kossuth appointed Lieutenant Colonel Sándor Asbóth to organize the factories. Though Sándor Asbóth did not accompany Kossuth on his tour of America, they kept in close touch by way of correspondence. An ammunition factory was also set up in Morningville, New York, and on Kossuth's authorization Major Gusztáv Wagner was appointed to oversee its operation. A leather factory was likewise established on the farm of the Polish immigrant, Count Theodore Dembinski, located at Weavertown, near Hoboken. The director of the latter was Major Lajos Csomortányi. [23] Based on Asbóth's report dated July 12, 1852, we know that all of these factories were doing well. [24] In the warehouse of Atlantic Dock No. 21 in Brooklyn, the following items were stored: 7,500 weapons in 375 cases, a field-printing machine with full equipment, 10 cases of saddlery, and 9 cases containing all sorts of weapons. Receipts also show that 365,220 shells in 130 barrels and other ammunition accessories were transported here from Morningville.

We do not know for certain what happened to all the stock stored here. We only know that they were never sent over to Europe; so using them in Hungary remained but an illusion. Later 6,000 guns were pawned by Asbóth on Kossuth's order.

More than half of the donations from America was spent on buying weapons. The rest was used at Kossuth's discretion, which caused considerable dissatisfaction among the Hungarian emigrants in Europe.

Kossuth's tour of America did not measure up to expectations. The money collected also fell short of the amount expected. More importantly, however, despite the ovations he received almost everywhere, Kossuth could not gain the political support he sought.

Having stayed in America for six and a half months, on July 14, 1852 Kossuth and his wife embarked for England, traveling under the pseudonym Mr. and Mrs. A. Smith.

From London Kossuth kept up regular correspondence with his former aide, giving instructions concerning the war materials stored, asking for information on the financial situation of the immigrants, and directing Asbóth to support certain Hungarians coming from Europe to America. Letters sent by ship were exchanged regularly. The fact that Kossuth was satisfied with Asbóth's activity is testified to by his letter of recommendation for Asbóth in 1853 (see Appendix No.2).

The hope of the Hungarian immigrants to launch a new war of independence was revived in 1853 during the Crimean War. Kossuth informed Lieutenant Colonel Asbóth of his plans to renew the struggle.[25] Expectations, however, fell through as Austria did not extend the help to Russia that would have embroiled her in a war against France, England and Savoy (i.e., Italy). Following the war the political situation in Europe came to a new standstill. This meant the renewal of the differences of opinions among the immigrants and their further alienation from one another.

1859 was once more a year of renewed hopes. Backed by the French, the struggle for the unity of Italy began. This struggle immediately embroiled the Habsburgs, for at that time much of Italy was under their rule.

Through Asbóth Kossuth got in touch with the immigrants in America again. "Bitter years have passed over my graying head since I last received word from you," Kossuth began his letter dated June 4, 1859. [26] In this letter he elaborated on the general political situation in Europe, its favorable and unfavorable omens, the growing unrest among Hungarian emigrants in Europe, and the public feeling in Hungary: "At home the spirit of the people is very favorable to us, and the hatred against the Austrians indescribable. While being transported to Italy, Hungarian soldiers often go so far as to sing: 'It is the train that takes us there, but we shall return with Kossuth...'." While making it clear to Asbóth that "the time has not yet come for you to leave America," Kossuth also entrusted him with various tasks, including taking stock of all "trustworthy patriots," and establishing a fund to cover the transportation expenses of those "who wish to serve their fatherland on the battlefields." In addition, he asked for reports on the still operating factories.

In his answer Asbóth assured "Governor Kossuth" of his deep-felt respect and trust, and indicated his readiness to be at his service again: "My only wish is to do my utmost and to serve guided by your wise leadership. As far as I am concerned, Governor, I am ready and willing to leave at any moment...."[27] Financial difficulties, however, imposed serious problems. In vain did Hungarian immigrants in America urge Kossuth's aide in New York to set up preparations and establish the date of embarkation. To encourage unrest was in line with the French Emperor's interests, but Napoleon III was not about to support a war for Hungarian independence. And Kossuth knew that in the absence of international help, it would be foolhardy to start such a struggle.

* * *

Some of the Hungarian immigrants sought to adjust their way of life to that of the United States and tried to make a living as best as they could. As we have seen, Asbóth was one of these.

Having Abraham Lincoln elected President of the United States, the southern slave-holding states convened in Montgomery, Alabama, on February 4, 1861 to declare the Confederate States of America. Jefferson Davis was elected President of the Confederacy. This development, together with the attack against Fort Sumter that summer, triggered the Civil War in America.

Of the four to five-thousand Hungarians in the United States, about 800 joined the Union Army.[28] At the same time, not more than a few are known to have served in the Army of the Confederacy. Close to 100 of those serving in the Northern Army were officers, including two major generals (Julius Stahel-Számvald and Alexander Asbóth), five brigadier generals, fifteen colonels, two lieutenant colonels, fourteen majors and fifteen captains.[29]

When the Civil War broke out, Asbóth, the former lieutenant colonel of the Hungarian War of Independence, immediately volunteered for military service to fight against the slave-holding southern states.

At the start of the war the Confederate Army had the upper hand both in military equipment and manpower, as well as in the number of well-trained officers. For this reason, experienced European immigrants were welcome into the Northern Army. Immigrants were especially favored by John C. Fremont, Commander-in-Chief of the Army of the West.

Having enlisted in New York, Asbóth was sent to Missouri and soon was appointed chief-of-staff and thus higher in rank to the former candidate for presidency. Besides him the following staff officers were Hungarian: Colonel J. János Fiala, Chief of the Engineering Corps, Major Károly Zágony, Chief of the Guards, as well as Colonel Albert Anselm, and Captains Leonidas Haskell and József Reményfi.[30]

General Fremont appointed Asbóth commander of the 4th Division. It was in that capacity that he gave evidence of his courage during the capture of Springfield in October, 1861. His troops were involved in the capture of Bentonville and Fayetteville in 1862.

In the Battle of Pea Ridge on March 7th, 1862, the troops of General Samuel R. Curtis—the second successor of General Fremont—won a smashing victory over the southerners. Fighting the enemy bravely while leading his division, Asbóth received his first serious wound in this battle when his left arm was hit by a shell. In recognition of his bravery and other merits, the U.S. Congress now commissioned him a brigadier general, as had been recommended by Fremont more than a year before. This meant the peak of Asbóth's military career in the United States. Although subsequent to this he still commanded major military units and governed large territories, never did he get a military post of similar importance again.

In May 1862, Asbóth was sent to Mississippi to command regiments that were to reinforce troops advancing towards Corinth. This transfer meant breaking off ties with a large number of Hungarians and other immigrants he had been associated with in Missouri and Arkansas.[31] Later he was in charge of the fortifications of Memphis, Tennessee.

In January 1863 he was assigned to Kentucky where he was to ensure communications and pacify the rear area for the troops of General Grant advancing against Vicksburg. He had a difficult time in eradicating guerilla attacks. His decision to break up the cavalry under his command into several small units was most unfortunate, for it only made things easier for the enemy.[32]

In early August 1863 Asbóth was commissioned chief of the 3rd Division of General William T. Sherman's 15th Corps. Later that year he was appointed a district military commander in West Florida, with headquarters in Fort Pickens near Pensacola. This sort of sidelined him, for that whole region was only of peripheral significance to major operations against Mobile, Alabama, and to campaigns farther north.[33]

Asbóth organized new regiments from among freed blacks and pro-Union whites. He established close cooperation with David G. Farrangut, head of the operations against Mobile. Despite being on the periphery of operations, Asbóth sought to lead attacks against the enemy. He asked for weapons and other equipment, as well as for a steamship to transport his troops to the military base. He often proposed detailed plans for a cavalry attack against the southern hinterland, because he believed that communication among the rebels should be continuously distracted.

During his stay in Florida only once did he lead his soldiers into a pitched battle, this being the second and last major battle of his military career in the Civil War. This happened in September 1864 when he led a cavalry unit into the northern sector of his district to capture rebel commandos and to free captured union soldiers.

Facing the enemy his soldiers first took to flight at Marianna. The second charge was personally led by Asbóth, and this cavalry attack resulted in an overwhelming victory. He captured a great number of prisoners, weapons, mounts, cattle, and much contraband. In this battle Asbóth was seriously wounded. His left arm was fractured by a musket shell at two places, and another shell lodged in his cheek bone to remain there forever.

In February 1865 Asbóth returned to assume his command once more, but with the war winding down, his services were not needed any more. He was promoted breveted major general in recognition of his merits on March 13th, 1865, [34] and then in August of the same year he was demobilized. In his somewhat de-heroizing recent article, Earl Hess characterized General Asbóth as follows: "He was a cavalryman at heart, operating at his best when dashing off on raids into hostile areas, as he had done before the Battle of Pea Ridge and during the Marianna Expedition. His superiors never fully realized that. Consequently, Asbóth spent most of his career commanding infantry units or geographic areas.... For his quick rise to upper command levels under Fremont, he could have thanked that undiscriminating general's preference for European officers.... his faults led to irritation rather than serious disaster." [35]

* * *

As a reward for his services rendered, President Grant, the former Commander-in-Chief, appointed him Minister of the United States to Argentina after the Civil War. He received his letter of accreditation in Washington in March, 1866, signed by Secretary of State William H. Seward.

Though he wanted to assume his post as soon as possible,

first he went to Paris—departing aboard the Fulton on June 6, 1866—to undergo an operation by a certain Dr. Nelaton, who had performed a similar operation on Garibaldi before. He stayed in Paris until late August, but in vain. Drs. Nelaton and Fouvel and their assistants were unable to remove the shell from Asbóth's cheek bone.

Fifteen years had passed since he left Europe. Now he was again close to his fatherland and longed to breathe Hungarian air once more. But, to quote one of his earlier biographers, "the proud Hungarian of the War of Independence subdued the desire of his heart. Hungary was not yet free and independent." [36] But Hungary did take note of him, for later that year several Hungarian newspapers mentioned Sándor Asbóth, the "North American general," who was also "his new country's plenipotentiary minister to Argentina." [37]

From Paris he went to London, from where he sailed aboard the "Oneida" to Rio de Janeiro, and then to Montevideo. From there he went to Buenos Aires on the American battleship "Shomokin" and arrived there on October 14th, 1866.

In the Argentine capital, Asbóth, having arrived ill after a long journey, was given a heartfelt welcome. As General Mitre, President of the Republic, was at the front in the war against Paraguay, Asbóth presented his credentials on October 20th to Vice President Marcos Paz. [38]

In Buenos Aires Asbóth stumbled into one of his old-time fellow-in-arms, General János Czetz, General Josef Bem's one-time Chief-of-Staff, who had been living there for years. Following the conclusion of Peace at Villafranca that ended the Austro-French War in Italy, General Czetz settled down in Buenos Aires. There he was commissioned to establish the Institute of Cartography and the Military Academy of Argentina, and also took part in directing the military operations against Paraguay.

In South America a war had been going on between Paraguay and the Triple Alliance of Argentina, Brazil and Uruguay for some time. Now, together with his American colleagues in Paraguay and Brazil, Asbóth was commissioned to bring the warring parties to conference table. [39]

Asbóth informed his superior in detailed reports about

matters falling within his jurisdiction, as well as on the social conditions in Argentina and on the difficulties caused by the war. He handed a memorandum over to Rudino Elizalde, Foreign Secretary of Argentina, in which he depicted the plight caused by the war to Argentina, pointing out that the United States would favor a conclusion of peace between the fighting nations as soon as possible. So as to promote the cause of peace, in October 1867 he was also appointed the United States Minister to Uruguay. Notwithstanding his good will, however, his mediation met with little success and the war dragged on for many more years.

APPENDIX
No. 1
Family Tree of the Asbóth Family[40]

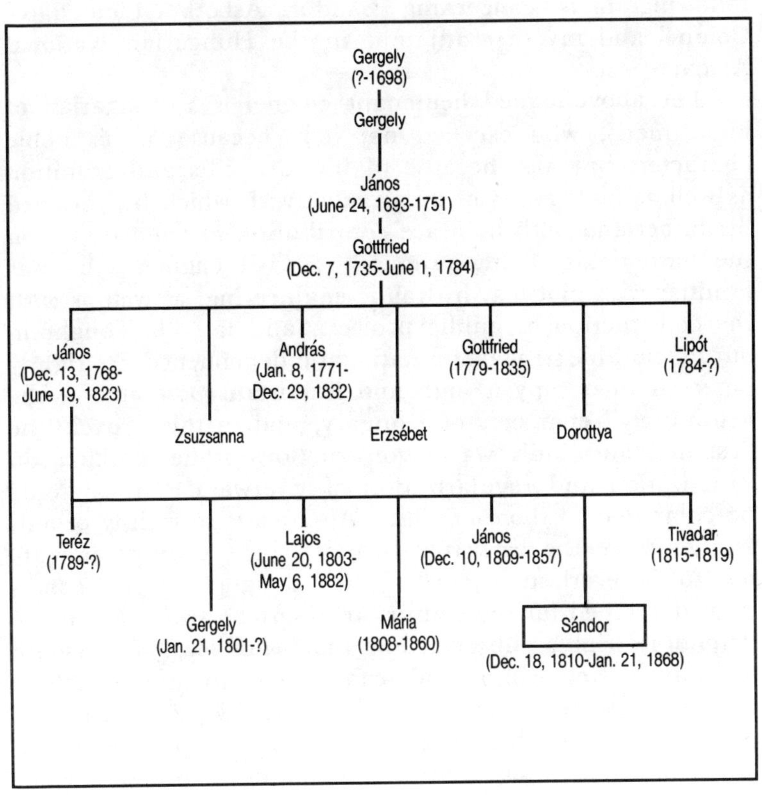

Although highly honored by his new country, General Asbóth never forgot his fatherland. He wanted to see Hungary once again, to visit his parents' grave, and to meet his relatives and friends. He felt, however, that he would no longer be able to undertake such a long journey because of his own deteriorating health. (See Appendix No. 3)

Asbóth died on January 21, 1868 in Buenos Aires and was buried in the city's Old English Cemetery.[41]

No. 2
Kossuth's Letter of Recommendation for Asbóth [42]

Whereby I, the undersigned, while fulfilling the duty to sincerely recognise patriotic services on the one hand and expressing my personal gratitude on the other, attest to the following facts concerning Sándor Asbóth, Lieutenant-Colonel and my first adjutant in the Hungarian National Army:

The above-named lieutenant colonel is a Hungarian of great merit, who excelled not only because of his noble character, but also because of his rare gifts and erudition as well as his services of great value with which he enriched his fatherland both in peace contributing to science and on the battlefields. Being originally a civil engineer, he was familiar with plotting, hydraulic engineering, as well as with the construction of public projects, and later he fought in our memorable struggle for national independence. He rightly deserved to occupy a high and important post among the leading civil engineers of Hungary, and in this capacity he designed and built water constructions while working on canalization and regularization of riverways that can only be compared to those of which America is so rightly proud, as they serve the perpetual benefit of the country and attest to the everlasting glory of their designers. When conditions developed for the country to resort to arms in order to defend its rights, liberty, and independence, Mr. Asbóth was immediately willing and ready to cast his life and blood and also his possessions on the scales. By exchanging his magnetic needle with the sword, he braved the enemy valiantly and relentlessly from the beginning to the end, while his personal merits gradually elevated him to the ranks of captain, major and lieutenant colonel respectively. He excelled first of all in the Battles of Tomasovácz, Kápolna, Kövesd, N.-Sarlós, and Komárom, where his valiance earned for him the military order of the 3rd rank. His rare skills as an officer of the engineering corps proved remarkable in several major events. He was present at many such dangerous situations, and a participant of all such undertakings. It was he who prepared perfect plans for the fortress of Temesvár and its environment, then in the hands of the enemy, for the upcoming siege; and it was also he who, though being watched by the enemy and amid strong and perpetual cannonade, bridged the Temes River at Tomasovácz in seven hours for our braving troops to advance against the entranched Serbian camp. It was he again who, without any kind of preparation, bridged the river Garam near Léva overnight, thus allowing our army of 40,000 to march to the glorious battlefield of Nagy-Sarlós that eventually humiliated Austria and forced her to find refuge in the arms of the Russian Tzar. It was again he who reinforced the roads near Babda and Szarvaskő before the Battle of Kápolna and designed the fortifications at Tiszfüred. Because of his excellence and competence he was singled out for the very important post of the chief engineer of the Fortress of Komárom to where he accompanied General Klapka as his adjutant when the latter was a Provisional Minister of Defense. Finally, I promoted him my own adjutant with the rank of Councillor of State, and with the assigned task to report on military affairs in the Council of Ministers on occasions when I chose to preside. Lieutenant Colonel Asbóth occupied this important post of trust until the last minutes of the war, performing his duties with constant zeal and enthusiasm for the cause to my utmost satisfaction, thus deserving that special trust I had put in him. This was his career as a patriot, fully deserving of my appreciation as the Governor of the Republic.

Then followed the period of personal devotion and friendship which entitles him to my everlasting gratitude toward him. When our joint fatherland met with sad trials which forced me to flee abroad as a miserable and homeless refugee, it was he who shared my adversities with touching devotion, accompanying me in my exile and truly standing by my side. Through all the trials of my arrest in Turkey he watched over my personal safety and calmed my soul by his self-denying care, always a true and loyal friend and brother, never wavering in his affections, not even in the saddest days of my life. May God remunerate him for all this should I not be able to do so, being still poor and homeless as I am. But I do hope that we shall still see better days, and that I shall be able to see them in order to prove my gratitude for his loyalty, the same way he had proved his loyalty, devotion, and friendship toward me. Finally, gaining his freedom through the generous mediation of the United States, Asbóth went on with all the activities in America I demanded of him within the given time and conditions, first to promote our fatherland's cause, and then to alleviate the hardship of his fellow immigrants. It is his deep-seated conviction that I may soon call upon him once more to help me achieve my greatest and sole aim, the liberation of our fatherland. In the meantime I truly and deeply recommend him to the good and generous graces of the people and government of the United States. I do so with complete confidence, for I know him to be as capable as any man to perform services and to create works for the huge projects and industrial firms aiming to facilitate transportation and communication between parts of this enormous union. I am convinced that he will bring the greatest honor to this country and constitute the most important means to make this land prosper. I consider the present certificate not only a testament to Lieutenant Colonel Asbóth's patriotic merits and rare gifts, but also a token of my respect, friendship, inclination, and gratitude toward him.

London, May 1st, 1853.

Lajos Kossuth,
Former Governor of Hungary

No. 3
Asbóth's Letter to a Friend, Dated June 25, 1867 [43]

Having suffered all the agonies of a long voyage by sea, I finally arrived in Buenos Aires in October last year. The field of diplomacy was again something new to me, but the civil management I headed besides my military leadership in the course of the war in several southern states meant good preparation, and thus I had some confidence in entering this new and slippery career. Having acted for six months as Minister for North America in the Argentine States, I was accredited to the same post in the neighboring Uruguay by my government and approved by the Senate. And thus, after undergoing so many trials in life, I finally received a position—thanks to the democratic republican institutions of my good home and to the renumerating trust of a populistic government caring for human strangers as well—in which, as a diplomatic representative of a great and free nation that acknowledges no superior authority over itself, I can look forward blissfully from my overcast past toward the happy termination of my days. And this is all the more so as recent events in Hungary permit me to hope that my beloved country, to which I have dedicated all my humble abilities and possessions both in the pride of my youth and in my manhood, will finally regain its ancient constitutional standing after eighteen years of manly patience; and will thus attain that for which we homeless refugees fell victim while fighting with dedication, conscious of our sacred rights. Deeply touched, let me also acknowledge, my dear friend, that together with this rising expectation there is also the deeply felt hope to see my fatherland once more freed from foreign yoke, to encounter the graves of my departed parents, to meet my good brother who has turned gray by now, and to see my only living sister and all those who, notwithstanding the long separation, have preserved the ties of friendship and nature. But fate seems to will it differently. For more than four months now, in painful sufferings, bound to my sick-bed in consequence of my old wounds, I daily witness the consumption of my vital forces. But abiding by an old maxim of mine, I hope for the best and prepare for the worst, while waiting for the wisest providence coming from above. If, helped by God's miracle, I could leave my bed and house behind, I would ask for a leave and depart to the mineral baths of Bohemia or of Hungary. In the latter case, this would mean revisiting my homeland again. If only I could see the land of my fathers and its people strengthened under

the protection of the Constitution, and all of you in brotherly
unity, happiness, and contentment.

No. 4
Will of Alexander Asbóth [44]

I, Alexander Asbóth, citizen of the United States and Minister Resident of the United States to the Republics of the
Argentine Confederation and Uruguay, being of sound
mind, in order to set in order all my affairs, do hereby declare and appoint in case of my death, that the Hon. M. E.
Hoolhester, Consul of the United States in this city, assisted
by Rev. William Goodfellow and by General John J. Czetz,
both of this city, shall take charge of all my personal property,
books and papers that may be found in this country, and
settle up all my affairs under the following general plan:
1. Let all books and papers and all articles of every kind
pertaining to this Legation be arranged in order, according
to the catalogue of them, and let them be placed in the hands
of the United States Consul for safe keeping and subject to
the order of the United States Government.
2. Let a list be made out of all my private property in order
to sell it at public auction, except such articles as are specified in a paper hereto appended, which are intended as
mementos to my friends.
3. Let all my debts be promptly paid, and let my man Burrill
receive five hundred dollars in gold, and my two black boys,
Edmund and William, are to receive the same sum divided
between them. If any or all these three persons desire to return to the United States, then their passage shall be paid
in a sailing vessel, and let them be commended to kind friends
there, who may be interested in them. In case they return
to the United States, then they are to secure there, the sums
specified.
4. After all the settlements shall have been made here, let
a list be sent to my honored and valued friend the Hon.
William H. Seward, Secretary of State of the United States,
of the balance of the property with the papers to be forwarded to him, all subject to his order pending the settlement of
my accounts with the United States Government. After these
accounts are properly arranged, I would request the Hon.

Secretary of State to have them forwarded to my brother Louis Asbóth of Lugos in the State of Krasso, Hungary. But if the Hon. Secretary of State should desire to retain for the government the papers connected with my military service he is at liberty to do so. Otherwise let them, with all the balance of my papers and property, be sent to my brother named above.

5. I declare to have my real estate in the city of New York disencumbered of a claim of $600 upon it, and the title to it I legally transfer to my brother, the above-named Louis. The property should not to be sold, but should be kept to become the possession of any of his family who may come to reside in it.

6. My real estate in the town of Radisa, in the State of Arad, Hungary, which I am informed was never confiscated, but was taken possession of by my friends to keep for me, is also bequethed to my brother as above named. I plan this on the condition that no rents shall ever be reclaimed for this property for the time in which it has been preserved for me and used by my friends.

7. When all business growing out of this Testament shall have been completed in this country, the gentlemen named above will make a complete report of all that they have done, to the Hon. William H. Seward, Sec. of State of the U.S., whom I respectfully and affectionately request to perform for me the service I here solicit.

Signed this twenty-fourth day of August one-thousand eight-hundred and sixty-seven, and given as my approved will and Testament.

A. Asbóth   Seal

Witnesses: John Langdon
               Berger

Notes

1. *Magyar Életrajzi Lexikon* /Hungarian Biographical Encyclopedia/, ed. Ágnes Kenyeres, 2 vols. (Budapest: Akadémiai Kiadó, 1967-1969), II, 58.

2. *Révai Nagy Lexikona* /Révai's Great Encyclopedia/, 21 vols. (Budapest: Révai Irodalmi Részvény Társaság, 1910-1935), II, 158.

3. Ede Lósy-Schmidt, "A szabadságharc magyar mérnökvezérei és mérnök-

vezetői" /The Engineer Generals and Engineer Leaders of the Hungarian War of Independence/, *Magyar Technika* (1948), p. 53.

4. Tivadar Ács, *Akik elvándoroltak* /Those Who Emigrated/ (Budapest, 1940), p. 20. The periodical *Hazánk és Külföld* /Our Fatherland and Foreign Lands/, no. 44 (November 4, 1866), p. 697, also gives 1812 as Asbóth's year of birth.

5. See József Antall's article in *Élet és Tudomány* (Life and Science/, vol. 21 (March 11, 1960), p. 435, where the author claims that the ancestor of the Asbóth family was a certain Protestant English knight, Gode-Jroy, who came to Hungary in the 16th century. Miklós Gaál's biography of Lajos Asbóth, however, claims that the Asbóth family settled in Hungary in the mid-17th century and became "naturalized" only in 1679. Cf. Miklós Gaál, *Asbóth Lajos emlékirata az 1848-iki és 1849-iki magyarországi hadjáratról* /Louis Asbóth's Reminiscences about the Hungarian War of Independence of 1848 and 1849/ (Pest: Ráth Mór, 1862).

6. Dezső Szabó, *A herceg Festetics-család története* /The History of the Prince Festetics Family/ (Budapest: Franklin-Társulat Nyomdája, 1928), p. 284.

7. On Lajos Asbóth's military career, see the above-cited *Asbóth Lajos emlékirata*.

8. See Ferenc Fodor, "Magyar vizimérnököknek a Tisza-völgyében a kiegyezés koráig végzett felmérései, vizi munkálatai és azok eredményei" /The Measurements, Water Projects, and Results of Hungarian Water Engineers in the Tisza Valley up to the Austro-Hungarian Compromise/, in *Műszaki Tudománytörténeti Kiadványok* /Proceedings of the History of Technical Sciences/, vol. 8 (Budapest: Tankönyvkiadó, 1957), p. 15.

9. Gábor Bona, *Tábornokok és törzstisztek a szabadságharcban, 1848-49* /Generals and Staff Officers in the Hungarian War of Independence, 1848-49/ (Budapest: Zrínyi Kiadó, 1983).

10. The claim in various American encyclopedias and handbooks that Asbóth allegedly served in the Austrian Army does not tally with the facts. See for example: *Who Was Who in America. Historical Volume, 1607-1896* (Chicago, 1963), p. 29; and *Dictionary of American Biography* (New York: Charles Scribner's Sons, 1928), I, 379.

11. There is also a largely unsubstantiated claim to the effect that, while fleeing to Turkey, Sándor Asbóth and his cousin, Adolf Asbóth, were the ones who hid the Holy Crown of Hungary near the southern Hungarian border town of Orsova. Cf. *Magyar Életrajzi Lexikon*, I, 58.

12. Ödön Vasváry cites Lajos Hentaller in his *Lincoln's Hungarian Heroes: The Participation of Hungarians in the Civil War, 1861-1865* (Washington, DC: Hungarian Reformed Federation of America, 1939), p. 123.

13. Imre Áldor cites these quotations in his *Vázlatok a magyar emigráció életéből* /Sketches from the Life of the Hungarian Emigration/ (Pest: Heckenast Gusztáv, 1870), pp. 16-17.

14. Gábor Egressy, *Törökországi naplói, 1849-1850* /Gábor Egressy's Diaries of Turkey, 1849-1850/ (Pest: Kozma Vazul, 1851), pp. 80-81.

15. "By the end of April 1851, the Hungarian emigrants had cost the Turkish Treasury sixty million piasters, and as the Treasurer of Constantinople had really no extra funds even in those days, he released this large sum with considerable reluctance. From this sum Kossuth received 9,000 piasters per month, the generals received 4,000 piasters each, and the others proportionately less while in Kütahya." Quoted by Áldor, *Vázlatok*, p. 34.

16. Quoted in *ibid.*, p. 35.

17. *1849-1866. Adalékok a kényuralom ellenes mozgalmak történetéhez. Az Asbóth-család irataiból 1848-1866.* /Documents Concerning the History of the Anti-Absolutist Movements. From the History of the Asbóth Family/ (Budapest: Ráth Mór, 1888), p. 58. Henceforth cited as *Asbóth Family.*

18. For a list of those traveling aboard the "Mississippi" see Áldor, *Vázlatok,* p. 38; and Dénes Jánossy, *A Kossuth-emigráció Angliában és Amerikában, 1851-1852* /The Kossuth Emigration in England and in America, 1851-1852/ (Budapest: Magyar Történelmi Társulat, 1948), II, pt. 2, pp. 684-686.

19. László Szabó, *Magyar múlt Dél-Amerikában, 1519-1900* /Hungarian Past in South America, 1519-1900/ (Budapest: Európa Könyvkiadó, 1982), p. 162.

20. Ács, *Akik elvándoroltak,* p. 21.

21. János Vadona, *Az öt világrészből* /From Five Continents/ (Budapest: Hornyánszky Viktor Könyvnyomdája, 1883), p. 230.

22. Quoted by József Balassa, *Kossuth Amerikában, 1851-52* /Kossuth in America, 1851-52/ (Budapest: Gergely R. Könyvkereskedése, 1931), p. 17.

23. Jánossy, *A Kossuth-emigráció,* pp. 698-727.

24. *Ibid.,* p. 930.

25. *Asbóth Family,* p. 76-77.

26. *Ibid.,* pp. 135-147.

27. *Ibid.,* pp. 154-156.

28. Jenő Pivány, *Magyarok és Észak-Amerika* /Hungarians and North America/ (Budapest: Offician, 1944), p. 9.

29. *Ibid.,* p. 9; Jenő Pivány, *Magyar-amerikai történelmi kapcsolatok a Columbus előtti időkből az amerikai polgárháború befejezéséig* /Hungarian-American Historical Connections from Pre-Columbian Times to the American Civil War/ (Budapest: Magyar Tudományos Akadémia, 1926), p. 48; and *Magyarország hadtörténete* /The Military History of Hungary/, ed. Ervin Liptai (Budapest: Zrínyi Katonai Kiadó, 1984), I, 576.

30. Pivány, *Magyar-amerikai,* p. 51; and Pivány, *Magyarok és Észak-Amerika,* p. 10.

31. Earl J. Hess, "Alexander Asbóth: One of Lincoln's Hungarian Heroes?" *Lincoln Herald,* vol. 84, no. 3 (1982), p. 184.

32. *Ibid.*

33. Antall's claim to the effect that Florida was "the target of General Lee's constant attacks" is erroneous. Cf. József Antall, "Asbóth Sándor, 1811-1868," *Élet és Tudomány,* vol. 21 (March 11, 1966), p. 438. See also Hess, "Alexander Asbóth," p. 188.

34. Vasváry, *Lincoln's Hungarian Heroes,* p. 124.

35. Hess, "Alexander Asbóth," p. 189.

36. Géza Kende, *Magyarok Amerikában. Az amerikai magyarság története, 1583-1926* /Hungarians in America. The History of Hungarian Americans, 1583-1926/, 2 vols. (Cleveland: Szabadság Kiadása, 1926-1927), II, 337-338.

37. See for example the following newspapers: *Hazánk és Külföld* /Our Fatherland and Foreign Lands/, vol. 44 (November 4, 1866), pp. 697-699; and *Vasárnapi Újság* /Sunday News/, vol. 50 (December 16, 1966), pp. 605-606.

38. Szabó, *Magyar múlt,* pp. 163-164.

39. János Ludwigh, "Asbóth Sándor és Paraguay" /Alexander Asbóth and Paraguay/, *Hon* /Homeland/, no. 66, March 19, 1868.

40. In addition to the already cited works on the Asbóth family, see also *Magyar Nemzetségi Zsebkönyv. II. rész. Nemes Családok, I. köt.* /Handbook of Hungarian Clans. Part II. Noble-Families, vol. I./ (Budapest: A Magyar Heraldikai és Genealógiai Társaság, 1905), pp. 7-13.

41. See Asbóth's obituary by Arnold Vértessy in the *Magyarország és a Nagy-világ* /Hungary and the Wide World/, March 22, 1868.

42. *Asbóth Family*, pp. 106-109.

43. Ács, *Akik elvándoroltak*, pp. 24-26. For recent works on Hungarians in America see Julianna Puskás, *From Hungary to the United States, 1880-1914* (Budapest: Akadémiai Kiadó, 1982); Steven Béla Várdy, *The Hungarian-Americans* (Boston: Twayne Publishers, 1985); *idem*, "Magyars in America," *The World and I*, vol. II, no. 3 (March 1987), pp. 462-477; and *idem*, "The 'Mystery of the Hungarian Talent'," *The World and I*, vol. II, no. 4 (April 1987), pp. 498-513.

44. United States Legation, Buenos Aires, Argentina, August 24, 1867.

Asbóth's house of birth in Keszthely, Hungary

Asbóth during his exile in Kütahya, Turkey

521

One of the "Kossuth Dollars" issued in New York in 1852

One of the illegal "Kossuth Forints" issued in London in 1860

General Asbóth at the Battle of Pea Ridge in the Civil War
March 7, 1862

General Asbóth in uniform during the Civil War

*General Asbóth's gravestone in the Old English Cemetery
in Buenos Aires, Argentina*

Leslie Konnyu:

24 / THE LEGACY OF ALEXANDER FINTA

The great Hungarian American sculptor, Sándor (Alexander) Finta was born June 12, 1881 in Túrkeve, Hungary, into an agricultural laborer family. The first-born son of Sándor Finta, Sr. and Rozália Hajdu brought with him the talents of his ancestors, and their hunger and thirst for knowledge and the arts.[1] Finta received his first education at his parental home and at the local elementary school. Because of the poor economic conditions of the big Finta family and the rebellious behavior of Sándor, he only finished the third grade. The young boy had to go to work. About his experiences as a shepherd boy, Finta wrote his first autobiographical book.[2] In Ecser *puszta* (a prairie land for grazing herds) Sándor became acquainted with the animals, birds and vegetation of the *Alföld* (the Great Hungarian Plain). First, he had to learn how to ride. For this purpose an old, skinny horse called "Mocskos" (Dirty) was assigned to him.[3]

On the *puszta*, Sándor became a self-made folk artist in wood carving. Since his younger brothers also showed talent for higher learning, around 1890 the Finta family moved to a thriving eastern Hungarian city, Nagyvárad (today Oradea Mare, Rumania). There Sándor finished four additional years of schooling, and then went to a technical high-school in Kassa (today Košice, Czechoslovakia). After graduation in 1900 he attended a railroad officer-training course, and then in 1902 became a certified railroad officer at Abony, a small town in central Hungary. Evidently he would have become an excellent railroad official if something unexpected had not happened.

In defense of the honor of one of his sisters, he was involved in a serious fight; in self-defense he stabbed his opponent. For this he was sentenced to twelve years of prison. [4] While in prison, Sándor decided to become a sculptor, just as one of his brothers, Gregory Finta, did under the wings of Auguste Rodin in Paris. He started to read and to study about art. His models and paintings reached the market of the prison town, Szamosújvár (today Gherla, Rumania). Soon newspapers published articles about the imprisoned artist. One of the celebrated Hungarian woman writers, Renée Erdős (1879-1956), who was living in Rome, sent him reports and photos about the events of the art world in the Eternal City. She called Finta the Hungarian Michelangelo. [5] Later she wrote a novel, *Szentgyörgy vára* /Fort of St. George/ in which she utilized the story of Sándor Finta. [6]

It was a proof of Finta's spiritual adulthood that he started to correspond with such outstanding figures as poet Endre (Andrew) Ady (1877-1919) and the novelist Zsigmond (Sigismund) Móricz (1879-1942), as well as with such other well-known personalities as Ady's mistress and muse, Léda (i.e. Mrs. Adél Diósi, 1872-1936). Finta sent many drawings and statue plans to Ady and Léda, which later were donated, together with the Finta-Pór correspondence, to the Finta Museum of his home town Túrkeve (Dr. Frida Pór of Boston, the donator of this material, also visited Finta in 1946 in Los Angeles, who then immortalized Frida with his "Pacific Ocean" composition). [7]

Finta was freed from prison on July 13, 1913, and took a study tour to Rome, where he visited with Renée Erdős the most important museums. [8] From there he traveled to Paris where his brother, Gregory (pseudo. Oscar Zádory), studied sculptoring from the great French master, Auguste Rodin. After his return home, Sándor Finta married a distant relative, Esther Finta, who bore him a son. But the marriage did not work, and they were divorced in November, 1918.

After serving for a time in World War I, Finta was wounded and was then transferred to work on war heroes' monuments in Hatvan, Nyitra, Pöstyén and Heves. His Nyitra monument, dedicated on September 21, 1918, shows Christ

as He lifts the body of a fallen soldier. The soldier's face
was Finta's father who was killed in that war. Of this statue
Charles (Károly) Lyka, one of the best art critics of Hungary
wrote: "With this statue Finta closed ranks with the best
Hungarian sculptors." [9]

On June 12, 1919, Finta married industrial artist Kata
Kántor. Since the young couple saw no hope for a successful future in Hungary that was dismembered after World
War I, they left their homeland and on July 26, 1920, they
arrived in Brazil. After a few months Finta won a contest
with his granite statue, "The Strength." He also created
for the Rio de Janeiro World Fair two more statues depict-
ing two tenth-century Hungarian heroes, "Botond" and
"Lehel." Finta also made an excursion into the Brazilian
jungle and learned about the life of the Brazilian Indians.
Later he wrote about his experiences in his book *Secret of
the Great Monkey*.[10]

It looked as if Brazil would hold a brilliant future for
the Fintas, but they could not stand the climate. In March,
1923, when Finta was 42 years old, they applied for an entrance visa to the United States. After some difficulties they
were able to immigrate. They settled in New York, where
Finta opened a studio at 601 West 164th Street. First, Sándor
worked on the design of the "Watchman of the Notre Dame"
and on smaller commissions. Finally in 1927 he received a
commission to create in carrara marble a bust of Cardinal
Patrick Hayes of New York. This statue found its way to
the Metropolitan Museum. Beside the paintings of Michael
Munkácsy (1844-1900), Finta's statue is one of the representatives of Hungarian art in that great collection.[11]

Around the time of the Hayes-bust, Finta also received
commissions such as the Whitman-relief for the house where
the poet wrote his immortal "Leaves of Grass" (the corner
of Cranberry and Fulton, New York), the Walt Whitman
Medal, and the plaque of Emory Holloway, the Pulitzer Prize
winner of Whitman's biography. Finta had great success
with his "Fisk Jubilee Quintet" for the anniversary of Fisk
University at Nashville, Tennessee. The script of the plaque
is the well-known Negro spiritual, "Swing low, sweet chariot,
Coming to carry me home!" [12]

On January 16, 1929, The United American Hungarian

Societies of Cleveland, Ohio, ordered a larger than life-size carrara marble bust of Sándor Petőfi (1823-1849), the great Hungarian lyricist, for the Cleveland Public Library. The price was one thousand dollars and was donated by the Rev. Joseph Herczegh, Mrs. Emery Király, Paul Nagy, Emery Olexo, and Alexander Finta himself. The sculptor did a splendid job and the bust was dedicated on May 15, 1929. Petőfi's bust is still in the Cleveland Public Library and is a fine contribution to American art. [13]

In the latter part of the 1920s Finta was commissioned for several federal projects: a memorial plaque of Robert Fulton, inventor of the steamship; a statue of President Ulysses Grant; a relief for the Washington Irving House of New York, (17th St.); a relief of Professor Wm. H. Park and Dr. Anna Williams, Health Department, New York; a statue of St. Stephen of Hungary (414 82nd St., New York; a bust for U. S. Senator Robert Wagner, New York; New York Plaques for Education and Pledge for Public School No. 82; a medal for Pittsburgh's mayor, Charles Cline entitled "Liberty Welcomes Hungaria." [14]

In 1929 Finta started a series of plaques and models of the Hungarian-American hero, Colonel Commandant Michael de Kováts (1724-1779), followed by bronze reliefs for the Museum of National History and the Colonel Kováts Square in New York, and The Citadel of Charleston, SC. In 1938 Finta sculptured another version of the relief for the City of Trenton, NJ. On January 24, 1940, one of his equestrian plaques was dedicated at the Hungarian Library at 19th West 44 St., NY. This was followed by another artistic relief at the Hungarian Reformed Federation of America in Washington, DC. In 1953 the American Hungarian Federation started a campaign for an equestrian Kováts statue in Washington, DC. Since not enough money was collected, the beautiful model was deposited for safekeeping at the Andersen Gallery in Washington, DC. [15]

Following their heart's desire, in the fall of 1939 the Fintas moved to Los Angeles, the land of eternal sunshine. There he started to work in high gear. He became a U. S. citizen and participated in many exhibitions. During these years he also produced a number of plans for major monuments, including the famous "Spirit of Columbia" in 1942, and a Civil War Memorial, which, however, was never completed. Its model was donated to the Finta Museum in Hungary. He was honored by his colleagues; in 1946 he was elected Vice President of the Artist Guild of Los Angeles. [16]

During World War II the Fintas were working for the war industries. After the war he started to exhibit again. In 1948 he received a commission from the United Hungarian Societies of Cleveland for a bust of the great Hungarian drama writer Imre (Emery) Madách (1823-1864). It was finished in 1949 and was dedicated in Cleveland's Gordon Park (Statuary of Nationalities) on July 22, 1950. [17]

For Finta another favorite group of sculptures were the Kossuth plaques and statues in America. On October 2, 1949, his Kossuth-relief was placed on the wall of the Sheraton Hotel of Pittsburgh (now Point Park College), where Louis Kossuth, former Governor of Hungary, stayed between January 22-23, 1852. Finta's other outstanding creation was the St. Louis Kossuth monument which, proposed by the writer of this paper, Leslie Konnyu, was placed in the St. Louis Fair Ground Park on Memorial Day, 1952. His famous Kossuth bust was dedicated on July 11, 1954, in the Los Angeles Exposition Park. [18]

Finta's last group of reliefs were created to commemorate Ágoston Haraszthy (1812-1869), the founder of the California wine industry. This relief was the crowning achievement of Finta, which was dedicated before his death in 1958. One bronze of this magnificent plaque went to Sonoma, California, where Haraszthy's wine garden and wine cellar are located. A copy of the relief went to the San Diego Hungarian House. (In 1850 Haraszthy settled in San Diego, became a sheriff of that town, and later a state representative of San Diego County.) Another copy of the Haraszthy plaque remained in the Los Angeles Hungarian Hall (1975 West Washington Blvd., Los Angeles, CA 90018). The third copy was ordered by Leslie Konnyu, the editor of the *American Hungarian Review*, who was the organizer of the Finta Centenary (1980) and the Haraszthy Jubilee (1981). [19]

Naturally, Finta also had many other creations and projects. He was a man of universal talents who, in addition to being a great sculptor, wrote poetry and fiction, and also authored studies on art and philosophy. Three of his main publications attracted considerable attention. The first of these is the *Herdboy of Hungary*, published by Harper and Brothers, New York, 1932. In this masterfully illustrated book he told the story of his youth, schooling, training for herdboy on the *puszta*, and his heart-warming friendship with the old, skinny horse, "Mocskos." Of course, as a writer, he over-emphasized his achievements, but this self-confidence was natural for a self-made man like Finta. [20]

His second book entitled *My Brothers and I* was also autobiographical in nature, and in a sense it was a sequel to his *Herdboy of Hungary*. Published by Holiday House in New York in 1940, this book is mainly about his own departure from the *puszta*. His natural scientist friend, Otto Hermann, made good his promise and acquired for him a scholarship in a reputable classical secondary school. But Sándor's father did not like the favoritism and he wanted all his six children placed at the same school. This, of course, could not be done; therefore, they all settled for a reputable grade school. In the rest of the book the author presents the problems and fights of the village kids against the city children. This book was also profusely illustrated by Finta.[21]

In 1938 Finta published his third book of this genre, the *Secret of the Great Monkey*. In this work he recalled his travels in the Brazilian jungle, his acquaintance with the Brazilian Indians, and his friendship with their chief Ita Giba whose bust he modeled. This book was rather successful, and it was also translated into Hungarian and published in Budapest in 1942. [22]

In the Finta Museum in Túrkeve, Hungary, there are beautifully executed ivory and buffalo bone carvings ("The Story of Attila," etc.) and a medium-sized, wonderfully carved chest with miniature reliefs from the Bible (e.g. "The Last Supper"). The chest is dedicated to Katalin Finta and is the last gift from Finta to his beloved wife who took care of her genius husband for half-a-century. This magnificent Renaissance miniature carving is the crowning achievement of the talented sculptor. [23]

Although Alexander Finta had a strong physique and worked long hours on his statues, on May 5, 1957, he had his first heart attack that slowed him down. On his way to recovery he finished a Haraszthy-plaque with two striking reliefs of planting and harvesting grapes, and began work on a number of small reliefs. These included the "Dancing Children," executed in a lovely Greek spirit, which turned out to be his last composition. A few weeks later came the terrible news from his hometown, Túrkeve, that his son, Dr. Sándor Finta, had died unexpectedly. That tragic event depressed his spirit and his health began to deteriorate. On July 23, 1958, he suffered another heart attack. He was taken to the hospital where he died on August 3, 1958, at the age of seventy-seven. His body was placed to rest in the Inglewood Cemetery in Los Angeles, on August 6, 1958.[24]

A long time before his death, Alexander Finta willed his art objects, drawings, and papers to his hometown, to establish a Finta Museum. In 1962, his widow sent crates of statues and drawings to Túrkeve, and in 1973 she traveled there personally to supervise the arrangement of her husband's artistic heritage at the museum. [25]

To keep Finta's memory alive, Los Angeles friends and admirers of the artist founded a "Sándor Finta Art and Literary Society," whose first president, until his death in 1978, was the noted physicist Géza Vajda (1898-1978). [26]

Because of space limitations, it was impossible to present a complete picture of Finta's life. It should be mentioned, however, that he had won thirty-six prizes in public monument competitions in eleven nations. Today he is well-known in Brazil and in the United States. But besides the New York and California statues, plaques, and his works in Hungary, there is one more new and very impressive depository of Finta's reliefs about which there is very little published in the annals of art history. Its story is as follows:

Not having proper place in his home, in 1956 Alexander Finta placed sixty-three of his original high relief master negatives in the custody of his friends, Dr. and Mrs. Géza Vajda (Lawndale, California) for safekeeping in their newly built exhibition room. After Finta's death, the Vajdas tried to give them to the Los Angeles County Museum, but the latter declined the offer under the pretext that they collected only "modern" reliefs. After Dr. Géza Vajda's death in 1978, his wife, Gizella Vajda, took over custody. She died in 1981. Her estate administrator, Ms. Viola Kleiner, gave the sixty-three art objects back to Mrs. Finta who, in turn donated them to the United Magyar House of Los Angeles.

The Los Angeles Magyar House displayed the collection properly in their club, and in the presence of Mrs. Finta they produced an impressive Memorial Program in 1981, on the 100th anniversary of Alexander Finta's birth. They invited Leslie Konnyu, writer of St. Louis, Missouri, to be their main speaker, and asked the Los Angeles Hungarian organizations to send representatives to the celebration. Everything seemed to be in good order until April, 1984, when Frank Nimrod, in the name of Stephaneum Scientific Academy of San Francisco, claimed the art objects. According to his statement, Mrs. Gizella Vajda willed the art objects to his organization. It is now up to the Superior Court of California to rule in this complicated matter. [27]

Today, two great California cities, Los Angeles and San Francisco, and two Hungarian American cultural organizations, United Magyar House of Los Angeles and Stephaneum Scientific Academy of San Francisco, are fighting for the possession of Alexander Finta's rich art legacy.

The following is a list of the sixty-three reliefs presently displayed at the United Magyar House, 1975 West Washington Boulevard, Los Angeles:

1. Daniel Szántai (10x16")
2. Lidia Vaskó (10x15")
3. Emery Király (10x15)
4. Jolán Király (10x15)
5. Julia Kemény (10.5x14.5)
6. Elizabeth Vaskó (10.5x15.5)
7. Cornelius Csongrády (11.5x15.5)
8. Rev. Louis Nánássy Tg. Dr. (13.5x18.25)
9. Holló (Raven), NY, 1939 (Edgar A. Poe)
10. Maria Réthy (11x15.25)
11. Dr. Géza Réthy (11x15.25)
12. Mother and Child (11x16)

13. Rev. Alexander Kalassay (13x18.5)
14. Gusztáv Varga-Irma (14.5x15; 10.5x14.5)
16. Michael Kosztin (10.5x14.25)
17. Ilona Bujdossó (9.25x13.5)
18. Julia Kiss (Spirit of Hungaria), (11x14.5)
19. John Kiss (11x15)
20. Faith and Cornelius Schusler (14.5x11.5)
21. Man and Woman (14x14)
22. Géza Gáspár (9.75x12.5)
23. Dr. Louis Kossuth Biriny (12x14.5)
24. Coloman Káldor (9.5x12.5)
25. Ladislas Szegedy (9.5x12.5)
26. Clarence Albaugh, M.D. (10x12.5)
27. Nicolas and Helen Nyirán (13.5x14.25)
28. **Pro Libertate Hungariae (15.25x22.5)**
29. **Pro Libertate Hungariae (14x22.5)**
30. Egy huszár (A Hussar); (circle with 7" diameter)
31. Harvest Scene (Haraszthy)
32. Original Haraszthy plaque
33-41. Nine small statues of different sizes
42. Portrait of Mrs. S. Finta (the artist's daughter-in-law)
43. Ida Bobula, Ph.D.
44. Christian and Sigma von Schneider
45. Frederic and Adele McKee
46. Leslie Kondorossy
47. Wm. P. Krehn
48. Landscape
49. Kossuth Plaque
50. L. Kossuth, L.A.
51. Ornament
52. Eleonore and Theodore Lukits
53. Ilona Lesko
54. Elda and Stephen Izant
55. Emblem
56. Dénes and Mary Fanchal
57. Woman's Portrait
58. Josephine's Portrait
59. Eva Hlozek
60. Kearny Sauer, M.D.
61. Maria's Portrait
62. Frieda Por, M.D.
63. George Szécskay's relief

Notes

1. Alfonz Lengyel, *The Life and Art of Alexander Finta* (Pittsburgh: Expert Printing), p. 6.

2. Alexander Finta, *Herdboy of Hungary* (New York: Harper and Brothers, 1932; reprint by the Hungarian Reformed Federation of America, Washington, DC, 1940).

3. *Ibid.*, p. 30.

4. Mária Egri and Lajos Győrffy, *A Finta művésztestvérek élete és munkássága* /The Life and Works of the Finta Artist Brothers/ (Szolnok-Túrkeve: Finta Múzeum, 1973), p. 1.

5. *Ibid.*, p. 3.

6. On Finta's relationship to Erdős, see László Könnyű, "A halott védekezik" /The Deceased Defends Himself/. Essay in the Los Angeles Hungarian Monthly: *Napnyugat* /Sunset/, April 26, 1974, p. 3.

7. Egri, pp. 178-179.

8. *Ibid.*, p. 21.

9. Lengyel, p. 92.

10. Finta, *Secret of the Great Monkey* (New York: Target, 1938); Hungarian edition: *A nagy majom* (Budapest: Forrás, 1942).

11. Lengyel, p. 26.

12. Egri, pp. 87-88.

13. *Ibid.*, pp. 100-101.

14. Lengyel, pp. 30-32.

15. *Ibid.*, pp. 44-48.

16. Egri, p. 176.

17. *Ibid.*, pp. 100-101.

18. *Ibid.*, pp. 181, 184-185.

19. Lengyel, pp. 48-49.

20. Egri, p. 129.

21. *Ibid.*, p. 173.

22. *Ibid.*, pp. 181-182.

23. Lengyel, pp. 54-57.

24. Egri, p. 188.

25. *Magyar Hírek* /Hungarian News/, July 1, 1973, p. 13.

26. *Californiai Magyar Élet* /Californian Hungarian Life/, July 24, 1959, p. 12.

27. Copy of court papers of Special Administrator, Robert N. Gary, for the Estate of Gizella Vajda.

Bibliography

Books

Egri, Maria and Győrffy, Lajos, *Finta művésztestvérek élete és munkássága.* /The Life and Work of Finta Artist Brothers/ (Szolnok-Túrkeve: Finta Múzeum, 1973).

Eminent Californians (Los Angeles, 1950).

Encyclopedia of American Biographies (New York, 1940).

Finta, Catherine. Interview by Leslie Konnyu, Los Angeles, June 13, 1981.

— — —, *Alexander Finta*: *A Biography* (Los Angeles, Manuscript, 1974).

Finta, Alexander, Catherine Finta, and Géza Vajda. Correspondence. Los Angeles, 1956-78. (In possession of L. Konnyu.)

Finta, Alexander, *Herdboy of Hungary*. (New York: Harper and Brothers, 1932).

— — —, *Kisbojtár* /Herdboy/ (Washington, DC: Amerikai Magyar Református Egyesület, 1940).

— — —, *My Brothers and I* (New York: Holiday House, 1940).

— — —, *The Secret of the Great Monkey* (New York: Target, 1938).

— — —, *A nagy majom titka* /The Secret of the Great Monkey/ (Budapest: Forrás, 1942).

Győrffy, L., Gy. Kaposvári and M. Egri, *A Finta Múzeum kiállítása* /The Exhibit of the Finta Museum/ (Túrkeve: Finta Múzeum, 1977).

Káldor, Kálmán, *Magyar Amerika írásban és képben* /Hungarian America in Words and Pictures/, 2 vols. (St. Louis: Hungarian Publishing, 1937).

Konnyu, Leslie, *Az amerikai magyar irodalom története* /A History of American Hungarian Literature/ (St. Louis: Az amerikai magyar írók munkaközössége, 1961).

— — —, *A History of American Hungarian Literature* (St. Louis: Cooperative of American Hungarian Writers, 1962; 2d enlarged edition, 1988).

———, *Külföldi magyar hivatásos képzőművészek* (St. Louis: American Hungarian Review, 1977).

———, *Professional Hungarian Artists Outside Hungary* (St. Louis: American Hungarian Review, 1978).

Lengyel, Alfonz, *The Life and Art of Alexander Finta* (Washington, DC: Hungarian Reformed Federation of America, 1964).

Póka-Pivny, Aladár and Zachar, József, *Az amerikai függetlenségi háború magyar hőse* /Hungarian Hero of the American War of Independence/ (Budapest: Zrínyi, 1982).

Who's Who in America (Chicago: Marquis, 1930-1956).

Who's Who in American Art (Chicago: Marquis, 1950).

Articles

"Leghívebben mindhalálig" /Most Faithful until Death/, *Magyar Hírek* /Hungarian News/, July 1, 1979, p. 7.

"Finta Sándor özvegyének látogatása" /The Visit of Sándor Finta's Widow/, *Magyar Hírek* /Hungarian News/, Sept. 1, 1973, p. 5.

Könnyū, László /Konnyu, Leslie/, "A halott védekezik" /The Deceased Defends Himself/, *Napnyugat* /Sunset/, April 26, 1974, p. 3.

———, "Finta Sándor centenáriuma" /The Centenary of Sándor Finta/, Memorial Address, Los Angeles Magyar House, June 13, 1981, pp. 1-8. (Unpublished.)

Máthé, István /Stephen/. "A Los Angelesi Magyar Házban őrzött Finta-művek listája" /The List of Finta's Reliefs Displayed in the Magyar House of Los Angeles/, MS., May 1, 1981, p. 1.

1.   Alexander Finta (1881-1958)

539

2. Cardinal Patrick Hayes

Marble by Alexander Finta
The Metropolitan Museum of Art, New York

3. The Hungarian Poet Sándor Petőfi (1823-1849)
White marble by Alexander Finta
Main Public Library, Cleveland, Ohio

4. Bronze plaque of Colonel Michael de Kováts
by Alexander Finta
New York

542

5. Bronze plaque of Colonel Michael de Kováts at the time of
his death at the Battle of Charleston in 1779
by Alexander Finta
New York

6. Model of the proposed "Spirit of Columbia"
by Alexander Finta
Finta Museum, Túrkeve, Hungary

7. Hungarian poet and dramatist Imre Madách (1823-1864)
Bronze by Alexander Finta
Nationalities' Park, Cleveland, Ohio

8. Bronze plaque of the Hungarian statesman Louis Kossuth
(1802-1894)
by Alexander Finta
St. Louis, Missouri

546

9. Bronze bust of the Hungarian statesman Louis Kossuth
(1802-1894)
by Alexander Finta
Exposition Park, Los Angeles, California

10. Bronze plaque of Ágoston Haraszthy (1812-1869),
father of the California wine industry
by Alexander Finta
Buena Vista Winery, Sonoma, California

11. "The Faun and the Nymph"
Wood carving by Alexander Finta

549

12. "The Pacific Ocean"
Bronze by Alexander Finta
Los Angeles, California

13. The Finta Museum in Túrkeve, Hungary

Susan M. Papp:

25 / DOCUMENTING HUNGARIAN-AMERICAN IMMIGRATION HISTORY: THE RUZSA COLLECTION AND ITS SIGNIFICANCE

The Ruzsa family played a significant role in the development of Hungarian Protestant institutions in North America. Five of the fifteen Ruzsa children were Lutheran missionaries in various Hungarian-Canadian or Hungarian-American communities, and the most prominent member of the family, Eugene /Jenő/ was the first Hungarian Lutheran minister in Canada. He began serving Hungarian immigrant congregations in 1933, and continued to do so until his retirement in 1969.

Rev. Eugene Ruzsa collected all documentation dealing with Hungarian immigrant life in North America, regardless of publication date, the nature of the document, and political affiliation. It was his greatest accomplishment that he succeeded in overcoming the differences among the various segments of the Hungarian community, whether generational or political, and brought them together for common causes.

His valuable collection will be housed in the Archives of Ontario through the Multicultural History Society of Ontario. The latter institution will also publish a biography of Rev. Ruzsa, together with a register to the collection.

The purpose of this paper is to examine, analyze, and to highlight the important aspects of the collection, and to present a general overview of its contents. For example, a significant part of the correspondence documents the difficulties Rev. Ruzsa experienced in compiling and publishing his *The History of Hungarian Canadians /A kanadai magyarság története/*. Inasmuch as this volume was the first history of this group in Canada, the documentation utilized by Rev. Ruzsa is of historical significance. Dedicated to his ministry, and to the Hungarian-Canadian community, Rev. Ruzsa participated in nearly every aspect of community life from the mid-1930s onward. Since he collected nearly everything he was involved with, his collection is a valuable addition to the body of knowledge concerning Hungarian immigrant community life in North America.

Rev. Eugene Ruzsa's Life and Activities

Eugene Ruzsa was born in 1899 in Nyiregyháza, where his father András was the principal of the local Evangelical Lutheran secondary school. The Ruzsa children were raised in a strict religious environment. Their mother (neé Julianna Babuz) died in 1905, when Eugene was only six years old. A few years later, in 1909, Ruzsa's father passed away as well, leaving the children entirely orphaned.

As expected, the children were tremendously affected by the death of their parents, and various sources indicate that they turned to their faith for spiritual strength. The eldest, István, temporarily took over care of the children until he decided to become a Lutheran minister. A few years later he emigrated to the United States to do missionary work among Hungarian Americans. Four other members of the family were to follow: Piroska and László in 1913, Juliska in 1915, and Eugene in 1929.

The dedication and zeal with which the family undertook religious work in the United States is indicated by their accomplishments. István became the first Hungarian Lutheran minister of North America. He is responsible for organizing the first Hungarian congregation in the United States, in Cleveland, Ohio, in 1906. The arrival of Piroska, László, and Juliska significantly augmented the work of Hungarian Lutherans in Cleveland. They founded an orphanage in 1914, which served not only orphans, but provided day care facilities for children left alone all day by working parents. An old age home was also established by the Lutheran congregation in 1916. Unfortunately the orphanage was closed

in 1923, due to state legislation which would no longer allow
the licensing of orphanages which operated in any language
other than English. The old age home, however, remained
an integral part of the congregation's activities for several
years afterwards.

Following the death of his parents, the ten-year-old
Eugene was taken in by an older married sister, who later
decided that the young boy would be better off in an orphanage. Consequently, for a while, Eugene lived in an institution with another brother who later died of bone tuberculosis.
The hardships of his childhood are reflected in stories he
related to his children years later. While in high school, he
was invited to a friend's house during the Christmas holidays. This occasion was the first time he ever slept in a room
by himself and he realized how alone he was in this world.
According to the story, Ruzsa felt God's presence at that
point and realized that he was not completely alone. When
his daughter related this incident, she was not sure whether
or not this was the first time her father thought of becoming
a minister.[1] Ruzsa's difficult childhood only made him more
enthusiastic about living a full life and serving others through
the ministry. Yet, he was never bitter about his childhood.
When telling stories to his children about his youth, he made
it sound like it was one of the happiest times of his life.

Another incident which, according to his children, had
an impact on the way he established the priorities in his life,
occurred just before the stock market crash of the late 1920s.
Ruzsa had received a tip that the price of a certain stock was
going to skyrocket; he bought a large number of the stock
just before the market crashed, and consequently lost all
his investments. Through this incident he learned about
the fleeting nature of money and was determined not to
rely on it for happiness again.[2]

Various stories exist as to why the third Ruzsa brother
to emigrate to North America settled in Canada, rather
than in Cleveland with the other members of his family. In
a report written to the Presbyterian Church Synod, Eugene
Ruzsa wrote that after arriving in the United States, he immediately joined the United Lutheran Church of America,
and together with his brothers, served the needs of
the church.[3] In that same year (1929) he was invited

by the United Lutheran Church of Canada Synod to serve
Canadian Hungarians, in light of the fact that there was
only one Hungarian Lutheran minister serving their needs.
However, according to the memories of his sister-in-law,
Mrs. István Ruzsa, Eugene could not gain admittance to
the United States because of the Quota System, and even
before he arrived in North America, the American Mission
Board had accepted him for theological studies in Waterloo,
Ontario.[4]

Eugene Ruzsa met Helen /Ilona/ Strompf at the Kitchener
Hungarian Club in 1930. They were married one year later
at the Windsor Hungarian Lutheran Church. On February
17, 1933 Eugene Ruzsa was ordained a minister of the
Lutheran Church and immediately set out to organize Hungarian Lutheran congregations in Kitchener, Hamilton,
and Welland. In the same year, the Ruzsa family moved
to Toronto, where the newly-ordained minister was appointed pastor of the recently-established Hungarian Lutheran congregation. He served the outlying communities of
Welland, Kitchener, and Hamilton until the difficult years
of the depression forced him to give up that work in 1937.[5]

The minister's activities, as well as his family's focused
on the smooth operation of the church. The Ruzsa children
recollected how, if their father received an appointment at
a congregation, they all had to help in whichever way they
could, such as playing the organ, teaching Sunday school,
and organizing the young people's club activities. Mrs. Helen
Ruzsa's role, as wife of a Lutheran minister serving a fledg-
ling immigrant congregation, was often just as demanding
as her husband's, sometimes even more. For example, in
1937 Mrs. Ruzsa embarked on a three-month trip touring
the various Hungarian Protestant congregations in the United
States and Canada in an effort to raise funds to build a Hungarian Lutheran church in Toronto. Helen Ruzsa went
alone, at her husband's urging, with very little money in her
pocket, relying on the hospitality and generosity of the
ministers' families and their congregations along the way.
She left her husband for this protracted period with four
small children, the oldest one being only four years old. The
trip included such cities as Hamilton, Welland, Windsor in
Canada, and Buffalo, Cleveland, Akron, Youngstown,

Bethlehem, Toledo, and Detroit in the United States. Mrs. Ruzsa collected only about $900 during her trip, which could not facilitate the building of a church, but assisted Rev. Ruzsa partly in the researching and writing of his book on Hungarians in Canada.[6]

Eugene Ruzsa's involvement with the community began nearly simultaneously with his arrival in Canada. He gave a March 15th commemorative presentation at the Hungarian Club in Kitchener in 1930. In Toronto he organized the first large-scale March 15th commemoration at the Labour Lyceum in 1936. He was a catalyst in the organization of the Toronto Hungarian House; the first meeting organized for this goal was held at the Ruzsa residence in 1939. According to a close associate, "He reached out to Hungarians in Canada, who felt like sheep without a shepherd, lost in this massive country.... He tried to establish a feeling of community in each area where Hungarians lived.... He achieved this because it was done in a Christian context, through a Christian church."[7] This view was reinforced by his daughter, who stated that the Hungarian community of the time needed a leader, and it really didn't matter what religion the person was as long as there was someone to help these immigrants who had little formal education and were unfamiliar with this country.[8] Ruzsa provided the leadership so desperately sought by the community. His activities were many and varied: from organizing community commemorations and handling individual immigrant's personal problems, to acting as liaison between the community and local and national government agencies. Out of his multi-faceted work with the community grew the desire to document many of the events which took place: the background as to how and why organizations were being founded, and the stories of individuals who were pioneers in Canada in one sense or another. In 1940, he travelled across Canada gathering research material for his book, while visiting every community where Hungarians lived in any sizeable number.

In 1942 the governing council of the Hamilton Hungarian Reformed Church invited Eugene Ruzsa to accept the vacant position of minister at their church. He accepted this position and remained in Hamilton until his retirement in 1969. The period in Hamilton was the time of Rev. Ruzsa's greatest community involvement. Moreover, he was compiling a second volume of Hungarians in Canada (from 1940 to 1970), but was never able to bring this second book to completion. He died in 1977, leaving behind a massive collection of personal papers, correspondence, and documentation on Hungarian community life in North America.

The Ruzsa Collection

The Ruzsa Collection is a significant addition to the archival material available on Hungarians in North America. Rev. Ruzsa collected all printed materials, correspondence and documentation dealing with community life, regardless of period, the nature of the document, or political affiliation. Because he was working on the history of Hungarians in Canada already in the late 1930s, he was already in the process of gathering documentation at this early stage. One of the earliest documents in the collection is a 12-page memoir by an early settler in Western Canada, Sándor Daku, who came from Hungary, via the United States, to join his parents in Saskatchewan. Daku was in the United States at the time when he learned that his parents had settled in Canada; they said they asked "every intelligent American they knew about Canada, but no one could tell them anything." They finally went to János Rizsák, a Hungarian banker in Passaic, New Jersey, who, while not handling immigration to Canada himself, helped them locate someone in New York from whom they could purchase a train ticket in Canada. Daku and his brother were very shocked to see snow on the prairies in May. He asked some Hungarians when sowing took place, for he was certain that the growing season must be very short. The answer he received was: "Don't worry son, the wheat grows so rapidly here that if you lie down at the edge of the field at night, you will hear the crackling of the growing wheat."

There is much correspondence and documentation surrounding the writing and publication of Ruzsa's *The History of Hungarian Canadians*. Since this volume was the first major publication on this topic, the sources amassed for it make this collection very valuable for students of Hungarian immigration history.

The most interesting and valuable aspect of the collection is the fact that Rev. Ruzsa worked with each wave of immigrants: the interwar, post-World War II, and post 1956-Hungarians. He was probably the only person in the Hungarian Canadian community who successfully resolved the generational and political differences among the various segments of the Hungarian community. Consequently, his papers reflect the organizational efforts of each of the three waves.

Writing the History of Hungarians in Canada

There are several versions of what motivated Rev. Ruzsa to write a book on the Hungarian communities in Canada. Each version is undoubtedly true in one sense or another, as there were probably various forces that moved Ruzsa to embark upon this great task with such relatively meagre resources at hand. One version holds that the Canadian Pacific Railway contracted Ruzsa to find out what Hungarian immigrants were doing when they went out West, and to ascertain whether the railway should expand its lines or consolidate what it already built.[9] Another source states that already in Hungary Ruzsa had realized the need for such a history, for when he was inquiring about Canada and her peoples, he could find practically nothing about the life of the Hungarian immigrants there.[10] Moreover, he wanted to document the experiences of the Hungarian pioneers who had settled out West while they were still alive to tell their stories. He realized only too well that people in Hungary thought Canada was a land of milk and honey. As one who had assisted hundreds of immigrants during the most critical period in Canada's history, the Great Depression, he wanted to ensure that his countrymen will read about some of the struggles Hungarian immigrants experienced in their adopted homeland. Finally, his motivation was also to inform Canadians about the contributions of Hungarian immigrants in building Canada. The final step towards the successful completion of this project would have been the book's translation into English to make it accessible to Canadians.

Eugene Ruzsa was given a further incentive to write the

book: The Hungarian consulate in Montréal verbally agreed
to purchase one thousand copies of the book once it was
published.[11] Diplomatic relations between Canada and
Hungary were severed, however, before this agreement could
be acted upon. Ruzsa hurriedly travelled to Washington
to try to arrange the transaction with the Hungarian Consulate there. The Consulate in Washington was amenable
to the situation, but once again diplomatic ties between the
United States and Hungary were broken before the transaction could take place. As a result Ruzsa and his family
were left with the entire financial burden of publication.

In a letter written during the latter part of the Second
World War to the former Hungarian Consul in Montréal,
Ruzsa wrote that he had decided to write the history of
Hungarians in Canada already in 1936, at the time of the
50th anniversary commemorations of the founding of Békevár. He felt that it was already almost too late to preserve
the history of the first settlers for future generations.[12] Ruzsa
further wrote that among the pioneer settlers only a few were
still alive and slowly all historical trace would be lost if
someone didn't take on the responsibility of gathering this
data and compiling it into written form. Ruzsa stated that
he had contacted "intellectuals" within the community who
were financially much better off, had fewer family obligations, or had a more prestigious position in society. Of those
contacted, no one was willing to take on the task.

The Lutheran minister departed for his research trip to
the West in 1940. He toured each province, and visited
practically every community where Hungarians had settled.
He received assistance from a few community leaders, in
particular from the editor of the *Kanadai Magyar Újság*
/Canadian Hungarian News/, who was of considerable assistance to him. Editor Gusztáv Nemes also lent him a typewriter with Hungarian type. Ruzsa happily wrote home that
he could even take the typewriter with him on his trip, without
having to purchase one.[13]

Ruzsa applied for and received a railway pass from the
Canadian Pacific Railway; however, it turned out that most
of the Hungarian settlements in Saskatchewan were along
the CNR and not the CPR lines. Ruzsa was already in

Manitoba when the misunderstanding came to fore, and had to send the CPR pass back to the head office before the CNR would issue another pass. Since Károly Winter, Consul General at the Hungarian Consulate in Montréal, was responsible in part for recommending Ruzsa to the proper authorities at the railways, Winter was also held accountable for the mistake.[14]

In a letter written to his family shortly after his tour began, Ruzsa wrote: "It has been very difficult to introduce the project; however, I believe that we have finally overcome the problems.... For sure, this work is hard and we will deserve God's blessing upon it, no matter what the final result will be.... The work is tiresome and involves much worry, trouble, and suffering.[15] Helen Ruzsa stayed in Toronto with their four children. They had very little money, and as Mrs. Ruzsa admitted later, had it not been for the kindness and generous support of the members of the Lutheran congregation in Toronto who knew about her husband's mission, they would have been unable to survive the four months while he was gone. In April 1940, while he was making the last stops on his journey, Ruzsa wrote to his family: "I believe this was my life's most difficult task, but I hope it will have God's blessing on it, and the product will prove to be serious and enduring; something that, when I close my eyes forever, not only all the children, but Mother will also be very proud of."[16]

The completion of the book was preceded by five years of research and preparation, much tiresome effort and financial sacrifice, and a 28,000 mile journey researching the various communities. Helen Ruzsa recalled that when Rev. Ruzsa was writing the manuscript, he entered into an agreement with the typesetter that the book would be set without interruption.[17] This meant that, because a certain amount of written material had to be at the typesetter's every day, on occasions Ruzsa had to stay up all night to finish the required material. Béla Bácskai Payerle, co-editor of the *Canadian Hungarian News* offered his assistance in proofreading the manuscript. He wrote: "I know what an ungrateful task it is, in a spiritual as well as financial sense, to compile such a book for publication. After it is published, it is even more painful to discover glaring mistakes, despite the fact that they may be explained through human error or errors introduced through the typesetting and printing." [18]

Ruzsa's *The History of Hungarian Canadians* was published in 1940. In the Epilogue, the author wrote: "As I dedicate the first history of Hungarian-Canadians to my countrymen, I do so with the request that it be received with goodwill...; that it not be placed under the microscope and scalpel of critics, because the writer is not a professional historian, only a very busy man, occupied with a large family and many problems; one who is in solidarity with and part of the Hungarian-Canadian community, and did what he did out of a great love for his ethnic group." [19] The book was well-received by the community. The minister's correspondence reveals that many of the orders for the book were accompanied by words of praise and gratitude to the author for compiling such a history. The reviews written about the book were generally complimentary, and even if certain aspects were criticized, the reviewers usually added that considering the many obstacles the author was forced to encounter while writing the book, it was the best anyone could have produced under the circumstances. Among those who wrote congratulatory letters, Watson Kirkconnell referred to the publication as a "mine of information." [20] Ödön Vasváry, Presbyterian minister and a scholar of Hungarian-American immigration history, wrote with admiration of the volume. He was particularly impressed in light of the fact that "as compared to the United States, Hungarian immigration to Canada was significantly smaller, more recent, and the immigrant communities more spread out over a much greater area." [21] Vasváry added, however, that because Ruzsa's work was the only book to document the accomplishments of the pioneers, more should have been written about their particular struggles and experiences. Another reviewer, Dr. Ambrose Czakó, editor of *Tárogató*, /Oboe Flute/ praised Ruzsa's work and summed up his opinion regarding the publication as follows: "It is the honest Hungarian work of a sincere man, originating from deep love of Hungarian culture and people, and from the desire to document its history. This work deserves the gratitude and respect of all Hungarians." [22]

Ministerial and Community Activities

In 1933, Eugene Ruzsa established the Hungarian Evangelical Lutheran Church in Toronto and nearly simultaneously set out to organize Hungarian Lutheran congregations in Kitchener, Hamilton, and Welland. The correspondence with The Board of American Missions (of the United Lutheran Church in America) documents the size and nature of these initial congregations. [23] According to reports of 1936, the congregation in Toronto had a confirmed membership of 114, the Kitchener Hungarian Lutheran congregation 59, and Hamilton 41. Eugene Ruzsa's salary was $840 per annum, on condition that the congregation pay $200, without parsonage. The correspondence indicates that Ruzsa's pleas for additional assistance were ongoing: the Hungarian immigrant congregations simply could not contribute enough. The congregation in Toronto was close-knit, but very small. They could hardly support a minister, let alone a minister with six small children. In one of the replies received from the Board of American Missions, the Executive Secretary, Zenan M. Corbe wrote:

> We realize, of course, that you have great difficulties in meeting your expenses with such a rapidly increasing family, but the additional support should come from the growth of the congregation. On looking over the reports from your congregation, it does seem to me they should do more for you, and in addition hereto you ought to secure more converts. [24]

It is not surprising that after experiencing so many difficulties with the Lutheran Board, Rev. Ruzsa accepted a permanent position as minister at the Hungarian Reformed Church in Hamilton. It was not an easy decision to make, however, as it required that Ruzsa break with the longstanding Lutheran tradition in his family and serve a Presbyterian congregation. While the changeover seems relatively insignificant to most, for Eugene Ruzsa, it required much thought and consideration. The financial security afforded by the new position made it possible for Ruzsa to concentrate even more on serving the needs of the community.

Eugene Ruzsa served continuously in the Reserve Army Division, Royal Canadian Army Medical Corps from September 3, 1942 until November 21, 1946. During wartime, his activities included acting as a mediator between the government and the community, promoting the Hungarian community as being dedicated to their new homeland, and defending the rights of those accused of misconduct. A fellow minister said of Ruzsa's wartime activities: "I think his greatest contribution was that during the war he was able to bring together an organization which stopped the anti-Hungarian movement at a time when it was very crucial.... His influence prevented a lot of discrimination and prejudice.... He was influential in obtaining a TV program on CBC where Hungarians could speak to Canadians and declare their loyalty.... His work had national influence." [25]

Ruzsa was vociferous in expressing his anticommunist views, so much so that threats were even made on his life. The Ruzsa children recalled that, on occasion, plainclothes RCMP officers were assigned to their home because of these threats. They remembered with amusement that, at the time, rather than being frightened, they thought this was exciting. [26] Despite his anticommunist views, however, Ruzsa often worked to prevent the deportation of Hungarian immigrants and circulated petitions in their behalf. Towards the end of the war, the Left and Right Wing of the community even worked together on a few joint projects, one of which was a national conference of Hungarian Canadian organizations to organize joint relief for war-torn Hungary. The conference was held in Hamilton on August 12, 1945 at the Royal Connaught Hotel; Rev. Ruzsa was an organizer and became part of the board of directors.

During the Second World War and in the years which followed, Ruzsa, along with many other priests and ministers in North America, was flooded with requests by Hungarian Displaced Persons living in Europe. The situation became so critical that in August, 1949, the Hungarian Ministers of the Presbyterian Church in Canada issued a circular in which they pleaded for the cause of European Displaced Persons, asking that one Sunday in September be set aside in all churches to pray for the cause of the DPs.[27] In another document, a Report of the Christian Settlement and Rehabilitation Board (August 1949), it was stated that Hungarians were the only people among the DPs.   In another document, a Report of the Christian Hungarian Protestant refugees in Western Europe; among them about 16,000 of the Reformed faith. There were 45 ministers, of whom 37 were Reformed (Presbyterian).[28] In light of such circumstances, it is understandable as to why Hungarian ministers of the Reformed faith were swamped with requests from DP camps in Europe. The new immigrants were completely different from the interwar immigrants. Rev. Kálmán Dóka, a close friend and colleague, said about Ruzsa's work during this postwar period:

> This group of immigrants was a completely different class than his congregation: they were upper middle class. There was tremendous tension between the earlier immigrants and the new arrivals—creating much conflict. This really wore him /Ruzsa/ out, as he worked day and night to overcome the conflicts and tensions. He was quite successful in bridging the gap—mainly inside the church. Beyond the church this was very difficult. He was mostly involved with setting up organizations—working ecumenically with all denominations. In fact, he was so involved in this category that he worked a great deal with members of parliament from this area, and the Dept. of Immigration. He was well-known in this field.[29]

The Ruzsa collection contains dozens of letters from hapless immigrants requesting aid in many forms, such as a letter dated February 14, 1951, from a Hungarian DP in Fort William, Ontario, who was employed by the Great Lakes Paper Co. The immigrant had been there since November of 1950, and had recently learned that his wife and child had been allowed to come to Canada; he wished to come to Toronto to join them. He wrote: "I am 160 km. away from the nearest city—it is impossible for me to look for other work. We work in waist-deep snow clearing the forest. One cannot even stop on Sundays or holidays because then one cannot get ahead. At first I thought I would get used to it, but now I must admit it gets harder and harder." [30] The letter from the Hamilton Cotton Co. requesting assistance with Hungarian DPs employed by the company, was only one of dozens of similar letters. [31]

The Post-World War II years brought about a noticeable change in the activities of Rev. Ruzsa: he was no longer only concerned with functions inside of the Hungarian community, but strove to organize activities with other ethnic groups on a larger scale, functions which would promote the good name of the Hungarians within the host society. He was instrumental in the founding of the Hungarian Committee of Cooperation in Canadian Citizenship. In 1946, he was chairman of the Hungarian Committee for the Hamilton Centennial Celebrations, and one of the directors of the "Nations in Revue" pageant, organized in conjunction with these celebrations. Ruzsa was co-founder of the Canadian National Unity Council (1947), and served for many years as one of the directors of this organization.

Whenever there was an event to be organized on a larger scale, Rev. Ruzsa was the person who was able to bring various factions of the community together for it. His personal papers contain much correspondence dealing with factional in-fighting within the community; Ruzsa always acted as mediator, as peacemaker. 1948 was the 100th anniversary of the Hungarian Revolution of 1848, and Ruzsa organized large-scale festivities to commemorate the event in Hamilton. His daughter Pearl said of the festivities: "I don't know if it has ever seen or would ever see its equal. Literally thousands of people attended and I don't know if it lasted for two or three days." [32] In 1956, Ruzsa organized a Commemorative Festival of the Fifth Centenary of the Noonday Bell and Hunyadi Victory of Nándorfehérvár /Belgrade/. The Ruzsa collection is full of correspondence and published material/ flyers regarding these events, and many similar functions.

During the 1950s, Rev. Ruzsa was involved in the founding of such organizations as the Canadian Hungarian Reformed Ministerial Association, the Canadian Hungarian Federation, Hungarian Helicon (Toronto), and the Free Hungarian Protestant World Federation. The collection contains much material from these organizations, but it is particularly valuable regarding the Protestant organizations in Canada, as materials concerning the other organizations may be found elsewhere. Ruzsa's correspondence with most of the other Protestant ministers serving Hungarian congregations is of particular interest, as they provide a valuable insight into the development of immigrant parishes in Canada.

After the outbreak of the Revolution in Hungary in October, 1956, the three Hungarian churches in Hamilton and other community groups were involved in organizing mass demonstrations. Ruzsa was involved in the work of the Hungarian Emergency Relief Fund, and the work of the Protestant Committee for Hungarian Refugee Children in Ontario (post-1956). The Ruzsa collection contains many documents regarding this period and the reaction of Hungarians in the diaspora to the crisis. There were tremendous cultural differences between the post-World War II DPs and the refugees of 1956. Many of these differences become evident in the correspondence of Ruzsa. In one report written by the Hungarian minister in Lethbridge in 1957, the minister complained that of 760 refugees who have thus far arrived in Lethbridge (sponsored by this particular church), not more than 30 have ever attended the Presbyterian church, and in the minister's opinion, only 20 or so will ever become members. [33]

In 1969, after 40 years of service as a minister, Eugene Ruzsa retired. During the 1950s and 1960s he was already active in compiling the second part of his history of Hungarian-Canadians. After retirement, he once again travelled across Canada, documenting the activities and organizations of Hungarian community life. He tried, unsuccessfully, to obtain Secretary of State funding for his second manuscript. Rev. Ruzsa died on January 4, 1977 in St. Joseph Hospital in Hamilton. One fellow minister said of him: "...There was no distinction between the religious and Hungarian aspect of his life-activities. He couldn't separate the two...He so loved his people...He was never in favor of developing an ethnic ghetto, that was never his approach... But he used his instincts, for example, when he appealed to the very ethnicity of the community in order to make it grow.... I feel he was psychologically ahead of his time in this regard.... He developed a community for the people in the church—used the church building to develop a wholesome community, a Christian community." [34]

Significance of the Ruzsa Collection

The Ruzsa collection is a valuable addition to the archival sources dealing with Hungarian immigration to Canada, in particular with the period from 1940 to 1970. The collection provides much insight into the activities of the Hungarian community during that period, and while there are smatterings of left-wing literature and content, it is overwhelmingly a collection documenting the activities of the religious, conservative segment of the community.

The collection is valuable in that it provides the background to the writing and publishing of the first history of Hungarian immigration to and settlement in Canada. Through the correspondence, the student of immigration history may gain excellent insight into the problems encountered by ministers in charge of immigrant parishes, as well as into the problems of the newly-arrived immigrants, and those seeking immigration to Canada. Moreover, the papers in the collection are over a long enough period that certain trends can be noted in the development of the community over the years. The organizations of the 1930s and early 1940s and their functions (mainly social and religious) were considerably different from those established after 1945 (most of which emphasized politics, education, and culture). Eugene Ruzsa could operate on both levels, and was accepted by all segments of the community. Thus, despite the fact that he was a convinced anticommunist, when members of left-wing groups were in serious trouble, they knew they could turn to Ruzsa and obtain help.

The Ruzsa Collection is most valuable because it transmits the feelings and hardships of individual Hungarian immigrants, the difficulties and joys of Hungarian Protestant ministers, and also sheds light on the development of Protestant congregations in Canada. It provides massive documentation of Hungarian community life, and of the efforts of a single Protestant minister who tried, sometime effectively and sometimes not, to elevate the status of his ethnic group in Canada.

Notes

1. Interview with Pearl Sojnocki, daughter of Rev. Ruzsa, conducted by S. Papp on August 23, 1979. (In Oral History Collection of Multicultural History Society of Ontario.)

2. *Ibid.*

3. Report to W. A. Cameron, Presbyterian Church Synod, by Rev. Ruzsa dated October 7, 1940.

4. Mrs. István Ruzsa *Emlékirataim* /Memoirs/ (Cleveland: Hungarian Lutheran Church, 1967).

5. Report to Rev. Cameron, *op. cit.*

6. Interview with Mrs. Helen Ruzsa, August 23, 1979 (In MHSO archives).

7. Interview with Rev. Kálmán Dóka by S. Papp, Feb. 21, 1981.

8. Pearl Sojnocki, *op. cit.*

9. Interview with Eugene Ruzsa (son of Rev. Ruzsa) August 23, 1979.

10. Dóka interview, *op. cit.*

11. Eugene Ruzsa interview. Also corroborated with correspondence in personal papers.

12. Undated letter to József Szentágotay, Royal Consulate General in Sweden in Charge of Hungarian Interests in Canada. The reply was sent Feb. 1947.

13. Letter dated Feb. 18, 1940 to wife and family written from Winnipeg.

14. *Ibid.*

15. *Ibid.*

16. Letter dated April 22, 1940 to wife and family from Saskatchewan.

17. Interview with Helen Ruzsa, *op. cit.*

18. Letter from Béla Bácskai Payerle dated Sept. 30, 1940.

19. Jenő Ruzsa, *A kanadai magyarság története* /History of Hungarian Canadians/ (Toronto, 1940), p. 505.

20. Letter from Watson Kirkconnell, dated June 15, 1942.

21. *Reformátusok Lapja* /Protestant's Weekly/ January 21, 1941.

22. *Tárogató* /Oboe Flute/, Feb. 6, 1941.

23. Letter dated Jan. 28, 1936 from the Board of American Missions of the United Lutheran Church in America.

24. *Ibid.*

25. Dóka interview, *op. cit.*

26. Pearl Sojnocki interview, *op. cit.*

27. Document dated August 27, 1949.

28. Document dated August 23, 1949.

29. Dóka interview, *op. cit.*

30. Letter dated Feb. 14, 1951.

31. Letter dated June 2, 1948.

32. Interview with Pearl Sojnocki, *op. cit.*

33. Letter from Lajos Vietorisz, Bethlen Hungarian Presbyterian Church, Lethbridge, dated May 15, 1957.

34. Dóka interview, *op. cit.*

Appendix A

The following Organizations and/or Institutions are represented significantly in the Ruzsa Collection:

Religious Institutions/Organizations

Békevár Presbyterian Church
Bethlen Hungarian Presbyterian Church, Lethbridge, Alberta
Canadian Hungarian Reformed Ministerial Association
Canadian Hungarian Reformed Elders' Association
Free Hungarian Protestant World Federation (U.S. Based)
Kitchener Hungarian Lutheran Church
John Calvin Presbyterian Church (Hamilton)
Protestant Committee for Hungarian Refugee Children in
    Ontario (1956)
Toronto Hungarian Lutheran Church
Windsor Hungarian Lutheran Church

Secular Institutions/Organizations

American Hungarian Federation
Canadian Hungarian National Federation
Canadian National Unity Council
Delhi and Tobacco District Hungarian House
Grand Council of Hungarian Churches and Organizations
    in Hamilton
Hungarian Centenary Committee
Hungarian Emergency Relief Fund (1956)
Hungarian Helicon Society
Hungarian "Turul" Sport Club
Hunyadi Anniversary Committee
Independent United Hungarian Society (forerunner of
    Toronto Hungarian House)
Kitchener Hungarian Club
Movement for an Independent Hungary
Toronto Hungarian House
Toronto Magyar Sport Club

Appendix B

The following newspapers are contained in the Ruzsa
Collection:

Large Collections (Complete annual issues collected)

Kanadai Magyar Újság /Canadian Hungarian News/
   (Winnipeg)
Kanadai Magyar Munkás /Canadian Hungarian Worker
   (Hamilton)
Kanadai Magyarság /Canadian Hungarians/ (Toronto)
Magyar Élet /Hungarian Life/ (Toronto)
Szabadság /Liberty/ (Cleveland, Ohio)
Képes Világhíradó /Illustrated World Review/ (Toronto)

Scattered Issues

Amerikai Magyar Református Lapja /American Hungarian
   Reformed News/
Kanadai Kis Újság /Little Hungarian News of Canada
   (Welland)
Egységes Magyarság /United Hungarians/ (Niagara Falls,
   Ont.)
Sporthíradó /Sport News/ (Toronto)
Csendes Percek /Quiet Moments/ (Hamilton-Ottawa)
Híradó /Hungarian Herald/ (Toronto)
Tárogató /Oboe Flute/ (Toronto)

N. F. Dreisziger:

26 / THE "JUSTICE FOR HUNGARY" OCEAN FLIGHT: THE TRIANON SYNDROME IN IMMIGRANT HUNGARIAN SOCIETY

It has been argued that the politics of interwar Hungary were dominated by the treaty that was imposed on the country in the wake of the First World War. This peace settlement, known as the Treaty of Trianon, disposed of Hungary's fate with severity unequalled in modern European history. It reduced the country to less than thirty percent of its former territory containing not much more than a third of its population. One of the pretexts for Hungary's trunkation was the principle of self-determination of nations, yet the settlement's provisions were not put to the test of plebiscites. In fact, the treaty violated the self-determination of close to 3.5 million Magyars who were placed under alien rule.

Hungary's dismemberment in the wake of the First World War has had a lasting effect on the Hungarian national psyche. "The shock of Trianon," argued Professor S. B. Várdy in one of his recent publications, "was so pervasive and so keenly felt that the syndrome it produced can only be compared to a malignant national disease." [1]

The role of the "Trianon syndrome" in modern Hungarian development has not been analysed in adequate detail and at sufficient depth until recently. In Hungary, conditions for a scholarly examination of this problem rarely existed. In the emotion-filled atmosphere of the interwar and war years, such examination was well-nigh impossible, and the shock of the harsh peace settlement paralysed even those Hungarian historians who, through emigration, had managed to distance themselves from the everyday influences of East Central European political life. [2] After 1945, the examination of the issue became difficult for another reason: Hungary's post-war regimes persistently discouraged the discussion of Trianon and its consequences on Hungarian national life. For obvious reasons, the scholarly analysis of this issue was also frowned upon in the neighbouring East Central European states, especially in those with large Hungarian minorities. As a result, the study of the "Trianon syndrome" has been left to a handful of students of Hungarian history in the West, and quite recently, to a few historians in Hungary who, defying decades-old traditions, began to write on this controversial issue. [3]

Notwithstanding the difficulties of studying this question, the literature on it has grown sufficiently, especially in recent times, to warrant some overall conclusions. In summing up these conclusions, it would probably not be unreasonable to say that historians have seen the Trianon syndrome as a negative factor in Hungarian national life, a neurosis that tended to incapacitate Hungarian diplomacy and to retard the pace of domestic political and social reform. The purpose of this essay is to carry the examination of the Trianon syndrome further, and to analyse its impact on a part of Hungarian society beyond the confines of East Central Europe, on the large Hungarian community in North America, with special reference to the Hungarian ethnic group in Canada. In many ways this will be a pioneering attempt, and its conclusions will be, by necessity, provisional. But they will suggest that it may well be that the impact of the Trianon syndrome on Hungarian immigrant communities in the various parts of the New World was similar to what it was on society in the mother country: it gave immigrant politics a narrow focus, and, as a result, it contributed to the impoverishment of immigrant community life. It did so particularly during a time when Hungarian ethnic life in North America, and especially in Canada, reached one of its peaks of development: the late 1920s and the very early 1930s. As the "Justice for Hungary" ocean flight was one of the outstanding episodes of that period, our examination will inevitably focus on that event and its historical context.

I

Though ostensibly a joint effort of the Hungarian immigrant communities of the United States and Canada, so much was contributed (mainly in terms of effort) to the success of the "Justice for Hungary" flight by members of the latter, that it seems appropriate to begin this study with an outline of Hungarian-Canadian society in the years leading up to the ocean crossing in 1931. A further reason for the appropriateness of starting this study with a survey of the Hungarians of Canada is the fact that, apparently, Hungarian-Canadian society was more "afflicted" with the Trianon syndrome than its American counterpart. The explanation for this seems to lie primarily in the Hungarian-Canadian immigrant community's tender age. A large majority of Hungarians in interwar Canada were new arrivals. As such, most of them had experienced the shock of Trianon before their departure to Canada, that is where it was most dramatically felt, in East Central Europe. It is not surprising then that the impact of the peace settlement was more keenly ingrained into the minds of these people than it was imprinted in those of their compatriots living in the United States, most of whom were pre-1914 arrivals.

According to Canadian census statistics, in 1931 Hungarians in Canada numbered 40,582. [4] Approximately three quarters of these had come to the country (or were born there) during the preceding ten years. Many of these recent arrivals had come via the so-called successor states: Czechoslovakia, Rumania and Yugoslavia. This suggests that for a large number of Hungarian-Canadians the Treaty of Trianon was not only some kind of a national humiliation, but a traumatic and often tragic personal experience as well. Having seen their homes transferred from their native country to a foreign one, they found conditions in the new political environment unpleasant enough to seek refuge in overseas emigration. Furthermore, not only did many Hungarian newcomers come to Canada via the successor states, but many who came from "trunkated" Hungary, were originally refugees from lands that had been detached from the country as a result of the peace settlement. Considering all this, it would probably not be an exaggeration to suggest that between a third and a half of Hungarian immigrants to Canada in the interwar period (nearly all of whom came between 1924 and the onset of the Depression years), stemmed from the territories assigned by the Treaty of Trianon to Hungary's neighbours.

Wherever they came from, the thousands of Hungarians who arrived in Canada in the mid- and late-1920s, brought new vitality to Hungarian ethnic life in many parts of the country. [5] This general revival of Hungarian-Canadian community life manifested itself in the birth of new centers of Magyar ethnic life, in the growth of others, in the appearance of a great many community institutions, both secular and religious. Included among these institutions were a few Hungarian-language newspapers and, after protracted preparations, an umbrella organization to serve as a nation-wide lobby of all Hungarians in Canada. This body was the Canadian Hungarian Federation /*Kanadai Magyar Szövetség*/, not to be confused with the present-day Hungarian Canadian Federation /*Kanadai Magyarok Szövetsége*/. It existed for a few years after 1928; its life spanned the gestation period of the "Justice for Hungary" ocean flight. Consequently, its history is quite relevant to our topic, and will be examined in some detail.

There is some historical evidence which makes it possible for us to gage to what extent the Hungarian-Canadian institutions that emerged in the mid- and late-1920s were imbued with the "spirit of revisionism," as the demand for the alteration of the terms of the Treaty of Trianon was known. The record of one influential institution from this period, the *Kanadai Magyar Újság* /Canadian Hungarian News/ is well known.

The *News* was established in the winter of 1924-25 in the town of Kipling, Saskatchewan. Although Hungarians constituted the largest ethnic minority in Kipling, the paper's publishers found it advisable to transfer operations to a larger urban center, to Winnipeg, Manitoba, a city of thriving immigrant life in the mid- and late-1920s. In its new home, the *News* prospered. In a few years it became a large, semi-weekly publication with subscribers in many parts of Canada. [6] It even managed to absorb a couple of Hungarian language papers started in Central Canada.

Within a decade-and-a-half of its founding, the *News* became one of the two viable Hungarian Newspapers in Canada. Its rival was the leftist paper, the *Kanadai Magyar Munkás* /Canadian Hungarian Worker/. Significantly enough, in 1941 an official of Canada's External Affairs Department described the *Worker* as the organ of Canada's Hungarian Communists, and the *News* of Winnipeg as the voice of the "Magyar-speaking refugees from the old Hungarian provinces that had been turned over to Jugoslavia (*sic*), Roumania and Czechoslovakia."[7] Indeed, the ardent revisionism of the *News* is also noted in a study that was done on its editorial policies by a young Canadian scholar a few years ago.[8]

It is not a mere coincidence that for much of the time under consideration in this paper the guiding spirit behind the *News'* operations was an intelligent, energetic young man, Béla Bácskai Payerle, who hailed from the region that had been transferred by the Treaty of Trianon to Yugoslavia. Other refugees from Hungary's "old provinces" made it to the leadership of other contemporary institutions. Indeed, it is hard to think of any Hungarian-Canadian leader of the 1920s immigration stream who did not have close personal ties to one or more of the provinces detached from Hungary. When the Canadian Hungarian Federation was formed in 1928, some of its top officers would be from this group of refugees; so were several of the most influential Hungarian-Canadian religious leaders of this period.[9]

Although the presence of so many newcomers from the detached Hungarian territories assured the prominence of "revisionist influences" in Hungarian-Canadian society, the Government of Hungary did not want to leave matters to chance and took pains to make sure that this spirit prospered among Canada's Hungarians.[10] Accordingly, contacts were established and cultivated with the conservative nationalist elements of Hungarian-Canadian society. These usually took the form of visits to Canada by Hungarian emissaries, often as a part of a larger North American tour. Among the Hungarian statesmen who visited Canada in the 1920s were Count Albert Apponyi and Baron Zsigmond Perényi. The former was Hungary's most respected elder statesman, while the latter was a Privy Councillor and a friend of Regent Miklós Horthy. There were also several visiting church dignitaries and a few journalists. An important role in influencing opinion among the newcomers was played by the staff of the two Hungarian consulates in Canada, the main one in Montréal and the other in Winnipeg. Through these contacts, the authorities in Hungary tried to guide the politics of the Hungarian-Canadian ethnic group, and reinforce its revisionist sentiments. While most of the time Budapest's efforts were confined to measures of persuasion, on a few occasions more direct methods were resorted to. One such step was the granting of a modest financial subsidy to the *News* of Winnipeg; another was the mediation which Baron Perényi undertook to resolve a quarrel between two major Hungarian-Canadian organizations in 1928.

II

The attempts of the Hungarian government to influence Hungarian ethnic affairs overseas encompassed the United States also. In fact, there can be little doubt that the main target of these efforts was the much larger Hungarian community of the United States. In 1930, that ethnic group numbered 274,450 Hungarian-speaking immigrants and a similar number of second-generation Hungarian-Americans. [11] There can be no doubt that the vast majority of these people were full of sympathy for Hungary, and agreed with the concept of treaty revision. The Hungarian-American community's attempts to forestall the Trianon settlement, and later to achieve its international condemnation, have been documented by historians. Dr. Julianna Puskás relates how in 1919-20 Hungarian-Americans lobbied in Washington and elsewhere against the proposed treaty, and how all political factions denounced its provisions later. [12] Although a fertile ground existed for revisionist sentiments among Hungarians in the United States, the situation there differed from that in Canada inasmuch as the leadership of the majority of Hungarian-American organizations remained in the hands of pre-1914 arrivals, or in those of second-generation Hungarian-Americans. Partly or perhaps even largely for this reason, the efforts of the Budapest authorities to woo the Magyar communities of the United

States, had limited success only. Although much money was collected from Hungarian immigrants for various causes pertaining to the welfare of Hungary and her residents, the expectations attached to the over half a million Hungarian-Americans by the government in Budapest were not achieved in their entirety. Nevertheless, when the Hungarian American Federation was revived in 1929 at a large gathering in Buffalo, a "revisionist" political platform was adopted, indicating the combined strength of these sentiments in Hungarian-American society, and the influence of Hungary's political elite over immigrant politics.

Though the revitalization of a nation-wide umbrella organization of Hungarian-Americans should have filled many members of this community with at least a partial feeling of satisfaction, it may not have been enough to counteract the sense of disappointment that had been bequeathed to them by an incident a year earlier, the so-called Kossuth statue fiasco. The story of this regrettable event is familiar. It all started with a campaign to collect money to erect in New York, a giant statue of the hero of the 1848-49 Hungarian War of Independence. Some $40,000 were collected, a bronze statue was cast in Hungary and was shipped to the United States. It was dedicated in the midst of much fanfare and festivities. Unfortunately, the statue's design proved defective and it had to be removed for repairs. [13] Undoubtedly this experience was taken as a national humiliation by many Hungarians who felt that more effective measures had to be taken to call national and international attention to the plight of Hungary.

III

The scheme that was eventually devised to achieve this objective was the plan of a non-stop flight from North America to Hungary. The undertaking may have been seen as a deed that would coincidentally correct the image of incompetence that some Hungarians felt that the Kossuth statue episode bestowed on them. The central protagonist of the ocean flight story was to be a certain Sándor Magyar. Magyar received his training as a pilot during World War I in Hungary. After the war, he spent some time in Germany. It was there that

he proved that he was a man of much bravado, and almost
lost his life in doing this. What happened was that on one
day Magyar learned that a well-known Hungarian actress
was involved in the shooting of some outdoor scenes for a
film near the airfield where Magyar was working. Anxious
to make a good impression on the starlet, Magyar borrowed
a small, reputedly rather unreliable plane from the airfield
and, with a bouquet of flowers in his hands, took to the air.
His intention was to throw the flowers to the film star, but
something went wrong with Magyar's plane, and he had to
crashland in a cemetery. [14]

After recovering from the injuries suffered as a result
of this adventure, Magyar emigrated to Canada. He spent
a few years in southern Saskatchewan, working on farms
during the agricultural season, and spending much of the
rest of the year in Regina. In 1928 Magyar left the Canadian West and settled in the industrial town of Windsor,
Ontario. It was here that he became a friend of the local
Hungarian Calvinist minister Jenő Molnár and his wife,
Rózsa Waldman (Waldmann?) Molnár. Rózsa was an intelligent, energetic woman who did much to help Hungarian immigrants in Windsor, especially members of her husband's congregation. She was a recent arrival from Hungary. Presumably, she sympathised with other recent arrivals such as Magyar, who often found it difficult to find
employment and must have felt despondent at times. It may
have been at a time when Magyar was particularly dispir-
ited and felt quite helpless that Rózsa suggested to him that
he should do something extraordinary, such as repeating
and bettering Charles Lindbergh's feat, by flying across the
Atlantic; not to Paris, but all the way to Budapest. Apparently, the idea that this deed should be used to call attention to the injustice of the Treaty of Trianon was also the
brainchild of this woman. [15]

To implement the plan, a campaign to collect money
for a plane was started. In Windsor, one of its early promoters was the Reverend Molnár, Rózsa's husband. One
of the first people to contribute to the campaign was an unemployed member of Molnár's congregation, István Rimaszombathy. He gave $30, probably all or most of his sav-
ings. [16] Soon, the campaign expanded. Postcards were

printed and were sent to prospective supporters of the venture, as well as to influential political figures in many countries. In distant parts of the continent campaign workers were recruited to manage the appeal in their respective regions. [17] In the United States, the cause of the ocean flight was endorsed by Géza Berkó, an influential newspaperman. Berkó's own paper, the *Amerikai Magyar Népszava* /American Hungarian People's Voice/, actively supported the appeal. [18] Yet, not enough money was coming in. By 1930, economic conditions for most immigrants, and especially newcomers, had become so bad that many people were not in a position to give more than what the postcards cost; and some people not even that much. The campaign stalled, and the flight had to be postponed.

IV

The campaign to collect money for the planned ocean flight was not the only major Hungarian-Canadian collective undertaking of the late 1920s. As has been mentioned in the introduction to this paper, these years also witnessed the creation of a nationwide umbrella organization of Hungarian-Canadians. The Canadian Hungarian Federation that resulted from these efforts was not the first such organization of Hungarians in Canada. There had been attempts to establish supra-communal organizations before, to be more exact, a few years prior to the outbreak of the First World War. These early attempts failed to create viable organizations; in any case, no such organization could have survived the war, as Hungarians were regarded as enemy aliens after 1914, and their political organizations had to disband. [19] With the return of normalcy in the 1920s, and the coming of thousands of new Hungarian immigrants from the countries of East Central Europe, the time became ripe to renew the efforts for the establishment of a Canada-wide organization of Hungarian-Canadians. The Hungarian government was also anxious to see Hungarians in their various countries of settlement organized into more effective lobbies, preferably under leaders that were sympathetic to the mother country's foreign and internal policies.

While the Budapest authorities were in favor of national

federations of Hungarian immigrants abroad, and had actively encouraged some Hungarian-American leaders to renew efforts at national unity in the U.S.A., there is no substantial evidence to prove that the efforts to this end in Canada were made on the initiative of Hungary's leaders. On the contrary, there is every reason to believe that the push for action originated with Hungarian-Canadian leaders. Perhaps the most prominent of these was the Reverend János Kovács, the minister of Western Canada's most active Hungarian Calvinist congregation located in the colony of Békevár, Saskatchewan. Kovács arranged for a preparatory conference to convene in 1927 in the city of Regina. [20]

In the meantime, a few hundred miles farther east, in Winnipeg, the idea of national Hungarian-Canadian union found another advocate in György Szabó, a ticket agent, as managers of travel agencies used to be known in those days. Others joined the bandwagon with the result that another "preparatory conference" was held in Welland, an industrial town with a large Hungarian colony in southern Ontario. This was followed by the "founding convention," held in February of 1928 in the bitter cold of Winnipeg. Here, the Canadian Hungarian Federation was established with much fanfare, amidst receptions, banquets, and the inevitable speechmaking. Problems came up only when the elections were held to the Federation's executive board, for it seems that people who were elected were not the ones who had planned and prepared the organization. As a result, the executive board was attacked, and an influential group of Hungarian-Canadian leaders, made up mainly of pre-1914 arrivals, established a rival federation at a convention in the city of Saskatoon, Saskatchewan. In the end, both federations selected Winnipeg as their national headquarters. [21]

There is no need here to go into the details of the reasons why the Canadian Hungarian Federation established early in 1928 was plagued with a multitude of problems. It should suffice to say that there were rivalries between two different streams of immigrants, the pre-1914 ones and those who came in the 1920s. There were also difficulties stemming from religious differences: some people denounced the Federation as a "Calvinist" organization. But the greatest source of mischief came from an unexpected quarter: from

Canada's two main railway companies. The fact was that both of these were deeply involved in immigrant affairs (not only as railway companies, but also as colonization agencies, as well as owners or partners in steamship lines carrying passengers from Europe and back). Naturally, both of them wanted influence within the budding federation, mainly through having their own men elected. The extent of the railway companies' meddling in the affairs of the just-established Federation is best illustrated by the fact that the headquarters of the two organizations were in the ticket offices of persons who were working for the Canadian Pacific Railway, and the Canadian National Railway, respectively. [22] The net result of these corporations' interference in contemporary Hungarian-Canadian politics was that the effort to create a national lobby was just about "railroaded."

The difficulties stemming from the railways' intervention were fortunately solved in the course of 1928. It was in this connection that Baron Perényi performed the useful function of mediation mentioned earlier. Partly or largely as a result of his efforts, the two rival groups resolved their differences, and at the Canadian Hungarian Federation's next annual convention, held early during 1929, managed to elect an executive acceptable to a large majority of those in attendance. The new leaders looked forward to the rest of 1929 with great expectations. Unfortunately for their cause, they were to be disappointed. To make the long story of the CHF's demise short, it should suffice to say that the organization, despite the valiant efforts of some of its leaders, never managed to become financially viable. It tried to collect membership fees of one dollar a year from Hungarian-Canadians, but what little was collected this way was not enough. The Federation also tried to sell life insurance, but this scheme, too, proved a financial failure. Without adequate finances, the Federation could not acquire a paper of its own (which was seen as useful, if not necessary). But what was much more serious, it could not repay the loans it took out when it began functioning. It did try to pay one loan off with another; but in the end its financial reserves became completely exhausted, its credit destroyed, and the organization disintegrated. Some of its provincial chapters continued to function for some time, but by 1931 the parent body was, for all intents and purposes, dead. [23] As shall be seen below, quite a different fate awaited the campaign to put the ocean flight scheme into effect.

V

There can be little doubt that, despite the dedication of many Hungarian immigrants to North America who, much like István Rimaszombathy, gave away most of their savings to support this cause, the appeal to achieve the "Justice for Hungary" flight would have met the same fate as the CHF had it not been for a few prosperous people who made substantial donations to the campaign. By far the most important of these was Emil Szalay of Chicago. Szalay came to America at the end of the nineteenth century as a young child of an immigrant family. He started out as a butcher's apprentice and, by the 1920s, had become a moderately prosperous man. Determined to help his country of birth, he decided to see to it that the ocean flight scheme was realized. He contributed enough money to the campaign to cover most of the cost of a suitable airplane, a Lockheed Sirius model. [24] The plane, constructed mainly out of wood, was named "Justice for Hungary." Much of the balance of the cost was apparently made up by an even richer man, an English friend of Hungarians, Lord Rothermere, the newspaper magnate. [25] With these donations, the preparations for the flight could begin in earnest.

The intervention of Szalay and the others came just in time. Not only was the campaign to collect money not yielding the desired results, but the venture was encountering opposition from various quarters. For some unexplained reason, the Reverend Molnár, one of the campaign's earliest supporters, changed his mind about it and withdrew his support. Another very influential Hungarian religious leader, Monsignor Pál Sántha of Stockholm, Saskatchewan, gave only lukewarm support to the project. [26] Still others, whose identity might forever remain unknown, began spreading derogatory rumours about Magyar and the campaign's chief organizers. These in turn attributed the attacks to Little Entente sources, believing that Hungary's neighbours had good reasons to prevent the flight from taking place. [27] In Hungary proper the plan was welcomed, and the Hungarian government dispatched György Endresz, one of Hungary's most experienced pilots, to take control of the flight (Magyar was to act as his back-up pilot and navigator). Test flights were made with the plane already in 1930. Then, alterations were made to it, including the addition of extra storage tanks to hold enough fuel for the long journey. [28]

The final preparations for the crossing were made in the late spring and early summer of 1931. Szalay had, in the meantime, left for Europe by steamship, hoping to be in Budapest when the "Justice for Hungary" plane arrived there. At this stage, only the weather forecasts were delaying the moment of departure from Grace Harbour, Newfoundland, the easternmost airfield of the North American continent. Finally, after delays that must have seemed interminable, Endresz and Magyar decided to risk the journey despite a not too promising weather forecast. [29]

The flight was not without some precarious moments. The first of these occurred right on takeoff. The plane, loaded with far more fuel than it was designed to carry, could hardly clear the obstructions near the end of the runway. A few yards farther away, it hit the top branches of a tree, yet it continued its flight and even cleared the top of a nearby hill, but only barely. Then it began its long journey across the ocean. At first, Endresz and Magyar flew very low, under the cloud cover. When the mist above the ocean enveloped them, they had to increase their altitude in order to avoid dipping too low and hitting the waves. Their primitive instruments made flying "blind" very risky. The plane took two hours to climb to an altitude of 6,000 feet. Here, they could see again; however, they could determine their position only by the stars, and through contacting steamships below them with their (for those days) ultra-modern radio equipment. Early next morning they encountered a storm. By this time they had entered the airspace over Western Europe. Leaving the disturbance behind them, they flew over the valleys and meadows of Germany, following notable landmarks at low altitude. Soon, they reached the western border of Hungary. A few minutes later, some 20 miles short of their intended destination, the plane's motor stalled.

The fuel in one of the aircraft's tanks was spent. There was
a little more of it left in one of the spare tanks, but Endresz
had switched not to this one, but to another empty one: the
plane was apparently not equipped with proper fuel gages.
By the time the mistake was discovered it was too late to re-
start the motor. Endresz and Magyar had to make an emergency landing in a field near the village of Bicske. [30]

Despite this anticlimactic ending, the ocean crossing was
a success. The "Justice for Hungary" had set a new record
for nonstop long-distance flying: it covered nearly 6,000
kilometers, and it crossed the Atlantic in record time. The
flight received a great deal of international attention. Endresz
and Magyar got a tumultuous welcome in Hungary. Even
though the plane failed to reach its ultimate destination,
everyone concerned was satisfied, at least for the moment.
After the passage of a few months, and even more so a year
or two later, the excitement of the summer of 1931 was gone,
and the ocean flight remained mainly a memory. Szalay
became disappointed in Hungary, or in her leaders. Perhaps
they did not accord him the reception he had expected and
felt that he had deserved. [31] Magyar returned to Canada
only to move to the U.S. later. The plane was repaired and
restored to service, mainly for publicity purposes; it was on
one such mission in 1932 that Endresz crashed with it and
lost his life. [32]

For most members of Canada's Hungarian community,
the ocean flight by this time had become little more than
history. After the excitement of the successful adventure,
life for these people soon returned to normal, if it is possible
to describe it as such under the difficult circumstances of
the 1930s. For most Hungarian immigrants to Canada, and
undoubtedly for the vast majority of those who came in the
late-1920s, "normalcy" by this time meant chronic unemployment, despair and poverty. [33] For their institutions, it
meant lack of progress at best and severe setbacks at worst.
For their community life it meant helplessness and aimless-
ness, and a lot of bickering between the conservatives (those
who still believed in religion and liberal democracy) and the
radicals (those who rejected both the churches and the ex-

isting political system). [34] There can be little doubt that, in view of the economic conditions of the times, much of this was inevitable. What might not have been inevitable was the near-total ineffectiveness of Hungarian-Canadian political life. Much of this ineffectiveness was caused by the lack of a viable Hungarian-Canadian umbrella organization. As it has been seen, there had been such an organization in existence for some time. If we discount the troubled first few months of the CHF's existence, we could still say that it "lived" for about two years. There was no valid reason why its existence could not have been prolonged.

The primary cause of the CHF's demise was the lack of finances. The Federation had trouble paying back loans amounting to a few hundred dollars only. This happened just at the time when tens of thousands of dollars were expended to get the ocean flight on its way. It must be admitted, most of that money came from outside of Canada; nevertheless, the demise of the CHF and the simultaneous success of the "Justice for Hungary" appeal clearly shows where the priorities of Hungarian immigrants lay.

It is evident beyond doubt that for Magyar newcomers to Canada, and probably also for many of their compatriots living in the United States, the fortunes of their only true Fatherland were more important than the fate of their ethnic community in their new country of residence. Indeed, the devotion of these people to their country of origin clearly indicates their true loyalties. That loyalty was not to anything associated with their new homeland, certainly not to their "ethnic group" in North America, but first and foremost to their one and only native country, Hungary. The fact that they conceived of their Fatherland as being mortally wounded through an act of international injustice, made their determination to come to its aid all the stronger. The desire to gain redress for Hungary's injuries became so powerful in them that they lost sight of their collective "ethnic" interests in the new homeland, and failed to take adequate steps to take care of these. To put it another way: Hungarian-Canadians became afflicted with the "Trianon syndrome" and, as the result of their excessive preoccuppation with the fate of the "old country," neglected to advance the cause of their immigrant community in their new homeland.

Notes

I wish to extend my thanks to the Directorate of Multiculturalism of Canada for the financial support they have given me over the years to cover the expenses of my research on the history of the Hungarian ethnic group in Canada. I also want to thank Mr. Ferenc Grob of Toronto, one of the main Canadian organizers of the campaign to collect funds for the "Justice for Hungary" trans-ocean flight, for the information he had given me a few years ago on this and other aspects of Hungarian-Canadian history during the interwar decades.

1. S. B. Várdy, "The Impact of Trianon upon Hungary and the Hungarian Mind: The Nature of Interwar Hungarian Irredentism," *Hungarian Studies Review*, Vol. X, Nos. 1 and 2 (1983), special volume on *Hungary and the Second World War.* p. 27.

2. Such as Oscar Jászi and Hugo Ignótus; see *ibid.*, p. 23.

3. Most prominent among them Péter Hanák. For a discussion of Dr. Hanák's ideas see *ibid.*, pp. 23-25.

4. Canada, Dominion Bureau of Statistics, *Census of Canada, 1931*, statistics on ethnic groups, introductory tables. Also, the introductory tables of statistics on ethnic groups in all subsequent censuses.

5. N. F. Dreisziger, M. L. Kovacs, Paul Bődy and Bennett Kovrig, *Struggle and Hope: The Hungarian-Canadian Experience* (Toronto: McClelland and Stewart, 1982), pp. 101-09. Unless otherwise indicated, references to this book are to the chapters by Dreisziger.

6. *Ibid.*, pp. 125f.

7. Copy of memorandum, Department of External Affairs to the High Commissioner for Canada in the United Kingdom, 7 November 1941; Record Group 25, G 2, file 2330-40c, accession 83-84/259, National Archives of Canada.

8. Carmela Patrias, *The "Kanadai Magyar Újság" and the Politics of the Hungarian Canadian Elite* (Toronto: Multicultural History Society of Ontario, 1978), pp. 38f.

9. Monsignor Pál Sántha's roots were in the north-eastern provinces. Ferenc Hoffmann, one of the most respected United Church ministers in Saskatchewan, had taught before the war at an agricultural institute in Kassa (today, Košice in Czechoslovakia). Sister Mary Schwartz, who later became the leading figure in the Hungarian Sisters of Social Service order, came from the Burgenland, a part of Hungary that was divided between that country and Austria as a result of the peace settlement.

10. Dreisziger, *et al.*, pp. 127f.

11. Julianna Puskás, *Kivándorló magyarok az Egyesült Államokban, 1880-1940* /Emigrant Hungarians in the United States, 1880-1940/ (Budapest: Akadémiai Kiadó, 1982), p. 388. See also S. B. Várdy, *The Hungarian-Americans* (Boston: Twayne Publishers, 1985), p. 103.

12. Puskás, pp. 326f.

13. Miklós Szántó, *Magyarok a nagyvilágban* /Hungarians in the Wide World/ (Budapest: Kossuth, 1970), pp. 124-27.

14. Ferenc Grob, "Kivándorlásom és szemelvények a kanadai életből, s életemből" /My Emigration and Observations on Canadian Life and My Life/, MS, pp. 20f. Copies of portions of this manuscript are in my possession, courtesy of Mr. Grob.

15. *Ibid*. In his recollections, Magyar gave a different story. His own account of the birth of the ocean flight idea is quoted in great detail in Kornél Nagy, "Igazságot Magyarországnak! A magyar óceánrepülés" /Justice for Hungary: The Hungarian Ocean Flight/, *Magyar Szárnyak* /Hungarian Wings/, Vol. X (1981), pp. 63-75.

16. Jenő Ruzsa, *A kanadai magyarság története* /The History of Canada's Magyars/ (Toronto: by the author, 1940), p. 274.

17. Ferenc Grob, who was a friend of Magyar from the time of the latter's stay in Regina, was in charge of the campaign in Saskatchewan.

18. Puskás, p. 371.

19. M. L. Kovacs, "The Saskatchewan Era," in Dreisziger *et al.*, pp. 78-83.

20. Dreisziger, *et al.*, pp. 28-30.

21. *Ibid*.

22. *Ibid.*, pp. 28f.

23. N. F. Dreisziger, "In Search of a Hungarian-Canadian Lobby, 1927-1951," *Canadian Ethnic Studies*, Vol. XII, No. 3 (Fall, 1980), p. 86.

24. Grob, pp. 22f.

25. Norbert Csanádi, Sándor Nagyváradi and László Winkler, *A magyar repülés története* /The History of Hungarian Aviation/ (Budapest: Műszaki Könyvkiadó, 1977), p. 140.

26. Grob, pp. 26f.

27. *Ibid*.

28. Nagy, pp. 66-68. Csanádi, *et al.*, p. 141.

29. Csanádi, *et al.*, p. 141.

30. *Ibid.*, pp. 141-43. Also, Nagy, pp. 69-71.

31. Grob, pp. 20f.

32. Csanádi, *et al.*, p. 144.

33. For details on this see Dreisziger, *et al.*, pp. 139-42.

34. *Ibid.*, pp. 155-57.

Ágnes Huszár Várdy:

27/ CHARACTER AND ROLE OF HUNGARIAN LITERARY AND CRITICAL JOURNALS IN NORTH AMERICA IN THE 1970s AND 1980s

In the spring of 1973 a new periodical appeared in Hungarian book stores across North America. Commemorating the 150th anniversary of the birth of Sándor Petőfi, the journal printed selections in honor of Hungary's greatest "poet of freedom" by prominent writers of the past and present. It was a symbolic moment for the launching of a journal that promised to provide a forum for the free expression of thought and ideas, to be free of all political and ideological constraints, and to promote the universality of Hungarian literature and culture. The journal wished to publish selections by Hungarian writers, poets, and intellectuals without regard to their places of residence. It was a journal whose ideals were long overdue, yet the founding of such a publication was a bold endeavor during the political climate of the late sixties and early seventies when contact among Hungarians in the homeland, the neighboring states, and those residing in the West was still in its infancy.

Hungarian language newspapers, beginning with the *Száműzöttek lapja* /Hungarian Exiles' News/, founded by one of Kossuth's followers in 1853, have always played a significant role in the social, cultural, and intellectual life of Hungarian-Americans.[1] Together with church almanacs, calendars, and the albums of fraternal organizations, they provided virtually the only opportunity for writers and poets to appear in print. But newspapers, even weekly and biweeklies are primarily

591

concerned with local, national, and international news and
commentary, and are frequently restricted by the political and
ideological orientations of their publishers, contributors, and
often their reading public.[2] One of the major goals of the
above-mentioned new publication was to provide a forum for
writers, and in the words of its publisher-editor, "especially for
the Hungarian diaspora's most talented group, those who live
in North America, but so far have not established an organ for
literary expression." [3]

The journal in question was the *Ötágú Síp* /Five-Branched
Flute/, an expression coined by Gyula Illyés, the almost
universally accepted contemporary doyen of Hungarian
letters. Illyés saw the five-branched flute as a symbol for the
five major areas where Hungarians live around the world
today: in the motherland, Romania, Czechoslovakia, Yugoslavia, and in the West. *Ötágú Síp* was the brainchild of Rev.
András Hamza, whose dedication and tireless efforts of
Hungarian literature and culture are well-known.[4] Promising
to publish 480 pages of material during the journal's first year,
Rev. Hamza stated: "If there is a need for such a journal, /i.e.
Ötágú Síp/, it will live. If not, it will cease publication within a
year."[5] The latter occurred. Despite his efforts and that of the
five members of the editorial board, the last issue, Volume II,
No. 1 of *Ötágú Síp* appeared in the summer of 1975. The
signal was clear, the verdict given. The Hungarian reading
public of North America felt no need to promote and to
support a literary/critical journal of the caliber and scope of
Ötágú Síp.

In the next decade, following the demise of *Ötágú Síp*,
several new publications appeared on the Hungarian-
American literary scene, virtually every year. Founded in
1978, and having similar intentions and content as *Ötágú Síp*,
the Toronto-based *Tanú* /Witness/ was published in the
format of a newspaper by Mihály Tar, and edited by Iván
Béky-Halász. Unfortunately, *Tanú* suffered a similar fate as
Ötágú Síp: It was forced to cease publication in 1980,
primarily due to a lack of support from the reading public.
Another literary publication appeared in 1979 in the form of a
yearbook edited by Gábor Bikich, who introduced many of his
own poems as well as that of János Csokits.[6] The years 1980
and 1981 saw the publication of two Hungarian-language

literary and critical journals, that of the Chicago-based *Szivárvány* /Rainbow/, and the Washington, D.C.-based *Arkánum*. In 1982 another publication of note was founded by István Miklóssi in Calgary, Canada, with the title *Nyugati Magyarság — Hungarians of the West*. Since its founding, this monthly newspaper that publishes both literary, historical, and cultural articles by Hungarian writers and intellectuals around the world, had its headquarters moved to Montreal, Canada. It is still published and edited by the capable István Miklóssi with the aid of Károly Nagy of Somerset, New Jersey, another well-known and active promoter of Hungarian culture in the United States.

Although founded in 1967, more than a decade earlier than the majority of the above-mentioned periodicals and newspapers, another publication called *Itt-Ott* /Here and There/ should be mentioned. It was originally founded to serve as a free forum of expression for the younger generation of Hungarian-Americans, who were denied the opportunity to express their views in the contemporary Hungarian-American press. The founders of *Itt-Ott*, Louis Éltető and Andrew Ludányi, who were at that time graduate students at Louisiana State University, are to this day the editors of the publication which is now published as a quarterly. *Itt-Ott* publishes articles, poems, and letters, and comments of interest to Hungarians around the world, and its contributors live in every part of the globe.

Since many of the publications discussed above are not (or were not) strictly literary and critical journals, the present study is limited to the examination of the character, content, and role of three periodicals only, namely, *Ötágú Síp*, *Szivárvány*, and *Arkánum*.

Besides their language of publication being Hungarian, one is hard-pressed to find significant characteristics common to all three journals. Two of them, *Ötágú Síp* and *Arkánum*, appeared with only five to six issues, while *Szivárvány* published twenty-two issues since its inception in 1980. The six issues of *Ötágú Síp* were published within a period of two years, from 1973 to 1975, while *Arkánum* published five issues in six years, the last one dated December 1986. *Szivárvány* and *Arkánum* publish book reviews, while *Ötágú Síp* printed lists of Hungarian-language books available on the contemporary market, similar to the lists *Szivárvány* prints on the back cover of each issue. While *Ötágú Síp* and *Szivárvány* publish (published) selections by writers and poets from Hungary, its neighboring states, and the West, with a few exceptions, the majority of the contributors to *Arkánum* come from the ranks of its North-American founders, Sándor András, József Bakucz, László Kemenes Géfin, and György Vitéz. However, *Arkánum* does publish reviews of books printed in Hungary and Yugoslavia.

The subject matter and scope of the selections published in these journals are natural outgrowths of their professed goals. Consequently, neither in their statements of purpose, nor in the overall content of the three journals are there similarities common to all three periodicals.

Wishing to be a free forum, *Ötágú Síp* openly expressed the desire not to place any kind of ideological straightjacket on its contributors. Its major concern was the promotion of an atmosphere of tolerance and harmony among the varied groups of the Hungarian-American community. The primary motivation of its editors, as expressed in the introduction to the first issue, was their love of the Hungarian language, their desire to assist the survival of Hungarian culture throughout the world, and to provide an opportunity for the expression of a wide-range of artistic, scholarly, literary, social, and political ideas. A high literary standard, dignity of expression, and the willingness to listen to and to accept criticism were cited as criteria for publication. [7]

Similar views were voiced by the founders of *Szivárvány*, Ferenc Mózsi and György Kontra. Although Mózsi named *Új Látóhatár* /New Horizon/, *Irodalmi Újság* /Literary Gazette/, and *Magyar Füzetek* /Hungarian Notebooks/, — all of which are published in Western Europe, — the godfathers of his journal, it is not at all inappropriate to consider the now defunct *Ötágú Síp* the North-American spiritual forerunner of the more vigorous and still functioning *Szivárvány*. Although wider in scope and more varied in its selections and contributors, *Szivárvány* definitely continues the literary heritage professed by the editors of *Ötágú Síp*. In fact, one of *Ötágú Síp*'s former editors, the linguist and poet Ádám Makkai, is now listed as one of the contributing editors of *Szivárvány*.

In the first issue of *Szivárvány*, Mózsi and Kontra emphasized that the journal's place of publication will in no way restrict its contributors and its readership to the Hungarians of North America. "Our journal's title, *Rainbow*," they wrote, "is suggestive of the ideological bridge that may serve as a binding force among the scattered groups of emigrants. In fact, the rainbow is symbolic of the wide spectrum of ideological and political convictions held by the journal's readers and contributors."[8] The editors expressed their wish to remain free from all trends and orientations, and viewed "an honorable 'Hungarianness,' writers' talent, and responsible humanity" as criteria for publication. "We believe," they stated "that direct and sincere words—even if they are seven-hued like the rainbow—are capable of achieving our real and supposed goals."[9] Expressed in slightly different terms, the goals put forth by the editors of both *Ötágú Síp* and *Szivárvány* definitely show basic similarities.

Not so the goals of *Arkánum*. The journal serves as the organ for a small group of writers, the Hungarian avant-garde of the West, and more specifically of North America. As such, *Arkánum* consequently lacks the considerably wider appeal of the other two journals. The poetry and prose published in *Arkánum* is hardly geared to the tastes and interest of the average, intellectually-oriented, educated reader. In their statement of purpose, the editors alluded to Count Miklós Zrínyi's dictum in his famous seventeenth-century epic *Szigeti veszedelem* /Peril of Sziget/, "impoverished is the Magyar tongue." /Szegény az magyar nyelv/. According to the editors, the Magyar language is likewise impoverished today, but unlike in Zrínyi's time, it cannot be cured by the injection of Turkish, Croatian, and Latin vocabulary, but "must be expanded on the level of meaning; it must be made translucent."[10] They believe that "in this language /Magyar/ there are certain things that cannot be printed; in fact, cannot even be written down. This language is blurred by a political, prudish, and nationalistic cataract, by religious censorship and self-censorship. It is encased in the filthy layer of respect for authority and prestige, finitism, an inferiority complex, and self-delusion."[11] They strongly profess that only by the "exposure of taboos" and the "removal of the veils of obscurity" can a writer or poet truly attain his independence.[12]

One of the founders of *Arkánum*, György Vitéz, stated that the journal wants "to make a statement, to shock, to disgust, to scandalize, and to arouse indignation in its readers." [13] Yet, the editors also expressed that literature (their literature) is designed to serve as medicine, as a kind of balsam that cures all ills. The majority of their selections, be they prose, poetry or book reviews do offend readers, and their deliberate wish to do away with time-honored, and respected trends is quite evident on the pages of each issue. Having read most of the selections that appeared in the five issues of the journal, the impartial and detached reader may legitimately ask the question of how shocking, disgusting, tasteless, and scandalizing words can have a soothing, medicinal effect on a reader's psyche. Their assertion is open to debate, and would require further explanation from the journal's founders.

Both *Ötágú Síp* and *Szivárvány* were or are engaged in the promotion of Hungarian culture throughout the world, and both strived or strive to reach a wide audience of the Hungarian-language reading public. *Arkánum*, on the other hand, gears its materials to a select few. Yet, this fact does not prevent its editors from urging readers to show *Arkánum* to their friends and to solicit new subscribers and new members to the "Arkánum Literary Society." One senses a definite contradiction here. A journal with such goals and content as *Arkánum* faces an even greater challenge to stay in print than any other Hungarian publication in the West. The journal's fifth issue, for example, appeared after two years of complete silence. The editors repeatedly ask for financial support, lamenting the "wide-spread ultra-conservatism" that according to them, is sweeping the cultural, artistic, and literary life world wide, making the survival of the ideas and ideals of the avant-garde writers especially difficult. As they state, "These are difficult times for avant-garde endeavors." [14]

Not only were the expressed goals of *Ötágú Síp* and *Szivárvány* quite similar in spirit, the contents also reveal many likenesses. Both publish (published) a wide variety of writings, including poetry, short stories, novellas, studies, essays, interviews, and obituaries. In terms of literary genre, poetry dominates the pages of *Ötágú Síp*, with György Faludy's poems appearing most frequently, followed, interestingly enough, by the more presentable poems of József Bakucz, one of the founders of *Arkánum*. In the area of prose, selections by the populist writer Imre Kovács and the Transylvanian-Hungarian writer András Sütő are the most frequent, and a column edited by Károly Nagy on the instruction of Hungarian language and culture abroad is of special importance. One of the most significant accomplishments of *Ötágú Síp* was the publishing of selections by Hungarian writers in the neighboring states of Romania, Yugoslavia, and Czechoslovakia, since during the mid-seventies these were not as well known nor as accessible as they are today. Other selections of interest are Imre Kovács's account of his conviction for his authorship of *Néma forradalom* /Silent Revolution/ which detailed the miserable existence of the landless peasantry on large estates in interwar Hungary. Ádám Makkai's study on the educational system of American colleges and universities and András Hamza's discussion of the image of 1848-1849 in contemporary American newspapers are also to be noted. [15]

The need for a journal such as *Ötágú Síp* was brought home by a letter addressed to András Hamza by Sándor Kelemen of Budapest, which was ironically, reprinted in what turned out to be the final issue of the journal. After expressing his congratulations for the goals and selections published in the journal, and wishing a much longer lifespan than the one-year probation period, he commended the editors for following the road of *Realpolitik*, and for placing the promotion of Hungarian language and culture above politics. Since one out of every three Hungarians today lives outside the borders of present-day Hungary, Kelemen re-emphasized the importance of Hungarian cultural activities abroad, especially in the diaspora.[16]

Although Sándor Kelemen's words went unheeded, and the short-lived *Ötágú Síp* is now only a phenomenon to be discussed in the evaluation of Hungarian-American cultural and intellectual life, it is also clear that the atmosphere of the 1970s was not yet ripe for the existence of such a publication. A lack of openness and trust, and perhaps a feeling of suspicion on all sides toward the idea of banding together regardless of political borders dominated the sixties and seventies. A more broad-minded attitude began to emerge in the 1980s. More Hungarian writers, poets, and intellectuals living in the West traveled to Hungary, more of their writings appeared in journals and in separate volumes in the homeland; while visits and prolonged stays by Hungarian writers, historians, and other professionals in America became more frequent. The current decade is significantly more ripe for the existence of a Hungarian language literary and critical journal than the previous ones. This does not mean, however, that co-operation, mutual tolerance and understanding dominates the cultural and intellectual life of Hungarians around the world. Yet, one may safely conclude that there are definite signs of improvement.

It is now appropriate to address the content of the journal *Arkánum*. Many of the selections that appeared on its pages do definitely shock, and not only do they often concentrate on the erotic, but in the view of most educated, intellectually oriented readers, they are obscene, while some are totally incomprehensible. In that respect, the journal attained its goals. The journal also printed hitherto unpublished materials. The publication of thirty-three pages of the poet Attila József's (1905-1937) unpublished writings is definitely in the category of obscenity, and can be added as another feather in their cap. What this selection adds to a better understanding and appreciation of Attila József's poetical works needs to be clarified. Considering the above, the journal *Arkánum* would not be quite the appropriate and ideal recommended reading material for the education of Hungarian youth, no matter where they happen to live.

Yet, noteworthy is the aura of openness that is evident in the review section of the journal. The works of highly regarded and often revered poets, the so-called "untouchables" of Hungarian literature, are openly criticized, and one must admit, not always unjustly.[17]

Of the three journals under discussion, the selections of *Szivárvány* are the most varied, have the widest appeal, and the contributors are the most widespread in terms of ideological and political convictions. One glance at any of the twenty-two issues reveals a wide variety of topics, and the contributors originate from every corner of the world where Hungarians live. One can find the poetry of György Faludy (Canada), Tibor Flórián (U.S.A.), Tamás Tűz (Canada), Győző Határ (England), Árpád Farkas (Romania), Géza Szőcs (Switzerland, formerly of Romania), the historical essays of

Péter Gosztonyi (Switzerland), Emil Csonka (West Germany), and Endre Haraszti (Canada), and the prose of István G. Fekete (U.S.A.), Mátyás Sárközi (England), Dezső Monoszlóy (Austria), Albert Vajda (U.S.A.), and István Csurka (Hungary); the list is endless.

Szivárvány is designated as a literary, artistic, and critical review, and true to its promise, it also serves as a forum not only for writers, poets, and critics, but for artists as well. Graphics, etchings, photographs, and drawings are included to illustrate each issue by such artists as Lajos Szalay, Béla Kondor, István Vígh, Gyula Varga, István Huszár, Éva Krump, and many others. In its desire to promote the works, of artists, *Szivárvány* follows the traditions of *Ötágú Síp* which also featured the works of artists such as József Domján, Lajos Szalay and János Tokay.[18]

The mere fact that *Szivárvány* succeeded in publishing twenty-two issues in seven years puts it into a category that no other Hungarian-language literary and critical journal in North America can rival. Its success is due to a large degree to the tireless efforts and great dedication of its editor-in-chief, Ferenc Mózsi, although in certain issues other editors were also designated, namely György Kontra and Elemér Horváth. The list of contributing editors has grown with the years, although the names do change. For example, the eighteenth issue lists six, instead of seven-to-eight in previous issues, while the last issue designates nine contributing editors. It is likewise to be noted that the number of contributors has grown significantly since the journal's inception, and at the present time stands between fifty and sixty. Special, commemorative events have also been featured, among them, the twenty-fifth and thirtieth anniversary of the 1956 Hungarian Revolution, the death of poet Gyula Illyés in 1983, the seventy-fifth birthday of the poet György Faludy, and the tenth anniversary of Cardinal Mindszenty's death.[19] Also of note are the publishing of an extensive study on Greater Moravia by Péter Püspöki-Nagy of Czechoslovakia, and Kálmán Szabolcs's (Los Angeles, California) impressions of religious life in Hungary. Lately, *Szivárvány* has also become involved in the printing of works by samizdat writers in Hungary, and has reprinted selections from *Beszélő* /Speaker/, and *Hírmondó* /Messenger/, two samizdat journals published in Budapest. For example, it printed the entire minutes of the Hungarian Writers' Guild's December 28, 1956 meeting, and also an extensive article that examines the state of affairs of Hungarian Jewry in present-day Hungary.

Of special importance is the fact that *Szivárvány* publishes material which is censored in Hungary. One example of this is an interview with the Viennese István Szépfalusy by Tibor Zalán of Győr, Hungary, the publication of which was declined by the journal *Műhely* /Workshop/, published in Győr. The journal's decision not to publish the interview is especially noteworthy, since it was *Műhely* that commissioned the interview in the first place. Another example of *Szivárvány's* significant role is the printing of an article entitled "Milyen szabadságról van szó?" /What kind of freedom is the one in question?/ by Dénes Csengey of Hungary who hoped that his discussion would spark a vigorous debate in the intellectual and cultural life of Hungary. However, he found it impossible to have his article published in a journal printed in the mother country. [20]

Szivárvány also publishes a relatively extensive section of book reviews which are extremely helpful in finding out what is available on the market. From among the principal contributors of the journal, besides the editor-in-chief himself, the writings and reviews of György Ferdinandy, Klára Györgyey, and Lajos Szathmáry appear most frequently. The perceptive and thought-provoking observations of these critics are important and valuable contributions to the journal.

Besides being the principal motivator and tireless worker in the publishing of the journal, in 1983 Ferenc Mózsi launched the publication of a book series called *Szivárvány Könyvek* /Rainbow Books/. It was originally founded to publish the writings of the journal's contributors, but later it was expanded to include the works of other authors as well. So far, thirteen volumes have appeared by such diverse writers and poets as Miklós Duray of Czechoslovakia, Peter Kaslik of Canada, János Makkai of Hawaii, Béla Hidegkuti of Australia, Nándor Ludvig of New York, Mózsi himself, and György Ferdinandy of Puerto Rico, whose second collection of short stories is one of the most recent additions.

The number, quality, and readership of a nation's literary,

historical, and cultural journals are to a degree indicators of its intellectual and cultural aspirations and interests. This is even more so in countries where such journals are not state-supported, but are independent endeavors. The continuing existence of such journals relies heavily on the dedication of their publishers, editors, writers, and the support of their readers. This state of affairs is so much more true of a nationality group that lives within the confines of a foreign land, whose native country does not subscribe to the concept of a free press, and its members are scattered around the world, as is the case of the Hungarians.

The role of such journals is especially great and far-reaching. They become significant and often irreplaceable organs for the dissemination of new ideas, for the discovery and introduction of new creative talent, especially if they adhere to the ideals of a free forum, as the journals *Ötágú Síp* and *Szivárvány*. Both journals were founded as organs of free expression, to promote communication and understanding among Hungarians throughout the world. *Ötágú Síp* was unfortunately short-lived, but *Szivárvány* continues to expand, to include an even greater variety of contributors and writings. Recently it published the poetry of five young poets living in Hungary, an important development that signals interest in the literary output of the next generation. *Szivárvány's* subscribers have grown from one hundred since its inception to over three hundred. Yet, this is a shockingly small number indeed, when, according to György Ferdinandy's calculations, it would take at least 1,500 active supporters to maintain an independent publishing house, to keep a journal viable, and in general signal to Hungarian authors in the West that there is indeed an educated reading public interested in their literary output, and in the problems that concern the entire nation.[21]

To be self-supportive, a journal such as *Szivárvány* would require at least five times more subscribers than it has today. Unfortunately, a grant by the National Endowment for the Arts that the journal enjoyed for two years has been withdrawn in 1986 because of lack of funds. The journal, at times does receive special support; for example, the issue that commemorated the thirtieth anniversary of the 1956 Hungarian Revolution was supported by a grant from the Illinois Arts Council. Yet, considering the total financial picture, the situation could seem to be hopeless. But from another perspective, one can sense a definite ray of hope among those who are engaged in the promotion of a universal Hungarian literature and culture. This optimism is the result of several new developments.

As it is well-known, even today, Hungarian-language writers and poets in the West exist in a virtually complete vacuum. They often compose for their desk drawers, perhaps for a few friends, or if they are able to scrimp and save enough to finance the publication of their own books, their volumes gather the dust of attics or cellars. Even the writings of such prominent literary personalities as László Cs. Szabó (1905-1984) have failed to reach a wider audience among the Hungarian communities in the West, especially in North America. This sense of hopelessness has been somewhat alleviated recently by the publishing of poetry and prose anthologies of authors living in the West both in Hungary and in Western Europe.[22] Also, with limitations, selections of Hungarian authors living abroad have appeared more frequently in periodicals in Hungary, and some writers, poets, critics and historians saw the publication of their works in independent volumes.[23] These are certainly encouraging signs. Another such encouraging development in the 1980s is the seven years of existence of *Szivárvány*, and in a more limited sense, the existence of *Arkánum*. Realistically, the exposure of the works of Hungarian writers living in the West to a significantly wider audience is a dream whose realization is far into the future. That is why the existence of a journal such as *Szivárvány* is of utmost importance. It has now grown into a publication that rivals its West European counterparts, and thus has emerged as a major contribution to the spiritual, intellectual, ideological, and political pluralism of Hungarian literature and culture throughout the world.

Notes

1. See Steven Béla Várdy, *The Hungarian-Americans* (Boston: Twayne Publishers, 1985), pp. 15, 151-163.

2. *Ibid.*, pp. 151-158.

3. András Hamza, "Beköszöntő," /Opening Announcement/ in *Ötágú Síp*, Vol. I, No. 1. (April 1973), p. 5.

4. Rev. András Hamza's sudden and unexpected death in 1983 at the age of 63 was a significant loss to the Hungarian-American community.

5. Hamza, p. 6.

6. For a short discussion of *Ötágú Síp*, *Tanú*, and the publication in question, see Miklós Béládi, Béla Pomogáts, and László Rónay, *A nyugati magyar irodalom 1945 után* /Hungarian Literature in the West after 1945/ (Budapest: Gondolat, 1986), pp. 43-44.

7. Hamza, pp. 5-6.

8. *Szivárvány*, (July 1980), p. 1.

9. *Ibid.*

10. *Arkánum*, No. I. (June 1981), p. 3.

11. *Ibid.*

12. *Ibid.*

13. György Vitéz made that statement to me in a telephone interview in March 1986.

14. *Arkánum*, No. 5, (December 1986), p. 108.

15. See Imre Kovács, "A falukutatás hőskoráról" /The Heroic Age of the Sociological Study of Village Life/, *Ötágú Síp*, Vol. I, No, 2 (June 1973), pp. 123-129; Ádám Makkai, "Az amerikai egyetemi rendszer és párhuzama az európai rendszerekkel" /The American University System and Its Parallel with the European System/, in *Ötágú Síp*, Vol. I, No. 2 (June 1973), pp. 153-168, and Vol. I, No. 3 (October 1973), pp. 228-241; and András Hamza, "1848-49 az amerikai sajtó tükrében" /1848-49 as Mirrored in the American Press/, in *Ötágú Síp* Vol. 2, No. 1 (Summer 1975), pp. 47-60.

16. Sándor Kelemen, "Levél hazulról" /Letter from Home in *Ötágú Síp*, Vol. 2, No. 1 (Summer 1975) pp. 33-37.

17. See László Kemenes Géfin's review of Sándor Weöres, *Ének a határtalanról* /Song of the Boundless/, in *Arkánum*, No. 1 (June 1981), pp. 100-101, and Sándor András's review of Gyula Illyés's *Szellem és erőszak* /Spirit and Tyranny/, in *Arkánum*, No. 2 (December 1981), pp. 115-117.

18. Together with such artists as Sándor Bodó, a leading engraver, István Juharos, a noted painter, and Endre Fazekas, creator of altar mosaics and *iconostas*, József Domján and Lajos Szalay have also been featured in the popular American press. See Steven Béla Várdy, "Magyars in America," in *World and I*. (March 1987 pp. 462 -477; and idem, "The Mystery of the Hungarian Talent," in *World and I*. (April 1987) pp. 498-513.

19. Cf. the following issues of *Szivárvány*: October, 1981, September 1983, May 1985, September 1985, and October 1986.

20. See *Szivárvány* (October 1986), pp. 132-135.

21. These volumes are as follows: *Nyugati magyar költők antológiája* /Anthology of Hungarian Poets Living in the West/, ed. by László Kemenes Géfin (Bern, 1980); *Vándorének* /Wanderer's Song/, ed. by Miklós Béládi (Budapest, 1981); *Nyugati*

magyar széppróza antológiája /Anthology of Hungarian Prose in the West/, ed. by György Ferdinandy (Bern, 1983); *Nyugati magyar tanulmányírók antológiája* /Anthology of studies by Hungarian Authors in the West/, ed. by Gyula Borbándi (Bern 1987).

22. See György Ferdinandy's reply to those Hungarian emigrés in the West who strongly criticized the London-based prominent Hungarian writer and essayist, László Cs. Szabó for consenting to have his works published in Budapest. (See Note 23 for titles of specific works). Ferdinandy's article is also an accurate appraisal of the pervasive lack of support of Hungarian language authors and their books by the general reading public of the West. *Szivárvány*, (May 1984), pp. 95-96.

23. A partial list of independent volumes published in Budapest during the 1980's is as follows: Győző Dojcsák, *A kanadai Esterházy története* /The Story of the Canadian Esterházy/ (1981); *idem, Amerikai magyar történetek* /American-Hungarian Stories/ (1985); István Deák, *Kossuth Lajos és a magyarok* /Lajos Kossuth and the Hungarians/ (1983); Gyula Gombos, *Hillsdale* (1982); Győző Határ, *Éjszaka minden megnő* /Everything is Bigger during the Night/ (1986); Lajos Kutasi-Kovács, *A mohikánok visszatérnek* /The Mohikans Return/ (1986); Kázmér Nagy, *Az elveszett alkotmány* /The Lost Constitution/ (1983); László Cs. Szabó, *Alkalom-esszék irodalomról és művészetről* /Opportunity-Essay about Literature and Art/ (1982); *idem, Közel és távol—Összegyűjtött elbeszélések,* /Near and Far—Collected Short Stories/ (1983); *idem, Őrzők* /Guards/ (1983); and Ágnes Huszár Várdy, *Karl Beck élete és költői pályája* /Karl Beck's Life and Literary Career/ (1984).

CONTRIBUTING SCHOLARS

Chászár, Edward, Ph.D. (George Washington University), is Professor of Political Science at Indiana University of Pennsylvania, and a specialist in national minority affairs. As the International Studies Association's observer at the United Nations Commission on Human rights in Geneva, Professor Chászár's articles concerning human and national minority rights have appeared in such periodicals as *The Middle East Review, The Hungarian Quarterly, Nationalities Papers*, and the *Documentation sur l'Europe Centrale*. He is also the author of *Decision in Vienna* (Astor Park, Fl. 1978), and *The International Problem of National Minorities* (Indiana, PA, 1988). Since 1973 he is a Member of the Árpád Academy of Hungarian Scientists, Writers, and Artists Abroad (henceforth Árpád Academy).

Clementis-Záhony, Botond R., M.A. (John Carroll University), is Legislative Director in Congressman Ernie Konnyu's office in Washington, D.C., and a past administrator of The John M. Ashbrook Center of Public Affairs at Ashland College, Ashland, Ohio. He is co-editor of Bálint Hóman's *Ősemberek-ősmagyarok* /Ancient Peoples-Ancient Hungarians (Atlanta, 1985).

Csizmadia, Andor (1910-1985), Dr. Jur. (University of Budapest), Dr. h.c. (Jagellonian University of Cracow), was Professor of Legal History and Dean of the School of Law at the University of Pécs, Hungary. His major publications include *Magyar városi jog* /Hungarian Urban Law/ (Kolozsvár, 1940), *Hajnóczy József közjogi-politikai munkái* /József

Hajnóczy's works on Public Law and Politics/ (Budapest, 1958), *A magyar választási rendszer 1848-49-ben* /The Hungarian Election System in 1848-49/ (Budapest, 1963), *A pécsi egyetem történetéből* /From the History of the University of Pécs/ (Pécs, 1967), *A nemzeti bizottságok működése, 1944-49* /The Functioning of the National Committees in 1944-49/ (Budapest, 1968), *Történelmünk a jogalkotás tükrében* /Our History in the Mirror of Legislation/ (Budapest, 1970), and the major post-World War II university textbook for Hungarian constitutional and legal history, *Magyar állam és jogtörténet* /Hungarian State and Legal History/ (Budapest, 1972). In 1981 Professor Csizmadia was elected corresponding member of the Austrian Academy of Sciences in Vienna.

Décsy, Gyula, Ph.D. (University of Budapest), Dr. habil (University of Hamburg), is Professor of Uralic and Altaic Studies at Indiana University, a former Professor of Finno-Ugric Studies at the University of Hamburg, a Member of the Árpád Academy (1968), and one of the most renowned practitioners of Finno-Ugric linguistics in the United States. He is also Editor-in-Chief of the *Ural-Altaische Jahrbücher* (1968-), and Editor of such other serials as the *Bibliotheca Nostratica* (1978-), *Arcadia Bibliographica Virorum Eruditorum* (1978-), and the *Transworld Identity Series* (1982-). Professor Décsy is the author of several hundred articles and reviews, as well as of over a dozen books. His most significant works include: *Einführung in die finnisch-ugrische Sprachwissenschaft* (Wiesbaden, 1965), *Die linguistische Struktur Europas* (Wiesbaden, 1973), *Spracherkunftforschung,* 2 vols. (Wiesbaden-Bloomington, IN, 1977-1981), and *Die Deutsche Universität im Schnittpunkt amerikanischer und sozialistischer Organizationsprinzipen 1965-1980* (Bloomington, IN, 1982).

Domonkos, Leslie S., Ph.D. (University of Notre Dame), is Professor of Medieval History and Renaissance Studies at Youngstown State University, and a Member of the Árpád Academy (1968). A graduate of the Medieval Institute of the University of Notre Dame, Professor Domonkos has been the recipient of several Ford Foundation, Fulbright and IREX Fellowships, and has done considerable research in Austria and Hungary. In addition to over a dozen studies in various periodicals, he is the co-editor of *Studium Generale: Studies in Honor of A. L. Gabriel* (Notre Dame, 1967), and *Louis the Great, King of Hungary and Poland* (New York, 1985), and the author of the forthcoming *The Political and Cultural History of Hungary in the Age of Matthias Corvinus*.

Dreisziger, Nándor F., Ph.D. (University of Toronto), is Professor of History at the Royal Military College of Canada, and a Member of the Árpád Academy (1973). The founding editor of *The Canadian-American Review of Hungarian Studies* and its successor the *Hungarian Studies Review*, Professor Dreisziger is a specialist in modern Hungarian diplomatic and political history and of Canadian immigration and ethnic history. He has published widely in Canadian and American periodicals, and has also received major grants from the Canadian Council as well as from the Social Sciences and Research Council of Canada. His most important books include *Hungary's Way to World War II* (Astor Park, FL, 1968), and *Struggle and Hope: The Hungarian-Canadian Experience* (Toronto, 1982).

Gabriel, Astrik L., Ph.D. (University of Budapest), Dr. h.c. (Ambrosiana Library, Milan), is Professor Emeritus at the University of Notre Dame and past Director of the Medieval Institute at that University. A specialist of the history of medieval universities, Professor Gabriel has served as President of the International Commission for the History of Universities (1974-1985), and President of the Catholic Historical Association (1973). He was member of the Institute for Advanced Study at Princeton (1950-1951, 1979-1980), and Stillman Guest Professor at Harvard University (1963-1964). At Notre Dame he directed the "Ambrosiana, Milano" Photographic Project for the University. Among his publications are: *Les rapports dynastiques franco-hongrois au moyen age* (Budapest, 1944), *Student Life in Ave Maria College, Mediaeval Paris* (Notre Dame, 1955), *Liber Receptorum Nationis Anglicanae (Alemanniae) in Universitate Parisiensi* (Paris, 1964), *The Medieval Universities of Pécs* *and Pozsony* (Notre Dame-Frankfurt, 1969), and *Garlandia - Studies in the History of the Mediaeval University* (Notre Dame-Frankfurt, 1969). Professor Gabriel is a Charter Member and first President of the Árpád Academy, Corresponding Member of the Bavarian, French, and Hungarian Academies of Sciences, and a Fellow of the Medieval Academy of America.

Gatto, Katherine Gyékényesi, Ph.D. (Case Western Reserve University), is Associate Professor of Modern Languages at John Carroll University, and since 1986 a Member of the Árpád Academy. A former Fulbright Scholar in Spain (1972-1973), Dr. Gatto's areas of specialization include Spanish language and literature and Hungarian Studies. She has published essays on the Spanish poet Frederico Garcia-Lorca and on the Hungarian poet György Gyékényesi. Currently she is working on a book on the medieval courtly poetry of Spain.

Konnyu, Leslie (Könnyü, László), M.A. (St. Louis University), is a poet, historian, cartographer, and geographer. He is the founding editor of *The American-Hungarian Review* (St. Louis) and the author of nearly fifty works of poetry, essays, and scholarly studies in four languages (Hungarian, English, French, and German). His most relevant works in English include: *A History of American Hungarian Literature* (1962; 2d ed, 1988), *Eagles of Two Continents* (1963), *Modern Magyar Literature* (1964), *John Xantus: Hungarian Geographer in America* (1965), *Hungarians in the U.S.A. An Immigration Study* (1967), *Acacias: Hungarians in the Mississippi Valley* (1976), and *Professional Hungarian artists Outside Hungary* (1978). He is Honorary Dean of St. Louis University, founder of T. S. Eliot Society, Fellow of the International Academy of Poets, Member of the International P.E.N. Club, and Member of the Árpád Academy (1976).

Kosztolnyik, Z. J., PhD. (New York University), is Professor of Medieval History at Texas A & M University, and Member of the Árpád Academy (1974). He is a past recipient of several scholarships and research grants, including a Fulbright Scholarship to the University of Vienna (1963-1965), and is a member of the Phi Kappa Phi Honors Society. A specialist of medieval Hungarian history, Professor Kosztolnyik has published nearly sixty articles and book reviews, and he is also the author of two books entitled *Five Eleventh Century Hungarian Kings: Their Policies and Relations with Rome* (1981), and *From Coloman the Learned to Béla II* (1095-1196): *Hungarian Domestic Policies and Their Impact upon Foreign Affairs* (1987).

Mihályi, Gilbert, O.Praem., Th.D. (University of Budapest), is the retired pastor of St. Stephen Hungarian Catholic Church in Chicago. Before that he served in the same position in St. Louis, and taught theology and political science at St. Norbert College in De Pere, Wisconsin. Father Mihályi is the author of numerous newspaper articles, as well as author or co-author of the following books: *Európa válsága és meg-mentése* /Europe's Crisis and its Reconstruction/ (Rome, 1956), *Az Egyház liturgikus élete* /The Liturgical Life of the Church/ (Rome, 1980), and *II. János Pál, a vasfüggöny mögül jött pápa* /John Paul II, the Pope from behind the Iron Curtain/ (Youngstown, OH, 1980). He is a Member of the Árpád Academy since 1966.

Papp, Susan M., M.A. (York University, Toronto), is a researcher and field producer with the National Television news department of the Canadian Broadcasting Company, and a past editorial assistant of the *Hungarian Studies Review* (University of Toronto). She is a specialist in North American social and immigration history, and the author of numerous articles on Hungarian immigration to the United States and Canada. Her most significant work is *Hungarian Americans and Their Communities of Cleveland* (Cleveland, 1981). She is also the editor and co-author of *Poliphony: Hungarians in Ontario* (Toronto, 1979-1980), and a contributor to the *Encyclopedia of Cleveland History* (Cleveland, 1987).

Rektor, Béla A., J.D. (University of Debrecen, Hungary), M.S.(California State University, Los Angeles), a specialist in the history of law enforcement, taught Hungarian lan-

guage at the Defense Language Institute, Monterey, California, and then Public Administration at the University of
Arizona. As a former member of the Royal Hungarian
Gendarmerie, Dr. Rektor's research interests center on the
history of law enforcement agencies, and in particular on
the history of the now disbanded Royal Hungarian Gendarmerie. He has published over four dozen articles and
two books on this topic. The latter include his *Federal Law
Enforcement Agencies* (Astor, FL, 1975), and *A magyar
királyi csendőrség oknyomozó története* /The Pragmatic
History of the Hungarian Royal Gendarmerie/ (Cleveland,
1980). Dr. Rektor became a member of the Árpád Academy
in 1977.

Somogyi, Lél F., M.S. (Case Western Reserve University),
is a computer engineer and a Management Information
Systems specialist, who currently is Director of Marketing
at Chi Corporation in Cleveland, Ohio. He is also involved
in the research and study of Hungarian and Hungarian-
American history, and has written and translated a number
of essays on those topics. He is the founding editor of the
quarterly *Hungarian Insights* (Cleveland), co-author of
*Faith and Fate: A Short Cultural History of the Hungarian
People through a Millennium* (Cleveland, 1976), and a
Member of the Árpád Academy since 1979.

Somogyi, Sarolta B., Dipl. (University of Pécs, Hungary),
the wife of Professor Ferenc Somogyi, has attended the József
Nádor University of Technical and Economic Sciences in
Budapest, and graduated from the Social Welfare Program
of the University of Pécs. She began her career with the
National Foundation for Folk and Family Protection, and
has also served with the Social Welfare Superintendancy
in Budapest and in Pécs. Since her departure from Hungary she has been active in Hungarian emigré affairs and
in various Hungarian-American organizations. She is the
author of a number of articles in Hungarian emigré periodicals, and is a Decorated Member of the Árpád Federation since 1972.

Sozan, Michael, (1938-1987), Ph.D. (Syracuse University) was Professor of Anthropology at Slippery Rock University. A winner of several national fellowships and research grants from such organizations as the National Institute of Health, Hungarian Academy of Sciences, International Research and Exchanges Board (IREX), National Academy of Sciences, and the United States Department of Health, Education, and Welfare, Professor Sozan has conducted field work in his native Hungary, as well as in Austria and India. Based on his field work, he published numerous research articles and a book entitled *A határ két oldalán* /On Both Sides of the Border/ (Paris, 1985). The final results of his research would have been a major two-volume work on comparative social systems. Professor Sozan is also the author of *The History of Hungarian Ethnography* (Washington, D.C., 1977), which is the first English language summary of Hungarian ethnographical developments.

Stroup, Edsel Walter, Ph.D. (University of Akron), is a specialist in eighteenth and nineteenth-century Hungarian history. He is the author of *Hungary in Early 1848: The Constitutional Struggle against Absolutism* (Buffalo-Atlanta, 1977), and the contributor of studies and reviews to various scholarly periodicals and collective volumes. For a number of years, Dr. Stroup had served as the Executive Secretary of the American Association for the Study of Hungarian History.

Szendrey, Thomas, Ph.D. (St. John's University, New York), is Professor of History at Gannon University, and a Member of the Árpád Academy since 1973. A former International Research and Exchanges Board (IREX) Scholar in Hungary, Professor Szendrey is a specialist in European intellectual and cultural history, and in the philosophy of history. His chapters, articles, and book reviews have appeared in many collective volumes and periodicals, and he has also authored a textbook on the general councils of the Catholic Church. He translated and edited Edith C. Mályusz's *The Theater and National Awakening: East Central Europe* (Atlanta, 1980), and co-edited Bálint Hóman's *Ősemberek - ősmagyarok* /Ancient Peoples - Ancient Hungarians/ (Atlanta, 1985). He is also the editor of the forthcoming *Historical Dictionary of Modern Eastern Europe* for Greenwood Press.

Szilassy, Sándor, J.D. (University of Budapest), M.L.S. (Indiana University-Bloomington), a former lawyer in Hungary, is Professor of Library Science and Director of the Libraries at Glassboro State College in New Jersey. He has held various professorial and administrative positions at Anderson College, Indiana State University, the University of Tampa, and Auburn University, as well as leadership positions in several professional library associations. Professor Szilassy is the author of *Revolutionary Hungary, 1918-21* (Astor Park, FL, 1971), and has published chapters and scholarly articles in such yearbooks and periodicals as *The Slavonic and East European Review, Ungarn-Jahrbuch, East European Quarterly, Hungarian Historical Review, Library Journal,* as well as in several Hungarian language annuals and journals. He is a Charter Member of the Árpád Academy (1966), and the President of the Academy's Department of Library and Archival Sciences.

Tar, Ferenc, Dipl. (University of Debrecen, Hungary), is a historian and a museologist at the Balatoni Museum in Keszthely, Hungary. His chief areas of research include local history and the history of Hungarians abroad. His most important scholarly publications have appeared in such Hungarian periodicals as *Élet és Tudomány* /Life and Science/, *Földrajzi Múzeumi Tanulmányok* /Geographic and Museum Studies/, *Múzsák* (Muses/, and *Új Tükör* /New Mirror/.

Várdy, Ágnes Huszár, Ph.D. (University of Budapest), is Professor of Comparative Literature at Robert Morris College, and also taught Hungarian language and culture at the University of Pittsburgh. Her areas of interest include Hungarian-American and comparative literature, with particular attention to Austrian, German, and Hungarian Romanticism. She has published extensively in various North American and European scholarly journals and annuals. Her books include *A Study in Austrian Romanticism: Hungarian Influences in Lenau's Poetry* (Buffalo, 1974), *Karl Beck élete és költői pályája* /The Life and Poetical Carreer of Karl Beck/ (Budapest, 1984), and the forthcoming *The Austro-Hungarian Mind* (New York-Boulder, 1989). She has also co-edited and co-authored *The Folks Arts of Hun-*

gary (Pittsburgh, 1981), *Society in Change: Studies in Honor of Béla K. Király* (New York-Boulder, 1983), and the present volume. She has been a member of the Árpád Academy since 1974.

Várdy, Nicholas Attila, M.A. (Stanford University), is an economist, historian, and a past Fulbright Scholar at the University of Economic Sciences in Budapest. Having also studied at the University of Heidelberg, Germany, Mr. Várdy is currently a student at Harvard Law School. He is the author of several studies on economic, social, and legal problems in such publications as the *Duquesne Law Review*, the *Review of Economic Sciences,* and *The Stanford Daily.* He is also the co-editor and co-author of the forthcoming *Stanford Guide to Study Abroad.*

Várdy, Steven Béla, Ph.D. (Indiana University-Bloomington), is Professor of History and immediate past Chairman of the Department of History at Duquesne University, an Adjunct Professor of East European History at the University of Pittsburgh, and the past Director of the Duquesne University History Forum. He is also a Member of the Árpád Academy (1968). A recipient of research grants and fellowships from the Ford Foundation, IREX, National Endowment for the Humanities, and the Carnegie Corporation of New York, Professor Várdy has lectured and/or researched in more than a dozen countries, and has twice served as Visiting Scholar at the Institute of History of the Hungarian Academy of Sciences and at the University of Budapest. He is the author of over two hundred articles, essays, and reviews, and of about a dozen independent volumes. His best known and most recent works are: *Modern Hungarian Historiography* (New York-Boulder, 1976), *The Hungarian-Americans* (Boston, 1985), *Clio's Art in Hungary and in Hungarian-America* (New York-Boulder, 1985), *Louis the Great: King of Hungary and Poland,* ed. (New York-Boulder, 1986), *Baron Joseph Eötvös: A Literary Biography* (New York-Boulder, 1987), *The Hungarian-Americans: The Magyar Experience in the United States and Canada* (New York, 1988), and the forthcoming *The Austro-Hungarian Mind* (New York-Boulder, 1989). He is also the co-editor of the present volume.

Varsányi, Julius (1912-1988), J.D. (University of Budapest), was Research Fellow in the Faculty of Law, Adelaide University, Australia. Having been trained in international law, before and during World War II, Dr. Varsányi had served in the Hungarian Office of Foreign Trade, and also held various diplomatic positions. In Australia, he continued his research in his two favored topics: the rights of national minorities, and the problems of regionalism and integration in Central and Eastern Europe. He published over two dozen articles in such international journals as the *International and Comparative Law Review, Revue Droit International de Sciences Diplomatiques et Politiques,* and *Studies for a New Central Europe.* His books include: *Quest for a New Central Europe,* ed. (Adelaide-Sydney, 1976), and *Border is Fate* (Adelaide-Sydney, 1982). He had been a Member of the Árpád Academy since 1976.

Wagner, Francis, Ph.D. (University of Szeged, Hungary), is a historian, and a specialist of Slavic Studies and national minority affairs. Having served as a Slavic specialist in the Hungarian Ministries of Public Education and Foreign Affairs, for nearly three decades, Dr. Wagner was an East European Specialist at the Library of Congress, where he continued his research and publications in his chosen field. He published over three-hundred monographs, periodical articles and book reviews, and has also written or edited over a dozen independent volumes. His best known and most recent works include: *The Hungarian Revolution in Perspective,* ed. (Washington, D.C., 1967), *Toward a New Central Europe,* ed. (Astor Park, FL, 1970), *Hungarian Contributions to World Civilization* (New Brunswick, NJ, 1977), *Eugene P. Wigner: An Architect of the Atomic Age* (Toronto, 1981), *Zoltán Bay, Atomic Physicist: A Pioneer of Space Research* (Toronto, 1985), and *Nation-Building in the United States: The American Idea of Nationhood in Retrospect* (1985). Many of Dr. Wagner's scholarly articles appeared in such major international journals as *Revue d'Histoire Comparée, Journal of Central European Affairs, The American Historical Review,* and the *Slavic Review.* Several of them were also inserted into the *U.S. Congressional Records.*

FINANCIAL CONTRIBUTORS

I.
Institutional Patrons:

-Hungarian Association (**Magyar Társaság**),
   Cleveland, Ohio
-Hungarian Central Committee for Books and
   Education, Cleveland, Ohio
-United Hungarian Fund, Cleveland, Ohio

II.
Patrons:

-Papp, Dr. Gábor, Cleveland, Ohio
-Roskó, Rev. László, Cleveland, Ohio
-Szirmai, Dr. Endre, Stuttgart, Germany
-Tihanyi, Dr. Sándor, Cleveland, Ohio

III.
Contributors:

-Burgyán, Aladár, Cleveland, Ohio
-Csia, Pál, Lakewood, Ohio
-Dömötörffy, Zsolt, Lakewood, Ohio
-Hollósy, Ervin v., Broadview Heights, Ohio
-Kondor, József, Broadview Heights, Ohio
-Kótai, Béla, Cleveland, Ohio

-Könnyü László /Leslie Konnyu/, St. Louis, Missouri
-Köteles, Béla, Broadview Heights, Ohio
-Lelbach, Andrea, Rocky River, Ohio
-Őszényi, Károly, Cleveland, Ohio
-Palasics, J.D. János (John), Shaker Heights, Ohio
-Rektor, Dr. Béla, Tuxon, Arizona
-Simonfay, Dr. Ferenc, Hankins, New York
-Tollas, Tibor, Munich, Germany
-Záhony, A. József, Clearwater, Florida